PRINCIPLES AND PRACTICE

OF

TOWN AND COUNTRY PLANNING

By

LEWIS KEEBLE, M.C., B.Sc., M.A., F.R.I.C.S., M.T.P.I.

Senior Lecturer in Town Planning
at the University of London

Formerly Lecturer in Town and Country Planning
at the University of Manchester

Vice-President of the Town Planning Institute

THE ESTATES GAZETTE LIMITED
28 DENMARK STREET · LONDON · WC2

FIRST PUBLISHED 1952
SECOND EDITION 1959
SECOND IMPRESSION 1961
THIRD EDITION 1964

TO MY MOTHER

PRINTED IN GREAT BRITAIN BY
WALKER & CO. (PRINTERS) LTD.
NORCUTT ROAD, TWICKENHAM, MIDDX.

PREFACE TO THIRD EDITION

SINCE THE SECOND EDITION was published a great deal has happened in Planning of which it is necessary to take account. The enormous growth of traffic and the acceleration of town centre redevelopment are obvious and conspicuous examples. There are, however, other much less conspicuous events and trends which greatly influence Planning thought and practice.

The resurgence of the inherently illogical linear town theory has been sufficiently marked to necessitate some treatment of it. Uncritical enthusiasm for "two-level" town centres is also great enough to merit some cold water. A campaign for very high residential densities conducted by an unholy alliance of architects and politicians has been sufficiently successful to imperil future environmental standards unless it is soon defeated. The machinery for the submission, approval and review of development plans set up by the Town and Country Planning Act of 1947 has now manifestly broken down, and seems unlikely to be capable of repair as distinct from reconstruction. Incoherent and illogical ideas about "pedestrian segregation" in residential areas have reached such proportions that ends and means are constantly being confused.

Worst of all, "planning by gimmick" seems almost to have become the rule. By this I mean that, far too often, the procedure is to think up some novel and exciting method of Planning and then to try to find economic and social reasons to justify it. This reversal of the proper order of things necessarily results in much strained, tangled and even preposterous thinking.

Never, in short, has there been a greater need for the establishment of rational principles, rationally connected with each other, in the field of land use Planning, and this edition of "Principles and Practice of Town and Country Planning" attempts, like its predecessors, to suggest, however sketchily and unevenly, the form which these principles might take.

In format this edition is very similar to the second edition, and special attention need only be drawn to two points.

Chapter 5 is a completely new chapter dealing with the concept of the urban region and its Planning, and attempts to fill an obvious gap. Second, the method of attempting to demonstrate the continuity of the Planning process by means of illustrations of proposals for different parts of the same area to different degrees of detail has been considerably extended. The whole Planning process can now be seen from a Regional Policy Plan in Fig. 16 and a more detailed Regional Plan in Fig. 17 through a Town Plan for a town within that region in Fig. 36 to two Supplementary Town Maps of the town centre and a residential area respectively within that town in Figs. 62 and 72.

The method of relating examples of various kinds of detailed design to the Master Plan of a theoretical new town is retained.

ACKNOWLEDGMENTS
Second Edition.

THE WORK OF MOST of the people who so kindly helped me with the first edition remains in the second edition in whole or in part, and it is with pleasure that I repeat my thanks for their aid.

Professor R. A. Cordingley, M.A., F.R.I.B.A., M.T.P.I., read most of the original proofs and made many valuable suggestions for their improvement, as well as contributing an introduction.

Mr. (now Dr.) F. W. Ledgar, M.A., Ph.D., M.T.P.I., gave me an immense amount of detailed help.

Mrs. M. Lock dealt very competently with a great mass of correspondence and typing.

Mr. G. B. Dix, B.A., Dip.T.P., M.L.A., A.R.I.B.A., A.M.T.P.I., was my mainstay in preparing many of the illustrations, including the majority of the most elaborate. His work survives especially in Figs. 6–13 of the present edition.

The following also prepared drawings, though I am not now sure which of these is still included:

Messrs. F. W. M. Crombie, J. Crothers, D. Hargreaves, I. C. Laurie, A. C. Smith, D. Thomas and D. J. Williams. (The latter drew the present Fig. 35).

For the second edition I was also fortunate in securing willing help of the highest competence.

Miss K. Backhouse and Miss B. I. Dickson did a very great deal of work, and between them typed practically the whole of the text.

Mr. L. C. Gale, F.R.I.C.S., M.T.P.I., gave me most valuable advice in revising Appendix III (Daylighting).

Mr. W. T. G. Wearne drew and redrew most of the drawing upon which Fig. 56 is based, and was most painstaking in devising methods of presenting it.

Mr. L. F. Baker M.A., F.R.I.B.A., A.M.T.P.I. drew Figs. 14 and 24–31, which seem to me quite outstandingly skilful examples of Planning presentation at an astonishingly small scale. He also helped and encouraged me in other ways too numerous to mention.

Mr. Colin Bridger, Dip. Arch., A.R.I.B.A., drew Figs. 51 and 62.

Mr. C. P. Andren, M.Sc., A.M.I.C.E., helped me greatly in the revision of Chapter 10 by his advice and by supplying much up-to-date information.

Dr. G. P. Wibberley, M.Sc., Ph.D., read most of Chapter 4 in typescript and provided very useful advice and criticism.

Dr. N. Lichfield read Chapter 1 in typescript and also helped with advice and criticism. I am further indebted to him for permission to reproduce extracts from his " Economics of Planned Development."

It is only right to make it clear that in a few respects I did not follow the advice given by the three last named, and they are not to be blamed for any of the opinions I have expressed.

My wife has wholly prepared a number of drawings, viz., Figs. 1, 2, 3, 5, 32, 48, 61 and 63, and has partly drawn a large number of others. She has also given inestimable help by preserving some semblance of order among a huge collection of drawings, many of which my subconscious seemed determined to lose or destroy.

I gratefully acknowledge permission to the following to publish extracts or reproduce drawings and make apology for any accidental omissions:—

Mr. C. B. Purdom: two illustrations from " The Building of Satellite Towns " (parts of Fig. 17). Professor R. E. Dickinson and Messrs. Routledge and Kegan Paul, Ltd.: illustrations from " City, Region and Regionalism " and " The West European City " (parts of Figs. 15 and 16). Messrs. C. D. Buchanan and D. H. Crompton: quotations from " Residential Density " published in the Proceedings of the Town and Country Planning Summer School, 1950. Mr. P. W. Smith and the Oxford University Press: illustration from " The Planning, Construction and Maintenance of Playing Fields " (Fig. 59). The Team Valley Trading Estates Ltd. (Fig. 50). The Stevenage Development Corporation (Fig. 45, part of Fig. 21 and written information). The Association for Planning and Regional Reconstruction: data relating to radii of railway curves etc., from " Town and Country Planning Textbook ". The Manchester Corporation: various tables from " The City of Manchester Plan, 1945 " and parts of Figs. 54 and 62. *The Manchester Corporation wish it to be made clear that the information given in the tables referred to is not necessarily representative either of the latest available information or the Corporation's agreed planning policy.* Professor R. G. Batson and Messrs. Longmans-Green: two drawings from " Roads " (Figs. 36 and 39). The Crawley Development Corporation: (Part of Fig. 21, Fig. 51 and written information). Mr. E. G. Robinson, B.Sc., Dip.T.P., F.R.I.C.S., F.A.I.: several extracts from our jointly written book " The Development of Building Estates". Messrs. Lund Humphries: (part of Fig. 17). The Worcester City Council and the authors of " County Town " (Part of Fig. 21). Mr. E. Maxwell Fry: illustration from " Fine Building " (part of Fig. 17). The Harlow Development Corporation: (part of Figs. 21 and 62 and written information). The Hemel Hempstead Development Corporation: (parts of Figs. 21, 54 and 62). The Town Planning Institute and the Royal Institution of Chartered Surveyors: various extracts from their respective journals, particularly from papers by Mr. R. H. Best, B.Sc., M.Sc. The Town Planning Review: extract from article by Mr. R. H. Best. The Town and Country Planning Association: (part of Fig. 17). I am specially indebted to Mr. Best for kindly allowing me to draw freely on the valuable material he has collected and presented from time to time.

A number of extracts have been made from H.M.S.O. publications with the permission of the Controller. Separate acknowledgment of each of these is made in the text. This applies also to a number of drawings reproduced from or based upon the Ordnance Survey.

I am again grateful for the help given by my publishers, particularly by Mr. F. P. Wilson.

Finally, my thanks are due to all the printers and blockmakers who have done their very best for me.

Third Edition. Additional Acknowledgments.

Miss Jane Linfield and Miss Madge Bridge have given me secretarial help of the most excellent kind. My wife has prepared many more drawings and has continued to keep the whole operation reasonably under control, while Mrs. Bridger, replacing her husband for this edition, has also contributed a number of admirable illustrations.

I am grateful for permission from Dr. P. A. Stone to quote, in Appendix II, from his work; from the L.C.C. to base a drawing (Fig. 20 (vi)) from their Hook Study; from the Cumbernauld Development Corporation to base a drawing (Fig. 20 (viii)) on the Master Plan for Cumbernauld and from the Controller, H.M.S.O., to base a drawing (Fig. 54) upon one in "Town Centres Approach to Renewal".

INTRODUCTION TO THE FIRST EDITION

By Professor R. A. Cordingley, M.A., F.R.I.B.A., M.T.P.I.

THIS IS NOT the first comprehensive textbook of Town Planning to be written, but it is different in kind from any that have gone before. It is as practical in character as it can be made. No pet theories are propounded or special pleas offered ; the author is not marketing untested ideas. His purpose is to render a factual, objective account of current practice—to review in as much detail as can be compassed in a single work the whole scope of legally-practicable Planning ; the mechanism of operation, the type and nature of the problems encountered and the methods and principles applied in their solution. History, as such, here finds no place, and there are no adventurous speculations on æsthetics. In so far as his convictions allow, the author refrains from intruding his own views. Throughout, it is the common or accepted practice he is at pains to discern and to explain. Hence the student will find in this book the authentic guidance he seeks and those in practice are given an unbiased comprehensive account of contemporary principle and method, and a trustworthy work of reference.

Because of its objective nature and comprehensive scope, this book stands, too, as a record of the achievement of modern Planning in this country to date. Despite the venerable history of the art, British Planning, universal, obligatory and touching social interests at almost all vital points, is young—almost completely new. Fifty years is a generous estimate of its age. What real progress has been made in this time ? How much of current activities is sheer mechanics and how much actually productive of the intended social good ?

It was no part of the author's intentions to concern himself with such abstract questions, but, indirectly, the answer emerges. Broadly, policy is well-established and general principles for the most part are implicitly accepted, but there is yet a good deal of irregularity in the practical application of principle in specific cases, especially in the matter of piecemeal development and in re-development. Some of the problems of Planning repeatedly occur, and there is now an accumulated experience in the solution of them ; others so far have only sporadically appeared and the specifics that have been applied consequently are sometimes found to have taken completely opposite trends. Again, when the general picture is presented there are seen to be quarters into which Planning principle has not yet penetrated. In all connections there is the further point that reliable factual data on which to base decisions all too frequently is lacking, since the field for research in Planning is very broad indeed and the modest resources so far available mostly have been concentrated upon the more pressing investigations.

From time to time, therefore, in order to present an entire and consistent account, the author has been obliged to relax his intention to confine himself to objective reporting and himself to bridge gaps in present experience or to arbitrate as to correct procedure whenever practice appears in conflict either with its own precedents or with general principle. In all such cases the grounds for his recommendations are fully stated.

Mr. Keeble writes from personal, first-hand experience. In all sections of his book he is on familiar ground and speaks with an authority allowed by an intimate knowledge of his subject. The breadth of his experience permits him to go directly to his points and to compress a very considerable body of skilfully sifted factual information within a small compass. Illustrations are drawn from a wide range, and in the course of his exposition many major Planning projects are submitted to comparative evaluation. Written in succinct, breezy style, revealing an irrepressible energy and humour, the book makes attractive as well as informative reading.

R. A. CORDINGLEY

CONTENTS

LIST OF ILLUSTRATIONS

*Drawings marked thus relate to the New Town used for purposes of illustration throughout Parts I and II.

PART 1

REGIONAL AND TOWN PLANNING

CHAPTER 1

DEFINITION, SCOPE AND OPERATION OF TOWN AND COUNTRY PLANNING

1-1. DEFINITION

TOWN AND COUNTRY PLANNING is not an easy subject to define. B. J. Collins, in " Development Plans Explained," calls it " the organising of building and land use in pursuance of an express scheme of urban or rural evolution." This is a clear, workmanlike definition which perhaps falls short of complete accuracy because a plan may, and indeed in some cases must, be prepared without there being any " express scheme of evolution " in existence. More lengthily, Town and Country Planning might be described as the art and science of ordering the use of land and the character and siting of buildings and communication routes so as to secure the maximum practicable degree of economy, convenience and beauty.

The name itself, however, is not altogether satisfactory, although it has so long been used in the titles of Acts of Parliament that it is well established and fairly well understood. B. J. Collins, in his presidential address to the Town Planning Institute, published in its Journal for December, 1957, pleaded for the shorter title, Town Planning, to be generally used, because it indicated the essential core of the subject matter concerned and was generally understood to include rural planning. There may be much in this argument, but there is the objection that rural Planning is already a neglected subject, and to omit reference to it in naming the activity of which it forms a part would be to invite further neglect. Other titles which have been used from time to time are: " Physical Planning", " Land Planning", and " Land Use Planning". The first of these hardly seems precise enough, and the other two both seem to leave out of account the more detailed aspects of planning.

Nearly all development of land is in fact in some sense planned, even if not set out on a drawing board before building operations begin. The trouble is that generally the area over which the planning is done is inadequate, the execution unsatisfactory and the Planning done in insufficient detail. The gradual development of a mediaeval town or of a village may often truly be said to be unplanned, but the rate of growth of these places has normally been so slow that each individual building can be erected as needed with full consideration of its relationship with other development. In conditions of this kind, unplanned growth may result in satisfactory conditions. By contrast, the 19th century industrial revolution town is an example of piece-meal Planning; each individual housing project had perforce to be drawn up beforehand in order that building operations could be organised, but these towns were unplanned in the sense that there was no co-ordination between individual projects and no consideration of the social needs of the inhabitants or of the eventual overall pattern of the town. The chaotic results are familiar to all of us.

Planning as a complete process, requires all aspects and implications of the physical development of land to be taken into account and fitted into a pattern devised with the object of making a region or a community as a whole into an effective and within limits, self-contained organism.

There are three characteristics of successful Planning which are of prime importance and to which, throughout this book, we shall constantly return. They are:

(1) The promotion of accessibility: accessibility of homes to work, shops, schools and entertainment, of industry to sources of labour, power and raw materials and so on. It would hardly be going too far to call Planning a study in accessibility.

(2) The employment of resources as economically as possible, so as to achieve the greatest possible measure of improvement with necessarily limited means.

(3) The separation of incompatible land uses from each other and the association of compatible or mutually helpful uses.

(4) The carrying out of all development in as visually pleasant a manner as is practicable.

1-2. SCOPE

Planning has both social and economic aims. Socially, successful Planning tends to make people's lives happier because it results in a physical environment which conduces to health, which allows convenient and safe passage from place to place, which facilitates social intercourse and which has visual attractiveness. The economic results of good Planning also, of course, conduce to increased happiness, but not quite so directly. A proper spatial relationship between the communities in a region and the constituent parts of a town, compactness of development, and an efficient arrangement of communication routes all result in human activities being carried on more efficiently and less wastefully, and thus increase wealth; but the results are not evident so far as they effect the welfare of a particular individual at a particular moment of time. This also applies to Planning provisions designed to conserve valuable woodland, to prevent the exploitation of valuable minerals being impeded or prevented by building taking place on the land above them or to secure that, where agricultural land is put to some other use, the less fertile is taken rather than the more fertile, where other and stronger considerations do not intervene.

For all that, it should be strongly emphasised that Planning, in the sense with which we are concerned with it, deals primarily with land, and is not economic, social, or political Planning, though it may assist greatly in the realisation of the aims of these other kinds of planning, and should obviously be made to fall into step with them. A source of considerable perplexity lies in the fact that Planning, even in the sense in which we are using the word, is likely to vary greatly in the range of its application. For example, in this country Planning powers are not used to regulate the change of use of land from one kind of agricultural use to another, nor to reorganise the re-grouping of farm units. They could possibly be so used, but it would require a change of national policy, expressed in legislation, for this to be done, just as such a change would be needed in those countries which do not, unlike Britain, control the appearance of buildings by means of Planning powers.

The kind of Planning which is done is in fact closely limited by political policy and by the form and extent of the legal powers given.

This leads to a variety of problems, which, though they will have to be discussed in detail later on, must be briefly touched upon here. Throughout this book I have assumed parliamentary democracy as the background to Planning. Obviously, under a dictatorship, many Planning problems diminish or disappear. In a country where extreme *laissez faire* is the rule, Planning may hardly be possible in any real sense. In any democracy, however, conscious or unconscious decisions have to be made about the legitimate limits and forms of public intervention in private lives. It is of the utmost importance that attempts should not be made to secure by means of Planning action social results which, though they may be desirable, are not within the accepted scope of public control.

With certain exceptions, a policy of what might be called " social neutrality " is followed in this country. That is to say, the individual is permitted to do as much as he likes, provided that he does not thereby do injury to the person or property of others in ways which the law has decided shall be illegal or evade the responsibilities, such as payment of income tax and jury service, which the law lays upon him. The border-line between those things in which the state concerns itself and those with which it does not is always shadowy and from time to time moves a little in one direction or the other; these movements, furthermore, are sometimes in advance of public opinion and sometimes lag behind it. Few would now question the desirability of compulsory education, many would dispute the propriety or need for any form of censorship of literature or art. Religious toleration is very wide; citizens are not compelled to attend places of worship and, on the other hand, religious sects are permitted freely to carry on their activities, provided they do not come into conflict with the general law of the land. Furthermore, such changes as take place in the law, so far as it affects the freedom of individual conduct, are for the most part the responsibility of Parliament and have not been the subject of delegation to Local Authorities, which can do nothing they are not expressly authorised by Parliament to do.[1]

It therefore seems clear, at least to me, that Local Authorities are under a duty to discharge their Planning powers in such a way that they do not seek to discriminate between land uses involving activities of which they do not approve and those of which they do approve. To take a simple example,

---

[1] Since this paragraph was first written a number of events have occurred which provide an interesting commentary upon it. The failure of the " Lady Chatterley's Lover " prosecution and the establishment of " That Was the Week That Was " as a national institution mark a decided trend towards greater freedom of expression which is immensely welcome to libertarians. The extraordinary exposures following the death of Rachman, on the other hand, have indicated the extent to which crime and violence can, almost unnoticed, underlie what is in many ways a highly civilised society if that society fails to make the provision of housing a comprehensive social service; while the ludicrous proposal of an ex-Archbishop of Canterbury to make adultery a crime suggests that the established Church still hankers for the restoration of a mediaeval authoritarianism.

many people would agree that listening to classical music is a more desirable activity than attending greyhound racing, but unless and until Parliament makes greyhound racing illegal, it is the duty of a Planning authority to consider an application for permission to establish a greyhound racing track as carefully and impartially as one to erect a concert hall. It is no doubt true that the effect on its surroundings of the former is likely to be so much wider and greater than of the latter that the number of sites suitable for it may be severely limited. This is a factor which can properly be taken into account in deciding the right use of land; the social desirability cannot.

I would, myself, extend the principle of social neutrality as far as to suggest that " Planning by demand " is the only safe means of ensuring that public control over the use of land is kept within proper bounds and does not encroach upon individual liberty. Restrictions upon economic activity are absolutely unavoidable in contemporary civilisation, and seem to me to be fairly clearly separable from interference with personal liberty. Obviously, any public exercise of Planning powers does involve substantial interference with economic liberty.

A simple exhortation to Plan by demand, to seek to arrange the development of land in such a way that it accords as closely as possible with the wishes of the majority, yet does as little as possible to affront those of minorities, does not really get us very far, for people do not always know what they want. Catherine Bauer has expressed this well in " Social Questions in Housing and Town Planning." " Conscious consumer wants are limited by experience and knowledge," she writes, " by and large, you can only want what you know . . . what we really want to know therefore, is what people would want if they understood the full range of possibilities on the one hand, and all the practical limitations on the other."

It is of enormous importance for Planning proposals to be based upon as reliable as possible an estimate of these notional wants rather than upon assessment of naïve wants, mere guesswork, or worse, upon the assumption that people should be given what they ought to want. In this connection, it is worth quoting from a paper by Professor T. S. Simey printed in the Journal of the Town Planning Institute for May, 1953. He mentions the opinion of a certain sociologist that " it is possible to coax people out of their inturned phase and on to shared local spaces, as there are fundamental human satisfactions in seeing neighbours and being seen by neighbours." His comment is: " this implies both that it is desirable that people should be ' coaxed ' to do what will give them ' fundamental human satisfaction ' and that the sociologist is well employed in associating himself with the process of judging what these satisfactions are. This is praiseworthy in itself, but it must also be recognised that it is dangerous as it is but a short step from ' coaxing ' to cajoling, and if the sociologist is to start laying down the law about what is a ' fundamental human satisfaction ' he is in a fair way to becoming a mastermind himself, and all that is implied by the phrase." (Earlier in his paper Professor Simey had enlarged upon the dangers of Planning being regarded as a field of operation for " masterminds".)

It may well be argued that it is unlikely that sociological techniques have yet reached the stage of perfection necessary to allow Catherine Bauer's admirable precept to be followed. It can also be urged that it is a poor set of governors who formulate their policies simply upon the immediate and un-informed wishes of a simple majority of their constituents; that it is indeed the duty of governors to govern, and that in a democracy they can easily be dismissed by the electorate if they fail to give satisfaction. This is true. And it seems necessary to add only that successful leadership depends upon leading without getting too far away from the led.

Not only may the range of Planning activity vary considerably; so may the degree of detail into which it enters. It would be possible to control the broad distribution of uses within a town without seeking to control the location of individual shops, or the detailed layout of a housing estate. It would be possible to control the appearance of buildings without bothering with that of fences and other means of enclosure; with the general location of rural housing without troubling about the siting of individual country houses. It must always be to some extent a matter of political decision what degree of detail of control is exercised; the main determinant will usually be whether the amount of public money spent and the amount of private irritation caused in exercising very detailed control is justified. This is another matter about which I shall have much more to say later on; it is another source of confusion and misunderstanding about which clear thought is necessary.

It has already been explained that no Planning can be carried out without the existence of the necessary legal powers; similarly, no positive Planning, which generally involves the execution of projects with the help of public money, is possible unless funds are granted by the appropriate authority. Much is said about " the cost of Planning". So far as the control of private development is concerned, the cost is no more than the cost of the staff engaged upon Planning, since this control is concerned with directing to the appropriate places and securing an appropriate form for development which would in any case take place. Any Planning which is being done competently would, in fact, save a great deal of money, if not for the individual, for society, since the shaping of development to secure compactness, accessibility, the appropriate location of various uses and safety must greatly reduce the cost of many human activities.

Public projects, such as the construction of main roads or the building of a town hall or swimming bath, do of course cost a great deal of money, and they may consist of development which, however desirable, is not absolutely indispensible for the life of the community. For the most part, however, they would, sooner or later, have been carried out, even in the absence of specific Planning proposals, though the existence of such proposals may well emphasise the need for them and accelerate their provision. It seems reason-able therefore to consider them from the point of view of cost in much the same way as private development.

It is worth noting here that, of course, nothing will be done to implement Planning proposals unless some person or persons, private or public, is able and willing to carry out the development proposed. Very detailed Planning proposals which include provision for particular buildings on particular sites are therefore quite often almost meaningless because they have taken no account of the improbability of a developer being found to implement them.

Conversely, the restrictive aspects of Planning proposals designed to prevent unsuitably located land from being built upon or inappropriate uses intruding in a particular area, depend for their success upon the ability and willingness of Planning Authorities to carry out the day-to-day control of develop-ment effectively. Success depends upon the tendering of right advice by Planning officers to their committees, the acceptance of such advice by the committees and, very often, support for those decisions by the Minister on appeal. Some writers on Planning have tended to wave away development control as a rather squalid affair. It is in fact a crucial link in the chain of Planning action. If it breaks, all is lost.

Some people still question the need for Planning, although one would have thought that the consequences of not Planning which lie all around us would provide sufficient answer—the ribbon of dwellings along the by-pass, the traffic jam in nearly every town centre, Peacehaven and many similar anarchic messes.

Planning is needed to prevent intrinsically bad uses of land, such as those just mentioned, but also to prevent the loss of valuable resources, such as woodland, minerals and fertile land, by reason of buildings being erected over them. Such action is needed to combat human folly and greed, but even in a community of saints (in a 20th century industrial society) public Planning action would still be necessary, if not to prevent wrong, at least to co-ordinate the activities of different developing agencies in order to produce a well-articulated whole. It is inconceivable that a satisfactory totality could be brought about without the operation of some definite and established agency for co-ordination. This, of course, would not necessarily have to be the kind of local authority familiar in this country; it could be an *ad hoc* body or even a private agency, provided that this had control sufficiently comprehensive and over a sufficiently large physical area. To allow the free play of econ-omic forces to determine the location of land uses, may, as already suggested, work well enough in a comparatively primitive community where there is no intense pressure on land, but is hardly possible in the circumstances now envisaged. One fact alone makes this certain. Many uses such as public parks, publicly provided schools, sewage works and the like do not earn profits, and in the absence of public Planning are bound to be outbid by profit-earning uses in respect of sites attractive to the latter, and forced on to sites which nobody regards as potentially highly profitable, which has deplorable results.

This leads directly to consideration of the whole complicated problem of compensation and betterment, which, though it has no direct effect upon Planning technique, has so frequently prevented the implementation of Plan-ning proposals that it cannot be ignored as a factor in the operation of Planning. The following discussion is confined to the bare essentials of the problem.

1-3. COMPENSATION AND BETTERMENT

The value of a particular piece of land may be regarded as divisible into two parts; its value for the purpose to which it is already being put, and additional value, often called development value, attributable to the likelihood of its being able to be put to some more profitable use. The most familiar example of this is land which as agricultural land may be worth no more than £100 an acre, but which because of the likelihood that it can be used profitably for building purposes, either immediately, or in the fairly near future, may fetch £1,500 an acre. In this case, its existing use value is £100 per acre, its development value £1,400 per acre.

Planning involves the restriction of use of some land so that its development value cannot be realised, and Planning projects involve the acquisition of privately owned land by the public. There has been an assumption in most times and places that in such circumstances the landowner who suffers loss should be compensated therefor, but from this simple and equitable principle many complications flow.

In the first place, if, as was the case in this country up to 1947, and is so still in many other countries, compensation has to be borne by the particular local authority in whose area lies the land to which restrictions or compulsory acquisition is being applied, it may often be that the areas in which the most stringent planning restrictions are needed, and hence the heaviest burden of compensation occurs, are those where the local authority has least resources to meet the burden, and that the restrictions imposed by no means only benefit local inhabitants but have regional or even national effects. The preservation of green belts around metropolitan areas is an obvious example of this. The remedy for this problem is a simple one. It is to make the burden of planning compensation a national one, and this was provided for in this country in the Town and Country Planning Acts of both 1947 and 1954.

There are complications less easy to deal with. Not only may public action deprive an owner of land or diminish its value to him, but it may also increase the value. The building of a railway, a main road, or a sewer, the provision of a water main, a school or a public park or the removal of detrimental industry are all examples of public actions which are likely to increase the value of land over a greater or lesser adjoining area. If, later, such land needs to be publicly acquired, it seems clear that there is no reason why the public should pay an enhanced price resulting from an increase in the value of the land brought about by public action and in no way due to the efforts of the owner, nor does there seem any reason why compensation for restriction on use should be greater because the development value attaching to the land has been increased by such action. Some would go further and say that when neither compensation for restrictions nor compulsory purchase arise, a levy should be made on the land to enable the public to reap a part at least of the increased land values it has brought about. Such direct levies have been visualised from time to time in legislation, for example in the earlier Planning Acts in this country, including the Town and Country Planning Act of 1932. They have not usually been very successful.

The extent to which such increases or " betterment " ought to be collected by the public is principally a political and financial one; the interest of the Planner is to be able to operate in conditions which enable land to be put to its most suitable use in the public interest without having constantly to consider whether any particular proposals are likely to involve a burden of compensation so crippling that they are unlikely to be implemented for that reason. It is therefore important in this connection to realise that unless some carefully arranged scheme for compensation is devised there is a strong probability that within a given area the total amount paid for compensation will in fact substantially exceed the total loss suffered by the owners compensated.

Consider the town shown in Fig. 1 (i). Within the surrounding cliffs it is assumed that all the land is about equally suitable for development and that the area concerned is sufficiently small for all the land within it to possess an appreciable development value. This is merely a convenient simplification of the situation more generally found where the development value of land gradually decreases as distance from the built-up centre increases, until it becomes negligible, which introduces further complications with which we need not here be concerned.

We have to imagine an energetic and enterprising local authority operating without the benefit of any scheme for coping with the problems of compensation and betterment. Each time the local authority acquires a piece of land it has to pay the full market value, including development value. Each piece of land so acquired reduces the supply of land available for private development, without reducing the demand, since aerodromes, sewage disposal works and cemeteries do nothing to satisfy the demand for land for houses and factories. The market price of land available for development can be expected to rise a little each time the supply is diminished, and eventually the local authority will be paying for land a price quite substantially enhanced by their own laudable efforts in improving the town's facilities.

In the case of a town with more normal topography there will be more land physically suitable for development than is likely to be needed for such purposes, and it may be impossible to forecast with any accuracy which particular pieces of land from the choice available will in fact be selected by intending developers. But landowners, when making claims for compensation will, naturally enough, urge the strong probability that their particular holdings would have been among the land selected for development but for the intervention of Planning restrictions, and will claim correspondingly high losses. It may be very difficult indeed for the authority concerned successfully to contest such arguments.

This was the thesis put forward in the report of the Expert Committee on Compensation and Betterment, known generally as the " Uthwatt Report ", in paragraph 23 of which it was suggested that the total amount of land for which claims for compensation could be made good might well be of the order of four times as much as the land actually likely to be required for development sufficiently soon for it to have an appreciable present value for development purposes. This conclusion has been challenged in some quarters. It has been said that in fact intending developers or land speculators when making bids for the purchase of land take into account the chances that it may never be possible to develop the land profitably. However this may be, it does seem clear that there is bound to be a strong tendency for the over-valuation of compensation in such circumstances, even though it may not reach the proportions assumed by the Uthwatt Committee.

The scheme for the solution of all these problems embodied in the financial provisions of the Town and Country Planning Act, 1947 was in principle simple but was rendered complex by numerous savings, exceptions and modifications. In essence the Act nationalised development value but left existing use value with the owner of land. As compensation for the loss of development value, a sum of £300,000,000 was allocated to meet all claims for loss. There was thus no guarantee that claims other than those by owners of " dead ripe " land and other preferential claims would be met in full, but as it turned out, had the scheme not been repealed, non-preferential claims would have received about 16/- in the £.

The £300,000,000 was to be paid out *in toto* by the 1st July, 1953. Since, under the scheme, landowners were to be compensated for the loss of development value out of the fund, there was normally no payment of compensation to be made for refusal of Planning permission, and compensation for compulsory purchase was limited to existing use value. On the other hand, when Planning permission was given, except for very minor development, the intending developer had to buy back the development value for the loss of which he was to be compensated out of the £300,000,000. This payment was known as a " development charge ". The intention of the Act was that where land

was developed by someone other than the owner entitled to compensation, the developer would pay the owner existing use value only and would pay the development value to the State in the form of development charge. Fig. 1 (ii) indicates the way in which payments and receipts relating to transactions in land were intended to be made.

Unfortunately, it was not made illegal to sell land at more than its existing use value, and the sanctions against doing so were slight and scantily used. In the exceptional conditions of the post-war years landowners were often able to sell land at its full market price, so that the purchaser, who also had to pay development charge, was paying for the development value of the land twice over. It was possible for a landowner to exploit the situation in this way, because, to take the commonest example, the restrictions on prices of new houses were such that while a new house might sell at £1,600, its close pre-war equivalent, on the selling price of which there was no restriction, might fetch £3,000 or more. In these circumstances, the fortunate possessor of a building licence did not worry too much whether he had to pay £10 for the plot of land on which the house was built, which might well be its existing use value, or £150 which might be its full value, including development value. When he realised what had happened and had to pay another £140 in development charge he was likely to grumble, but his grumbling was more often directed at the Government, who imposed what he regarded as a tax, than at the previous owner of the land. This was one of the more potent causes (another was what often seemed to be unimaginatively excessive assessment of development charge, which lent colour to the " tax " theory) which turned public opinion against the 1947 Act scheme and led to the substitution for it of the scheme contained in the Acts of 1953 and 1954.

This is less radical and less simple. Development charge is abolished, as is the once-and-for-all-payment of the £300,000,000 fund. Compensation both for Planning restrictions and compulsory acquisition becomes payable when loss is suffered, and not before, and is limited to any admitted claim on the £300,000,000 fund, plus 1/7 accrued interest, to which, in the case of compulsory acquisition, existing use value is of course added. Furthermore, compensation is not payable for what has been called " good neighbour " restrictions, nor for restriction of development to one profitable use rather than another. If the erection of shops is refused but houses would be permitted, then no compensation is payable, for example. In general, in fact, compensation is only payable where the development of land is prevented rather than restricted, and since compensation is restricted to land in respect of which there was an admitted claim under the 1947 Act, no compensation is payable for prevention of building on land so remote from existing development that no claim for loss of development value could have been substantiated in 1947. Compensation for compulsory purchase is limited in the same way.

Where land is sold privately there is no limitation, direct or indirect, imposed by the Act on the price charged, which leaves the vendor free to reap the full market value of the land which in many areas has risen enormously since 1948, partly as a result of depreciation in the purchasing value of the pound, partly as a result of greatly increased effective demand for houses

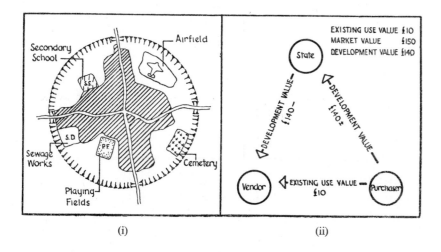

(i) (ii)

FIG. 1 (i) Successive public acquisitions in a town with limited room for growth diminish the supply of land for houses and other building uses without reducing the demand for it, and hence the price of land rises with each acquisition.

(ii) The assumptions upon which the financial provisions of the Town and Country Planning Act, 1947 were based. Upon the sale of a piece of land for development the transactions shown above were supposed to take place, leaving all parties in the same financial position as they would have been but for the passing of the Act, but making the payment of compensation a national charge, and so enabling Planning to be carried out without concern for the values of particular areas of land.

but largely as a result of the redistribution of land values brought about by Development Plans. This is the principal difference between the 1947 and 1954 schemes. The former, by means of the development charge (which could be raised above 1947 development value where an increase had occurred meanwhile) reaped for the public all increases in land values since 1947; the latter does so only where Planning restrictions or public acquisition are involved.

On the other hand the 1947 scheme provided for compensation in *all* cases where an owner was prevented from reaping development value; the 1954 scheme only compensates him for restrictions more onerous than those of the " good neighbour " type.

The merits of the 1954 scheme are that no very large payment, with possible inflationary effects, is made at any one time; payment for loss is only made when loss is actually suffered, and there is, as noted, no compensation for restrictions designed to secure reasonable disposition of land uses in relation to each other. The 1947 Act scheme did not possess any of these advantages.

The disadvantages of the 1954 scheme, though less definite, are however probably more serious. In the first place, it becomes financially disadvantageous for a landowner to be refused permission. Under the 1947 Act it made no difference to him unless he went in for the kind of exploitation mentioned above, and it is very likely that the easing of housing shortages would have made it no longer possible to do this within a few years. Since a landowner is now financially aggrieved by refusal of planning permission it is all too possible that Planning policy may in particular cases be distorted by sympathy for individuals, which is the very thing that any comprehensive scheme of compensation and betterment ought to avoid.

It seems, too, a bad principle that where permission for development is refused, or development is undertaken by public bodies, the betterment which has accrued since 1947 should be taken by the public, but that where private development takes place, the public reaps no betterment. Surely all should forfeit betterment, or all should reap it.

If the 1954 Act substituted a rather involved and weak Conservative solution to the problem for a strong and simple, if slightly crude, Labour solution, the Town and Country Planning Act of 1959 must be regarded as a singularly disastrous attempt to improve the former. Subject to certain provisoes, it restores full market value as the basis of compensation for compulsory purchase of land, and casts the burden of paying for the difference between 1948 value and current value upon the acquiring authority. The reasoning behind this deplorable measure is confused; it seems to stem from the assumption that an owner whose land is acquired compulsorily is at a disadvantage in comparison with the owner who is refused permission to develop but is able to keep his land and so should be more fully compensated. There is no logical basis for this view.

The results of the 1959 Act and of its successor the Land Compensation Act of 1961, which substantially re-enacts its provisions, have been regrettable on at least three counts:

(1) A great deal of money which should have gone into the public purse has gone into private purses.

(2) In numerous cases acquiring authorities have abandoned sites reserved for public open spaces in Development Plans, because of the great additional cost involved, while it is now common form to place both schools and open spaces on the outskirts of towns, where land may be expected to be cheaper, instead of in the positions which Planning requirements suggest to be the best in the interests of accessibility. The avoidance of such a state of affairs is one of the most important reasons for ensuring that there is a sound system for dealing with the compensation-betterment problem.

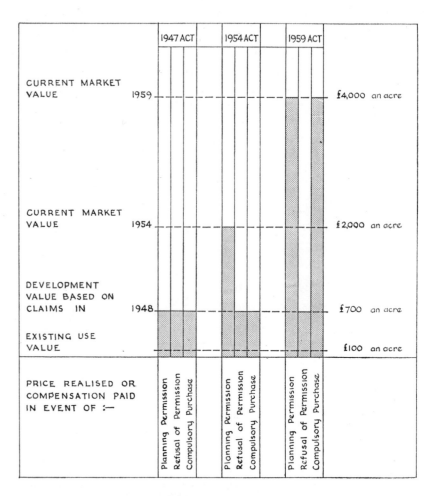

Fig. 2. Comparison of the basis of compensation under successive Planning Acts.

(3)   The basis of compensation is current market value subject to the provisions of any development plan in force, and owners have to obtain a "certificate of alternative development" before claiming compensation. This certificate is, essentially, the answer to the question: "For what purpose would this land be allocated if it were not required for a public purpose?"   Within the general built-up area of a town the answer must usually be "residential" or "industrial" but near the edge of a town it becomes debatable.   It is sometimes possible, in the case of a secondary school site, for example, for the Local Planning Authority to say with some show of reason that if the site had not been required for secondary school purposes it would not have been allocated for any development at all but would have been left as "white land" or even included in a green belt, thus limiting compensation to 1947 Act claim levels.   In order to reinforce such arguments Green Belt notations have therefore often been applied to land which it is grotesquely inappropriate to describe as being part of a Green Belt.

This practice breeds public suspicion of the good faith of local authorities, and leads to distrust and dislike of Planning.   It is deplorable that the Ministry has seemed, in decisions on appeals, to support it.

1-4.   FUTURE OPPORTUNITIES

One of the greatest difficulties in deciding Planning policy is to distinguish between the physically and economically practicable and the psychologically, legally, and administratively practicable.   There are many desirable Planning activities which do not involve any great technical difficulty, but which nevertheless do not get carried out, simply because it is impossible to secure agreement, or even sufficient initiative, on the part of the agencies concerned. There is a great difference between the technical problems of how to apply human effort in the field of land development in the best way and that of securing administrative and economic organisation of a kind which allows the effort to be made.

Since the enormous development of technology of all kinds during the war it has been apparent that we were standing on the brink of a new technological revolution, which would in turn bring about a second industrial revolution. During the last two or three years the rate of technological progress has increased sharply.   The physical possibilities which confront the human race, are, as almost every politician has wearisomely reiterated, practically limitless. Political, administrative and economic organisation has shown no comparable advance.   Ignoring all the appalling international failures of understanding and the menace of annihilation which confronts mankind, and taking an optimistic, domestic view, it is still hardly possible to say more than that the graph of administrative progress in this country is a straight line inclined in a very slightly upward direction.

This is highly unsatisfactory.   Although knowledge about Planning is, by scientific standards, rudimentary, it is still so far ahead of the opportunites available for using it that one sometimes feels that it would be better to call a halt to technical Planning research for a fairly long time, and for efforts to be concentrated upon improvement in administrative arrangements.

It is my personal view that the domestic and the world situations are closely linked, and that if humanity is to survive the nuclear menace, which will surely be settled one way or the other within a comparatively few years, it is likely to survive it gloriously and to proceed to a fulfilment of technological possibilities greater than it is easily possible to imagine.   It seems certain that if this comes about it must inevitably be accompanied by an enormously rapid advance in social organisation to enable technological resources to be adequately deployed.

This involves something of fundamental importance to Planning thought and Planning method.   A great deal of the material in this book deals with policies which are unattainable at the present level of organisation.   This is particularly so in the field of Regional Planning.   Although a good deal of the reorganisation involved in pursuing such policies is also at the time of writing physically unattainable except over a very long period, the full application of technological ingenuity and inventiveness to building and road construction, combined with a reorganisation of political and administrative processes designed to secure full play for the former, could easily increase both the scope and speed of physical reconstruction to a prodigious extent.

If we were able to multiply the productivity of building labour several times and also to secure the land needed for comprehensively planned development and redevelopment immediately and without considerations of price intervening, the remotely impracticable would become the immediately practicable in many cases.

We should be able to Plan with the needs of true economy uppermost. We should be employing the inventions of technology and the ingenuity of designers within a proper framework instead of within a cramped and twisted framework imposed by prejudice and defective economics.

But even if these very desirable changes came about we should still be unable to take full advantage of them unless we had also meanwhile vastly improved the general level of competence in applying Planning techniques, and, in many cases, the techniques themselves.   On the whole, only a small proportion of existing knowledge about Planning is applied by Local Planning Authorities or by the Ministry of Housing and Local Government; still less are effective steps taken to accumulate the necessary information and devise appropriate techniques to deal with the alarming number of important Planning matters concerning which information and technique are gravely deficient.

Above all, it is a matter of failing to devote sufficient resources to a subject of great public importance.   (It was calculated that the cost of Planning administration in Kent for the 10 years ending in 1959 averaged annually the product of a $1\frac{1}{4}$d. rate or $0 \cdot 15$ per cent of the value of development undertaken in the county during the same period, taking account only of development the value of which could be readily ascertained).   Thorough and successful land use planning can immensely increase national prosperity and happiness but needs resources in brains and equipment to be devoted to it much greater than at present, though still insignificant in relation to the benefits to be secured.

For example there can be little doubt but that nearly every town plan should be subjected to thorough traffic forecast analysis, the preparation of Planning balance sheets on the lines suggested by Dr. N. Lichfield and, as part of these, the drawing up of "food replacement" calculations as suggested by Dr. G. P. Wibberley. (Both of these are described elsewhere in this book.) To use these techniques with any thoroughness frequently involves the comparison of innumerable different arrangements of roads, land use patterns and of alternative sites for new development. Such comparison can only be done with the aid of electronic computers specially programmed for the purpose. These should by now, if Planning were treated with appropriate thoroughness, be in use by every Local Planning Authority; they are not.

The consideration of Planning problems does not, on the whole, at any level receive, either quantitatively or qualitatively, anything like adequate attention. Perfunctoriness and sheer inferior thinking are regrettably prevalent. A recent example within my own experience well illustrates the point, as well as indicating a quite alarming lack of liaison between adjoining local authorities. The particular circumstances of the case produced exceptional and startling evidence of inefficiency of a kind which flourishes less dramatically most of the time in many places.

The developed area of a fair sized but not gigantic town fell within the boundaries of no fewer than three Local Planning Authorities, and was covered by four town maps. All the town maps were old, and manifestly out of date, and one of them was (? illegally) out of print. None of the Local Planning Authorities concerned seemed to have considered the Planning of the town as a whole, and certainly no map had been drawn up showing the proposals of all the four Town Maps, and thus their total effect.

An application to develop some 50 acres of land shown as "white" on one of the Town Maps had been refused permission, principally on the grounds that the land had not been allocated for development. An appeal was made, and an attempt made on behalf of the appellant to do what the Local Planning Authorities concerned should have already done themselves, namely to determine the adequacy of the land allocated for development in the light of the Planned population for the town stated in the relevant Development Plans and to assess the relative suitability for development of various areas of land not allocated for development should it appear that more was needed. This was a difficult task because of the lack of information available but there seemed to be a deficiency of at least 1,000 acres in the land allocated for development and the appeal site, on the available evidence, appeared to rank very high as land suitable to make good this deficiency.

At the hearing, (attended by only one of the three Local Planning Authorities affected) no serious effort was made to rebut the appellants' evidence, and no alternative assessment of the town's land needs was put forward but the inspector recommended that the appeal should be dismissed, expressing himself as not being convinced by the appellants' evidence and unable to assess its accuracy. The wording of his report made it clear that he had not troubled to give any serious thought to the appellants' case. He made no suggestion that there might be anything amiss with the administration of Planning in the area concerned; nor did the Minister, who accepted his recommendation. It is hardly possible for effective Planning to take place in an atmosphere of official apathy as stifling as this.

The L.C.C.'s Hook New Town project, published in "The Planning of a New Town" (Tiranti, 1961) is certainly no example of apathy or laziness; it is full of vigour and enthusiasm. Unhappily it is an almost ideal example of illogical thinking. In relation especially to the design for the Plan as a whole, totally fallacious arguments are used in profusion to justify a particular theory of design. While it is disturbing that enthusiasm should so distort reasoning this is to some extent pardonable on the part of the authors. What is much more disturbing is that the frequently quite ludicrous ideas about Town Master Plan design advanced in "The Planning of a New Town" have received no general condemnation at the hands of the Planning profession. The reason for this, I fear, is that although the design of Master Plans for towns is the central subject matter of Town and Country Planning it receives at present very little serious attention because the procedure for the preparation and approval of Town Maps is so cumbersome, and the prospect of carrying out the extensive redevelopment needed to bring about any appreciable change in the basic structure of a town has, until recently, seemed so remote that discouragement has diverted attention. In point of fact most of the operative Town Maps in this country represent work carried out in the late 1940's and early 50's and are, even so, not very enterprising because of reluctance to include anything which might attract heavy compensation.

If Planning is to be successful this will have to change rapidly, for it is quite impossible to carry out sound detailed Planning within an unsound and outmoded framework.

Although it may often be fatal, in Planning, to set one's sights too high, because the attempt to implement an impracticably perfectionist Plan may well produce almost total failure—a result much inferior to the successful implementation of a less ambitious plan, it is also fatal to set sights much too low. Almost all current Town Maps may fairly be said to represent sights set much too low.

However, it is encouraging to reflect that, although the creation of Planned new towns is an activity as old as civilisation, the attempt at comprehensive reshaping of existing towns to accord with current and envisaged future needs is a completely new activity, a phenomenon which has only appeared since the Second World War, for no previous Planning legislation or machinery attempted nearly as much. It is hardly surprising if this brave endeavour does not meet with complete and immediate success, though this reflection ought not to make us relax our efforts or curb our dissatisfaction.

The results to be expected from really thorough, comprehensive physical Planning, successfully achieved, have seldom been expressed, although every Town Planner must have a vision, however vague, of what he is trying to work for. It seems, therefore, worthwhile to try to set out a personal picture of the realised objective, for this may assist in some measure to connect the mass of only slenderly related topics dealt with in this book.

Agricultural land should be entirely devoted to agriculture; though changing agricultural methods and requirements may very well mean a less picturesque appearance than that of the traditional English farming country-side, one need not fear they will bring about unsightliness, provided that the same requirements of good design and siting are applied to agricultural buildings and appurtenances as are sought to be applied at present to other kinds of buildings. Wild country should remain wild country, a place of refreshment for the human spirit, where indigenous plant and animal species can flourish and contribute their own part to the essence and beauty of the country. There have to be non-agricultural uses in the countryside, and in a densely populated country in modern times it is unfortunately unavoidable that they shall make an appreciable impact. If they cannot be hidden, they should be superbly designed and proclaim themselves boldly, as in the case of dams and viaducts. If they can be hidden they should be hidden by means of actual concealment in folds of the ground, or camouflaging by means of skilful landscaping, or both. Such unavoidable intrusions should, further-more, be brought together and localised as far as possible, rather than scattered about pell-mell.

The country needs to be traversed by an adequate system of roads, well engineered, well designed as to details such as bridges and so on, and well landscaped. It ought to be possible, once having reached a main road, to travel from any town in the country to any other without going through a built-up area, an objective which may seem wildly idealistic at the present time but which is surely a bare necessity if anything approaching the full potentiality of the motor vehicle is to be realised.

The countryside is punctuated—pretty frequently punctuated in areas of high occupation—by towns and villages of various sizes, and the most im-portant thing, looking at them from the outside, is that they should have clear, clean edges, without peripheral clutter at their approaches and deliberately designed silhouettes.

Not only should one be able to drive about the country without entering built-up areas, but one should be able to drive right to the heart of a town, or to any of its principal component parts, along roads not congested and made dangerous by riparian accesses and uncontrolled intersections with minor roads. This, too, may seem idealistic but it is a basic requirement for good Town Planning.

The most important requirement for a town is that it should be able to provide employment for all its own workers, and on the other hand should not need to import workers from elsewhere. This is what is meant by "balancing population and employment", and its attainment means nothing less than the conquest of one of the most cruelly repressive and widespread of contemporary social ills—the mass journey to work over long distances. This, of course is not so much a matter of physical planning as of wisely governed economic policy, but this and physical planning need to go hand in hand.

The town ought to have a clear structure: a pattern of uses and com-munication routes designed for maximum accessibility and minimum congestion and danger, in which uses whose juxtaposition, such as those of homes and open spaces, improves living conditions are placed together, and those, such as industry and homes, where the reverse applies, well separated.

The town centre, places of employment, schools, playing fields and subsidiary centres for shopping and other facilities need to be located, designed and related in such a way as to meet fully and conveniently the daily needs of their users. An important element in this, of course, is a well articulated minor road system within the general framework of the major roads.

A well-designed system of main roads will in itself have avoided gross congestion in the town centre, but the present trend towards providing pedestrian precincts, in particular for the shopping parts of the town centre, should be persisted with and made general so that the mutually incompatible activities of shop gazing and traffic avoidance are kept apart.

Playing fields need to be provided so that all who wish to play outdoor games can have a reasonable opportunity for doing so without exhaustingly long journeys, and the same applies to every other kind of open space, from the formal flower garden to sit in for the odd half-hour to the wild landscaped park.

Great advances have been made in the design of industrial areas, and if every industrial area came up to the standard of those created in the New Towns, little more could be asked for.

The prerequisite of the residential area is that it should contain homes of all kinds in such proportions that every family has a good chance of securing a home of the size and kind it wants, whether flat, house or bungalow, with outdoor space of the size and kind it wants, whether individual private garden, common garden, or merely drying space.

These, in barest outline, are the functional needs of the good town. Visually, it is necessary that every building should be well designed, not only as regards its own intrinsic properties, but in relation to the buildings and other objects seen with it, the new respecting and blending with everything of merit in the existing without in the process losing its own vigour and originality.

But it is not only buildings which make up the urban scene. There are other elements, both vertical and horizontal: trees and bushes, gates, walls, fences, hedges, pillar boxes, road names and traffic signs and the whole "floor" of the area, both soft and hard, in varying colours and textures. The proper design and integration of these items is usually almost totally neglected, but they are of great importance in contributing to the whole resultant visual effect.

Everything I have said about the town applies, of course, with some modification, to the village.

Nowhere has the kind of comprehensive Planning at all levels which I have just sketched been applied with sufficient thoroughness for the Planning to show through the non-planning strongly enough to give the predominant impression. Even in a New Town, the non-planning has usually so far been strong enough substantially to spoil the effect of the Planning, so that to some extent Planning remains an act of faith, a hope of unrealised possibilities. Its full achievement would be an event of colossal importance and hopeful-ness in the history of the world; it would give such sheer joy to all who saw it that no civilised country would thereafter remain content until it had secured similar conditions for itself.

This is a large claim, but I do not believe it to be overstated. Consider what is probably the finest piece of comprehensive Planning in this country, tiny though it is, namely the shopping core of the centre of Stevenage New Town. Imagine the same degree of consideration for functional and architectural design and the same attention to detail applied to the whole of a region. Think of a region where *all* the main roads were as efficient and as beautifully detailed as the best of the German Autobahnen. Think of *all* residential development being as good as the best in the New Towns, or Roehampton. Think of every area of public open space being as good as the Hampstead Heath extension or Didsbury Park, Manchester, or the parkway approach to Brighton from London. Think of as many more examples as you can of what you regard as admirably designed development, then think of the effect of that level of quality existing generally and you may well agree with me.

CHAPTER 2

THE CONTINUITY OF THE PLANNING PROCESS AND THE PLANNER'S SKILLS

2-1. CONTINUITY

THERE MIGHT POSSIBLY be Planning, in our sense of the word, of sub-continental regions as a whole, or of countries. As yet Planning has hardly been applied in a full sense to any larger unit than the county. But in order to illustrate the thesis that follows, that of the continuity of Planning from the broadest process to the most detailed, it is necessary at least to suggest what might be applied in national Planning if it were undertaken.

Although we have no national Plan as such in this country, embodied in a coherent series of maps, diagrams and written statements, there is a somewhat shadowy national Planning policy of which plans for trunk road improvements, policy on the distribution of industry and adumbrations of policy on such matters as density and the relief of metropolitan congestion form parts. It is at least arguable that it would be beneficial to collate these into a single set of documents comprising an outline national land use Plan, if only because doing this would suggest the need for further development of policy and might easily reveal discrepancies between the aims of the different ministries primarily responsible for various aspects.

It is important to stress here that at this very general level the contribution of the Planner, in our sense, would necessarily be somewhat limited. Many of the decisions to be incorporated in such a Plan would have to be made primarily on the advice of economists and geographers, and would be based on economic considerations far removed from land use, the determination of which would be the last link in a fairly long chain.

At this stage the role of the Planner might well be limited to the collation of information and its expression in graphic form, and to tendering advice upon the land use implications, favourable and unfavourable, of various alternative policies relating to the distribution of industry, the arrangement of the national transport network, the exploitation of natural resources and the location of power generators and reservoirs.

At the regional Planning level the Planner comes into his own to a much greater extent. Regional Planning, sensibly defined, involves proposals for the distribution of population and industry, the location of main transport routes, the distribution of rural services and the location of large non-agricultural uses in open country to a greater degree of detail than would be comprehended in a national Plan. These proposals should fit in with the requirements of such a Plan, but still be confined to very broad decisions as to quantities and locations rather than the choice of particular sites for particular uses.

It is reasonable to suggest that much of this work falls within the province of the economic geographer, but that considerable knowledge of town Planning technique is also necessary in order to avoid, for example, the selection of communities for considerable expansion which are not in fact capable of absorbing such expansion satisfactorily. It is here the Planner's synoptic function, his ability to weigh, and discover a satisfactory resultant of, the physical, economic and social factors involved, comes into play.

Here then is the first clear indication of that strong connection between the various stages of the Planning process which I believe to be fundamental to any real understanding of Planning as an art and a science. The essence of this is that at any given stage in the Planning process, except at the first and the last, it is necessary not only to look at the particular job in hand but to look back to the requirements imposed by some more comprehensive Plan covering a larger area, to interpret these requirements intelligently for the immediate task and also to look forward to the next stage in the Planning process, the next more detailed stage, so that the proposals currently being drawn up shall be so arranged as to allow detail to be filled in satisfactorily.

This process of looking simultaneously backwards and forwards is perhaps most fully exemplified at the next stage, of which the most typical instance is the preparation of a town Plan. At this stage a new factor has to be taken into consideration; the need for remedial measures to heal the town's sickness, whether of congestion, maldistribution of land uses, defective road system, or all three. In preparing the Plan it is necessary to ensure not only that appropriate amounts of land are allocated to residential and ancillary uses and industry to fit in with proposals in the regional Plan for the distribution of population and industry, and to rectify congestion and shortages in existing allocations, but to ensure that the shapes and locations of these areas are such that, at the next more detailed stage, a good example of which is the neighbourhood plan at a scale of perhaps 1/2,500, a well arranged road skeleton and a satisfactorily related system of minor service centres and open spaces can be designed. It is seldom practicable at the stage of preparing the town Plan to do all the detailed work involved in preparing neighbourhood Plans and to generalise these back as it were, into a town Plan, although it would no doubt ideally be desirable to do this. This I have found is a point of particular difficulty to students, who often find themselves at sea when asked to produce a town Plan without being given time to work out fully detailed designs for its various parts.

The neighbourhood Plan and others belonging to the same stage—the village Plan and the town centre and industrial area Plans—having been prepared, the final stage in the Planning process is the actual location and design of individual buildings and groups of buildings, and the provision of minor roads to serve them. It is a matter of argument at what precise point the proper boundary between Planning and architecture, landscape architecture and civil engineering should be drawn, but it is obvious that the more detailed the proposals being considered the more predominant become the roles of these specialisms.

Another aspect of this detailed stage of the process is of course the application of development control to problems involving the use of land which are more detailed than can be dealt with in a development Plan of even the most detailed kind.

Most people would probably agree that it is reasonable to give predominance to the economist and geographer at the most general Planning level and to the architect and other specialists at the most detailed level, but there is far from general agreement about what seems to me an equally obvious fact, namely the need at the intermediate levels, particularly at the town Plan level, for the predominance of the town Planner. The work involved at this stage is not comprehended to any appreciable extent by any of the specialists mentioned, being something entirely different in kind and not merely in degree. One sometimes hears of a town Plan having an " architectural " quality or being an " engineers' plan ". Rightly regarded, such Plans, it seems to me, merely give evidence of the insufficient scope or balance of their author's knowledge and experience.

2-2. SKILLS

The qualifications necessary for those engaged in the practice of Town and Country Planning have long been a matter of controversy. In the earliest days of Planning in this country the men engaged in it were of two main types: first, those who had no special technical knowledge but a great interest in the subject, derived usually from a zeal for social reform, and, second, technical men, such as architects, engineers and surveyors, whose interest sprang mainly from their professional activities. As time went on, Planning began gradually to be recognised as a semi-independent profession. The Town Planning Institute was formed, and qualifying examinations for Corporate Membership were devised, but, partly because of the origins of the profession, partly because of the uncertain economic future of those engaged whole-time in it, until very recently the great majority of Planners have also been either architects, civil or municipal engineers or chartered surveyors. This tendency was strengthened by the fact that until very recently examinations of the Town Planning Institute were conducted by a Joint Board with members drawn from the above professions. As the result of the grant of a Royal Charter to the Town Planning Institute, the Joint Board was dissolved, and the Institute now conducts its own examinations.

Up to the late war, no one could be quite sure that the Planning profession was viable; there seemed to be a distinct chance that the vagaries of economic or political fortune might blow it into oblivion. Young men, therefore, even though they might decide at a very early stage in their careers that they wanted to be Planners, usually took the examinations of one of the so-called basic professions of architecture, engineering or surveying before proceeding to qualify for Corporate Membership of the Town Planning Institute by taking the Joint Board Final Examination, a procedure which not only provided them with an alternate means of earning a livelihood if Planning failed them, but also exempted them from the Intermediate Examination of the Town Planning Institute. This precautionary measure has, in some quarters, been elevated into a principle, and plenty of architects, surveyors and engineers are to be found who roundly declare that the only appropriate entry into Planning is by practice and qualification in their own particular profession.

However, in the late thirties an increasing number of people were appearing on the scene who had not taken the conventional line but who, braving the possible economic consequences, had decided to be Planners first, last and all the time, and had proceeded to Corporate Membership of the Town Planning Institute via its Intermediate Examination. Some of these, who had risen from the ranks of draughtsmen and clerks, were able to take advantage of the exemption from the Intermediate Examination given until recently to those over 35 years of age and possessing practical planning experience. Their practical training had usually been in a local authority office or with a planning consultant, or both.

Preparation for Planning examinations was varied. Many, probably the majority, studied by means of correspondence courses, and found that these, reinforced by office experience, enabled them to meet the then somewhat less stringent requirements of the Institute and Joint Board examinations. Others took the Diploma Courses, giving exemption from the Joint Board examination, offered by Universities and other bodies (but few of these were open to candidates who had not already qualified in a basic profession), while a few relied on their own undirected reading.

Since the war the Universities of Durham and Manchester have instituted five-year Honours Degree courses in Planning,[1] which claim to provide a comprehensive undergraduate education for the Planner, and which give graduates a qualification of higher status than a diploma, which was the only one previously available to those who wished to concentrate on Planning from the start.

The claims of graduates in geography, economics and some other subjects to be entitled to take the shorter post-graduate courses available to members of the basic professions and to be exempt from the Intermediate Examination of the Town Planning Institute have now been met, while increasing numbers of students without a degree or a qualification in one of the basic professions take the Intermediate Examination and then proceed to a part-time Diploma course. Their numbers seem likely to increase, since passing the Final Examination of the Town Planning Institute by correspondence course or independent study has been, since the adoption in 1950 of a new syllabus, extremely arduous.

Yet others take part-time preliminary and certificate courses at a recognised school, success in which secures entry to a Diploma course.

The increased importance of Town and Country Planning led to the appointment in May, 1948, of a Committee under the Chairmanship of Sir George Schuster, with the following terms of reference: " To take account of the present and prospective scope of Town and Country Planning and to consider and report what qualifications are necessary or desirable for persons engaged in it and to make any recommendations affecting those persons which appear to the Committee to be relevant." The Committee's report was presented in September, 1950. Its recommendations are somewhat diffuse, and thus not easy to summarise. The Committee considered that Town and Country Planning included two principal activities, synthesis and design, and

---

[1] These have recently, and perhaps only temporarily, been reduced to four years.

that the second was subsidiary to the first. It defined " design " as " setting out on a drawing board a pattern of physical features", and contrasted this with " the creation of a synthesis " (although, in fact, the creation of such a synthesis would appear to differ from other kinds of design only in the magnitude of its subject-matter, while design, even as defined by the Committee, certainly includes synthesis). Nevertheless, the Committee appeared to think that this synthesis was more of an administrative than a design process, and went so far as to express the view that a chief planning officer need not be skilled in design, but must merely be capable of appreciating good design.

The Committee did not come down heavily in favour of any particular method of training for the Planner, except to express a strong preference for Planners to have received a University education. It held the view that Planning should be undertaken as a post-graduate rather than an undergraduate study, though it noted the full-time undergraduate courses begun by Durham and Manchester with benevolent if cautious neutrality. It did not exclude qualification in one of the so-called basic professions, particularly if taken as a University study, as a preliminary to post-graduate Planning study, but, equally, did not express preference for them or for any one of them compared with any other course of study.

The Committee cast a somewhat distasteful look upon preparation for qualification by means of correspondence courses, but evidently recognised that the existing geographical distribution of Planning schools made it certain that correspondence courses would have to provide the training for a fair number of potential Planners for many years to come. The principal effect of the Schuster Report has been to make entry into the Planning profession easier for geographers and economists.

Let us now turn to an impartial consideration of the subjects a knowledge of which is necessary for a competent Planner. It has often been said that the complete Planner requires a knowledge of so many subjects that it is quite impossible for any one person to compass them all, but I do not believe that it is impossible at least to approach within striking distance of such an ideal. Even less do I accept the notion sometimes heard that the comprehensive training of a Planner as such is futile, and that, *faute de mieux*, initial training and experience in one of the basic professions, giving a thorough grounding in one of the subjects related to Planning, is the best course to pursue, with subsequent specialisation in Planning.

It is not often possible in the course of general professional conversation with a Planner of experience and standing to tell from which, if any, of the basic professions he has sprung. He has become a Planner, indistinguishable as regards the content of his knowledge from others of comparable experience in the profession, whatever their origins, and this has not usually occurred through assimilation of a carefully prepared course of instruction, but in the course of his day-to-day duties, from which he has acquired a working knowledge of the skills most directly relevant to the work of the Planner; most of these skills will be quite outside the scope of his basic qualification. If, as I contend, so rough and ready, casual and unorganised a method of acquiring a large body of diversified knowledge has proved reasonably successful it seems likely that carefully organised courses of instruction

directed to the same end and supplemented by similar experience ought to give even better results.

Certainly, study and practice as an architect, surveyor or engineer will teach a man a great deal which it is useful for him, as a Planner, to know, but it will also teach him even more which is of no discernible use at all for such purposes, and the time spent in acquiring it could have been much better spent in learning about Planning. For example, a junior assistant with a firm of chartered surveyors may learn much about housing, social conditions and building construction which will help in his Planning work from the time he spends collecting rents and carrying out surveys of dilapidations, but it seems almost certain that the useful knowledge thus acquired could better have been compressed into a much smaller space of time and some of the remainder at least spent in acquiring, for example, an appreciation of the visual qualities of buildings, which is indispensable to the Planner, and seldom learnt through the work of a chartered surveyor. One could readily give similar examples in the case of the other basic professions.

The emphasis of what may be termed the basic profession school of thought seems to be on the need for the Planner to have acquired practical experience and practical, rather than theoretical, knowledge, and this school might well reply to the previous sentence that it is impossible to avoid administering a good deal of chaff with the grain. But in preliminary training for Planning the grain should bear a higher proportion to the chaff than is actually the case.

But the main weakness in the basic profession case is that it assumes Planning to be a specialisation, something related to but narrower than each of the basic professions. This is almost self-evidently not so, as witness the " jack of all trades and master of none " accusation often directed at Planners, which at least recognises the wide scope of the subject, even if its deductions are erroneous. In fact, the scope of Planning is a great deal wider than architecture, engineering or surveying, and none of the three can cast light upon more than a very small part of the Planning field; it is they which are the specialisms. Since almost every educational course proceeds from the general to the more specific, it is difficult to think that in the case of Planning the opposite is desirable.

At the time of writing (Autumn, 1963) a good deal of discussion is going on concerning the need for " generalists " and " specialists " within the Planning profession. Although this may well prove to be an ephemeral topic it has created a good deal of confusion, and raises some matters of considerable importance, so some attempt at clarification may be desirable.

As has already been suggested, the economist and the geographer have, by virtue of their initial training, a special knowledge of much of the subject matter of regional planning. One might therefore expect such people, when qualified as Planners, to tend to seek and be appointed to posts in which the majority of the work will be concerned with the regional aspects of Planning rather than with, for example, detailed residential layouts. Conversely, one would expect Planners who had originally qualified in architecture to tend to be employed in work dealing more with the detailed than with the broad aspects of Planning. But this does not in the least mean that a Planning department can appropriately be staffed wholly or even mainly with specialists. For one thing, neither the preparation of town Plans nor the bulk of the work involved in administering development control relates to any appreciable extent to the subject-matter of any recognised discipline other than that of Planning itself but also, almost all senior Planning posts require a knowledge and experience of the entire field of Planning.

It is essential that the great majority of entrants into the Planning profession should have been trained as generalists, otherwise a very large proportion of the necessary work will not be done as well as it should be. To this end, it is therefore desirable that Planning schools should principally offer courses which will provide a general training in Planning, even though some may, properly enough, place particular emphasis on one or more branches of the subject and each, it is to be hoped, will have its own specialities which give it distinctive character.

Nevertheless there is undoubtedly a need for trained specialists to work on Planning. These fall into two categories whose functions are in principle quite distinct though they are easily and frequently confused.

There is, first, the man who, by taste and aptitude, is intensely interested in part of the field of Planning but comparatively uninterested in the remainder. An obvious example of this class is the architect who wishes to devote himself to the detailed design of town centres and residential areas but who has neither the desire nor the ability to concern himself with town or regional Planning. At the present time in this country there is certainly no lack of posts for anyone trained in detailed planning only, yet, as things stand, there is no academic or professional means by which he can secure recognition of his competence short of passing the final examination of the Town Planning Institute or obtaining a Degree or Diploma of a recognised Planning school.

It would be quite wrong to accord corporate membership of the Town Planning Institute and the right to use the designation " Chartered Town Planner " to anyone who had not taken a qualifying examination of a broad kind : medical specialists rightly have to qualify first as general practitioners, so that some special course leading to a special qualification not entitling its holders to such a designation seems called for. This would enable the genuine specialist to secure recognition without having to be led unwillingly through masses of material irrelevant to his needs and alien to his temperament.

The second class of specialist is quite different; the man whose knowledge and skill is important to the assembly of the necessary data for the preparation of Planning proposals, and for whom there may be a post in at any rate the larger Planning department, but who need not have any substantial knowledge of Planning in order to make his contribution. There is really no problem here; such people need no more than their own specialist qualifications, with perhaps some quite elementary familiarisation course to help them to understand the scope of Planning and the relevance of their contributions. Sociologists and statisticians are obvious examples of specialists of these kinds.

What I have said in the last two paragraphs does not of course imply that architects on the one hand or sociologists and statisticians on the other cannot become perfectly good Planners if they wish to do so and take an ordinary Planning course, indeed they are no better and no worse equipped to do so than anyone else. The point I wish to make clear is that they can effectively contribute to the Planning process as specialists without, in the case of the architect, acquiring a full qualification or, in the case of the economist or statistician, without taking any Planning course.

Planning is concerned with land; all information concerning land, its shape, fertility, appearance and value, is of direct interest to the Planner. This includes geographical, economic and visual matters, and these are the three main divisions which appear and re-appear in all the subjects involved, with the addition of a fourth, the social aspect, which is mingled with, but distinguishable from, the economic aspect. Sir William Holford, in his Inaugural Lecture, delivered at University College, London in 1948, says . . . " we want people with a broad cultural background, able to understand the point of view of scientist and humanist, and interested in society at all levels. That is easy to say, and it is too general a statement to be of much value. Suppose we break up this cultural activity, prismatically, into its components. From left to right there will be a succession of columns or activities, each fusing imperceptibly into its neighbour, but each distinguished as a separate colour in the spectrum. Out of the whole spread or range of activities let us take two as representing the subject we are discussing—town and country planning. I will call one column Administration and the other Technical Planning and Design. Their boundaries touch, and at the margin it takes a spectroscope to measure where one ends and the other begins; yet in the centre of their columns they are distinctive and different. To the right of the administration column are activities of a colour still further removed from design. They include other types of administration and management, economic planning, political science, government and law.

" To the left of the technical planning columns are the scientific and research activities—and architecture and civil engineering—a long list ranging through the applied and natural sciences and specialist technologies. They include statistical method, social survey, demography, many branches of geography and surveying (including photogrammetry), economic theory, agriculture and agricultural biology, horticulture, forestry, hygiene, building construction and traffic engineering.

" These four columns represent the essential and the contributory elements of town and country planning."

This illustrates extraordinarily well the relationship between the various activities connected with the Planning process. A slightly different way of looking at the matter is given in Fig. 3 (i), which shows the relation of Planning as the central subject to all the allied activities which contribute to it and to some of which it, in turn contributes and in Fig. 3 (ii) which distinguishes between those huge subjects, such as sociology, economics and geography, even bigger in their scope than Planning, from which relatively small parts can be taken for use in the service of Planning, and those narrower specialisms such as architecture and civil engineering, which are exercised within the general framework of Planning, the limitations and requirements of which need to be studied and allowed for in framing Planning proposals.

Before going on to discuss the contribution to Planning knowledge made by various specialisms it will be well to examine and dispose of a concept which

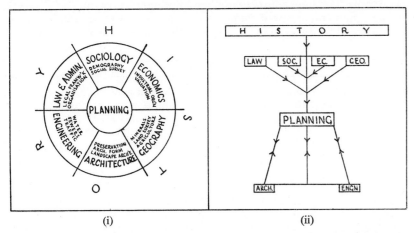

FIG. 3. Planning considered (i) as the centre of a field of study, showing the contributions which various other subjects make to it and (ii) in relation to other Arts and Sciences, showing the contributions made by and to Planning.

has been much misused, even though it has already been partially dealt with a little earlier when discussing the roles of " generalists " and " specialists ". This is the idea of the Planning team, and is often used to pour oil on troubled waters when the claims of some particular specialism to dominance in the Planning field are being argued. Some liberal minded person usually winds up the discussion by saying " after all, Planning is a team job." So it is, but not in the sense in which the term is generally employed in this context.

Let us take as an example the preparation of a town Plan; the drawing up of proposals for the rectification, improvement and extension of an existing town. Information about a large number of matters will be needed which can only be obtained by relying on the skilled investigations of specialists who, if they work together well, may reasonably be called a team; but the assembly, comparison, and final evaluation of all the correlationships, opportunities and conflicts revealed by these investigations can only be done with full expectation of success by those whose principal experience and knowledge lie in town Planning. The Plan produced is bound to be, if it is worth anything, the product of one mind—of the senior Planner with the task of preparing the town Plan. He may well delegate to his juniors the working out of the details of his broad conception, and the exploration of possible alternatives, but none of the specialists, *qua* specialists, engaged on the production of information will be equipped to do this. *Their* further role after the draft Plan is produced, is to criticise it constructively in the light of the requirements of their specialisms, so that if the Planner has

failed in any particular to make proper use of the specialist information provided this may be pointed out and the matter further considered. Any other procedure is almost nonsensical. The notion that such a Plan can be prepared by a number of specialists sitting round a table, each contributing to the Plan those aspects of it covered by his own speciality, is fantastic.

It often seems to me that this subject is made even more confusing than it need be because discussion of it tends really to be about development rather than about Planning. It is perfectly true that innumerable specialities are involved in the actual processes of development, and that in many circumstances no single one predominates over another, but Planning is not the carrying out of development, it is the creation of a framework into which development shall fit. Admittedly the boundary between the two is not sharp: very large development projects may be indistinguishable from very detailed Planning, but except at this frontier the distinction is clear.

It should now be possible to look at some of the professions and skills connected with Planning, to consider how they contribute to the Planning process and the extent to which the Planner himself needs to have knowledge of them.

Architectural Design and Building Construction

Most changes in the use of land involve the erection of buildings, and although a Planner need not be an expert designer of buildings or be capable of working out in detail such problems as the load-bearing capacity of structures, he needs to know enough to understand the architect's problems and to produce designs which, in terms of shape and size of sites and of road layout, enable the architect to give of his best, to forecast what kind of buildings can successfully be erected on a given site, to appreciate the constructional factors which affect the shape and size of buildings and which limit the choice of building materials. He must also understand the relationship between internal design and external appearance so that he is not led into suggesting architectural absurdities.

Above all, of course, a general sensitiveness to the effects capable of being produced by the massing of buildings in various ways and an appreciation of the role of buildings as enclosures of space is essential.

What has been said about architecture applies so similarly to landscape design that this need not be discussed separately.

Valuation

The value of land and buildings for different purposes also concerns the Planner, since, as already suggested, he must not put forward proposals for the use of land which will not pay, unless they are uses, such as open spaces, playing fields, schools or civic buildings which by their nature can hardly be economically self-supporting. To this end he should have some knowledge of valuation theory and practice, but here it is necessary to digress in order to explode a widely accepted fallacy.

This may be stated as the belief that land values dominate Planning proposals, that the valuer can appropriately be regarded as a dominant influence in formulating such proposals, and that the Planner requires a profound knowledge of valuation. The boot, it seems to me, is on the other foot. Sound Planning involves the allocation of land uses in such a way that a convenient and well-integrated pattern of uses is created, a pattern which will attract residents, in which, because of its attractiveness and convenience, they will gladly live, and one which provides commercial sites well located to exploit the consumer demands of the residents thus attracted. In other words, the measure of successful Planning design is the degree of satisfaction of all who live and work within it. The valuer is well qualified to express this degree of satisfaction in terms of money and his experience also enables him to predict the amount of satisfaction likely to be occasioned by a particular scheme, but he is not qualified to create the design any more than the printer is qualified to write the book or the art dealer to paint the picture. The skills of the Planner are infinitely more varied and complicated, and require creative ability quite irrelevant to that of the valuer.

This fundamental difference exists also as between the Planner and the geographer, the economist and the sociologist. Profoundly valuable though the knowledge of all of them is to the Planner in providing background data, it does not assist him in acquiring the vital ability to design.

There has, however, lately emerged one particular valuation technique of very special importance to the Planning process. This is summed up in the term " the Planning balance-sheet", and is ably and fully set out by N. Lichfield in his book " Economics of Planned Development". Very briefly, the argument which Dr. Lichfield states is that although there are many advantages and disadvantages attaching to alternative methods of developing a particular area which cannot be reduced to money terms, there nevertheless are a great many which can be so expressed, and that these, when set out in appropriate form so as to be fully comparable, enable Planning policy to be drawn up on a basis of fact rather than of intuition or prejudice. Though Lichfield would, I think, be the last to deny that financially non-measurable aspects may sometimes properly prevail over the financially measurable, this is a technique of the utmost value, as yet in its infancy but worthy of the greatest attention and development.

Sociology

The contribution of the sociologist to Planning is clearly, potentially at least, very great but words in which to define it prove elusive. I do not believe that Planners have yet made clear to sociologists the ways in which the latter can best help them. It seems to me that the most valuable aid which the sociologist could render to Planning would be to provide answers to the question mentioned in Chapter 1: What would people want if they knew the full range of possibilities and limitations? Adequate answers, which Sociologists should be able to provide by using some of the extremely ingenious techniques at their disposal, could do much in helping to decide the relative numbers of houses and flats which should be provided, preferences for garden sizes and types, forms of layout and many other matters. This is in addition to the wealth of material regarding population composition and changes which can be supplied by the demographer.

There is also a mass of less well defined sociological data by which the

Planner can profit, all casting light upon the problems of what lies behind apparently motiveless behaviour. So far as the Planner himself is concerned, it is clear that no reliable information which helps him to understand human beings and their likes and dislikes is superfluous, and though he will be wise to hesitate long before himself attempting to carry out social surveys, with the innumerable pitfalls which they conceal, an understanding of the techniques and methods of evaluating social surveys is most desirable.

Statistics

Much sociological and much economic study depends upon elaborate statistical work. The extent to which the Planner will have to prepare his own statistical material obviously depends upon many circumstances but, at the very least, he should know enough about statistics to avoid the numerous howlers which can so easily be perpetrated. He should be able to carry out comparatively simple statistical investigation reliably and with knowledge of the limits of validity of his findings.

Engineering

The provision of buildings involves also the provision of the necessary services to convey power and water to them and to conduct wastes from them, and of roads to give access to them. This is the province of the engineer, and again, although the Planner need not have intimate knowledge of the detailed processes of road and sewer construction, or of water, gas and electricity supply, he must know the limiting factors governing their provision and the relative costs of different methods. His knowledge of sewerage should, for example, go sufficiently far to enable him to calculate the sizes of sewers necessary to serve a given amount of development, but certainly need not extend to expert knowledge of the processes of sewage purification.

Traffic engineering or traffic planning has now assumed such importance, and is so intimately linked with Town Planning that it is hardly possible to draw a definite line between the two. It is in itself a subject of such complexity, involving much abstruse mathematics, that the Planner can hardly hope to acquire a very thorough knowledge of it—there is no reasonably simple book at present which would help him to do so. It has already been suggested in Chapter 1 that nearly all town Plans need to be subjected to thorough traffic analysis for their validity to be tested. As with many other subjects, the best that most Planners can probably hope for is to know enough of the subject to avoid putting up proposals which have serious drawbacks from the point of view of traffic planning. For this purpose he needs especially to know which of the roads he provides for in his plan are likely to bear so much traffic that they need to have dual carriageways and which of his junctions and intersections will, similarly, bear enough traffic to necessitate being constructed in multi-level form.

Geology

This is a subject which, although it is both literally and metaphorically fundamental to Planning, has comparatively little direct influence upon

Planning proposals. Although the Planner will find it useful to know the general characteristics of most common types of soils and rocks, their strength, permeability and fertility, any detailed specialist knowledge would be likely to be comparatively little used. In the field of applied geology understanding of the characteristics, location and methods of winning minerals by surface working is, of course, invaluable.

Agriculture

The Planner has at present little direct influence on agriculture; though he can help to maintain a satisfactory distribution of agricultural population by encouraging the creation and enlargement of adequate rural centres, and he can have a large say in determining the siting of individual agricultural workers' houses, he is not in a position to bring about changes in the structure of the industry. It has been said, for example, that the agricultural productivity of this country could be greatly increased by a drastic rearrangement of the boundaries of farm units, and the bringing about of this might reasonably be considered part of the function of the land Planner; in point of fact legislation has not yet given him any say in the matter. There is an aspect of agriculture, however, with which he is intimately concerned, and that is the choice of agricultural land to be sacrificed to other uses. Although he will receive a great quantity of expert and semi-expert advice on the subject whenever he proposes that land should be so sacrificed, it will nevertheless save the Planner much time and trouble if he has sufficient knowledge of the agricultural system to ensure that he is aware of at least the main agricultural implications of his proposals.

Law

The law is one of the Planner's tools; he must know the extent to which it limits his activities both in kind and in degree. No intimate knowledge of legal detail is necessary except as regards the limitations on control of development imposed by, e.g., the General Development Order and the Use Classes Order, since he will have to resort to qualified legal advice before taking any action with legal implications, but, as with agriculture, he will save himself much grief if his knowledge of the law is sufficient to prevent him making recommendations which are legally impracticable.

Government Structure

A knowledge of the machinery of Central and Local Government is of great importance. Consultation and co-operation with many Central and Local Government Departments is indispensable and often obligatory, and a clear understanding of the powers, constitution and duties of each of them is vital. A lively appreciation of the spirit of British constitutional practice is, too, among the most important of the Planner's needs.

Geography

It should be obvious that physical, economic and human geography are all directly and intimately linked with Planning and can provide the Planner with a very large proportion of the basic knowledge he requires. Among the subjects suitable for study preliminary to Planning, geography must hold a very high place.

Economics

This, too, is basic to Planning. What is required is something more than the economics of land values. An appreciation of the general economic problems of industry, the site, labour and transport requirements of different industries, at least in general terms, an ability to interpret statistical information and an understanding of the complicated economic linkages between different activities are all of enormous importance. In particular, the Planner needs to be in a position to indicate not merely the activities which would be harmless on a particular site, but those which would be most successful there and, conversely, to be able to select suitable sites for particular activities.

Finally, the Schuster Report rightly emphasised the need for Planners to be people of wide culture, and this ought, perhaps, more specially to include a knowledge of the world and its ways, a sense of history and of human destiny.

It follows from this very condensed summary that much of the design skill necessary to the Planner depends for its successful exercise upon his ability to evaluate and synthesise the information relating to whichever combination of the subjects mentioned applies to a particular Planning problem. Indeed, Planning design springs so directly from this synthesis that it can hardly be separated from it, hence the doubtful validity of the Schuster Report's view that it partakes more of administration.

Nothing has yet been said to refute the common allegation that the Planner is a jack of all trades and master of none or to indicate the nature of any special skill he possesses which is not merely derived from knowledge of the background subjects listed. It lies, I suggest, in the ability to determine the appropriate relation of land uses spatially and quantitatively and to create a design which expresses this relation without violating other needs. This is the core of Planning skill; to reach the highest levels it needs to be accompanied by the ability to discern those aspects of a particular subject which are of particular Planning importance and to master these in some detail, together with the broad appreciation of the subject as a whole which such mastery entails. There is nothing superhuman about this ability; it is one possessed, in somewhat different fashions, by the barrister and by the able journalist, and there is nothing superficial or meretricious about it.

I cannot conclude this chapter without recording my belief that, for those who are able to take one, a course of full-time undergraduate study of the kind provided at Newcastle and Manchester is likely to be the most satisfactory preparation for a career in Planning, and I do not share the Schuster Committee's doubts about this. Planning is a subject which requires great width and depth of study. There seems little point in spending several years taking a degree in some subject of general educational value when an adequate preparation for Planning itself involves a variety of subject-matter, related always to human needs and human character, sufficient to constitute a liberal education, and which, even if the graduate eventually decided to take up some other career, would give him a framework of knowledge more than ordinarily useful as a foundation for many kinds of more specialised learning.

Below is a summary of the newly revised examination syllabus of the Town Planning Institute which comes into operation in 1964. It is given in very general form, since it is liable to changes in detail at any time, and the printing here of more detailed summaries might, therefore, lead to confusion. The syllabuses of Planning Schools recognised by the Town Planning Institute include a similar range of subjects, with, naturally, fairly wide variations in arrangement and emphasis.

Town Planning Institute Examinations

INTERMEDIATE EXAMINATION

Open to candidates over 18 who have a General Certificate of Education with passes in three subjects at ordinary level and two at advanced level.

Part I

Testimonies of study including measured drawings, an analytical study of a group of buildings, a land survey and a set problem in design.

Part II

Written examinations in:
   Elementary Design of Buildings, Roads and Bridges.
   Surveying and Levelling.
   History and Principles of Planning.
   Central and Local Government and Outlines of Law in Relation to
      Planning.
   Outlines of Social and Economic Organisation.
   Survey and Analysis.
   Drawn Analysis and Design.

FINAL EXAMINATION

Open to candidates over 21 who have passed the Intermediate Examination of the Institute or the Final Examination of the R.I.B.A., the I.C.E., the I.Mun.E. or the R.I.C.S. (or an examination carrying exemption therefrom) or who hold an approved University degree in any of a wide range of subjects.

Part I
Testimonies of Study

General: Three drawn exercises in design or an essay of about 5,000 words on a subject related to economic, geographical, social or other aspects of Planning. The subjects in all cases are set by the Institute.

Special: A Survey and Analysis, Plan and Design and Programme of Development for an area chosen for himself by each candidate.

Part II

Written examinations in:
   Historical Development of Planning (Holders of T.P.I. Intermediate
      are exempt).
   Architectural and Landscape Design in relation to Planning. (Architects
      are exempt.)
   Civil Engineering and Surveying in relation to Planning. (Engineers
      are exempt.)
   Economics of Land Use. (Chartered Surveyors are exempt.)

Part III

Written examinations in:
   Planning Theory.
   Planning Practice.
   Law in Relation to Planning.
   A sketch plan and report also has to be made after a site inspection.

Parts I, II and III can each be taken on different occasions, and need not be taken in any particular order.

CHAPTER 3

VISUAL PRESENTATION FOR PLANNING PURPOSES

3-1. INTRODUCTORY

IT IS IMPORTANT that visual information relating to Planning should be attractively presented. The first essential is that its general meaning should be speedily apparent and that, on further inspection, its details should be capable of being easily and accurately read. If a map, for example, meets these requirements it is almost certain to have a crisp and attractive appearance, for they necessitate the maximum legibility and appropriate variation in size and style of lettering, harmony between colours, proper weight of hatching, and cleanness of line. However, something more than this is needed; touches of artistry going beyond mere clarity and efficiency arouse and sustain the interest of the viewer, which otherwise flags all too speedily, particularly when a number of different maps have to be inspected at one time.

Most of this chapter applies to the presentation both of Planning proposals and of survey data, but the latter present more diverse and difficult problems in presentation than do the former.

The most convenient arrangement will be to deal first with maps and diagrams in map form, second with diagrams not in map form and finally with models and other methods of three dimensional representation.

3-2. MAPS AND DIAGRAMS

These are the most frequently used forms of presentation; great variety is possible in the techniques employed.

The kinds of maps required from the point of view of the different presentation techniques they demand, fall naturally into five classes: those showing:—

(1) Factors or areas of different character but of approximately equal importance, e.g. Land Use, Farm Units.
(2) Factors of the same kind but of differing intensity, e.g. Density, Age of buildings
(3) Flows, e.g. Traffic, Population movements.
(4) Distribution of Service Centres combined with representation of their service areas, e.g. Shops, Schools.
(5) Comparison of different subjects, e.g. Land Availability sieve, Comparison of Density and Disease Incidence.

To solve the problems of presentation which these pose, the means available can be classified as:—

(1) Hatching and Stippling.
(2) Borders.
(3) Colour washes.
(4) Symbols.
(5) Directional signs.
(6) Overlays.

These items can be combined in numerous ways, and it is safe to say that the complexity of a satisfactory map is limited, not by the total number of items which can be distinctly shown, but by the variety which the human mind can comprehend without becoming confused.

It is also necessary to distinguish between the purposes intended to be fulfilled by maps, which greatly affects the techniques used. A completely clear-cut classification is hardly possible, but the following indicates the most widely differing purposes :

(1) Maps which merely record information without trying to present a vivid, comprehensive picture, e.g. Routes and capacities of Public Utility Services.
(2) Maps, primarily for the perusal of laymen, which attempt to present the facts dealt with in the simplest, most quickly assimilable fashion possible.
(3) Maps which aim at the maximum clarity, but also present their information in considerable detail.

The most successful examples of this third type are so arranged that their essential meaning is at once apparent but, without detriment to this, yield further, more detailed information when closely studied. Most of the survey maps actually used as the basis for formulating Development Plans and Development Plan maps themselves fall within this class.

Base Maps. The success or failure of a set of Planning maps depends to a very large extent upon the suitability of the base maps used. A base map may be defined as a map which shows the existing physical pattern of land, upon which survey information or Planning proposals are superimposed.

The perfect base map is one which gives just enough detail, but no more, to make the information superimposed on it fully comprehensible.

The Ordnance Survey of Great Britain publishes maps at various scales and provides a map coverage of the country which is unrivalled anywhere in the world. The reader is assumed to be familiar with the use of maps and to have some knowledge of Ordnance Survey maps, but full information about them, including examples, can be found in the Ordnance Survey explanatory handbooks published by the Stationery Office.

Many published Plans and surveys have been prepared with far too little regard to the importance of using suitable base maps; in fact, quite often, almost any map which happened to be immediately available seems to have been utilised. No published Ordnance map is ideal as a base map for Planning purposes—although many are good—since they are produced for the benefit of a variety of users who have different requirements, and the total amount of detail shown is excessive for Planning purposes; nor is any one base map ideal for a whole series of Planning maps, since different subjects demand the inclusion of different degrees and kinds of detail.

Wherever possible it is most desirable to prepare special base maps in the form of traced adaptations of published Ordnance maps.   This is not usually as huge a task as it seems to be at first sight but, in any case, the expenditure of quite a large amount of draughtsman's time is justifiable since it is capable of producing quite disproportionately large benefits.

It is not, of course, *always* possible to produce special base maps; time or money as limiting factors may preclude this being done, and in the case of maps for a very large area which have to be produced on a large scale the sheer volume of work may be too fearsome to contemplate.   Where this is the case much can, nevertheless, be done with comparatively little expenditure of time by judicious touching up—strengthening the main roads, emphasising the most important place names by underlining them and similar minor improvements.

The essential purposes of a base map are to enable the location of one set of Planning information to be identified in relation to that on other maps and to show the relationship of the general character of the area to the Planning information superimposed.   The map may be so devised that this identification is either quite precise or merely general, the choice depending on the type of information intended to be shown.   The more detailed the base map the less will be the degree of clarity with which the information superimposed on it can be shown, but the more easily and precisely can this information be located.

It may be helpful, before making positive suggestions for the preparation of base maps, to cite examples of well-known works which, in one way or another, have failed to meet the requirements already mentioned.   That the time and circumstances of some of these works, rather than lack of skill or foresight, must largely have accounted for these defects does not of course invalidate the conclusions drawn.

The base map of the Master Plan in the Greater London Plan is simply the War Department's wartime 1/25,000 map, which itself suffered from excessive reduction of scale, much further reduced.   The results are that, in steeply sloping areas, the contour lines fuse together into black masses, a very large proportion of the minor place names are completely illegible and, in many places, the road pattern cannot be followed.   The total effect is a barely differentiated, dark grey background which greatly diminishes the clarity of the superimposed colours.   In the early stages of post-war Planning the hearing of appeals against development control decisions based on the Plan was often rendered difficult by the inability of the parties concerned to agree upon the boundaries between zones shown in it.

At the other extreme, the base maps used in " English County " (Hereford-shire) are so skeletal that, while they certainly do not in the least obscure superimposed colour, they give hardly any assistance in fixing location.   In fact, in nearly every case, the base map consists simply of the County Bound-ary and a few circles indicating the positions of the principal settlements.

Here is a case in which no class of reader is adequately catered for.   The Planning information given is far more detailed and extensive than the casual lay reader could possible be expected to absorb, yet the form in which it is presented renders it practically unusable for the professional Planner, land-owner or anyone else really wanting to appreciate it in detail.

The base map used throughout Gordon Payne's " Survey of Gloucester-shire " is imperfect in another quite different way.   The amount of detail shown is insufficient but, quite apart from this, what is shown is indefinite. The adoption of a free, somewhat irregular style of draughtsmanship may often not only save a great deal of time but may, in its own right, be highly effective; this, however, is different from indefiniteness.   On the Gloucester-shire base map the physical extent of communities is shown by weak, ill-defined areas of stippling which frequently disappear beneath the colouring applied.   The lettering of the place names, somewhat sprawling and following no discernible convention, leaves one often in doubt as to which stippled area a name refers.

Finally, the base map used for most of the illustrations of " A Planning Basis for Kent " is a brave attempt to make the best of both worlds, which must on the whole be accounted a failure.   Here a very faint grey base map is used, a reduction of a small scale ($\frac{1}{2}''$ to one mile) Ordnance Map.   In addition, for certain survey maps, specially important items on the base maps are picked out in a thicker black line for emphasis.   The failure lies in the fact that, while it is just possible, with infinite patience and a magnifying glass, to fix the location of survey items by reference to the grey base, this is so faint that when the map is inspected in the ordinary way in order to gain a general impression, it has no effect on the eye, while the items picked out in black are insufficient to form an adequate base map in themselves.

I do not believe that the use of a faint detailed base map is desirable.   If it is faint enough to enable superimposed information to be clearly read it can hardly have enough strength to form a proper base map, since, for most purposes, it is desirable to read superimposed information in relation to the physical pattern of the area.   It might indeed be possible to devise a satisfactory method by which map detail was shown in a faint tone and the outline information necessary for a general appreciation of pattern, varied to suit the special needs of particular base maps, emphasised, but the technical difficulties would be great, particularly in securing sufficiently exact register at a small scale.

The soundest policy generally seems to be to devise base maps so that they consist of the minimum number of lines necessary to achieve their purpose but to print these lines at normal intensity, though some lines may appropriately be stronger than others.

The standard of clarity of many official Development Plan Maps is deplorable. Though the reasons for this are often complex, unsuitable base maps are often the most important.   For example it is by no means un-common to find County Maps on which it is impossible to read the names of towns and villages (an elementary requirement!) because the faint grey colour and the small lettering of the place names result in their being obliterated by superimposed rendering.

Town Maps, for similar reasons, are frequently indecipherable in detail; in particular it may often be literally impossible to read street names.

It will be evident that the actual content of base maps will vary not only according to the subject matter to be applied to them but also to the scale at which they are drawn. Thus, for Regional purposes, the scale used might be anywhere between ¼″ to one mile and 1/25,000, for Town Planning between 1/25,000 and 1/2,500 and for detailed Planning between 1/2,500 and 1/500. At the same time, the particular scale used, even within one of these general ranges, will, at least in part, be determined by the use to be made of the map. For example, the Diagrammatic base map described below could more appropriately be drawn at ¼″ to one mile than at 1/25,000, while the General Purposes base map would not normally be drawn at less than 1/25,000, though, in some circumstances, with the omission of enclosure boundaries, it would be useful at 1″ to one mile. The factors of size, time and money and the character of the area under examination may all operate in different ways to affect the choice of scale.

The problems of maintaining clarity in the event of Planning maps having to be reproduced for publication at a smaller scale are considerable and are not of course confined to base maps. The sizes of symbols, thickness of lines and intervals between lines, together with the size of any lettering added subsequently to the base map, must all be taken into account.

Any important Planning project is quite likely to be published sooner or later; it is most desirable that, from the first, drawings shall be prepared with this possibility in mind. A map which will be suitable for a large degree of reduction is likely to be thereby rendered less than perfect at its original scale, but not to any serious extent. Since the requirements for suitability for reduction lead to some excess of boldness of presentation at the original scale this results in faults on the right side if the originals are exhibited to the public.

The best example which I know of unfortunate results following from failure to anticipate the need for publication is to be seen in the " City of Manchester Plan, 1945," an exceptionally able and important work on Planning. In this book a number of the illustrations are full-colour lithographs, obviously taken from intensely coloured 6″ maps. The colours are often too complex to be easily read, partly because the grey colour of the detailed base map dulls them. The base map itself is useless; one cannot identify locations from it except with the greatest difficulty. One can feel tolerably sure that in this case it would have been cheaper and certainly much more satisfactory, even after the preparation of the original maps, to prepare fresh ones for publication with a bold outline base and a simple colour notation.

At the Regional level there should ideally be four base maps :—

(1) *Diagrammatic*, to show in barest outline the pattern of the area, on which would be presented data such as flows and service areas, for which extents and boundaries only are of importance and intervening detail is no more than a distraction.

(2) *Physical Features*, which emphasises the natural at the expense of the artificial pattern, on which would be shown principally topographical data.

(3) *Man-made Features*, on which the emphasis is the reverse of that on (2). This would be used for more detailed information regarding service areas and accessibility than could be shown on (1) but its most important use would be for the presentation of outline Planning proposals and survey analysis in cartoon form for special purposes.

(4) *General Purposes*, for presenting subject-matter without any special bias towards natural or artificial features. Outline Land Use and Planning proposals are examples of the subjects for which this base would be used.

At the 1/25,000 scale this map would be so similar to the published Ordnance Maps, with the omission of some detail irrelevant to Planning purposes, that one hardly would be justified in preparing such a map for a very large area because of the great amount of work entailed.

Careful forethought should enable substantial economies in time to be effected in preparing different styles of base map for the same area. The principle is to draw first the material common to all four and have transparencies made of this, adding further material required for each different base. The following table gives an indication of how this might be done.

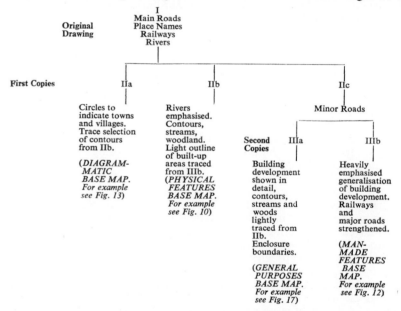

It will be seen that some items have to be strengthened on some of the copies, but this can be done very rapidly when the lines are already shown on the drawing; again, some items have necessarily to be traced twice, but these are taken from the tracing already made, and it is much easier and quicker to retrace from a selective tracing than from a fully detailed ordnance map. With great care, it might be possible to reduce even this amount of duplication of work; provided perfect register could be obtained, any item which did not appear on all the versions could be drawn on a separate piece of material and overprinted on to the versions in which it was required. The only duplication of work which would then remain would be the emphasis of some items on some of the base maps.

It should be noted that the complete mechanisation of this kind of work is hardly possible. Various items require different degrees of exaggeration in size and thickness of line, and, in adding items to material previously traced and printed, a certain amount of erasure and adjustment will inevitably be necessary in order to obtain well balanced appearance. It is, for example, very difficult to position the place names on the first drawings in such a way that none of them will be obscured by detail subsequently added to one or more of the copies.

It must be mentioned at this point that the present method of publishing 1″ to one mile and 1/25,000 Ordnance sheets greatly reduces their usefulness as base maps, even if it is considered that for some purposes they are close enough to the ideal to justify omission of specially drawn maps. It is not possible to add further colour to the coloured edition and obtain satisfactory results, while the outline edition has no contour lines. In order to use these maps it is therefore necessary to undertake the considerable labour of copying the contours on to the outline edition.

At the Town Plan scale base map requirements are less complex. Enlargements to 6″ to one mile of the appropriate portion of the Regional Man-made Features Base will provide a satisfactory cartoon map for discussion of proposals, while for most other purposes, so far at least as urban areas are concerned, a base map of the type shown in Figs. 29 to 38 but with the street names added will be perfectly satisfactory.

A word of explanation is desirable regarding the omission of buildings from this map. At 6″ to one mile buildings cannot be shown with perfect accuracy, some generalisation and distortion of shapes being inevitable, and indeed the published Ordnance maps at this scale increase this distortion because street widths are exaggerated in order that names of easily legible size can be printed along them. Buildings have to be hatched, stippled or tinted distinctively in order that they shall show up clearly, and the result is a close knit pattern, except in areas of low density housing, which blurs, and in turn is blurred by rendering of any complexity applied over it. Since the scale is too small to allow positions to be pin-pointed by reference to buildings, any use of it for maps which show boundaries which are legally binding is inappropriate. It therefore seems best to exclude buildings from the map, leaving a relatively simple base upon which rendering can be superimposed with great clarity. The framework of roads enables sites to be readily identified to a degree of accuracy quite sufficient for the type of information which can be shown at the 6″ scale, and ease of identification is of course greatly increased if all roads are named.

Outside built-up areas the ordinary pattern of field boundaries can be shown, while both inside and outside these areas there is every justification for aiding legibility by showing important isolated buildings as reference points.

Naturally, the orthodox type of 6″ map gives a better general picture of the character of the town since it provides a rough impression of relative building densities, but as a base for individual surveys and for proposals, that just described is preferable.

General considerations governing Technique employed

The advantages and disadvantages of the different methods of presentation will now be considered in order to clear the way for discussion of the best ways of presenting the five principal classes of maps previously listed.

There are, however, two broad sub-divisions which cut across this classification: first, between monochrome and colour technique and, second, between the use of series of overlays and of single composite maps for the purpose of comparing a number of factors.

Monochrome presentation, as its name implies, does not rely upon colour contrast to denote differentiation but secures the desired effect solely by variations of density, texture and/or direction in the lines, edgings and symbols used. Its principal advantage is that once the first copy of a map has been made an unlimited number of reproductions can be obtained without further drafting work. The principal disadvantage is that there is a limit to the number of different kinds of information that can be shown on a single monochrome map, whereas, with the use of colour, the changes that can be made by combining backgrounds of one colour with edgings of another, varying the depth of tone of each tint, and combining variety of colour and variety of density and direction in the hatchings etc. used are practically infinite.

Fig. 15 is an example of monochrome technique stretched beyond the limit of full effectiveness. While it is possible that further experiment with and revision of the notation used would effect an improvement, it could still not approach the clarity attainable with a coloured notation.

It might well be possible to devise notations which would serve for both coloured and monochrome maps. The object would be to prepare full coloured maps as master copies which would embody the highest possible degree of clarity and interest, but with the colour schemes so devised that, when photographed in monochrome, each separate colour would show up as a distinctive tone. The use of coloured Zippatone stipple tints on a transparent base, from which monochrome prints could be made in quantity seems in principle perfectly feasible.

It is often possible to add one or more coloured areas to a monochrome map with great effect and quite rapidly, the boundaries of all factors having already been plotted in monochrome. One purpose for which this is particularly useful is the emphasis of a particular use on a Use Survey Map. It is sometimes desired to show the distribution within a town of each of a number of uses, and this can conveniently be done by preparing a Monochrome Use Map, taking from it as many prints as the uses to be isolated, and colouring appropriately on each of them all the areas devoted to one such use.

The disadvantage of colour used merely as flat washes, with or without edgings, is that it gives little scope for indicating the overlapping of factors. When a blue area and a yellow area overlap, the overlapping portion will of course show up clearly as green, with an obvious affinity to each, but the extent to which this technique can be applied without loss of clarity is very limited.

Turning to the relative merits of overlays and composite maps for the purpose of comparison, the first point to note is that overlays have numerous theoretical advantages. Each separate survey subject, drawn in monochrome or on a transparency, can be treated as a map in its own right, be reproduced on ordinary prints and coloured if desired. Or it can be placed over a base map, together with any combination of other subjects desired, and compared with them; by experimenting with different combinations significant correlations of data apparently unconnected may reveal themselves. Any interesting combination of subjects can be printed to form a composite map.

These advantages appear overwhelming but the difficulties of securing and maintaining perfect register simultaneously between a number of overlays and a base map are sufficiently great to discourage much light-hearted shuffling in order to discover interesting relationships; even if differential expansion or contraction of the sheets does not upset the register it is hard to fix a number of them precisely in position one above the other. However transparent the material used for the overlays it always seems difficult to read the lowermost when a number are superimposed. Finally, the notations for a number of overlays must be worked out systematically beforehand if they are not to clash and obscure each other.

In my opinion it is better to confine the use of overlays to rough preliminary work, when indeed they may prove interesting and revealing. If, for any reason, the use of overlays in finished form were considered essential, it would probably be more successful to begin with a composite map and then, by copying each factor on to a separate sheet, to " explode " it into overlays, but this procedure would of course entirely eliminate the saving of time claimed for overlays.

The terms "hatching", "stippling", "washes", and "symbols" are not entirely mutually exclusive. "Wash", as used in this chapter, means an area of uniform colour or an area treated to give that effect. A more familiar word is "tint", but this might give rise to confusion, since, in the printing trade, "tint" often means a fine stipple. A very fine coloured stipple gives the effect of a wash, a coarse stipple is virtually the same as a close pattern of symbols, as is hatching with widely broken lines. This being understood, it is sufficient to say that the following observations relate to average examples of each of these types of rendering rather than those which are close to merging with another.

Hatchings may be differentiated from each other in a number of ways; the lines, or more accurately bands, may be of varying colour, width, direction or texture, and the spaces between them can also be varied in width. (See Fig. 4). There is in fact almost no end to the number of different effects which can be obtained; the practical limit is set by the limited number of directions possible and by the fact that two or more sets of parallel or nearly parallel bands produce visual confusion. It is a good rule to stop well before

this begins and to turn to other means of indicating the remaining factors which have to be shown.

A particularly effective way of using hatchings, though very laborious to draw unless mechanical aids are used, is to cover the areas to be shown with a series of very fine lines drawn close together; if the colour and direction of these lines are both varied a very sharply differentiated effect is given.

Patterns of symbols are especially suitable for items covering a large proportion of the map. They may consist of squares, oblongs, triangles, circles or in fact any shape capable of being drawn quickly and accurately in large numbers. A variation of this is to use symbols which suggest the character of the area they cover—e.g. ears of wheat for arable land. If this is

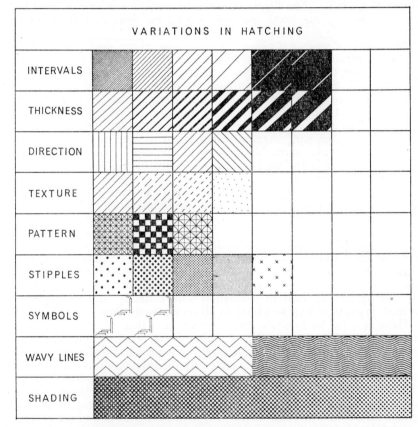

Fig. 4. Some of the numerous variations obtainable by means of hatchings.

done it is necessary to cut stencils so that the symbols shall be uniform; this method can be very effective if used with restraint, but it is all too easy to give the map a florid and somewhat absurd appearance. If the sizes of the actual symbols and their spacings are carefully balanced the areas so delineated can be shown up prominently, yet underlying information is only very slightly obscured.

Stipples are midway between washes and patterns of symbols. The actual areas of colour are reduced to little more than points, yet their spacing is close enough to give the effect of a light toned wash.

It is desirable that every area distinguished by hatching, symbols or stipple is appropriately edged. Even with a very close hatching the shape of the area enclosed by it appears blurred and uncertain unless it is also edged. The edging should, of course, be of the same colour as the hatching etc., but its width should also be related as closely as possible to the width of hatching or size of symbols. The edging need not be a continuous line or band but, if discontinuous, the blank portions should be short in relation to the solids.

The edging of washes is not of the same importance, since, although this certainly increases clarity, it is simply a matter of competent draughtsmanship to create clean, definite boundaries between coloured areas which will ensure sufficient definition for most purposes. Edgings to washed areas have a different function; they can be used to increase the range of variation. For example, on a Land Use Map, a single colour might be used to indicate a series of allied uses, edgings in other colours being added to indicate the precise use of each site. Again, washes might be used to show residential density and edgings to show the condition of buildings. This device is on the whole more suited to the rapid production of maps for *ad hoc* purposes than to those in the main series.

One other general aspect of the use of coloured areas deserves mention. It has already been noted that very close spaced fine hatching gives an effect of solid colour, and, of course, variations in the thickness and spacing of the lines affect its apparent depth of tone. When maps are produced by mechanical means (it is hardly feasible to do this by hand) and include variations in the depth of tone of one or more colours it is more economical and more satisfactory to do it by this means than by using areas of continuous colour. The substantial number of people who have partially defective colour vision are also thereby enabled to distinguish with certainty between slight differences in depth of tone which might otherwise escape them.

There is a use of symbols quite distinct from that already discussed in connection with patterns. The distribution of workers, factories, road accidents etc., is often shown, particularly on maps intended for popular use, by means of symbols representing pictorally the subjects dealt with. Quantitative variations are indicated either by the number of such symbols or their size at each point of occurrence. For example, the distribution of mine-workers in North West England might be indicated by placing on the map against each town concerned a little isotype or pictogram of a miner swinging a pick for each 500 mineworkers employed there, or alternatively by means of a single isotype for each town, its size depending on the number of mine-workers employed.

I am not enthusiastic about either of these methods, believing that better results can generally be obtained by simpler means, such as coloured bars of varying length. Nevertheless, they have the not unimportant merit of presenting an immediate vivid impression if they are kept within bounds. Generally speaking the second alternative is preferable, for, with the first, it is often very difficult to keep platoons of miners, clerks, milkmaids or oast-houses sufficiently compact for any real sense of location to be preserved; frequently they seem to sprawl all over the map, and it is very hard to understand to which town or village a particular group of symbols relates. When an attempt is made to indicate on one map the distribution of a number of different items, this method nearly always fails.

The second method avoids the lack of compactness of the first provided one subject only is dealt with, but when an attempt is made to summarise a series of subjects on one map the effect is often ludicrous, with gigantic milkmaids, tiny miners and medium-sized brewers' draymen jostling each other in wild abandon. One rule needs to be observed. Since the symbols used nearly always represent three dimensional objects their heights and widths should vary as the cube root of the total amounts represented. Thus a symbol representing 27,000 transport workers will be 3 times, not 27 times, as high as that representing only 1,000.

Little can be said about what, for lack of a better name, have been referred to as directional signs. They range from the precisely measured strips which indicate the amounts and routes of traffic determined by an origin and destination census to the tentative, many-headed arrows which seek to give an impression, unconfirmed by full survey, of the different service centres used by the inhabitants of a residential area. This perhaps suggests the only firm principle which can be advanced; that the definiteness of such signs should be proportionate to the reliability of the information they give.

Materials

Various media can be used for rendering maps with colour; the most generally used are water-colours. These are cheap, available in a wide range and do not obscure the map detail beneath, but they have to be mixed with water to the required strength, and where the whole of the area for which a particular colour is required cannot be coloured at one sitting it may be a matter of some difficulty to match up when resuming work.

This difficulty is overcome with the Planning dyes specially prepared for colouring Planning maps. These are ready mixed and need no dilution; their other characteristics are similar to those of water-colours, but they are much more expensive and they have a marked tendency to " creep " into each other along the boundary between different colours, which sometimes makes it difficult to obtain a clean and crisp effect. Both water-colours and dyes are, in some colours, very difficult to apply evenly, because in the case of water-colours, of sedimentation taking place, and, in the case of dyes, of over-rapid drying.

Drawing inks are useful for some purposes; many of them are waterproof, which dyes and water-colours are not, but many of them are impossible to apply evenly over a large area. The number of different colours made is limited, and, owing to their chemical composition, a good many of them cannot be mixed satisfactorily. Their usefulness is greater for line work than for colouring areas.

Poster colours are extremely vivid but are opaque, completely hiding the map detail beneath, which disqualifies them for all but a very few Planning purposes; also, after application, they tend to flake away from the surface of the paper.

Coloured pencils and crayons are useful for rapid, sketchy work, but their lack of permanence and evenness make them unsuitable for maps for which a first-class finish is required.

Very interesting effects can be obtained by spraying colours on to maps, either with a mouth-operated spray or with an air brush By these methods the intensity and texture of colours can be widely varied. Further, with sprays it is possible to a limited extent to indicate the overlapping of different factors, which cannot be done successfully by means of colour applied in the ordinary way. The use of sprays produces a very lively map, and interest is enhanced if some of the smaller areas are coloured in the normal fashion, sprays being used only for the larger areas. This has the advantage of reducing the number of masks that have to be prepared. The need of masks is, in fact, the principal disadvantage of spraying; they have to be cut with great precision so that all parts of the drawing not required to be rendered with a spray are covered. For ease of working, masks are usually made of paper, which is liable to stretch as it becomes impregnated with sprayed colour, so that after a mask has been used several times it becomes useless and has to be replaced. It is, therefore, impracticable to prepare many copies of the same drawing by this method; its use is generally confined to a few display maps for which a particularly high standard is required. The use of both hatchings and colours on the same map is another method of producing a specially lively effect.

In recent years, one particular form of mechanical aid has been much used in the preparation of Planning maps, namely a transparent plastic material adhesive on one side, sold in convenient sized sheets printed with a large variety of hatchings and symbols. This is obtainable under various proprietary names, such as " Zippatone " and " Plastitone ".

This material is available both in black and white form and in colours, and the colours are in the form of solid " washes " as well as of stipples, etc. It is, for the nimble fingered, very easy to use. A sheet of the appropriate type is applied gently to the area to be rendered and is cut to shape with a razor blade or a special pointed cutter, after which the surplus is detached and the material is made to adhere firmly to the drawing by applying pressure. The material can be applied to opaque bases as well as transparent ones, and in the latter case prints can be made in the ordinary way.

Application of the principles suggested to basic types of Planning Maps

These types were set out on page 27 and are now dealt with in the same order :

(1) *Maps showing factors or areas of different character but of approximately equal importance.* In order that a true picture may be presented it is essential that the notation used shall not unduly accentuate any particular area. Thus, if colours are used they should be of about equal intensity, hatchings should be differentiated by changes of colour, direction and texture rather than by variation of spacing or width of line, this rule being applicable also to stipples and patterns of symbols.

In the case of Land Use Maps the matter is rendered more complex because intensity of use needs to be given some visual expression even though it may be difficult to assess, and on the other hand many quite different uses are of equal importance. The very large number of items required for this map, with the consequent elaboration of notation entailed, makes it difficult to pursue a consistent and straightforward policy.

(2) *Maps showing factors of the same kind but differing intensity.* In this case, clearly enough, the considerations which apply are almost exactly the reverse of those in the previous one. Variety in the intensity of the rendering applied is to be desired rather than variety of colour, shape or direction. Nearly every map of this kind is in essence similar to an ordinary physical contour map except that in some cases the grading is discontinuous rather than continuous.

The exact technique adopted depends mainly upon the number of different grades which have to be distinguished. If colour is used and the number of grades is large it may be necessary to use several related colours of increasing intensity instead of the more satisfactory device of restricting use to several intensities of a single colour. For example, raw sienna, burnt sienna and burnt umber is a range of colours which can be used to give an effect of continuity.

Similarly, if stipples are used, the number of readily distinguishable intensities which can be achieved simply by varying the spacing of the dots is limited and it may become necessary to use dots of a different size.

The logic of this, no doubt, is obvious but it is surprising how many maps in this class are produced with entirely unrelated colours of similar intensity, so that the key must be constantly consulted in order to interpret the map.

(3) *Flows.* These will most often be represented by the use of direction indicators; the greatest need is simplicity. Such maps are never easy to interpret, and elaboration beyond what is absolutely essential is usually fatal. A great aid to simplicity is the use of the simplest possible base maps such as the diagrammatic base described earlier, since the details of the country over which the flows take place are seldom of importance and, in fact, the position on the map of the indicators may not even correspond to the physical routes along which such flows take place. It is of great importance, where a number of unconnected flows have to be shown on the same map, particularly if they cross each other, to use a different colour or texture for each indicator.

In the case of maps showing traffic flows it is often desirable to prepare a simplified version for the purpose of making an appreciation of the fundamental problems involved. A form of presentation which distinguishes between several different types of traffic may be invaluable for the analysis and solution of detailed problems, but it seldom enables a general impression to be easily gained.

Other maps showing movement require different treatment because the movements concerned are not from one specific point to another, but consist of a gradual redistribution. A typical example is a map showing changes in the density of population in different parts of an area. The most usual way of presenting this is to show increases in red, decreases in blue, the intensity of the colour in each case being related to the degree of change. Alternatively, where the situation has to be shown also at one or more intermediate stages, the best method is to use several diagrammatic maps of the smallest practicable scale, mounted on a single sheet, and to show the densities prevailing at a given stage on each. Provided the units over which density is measured are the same in each case comparison is simple.

(4) *Distribution of Service Centres and extent of Service areas.* This is another subject for the representation of which symbols are often used—a mortar board for a school, a bed for a hospital and so on. Used with great restraint these symbols may be useful, but if, as is often the case, it is necessary to indicate the presence or absence of a considerable number of service facilities it becomes difficult to devise sufficient self-explanatory symbols—and unless they are self-explanatory they are useless. In these circumstances it is better to use a grid or similar device, each sub-division of which represents a particular service; where a particular service is available the appropriate sub-division is filled in, otherwise it is left blank. Frequent reference to the key to discover which sub-division refers to which facility is entailed at first, but after quite a short time the positions become fixed in the memory. A refinement would be to draw a very small symbol within each sub-division to remove this necessity, but it is doubtful whether the considerable extra work involved would often be justified.

There are two methods of indicating the areas served by centres. The first, is to draw rays from each minor community to the place or places on which it relies for the services it cannot itself supply; this may be sufficient but can be reinforced by outlining the boundary of each service area (they will usually overlap considerably) with a distinctive band. The second is to hatch or colour each area of influence distinctively.

For all maps of this kind an outline diagrammatic base should be used, as the physical characteristics of the area are only important as regards their broader aspects—ranges of hills, rivers and other physical barriers tending to distort service areas, which will be shown even on an outline base.

(5) *Maps dealing with several subjects.* " One subject one map " is a very good rule, so that it is not surprising that maps of this kind, usually sieve maps, which are a deliberate violation of the rule, entail the most difficult problems of presentation.

The term " sieve " is used metaphorically. It is assumed that all the land under examination is " passed " through a series of sieves, each of which represents some characteristic rendering land unfit for the particular purpose being considered, often, as in the example described below, large-scale building development, although the method can be applied to many other subjects. Any land possessing characteristics represented by one or more of the sieves is " caught ", while that which passes through all of them is prima facie suitable for the purpose concerned.

Sieve maps constitute a most valuable means of summarising and analysing survey data.

Discussion will be confined to colour notations, and should be understood to refer principally to sieve maps showing the suitability of land for large scale development.

There is endless scope for ingenuity in working out the details of such notations but, as regards the general basis, only one method has so far been devised which is wholly satisfactory.

The map creates formidable presentation problems. It is necessarily extremely complicated; the boundaries of each of numerous overlapping areas must be absolutely distinct and the hatchings, etc., which cover them must be arranged so that they do not coincide. No very specific suggestions can be made for the design of a notation, since this will be affected by the number and prevalence of the factors affecting a particular region, but four general principles should be observed :—

(*a*) The areas affected by each factor should be indicated both by an edging and by a hatching or pattern of symbols.

(*b*) The larger the area affected by a particular factor the wider should be the spacing of the hatching etc., and the more important the factor the more prominent should it be.

(*c*) The land in each area should be washed in a lighter shade of the colour used for the edging and hatching of the most strongly disqualifying factor affecting that area. For example, assume the strength of disqualification to be, in descending order, steep slopes, high agricultural value, high landscape value; then all areas subject to steep slopes would be washed in the steep slope colour, areas not subject to the steep slope factor but subject to the other two or to agricultural value only would be washed in the high agricultural value colour, and areas subject to high landscape value only would be washed in that colour. This means that in any given area the dominant factor is indicated both by edging and hatching and by a wash, and the lesser factors by edging and hatching only. This treatment greatly increases the intelligibility of the map.

(*d*) Only areas *unsuitable* for development must be shown; any mixture of favourable and unfavourable factors reduces the map almost to illegibility. It would, no doubt, be possible to prepare a positive rather than a negative map, i.e. one showing degrees of suitability for development rather than of unsuitability, but it would necessarily be less definite and selective, since most disqualifying factors cover only a comparatively small proportion of the total area, and by this method the most suitable areas, instead of being left blank, would be covered by so large a number of hatchings that differences between them would not easily be appreciated.

To make clear what is meant by a mixture, suppose that there are, among other factors, a few areas of steep slope in a survey area and only a few areas capable of being readily sewered. The obvious way to indicate these is to hatch both types of area, but this is wrong; it would result in the two hatched areas meaning opposite things. The steep areas should be hatched and all the areas not readily capable of being sewered; the hatched areas then both indicate unsuitability. This may seem a very obvious point, but it is surprising how often it is overlooked.

It is practically essential to prepare a " mock-up " in some detail before embarking on the drafting of a complicated sieve map, for it is very difficult indeed to visualise the exact effect which will be produced by the addition of a particular kind of rendering to a map which already has several drawn on it, and if a mistaken decision is made amendment is usually impossible.

The main difficulties are to ensure that the spacing of the hatching or other rendering used for each factor shall be sufficiently close to show up on the smallest area to which it applies, yet not so close as to prevent other factors present being visible, to avoid any hatching or symbol coinciding with another and to make sure that no factor is shown so unobtrusively that it vanishes under the weight of others.

The first can be very awkward. It is absolutely essential that the spacing for the rendering of any particular factor shall be constant throughout the map and not, as can often be done with less complicated maps, moved about to suit the positions and shapes of detached areas (for to do this would make it impossible to solve the second difficulty), and it is difficult to position hatching so that every small detached area affected shall have a line running through it.

The second merely demands care. If a sub-divided geometrical grid is placed over the map and the spacing of each hatching, symbol etc., determined by reference to it, it should be easy to ensure that no clashes occur. They must not; even minor coincidences which one would not expect to have any appreciable effect are liable to impair the legibility which is so important and difficult to maintain.

The third cannot always be guarded against in advance but can usually be corrected by strengthening after the map has been completed. This may in fact be necessary for more than one factor.

Diagrams not in map form. These are principally of use in providing a visual summary of information which does not relate to land, or at least not to specific parcels of land, and so cannot be shown in map form, but which can be more readily assimilated if presented graphically. This in fact applies to nearly all quantitative statements except the simplest.

A simple example of the advantage of this form of presentation is to imagine a list of fifty parishes with the acreage of each beside it. If in written form it would, at best, require several careful readings before its principal implications could be appreciated. But if a bar of length proportionate to the acreage of each parish were substituted for or supplied in addition to the figures one could, almost at a glance, see which Parishes were the smallest and the largest and gain a very good idea of the mean size.

There is seldom any need to adopt a much more complicated technique than this though minor adaptions and elaborations may sometimes be helpful.

It remains only to mention subjects which suggest themselves as especially suitable for presentation in this way, such as comparisons of the total area occupied by each use in a town, employment structure, comparison of household structure with house sizes, proportion of dwellings in bad and very bad condition, areas of land required to relieve congestion and establish satisfactory open space standards, areas of land suitable and moderately suitable for general development. Fig. 35 is a graphic representation of the areas of land needed to implement Planning proposals of several kinds. Though in this case partially related to a map it is essentially an example of the technique under discussion.

Notations for Planning Maps

A comprehensive code has been worked out over the years by the Ministry, now called the Ministry of Housing and Local Government, and is contained in the following circulars: Ministry of Town and Country Planning Circulars Nos. 40, 59 (as amended by Circular 70), 63 and 92. Three scales of map are used for most purposes: 1″ to the mile for county surveys and proposals, 6″ to the mile for town surveys and proposals and 1/2,500 for more detailed proposals such as supplementary town maps and comprehensive development area maps. The principle used is to treat the existing land use maps at each scale as reference points to show the conditions obtaining now as compared with the conditions which it is hoped will exist at the end of the plan period (usually 20 years). The latter are shown on development plan maps, which might be described as prophetic land use maps—maps of the land use as it is hoped it will be in 20 years' time. This sounds reasonable, but it is in my view an unsatisfactory method, since proposed changes can only be understood for a particular piece of land by first identifying it and noting its use on the existing land use map and then turning to the development plan map to see whether the use is intended to change. This is not particularly convenient even in the case of one piece of land, but is practically impossible to get an overall understanding of the changes proposed by means of it.

The official system is more fully explained in Appendix I.

A very much better method, which is shown in Fig. 36, is to treat the development plan map as a self-contained document and to show on it existing areas of use which it is intended to retain in an intense colour or hatching, and proposed new areas of each use in corresponding notations of decreased intensity. In practice this method works well, and it is very difficult to understand why it was not adopted by the Ministry, especially since it is used for areas of existing and proposed urban development shown on County Maps. Its only defect is that, where a monochrome notation is used, it is still not possible where one building use is intended to be changed to another building use on a particular area of land, to tell what the present use is without reference to the existing land use map, but this difficulty applies to only a minority of proposals, whereas the official method applies to all. Where a coloured notation is used even this drawback disappears if a monochrome map showing existing land use is used as the base. The existing use appears in black and the proposed new use as a colour. This method can be used for what are referred to in this book as Second Stage Regional Plans, Town Maps, Supplementary Town Maps, and Comprehensive Development Area Maps.

When one gets to the stage of detail at which individual buildings, small open spaces and the like have to be portrayed the problems of presentation become exceedingly difficult. It is easy enough to show an area as it is hoped it will be after development has been carried out, by means of a coloured or monochrome drawing prepared in ordinary architectural fashion, but this does not enable the pattern of land uses to be shown clearly if the design qualities of the proposals are also to be given full emphasis, nor does it enable a quick comparison to be made between the area as it is and as it will be, with particular reference to the buildings which will have to be demolished and to the extent to which the existing road system is retained.

As is explained elsewhere in this chapter, it is normally desirable that both the existing state of affairs and the proposed alterations should be shown on the same drawing, but in this case it is difficult. For a residential area the best solution is probably to prepare one map as a straight-forward zoning map which shows existing uses to be retained and proposed new uses, in just the same way as I have suggested for a town map, and another of the normal architectural kind; where practicable it is helpful to prepare the former at a much smaller scale than the latter so that both can be mounted on the same piece of paper to facilitate comparison. In the case of the redevelopment of a town centre, a zoning map may or may not be useful, since zoning may be by means of horizontal rather than vertical divisions. Where the division is mainly vertical an excellent method is to show the Town Centre as redeveloped, on an axonometric projection instead of a plan and to distinguish the different uses at different levels by means of colour.

For residential areas in which some redevelopment as well as new development is involved, as well as for Town Centres, it is also desirable to prepare architectural type drawings, showing as clearly as possible the intended eventual form of the area concerned and, in addition, the proposed new buildings, streets, open spaces, etc. lightly superimposed upon a base map showing existing conditions. The latter will afford a ready means of appreciating in greater detail than the zoning map precisely what demolitions are entailed.

3-3. METHODS OF THREE DIMENSIONAL REPRESENTATION
Models

The cleverest rendering of maps can only produce an illusion of three-dimensional reality, since, to provide a blinding glimpse of the obvious, a map is only a flat sheet of paper. Quite crudely constructed three-dimensional models can give an altogether more vivid impression of the shape of an area than even the best of maps.

Models can be prepared to scales as widely varying as those of maps, and there are several kinds.

Landscape models aim at giving a more or less literal impression of a stretch of country, the only departure from accuracy being the exaggeration of differences in level, which are often almost imperceptible if this is not done. A point sometimes overlooked by the tyro model-maker is that though it might seem logical to exaggerate the heights of buildings, trees, and so on, in the same proportion as differences in the level of land, this, in fact, leads to disaster. Models of this kind are generally familiar; they are often extremely beautiful pieces of work, but when highly finished they are likely to be unduly expensive; almost equally good effects can be obtained by less elaborate means.

" *Map* " *models* consist simply of maps stuck to sheets of plywood or cardboard and placed on top of each other in layers, each successive layer including all the land above a given contour line. The final result is a stepped model which, while it lacks the literal realism of the other kinds, gives a startlingly clear picture of land relief. The 1/25,000 Ordnance maps (fully coloured edition) are particularly suitable for models of this kind. The method of leaving steps between successive contours, which is unavoidable when maps are used, is sometimes employed for the other type of model. It simplifies construction and emphasises relief, while it does not reduce realism nearly as much as might be expected.

It is often very effective to present a Town Map in model form, proposals being shown exactly as they would be on a map. This method can often make clear the reasons for the locations of the various uses better than any other.

Another kind of model consists of aerial photographs specially treated and stretched over a previously prepared surface shaped to the relief of the area. A model of this kind has obvious and great advantages but is clearly more suited to comparatively small scales, at which the lack of third dimensional treatment of buildings and trees does not matter.

Recently there have begun to appear models of a novel kind which have not, so far as I know, yet been used for planning purposes but which have great possibilities. These are in two slightly different forms. Each consists of a sheet of plastic stamped to shape on a matrix, but one form is limp as a roll of cloth and can be folded up and carried about under the arm while the other, although almost light as paper, is rigid.

Most models are heavy, difficult to transport and fragile, disadvantages which these overcome altogether. If reasonably adequate resources were devoted to Planning there can be little doubt that these plastic models would soon become widely used.

An extremely ingenious and economical use of contoured models to produce a striking form of presentation has recently been developed by postgraduate students of the Town Planning Department of University College, London. They prepared a map model of a study area, and superimposed upon it a number of sheets of glass upon which survey information, survey analyses and diagrammatic proposals had been directly drawn. Each of these in turn was photographed, the model being appropriately lighted to show up the contours, and slides made of the photographs.

The making of first-class models is a complicated art, but quite satisfactory ones can be made with very little experience. The basis for each is the superimposition of layers of plywood or other material and, except with the stepped type, these are covered with plasticine, plaster of Paris or modelling clay to reproduce the natural slopes of the land and to provide a base for the application of ground colour, buildings, trees, roads, hedges, etc.

It is possible and very effective to employ for display to the public the kind of map sometimes found in hotel foyers, on which certain features consist of transparent material, the remainder of the map being opaque. Various selections of items can be thrown into prominence by switching on a series of small lamps placed behind the transparent areas, sometimes in different colours for different kinds of items. Obviously this kind of presentation would be costly and take a great deal of time to prepare, and would only be justified for a major piece of presentation.

Aerial Photographs

Vertical aerial photographs are available in two principal forms:—

(i) Series of small overlapping photographs which, when any two are looked at through a stereoscope, give a brilliant three-dimensional picture.

(ii) Mosaics at a scale of 6″ to one mile. These are printed on sheets based on National Grid squares. They cannot be used stereoscopically and lack the definition of the smaller photographs, but they are much more useful for general purposes. The smaller photographs, because of the very large number required to cover an area of any size, are somewhat confusing to use and are much more useful for studying detailed problems than for making broad appreciations.

Aerial photographs show the distribution and character of vegetation very clearly, while few maps show it at all except for woodlands and orchards.

Oblique aerial photographs are not so generally useful as vertical ones, since they are not true to scale, but they provide excellent panoramas and are much more readily understood by laymen than maps or vertical photographs.

Anaglyphs, though not in general use, are potentially of enormous value. They consist of two photographs of the same area which do not quite coincide, one printed in red, the other in blue, upon the same sheet of paper; when viewed through eyeglasses of plain glass or plastic, one red, the other blue, a three-dimensional effect is obtained almost equal to that given by a stereoscope used with ordinary aerial photographs, but covering a much larger area. Thus, by issuing a pair of these inexpensive eyeglasses to each spectator, an anaglyph can effectively take the place of a model, but is more easily portable and also saves the large amount of laborious manual work which the preparation of a model requires.

Another development with exciting possibilities is the " artificial anaglyph ", which consists of line drawings superimposed in exactly the same way as in the case of the photographic anaglyph. The best known example of this is

the drawing prepared for the London County Council's proposals for the redevelopment of the South Bank, which gives a startlingly vivid impression of buildings, at the cost, one would suppose, of much less effort than that required to construct a model, and with the advantage of portability. It was published in the " Architect's Journal " of 21st January, 1954.

3-4. REPRODUCTION OF DRAWINGS

Much of the foregoing has been concerned with the technique of preparing drawings in a form suitable for reproduction, something must now be said about the various processes used for reproduction. The subject is a specialised one and it is beyond the scope of this book to attempt to treat it in detail. " Processes of Graphic Reproduction in Printing," by Harold Curwen (Faber and Faber) gives a clear and authoritative account.

A distinction must be made between the reproduction of drawings in limited numbers for office or committee use and production in quantity for publication. Quite different methods are used for these two purposes.

Reproduction in limited quantities

Three principal methods are available :

(i) Dye-line prints

These are produced by laying a transparent original over sensitised paper, exposing both to strong light and then immersing the sensitised paper in ammonia fumes. This process is quick and cheap, and the apparatus is sufficiently simple and inexpensive to be installed in a fairly large drawing office. The prints obtained have a dense but not perfectly black line; they can be coloured, but the paper is rather spongy, which makes first-class work difficult, and any erasures which may be necessary cannot be coloured over successfully; moreover, dye-line prints are not permanent; the lines gradually fade away, and this happens fairly quickly if prints are kept where they are exposed to strong light. A print pinned to a wall on which sunlight plays may, in the course of a year or two, be reduced to a blank sheet of paper. Nevertheless, for the quick reproduction of drawings required to be in use for only a short time, dye-line prints are extremely useful.

(ii) True-to-scale prints

These give prints with firm black lines indistinguishable from those hand drawn in Indian ink. They are produced by making on gelatine an impression of a special print taken from the original drawing; the gelatine surface is then inked, and the true-to-scale prints are obtained by placing sheets of paper one by one on the gelatine and passing a roller over each. Any type of ordinary drawing paper may be used, so that hand colouring of the prints is much more satisfactory than for dye-line prints. It is possible, though expensive, to have the prints made in a simple colour notation when the work involved is too great to be tackled by hand colouring in the drawing office, but the number of copies required is too small to justify the more elaborate processes about to be described. It is however, difficult to obtain a high degree of accuracy in coloured "time to scale" prints. The true-to-scale process is rather more expensive than the dye-line one and can only be carried out by specially trained operators.

(iii) Photographic prints

These are simply photographs of drawings. They have several advantages not possessed by the dye-line and true-to-scale processes; the original need not be transparent and the prints need not be made to the same scale as the original. Colours on the original will appear as different tones of grey on the prints, and this can be deliberately used to advantage if the colours chosen are light and carefully contrasted; heavy colour, on the other hand, will print as black and obscure underlying detail.

Since the prints are made on photographic paper of various kinds, the satisfactory application of colour to them is difficult, although small areas of special significance can be picked out effectively in colour. The cost of this method varies considerably with the degree of enlargement or reduction required; on the whole it is rather more expensive than either of the two previous methods, but it has the advantage over them that, because of the different tones which can be produced, more complicated information can be shown clearly.

One extremely valuable application of the photographic process is its ability to reproduce an opaque original on transparent material. If such an original is of a complicated nature this may save a great deal of labour, since the reproduction can be altered as desired and subsequent prints taken by the dye-line or true-to-scale methods, and coloured by hand. In the absence of a photographically produced transparency many hours might have to be spent in making a tracing of the original.

Reproduction in quantity

Three methods are in general use; all three can be used for black and white or for colour work and need not be to the same scale as the original drawing.

(i) Line blocks

The original drawings are photographed and transferred to zinc blocks; a separate block must be made for each colour, and if many colours are used the cost is likely to be prohibitive. Some economy can be effected by combining primary colours to form secondary colours, e.g., areas to be coloured purple would be printed on both the blue and the red blocks. Some variety of tone can be obtained by placing finely hatched or dotted screens over those portions which it is desired to print lighter than the remainder; the pattern on the screen prints white and dilutes the colour. This process cannot be used to produce a continuous gradation of tones, but must be limited to two, or at most three, tones of the same colour if they are to be distinct. Screens can also be used with black and white drawings to produce varying tones of grey.

(ii) Half-tone blocks

These are produced by an entirely different process. A continuous gradation of tones can be produced, and, in fact, a fairly close approximation to a complicated painting can be obtained. Since, however, the colours are built up from a vast number of blue, yellow, red and black dots of different sizes, spaced at varying intervals, it is impossible to obtain quite the sharpness and clarity given by a good line block, and, since planning maps seldom or never require continuous gradations of tone and colour, line blocks are generally to be preferred.

(iii) Lithography

The lithographic process gives results similar to, but not quite so sharp as those from line blocks, but where the area of the reproduction is to be greater than about one square foot lithography is cheaper.

It is highly desirable, before embarking on any programme of work involving the reproduction of planning maps by any of the three preceding methods, to consult the firm which is to make the blocks and plates. This should be done before the original drawings are made, as much expense can be saved and greatly improved results obtained by following expert advice on details. In the case of line blocks and reproduction by lithography in colour, it is necessary to supply the firm with the following :

(1) A fully coloured copy of the original drawing showing as precisely as possible the effect desired in the reproduction.

(2) An uncoloured print showing the black lines (i.e., normally the base map) and any black areas only.

(3) An overlay for each colour to be used with the areas over which that colour is to be printed, and those only, blacked in.

The above procedure avoids errors through misunderstanding and lightens the task of the printer.

It is obvious that where the original is to be reproduced to a different size the scale must be drawn on it and not stated in figures or as a representative fraction.

It is important that all lines on drawings to be reproduced should be firm and even, otherwise some lines or portions of them may not show up on the reproductions.

3-5. CONCLUSION

It is all too easy for slick presentation to be used in such a way as to conceal, at least from all but the most perceptive of viewers, shortcomings in the proposals portrayed. Conversely, very inept presentation may do precisely the same thing. Many Town Maps, drawn up in the drab "monochrome" notation of Circular 92, rendered drabber by slovenly draughtsmanship, approach so close to illegibility as to conceal from nearly everyone the absence of ideas or, in some cases, the abnormality of the ideas contained in them.

In recent years standards of presentation in this country, which used to be very high, have deteriorated badly. Nowadays one would usually look to German, Italian or Scandinavian sources for really good examples. This is a great pity, for, while good presentation can do nothing for poor proposals, it can do much to aid understanding and acceptance of good proposals.

Undoubtedly, the insistence by the Ministry upon use of the Circular 92 notations, at best uninspired, at worst incomprehensible, has discouraged

enterprise and resourcefulness in developing new techniques. It is high time that some of the more energetic planning authorities refused to submit to Ministry pressure, and insisted upon developing and using a better system.[1]

---

[1] As this book goes to press a revised system of notations is emerging. This is based entirely upon edgings and letterings, hatching being entirely eliminated. This system is at least legible; it enables a given site, and the land use allocated to it, to be identified with ease, but gives even less good a general idea of the Plan than the system it is displacing.

CHAPTER 4

REGIONAL PLANNING

4-1. INTRODUCTORY

REGIONAL PLANNING, as distinct from town or local Planning, involves primarily, as has been suggested in Chapter 1, the selection of some communities rather than others for change or growth, the general determination of locations for large non-urban uses, and the working out in general terms of a satisfactory transport network, rather than the specific selection of particular sites for particular uses. These processes can be described more fully as :

(1) The balancing of population and employment so that no daily mass movements of population to and from work and home are necessary.

(2) The improvement and rationalisation of transport routes to take the best advantage of existing facilities and to make the most effective use of the resources available for constructional improvements.

(3) The strengthening of the pattern of service centres in such a way as to secure for the great majority of the population concerned a reasonable accessibility to all grades of service.

(4) The location of large non-agricultural uses of land in the open country in such a way as positively to make the best use of natural resources. (Areas to be reserved for afforestation, reservoirs, areas of natural beauty and nature reserves are obvious examples of these) and, negatively, to secure that both these and unproductive uses such as military training grounds are placed so as to disrupt the agricultural pattern and the communications of the region as little as possible.

Regional Planning has nowhere been practised very fully. There have been innumerable advisory regional Plans, mostly quite incapable of fulfilment. There have been great experiments in regional development such as the Tennessee Valley Authority's, but these have either been unrelated to practical possibilities or else have had little connection with Planning as we have agreed to use the word, however impressive they may have been in other ways.

It would, in fact, probably only be possible to practise regional Planning fully in a community more politically advanced than any at present existing. The advance beyond present political and administrative standards might not have to be great, but it would have to be appreciable, since the full practice of regional Planning involves the complete abandonment of parochialism and rivalry between communities and the submission of land use problems to dispassionate public decision.[1]

---

[1] The ludicrous, but successful, campaign to prevent the amalgamation of the County of Rutland with its neighbours is a good example of the obstacles to administrative rationalisation which stand in the way of creating a system within which fully effective Regional Planning could be applied.

The Town and Country Planning Act of 1947 paved the way for regional Planning in this country, but it is beyond doubt that it is at the regional level that Planning has so far had least success. Sixteen years after the coming into operation of the 1947 Act, fundamental problems of regional Planning which ought long since to have been settled and incorporated as parts of outline regional Plans are still a matter of acute controversy. Perhaps the most flagrant example of this is the question of where over-spill from the Manchester region should be accommodated. Indeed, in no part of the country has the pattern of future distribution of population and industry been determined to an acceptable degree of definiteness. The mere fact that decisions on such matters are still constantly being made the subject of public inquiry and fought out *de novo* is itself an indication that regional Planning by means of an orderly sequence of survey, preparation of outline Plans, consultation and finally the preparation of more detailed Plans is not taken seriously by the government.

I have said that the 1947 Act provided the basis for regional Planning, and this is true inasmuch as it made County Councils and County Borough Councils the local Planning authorities for the country and included provision for the Minister to set up Joint Boards to deal with the Planning of any two or more of these, where desirable. At the time of writing no Joint Boards have been formed except for the purpose of National Park administration. By no means all Counties are suitable units for regional Planning, even if the County Boroughs which they contain were included. When the County Boroughs are taken away and made independent Planning authorities the idea of regional Planning tends to become a mockery in the absence of Joint Boards.

It is true that proposals are in hand for the creation of a Greater London Council and for regrouping and rationalisation of authorities in the Newcastle-upon-Tyne area and elsewhere, but in the case of London it is doubtful, to say the least of it, whether the new arrangements will in fact bring Regional Planning in a real sense much nearer to reality. Even if the Greater London Council sets up a suitable Regional Planning organisation there appear to be grave doubts as to whether effective steps can be taken to ensure that the new London Boroughs will implement the Regional Plan it prepares.

It is necessary to distinguish between Regional Planning and Regional Development, for they are often confused. Regional Planning need involve no more than the control of development in accordance with a Regional Plan, by whatever agencies it is carried out, but Regional Development is usually taken to mean the organisation of all or most forms of development, production and power by a Regional Authority. Though this is a concept which has much to commend it, and I personally would strongly support it, Regional Planning in the more limited sense is perfectly possible, if admittedly a good deal more difficult, under the present economic arrangements.

Let us now turn to consideration of what constitutes a region, and what kind of area makes a satisfactory region for Planning purposes. A Region in a general sense is an area of land possessing characteristics which make it a readily identifiable entity; these characteristics may be physical, economic or social, and, in the case of a region with strongly marked identity, several are likely to apply to it.

What is needed for Planning purposes is an area which is large enough to enable substantial changes in the distribution of population and employment to take place within its boundaries, yet which is small enough for its Planning problems to be comprehended as a whole.

A provincial metropolis such as Manchester or Birmingham and the towns, villages and area of open country which look to it for regional services, or a group of towns linked industrially, together with their rural hinterlands, such as the Potteries, comprise Planning regions with obvious advantages.

In less densely populated areas the service area of a local capital (defined later in this chapter) would be suitable, and in fact corresponds roughly with the boundaries of some of the more rural English Counties.

As a matter of practical policy it is also desirable that the physical extent of a region should not be too great for it to be possible to reach all parts of it from its centre and to return to the centre within a day, leaving adequate time for work to be done, or, from another point of view, for it to be possible for the senior Planning staff to acquire sufficient knowledge of the whole region for each community in it to be something more than a mere name to them. These may possibly seem trifling factors, but they may make the crucial difference between efficient and understanding Planning work and a mere lifeless process of pattern-making.

The determination in detail of suitable boundaries for a Planning unit is a matter of considerable difficulty. Existing administrative boundaries are rarely ideal, but to ignore them entirely would create hopeless confusion. Professor Eva Taylor has suggested in the A.P.R.R. " Town and Country Planning Textbook " that after determining the general extent of the region the detailed boundary should be built up by using the outer parts of the boundaries of those parishes which lie on its periphery. She suggests that, although parish boundaries may cut across functional or geographical units, the short lengths of boundary involved for each individual parish should reduce such drawbacks to a minimum. Although Professor Taylor does not specifically link this method of fixing the boundary with the selection of a general area based upon the area of influence of a provincial metropolis or group of towns it would seem that the two could readily be combined and that the result would probably be a region possessing physical as well as economic and social unity. The boundaries of areas of influence generally follow marked physical features such as watersheds because of the obstacles to transport which these form. They are commonly respected to a considerable extent by parish boundaries.

Areas bounded by watersheds form satisfactory units as regards agricultural structure and drainage, although, where a watershed does not form a very pronounced barrier, social and economic influence may be little impeded.

It has already been said that existing administrative boundaries are rarely ideal for the purpose of Planning units, and this applies in varying degree to all grades of units from counties to parishes. The historical development of these units has been so profoundly influenced by strategic, ecclesiastical and political considerations that they have often lost all administrative convenience, and this has been accentuated by the immense changes in the distribution and areas of influence of centres of economic and social im-

portance caused by the Industrial Revolution, the railways and the internal combustion engine.

Dr. Dudley Stamp and S. H. Beaver in " The British Isles " describe, for example, the way in which parishes in mediaeval times became unwieldy and irregular in shape because of the efforts of monasteries to increase their tithe income by combining several parishes surrounding a parish church belonging to a monastery.

They also contrast the counties, such as Kent, Sussex, Norfolk and Suffolk, which were originally kingdoms and which, on the whole, still form convenient units, with those, such as the Midland shires—Bedfordshire, Northamptonshire, Oxfordshire and so on—which originated later as arbitrary sub-divisions in the course of wars between Wessex and the Danes and which today are in many cases administratively unsatisfactory.

Later developments of local government units have often produced situations as anomalous as those which arose earlier. Perhaps the most striking example is the Manchester area, in which the County Borough of Manchester itself is a comparatively small part of the main built-up area, in which are included also the County Boroughs of Salford, Oldham and Stockport and the Boroughs of Stretford, Sale, Middleton, Prestwich and Eccles, together with several urban districts and parts of rural districts. To complete the chaos the county boundary between Lancashire and Cheshire runs through the midst of this area.

As noted earlier, the Town and Country Planning Act, 1947 theoretically enables any Planning region considered suitable to be created by the setting up by the Ministry of a Joint Board, which may embrace the whole or parts of any two or more counties and/or county boroughs, but, except for the purpose of administering National Parks, no Joint Boards at all have been established, not even for Lancashire, the numerous county boroughs within it, and Cheshire, or, at the other extreme, for Kent and Canterbury, the latter the smallest county borough in the country with a population of little more than 20,000.

It therefore appears that the notorious inability of local authorities to co-operate with each other has been officially considered impossible of cure. The Act also enables joint advisory planning committees to be established, but the prospect of these operating usefully is even dimmer than for executive Joint Boards.

Meanwhile, the administrative counties are in effect the Planning regions; where there are no county boroughs and where the counties are reasonably large and their boundaries follow those of geographical units, however approximately, they form not wholly inappropriate units provided that a reasonable degree of collaboration takes place between adjoining authorities in respect of border areas which are on the wrong side of the boundary for Planning purposes. Even in the absence of such collaboration the co-ordinating functions of the regional offices of the Ministry of Housing and Local Government might suffice if energetically performed.

These regional offices, it should be noted, do not relate to regions in the sense in which the word has far been used in this chapter. The Ministry regions are merely groups of adjoining Local Planning Authorities, each capable of being administered, so far as the regional offices' functions are concerned, from a central point. These functions are supervisory and co-ordinating, and little concerned with Plan making.

It has become evident that, if Regional Planning is to become a reality in this country, the impetus must be provided by the Central Government both in the form of an outline National Plan to give a framework of general planning assumptions within which each Regional Planning Authority can work and also to set objectives. The present County Plans are meagre and uninspired, and are becoming more so (see Appendix I); they contain none of the dynamic needed for real Regional Plans.

4-2. THE DISTRIBUTION AND SIZES OF SETTLEMENTS

Just as many administrative units were created to meet circumstances which no longer exist, so the sizes, types and distribution of human settlements which exist today are largely the result of factors which have become altered in many ways.

The basic pattern. Human settlements form a pattern, albeit usually a highly irregular one, and are not arbitrarily scattered. The pattern can best be conceived as a primitive distribution of settlements, based upon food gathering and marketing, which has, in areas of dense population, been overlaid and distorted by a series of subsequent events.

There is a reason for the location of any human settlement. In primitive times, after the introduction of animal husbandry and crop cultivation had rendered possible a degree of specialisation and density of population greater than that attainable by the nomadic hunting tribes of the earliest men, prosperity and, indeed, survival must have depended directly upon local agricultural productivity to an extent which, in a modern urbanised and industrial country with highly developed transport resources, it is difficult to imagine fully.

Primitive settlements, therefore, were necessarily sited near fertile land so that it was physically possible to carry the fruits of the land to the community for its consumption. A sufficient, reliable and pure supply of water close at hand (a singularly difficult substance to transport in primitive times) was also essential, and, frequently, local conditions made it essential that the site should be capable of being readily defended. The population of any particular community was automatically limited by the number who could be fed from the produce of an area of land with a radius sufficiently small to enable the food to be gathered and brought to the settlement without the expenditure of more labour than could be spared from actual food production—a simpler version of our own problem of combining directly and indirectly productive labour in satisfactory proportions.

Much later, the improvement of communication routes, the introduction of wheeled transport and the centralisation of administration resulted in a pattern which, although based upon the simple original distribution of communities, was a great deal more complicated. The elements in this pattern, as it exists today in this country, may be summarised as follows:

(i) *Provincial capitals.* Towns such as Manchester, Birmingham and Bristol with populations of half a million or more. These provide services of many kinds for the inhabitants of a very large area. Characteristically, they possess a daily newspaper, a university, regional government offices, a stock exchange and a large general hospital, and are the nodes of main transport routes of all kinds, which make them easily accessible to the inhabitants of large areas.

(ii) *Local capitals.* These are often, but not always, county towns. They have, typically, populations of 50,000 upwards and possess urban facilities which, although they do not include those mentioned in the preceding paragraph, constitute a set of services complete except for those which require an extremely large population for their support. Typical institutions not found in towns of a lower grade are a weekly newspaper circulating over a wide area, an assize court, a repertory theatre, an ancient grammar school and department stores. Many towns of this class are cathedral cities. They, too, are points of convergence for transport routes, and have often grown from market towns of very modest size because their geographical position made them specially accessible. They are found at widely varying intervals but are often spaced about 25 miles apart in regions of dense and fairly uniform population, conditions to which the average intervals given here for places of lower status apply.

(iii) *Fully-fledged towns.* These vary in size around 10,000 population and possess facilities meeting all but the occasional needs of the majority of people. A. E. Smailes, in the A.P.R.R's "Town and Country Planning Textbook," has suggested that to qualify as a fully-fledged town a place must possess the following :

> Three or four banks.
> A secondary school.
> A cinema.
> A weekly newspaper.
> A hospital.

One would also expect to find professional and insurance offices, multiple shops such as Woolworth's and minor Government offices, while most such towns still have weekly stock and produce markets. These towns occur at intervals of about 15 miles.

(iv) *Urban villages or major rural centres.* These, typically, have a population of 1,500 or more; they do not normally possess a newspaper or a hospital, but have at least one bank, a fairly wide range of shops and usually a cinema and a secondary school. Frequently they are the headquarters of the administration of a rural district, and occur at intervals of about six miles.

(v) *Villages or minor rural centres.* Villages vary greatly in size, but, as used here, the term means a place with a church, a primary school and several shops. The population of such a " fully-fledged " village, which can appropriately be described as a minor rural centre, and has a social and economic influence extending some distance beyond its area of compact development, is often about 500 within such area, although the texture of villages varies greatly and is often so loose that it is hard to decide where the village proper ends and its more thinly populated hinterland begins. A common interval between villages is about four miles.

(*iv*) *Hamlets*. These are the smallest communities, and may consist of no more than a dozen households, together with a pub, a general store and sometimes a church. Occurring at intervals of two miles or so, they provide some very small degree of community services to those outside them and are, in this respect only, distinguishable from

(*vii*) *Isolated farmhouses and agricultural workers' cottages*, which are entirely dependent for services upon communities and which, together with the hamlets, contain the outside population served by the minor rural centres.

Places of each of these classes, except the last, possess some degree of centrality, i.e., are places to which people other than their inhabitants tend to converge; all, therefore, also possess some degree of nodality. They are almost invariably situated at or very near a junction of transport routes or change in means of transport—a cross roads, the point at which a river ceases to be navigable, or a harbour. This is true of even the smallest settlements, although the junction in such cases may be no more than that of a road with a much-used footpath.

It is by no means always easy to decide to which class any place belongs. Many places possess characteristics almost exactly intermediate between two of the grades listed above, and in the last resort it is the functions that they perform rather than their populations and visual characteristics which determine their positions in the scale. Many different classifications of the grades of place have been adopted by various authorities for different purposes, each with different sets of names; the above has been chosen as distinguishing those which for Planning purposes require to be treated distinctively.

Moreover, the functions of places change as inventions increase accessibility or self-sufficiency. Just as the introduction of the railway, as noted a little later, led to the decline of a proportion of market towns so the modern rural bus service and the wide availability of private motor vehicles may well be breaking down the distinction between the ordinary village and what I have called the urban village. As the towns proper become more and more accessible the usefulness of the urban village as a distinct level in the heirarchy seems certain to diminish.

The spatial distribution of centres of different grades tends to form a pattern the regularity of which is proportional to the simplicity and uniformity of the land area concerned. Thus, in an area without natural obstacles, of uniform fertility, with an evenly meshed transport network and hence a fairly even distribution of population, a pattern of remarkable regularity can be observed, provided that agriculture remains the dominant industry. Manufacturing industry, geographical obstacles, greatly varying fertility and irregular spacing or varying importance of traffic routes are all distorting factors which push and pull the pattern of settlements out of place until it may become indecipherable.

In numerous small areas and over most of Lincolnshire, Norfolk and Suffolk the pattern is still remarkably regular, but elsewhere distorting factors are extremely prevalent, so that the practical applicability of any theoretical statement regarding the distribution of communities must be limited unless some method can be found of measuring the distortion to be expected from any particular factor.

The most comprehensive and detailed theory has been produced by a German, Walter Christaller, whose work is based on a study of Southern Germany. For Christaller, what matters about a place is its centrality—the facilities it provides as a centre for services and the population which make use of these services. The resident population of any particular place may not be proportionate to its centrality, and thus a map of a region which indicates the population of each place may not show its true relative importance as a service centre. The pattern may only emerge clearly when the centrality has been measured and compared with that of other places, allowance being made for distortions. Nevertheless, Christaller sees some connection between centrality and resident population, since he assigns typical populations to places occupying distinctive positions in the hierarchy of communities.

As a yardstick Christaller takes the telephone, and derives the degree of centrality of a place—that is, the amount of the services it performs apart from those relating to the needs of its own inhabitants, by means of the following formula:—

$$\text{Centrality of place} = \text{Number of telephones in place} - \left\{ \text{Number of inhabitants in place} \times \frac{\text{Number of telephones in area served by place}}{\text{number of inhabitants in area served by place}} \right\}$$

It is claimed that this formula enables the relative importance of places as service centres to be assessed, and thus for an optimum distribution of services to be determined.

Within the service area of a town with half a million inhabitants Christaller distinguishes six other grades of centre, with approximate populations in descending order of 100,000, 30,000, 10,000, 4,000, 2,000 and 1,000, the last-named being $4\frac{1}{2}$ miles apart.

In a regular theoretical system the service area of each place would be a perfect circle but these circles would intersect, indicating dual influence within the intersecting portions. Straight lines bisecting these intersecting areas would build up into a series of regular hexagons, as shown in Fig. 5, each hexagon representing the service area of a place. On this basis a place provides services of a given order for itself and for an area totalling one-third of the service areas of the places of next lower grade surrounding it. This series of regular hexagons necessarily involves a regular interval between neighbouring places (irrespective of their grade) and that the distances between places of equal grade increases $\sqrt{3}$ times for each successive upward step of grade. Thus, if the distance apart of all places irrespective of grade is $2\frac{1}{2}$ miles, places of equal status in the hierarchy will be, in ascending

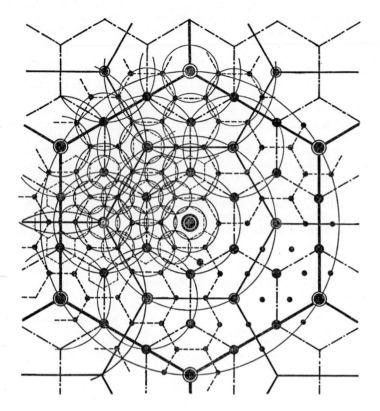

THE CATEGORIES OF CENTRAL PLACES		INTERVALS MILES	TYPICAL SIZE	BOUNDARIES OF AREAS SERVED
HAMLET	•	2	50	----------------------
VILLAGE	◉	4	500	---------------
URBAN VILLAGE	◉	7	1500	— - — - — - — - —
FULLY FLEDGED TOWN	◉	13	10000	————————
LOCAL CAPITAL	◉	22	50000	———————

SCALE   0   5   10   15   MILES

FIG. 5.   Christaller's theory of service centres applied to English conditions.

order, 2½ miles, 4⅓ miles, 7½ miles, 13 miles, 22½ miles, 39 miles and 67½ miles apart.   This does not agree exactly with the intervals suggested earlier in this chapter as being general in this country, which were rough averages for each grade for the country as a whole, but it is close.

Above the level of the local capital the theoretical grading breaks down so far as England is concerned, for the inhabitants of towns with a population of about 50,000 do not in fact normally look to towns of 100,000 for such central services as would not be found locally, but rely almost entirely upon a Provincial Capital.   A probable reason for this is the very high degree of accessibility possessed by English Provincial Capitals, because of the close communication network, resulting in a greater concentration therein of central services than would take place in a theoretical system.

Even though it is not possible to give the Planner a formula for calculating the services which ought to be provided in each town and village, the hierarchic concept of settlements is essentially valid and important, and should be incorporated in all regional Planning proposals.

Before leaving this subject it will be valuable to compare the views of geographers regarding the spacing of towns.   R. E. Dickenson, in " City, Region and Regionalism," refers to Christaller's figure of 7—9 kilometres (4½ to 6 miles) as the average distance apart of places, and states that this is " a basic determinant of the distribution of villages and small country towns all over the Old World in closely settled areas."   He points out that this spacing provides a local service area which takes about one hour to traverse from circumference to centre—i.e. 2½—3 miles.

Professor Eva Taylor, in the A.P.R.R. Textbook, gives the traditional distance apart of market towns as 10 to 12 miles in comparatively fertile lowland areas, an interval which made possible the carrying of produce or driving of stock to a morning market.

Dr. Dudley Stamp and E. H. Beaver, (" The British Isles ") consider that in mediaeval England 7—10 miles was the normal distance apart of market towns, and that, as a result of the introduction of railways and the improvement of roads in the nineteenth century, fewer were required and approximately every other one decayed.

It is now necessary to consider what possible changes might take place in the sizes and distribution of settlements in this country in order to bring about a more satisfactory arrangement.   A very large number of people live in conditions which may be described as congested, and this congestion may involve any or all of four different sorts of deprivations:

Insufficient living space within and around the dwelling.
Inadequate facilities for games and other outdoor recreation within a reasonable distance of the home.
A lack of schools and/or adequate school sites.
Sheer physical inaccessibility of the open country.
Nevertheless, as I shall show, congestion is more a matter of maldistri-

bution of development than of actual shortage of space even in this country which is very densely populated.

The following comparison of population densities in persons per square mile is interesting although such crude figures are apt to be misleading

since they give no indication of the proportion of virtually uninhabitable land in each case.

Netherlands	855	France	215
England and Wales	794	China	190
Belgium	775	Spain	159
Japan	657	United States	51
W. Germany	562	U.S.S.R.	25
India	369	Brazil	20
Israel	270	Australia	$3\frac{1}{2}$

At a density of 15 persons per acre, it is possible, as will be explained in Chapter 7, to accommodate all urban land needs with a fair degree of spaciousness. This does not allow for large cemeteries, golf courses, sewage disposal and refuse disposal works, nor for areas for mineral working or service department land. Whatever the present amount of land used for these purposes may be it is likely to shrink. The increased practice of cremation, modern techniques of sewage and refuse disposal which involve less lavish use of land, probable eventual drastic reduction of service land needs, the opportunity for restoring to productive use much of the land used for mineral working all support this view.

The land surface of England and Wales is 37,132,358 acres, or 58,019 sq. miles, within which live about 45,000,000 people at an average density of 776 per square mile. At 15 persons per acre they require for urban purposes 3,000,000 acres, which can be contained within a circle with a radius of about 38·6 miles (see Fig. 6). It is worth noting that if the population rose to 50 million the circle required to accommodate them would still be only 40·7 miles. If, on the other hand, one assumed an average density of 20 persons per acre for 45 million people, which is not an impossibly high figure, the radius of circle required to accommodate them would diminish to about 33 miles. These figures may seem incredibly small but their correctness can be checked in a few minutes by anyone with a knowledge of elementary arithmetic. A clue to their conflict with everyday observation of the actual pattern of development in Britain can be obtained from another calculation. If the 45 million people at 15 persons per acre were accommodated in the form of ribbons of development 100 yards wide, these ribbons would have a total length of 82,500 miles—(three times around the World!).

The hexagon shown in Fig. 5 with a local capital at its centre has an area of 439 square miles. Assuming the size of each settlement is as set out below, it contains a total population of 100,700 people.

Local Capital	60,000 × 1	=	60,000
Town	10,000 × 2	=	20,000
Urban Village	1,500 × 6	=	9,000
Village	500 × 18	=	9,000
Hamlet	50 × 54	=	2,700
			100,700

FIG. 6. The present population of England and Wales, 45,000,000 in round figures, could be accommodated at 15 persons per acre within a circle with a radius of 38·6 miles. At an overall density of 15 persons per acre all urban land uses can be provided at comfortably spacious standards.

This gives an average population density of 229 persons per square mile for the hexagon, far lower than the national average. It is therefore clear that with our present level of population it would be quite impossible to do away with all cities, as some people would like to do, and to house the entire population in towns and villages, with no town larger than about 60,000.

About 17,000,000 people live in the great conurbations of England and Wales. If we left the total for conurbations at this level but redistributed the population so that all enjoyed a space standard of 15 persons per acre, then these conurbations would occupy 1,770 square miles. Many more people than this work within the conurbations, commuting unreasonable distances to do so.

There is an area of something like 7,000 square miles in England and Wales, which because of its height above sea level and general character, is hardly practicable for occupation above a very low level of intensity and which, in any case, ought not to be so occupied since much of it consists of national parks.

Deducting these two figures from the total land acreage of England and Wales, the remaining area of some 49,249 square miles would be occupied by the remaining 28,000,000 people at an average density of about 568 per square mile, so that even outside the conurbations it is necessary either to have a considerable number of towns substantially larger than 60,000, or else to space them very much closer than the existing network.

It is clearly desirable to group communities in such a way that there is ample distance between them, not only for enjoyment of the countryside to be possible, but also because at the border between urban use and agricultural use urban dwellers inevitably, by trespass and disturbance, greatly reduce the productivity of agricultural land. A very close network of small settlements is therefore not so good as a wider network of larger ones, though none should be so large that its physical size makes the countryside inaccessible to any of its inhabitants or produces a brutal, overwhelming effect.

Supposing, therefore, that, retaining the present basic network, the conurbations and the 7,000 square miles of virtually unused land, we introduce two additional grades above the local capital level, namely, towns of 225,000 and towns of 500,000 at distances apart of 39 miles and 67½ miles respectively, and increase the sizes of lower grade settlements as shown below. " Super-hexagons " are formed, each containing :—

				Interval
1 Town at	500,000	=	500,000	67·5 miles
2 Towns at	225,000	=	450,000	39 miles
6 Towns at	80,000	=	480,000	22·5 miles
18 Towns at	30,000	=	540,000	13 miles
54 Urban Villages at	3,000	=	162,000	7·5 miles
162 Villages at	1,000	=	162,000	4·3 miles
487 Hamlets at	50	=	24,300	2·5 miles
	Total		2,318,300	

This "super-hexagon" occupies 3,949 square miles with a population

density of almost 587 per square mile, which corresponds comfortable with the requirements.

It is quite clear therefore that it is physically possible to accommodate the whole population of the country at living standards which avoid the necessity of providing tall blocks of flats for any considerable proportion of the population, without in any way violating a reasonable spatial relationship between town and country.

In addition to the conurbations, 13 super-hexagons would be needed for the whole of England and Wales.

The radius of each of the towns and villages in the super-hexagon would be as follows, at 15 persons per acre:—

Population	Radius
500,000	4 miles
225,000	2·73 miles
80,000	1·65 miles
30,000	0·99 miles
3,000	0·32 miles
1,000	0·18 miles
50	0·04 miles

The hamlets can reasonably be regarded as punctuations of the landscape rather than interruptions of it, and, ignoring these, a replanning on radical lines of England and Wales would result in a distribution of settlements with spacious density standards in such a form that nearly four miles of open country would separate settlements.

To complete the picture, suppose that as a result of some extraordinary circumstance it became practicable to break down and disperse the conurbations and distribute the whole population of the country in super-hexagons, leaving the 7,000 square miles of moorlands and national parks undisturbed. We should require to accommodate 45 million people in 51,019 square miles at a density of 882 persons per square mile. This could be done by means of the following distribution in each super-hexagon:—

1 Town at	1,250,000	...	1,250,000
2 Towns at	300,000	...	600,000
6 Towns at	100,000	=	600,000
18 Towns at	35,000	=	630,000
54 Urban Villages at	3,500	=	189,000
162 Villages at	1,200	=	194,400
487 Hamlets at	50	=	24,350
	Total		3,487,750

The 1,250,000 town would have a radius of a little under 6½ miles.

The truth behind all these figures, which may seem incredible to anyone who travels about the main roads of the country and perceives the almost unbroken threads of development existing in many parts, is quite simply that, in innumerable ways, some of which will be discussed later, prodigious quantities of land are either totally wasted or seriously under-utilised, thus producing local congestion within a general framework of low intensity of utilisation; and also that the actual distribution of development since the advent of the motor car has tended to assume a ribbon form so universally that one does indeed get the impression from a motor car that nearly all the whole of south-eastern England, at least, is built up. A view from the air or even from a railway train, since development is not so strongly attracted to railway lines as to main roads, shows a truer picture.

It is clear that a properly organised distribution of settlements of various sizes at proper density standards can be attained in a large variety of ways. There is no limit to the extent of metropolitan decentralisation possible in terms of space for communities. It follows that the menace to the conservation of agricultural land and to the maintenance of sufficiently large stretches of open countryside arises not from the density at which new development or redevelopment may take place, but rather from the present strong tendency for development to take place on virgin sites, which eat up both agricultural land and countryside, and to leave under-developed areas of land unchanged.

There is a danger that this may eventually lead to an absurd situation in which there exist at the same time both substantial numbers of central area flats at an inhumanly high density, and vast stretches of under-developed land unsatisfactory by reason of lack of compactness, so rendering a proper provision of central services difficult or impossible. The ultimate possibility is that when housing demands are saturated, as they may well be within a comparatively few years, intensity of occupation will fall away in both these categories of development and become concentrated in the remaining kind, that is to say, the well-knit areas of moderate density well served with social facilities. If this happens, we shall have embraced both of two alternative evils: we shall have wasted a great deal of capital on building high, dense buildings which do not meet human needs, and we shall also have spoiled the countryside of Britain by dispersing dwellings over it. It should be one of the chief aims of Planning to avert this disaster.

To turn from land requirements to land use facts, R. H. Best and I. T. Coppock in "The Changing Use of Land in Britain" give an estimate of the total amount of land in urban use in England and Wales in about 1950 as 3,601,908, while their analysis of all Land Uses in England and Wales at that time is as follows:—

A New Classification of Land Use for England and Wales in 1950

Land Use	Area	Proportion[1]
	'000 acres	%
Agriculture:[2]		
Arable	13,949	37·6
Permanent grass	10,496	28·3
Rough grazings...	3,969	10·7
Total	28,414	76·6

Land Use	Area	Proportion[1]
Brought Forward ...	28,414	76·6
Multiple and special uses:		
Common rough grazings	1,502	4·0
Service departments	850?	2·3?
Water gathering grounds[3]	500?	1·3?
Opencast mineral workings	150?	0·4?
Unclassified	250?	0·7?
Total	3,252	8·7
Woodland:		
High forest	1,266	3·4
Other woodland	1,107	3·0
Total	2,373	6·4
Urban development:		
Cities and large towns[4]	1,812	4·9
Small towns and villages[4]	717	1·9
Isolated dwellings	534	1·4
Transportation land[5]	574	1·6
Total	3,637	9·8
Grand Total	37,676	101·5
Total land area	37,133	100·0

[1] Of total land area.
[2] Land in sole occupation used primarily for agriculture.
[3] Of water undertakings with large impounding reservoirs.
[4] Of over and under 10,000 population, respectively.
[5] Outside built-up areas and including civil airfields.

They conclude that the rate of turnover of agricultural land to urban development in England and Wales was greatest in the 1930's when the net annual diminution was over 60,000 acres. Since the war the net loss has, in contrast, been only about 38,200 acres a year. Information from a number of sources suggests that in the twenty years up to 1971 a total of between 500,000 and 700,000 acres is likely to be taken from farming use for urban purposes, though it might possibly amount to as much as 750,000 acres.

The urban area, they emphasise, though far less extensive than is generally appreciated, has nevertheless grown even faster than is usually realised; but in spite of an ever diminishing area of farmland the efforts of both farmers and scientists have meant that a large expansion in food output has still been secured over the last two decades.

It is important to get the problem of conservation of agricultural land into proper proportion. A comprehensive Planning policy could, in the long run, result in bringing back the total of urban land to about 3 million acres, assuming a population of about 45 million, to which must be added a certain amount for reservoirs, sewage works, etc., and opencast mineral workings. The land of service departments, one feels confident in predicting, will eventually fall to a very small figure if civilisation manages to survive.

It is certainly of great importance that no agricultural land should unnecessarily be taken and converted to other uses, but it would be quite wrong to have regard to alarmists' views, and stint ourselves of land for urban purposes for this reason. As explained in more detail in Chapter 17, there is strong evidence for believing that, incredible though it may seem, reasonably low density housing is capable of producing more food from the gardens than is medium quality farmland, and that within certain limits the reduction of housing density more than proportionately increases the output of garden food.

It may be challenged whether, in our present national circumstances, the maintenance of a high level of agricultural production is of very great importance, having regard to the certainty that we shall always in part be dependent upon imported foodstuffs, and to the probability of increased efficiency in the disposition of land uses and communication routes, at some cost to agricultural land, resulting in increased industrial efficiency, and hence a greater of volume of exports with which food can be paid for. It is still more open to question whether the mere maintenance of as large an acreage of agricultural land as possible is of great importance. The opportunities for improving the output of agricultural land by the investment of capital on buildings, drainage and fertilisation are very great, and, as has been pointed out by many authorities, the capital at present devoted to special subsidies for high density flat development would, if devoted to the improvement of agricultural land, result in immensely greater increases of food production than any possible increase from the small amount of agricultural land saved by building at very high densities.

4-3. FACTORS IN REGIONAL PLANNING

Balancing Population and Employment. The balancing of population and employment is a complex process depending on many different factors; Planning action alone cannot do more than create conditions which render the achievement of a satisfactory degree of balance physically possible and reasonably probable.

Just as, in the long run, the imports of a country must be balanced by its exports, so must those of a town. Unless a town, in which is included the areas directly dependent upon it, exports valuable products, whether these consist of minerals, manufactured goods, food or professional and business skill, its inhabitants will be in much the same position as those of the mythical islanders who earned their livings by taking in each other's washing. In other words, they will be able to consume only the produce of their own area, a state of affairs inconceivable in this country, where the ordinary daily menu includes items from all parts of the world.

The goods and services which a town exports are its basic industry, the return derived from which enables it to obtain the goods and services which it cannot itself produce.

The complicated and often indirect ways in which a town exports commodities, through the medium of numerous private concerns and individuals and with the intervention of middlemen and distributing agencies, need not be pursued, being a matter of elementary general economics, but a word of explanation regarding the meaning of the somewhat misleading word " export " may be useful. " Export", in the sense in which it is here used, means *providing* goods and services to the outside world; it does not necessarily mean that they are *sent* outside.

The tourist trade enjoyed by an historic city such as Chester—the money spent in the city by those who come to look at its historic monuments and buildings—is an export. The entertainment provided by Brighton is an export. The income derived by a solicitor from the written advice which he sends to a client in another part of the country is derived from export. Even the income of the London businessman who lives in a country town is part of that town's export income.

Service industry, on the other hand, is that which is carried on for the benefit of the inhabitants of the place in which it is situated—the " taking in of washing "—and, curiously, laundries are a very characteristic service industry.

In Planning a region, therefore, it is essential to plan for a state of affairs in which there will be sufficient basic industry in any town to balance its necessary imports. Such Planning cannot, of course, be done in detail; as already indicated, economic transactions are so diverse and multifarious that it would, in any case, be beyond human power to do so; what it comes down to in practical terms is that the Plan must allocate sufficient land for uses which will provide jobs for all or most of the inhabitants of each town, otherwise they will have either to go elsewhere to live or work elsewhere.

It must also be remembered that people will not permanently live in places where public services and social facilities are defective, where the general habits of life prevailing are displeasing to them or where there is not a reasonably assured prospect of congenial work, although in conditions of acute housing stringency they may go almost anywhere to get a house.

The Transport Network. However well the distribution of homes and places of employment is devised, innumerable journeys will, of course, still need to be made within the region as well as into it and out of it. A large part of planning is concerned with securing the elimination of unnecessary journeys, but another large part is concerned with facilitating necessary journeys. Necessary journeys are of course here to be understood as including any journey that anyone definitely wishes to make, not simply " useful " journeys.

Journeys into and out of and through a region ought to be on trunk routes generally determined by a national plan, though modified as to their details by regional considerations. They should provide the skeleton upon which to superimpose routes which are concerned with journeys only within the region.

This part of Regional Planning is concerned with two rather different items: the actual physical improvement of existing routes, such as roads, whether by means of widening, by-passing or building completely new lengths of road, and also the co-ordination of different methods of transport in order to promote more flexible means of travelling by creating interchange points between road, rail, air and water transport at suitable places.

This is a subject, of course, which goes much beyond physical Planning in its scope. The co-ordination of time-tables, the issuing of tickets which can be used on more than one kind of vehicle and so forth are matters for transport undertakings rather than Planning authorities. At the same time, given a suitable administrative machine, there is not the slightest reason why these activities should not be inter-related for the benefit of all. Unfortunately, life being what it is, this seldom happens, and it would be unrealistic to suppose that at any level of physical Planning complete co-ordination with agencies concerned with kinds of planning other than land Planning can normally be assured.

Nevertheless, a reasonable degree of co-ordination is absolutely essential. I am not the first to point out that the Beeching Plan for the re-organisation of the railway system, however skilfully prepared and however valid within its own terms of reference it may be, is to a large extent useless and even harmful, because it fails to take account of the obvious fact that public transport in this country needs to be regarded as a co-ordinated activity rather than as the independent activities of a number of undertakings which happen to run different kinds of vehicles on different kinds of tracks. It is also, in part at least, futile because it was undertaken before instead of after the preparation of Regional Plans, which, for many reasons quite independent of transport, might well postulate a distribution of population, employment and service centres very different from what exists at present, different even from present discernible trends, and therefore demanding a quite different distribution of rail services from that postulated in the Beeching Report. If this kind of disorganised, piecemeal national planning goes on, we may yet see the day when a particular length of railway line which has been closed and torn up under the recommendations of the Beeching Plan becomes vitally needed as the result of the planned expansion of some of the places which it used to serve.

In planning the improvement of a regional transport network finance is even more important than in other parts of Planning. It takes very little skill to plan an excellent, even an ideal distribution of transport routes in a region if no limitation is placed upon the mileage of routes to be constructed or improved. But in any conceivable circumstances there will be severe limitations on the money that can be spent in this way; successful planning depends upon making the greatest possible improvements within the limitations of the finance likely to be available for the purpose over a given period. The Planner is inevitably handicapped because it is seldom possible to get any reasonably firm or definite statement as to what this sum will be; the more he is left in the dark the less useful in this direction can his activities be.

A further severe and insurmountable difficulty is the lack of any means to forecast likely changes in methods of transport, as the result of new inventions or of new methods of exploiting existing ones. The helicopter and the hovercraft may yet completely transform modes of travel in this country, and demand the preparation of regional transport plans totally different from those appropriate to the present situation. There is little or nothing that the Planner can do about this, but he and those who employ him are at least under a duty to try to meet changing requirements when they become apparent, instead of waiting till such changes have produced conditions of almost insoluble difficulty, which is what has happened in the case of all previous changes and improvements in the transport system.

Distribution of development and Services. The purpose of a regional Plan is not merely the balancing of quantities of employment and population; it involves, too, an appropriate spatial arrangement of these and of all community services.

This spatial distribution may take the form of creating settlements, such as new towns, or of altering the size and/or the status within the hierarchy of service centres of existing settlements.

The population of a place, as has previously been suggested, is not necessarily proportionate to the amount of service it performs for its tributary area, particularly in the lower grades of settlement. An alteration in the status of such a place may therefore be effected by the addition or subtraction of Service institutions without a corresponding change of population. Nevertheless, the greater the nucleated population of a place the greater the services it can perform and the more economically secure will be its Service institutions, since, although various changes of circumstances may result in the population of parts of the tributary area transferring their allegiance to other supply centres, the population within the place itself is hardly likely, for reasons of physical convenience, to do this to any serious extent. Save in quite exceptional circumstances it is therefore desirable that nucleated populations in various places should be roughly proportional in numbers to the services rendered by the place.

Changes of status within the hierarchy of settlements may theoretically involve either upgrading or downgrading.

Places down to and including urban villages are mostly so well established and have survived so many vicissitudes over a long period that it is improbable that a development Plan would seek to downgrade any of them, while it will often be appropriate to provide for the relocation of population in such a way that one or more of them is upgraded. Similarly, it will often be appropriate to transform a number of villages into urban villages.

On the other hand, it may well be desirable to provide in the development plan that some towns which are well balanced industrially or which have a deficiency of employment shall not increase in size because an increase would involve the provision, concurrently, of additional central services, which would fit better into the regional pattern if located elsewhere, or because the limited amount of increased population to be expected in the region needs to be located elsewhere to remedy labour deficiencies.

Requirements of this nature are seldom appreciated by the elected representatives of places which it is not intended to expand, even though the amount of land suitable for building is insufficient to accommodate the overspill resulting from the redevelopment of existing areas of congested development. It is this failure to rise above parochialism which makes the existence of a strong and independent Local Planning Authority particularly necessary.

When one considers the smaller villages and the hamlets, the need for changes of status becomes more frequent. Most of these settlements arose when walking and horse-riding were the only means of travelling, and long before the days of conveying water and power by pipe or wire. These services and the motor bus have effected a transformation in the pattern of settlements required in rural communities in order to take full advantage of them. On the one hand, the motor bus makes it much less necessary for social and marketing facilities above the level of daily needs to be made available within walking distance of every home, and makes it possible for higher services to be provided in a more effective form than previously in a smaller number of larger communities. On the other hand, to make the provision of piped and wired services economically possible a very much closer texture is required within the individual rural community than exists in many cases.

This leads to the inescapable conclusion that development Plans should in most areas provide for fewer but more compact rural settlements than exist at present, and this is a view which has received the general support of informed opinion from the publication of the Scott Report in 1942 onwards.

At the present time a stage of peculiar difficulty and uncertainty has been reached about the appropriate policy for village change and growth in this country. Villages other than fishing villages, mining villages and a few others founded for special purposes came into being in order to serve the needs of agriculture. In fact it is a healthy corrective to an unduly romantic attitude about villages if one regards them as industrial settlements.

Although agricultural production has increased and continues to increase, modern methods of agriculture require fewer and fewer workers to cultivate a given area, so that a decrease in the number of village inhabitants directly concerned with agriculture is inevitable, and in itself perfectly healthy. But apart from the general psychological disadvantages attached to life in a numerically declining community, there are the far more definite social and economic disadvantages.

To select what may often be the crucial item, since children of school age form about 1/60th of the population for each year of age, a total population of some 1,200 is needed to support a school, with a separate class for each year of age and with no class having fewer than 20 children in it. This is probably somewhere near the lower limit for an efficient and economically run primary school. Since the mean size of village (excluding hamlets) is probably about 300, it is clear that only a small proportion of villages can support their own primary schools if these are to be efficient and economical. The fewer the villages with primary schools, the larger the proportion of children who have to make tiring and costly journeys to school. At the same time, the enormously increased availability of personal motor transport has made the agricultural worker far more mobile, and in this connection it needs to be remembered that the nature of his work is such that, wherever he lives, he may have to travel a substantial distance to the actual site of his day's work.

Villages have always supported an appreciable population not directly linked to the land—shop keepers, parsons and schoolmasters, while in the more attractive and accessible villages these have over the last generation or so been increasingly augmented by people whose work is in no way connected with the village in which they choose to live and who are often referred to as " adventitious " population.

During the last decade this increase in adventitious population has accelerated. The reasons for this are no doubt partly the increased congestion and unpleasantness of city and town life, partly the relative cheapness with which building sites in villages can be obtained and partly highly restrictive zoning in towns which has meant both that prices of building plots have been unduly inflated and that there has been an absolute shortage of land for houses in some towns.

A large increase of adventitious population in villages has both advantages and disadvantages. It makes for greater prosperity among local traders, and may indeed even make possible the provision of more ambitious services than otherwise. It injects life into the village and prevents it from becoming excessively inbred. On the other hand there are certain disadvantages which may or may not be permanent. Adventitious populations are frequently accused of taking little or no part in the life of the village, or, if they do, of doing so in a condescending and officious manner. It is no doubt true that they tend not to send their children to the village school, and thus fail to provide support for the enlargement and improvement of this vital service. They are said drastically to raise the seduction rate among the local girls. It is obvious that for good or ill, beyond a certain point, the increase in adventitious population in a village will transform its social character, and that, correspondingly, a large number of new houses will equally transform its physical character. Much more will be said about this aspect in Chapter 18.

It will be clear from what has been said earlier in this chapter about possible methods of redistributing the population of the country to relieve metropolitan congestion, that, in the more densely populated parts of the country at least, many villages will need to be so enlarged as to acquire the status of towns; there can be no doubt about this. As regards other villages, some definite policy needs to be adopted, and the difficulties of choice involved may perhaps be most clearly presented by setting out the two ultimate extremes.

One policy would be to prevent all new buildings and even replacements in villages not destined to become upgraded to towns, so that eventually they became abandoned, and to concentrate all new development in towns, thus requiring agricultural workers to travel some miles to work but providing them and their families with full urban facilities in the form of shops, schools and places of entertainment close at hand, concentrating urban areas and preserving the countryside from numerous intrusive patches of development.

The opposite policy would be to permit and encourage every village to expand to a population of 1,200 or even more in order to raise the level of facilities to rural dwellers, prevent the undue growth of towns and generally to prevent the physical decline of villages.

To state these alternatives is to make it clear that neither, in full stringency, is correct or practicable. The proper policy must clearly lie somewhere between. It is highly unlikely that any policy will be adopted which postulates the abandonment of reasonably attractive and flourishing settlements.

It is also obvious that there are many quite small villages of great charm which are worth preserving even as museum pieces, and that there will be no lack of people willing and even anxious to live in them. But it is extremely difficult to know the position of the optimum point on the scale. At present a great many villages are growing substantially for no obviously sound reason, while the growth of others is severely discouraged for no clear reason. It would hardly be unfair to suggest that in many areas county councils seem to have no real policy, but strive to resist or damp down development almost everywhere, with varying success, instead of welcoming development in some places and resisting it as strongly as possible on definite grounds elsewhere.

It is worth pointing out that the hope of finding a simple rural environment and closer contact with the countryside is to a considerable extent illusory. When a village grows beyond quite a small size a considerable proportion of residents in its new houses will be surrounded on all sides by other houses, and will from their homes see no more of the countryside than they would if living in the town, while anyone living near the outskirts of a town is as close to countryside as a person living in a village. As is so often the case in Planning problems, attractive possibilities disappear when they are taken advantage of by large numbers of people. It is difficult to avoid the conclusion that a good many residential estates recently built in villages would, economically, socially and visually, have been better placed in the nearest town. No one would have been subjected to a less favourable environment if this had been done, and very great economies would have been achieved in the provision of numerous central services and in the reduction of journeys.

Other factors in the pattern. Consideration must now be given to the various forms of development which have been superimposed on the ancient pattern of agricultural communities.

Manufacturing industry. First among these is manufacturing industry, which is entirely independent of the agricultural pattern. During the industrial revolution industry became established in quantity wherever access to raw materials, power or transport facilities gave it the best opportunity of flourishing.

The story of the mushroom growth of the industrial towns of Britain, the crowding of houses, their intermixture with factories, the lack of open spaces and of provision for social services, will probably be familiar to every reader, and need not be repeated here. Although some of the deficiencies have gradually been made up, the typical industrial town, which frequently has not evolved from an ancient original of any considerable size—Middlesbrough, for instance—presents Planning problems which are different in kind from those associated with towns rooted in the past and which have grown steadily and organically through the centuries. This problem is greatest in the case of the fused masses of industrial towns known as conurbations, such as Greater Manchester, Greater Birmingham and the West Riding Woollen towns. Sheer lack of space and the vast quantity of capital investment in existing buildings precludes rapid solutions in their cases; the best that can be

done immediately is usually to set standards which fall short of but approach as closely as possible to the satisfactory.

Modern transport developments. The coming of the railways after 1830 resulted in unprecedented growth of many towns and villages on sites which had previously been occupied by only the smallest of settlements. These places owed their growth to the advantages attaching to the increased nodality afforded them by the railway, which increased their importance as centres of exchange, junction points (Crewe is a fine example of this) or suburban centres for the more well-to-do inhabitants of near-by industrial towns. It must be remembered that the fourfold increase in the population of the country between 1811 and 1911 enabled these increases to take place without corresponding decreases occurring in other places.

Most places created or greatly enlarged by the influence of the railways have, by now, been fairly well absorbed into the pattern of communities and cause no special Planning problems because they always possessed latent advantages of position which the railway enabled them to realise. But this emphatically does not apply to many of the places created by inter-war growth in the use of the internal combustion engine.

The motor-bus virtually destroyed the limiting factor of time which had hitherto kept most settlements reasonably compact, whatever their other defects might have been, and which had confined suburban growth to places accessible to railways. Desire to escape from the grimy and congested inner urban areas and to get into close contact with green fields caused many to make enormous sacrifices of time and money, and they were enthusiastically aided by the speculative builder, who, since public services had usually been installed in the main roads leading out of town, tended to confine his operations to the land fronting them, and so created the ribbon development which now forms the approaches to most towns. The depressed state of agriculture, leading to the ready sale of land for building purposes and the growth of the building societies, which financed much of this development, were strong contributory factors.

For those owning motor cars the choice was much wider. They could live on pleasant sites near or adjoining villages or in houses, either isolated or built in groups, in the open countryside. In the home counties, particularly, this kind of development, combined with the urban ribbons, has resulted in vast, amorphous areas thinly scattered with houses but with no development of other kinds. These are neither town, village nor countryside; possess many of the disadvantages of each with but few of the advantages.

It is virtually impossible for most of these areas to be welded into coherent communities and their decay and eventual disappearance is the best that can be hoped for (see Chapter 20).

Another kind of development less directly connected with the development of transport, although to a considerable extent dependent on it, is the shack town which is commonly associated with large industrial towns. This has generally been created by the demand of low-paid workers who have been financially unable to escape into ribbon development or sporadic country development, but who have nevertheless determined somehow to live in the country. Houses in these areas are often of the " home-made " kind, including converted sports pavilions, Nissen huts and flimsy structures which resemble houses, but comply with no by-laws. Drainage is usually extremely sketchy —a cesspool with an overflow, or non-existent. Water is obtained from various sources.

Little blame rests on the people who took advantage of the opportunity to acquire the poor man's version of a country seat, but what is almost incredible is that local authorities should not have devised more effective means to stop development which breaks all laws of hygiene. When it is extensive and particularly when, as sometimes happens, it is on a water-gathering ground, it is a constant danger to public health, and, in any case, it causes wasteful expenditure of public money in the provision of services such as postal deliveries, cesspool emptying (when cesspools exist), the visits of doctors, midwives, and ambulances and many others, because of the scattered nature of the development and the frequently impassable nature of the roads. These circumstances, conversely, often make it extremely difficult for children to attend school regularly.

Most of these objections also apply to the more ordinary kind of sporadic development in rural areas, which, in addition, necessitates a good deal of road improvement which would otherwise be unnecessary, but in this case, local authorities were powerless before the existence of adequate Planning legislation.

Service establishments. These take many different forms. They may be long established and be the dominant form of development in a town, as in Aldershot, in which case it is necessary to adjust the whole form of development of the town to their needs, or they may merely be extensive tracts of open country in which practice is given in using live ammunition and manoeuvring vehicles, in which case consideration must be given to the extent to which the agricultural economy is affected by the loss of farmland and to the way in which the rural settlement pattern needs to be adjusted to changed circumstances.

Establishments which often present the most difficult planning problems are barracks and airfields in rural areas, with married quarters attached. Although the rations officially supplied, the N.A.A.F.I., and camp concerts provide a partial substitute for shops and social services in such places, their existence is likely to cause a substantial increase in the use, and sometimes a need for increased provision, of shopping and recreational facilities in near-by towns and major rural centres. The spectacle of wives and children trailing along the road to the village a mile or more away emphasises the absurdity of not locating living accommodation for all except operational personnel within existing communities, and it is regrettable that Planning Authorities have not had more success in securing this.

Other uses of large areas of open land. Just as firing ranges may upset the balance of a rural settlement pattern, so, of course, may many other less sterile uses: the inundation of agricultural land to make a reservoir for the water supply of a city, the surface working of minerals, an open-air zoo like Whipsnade, or a civil airport may all take up areas of land extensive enough to upset the agricultural economy in their vicinity, while in recent years power stations have become large users of open land.

The extractive or quarrying industries are, in many cases, very large land users and the Planning problems they create are great. Minerals lie where nature has placed them, and in the case of many minerals the supply, or at least that part of it which it is economically possible to use, is less than the demand. Although quarrying is frequently open to grave objections, including the destruction of natural beauty, the use of fertile agricultural land and of land which is needed for building or other urban uses, it is frequently necessary in the national interest to override these objections and permit quarrying, subject to whatever safeguards can be imposed with regard to manner of working and restoration of the land to a state in which, after the minerals have been extracted, it can be put to other purposes.

Residential and resort towns. A good many towns have little connection with agricultural or manufacturing industry but cater almost entirely for holiday-makers, the retired, or those who work in other towns.

Resort towns are, in effect, industrial towns of a very special kind, and have their own peculiar needs as regards the allocation of land for various purposes; they range from garish joy-towns, catering for those who want short holidays crowded with incident, to sedate places, like Bournemouth or Folkestone in which quieter attractions are popular and in which the requirements of holiday-makers and of the retired coincide happily, so that such towns perform a dual function. Much the same applies to inland towns favoured by the retired, such as Tunbridge Wells and Malvern, although the holiday-making side of these places is usually smaller proportionately than in the case of the seaside towns.

The problems of most of these towns is to maintain the characteristics upon which their income depends and yet to provide their working resident populations with sufficiently varied occupations, so avoiding the disadvantages associated with single industry towns, which are vulnerable to unemployment in the event of depression in the single industry, and lack opportunity for the employment of varied talents. A particular difficulty is the seasonal unemployment which inevitably afflicts towns which depend principally upon summer holiday-makers.

Having now briefly explored the nature of Regional Planning and some of its especially perplexing problems we now turn to the most intractable problem of all, the Conurbation, City Region or Urban Region, which demands a chapter of its own.

CHAPTER 5

URBAN REGIONS

THE TERM "CITY REGION" was coined by Professor Myles Wright to describe those vast areas of continuous or nearly continuous development too large to be considered as a single city, however big, because of their physical extent and because they contain within them the whole range of activities and facilities found within a normal region. But in "Land Use in an Urban Environment", edited by Professor Myles Wright, the term Urban Region is preferred, as it is by Peter Hall in "London 2,000". Whatever the name used, the essential nature of such an area is that at its core is a very large central area which exerts a dominant effect over a large number of smaller settlements which are hardly separated from it or from each other. The Urban Region is obviously closely related to a conurbation, but can be distinguished from it because, both officially and unofficially, "conurbation" is taken as referring to a considerably more limited area than comprises the Urban Region, properly understood.

It is, of course, very difficult to define in any decisive way the boundary of an Urban Region such as Greater London, Greater Birmingham or Greater Manchester. The influence of the central area at its heart extends for a very great distance. For example, since Brighton and Hastings, among other coastal towns, act to a considerable extent as suburbs of London because of the large number of daily commuters who live in such places, they may to some extent be regarded as part of the Urban Region of London.

So to include them, however, would be extending the meaning of the term further than is useful. At some distance from the centre there comes a point at which towns begin to have an independent existence, which justifies them being treated as independent entities. In the absence of some more reliable index one might as a crude suggestion think that this point was reached if a majority of the working population of a place work in it rather than in the main centre of the Urban Region.

Urban Regions have certain definite characteristics which make them what they are. They are highly condensed. The communities within them are physically closer together and thus more closely related than in a normal region. For this reason a community within the region containing a given population will normally only be able to sustain a lower level of services and facilities than a community of similar size in a normal region, just as an urban neighbourhood of 5,000 people cannot support nearly as high a level of such facilities as a detached small town of similar population. As the centre of the Urban Region is approached communities are not merely very close together but become fused, and without recognisable physical boundaries. In these circumstances, any large measure of real identity is lost, and the effective boundary of a place is the mean of the boundaries of

its service areas for various purposes, which in turn are determined by the main road patterns, bus routes and physical interruptions and obstacles, such as railway lines and open spaces.

Another common characteristic is congestion, both in terms of traffic and of living conditions. Near the centre of, and indeed, to an increasing extent throughout, an Urban Region, severe traffic congestion prevails, and the confused pattern of streets and of large and costly buildings renders amelioration extremely difficult. Traffic congestion, moreover, is not limited to traffic on the move but extends to the parked vehicle, provision for which is universally insufficient. Congestion of living space is of two kinds; a large proportion of the population have to live in conditions which are attributable roughly, in terms of Chapters 8, 9 and 10, to excessive net density and/or to excessive gross density. As regards the former, a large proportion of homes have rooms of inadequate size, inadequate privacy and daylighting and inadequate or even no personal outdoor space. In terms of the latter these conditions, bad in themselves, are commonly associated with a very serious shortage of land for schools and open spaces.

Add to this that most of the homes concerned are approaching the end of their physical lives, were never very attractive, and in most cases have not been properly maintained for some long time, and that intrusive and incompatible uses are mingled with them in completely promiscuous fashion, and one has a picture of utterly unsatisfactory living conditions which no one puts up with unless he has to. More optimistically, however, one also has a picture of huge outworn areas which, come what may, are virtually certain to be redeveloped within a comparatively few years, and which offer incomparably greater opportunities for large scale improvement than have ever before been seen.

Looked at less optimistically, this is also a moment of crucial challenge because the inevitability of large scale redevelopment brings with it also the possibility that this will take place on completely unorganised lines, leaving behind a new scene superior to what was before it in terms of light, air and living space, but in other ways almost if not quite as disorganised.

The generally excessive density of the inner residential parts of Urban Regions brings with it a corollary which may well be stated as yet another general characteristic, namely, that, failing some substantial decrease in the level of population, more land *in toto* will be needed for building and allied purposes than at present; a daunting requirement when one considers the already grossly excessive size of continuous built-up area within the inner parts of Urban Regions.

But the impression of huge, continuous, fully built-up areas is to some extent a misleading one. Anyone inefficient at packing a suitcase or trunk will have noticed how much more a really good packer can get into the same cubic capacity than he can. This is a very valid comparison; the efforts of the skilful packer, given a chance to show his skill, are very similar to those to be expected from the skilful Town Planner given a similar chance.

Unless he is given reasonable opportunities in several different ways he has no chance of doing anything very much. This is true everywhere, but especially true in the Urban Region, where all the problems of Town Planning are seen at their most complicated and acute. For the Planner to have a reasonable chance there has to be genuine control of land use, not merely wide statutory powers. By genuine control I mean the ability for a developing authority to obtain all the land needed for its purposes without excessive delay and without being put to impossibly high levels of expenditure, especially as regards the taking over of existing use rights in areas needed to be put to some relatively or absolutely unprofitable use and the extinguishment of " third schedule rights ". This is, of course, a national political problem, not a local one, and its solution depends upon thorough and realistic legislation.

Another requirement needed to give the Planner a proper chance is the placing of the whole Urban Region area under a single Planning Authority.

Only by tackling the problem in this way will it conceivably be possible to sort out our formless and squalid Urban Regions into places fit to live in. A prerequisite for doing this is to be able to produce, discuss, publish and implement Development Plans which postulate a real solution. Partly because of their age, partly because of the bogey of compensation for extinguishment of existing use rights, current Development Plans are in many ways useless. For example—this is merely one out of hundreds that one could take—practically the whole main road frontage from Hammersmith to Gunnersbury is zoned in the London and Middlesex County Development Plans for shopping purposes, a total distance of well over two miles. No sane theory of Planning could possibly assume this to be a sensible form of development for the area concerned. What would either of the authorities concerned say if large scale redevelopment proposals conforming to their Development Plans were submitted by intending developers? One feels confident that their reaction would be one of horror; they would earnestly beg the intending developer to do something else! A Development Plan which would fill its authors with horror if someone tried to implement it is indeed a strange one! I am not here, of course, pouring derision on the unfortunate county councils of London and Middlesex, but merely pointing out that through force of political and financial circumstances, their Development Plans are in many ways nonsense.

The relevant facts are that almost all current Development Plans are hopelessly out of date, were first prepared when post-war Planning ideas had not yet had time to mature and crystalise, have been reviewed belatedly and in such a way as merely to tidy up errors, inconsistencies and anachronisms, and have been dominated by the need not to attract crushing compensation by zoning land uses in accordance with need and sensible Planning design. Instead, they are simply a reflection of existing land use patterns with very minor modifications, which mostly relate to projects of comprehensive development to be carried out in the comparatively near future.

To rub the lesson home a little further, one needs only to draw attention to the fact that the L.C.C. Development Plan incorporates no road plan. Nothing is done but to show as main routes those which are already main routes and a few improvements imminent or already carried out. A Development Plan for part of an Urban Region which makes no attempt to deal with its traffic problems is not even worthy of the name of a plan. To give just

one example of this, Victoria Street is quite evidently a main traffic artery at present, and if it is to remain so every possible effort should be made to remove the need for local traffic to use it, yet there are no proposals for a main route to act as an alternative to Victoria Street, while at the present time redevelopment of offices on a colossal scale is taking place on both sides of it and more is about to take place. Unless something drastic is done we shall soon have an example in the most acute possible form of a road of the kind which has been condemned universally by Planners, namely, one which has to carry large quantities of access and local traffic as well as large quantities of through traffic.

In considering the requirements for the Planning of an Urban Region it is first necessary to dispose of the joint myths of the " city dweller " and of " an urban way of life ". The city dweller is not a species distinct from *homo sapiens*, he is not even a recognisable sub-species; he is a perfectly ordinary person who has to put up with living and transport conditions much more crowded than those of most of his fellow citizens. It may be some compensation to him that he also has accessible to him a far wider and higher range of facilities of all kinds than the majority of his fellows, though if he happens to be a housewife with five children the knowledge that there is a West End entertainment centre, the British Museum, the National Opera House and suchlike only three miles down the road, is not likely to do much to counteract the miseries of a damp, leaking, draughty, ill-heated, ill-ventilated poky house.

Much the same applies to the " urban way of life ". The romantic view of this is that the sophisticated and cultivated city dweller engages in large quantities of intercourse (both social and sexual), imbibes deep draughts of culture and pursues his daily journeys in rapt contemplation of those architectural and sculptural splendours of the metropolis which lie athwart his path. He is thus, it is claimed, neither needful nor desirous of a spacious home or of personal space around it, the possession of which would indeed reduce the compactness and accessibility of his environment and reduce the opportunities for intercourse afforded.

Like most errors, this contains some truth. Life in a big city has attractions not available to those who dwell elsewhere, and vice-versa. This undoubtedly justifies the assumption that slightly more compact living quarters may generally be acceptable in cities than elsewhere, but it emphatically does not justify any extreme move in this direction. The ordinary family with children has much the same needs and desires whether it happens to live in St. Pancras or St. Ives, and beyond the obvious need to exclude extremely low density housing near the centre of an Urban Region there is no justification for adopting standards less spacious than those elsewhere. Far more detailed discussion of dwelling needs and densities will be undertaken in Chapter 17; all that needs to be emphasised additionally here is that it is only the distorted economics of private enterprise capitalism of the mid-twentieth century which dictates excessive densities in Urban Regions, not genuine physical requirements.

The essential problem of Urban Region Planning is that of traffic. By and large, in all Urban Regions, far too many people are trying to get into or out of the centre at the same time for the transport system to be able to deal with them, and very probably for any improved transport system within economic limits capable of being tolerated to do so. In some cases, indeed, it is doubtful whether, apart from economic considerations, it is physically possible to do so. The creation or restoration of a rational hierarchy of service centres in order to take pressure off the main centre is therefore at least as important an aid to relief of traffic congestion as is road building, and probably a good deal greater.

It is difficult to think that at present at any level a serious attempt is being made to formulate policy concerning Planning techniques, economics, law and administration capable of providing a solution for the problems of the Urban Region, which is one of the most serious problems, apart from the hydrogen bomb, with which contemporary society is faced. A solution of it would probably of itself bring about a solution or at least a substantial diminution of other worrying current problems such as those of armed robbery, juvenile delinquency and so forth. It is therefore no use pretending that the following discussion of Urban Region Planning technique is closely linked to contemporary law, administration and practice. To be fruitful it cannot be.

The first objective in Planning an Urban Region must be to determine and create a suitable hierarchy of centres and sub-centres. The main characteristic of the present Urban Region is that although it contains a population and economic activities comparable in quantity to those of an ordinary region, they are compressed into a smaller area, and the main centre at the heart of the conurbation contains too large a proportion of employment, entertainment, etc. It is essential, therefore, to move out to sub-centres as much of these things as is not irrevocably committed to a situation there.

The main point about excessive concentration in a single centre is that (a) it makes it impossible, or certainly impossible without inordinate expenditure, to devise means of getting all the people who work in it or wish to visit it into it in the morning and out at night, and (b) it has to occupy too large an area for movement within it to be reasonably convenient.

An essential piece of Planning research is to determine which activities are forced to remain within the main centre if they are to be able to operate properly and which can move elsewhere. When this has been discovered it will be possible to decide appropriate methods to encourage dispersal. This is not the place to discuss such means in detail, but it may be mentioned that a swingeing payroll tax on all offices in the main centre which are not of a kind to require inescapably to be there, coupled with a generous bounty on similar lines for all decentralised offices is an obvious method. Others are the establishment of a system of office development certificates on the lines of the familiar industrial development certificates, and combinations of these methods. " The Paper Metropolis ", published by the Town and Country Planning Association in 1962 contains a valuable explanation of this subject.

A chain of beneficial events would follow from successful implementation of a breaking down of the monolithic Urban Region central area. In the first place, the main centre itself could be sufficiently relieved of congestion to function properly, and could specialise effectively in providing those services which it is especially fitted to perform, namely services of the very highest level in terms of business activities, professional services, educational facilities, shopping and entertainment, as well of course as being the headquarters of government for the region concerned.

Employment which is removed from the main centre should be linked with, and, where possible, actually physically adjoin, existing subordinate centres containing shopping and entertainment facilities, which may or may not already contain a certain amount of employment. Though, for the most part, in the ordinary Urban Region such existing centres will be more than sufficient in number to provide locations for expanded sub-centres, in exceptional circumstances it may be justifiable to start such a centre on a site where at present there is none.

The result of such multiplication of employment nuclei would obviously have the immediate beneficial effect of bringing their work within walking distance for a far larger proportion of people than where the vast majority of employment is concentrated in a single main centre.

In saying this I am not falling into the error of supposing that people will automatically and speedily undertake a general moving of homes in order to bring them within easy distance of their places of employment. This is something which can only happen gradually and partially. Obviously, however, there must be a tendency, however feeble, for this to happen, and the effects must cumulatively become more effective over a period. It is worth noting that mobility in the location of homes would be substantially accelerated if (a) the total supply of homes more nearly approached the demand for them than it does at present and (b) if the buying and selling of houses were made simpler and cheaper than it is and if it were easier to rent a house instead of buying one.

But even before a general shifting of homes had taken place the multiplication of employment nuclei would have had highly beneficial results on transport congestion. Even at the cost, perhaps, of some exacerbation of congestion in places other than the main centre the net improvement would be great. For in place of one enormous tidal surge to and from the centre each day, incapable of being dealt with effectively, there would be a large number of much smaller tidal movements capable of being dealt with by normal traffic control methods.

Another result would be the creation or restoration of individuality for the many districts making up the inner parts of the Urban Region which at present give the appearance of an almost undifferentiated urban mass. The mere addition of considerable numbers of buildings of substantial size at selected points would do this, but, also, a large increase in daytime population would enable considerable improvement in the range and quality of shops and entertainment to be provided locally to be made.

One would therefore have a large number of nuclei of employment, shopping and entertainment spread over the Urban Region, all except the main one substantially bigger than at present, though the actual sizes would have to be worked out carefully in relation to many factors, including capacities of transport, the ages and densities of existing buildings and so forth.   Complementary to this would be the sorting out and re-organisation of land uses within each of the districts serving and served by each centre.

The logical way of doing this would be for the residential area surrounding each such centre to have on its outer side a ring of public open space, the larger school sites and institutional and other uses with a substantial proportion of the site unbuilt.   This is justified by normal planning principles in relation to accessibility, but would also have the important benefits of reinforcing the differentiation, character and individuality of different parts of the Urban Region already achieved in part by the building up of sub-centres.   It would also, and this perhaps is the greatest benefit although the one least capable of being defined and quantified, alleviate what is at present in many ways the most distressing feature of all our conurbations, namely, the feeling of continuous buildings rolling on for many miles, giving a largely justified feeling that however much one may wish to escape for a while from one's fellow men it is impossible to do so.

A belt of open public space, however generous in quantity and augmented by schools and the other uses mentioned, would not, of course, in any way amount to an adequate substitute for genuine open countryside close at hand, but it would at least provide within reasonable reach of everyone an area where substantial stretches of green could be observed and in which it would be possible to walk out of sight of buildings.   Naturally, continuous pedestrian routes should be provided through all such open areas, even though not all of them could be thrown open to the public.   As will be mentioned in Chapter 15, an open area can make its visual contribution even though it cannot actually be entered by the public.

Obviously it would frequently be appropriate for the network of main roads to run through or adjacent to the open space system, forming a loosely reticulated system of main communications constructed on motorway lines and leading to the normal hierarchy of roads described in Chapter 11 within each district.

The end result would be, in effect, a series of towns, each to some extent dependent upon its neighbours, each looking for its highest facilities to the main centre of the Urban Region, but each for many purposes self-contained and having physical definition.   It is not feasible, one feels sure, to upset the existing structure of a conurbation completely; it is too well established and has had such vast sums of capital investment poured into it that a complete change would be impracticable.   One can perhaps best express the result to be aimed at as something falling far short of what would be attempted if (a situation difficult to conceive) one had the opportunity of carrying out from scratch physical Planning for a densely populated, highly industrialised community.   But conditions would be quite reasonably good, and, with the development of an effective road system, access to genuine countryside should be sufficiently easy to make the artificial open space system adequate for daily needs of refreshment and seclusion.

Because of the existing pattern, the towns or districts nearest the centre of the city region would be very close to each other indeed, separated, in fact, merely by public open spaces and schools.   Gradually the distances apart would increase, agricultural land beginning to take its place as part of the

separation, until, almost imperceptibly, the outer parts of the city region blended into the normal pattern of town and village in the hinterland.

In this connection it is worth mentioning that the strengthening of service centres for the benefit of the Urban Region also has its benefits for the

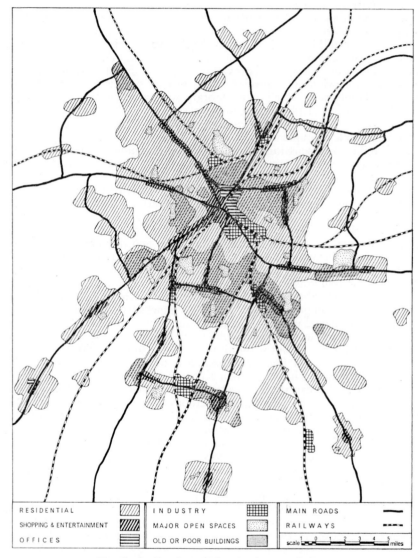

FIG. 7. An imaginary Urban Region as existing.

outside world in providing near the periphery strengthened service centres for the use of the population in the normal areas beyond.

Densities within the Urban Region should be normal densities. Though it would no doubt be necessary on many grounds to exclude from the more

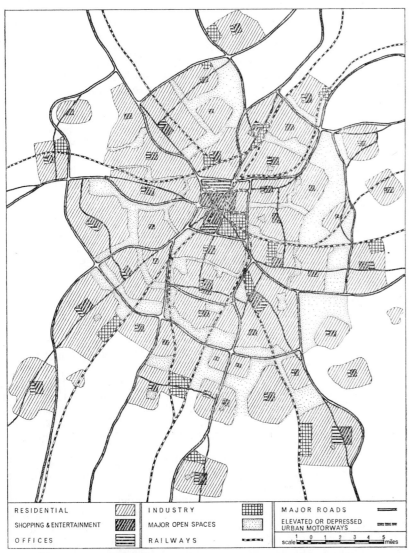

RESIDENTIAL		INDUSTRY		MAJOR ROADS	
SHOPPING & ENTERTAINMENT		MAJOR OPEN SPACES		ELEVATED OR DEPRESSED URBAN MOTORWAYS	
OFFICES		RAILWAYS		scale	

Fig. 8. An outline plan for the Urban Region shown in Fig. 7.

central districts very low density housing, there is, as explained earlier in this chapter, no reason whatever for imposing on the inhabitants of an Urban Region densities greater than those normal elsewhere.

The foregoing picture of the logical Planned form for the Urban Region, illustrated in Figs. 7 and 8, would clearly, in relation to existing law and administration, entail colossal expenditure because of the wholesale extinguishment of existing use rights which would be necessary. To produce a rational Planned pattern, much land devoted to shopping and business use would have to be put to other purposes, much land at present used for housing would have to become schools and open space. Conversely, however, even in the comparatively densely developed inner part of the Urban Region appreciable areas of land not so far built upon would need to be built up to bring about an appropriate relationship of uses. Given a proper resolution of the compensation-betterment problem, the real cost, however, would be nil, except to the extent that, as a matter of urgency, the demolition of a certain number of buildings before the end of their physical lives would be necessary. Not only would the real cost be nil, but the benefits, economic and social, would be enormous.

All this is, of course, entirely at variance with the views of those who would more or less leave the Urban Regions alone, except for small local ameliorations, and would not greatly interfere with " natural " tendencies or seek to reduce commuting drastically. This is really what present official policy seems to amount to. On the other hand it is equally alien to the ideas of those who would " roll back " the city on itself, and seek to create a very dense compact, highly mechanised city. The ideas of those who incline to this policy are seldom very clearly expressed. They tend to relate more to individual pieces of development (even if large ones) rather than to a comprehensive picture of what would happen to the region as a whole. Little can be said about the former policy except that it is quite unlikely to lead to a state of affairs recognisable as a success. As regards the latter, some exploration of its implications is necessary.

For modern technology almost anything is possible if sufficient resources are expended. Frank Lloyd Wright proposed the building of a structure a mile high and Kevin Lynch, in " The Future Metropolis ", visualises the possibility of city centres composed of solid buildings several cubic miles in capacity.

The access of daylight to buildings is not a physical necessity, nor is direct access to fresh air. Artificial daylighting, air conditioning and ultra-violet and infra-ray lamps could no doubt form almost complete substitutes for natural supplies. Buckminster Fuller has suggested the enclosure of whole towns under space domes. The provisions of kitchens placed internally, without access to air or daylight has been seriously proposed for some of the flats in the Barbican. If such conditions proved psychologically distressing, much could no doubt be done to simulate an outlook on the outside world by projecting films of landscape, complete with waving trees, moving vehicles and passers-by, onto walls, and if three-dimensional techniques were used the effect might be very convincing. Substitutes for reality, if they are sufficiently complete, may indeed raise interesting philosophical questions about the nature of reality.   For a fantastic and amusing exploration of this field the reader is referred to " The Big Ball of Wax ", by Shepherd Mead.

What, however, would be the object of carrying out such extremes of intensity in development?   It is difficult to say.   One feels safe in saying that the amount of land required to provide the food supplies of a given population is always likely to be so much greater than the amount required for building purposes for that population, even at very generous standards, that the employment of the gigantic resources required for the measure of intensification imagined above could never be justified.   A minute fraction of the resources employed would suffice to reclaim or increase the fertility of barren land to an extent sufficient to cancel out the land saved by extremely intensive development.   In fact, it is difficult to ascribe to such a trend any motive more sensible than an obstinately exaggerated regard for the sacredness of land values.

We are in some respects approaching sufficiently closely to some of the fantastic possibilities suggested for it to seem desirable to draw attention to the danger of lavishing colossal efforts and making great sacrifices in order to produce tolerable conditions in exaggeratedly intense development when excellent conditions could be produced by normal methods of development by means of the exercise of a quite moderate amount of technical, administrative, economic and legal common-sense and ingenuity.   We should never forget that in America, after mechanically-operated car windows had been popular for some time, a new model with a novel gimmick was advertised: "Do it yourself windows; wind them up and down yourself just as you like ". And that, more recently, " vocal dialling ", i.e., asking the operator for the number, has regained some ground there.

In many ways the capacity of roads is a severely limiting factor in Town Planning.   It is especially so in relation to realistic Planning of the Urban Region.   Another limiting factor, as already suggested, is that of density. In considering therefore, as one is bound to consider very seriously in relation to the Urban Region, appropriate upward limits of size for each district or town, road capacities tend to be predominant, even though many other factors are important.

Parking standards and the capacities of road intersections are peculiarly important and sensitive items in making such an assessment.   What I have to say in the following paragraphs is extremely tentative because little of the necessary information to make more definite assessments has been assembled. I have therefore deliberately refrained from quoting sources for the various figures I give; this, in part, is because some of these sources are confidential, but mainly because I wish merely to indicate the direction in which I think inquiries should take and the basis on which decisions should be made, rather than to suggest validity for the actual figures quoted.   To give sources would encourage reliance to be placed on data which could not support it.

The crucial test in trying to determine town size is whether the central area can (a) absorb into itself the number of people and vehicles which it attracts, (b) whether the buildings serving these people and the spaces for their parked vehicles can be placed within an area sufficiently small for the central area to be reasonably convenient, and (c) whether the forms of construction involved in order to produce physically effective solutions for given levels of population are economically bearable or justified.

In other words, it has become apparent that a single main centre for all the needs of an Urban Region of several million people cannot be planned in such a way as to work effectively or even tolerably.   No one yet knows what is the maximum population which can be dealt with by a single central area. In planning an Urban Region it would obviously be wrong and futile to plan the towns and districts in such a way that any of them were above the size for which a properly working centre could be provided.

This is an insurmountable limitation which ought to be the root consideration in all decisions about town size.   It is extraordinary that this is as yet barely recognised, and certainly does not receive the attention which it should.   If it did so, there would be firm data to provide in place of the imprecise suggestions, which are the best that I can offer.

Travel to a central area is governed by many factors which are extremely difficult to assess.   The proportion of workers and visitors using rail transport, public road transport, their own motor vehicles or who walk and cycle is governed by a multitude of factors related mainly to existing conditions, layout and facilities, about which it is difficult to generalise.   In any case, modes of travel are likely to vary in their proportions from day to day.   Those who normally walk may very well decide in bad weather to drive.   Furthermore, congestion itself acts as a limiting factor.   Experience of conditions of chronic congestion may discourage large numbers of people who would otherwise drive to the centre from doing so, which leads to a lessening of congestion and this in turn to an encouragement to drive, leading to a second phase of acute congestion.   In fact, there may well be alternating phases of acute congestion and relatively mild congestion between a mean level of heavy congestion.

Nevertheless, recognising all these difficulties, some general assumptions and calculations can be made.

It is likely that something like 45% of the total population of a town will go out to work, and that, of this, 40%, or 18% of the total population, will work in the town centre.

If all go to work by car, at an average vehicle occupancy of 1·5 persons, then a total of workers' vehicles equivalent to 12% of the total population of the town will approach the centre in the morning and leave again in the evening.   To this must be added a possible 25% of non-work peak hour traffic, making a grand total vehicles equivalent to 15% of the total population of the town.

Assume that peak traffic flow will be confined to a period of one hour in the morning and one hour in the evening, and that the town centre can be approached by any of four road intersections.

If these four intersections are " at-grade " roundabouts, the weaving sections controlling entrance to the town centre have a capacity of $4 \times 4,000$ vehicles per hour, making a maximum of 16,000 vehicles per hour.   In practice, however, some vehicles will execute 270° turns, and it is unlikely that all junctions will be equally loaded, so that the actual number of vehicles which could enter would be limited to about 12,000 vehicles per hour.

If this figure represents 15% of the population, that population will be 80,000.[1]

More complex junctions will permit the handling of greater volumes of traffic, but the maximum volume of traffic will be governed by the capacity of the direct crossing radial roads—about 5,000 vehicles per hour for each four-lane carriageway—plus approximately 2,000 vehicles per hour for each ramp; making a total of 9,000 vehicles per interchange, giving a population limit of about 250,000 for four such intersections. Whether the street system within the central area can handle the discharge from dual six-lane carriageways is another matter; even the problems created by the discharge from the roundabouts (dual three-lane carriageways) may be such that the capacity of the system is governed by the distribution and terminal facilities of the internal street system rather than the capacity of the entrance/exit junctions.

It is worth noting that the cost of a single level intersection is of the order of £20,000, of a two-level intersection of the order of £100,000 and that of a three-level intersection of the order of £500,000, while that of the most elaborate might well be of the order of £1,000,000. These estimates omit land costs entirely as well as site difficulties, diversion of services and so on, all of which may increase the cost by anything up to four times.

There are, however, a number of variables which might enable a satisfactory Central Area to be designed to cater for a higher level of population than 250,000. Suppose that the number of entries to the Central Area was eight instead of four (this would only be possible with very large Central Areas because of physical limitations of spacing); the limit of population would then be about 500,000—the limit suggested by Dr. Smeed at the " People and Cities " Conference, 1963.

Some increase might also be possible because of the number of people who found it convenient to walk to work, but the limitations upon this source are very severe because, although the numbers concerned might be significant in the case of a small town, the bigger a town is, the smaller the proportion of its inhabitants who can live within reasonable walking distance. At the size range of which we are speaking here they could hardly amount to more than 10%.

Further increases would be possible if any substantial number of workers used public transport, because of the relatively very economical use of road space made by large buses and because trains operate independently of the road system. It is hardly possible to estimate the feasible increase which might result from this but I think it would be unwise to rely very much upon it for long-term Planning. The personal motor vehicle, produced at prices which have put it within reach of increasingly large numbers of people, has conferred such enormous benefits that it seems to me highly improbable that its use will be voluntarily curtailed to any appreciable extent and perhaps even more improbable that public opinion will allow it to be curtailed by legislation.

The motor car takes one in comfort from point of origin to destination,

---

[1] This is, it happens, the figure suggested in the Buchanan Report as the population above which road provision becomes complicated.

free from the effects of all but the most drastic weather conditions, free from timetables and waiting on platforms, free from the physical discomfort of crowded trains and buses, and will accommodate a considerable quantity of personal baggage. It not only takes one to work, it takes one to play; it takes one to holidays abroad, and has conferred the ability, hitherto not even available to kings, of a continuous ever-changing view of 500 miles of landscape within a day's drive. It hardly seems sane to Plan for its reduced use unless the problems it presents can be shown to be insurmountable. No evidence so far produced suggests that they are insurmountable if the public control of land use is exercised with full determination and efficiency.

The practicable maximum population to be served by a single centre is not governed entirely by the capacity of the road system, it is also limited by the physical extent of the centre. A centre so large that travelling between different destinations within it is a serious problem cannot be said to be an efficient one. It would be reasonable to set one square mile as a rough upward limit for a centre, which could easily be walked across in twenty minutes.

The most important determinant of central area size is likely to be the space needed for parking vehicles. Since a total number of vehicles equivalent to 15% of the population of the town may have to be accommodated at any one time in the town centre, then at 250 square feet per car or 175 cars per acre, one acre of parking space will be needed for approximately every 1,150 of the town's population.

Turning to building space, for shopping something of the order of 4,000 square feet is likely to be needed per thousand of the population of the town.

For offices it has been estimated that about half the workers in the town centre will work in offices and half in shops, and assuming 125 square feet gross floor area per office worker, about 11,250 square feet of offices will be needed per 1,000 of the town's population.

Shops and offices, using each term in the widest sense, are far and away the most important town centre uses. To them must be added places of entertainment, education and worship, the space needs for which are exceedingly difficult to estimate. If 10% of the combined shop and office floor space is added for these purposes it is likely to be adequate.

Total town centre floor and parking space per thousand people can then be tabulated as follows:

			Square feet
Cars ...	...	...	38,000
Shops ...	...	...	4,000
Offices ...	...	...	11,250
Places of entertainment, etc.		...	1,500
Total ...		...	54,750 sq. ft. of floor and parking space.

This space can be arranged in a considerable number of different ways. Let us take one fairly simple method and see what emerges.

Omitting the area of road outside but adjoining the centre, which is difficult to calculate on generalised assumptions, but which is likely to be negligible, we might well assume that nearly all the shopping and entertainment, etc., would be on one level, that offices would be built in the form of six-storey blocks, that parking would be on one level and that pedestrian ways between shops could be provided out of the total allocation of shop space.

On this basis the area of the Town Centre, per 1,000 people, would be:

		Square feet
Shops		4,000
Entertainment, etc. ...		1,500
Offices		2,000
Parking		38,000
Total		45,500 square feet

Some or all of the office accommodation might well be built directly above the shops so that, in round figures, we should need one acre of land for Central Area purposes per 1,000 population. This is an example of those traditional figures of space needs which are met quite often, and which, though they seem originally to have been arrived at by a process somewhat resembling guesswork, maintain an obstinate validity.

Accepting, for the moment, one acre of Central area per 1,000 population, it is clear that, if the Centre is not to exceed one square mile in area, the population it serves must be limited to 640,000; this corresponds tolerably well with the estimate of 500,000 as the probable ultimate limit set by the limitations of capacity of road intersections, assuming eight of these to be provided.

If the overall urban density in the area served by the centre were 20 persons per acre, this area would be 25,000 acres in extent, a circle with a diameter of about seven miles, a large but not oppressively great urban spread.

Since the limitations of road capacity appear to be more drastic than those of town centre size it may not be very important to consider the possibilities of reducing the latter. Nevertheless some thought about this subject may be worth while.

Tremendous interest has been shown in the last few years in the possibilities of multi-level town centres, in which, speaking in the simplest terms, vehicles would be circulated and parked and buildings serviced from the vehicles at ground level while all pedestrian circulation and access to buildings would be from a raised platform—an idea which will be discussed further in Chapter 12.

If the ground area needed for parking on the one hand, and for buildings and pedestrian space on the other, is roughly equal then, clearly, the total land needed for the central area is halved if this method of development is adopted. In the well known Hook project, for example, the Central Area,

for a population of 100,000 is 100 acres on plan. Of this, however, not much more than half (one cannot tell precisely) seems to be devoted to genuine central area uses. On the lower level 56 acres is devoted to parking; a rough one-to-one ratio between central area buildings above and parking below thus emerges. This may be valid in terms of a town of 100,000 but the calculations made a little earlier in this chapter give a 1 to $2\frac{1}{4}$ ratio between floor area and parking area, which becomes 1 to 5 when floor area is condensed into building area.

The discrepancy, on the information available, cannot be fully resolved but a large element in it is accounted for by the fact that the parking space for Hook is based upon accommodation for about 8% of the population as against the 15% assumed in my calculations.

A far smaller proportion of the working population was assumed to be working in the town centre in the case of Hook, and 27% were assumed to walk. In relation to an Urban Region, with larger centres and with a very high proportion of office workers, my assumptions are probably more appropriate.

If a space ratio of the order of 1 to 5 between ground area and parking area for large centres is correct, it is apparent that a simple two-level form of centre is not appropriate—the cars would stick out all round! Multi-level parking, either below ground or above, in the form of parking buildings, or both, becomes necessary to secure any significant reduction in town centre size.

A few figures are significant. Assuming that the compensation-betterment bogey has been removed, which is indispensable to any proper Planning of an Urban Region, then, since land costs will not enter into the matter, the conservative cost of creation of a pedestrian deck is about £50,000 an acre. If about half an acre per thousand population is needed for the town centre, this will mean a cost of £25 for every inhabitant of the town: no small sum.

In relation to road intersection costs, then, above the critical figure of 80,000 population, the cost of each of the four town centre road intersections rises from £20,000 to £100,000, an increase of £80,000 or, for the four, £4 for each member of the town's population.

These data indicate that very careful consideration indeed needs to be given before a decision about town population is taken which would lift its population above any of the critical levels mentioned. This is not to say that to do so will never be justified, but many factors come into the count. It may be that the greater compactness of a two-level town centre, for example, may make it so relatively attractive that the rents which can successfully be asked of shopkeepers and office employers can be raised to a figure making a reasonable return on the extra capital costs, but is by no means certain that this will be so. This is a subject which will be further discussed in Chapter 12.

Attention has been focused upon the capacity problems of the Central Area because these are likely to be the most acute problems encountered. Similar problems will of course arise in relation to industrial areas, but they are unlikely to be quite so difficult unless the industrial area and the central area are so related spatially that the traffic approaching each has to share road intersections.   In this case the workable size limits of a town or district will be drastically reduced.

In conclusion, I wish to emphasise again the slenderness of the data upon which the argument in the latter part of this chapter has been based.   Further research might well profoundly modify the provisional conclusions reached. I can only say that I shall be extremely pleased when sufficient information is available for confident predictions to be made.

CHAPTER 6

REGIONAL SURVEYS

6-1. PRELIMINARY

THE TERM SURVEY, as used in connection with Town and Country Planning, means the collection, interpretation, arrangement, combination, and presentation in the most readily understood form of all the information likely to influence the proposals to be included in a Development Plan. Survey is necessary for any Plan, from a national Plan right down to investigation leading to the selection of a housing site, although naturally the subject-matter for inquiry and the degree of detail entered into vary widely with different kinds of Plan.

The need for preliminary investigation before preparing Plans has long been recognised, Patrick Geddes being known everywhere as a pioneer in this field. His untiring reiteration of the need for such survey did much to stimulate the many excellent county and regional surveys, usually including also advisory Plans, carried out during the inter-war period. These helped to make clear the principles upon which land for different uses should be selected and the ways in which wise action could alter for the better the numerous ways in which the constituent units of the pattern of human settlements affect each other; but the lack of any sufficient legislation to enable the obviously desirable action to which they pointed to be taken lent them an air of unreality. If anyone had tried to prepare a town or rural Planning scheme in such a way as to give effect to the findings of a regional survey it would have been practically impossible to do so without incurring liability for stupendous amounts of compensation, even if the approval of the Ministry of Health (then responsible for Planning) could have been obtained for any really effective proposals.

Nevertheless, these surveys and advisory Plans, often beautifully presented, provided to a great extent the stimulus for the necessary legislative sanction for effective Planning.

Those preparing statutory Planning schemes under the 1932 Act did *some* survey. It usually took the form of travelling about the area concerned and making notes of such relevant factors as took the eye: an area of marsh, a fine view, a patch of unsightly development or a group of trees worth preserving. In this way the trained eye could rapidly give the skilled brain an excellent general impression of the salient characteristics of an area. This impression was reinforced by the study of ordnance maps and of the local authority's maps showing the distribution of sewers and gas, water and electricity mains.

On the whole, however, this rough and ready survey existed chiefly in the planner's mind, reinforced by a few cryptic notes on dog-eared ordnance sheets, and was not available to his successor if promotion, retirement or death called him elsewhere. The survey lacked any coherent visible expression which could be produced at will to assist in discussion or to confound opposition.

It is true that the Ministry of Health did require a sort of survey map to be submitted with the Planning scheme, which showed broad divisions of land use, areas sewered and provided with piped water supply, and areas to which these services could readily be extended, but there was, as far as one recalls, no suggestion that the plan should have been based upon this information.

The present system of Planning survey, on the other hand, is, or ought to be used, *first*, to give the requisite information upon which to base proposals, *second*, to provide members of the Local Planning Authority, and subsequently the Ministry, with information upon which to judge the merits of the proposals; and, *third*, to convince owners and intending developers of the rightness of the proposals to which they are being asked to conform.

This new attitude towards survey emerged gradually towards the end of the war. There was a tendency at this time somewhat to exaggerate the desirable scope and degree of detail of Planning survey. In some quarters it was virtually suggested that a really thorough survey practically removed the necessity of doing any Planning; the survey would reveal unmistakably what proposals were required. This, of course, is nonsense, but, on the other hand, it is certain that a really well prepared and presented survey will often indicate in general terms the solutions to various problems which, without such aid, might never have been arrived at, and would, at best, have necessitated a much greater amount of thought and worry than that involved in preparing the survey.

Before and shortly after the passing of the 1947 Act many admirable Planning surveys had been prepared by various agencies in anticipation of the need for such work as a basis for real land Planning. In their very different ways the surveys for Hereford, Kent, Lancashire and East Suffolk among the counties, and of Manchester and Middlesbrough among the towns, are especially interesting. It is noteworthy that some of them enter into much greater detail in some directions than is required for official purposes, but that, on the other hand, none of them entirely covers official requirements.

Unhappily, the process of survey, which should be dynamic and imaginative, has, with too many Local Planning Authorities, hardened into a rather dreary process of going through the motions prescribed by Circulars 40 and 63, in order to meet the Ministry's formal requirement for approval of a Development Plan, with little or no consideration of whether all the surveys prescribed are, in any particular circumstances, necessary or in the best form for the project in hand, or whether additional and quite different surveys might be desirable. In a good many cases I feel fairly sure that no one either in the Local Planning Authority or the Ministry has any clear idea of what use some of the surveys carried out are likely to be.

On the other hand some Local Planning Authorities carry out excellent surveys, employing methods far in advance of the rather crude techniques suggested in the Ministry Circulars.

It is essential before embarking on a Planning survey to be as definite as possible about the terms of reference: the problems about which information is required and the *kind* of action possible to solve them. Thus, although the ideal method of conducting a survey might be to collect and correlate as much information as possible about every subject which could possibly have a bearing upon the Planning of the area concerned, time and expense both render such a course impracticable. It is necessary to confine the survey to such subjects as commonsense and experience suggest are likely to assist in formulating proposals for which there is legislative sanction.

This statement needs to be qualified. An all-out investigation into the problems of land use without regard to the immediate practicability of translating its findings into action may itself eventually help to stimulate the necessary legislation, or an investigation of some special aspect may reveal the need for more drastic and far-reaching proposals than are possible within the existing framework.

There is also a great but insufficiently recognised need for all information dealing with social and economic subjects which relates to land use, population growth and migration, employment, etc., to be obtained and interpreted in such a way as to be capable of being directly compared in order to form a continuous body of knowledge throughout many fields.

No hard and fast line can be drawn; there are several subjects the direct relevance of which to statutory Planning the average Planner might have difficulty under cross-examination in establishing, yet without a knowledge of which he would feel himself lacking the essential information. The best example of this is the general history of the Planning area (as distinct from such special aspects of it as the preservation of ancient monuments and buildings of historical or special architectural interest), which may have practically no discernible influence upon the Development Plan, but of which no planner would care to be ignorant because of the general *understanding* of the area, an understanding which might almost be called emotional, which a knowledge of it gives.

In these chapters, in order to keep treatment of the subject to a reasonable length, I have confined myself almost entirely to those subjects which have a direct bearing upon the preparation of the Development Plan.

The scales of the maps used, the subject-matter and the degree of detail entered into necessarily differ between various surveys. We cannot here be very greatly concerned with national surveys, which lie outside the scope of this book, but mention must be made of the series of 1/625,000 maps (about 10 miles to 1 inch) prepared under the auspices of the Ministry, which constitute a sort of vague beginning to a survey for an outline National Plan.

Regional surveys can be prepared to larger scales than a national survey, and town surveys to still larger scales. Some subjects may have to be dealt with on all three levels, and one of the 1/625,000 series illustrates this point. The Land Utilisation Survey is a generalisation from the 1 inch to 1 mile series published by the Land Utilisation of Great Britain, and this in turn, is taken from 6 inches to 1 mile field sheets. The first two of these also illustrate well the principle that where the same subject-matter is dealt with on different scales the notation on each should, as far as possible, be the same, or, where this is not possible or appropriate, sufficiently similar for the connection between the two to be immediately apparent. (The 6 inches to 1 mile field

sheets were not coloured, the use of each parcel being noted in writing.) Both the 1/625,000 and the 1 inch to 1 mile Land Utilisation Maps can, incidentally, be commended as among the most effective and beautiful maps ever made. Looking at the 1/625,000 map one probably gets as vivid a picture as is possible of the contrasting patterns of land use in different parts of the country.

The inter-war Land Utilisation Survey is at present in course of being revised and is being republished at 1/25,000 scale. The specimens so far seen are even better than their predecessors, quite superb examples of cartography.

Regional Surveys can conveniently, though rather loosely, be divided into three broad classes, those dealing with:—

    (a) *Physical factors*
    (b) *Physical and economic factors*
    (c) *Social and economic factors.*

6-2. PHYSICAL FACTORS

(1) Topography

This may be presented in the form of a model, map or anaglyph. Models and anaglyphs have already been mentioned in Chapter 3. If it is decided to construct a model the most suitable method for this purpose will probably be to make a stepped model using fully coloured 1 inch to 1 mile or 1/25,000 Ordnance sheets in their published form without any rendering. The vertical interval of the steps must to some extent be dependent upon the time available and the skill of the model makers; the smaller the vertical interval the more detailed and accurate will be the picture given. The vertical scale should be some three or four times greater than the horizontal scale in order to emphasise the relief adequately.

If a map is used the base map should be No. IIb (see page 29), and if it is to be rendered in colours it is necessary to work out some simple gradation. It is usual to colour the lowest land lightly and higher land progressively darker, but there is no particular reason why the opposite should not be done.

A monochrome notation is hardly suitable for a large contour map, but can be employed very effectively on a small generalised map on which only broad differences of level are indicated.

(2) Physically difficult land

This survey is sometimes presented in combination with the preceding one, but is much better dealt with separately. On it is shown all the land which, because of its characteristics, is relatively or absolutely physically unsuitable for the purpose of large-scale building development, the land subject to each particular factor being distinguished. Among the characteristics tending to make land physically unsuitable for such development are:—

(i) *Excessive height*
In this country the climatic conditions of land within a few hundred feet of

sea level are generally mild, but above a certain height they become severe; this severity increases progressively until a second point is reached above which development is undesirable.

The selection of actual datum heights is necessarily somewhat arbitrary, since the change of severity is gradual and not abrupt. Seven hundred feet and one thousand five hundred feet have been suggested as suitable heights in average circumstances, but these circumstances are subject to considerable local variation; the critical heights, for example, may be considerably lower where the aspect of the land is northerly. It is improbable in the extreme that anyone would accidentally select a site for a new town in this country 2,000 feet above sea level because no survey map picking out high land was available! Nevertheless, abroad, in mountainous country, such information conveniently plotted might be very helpful, and even here it can occasionally have its uses.

(ii) *Excessive slope*

Steeply sloping land, however delightful it may be for the siting of a few houses, is unfavourable for large-scale development in several ways:—

(a) The costs of roads and buildings are increased because of the amount of excavation and building-up required.
(b) Traffic danger is increased.
(c) Flexibility in the siting of buildings is decreased.
(d) Playing fields and other uses requiring flat sites may have to be located inconveniently far from the population they serve.

It is, of course, unlikely that the whole of a site under consideration for extensive development will consist of steeply sloping land, and, in weighing up its merits from this point of view, it is necessary to consider both the proportion of steeply sloping land to the whole and its distribution; it will usually be possible to accept a higher proportion of steeply sloping land if it consists of a few fairly large masses than if it is, on the one hand, confined to one very large area, or, on the other hand, is greatly fragmented. In either of these two latter cases flexibility of siting will be very greatly reduced and, where there is great fragmentation, areas of comparatively level land surrounded by steeply sloping land may be virtually undevelopable either because they are too small in extent or because access and drainage are rendered unduly difficult and costly.

As with height, it is useful to distinguish two degrees of steepness: first, the point at which slope begins to create difficulties, and, second, the point at which those difficulties become so severe as to preclude development unless no better alternative site can be found.

Again, a more or less arbitrary choice has to be made of critical slopes for purposes of differentiation, and opinions on this subject vary considerably. In the West Midlands Group's " English County " 1 in 10 and 1 in 7½ are chosen, while in the A.P.R.R. Textbook on Planning 1 in 20 and 1 in 7 are suggested. The particular slopes chosen must necessarily depend to a great extent on the characteristics of the area being surveyed, and it is important to choose ones which will effectively distinguish between suitable and unsuitable sites. For instance, in an area where a large proportion of the land was at

gradients of between 1 in 9 and 1 in 8, the choice of 1 in 10 and 1 in 7½ would clearly be inappropriate since, on this basis, there would be very little differentiation between somewhat unsuitable and very unsuitable land.

There are one or two points to be borne in mind when working out areas of excessive slope. The actual process is simple enough, though tedious. Suppose that areas with a slope in excess of 1 in 10 are being plotted; a distance, at the scale of the map being used, equal to ten times the vertical interval between contours is marked on a piece of paper and, by measuring with this, all the land between successive contours, along those portions of their length where they are closer together than this distance, can be shaded or otherwise marked off; the result, even after smoothing out curves, is usually a series of shapes of great complexity, and at the Regional scale there is no objection if these are generalised somewhat. But, since the 1/25,000 maps give the most detailed contour information likely to be available over an area of any considerable size, and since information concerning steep land is a survey item which recurs at all scales of survey, it is certain that at some stage, even if a smaller scale is being used for the regional survey, the areas of steep slope will have to be plotted on the 1/25,000 scale for the sake of the extra detail. It will save labour if they are worked out on the 1/25,000 map in the first instance and transferred to the smaller scale map.

(iii) *Unfavourable Aspect*

Land which slopes in a generally northerly direction suffers from a diminution in the intensity of the sunlight falling upon it, from exposure to cold winds and from a reduction in the potential number of hours of sunshine which it enjoys. The incidence of this disadvantage is difficult to determine because any precise definition of the areas affected is complicated in areas of intricate topography by the overshadowing of some areas by others in a manner which is not simply related to aspect. However, experiment suggests that where the general slope of land is in a direction between north-west and north-east and is also steeper than one in ten the disadvantageous effects are significant. The areas of unfavourable aspect shown in " English County " appear to have been plotted on this basis. If this standard is used, plotting is, of course, extremely simple and consists merely of selecting those portions of the areas with slopes in excess of one in ten which have a general direction between north-west and north-east. It is unnecessary to exclude small areas within a hill feature which have some other aspect, since they are likely to be so overshadowed by other land that they enjoy little or no advantage compared with the remainder.

(iv) *Land liable to flooding or waterlogging*

It hardly seems necessary to point out the disadvantages of such land, which include physical inconvenience, costly construction and unhealthiness. It is, however, a matter of some difficulty both to determine the standard which should be used to determine the degree of flooding or waterlogging which constitutes a serious disadvantage to development, and, when this has been done, to define the areas affected. Gordon Payne, in his Survey and Plan for Gloucestershire, quotes the opinion of the Medical Officer of Health for Gloucester that development is undesirable where the level of underground water rises to within 10ft. of the surface, a standard which at first sight seems extremely severe. Under the Land Drainage Act of 1932, drainage authorities have to determine areas within which occupiers are liable for drainage rates. These areas usually comprise land not more than 8ft. higher than the highest known flood level. There is a fairly close relation between these figures, and, since the extent of these areas is defined on maps and is, therefore, readily ascertainable, there is considerable advantage in using them.

However, some caution must be exercised. It may be appropriate to exclude such areas from consideration as New Town sites, for example, but it would obviously be futile to attempt to prevent all building within them, since many towns and their potential development areas lie wholly within such limits. The flood areas on which drainage authorities base their rating areas are, too, open to some suspicion, since, in many places, they are prepared from " oldest inhabitant " information. The incidence of flooding is by no means an unchanging factor; the activities of drainage authorities may reduce the affected area considerably. Building development may itself operate to reduce the incidence of flooding; the provision of road channels and surface water sewers enables rainwater falling on the area to be taken away rapidly without causing flooding.

Enough has perhaps been said to indicate that great care is necessary in basing Planning decisions upon survey data. At the regional scale the drainage authorities' flood and rating areas, suitably differentiated, may provide a useful guide; for more detailed purposes they will need to be supplemented by recent local information, aerial photographs, study of the distribution of moisture-loving plant species, and any other available source. It goes without saying that land permanently covered with water should also be shown on the map.

(v) *Large excavated areas and spoil heaps*

These will have to be very large to be significant at the Regional scale, but where very large ones exist they should be shown. Normally the sides of excavations will be too steep for road access to be practicable, and this alone rules them out as sites for development.

(vi) *Land liable to subsidence*

The land above underground mineral workings is often unstable and liable to subsidence to an extent likely to cause serious damage to buildings and services. It is often a matter of great difficulty to ascertain the boundaries of areas liable to subsidence, but it is clearly of importance to do this as accurately as possible.

(vii) *Large areas of land used for the disposal of sewage or refuse*

These are self-evidently unsuitable for building development, at least until such a use has ceased for a considerable number of years. It may be asked why these particular public uses should be selected for attention on this map out of the large number of other such uses which preclude general development. The factor which distinguishes them is that they are virtually the only ones which adversely affect the land itself from the point of view of prospec-

tive building development; obstacles to development in the case of other public uses are the importance of the existing use, the cost of changing its location, the legal complexities involved in making a change of use or straightforward reluctance on the part of the owning authority.

(3) **Geology**

This is a subject which provides the Planner mainly with background information; that is to say, although the geology of the region has the most profound effect upon its agriculture, landscape and local building materials, and although no Planner can afford to be without a knowledge of it, the occasions upon which he will have to go right back to fundamental geological facts upon which to base any particular Planning decision are likely to be rare; more commonly, knowledge of the geology of the area will tell him what problems to expect.

Published geological maps need expert interpretation, for the categories shown on them are sometimes misleading. For example, the Weald Clay though much of it is in fact clay, contains also sizeable areas of sandstone which are not shown on the map.

The most useful geological map for planning purposes is a lithological map, which shows merely the distribution of rock types—sand, clay, chalk, etc., and does not concern itself with the particular geological formation to which each belongs. Once more it must be emphasised that it is essential to obtain expert advice when preparing such a map.

Those unacquainted with geological maps must be careful to distinguish between solid maps and drift maps. The former show only the underlying bedrock, while the latter show any overlying strata deposited on the bedrock by the action of wind and water. Even the drift maps do not show the character of the topsoil, normally no more than a foot or so in depth, which is mixed with humus (decaying organic matter) and may vary in character much more widely than the drift of which the subsoil is composed. However, important superficial deposits, such as sand, gravel and brickearth, are shown by means of symbols where they overlie drift of a different composition, the latter being identified by colour.

(4) **Landscape**

Few would deny the need to preserve unspoiled the beauty of as much as possible of our countryside, and the attainment of this object can be substantially assisted by the collection and presentation of appropriate survey data. In order to understand the basis upon which the Survey should be carried out it is necessary to make certain fundamental assumptions; opinions may differ about what these should be, but the following appear to me to be reasonable:

(i) The countryside is not a museum-piece but a vital part of the national life, much of it the workshop of the agricultural industry; it would be foolish, in any area, to attempt to prevent any economically or socially essential development, but much can be done to steer it to sites where it will do the least harm to the landscape.

(ii)   Notable landscape is of three principal kinds:

   (a)   That which forms part of a stretch of magnificent scenery visible from one or more viewpoints.

   (b)   Landscape which, because of its topography, vegetation pattern, and, sometimes, design, is exceptionally beautiful, but does not give rise to any particularly sweeping or dramatic views.

   (c)   Small-scale landscape of superlative quality—small, wooded valleys, strips adjoining rivers and streams and so on.

Of these (a) may cover the best part of several counties and it would obviously be both absurd and impracticable to attempt to prevent development in the whole of such an area. Apart from anything else, it is quite likely that much of it will have no great intrinsic beauty at close quarters. The important thing is to prohibit all except the most essential agricultural development in the immediate vicinity of the viewpoints themselves and the foreground of the view. The depth of foreground which it is practicable to preserve against development will vary considerably, but it seems reasonable to assume that any development more than two miles from a viewpoint will, if reasonably well designed, be sufficiently softened by distance for its injury to the landscape to be greatly minimised. Such a policy will also protect the skyline, and the slopes leading to it, of the feature on which the viewpoint is situated, which may well form as fine a landscape feature from the lowlands as the lowlands do when seen from the viewpoint.

As regards (b) it is important that only the very finest landscape should be selected for complete preservation; so much English countryside is extremely attractive that there is a temptation to try to preserve all of it against development—a policy bound to be self-defeating. Within such areas as are eventually selected the objects will be to prevent any large-scale development and to control small amounts of development with special care. The selection of these areas must necessarily depend upon personal opinion, and it is desirable to make use of the agreed choice of several people.

As regards (c) it will, of course, be necessary to prevent development within the area concerned and of any land close to and visible from it.

It is appropriate to include on *the landscape map* the areas proposed as nature reserves or areas of special scientific interest under the National Parks and Access to the Countryside Act, 1949. In addition to Nature Reserves proper there are certain geological monuments—examples of rare or specially interesting geological formations which are exposed to view and which should also be included.

It is also convenient to indicate areas of woodland which it is considered should be preserved on account of their appearance. The factors governing the selection of these are discussed in Chapter 20.

During the war the Admiralty developed an instrument called a Landfall Projector, which enables the area of land visible from any particular spot to be plotted from a contour map. I have no knowledge of the speed at which this work can be carried out, but if it is not excessively slow it is obvious that this instrument could be of great value in determining areas for preservation. It

could also be of value in finding unobtrusive sites for inevitable intrusions in the landscape.

An account of the instrument and its operation is given in the Journal of the Town Planning Institute for March-April, 1947.

6-3. PHYSICAL-ECONOMIC FACTORS
(1) Agricultural value

Maintenance of the welfare of the agricultural industry by preventing the loss to agriculture of as much good land and as many productive farm units as possible is an important Planning aim. The factors involved are numerous and complicated, and it is not possible entirely to separate the regional and local aspects of the matter.

Eight factors which affect the agricultural value of a given area of land as compared to other agricultural land are of special importance. They are as follows:—

   (i)   The inherent fertility of the land due to the composition of its soil.

   (ii)   The local climate; differences of height and aspect and the prevalence of frost pockets may cause wide changes in the productivity of land within quite a small area.

   (iii)   The prevalence of steep slopes and broken land.

   (iv)   The thoroughness with which the land can be drained.

   (v)   The condition of the soil, buildings and fixed appliances as the result of the skill of the farmer and the amount of money spent on maintenance and improvement.

   (vi)   The extent to which the farm is a satisfactory unit as regards size, shape, internal communications, position, size and design of buildings, balanced variety of soil types within the holding, etc. When considering, on the local Planning level, the relative importance of retaining in agricultural use several small areas of land each comprising only part of a farm unit, the intricacy of the factors involved becomes very great. Two fields of approximately equal acreage forming parts of one unit may have totally different degrees of importance to the economy of the unit; the loss of one may be negligible, that of the other crippling.

   (vii)   The position of the land in relation to transport routes and markets.

   (viii)   The availability of sufficient agricultural labour, including the various specialist workers required.

The Planner, unless he is also an agricultural expert, must inevitably be ignorant of the relative weight to be attached to these numerous factors, and in any case their collection, interpretation and mapping would be a task of impossible magnitude for a Local Planning Authority to carry out in connection with a Planning survey.

It has nevertheless been suggested that, within areas in which substantial development is possible, the relative agricultural value of each parcel of land should be assessed according to the incidence of all the relevant factors, such as those mentioned above, so that an intelligent selection could be made to minimise the agricultural loss caused by development. Clearly such a survey would be a very large task, would have to be carried out by agriculturists, and would need frequent revision, since the incidence of some of the factors may change fairly rapidly. Since the Planner is concerned with relatively long-term values, it would be best from his point of view for such an assessment to be confined to the comparatively unchanging factors.

For the purposes of regional survey two maps will probably suffice; a map showing, broadly, *areas of relative fertility* and a *farm unit map*. The former, in the absence of more detailed information, can be based upon the classification adopted for the 1/625,000 Land Classification map. This map is itself at too small a scale for accurate plotting to a larger scale to be made from it, but the same information, plotted to a larger scale, can be obtained from the Ministry of Agriculture. This survey distinguishes ten different categories of land, which is excessive for the purposes of the map under discussion. They may be boiled down to areas of good, moderate and poor farmland and mixtures of these. In " English County " it is suggested that categories 1 to 4 may be regarded as good quality land, categories 5 and 6 as moderate land, and categories 7 to 10 as poor land. These categories are based upon depth and character of soil and drainage.

Unfortunately, the information given by the Land Classification Survey is so general that for Planning purposes it is sometimes misleading; there may be widely varying types of land within an area shown as falling within a single category and some areas are shown as combinations of two or more different categories, which makes the information even more general. It is not uncommon for very large areas of excellent land to exist within an area shown as of moderate quality and vice versa. More detailed surveys have been carried out by various bodies in some parts of the country, and where one is available and its reliability assured it should be used. Even so, it is likely that in parts of the survey area there will be such wide variation of quality within a small area that a mixture will have to be indicated on the map.

The Farm Unit map should distinguish clearly the boundaries of each holding, a farm unit or holding being an area occupied and managed as one unit. Where a holding is severed into two or more portions they should be linked by ties, since this map is normally so complicated that merely to indicate the different portions in the same notation will be insufficient to make clear the relationship between them. The position of the principal group of farm buildings, or farm headquarters, of each unit should be shown by a symbol, since the loss of these buildings or their severance from the remainder of the holding will often be much more serious than the loss of even a substantial part of the land.

Although knowledge of the Farm Unit pattern is most important in the vicinity of town and villages, where development involving the loss of land to agriculture is most likely to arise, proposals for main roads, airfields, W.D. training ground, etc., may affect land anywhere in the region, and it is well worth while to do the small amount of extra work involved in mapping the farm unit boundaries over the whole area.

The Ministry of Agriculture has full information regarding farm unit boundaries, although this is not everywhere completely up to date. Unfortunately, access to this information is uncertain. It was originally obtained from the Ministry of Agriculture from farmers on the understanding that it would be treated as confidential. The extent to which officers of the Ministry of Agriculture regard the passing of this information to the Local Planning Authority as being consistent with this undertaking varies in different parts of the country, notwithstanding that it is an item in the official notation for land use maps. It would not, of course, be a task of insuperable difficulty, though it would be one of some magnitude, for the Local Planning Authority itself to acquire the necessary information by local investigation on the part of its officers, though to do this when the information has already been mapped by the Ministry of Agriculture would involve a quite indefensible duplication of work.

(2) Mineral resources and water-gathering grounds

For information on these subjects, which can appropriately be shown on the same map, the planner is very much dependent upon information from outside sources. The location of commercially valuable minerals is often not precisely known, still less the areas in which they exist in an economically workable form or in the requisite degree of purity. It is the responsibility of the Ministry of Housing and Local Government to supply Local Planning Authorities with information on these subjects, but additional information by any other reliable source is likely to prove useful,

Generally speaking, it is desirable to map all areas in which it is reasonably certain that economically workable minerals exist, with notes in as much detail as possible regarding the type, quality, depth below surface and depth of mineral-bearing formations. The presence of such minerals is not, of course, an absolute bar to development; the need for them to be worked has to be balanced against the need for the land to be used for other purposes, but, since the supply of many minerals is less than the demand, it is preferable to locate other forms of land use elsewhere if this is possible.

Water may be regarded as a special kind of mineral; in some circumstances it is collected into usable concentrations from the surface of the ground, sometimes it is obtained from underground. In both cases there is need for protection from land uses liable to pollute the water supply. In the case of underground supply an area surrounding the points at which the supply is tapped, depending in size upon the geological structure of the area and the amount of water extracted, will need protection. The necessary precautions may not prevent development, but may consist merely in the prohibition of development not connected to a sewer or likely to result in harmful substances percolating into the ground.

There seems to be no agreement about the degree of protection which is required for surface supply. Current practice varies greatly.

As regards potential future sources of supply, such as that which would be required for a new town, the investigation needed is too specialised and arduous a task to be included in an ordinary regional Planning survey, but should be undertaken as a special project. The number of sites suitable on other grounds for a new town is likely to be extremely small, and water can be conveyed for considerable distances by pipe, so that the nearness of sources of water supply is not necessarily a severely limiting factor.

(3) Areas provided with public services

A map should be prepared to show the road frontages which are served by sewers, gas, electricity and/or water.   The best way to show the information is to colour a strip of arbitrary width on either side of the road served, varying the colour according to the degree of completeness of the services existing. Thus, lengths of road in which there are a sewer, a water main and gas or electricity mains (gas and electricity may be regarded as alternatives for domestic purposes) might be coloured brown, lengths with a water main and gas or electricity but no sewer, orange, and lengths with a water main only, blue.   There may be a few lengths of road without water but with a gas or electricity main, and these should be indicated separately.

Care should be taken only to show tappable lengths of main in the fashion indicated above, any trunk lines not capable of being tapped for purposes of small-scale development being shown separately.   The position of sewage disposal works, power stations, gas works and reservoirs should be shown.

Another map should indicate areas which cannot be economically served by the existing sewerage system so far as they can be determined at this stage, and on it should also be shown any land which, because of insufficient head of water, cannot economically be provided with water supply.   It is hardly practicable to indicate areas which cannot be served by gas or electricity, since almost the only consideration which applies is distance from existing sources of supply, and the distance beyond which the provision of a new service becomes uneconomical varies according to the amount of development to be served by it.

The principal purpose of these maps is to help decide the areas in which small new settlements, comparatively minor additions to existing towns, additions to villages and such isolated rural dwellings as may have to be permitted can suitably be located.   The location of new towns and major extensions to existing towns, which may require the constructions of new sewage-disposal works and reservoirs and of trunk mains, cannot be determined in this way; their service requirements need special investigation (as suggested when dealing with sources of water supply under (2) above), which can most easily be undertaken after possible alternative sites suitable on general planning grounds have been determined.

(4) Transport

The facts concerning transport facilities which directly concern regional Planning and upon which Planning action can be taken are comparatively few.   Many regional surveys contain large quantities of complicated data on the subject, which, interesting though they may be and valuable to those concerned with organising public transport services, mainly consist of information which the Planner himself cannot turn to account.

Two maps will normally suffice for the purpose of regional survey:

(a) *Existing Facilities:* a map showing as clearly as possible the existing network of roads, railways, canals and navigable rivers and the position of civil airfields.   Much of this information is shown on Ordnance maps, and all that needs to be done is to reproduce it on a map in such a way as to emphasise strongly the pattern of the transport system and the relationship of one form

of route with another, so that the points at which improvements are needed can be clearly seen.   A useful refinement is to differentiate between roads in respect, not of their Ministry of Transport classification, but of the width of their carriageway; obstacles such as low bridges and sharp bends should be noted.   The depths of canals and navigable rivers might well be shown.

(b) *Traffic Density:* a map showing, by bands of varying widths, the amount of traffic using various main roads.   Differentiation between weekday and weekend traffic, industrial or commercial traffic, and private cars, and cycles is also helpful.

6-4. SOCIAL-ECONOMIC FACTORS

(1) Areas of influence of towns and villages

" The hierarchy of service centres " is a phrase often used to describe the pattern of human settlements, which, from metropolis down to hamlet, all provide services of a commercial, social, and often educational character, not only for their own inhabitants but for those of a surrounding area as described in Chapter 4.   One of the principal objects of regional Planning is to work out the positions and amounts of the additional supply services which should be provided in order to attain a well-graded hierarchy, but the Planner is not in a position to influence directly the choice of settlements by banks, insurance companies, shopkeepers and other suppliers of services; on the other hand, he can at least have a large say in determining which of the smaller villages are chosen for the establishment of new primary schools and which of the larger villages for secondary schools, and, since supply services depend upon the existence of a central population as well as of a surrounding one, he can exercise a powerful indirect influence by providing for the greatest increases of population in those communities in which the greatest increase of supply services is needed to secure the optimum pattern.

Information regarding the existing pattern can be presented in a variety of ways and with greatly varying degrees of detail.   For example, it would be theoretically possible to map the areas supplied by every important service in every town and village, and from these to plot the mean area of influence of every such place.   However, it is neither practicable nor necessary to go into such detail; in practice the selection of one specially important service, with perhaps the addition of another as a check, is found to be satisfactory.

Shopping is a particularly suitable service for this purpose.   There are some shopping facilities in almost every place where there is a demand for them because the provision of rudimentary shopping facilities requires the outlay of comparatively little expenditure—no more than a counter across the front room of a house in extreme cases—and is in such cases only a supplementary source of income.   Prospective shopkeepers are not, therefore, likely to be greatly deterred by the possibility of demand proving insufficient to support a business, and the situation is not greatly complicated by the vagaries of choice of capital investment.   Also, shopping can be divided into three fairly distinct types :

(a) The daily, or at any rate very frequent, purchase of small articles such as loaves of bread, milk, cigarettes, and meat.   These have necessarily to be purchased from close at hand.

(b) Purchases made weekly or at other fairly regular intervals of articles not obtainable, or of which there is not a wide choice, at small local shops. These purchases involve, for those living in the country and in the outer residential areas of towns, shopping expeditions which are often combined with a visit to the cinema, "window shopping," changing library books, and visits to multiple stores.

(c) Occasional important purchases, some of which may be made only once or twice in a lifetime, carpets, suites of furniture and pianos, for example, and others, such as tableware and crockery, clothes and television sets, which, although they may be made more often, involve laying out sums of money sufficiently large to make this something of an event. The prudent purchaser may decide that he can only obtain a sufficiently wide choice in the large and numerous shops of the local capital.

By determining and mapping the shopping centres used by every community in the region for each of these three purposes a good picture can be obtained of the areas of influence of the larger centres. The necessary information is not particularly difficult or laborious to obtain. It would be sufficient to question a number of housewives in each community. They would not necessarily all give the same town as the place to which they went for the weekly shopping expedition, and this would indicate that the particular place concerned was within the influence of two or more larger places. The results of such a survey can be mapped in two ways:—

(i) By drawing lines joining all the places served by a particular shopping centre and distinguishing between places visited for weekly and occasional expeditions (the service area of a centre used for daily shopping will seldom be large enough to be significant at the regional scale), which will give a number of overlapping areas of approximately circular shape, and

(ii) by drawing rays from each place to the place or places used by it for shopping purposes.

If, in answer to the questions asked, any clearly atypical answers are given, e.g., the use for weekly shopping purposes of a town much further away than those given by the other people questioned, they should be ignored in plotting the results of the surveys, but where such answers are obtained precautions should be taken to check that they are truly exceptional and due to individual whim rather than to any special advantages, not immediately apparent, of the places so named.

The use of shops to determine areas of influence is not a perfect method. Local deficiencies in public transport and variations in the attractiveness of towns as shopping centres, both non-permanent factors capable of being changed comparatively quickly and easily, may cause distortions of the pattern which would otherwise be formed. But it has the great advantages that shopping is an almost universal activity not restricted to particular categories of people and that the choice of shopping centre is not influenced by restrictions artificially induced by extraneous factors such as admin-istrative boundaries. Where there is any reason to doubt the reliability of the results given by the survey a check could be made by carrying out some completely different survey, such as the areas served by local newspapers (approximately equivalent to the weekly shopping area).

Another map which is required, either separately or, preferably, in combination with the areas of influence map, is one showing *the existing population* of every community and the principal services supplied by each. The necessary information can be shown in many different ways; there are a few points of importance regarding the content which require special attention:

The populations of towns can be obtained from the Census but this is compiled in terms of local government units; developed areas which are physically, economically and socially part of a particular town but which happen not to be within the borough or urban district boundary, are not included. Since such areas may form quite an important part of the town's population, it is necessary to decide the boundaries of the development which ought to be included within the town and then to calculate the population living within them but outside the urban authority's area.

There are several ways in which this can be done, short of a house-to-house count of population. The first and most common method is to count the number of houses involved and to multiply the total by the local or even national average number of persons in a house. This may often serve well enough, but in areas which are exceptional in any way may give rise to considerable error.

Another method is to count from the electoral rolls the number of voters within the areas concerned, and, in order to arrive at total population, to multiply this by the Census figure of the total population of the rural district, and divide the result by the total number of voters in the rural district. This generally gives a better result than the previous method, since it is unaffected by local variation in house size, but it ignores the possibility of the local distribution of age groups being abnormal because it assumes a constant proportion of people under 21 years of age to people over 21.

A third method is to conduct a sample census by making personal inquiry as to the number of people living in each house visited, and arrive at an average from the answers obtained. The number of houses visited need not be very large in proportion to the total, but it is necessary that it should be a truly random sample and that any houses on the list which are clearly inhabited, but where at first visit no one is at home, should be re-visited until success is achieved, since these may be the houses occupied by the smallest number of people, and to ignore them would result in too large an average figure being obtained.

The same methods are applicable to villages. Some such calculation is essential for these since no population figures are published for villages but only for parishes; a given parish may include two or three villages or hamlets and also areas of semi-urban development, so that parish population totals are frequently useless. It is often a matter of considerable difficulty to determine the appropriate limits of a village, since many villages are extremely loose in texture, and merge almost imperceptibly into the scattered development of the open countryside.

The services supplied by a place fall into two main categories: those which arise from the existence of buildings—shops, churches, village halls and pubs., for example, and those provided by organisations such as women's institutes, amateur dramatic societies, etc. It is important that they should not be confused; whatever notation is used the two should be sharply distinguished. Buildings are the permanent equipment of a place, which can only be diminished by demolition and added to by construction; their number, size and equipment are a measure of the adequacy of the place to support social institutions in comparison with its population, while the institutions themselves, several of which may use a single building, are apt to be not nearly so permanent as the buildings. They may rise and wane, come into existence and disappear quite independently of the buildings they use. The number and size of the institutions are nevertheless a measure of the social virility of a place and of the likelihood that additions to the building equipment are likely to lead to satisfactory use. Together, the buildings and institutions indicate the strength and adequacy of the place as a service centre. Comparison of these different places and of their comparative populations can give substantial assistance in deciding which places should be encouraged to extend, both as regards population and buildings providing services, to bring about the optimum spatial distribution of such services.

While all the principal services provided in villages should be shown, it is quite unnecessary at the regional scale to show the smaller urban ones which cater entirely for a town's own population. Attention should be confined to those, such as libraries, cinemas, secondary schools, hospitals, etc., which are used by people living outside the town.

(2) Employment

A map should be prepared showing the total number of workers employed in each community, subdivided into different kinds of employment.

Where any substantial number of people work in a town or village other than that in which they live the origins and destinations of journeys to work should be shown diagrammatically. In Britain this information can be obtained from the Usual Residence and Place of Work volume of the 1951 Census; elsewhere, or where it was desired to obtain more detailed or up to date information than that provided by the census, the normal methods of sampling could be used.

Surveys under this heading are capable of indefinite elaboration; one could, for example, go on to examine the types of employment in which people working outside their home towns were employed, or, conversely, the locations of the homes of workers in each particular kind of employment in each town.

It will be well to consider carefully what guides to Planning action are likely to be found from such further investigations before beginning them, having regard to the limited powers of control available.

Where important changes in employment structure appear feasible in pursuance of Planning policy or inevitable in the light of economic exigencies, such additional surveys may, however, be of great importance in helping to redistribute employment with as little upset as possible. An investigation of

the extent to which particular industries in an area are tied to a particular location or can, on the other hand, move with comparative ease is likely to be of special value where it is sought deliberately to bring about wide changes.

(3) Population Changes

It is useful to know what changes of population have taken place within the region over the last twenty years or so. This can best be done on a local government area basis, breaking the rural districts down into parishes. Distinction should be made as follows:

Static areas (less than 10 per cent. increase or decrease).
Areas of moderate increase   ...   10 per cent. to 25 per cent.
Areas of great increase   ...   more than 25 per cent.
Areas of moderate decrease   ...   10 per cent. to 25 per cent.
Areas of great decrease   ...   more than 25 per cent.

Often the map will show nothing that could not readily have been anticipated—increases in and around town and decreases in the poorer and more remote country areas; but anything not fitting in with this pattern may provide a pointer to unusual conditions capable of being remedied or taken advantage of by Planning action.

In order to avoid undue significance being attached to numerically very small changes which have taken place in thinly populated parishes, which appear on the map as great increases or decreases, the actual numbers of people involved in each unit should be shown on the map.

6-5. GENERAL

(i) Land Use Map

This indispensable map will be a generalisation of the land use maps of towns and villages if these have already been made; otherwise special surveys will have to be carried out to a degree of detail no greater than that required for the appreciation of land use distribution at the regional Planning stage.

Many of the surveys already described have indicated the distribution of land uses as between different places; the land use map itself shows the geographical position and extent of each major use.

Such a map has to be used with care, since it must be realised that the importance of a use is not necessarily to be measured by the area of land it occupies—e.g., an industry using a very large site at an unusually low intensity. Conversely, some extremely important uses which take up little space may be impossible to show at the regional scale, so that the limitations of the map must be realised, and its use combined with that of the other regional surveys.

It is important not to overcrowd the map with information; the local use surveys will provide detailed information wherever considerable general development is likely to occur.

Building uses can probably best be divided simply into the following categories:

Residential;
Business;
Industry;

Public Buildings (Schools, Hospitals, Town Halls, etc.); only substantial areas of each being shown.

Some public buildings occupy sites so large that they are virtually a special kind of private open space and should be so indicated.

Open spaces should be divided into:

Public open spaces—parks and playing-fields, to which the public in general has access at all or most times without payment, irrespective of ownership.

Private open spaces—golf courses, large grounds of institutions, etc., privately owned playing-fields, large areas of allotments.

Sewage disposal works of large extent, large areas used for military, naval and R.A.F. purposes, and land being used for the surface working of minerals, all of which may be located in the open country, should be separately indicated, and also areas to which the public have access under the National Parks and Access to the Countryside Act, 1949.

(ii)   *Sieve Map for selection of large areas for development*
The following items should be shown:

All on the physically difficult land map (i.e., areas subject to excessive height and slope, unfavourable aspect, flooding and waterlogging, excavated areas and spoil heaps, areas liable to subsidence, areas used for sewage or refuse disposal).
Land of the highest landscape value.
The most valuable agricultural land.
Areas in which minerals to be won by surface working lie.
Areas of commercially valuable woodland.
Water-gathering grounds.
Areas which cannot readily be supplied with water.
Areas which cannot readily be sewered.
Land comparatively remote from existing communities.

Some explanation of the use of this map is necessary. It is only useful for the selection of areas for really large-scale development, a neighbourhood unit being probably the smallest area in connection with which it can be appropriately used.

Isolated houses and small extensions of existing communities cannot be sited by reference to it because many adverse factors may apply to the whole of such a community and the surrounding land, so that if any further development is necessary, the adverse factor must be accepted; many villages, for example, lie wholly within areas of the highest agricultural value or areas liable to flooding.

Some factors, such as uneconomic levels for sewerage and large areas of very steeply sloping land, may constitute an absolute or almost absolute bar to large-scale development, while others, such as high landscape or agricultural value, are only disadvantageous in comparison with other areas.

If the factors have been correctly selected and appraised, areas which are subject to no absolute and few or no relative disqualifying factors are those which should first be considered as sites for development, and only if these prove unsuitable on general planning grounds should search be made among areas more strongly disqualified.

It is necessary to stress the proviso that suitability on general Planning grounds is a prerequisite for selecting an area for development. Land subject to slight disqualifying factors should, of course, always be selected in preference to land subject to none if it is suitably located in relation to existing development and the latter is not. As regards new towns, the layout of the transport network and the location of other towns may make it necessary to select a site other than that indicated as the most suitable by the sieve map.

The map must in many respects be regarded as merely a guide to the tentative selection of areas for development; on the evidence it gives there may well be several sites of apparently equal suitability for a particular piece of development; this evidence narrows down the area of search to these areas, and more detailed investigation then becomes necessary in order to choose between them.

Nevertheless, in spite of these reservations, a sieve map of this kind is of enormous value in summarising and focusing the land suitability problems of a region and is, indeed, in my opinion, the only means available of reducing the numerous and complicated factors involved to comprehensibility, which makes it all the more remarkable that the Ministry of Housing and Local Government neither require its submission nor specifically recommend its preparation.

The preparation of a map of this kind is explained in Chapter 3, page 34.

Figs. 9 to 15 are examples of some of the most important Regional Survey maps.

FIG. 9. PHYSICALLY DIFFI-
CULT LAND. This is the first
of a series of illustrations showing
important regional surveys.   The
area included does not comprise a
complete region because of difficulties of scale.   This illustration
shows land which, for purely
physical reasons, it is difficult,
costly or undesirable to use
extensively for building purposes.

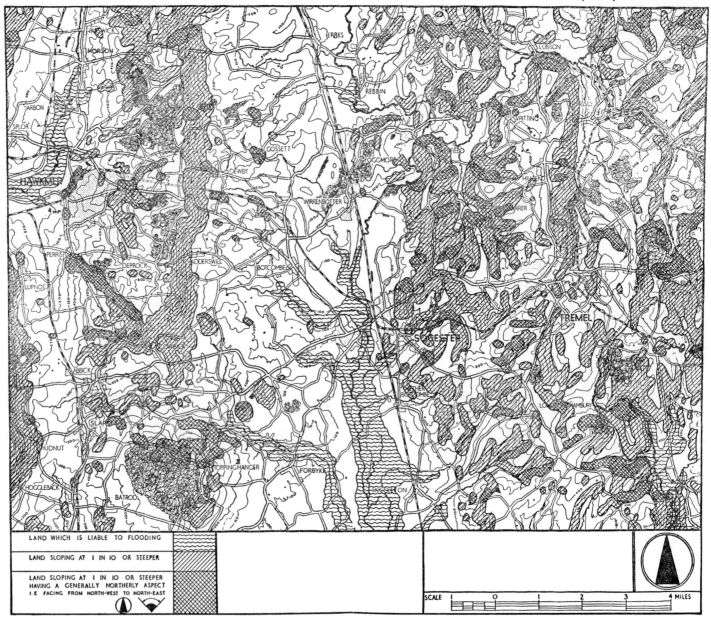

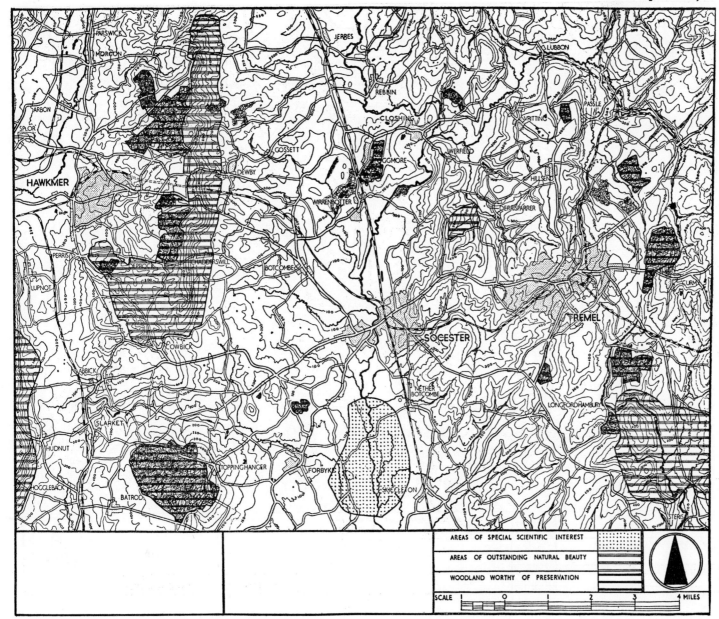

FIG. 10. Areas which, for visual or biological reasons, deserve to be protected.

AREAS OF SPECIAL SCIENTIFIC INTEREST

AREAS OF OUTSTANDING NATURAL BEAUTY

WOODLAND WORTHY OF PRESERVATION

SCALE | 1 | 0 | 1 | 2 | 3 | 4 MILES

FIG. 11. Diagrammatic representation of the distribution of
existing public services.

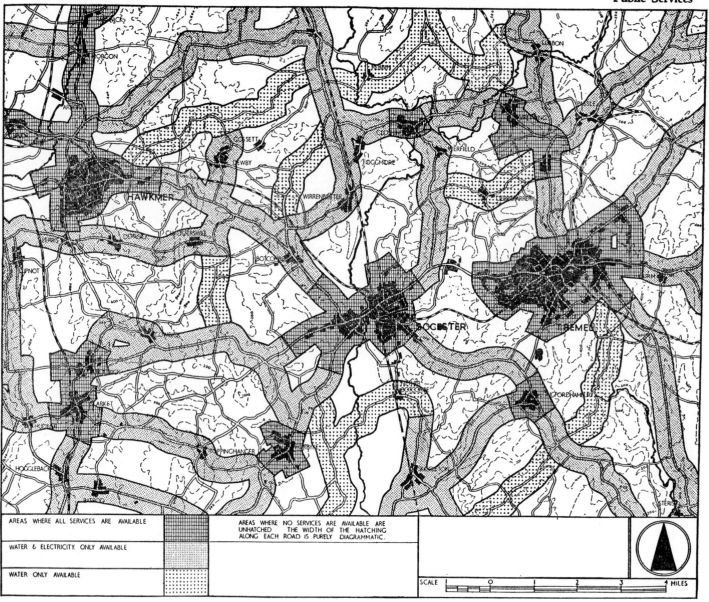

AREAS WHERE ALL SERVICES ARE AVAILABLE		AREAS WHERE NO SERVICES ARE AVAILABLE ARE UNHATCHED THE WIDTH OF THE HATCHING ALONG EACH ROAD IS PURELY DIAGRAMMATIC.
WATER & ELECTRICITY. ONLY AVAILABLE		
WATER ONLY AVAILABLE		

SCALE
MILES

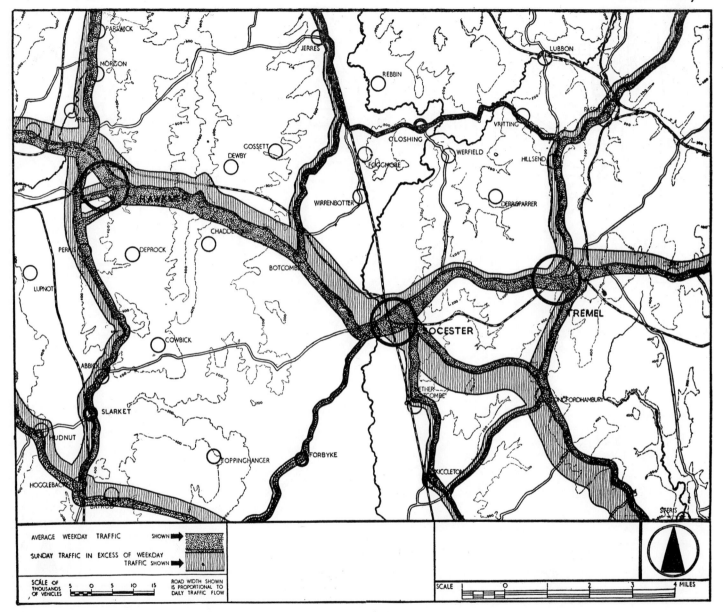

Fig. 12. THE MAIN
PATTERN OF TRAFFIC
DENSITY. Note that this shows
density of traffic, not its origin and
destination.

AVERAGE WEEKDAY TRAFFIC SHOWN

SUNDAY TRAFFIC IN EXCESS OF WEEKDAY TRAFFIC SHOWN

SCALE OF THOUSANDS OF VEHICLES   5   0   5   10   15

ROAD WIDTH SHOWN IS PROPORTIONAL TO DAILY TRAFFIC FLOW

SCALE   0   2   3   4 MILES

FIG. 13. AREAS OF INFLU-
ENCE. This map shows existing
populations of towns and villages,
the most important and distinctive
central services available in each
and the areas of influence of
towns in relation to the "weekly
shopping visit" level of services.
For higher services the area of
influence of Tremel would no
doubt spread much wider.

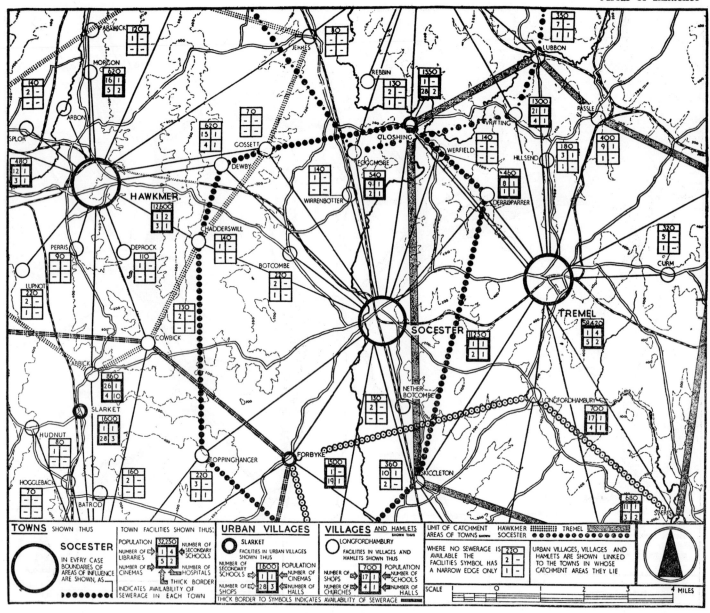

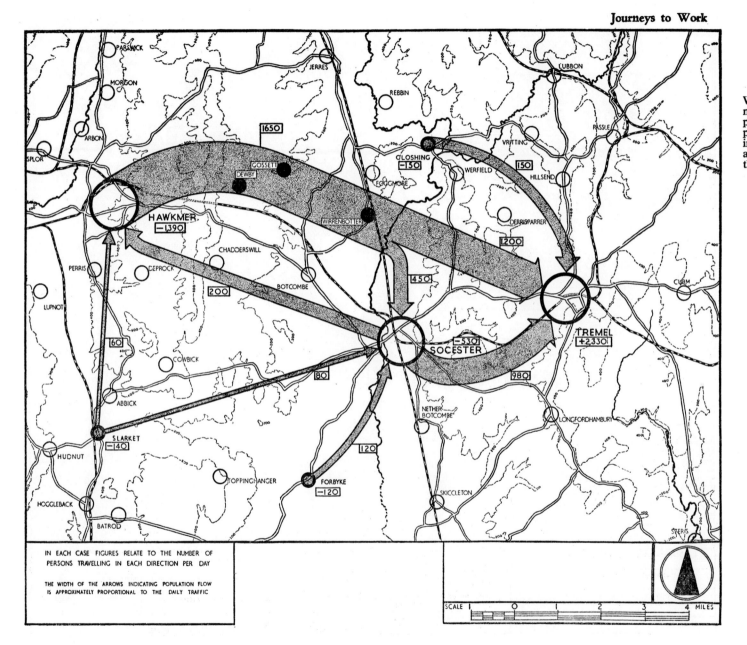

FIG. 14. JOURNEYS TO WORK. The main daily movement of workers between different places in the region. Figures preceded by a plus or minus sign indicate respectively net inward and net outward movement for the place concerned.

FIG. 15. **FACTORS LIMIT-ING DEVELOPMENT.** The information shown on Figs. 9 and 10, together with information relating to agricultural value, mineral bearing land and water-gathering grounds and areas not capable of being economically sewered is combined here to form a sieve map. It is to be emphasised that this map is mainly useful in selecting areas for extensive development.

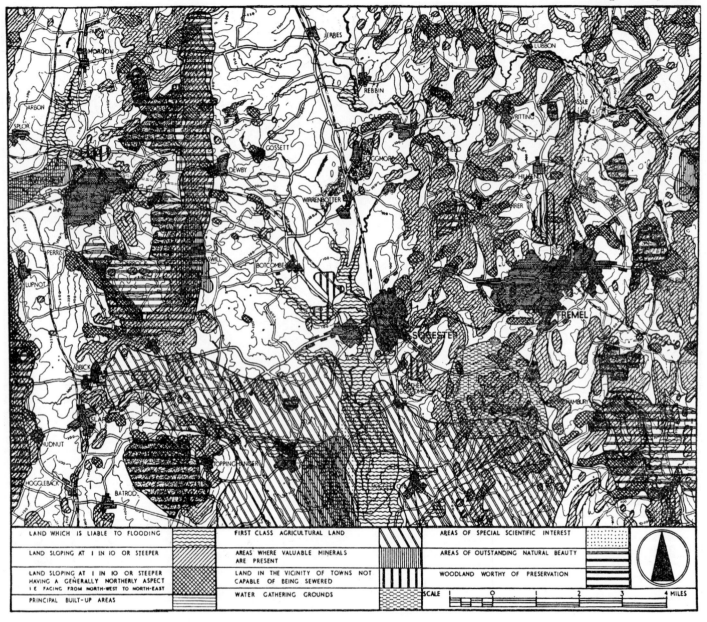

LAND WHICH IS LIABLE TO FLOODING	FIRST CLASS AGRICULTURAL LAND	AREAS OF SPECIAL SCIENTIFIC INTEREST
LAND SLOPING AT I IN IO OR STEEPER	AREAS WHERE VALUABLE MINERALS ARE PRESENT	AREAS OF OUTSTANDING NATURAL BEAUTY
LAND SLOPING AT I IN IO OR STEEPER HAVING A GENERALLY NORTHERLY ASPECT I E FACING FROM NORTH-WEST TO NORTH-EAST	LAND IN THE VICINITY OF TOWNS NOT CAPABLE OF BEING SEWERED	WOODLAND WORTHY OF PRESERVATION
PRINCIPAL BUILT-UP AREAS	WATER GATHERING GROUNDS	SCALE 0 1 2 3 4 MILES

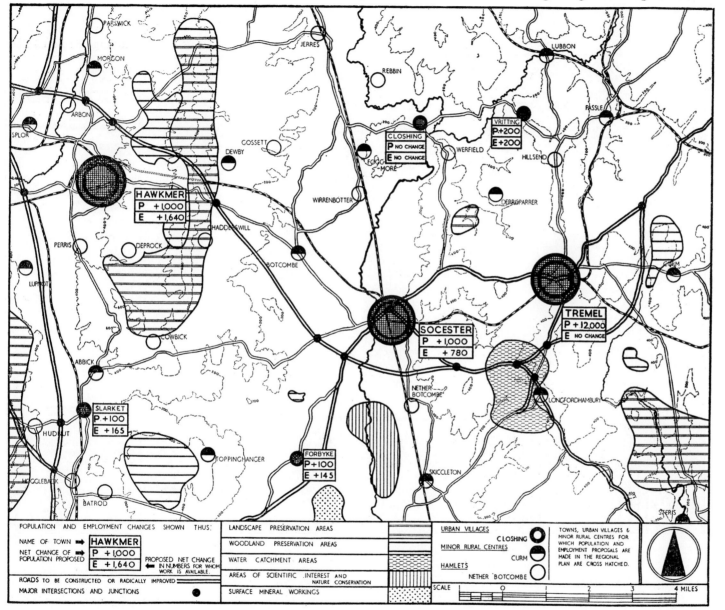

FIG. 16. OUTLINE REGION-
AL PLAN (or First Stage
Diagram). It is assumed that
the population of this part of
the region is intended to increase
by about 14,500, as the result
of metropolitan decentralisation
added to natural increase. The
most important proposals are for
the redistribution of population
and industry. In particular,
Tremel, which at present imports
large numbers of workers, can be
substantially enlarged without
need to increase facilities for
employment. Both Socester and
Hawkmer are also slightly enlarged, but with a more than
proportional increase of employment facilities, so that they shall
no longer need to export workers.

80

FIG. 17. SECOND STAGE
REGIONAL PLAN. Part of the
area shown in Fig. 16, illustrating
the transition from "diagram" to
"map" representation of proposals. This map should be compared
with Figs. 29-37 in order to see
how the degree of detail of Planning proposals increases step by
step.

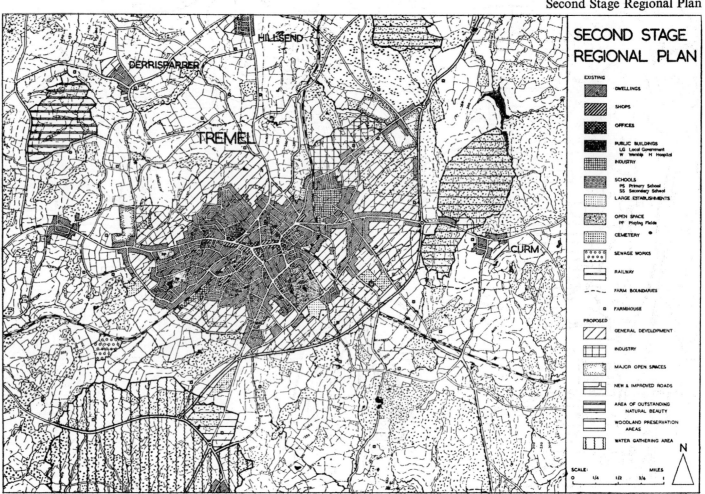

CHAPTER 7

PREPARATION OF THE REGIONAL PLAN

7-1. CONTENT

IT IS BY no means easy to describe definitely or succinctly the actual processes which need to be gone through in preparing a regional Plan. It is seldom indeed that a regional Plan can be prepared in a straightforward and orderly fashion, uninfluenced by either previous partial attempts or the immediate, pressing problems of detailed Planning, the solution of which cannot await the working out of the full Planning process. However, for purposes of discussion and exemplification, at least, such orderliness can be assumed.

Obviously any national Plan which may exist will have to be taken into account when preparing a regional Plan. It may well be necessary, if it has not already been done, to discuss and debate with the authority preparing the national Plan the exact meaning and implication of their proposals. No more need be said on this subject.

Assuming that adequate surveys have been prepared for the region, the next step is to interpret them, both individually and in relation to each other, in order to obtain the clearest possible picture of the region's requirements, potentialities and shortcomings from the Planning point of view. The culminating stage in this should be to draw up a list of the principal Planning problems of the region; this may well suggest the need for the amplification of certain surveys to assist in discovering the appropriate solutions.

Usually the main problem will relate to the balancing of population and industry, and it is likely that other aspects of the Plan will depend upon the solution adopted, for both the arrangement of rural services and improvements to the road system will necessarily be influenced by the general disposition and relative sizes proposed for the main centres of population and employment in the region, though it may well be that the latter two items will in their turn suggest modifications of the first. For example, the opportunity to secure a better balanced distribution of urban services may well prove the deciding factor in selecting one town rather than another for substantial expansion and the same may apply where one or more towns already enjoy particularly advantageous communications.

The proposals for the redistribution of population and industry call for the most careful and earnest investigation, and it will be necessary to work out in as great detail as practicable the implications which follow from each of a number of alternative solutions, for it is most unlikely that any single solution will show itself as having clear-cut advantages over all others.

The general principle to be followed is clear enough; that any towns importing large quantities of labour should receive additional housing sufficient to increase the labour force to the figure required by the town's employment resources and, conversely, that any town exporting large quantities of labour should receive additional industry sufficient to provide employment on the spot for such export, an attempt being made to reach an overall balance. It is obvious that this is an over-simplification of what is actually possible. It would be absolutely impracticable to carry out development in pursuance of such a policy in such a way that large numbers of houses became untenanted because homes had been provided for their original occupants much closer to their places of work, nor indeed is it ever possible to secure more than a rough balance. Under the most perfect conditions imaginable, it would be necessary for appreciable numbers of people to travel long distances to work, either for purely personal reasons, or because of the location of specialised forms of employment which could not be spread over the whole of a region.

The balancing process is of course facilitated where, as a result of a policy of metropolitan decentralisation, it is intended that a region shall receive substantial quantities both of additional population and of additional industry. Within limits, it is then possible to distribute these in such a way as to secure balance without wastage of existing homes or workplaces.

Nevertheless it would be wrong as a long-term policy to rule out entirely the possibility of a net reduction of homes and workplaces in particular towns, where the buildings concerned in either or both categories were in bad physical condition and there were no strong economic or social reasons for replacing them.

It is absolutely essential to make sure that any town selected for increases of homes or workplaces should be physically able to receive them; that, in particular, there is sufficient land physically suitable and appropriately located for the purposes required. It may often be necessary where any doubt exists about this to carry out at once some at least of the surveys normally carried out when preparing the town Plans in order to resolve the matter.

The substantial expansion of a town may have important social consequences; it is essential to consider, when making decisions about relocation of population, whether the towns tentatively selected for expansion are of a character likely to provide a congenial environment for the population to be imported, whether the existing population is likely to take kindly to " invasion " and, if not, whether the economic need involved is important enough to justify ignoring the resentment and possible exodus in considerable numbers of existing population. This, of course, is a political rather than a technical matter the final decision upon which must be made by elected representatives, guided by their professional advisers, but not so completely dependent upon that advice as they ought perhaps to be in other matters.

Next comes consideration of the proposals for improvements of communications to be included in the Plan. These, as explained in Chapter 4, are likely, so far as this country is concerned, to be confined almost entirely to proposals for the improvement of roads. Probably the most important consideration here is to decide upon the best way of allocating the resources available for work of this kind, which, even in the best circumstances imaginable, are likely to be far less than those required. It is not a difficult matter to draw up an ideal Plan for the improvement of the main road system of a region; all that is necessary is to decide upon the principal traffic routes existing and future in the light of traffic surveys and proposals for the re-distribution of population and industry, to show lengths of new road where necessary, and lengths of road to be improved where they already exist but are not constructed to a sufficiently good standard for modern requirements. Proposals in this form are, however, practically useless. It is necessary to prune them by limiting them to what is essential, to look at this from the point of view of doing such work as will lead to an overall improvement in the quality of the road system rather than the construction of a few lengths of magnificent road to the neglect of the remainder, and to work out an order of priority for the works of improvement selected so that not only will the results at the end of the Plan period be as good as possible but that improve-ment is progressively achieved throughout the period.

This involves a great deal of careful and complex consideration, for it is necessary to decide the priority to be given to a very large number of almost equally urgent requirements and to visualise each possible item of work not only in terms of the local improvement of conditions to be secured by it, but in relation to the road system as a whole. For example, it may well be less advantageous to construct 12 miles of new dual carriageway road where the existing road is seriously inadequate, if at each end there are still left skew bridges and lengths of narrow and winding carriageway, than to carry out comparatively minor improvements along the whole of a particular route where it traverses the region if by so doing road conditions throughout its length can be made tolerable, if not ideal. This is not to say that it is not desirable to include in a regional Plan all very important road proposals, however remote of attainment they may seem, for it is also necessary to relate comparatively short-term proposals to the ultimate pattern envisaged so that the former may make the greatest possible contribution to the latter, and not conflict with it.

It is almost impossible to generalise about the proposals which may be required regarding the redistribution of services in rural areas, for the complexities involved defy classification. But one may perhaps safely say that as even a distribution as possible should be sought over the region as a whole, though locally the concentration of facilities in fair measure at a limited number of points is better than to seek a diffusion over the largest possible number of settlements. It is quite impossible for every village and hamlet in the country to be provided with even a reasonable measure of public services and facilities (though there seems to be no settlement whose inhabitants are willing to acknowledge that it is one to which this principle should be applied). It may also be said with some confidence that within limits a settlement selected for the introduction or improvement of any particular facility should also receive others, rather than its neighbours, for the different facilities tend to supplement and strengthen each other, pro-viding a total level of convenience much higher than the sum of each. Even so, it may be necessary, where a particular village is in very dire need of some particular item, to provide it, even though this may not fit in with the best general arrangement.

Schools and shops constitute the urgent, irreducable needs of all rural settlements, but though it may be possible for every settlement to have some shopping facilities, however slight, the provision of a school is limited by the existence of sufficient population within an accessible distance to provide sufficient pupils for it to be a reasonably economical proposition for the education authority. This means that under present conditions there must be fewer primary schools than there are villages, and correspondingly fewer secondary schools than villages.

The regional Plan can only take account of those demands for the use of open country for non-agricultural purposes which are fairly definite. These can seldom be accommodated without some damage to the rural structure, and the best that can be done is to make a very careful selection, in the light of all the survey information available and of the known land requirements of particular users of the land best suited to receive them. It is also of great importance to extend this inquiry so as to be in a position later on to make positive suggestion for demands which may then arise, rather than to be faced with a demand for a particular site without being able readily to suggest alternatives.

It is necessary to understand clearly the ways in which regional Planning proposals can be implemented and the severe restrictions upon this which exist. If a town is merely shown on a Plan as intended to receive an increase of population or industry, or a village shown as intended to be up-graded to a major rural centre, this will have absolutely no effect upon these places in the absence of steps to promote the development required, or in other cases to prevent that not desired. There are broadly three ways in which the desired results can be brought about, none of them infallible. The first is to zone sufficient land for, for example, residential and industrial purposes to accommodate the development required in particular places, and both to refrain from zoning land and firmly to resist development elsewhere. The second is for public authorities themselves to carry out particular forms of development in the areas selected for it in the Plan. The third is, by means of financial inducement, to encourage private developers to carry out develop-ment in one place rather than another.

As regards the first method, it is obvious that if large amounts of land are zoned for residential and industrial purposes in all towns there is absolutely no guarantee that development will in fact occur in the places and in the quantities demanded by the proposals of the Plan. It is also clear that even where proper zoning is carried out, development will still not take place unless the site zoned provides conditions satisfactory to prospective develop-ers, though the more restrictive the zoning the greater will be the chances of attracting development, for houses and factories will be built on com-paratively unattractive sites if they are the only ones obtainable.

As regards the second method, its limitations depend upon the current policies of the authorities concerned, though no authority will willingly carry out development which involves too wasteful an employment of resources. For example, education authorities are often compelled, in thinly populated rural areas, to provide schools far smaller than can be economically staffed and administered because only by doing this can they provide a reasonable degree of accessibility to a school for the population concerned. But private developers are not concerned with these considerations, and as regards those types of development normally provided by private enterprise, of which shops are a convenient example, even the most rigid selective zoning will be of no avail unless there are also proposals to secure that in, for example, the villages where it is intended to permit shops to be erected, there is also enough land zoned for housing to accommodate sufficient people, together with those already in the village, to make the provision of shops an attractive proposition. Broadly, therefore, the provision of facilities of all kinds must be linked to residential zoning proposals, though publicly provided facilities are less severely limited by this than private ones.

The third method has not been extensively applied in this country, the most familiar example of it is the financial advantages offered under the Distribution of Industry Act by the Board of Trade to developers willing to build factories in the Special Areas. It could theoretically be applied to such things as the provision of shops in rural areas by offering subsidies or rate rebates to new shops in selected villages, and would then do something to narrow the gap between the limitations on publicly and privately provided facilities in the previous paragraph.

The decisions on all these matters should first be embodied in an outline regional Plan.

7-2. PRESENTATION

There seems to be wide support for the idea that regional Plans can best be presented in two stages, first a diagram showing no more than the positions of the main proposals, and, second, a map, drawn to a larger scale and showing, as far as possible, the extent of the areas proposed to be used for various purposes.

The First Stage Diagram. Several excellent examples of such diagrams have been published. The diagrams in the Preliminary Outline County Plan for Kent, in the Tay Valley Plan, in the Preliminary Outline Plan for Hertfordshire and in the Preliminary Plan for Lancashire are particularly good.

The Kent diagram shows by means of symbols the predominant characteristics and present and intended future populations of each town, while villages intended to be major and minor rural centres are differentiated. It also indicates areas for landscape preservation and conservation and the future pattern of the principal roads. The Hertfordshire Diagram is similar, while the Lancashire one, confined to proposals for the decentralisation of population, is a splendid example of the way in which a diagram can clearly portray complicated subjects.

A typical list of items to be shown on a first stage regional diagram might comprise the following :

Present and intended future population and predominating characteristic of each town, together with an approximate indication, expressed

in numbers of employees, of the extent to which employment facilities should be increased or reduced to secure industrial balance.

Major rural centres: the intended population of each and the principal services, existing and proposed.

Minor rural centres.

The proposed main communication network.

The location of large, or otherwise specially important, areas for :—

Landscape preservation.

Nature conservation.

National and regional parks.

Public access to countryside.

Woodland preservation and afforestation.

Smallholdings.

Reservoirs and water catchment areas.

Manufacturing industry outside towns.

The surface working of minerals.

Military use.

The scale of such a diagram could generally be a quarter of an inch to one mile, and the minimum of detail should be shown on the base map. (See Chapter 3.)

Many proposals for the use of large tracts of land for reservoirs, military training, etc., are of course, likely to be made after the preparation of the regional Plan and cannot be foreseen; the problems connected with *ad hoc* proposals of this kind are dealt with in Chapter 20.

Fig. 16 is an example of a first stage diagram for part of a Region.

The Second Stage Map. The Greater London Plan Master Plan is, both in content and form, such a map, but since the area concerned is so predominantly urban, it is hardly typical. " County Palatine, a Plan for Cheshire," contains a map to a scale of one inch to one mile, which shows the proposed extent of urban land uses and of various kinds of rural reservation in some detail, but as regards rural communities it is more in the nature of a first stage diagram, since it indicates their proposed status in the hierarchy of settlements but does not prescribe areas of development for them.

Many maps which fulfil the suggested requirements of a second stage map were prepared by Joint Planning committees before the Town and Country Planning Act, 1947, came into operation.

The second stage map is of great importance, even though its preparation is not statutorily required, for it gives a comprehensive picture of the spatial relationships of land uses, including size as well as relative positions. It also provides a framework which enables the merits of applications for permission to develop land to be judged on something better than a mere *ad hoc* basis until more detailed local Plans have been prepared.

An appropriate scale for the second stage map is 1/25,000. This is the smallest scale at which enclosure boundaries can be clearly shown, and hence at which the boundaries of areas devoted to various uses can be shown with any degree of accuracy. Although its size is likely to be such that it will have to be prepared in sections, the first stage map, at about one-tenth its scale, serves as a key to it which should enable the contents of each section to be related to the whole quite easily. The size of each section should be determined by the sizes of the walls and tables available.

The second stage map need not include the statistical information such as proposed populations, etc., shown in the first stage diagram but can be confined to depicting areas of use and communication routes.

A typical list of items for inclusion in the second stage map is as follows :—

> The main areas to be used for business, industry, dwellings, major public uses and major open spaces in each town, areas of existing and of proposed use being distinguished.

> Similar information, so far as may be necessary, in respect of each village. Normally there will be little or no segregation of uses, and all that need be done is to indicate a single area within which it is intended that development should be confined.

> All the areas for specific uses shown on the first stage diagram, but in greater detail.

> The future communication network in similarly greater detail, distinguishing portions which exist and are not intended to be altered, those to be improved and to be created and any intended to be discontinued.

The areas of use shown on the second stage map will still necessarily be approximate in most cases, for it should normally be prepared before the survey information necessary to establish them precisely has been obtained. This applies especially to areas for future residential development and the uses ancillary to it, such as primary schools, local shopping centres, minor open spaces, etc., in towns and major rural centres. It will not usually be practicable to show anything but the total area likely to be required for all such uses, without differentiating between them, the most suitable land for development being selected.

Even this can only be done very approximately because calculations (see Chapter 10) based upon detailed surveys are necessary in order to arrive at a firm figure.

A rough estimate can be made by calculating the total area at present taken up by residential and ancillary development. By dividing this figure into the total population the existing gross density is obtained. Where this is excessive the additional area required to reduce it, by redevelopment at lower densities, to an acceptable figure can easily be found, and this, added to the area needed to house any proposed increase of population, makes up the total figure. It will be apparent, after reading Chapters 9 and 10 that such a method gives results which may later have to be considerably modified.

Nevertheless, this calculation is of great importance, for when an attempt is made to select land for future development it may well appear, in some particular case, that the amount of suitable land which is available is insufficient, and that a detailed check must be made. If this check confirms the original estimate it will clearly be necessary either to raise densities or, if

the land deficiency is too great, to revise the regional Plan in order to provide elsewhere for the population for which room cannot be found in the town under examination.

Such calculations are neither necessary nor possible for minor rural centres. Increases of population are unlikely to take up any large area of land; all that need be done is to select an area of land suitable for development and of a size which is likely to be ample for all needs, yet not so large as to encourage scattered development. (See Chapter 18.)

Areas for development shown on the second stage map should not carry an express or implied right to carry out development anywhere within them; they should rather indicate the limits outside which permission could only be contemplated if an unanswerably strong case were established; proposals for development within them should be examined carefully to see whether they enable a reasonable programme of development to be followed.

The second stage map is primarily an interim Plan used to avoid major errors being committed and to relate individual proposals to a framework. Fig. 17 is an example of part of a second stage Regional Map.

After the preparation of the outline Plan, it will be necessary to enter upon exhaustive consultations with all the numerous bodies affected by the plan. This is part of the political aspect of Planning with which we need not be concerned, except to say that it is likely to be protracted and that the Plan may well emerge from it somewhat battered.

The method of presentation here suggested for the regional Plan is of course very different from that adopted by the Ministry in the Development Plan Regulations, which are, in this respect, I have no hesitation in saying, markedly inferior. They involve the preparation of a County Map, at a scale normally of 1 inch to 1 mile, which is a curious and unsatisfactory blend of both the first stage and second stage maps described above, but does not clearly set out nor include the full contents of either. They provide for the delineation of road proposals, the location of rural services and of the major non-agricultural uses in the countryside, but do not require areas in villages in which development is intended to be permitted to be shown, and only for those towns for which a Town Map has been prepared and is submitted at the same time as the County Map, thus entirely failing to provide for the " holding operation " which is the principal purpose of a second stage map, for proposed development areas are to be shown in outline only for those places for which they have already been worked out in detail to a larger scale. On the other hand, proposals for changes in the population and employment of towns are not required to be shown. It appears that the need to prescribe areas for permitted development in villages has at last been realised, for in Circular No. 50/57 provision is made to map development areas at a scale of 1/25,000 for villages where a limited measure of expansion is contemplated.

7-3. PROGRAMMING

Programming consists of deciding the order in which the development to implement a development Plan is to be carried out and calculating, as far as possible, the time within which each stage may be expected to be completed.

The first half of this task is relatively straightforward and, at least as regards the local programme, is no more than a necessary extension of the technique of Planning design itself; the second half is extraordinarily complicated; its successful performance depends upon the correct prediction of many trends, economic, social and technological, so that any approach to accuracy is improbable. Fortunately, the first half, as well as being easier, is a good deal more important.

Programming is important for three special reasons. First, it is essential that development of various kinds should be so co-ordinated that there is a reasonably balanced state of affairs in existence all the time. It is hopeless to stage a Plan so that, although conditions may be confidently expected to be well nigh perfect in 1980, between 1965 and 1975 they are sure to be wretched, large numbers of people having no shopping facilities or schools reasonably near their homes and having to travel a long way to work. Most Planning involves some present sacrifice for the sake of future benefit, but this should be reduced to a minimum, not only with the simple object of making life as pleasant as possible for as many people as possible during the long period of implementation, but because no programme which involves too great a measure of present sacrifice will be carried out but will be modified or abandoned by public demand.

Second, a target is psychologically necessary, so that if it is exceeded there will be satisfaction, and, if it is not met, disappointment and a spur to greater endeavour. Most human enterprises have to be divided into stages if the best results are to be achieved, and this is particularly so with those which may stretch over the greater part of a human lifetime.

Third, in order to prevent capital lying idle, it is necessary to have a fairly clear idea of the time at which any particular development is likely to become necessary, so that where public acquisition is involved this shall not be done prematurely.

Programming needs to be carried out at scales and in degrees of detail comparable with those of the development Plan itself. At the regional scale it is necessary to know in what order and quantity the various steps necessary to redistribute population and industry are to be taken.

Programming can be implemented, so far as public development is concerned, simply by the various public bodies involved harmonising their activities with it. With private development all that can be done is to release appropriate amounts of land at the right time and the right place and to resist premature development.

It is not possible entirely to separate the programming of the regional and of the local Plan. At first sight one might suppose that it should be possible to decide the places within the region in which development should take place first, and the amount to be allocated to each, in order to secure the most satisfactory interim distribution of population and industry, but the mobility of building and other constructional labour within a region is not complete, and, therefore, the speed of development in a particular town must necessarily be dependent in part upon the strength of the local labour force. Also, optimum distribution of population and industry must, in some cases, wait upon the relief of bad living conditions. Thus, a town from which it was intended to remove a considerable amount of population might nevertheless require a great deal of development to be carried out at an early stage because of the large number of houses unfit for habitation which it contained.

The relative importance of increased production and reduced waste attributable to improved location of population and industry, and of greater health and happiness, due to the amelioration of housing conditions, is a matter which cannot, of course, be determined entirely in the light of land Planning principles, but must largely be a matter for political decision.

While, therefore, it is most desirable to prepare a regional programme designed to remedy defects in the balance of population and industry in the approximate order of their magnitude, it will have to be recognised that such a programme is likely to need substantial revision as the detailed needs of individual towns become known, and that the incomplete mobility of labour (as well as local feelings!) will make it necessary for some development to be going on all the time in every town rather than for work to be entirely focused on a few places in the early stages.

The regional programme is influenced not only by the rate of building construction possible but by other development required to implement it. For example, the increase of population proposed for a town may be impossible to attain unless it is accompanied by an improvement of transport routes so radical as to be incapable of achievement for many years.

The regional programme must be concerned not only with the order in which population and industry are redistributed but with the consequent rearrangement of central services needed. Every increase of population within the service area of a place throws some additional burden on its supply services; though they will normally be sufficiently flexible to prevent this burden being seriously felt for some long time, additions will eventually be required because of the increased importance of the place as a centre, irrespective of any increase in its own population.

The regional programme, as it affects the rural parts of the region, poses less difficult problems of decision than those of the urban parts, because the scale of development is smaller and the interaction of different operations less complex, but the implementation of such a programme may present appalling difficulties.

Rural development should aim at providing central services of the simpler kinds as quickly as possible for those areas whose deficiency is greatest; this will frequently entail, paradoxically, provision for increased *population* in certain centres, so that there may be sufficient local support for services supplied to a large and sparsely populated area. Schools, village halls and shops will be the forms of building development most required for increasing services, while local increases of population will often be dependent upon the provision of piped water and sewage disposal works.

Conclusion

The foregoing account may, perhaps, suggest that the preparation of a regional plan is a somewhat haphazard process, and that there can be no certainty of producing a sound set of proposals, but this would hardly be a correct assumption. A thorough survey of existing conditions, if its findings are incorporated in the Plan, is in itself a safeguard against serious errors. A multitude of Government Departments, local authorities and statutory bodies, as well as private persons and associations, all have the opportunity of offering comments and criticism either at the public inquiry into the Plan or beforehand, and the Minister has at his disposal a wealth of technical advice upon which to draw before deciding whether to approve the Plan.

Hence there is every likelihood that any fundamental error in the proposals will be detected and exposed by one or more of the various interests whose activities would be prejudiced by it. It is true that a choice may sometimes have to be made between two opposed policies, but this should only occur when the technical evidence available shows the balance of advantage to lie evenly between them, in which case it is unlikely that either will lead to disaster, however much this may be prophesied by supporters of the opposite policy.

CHAPTER 8

THE PLANNING OF TOWNS

8-1. GROWTH AND CHANGE

WE HAVE SEEN in Chapter 4 that human settlements form a hierarchy of service centres. At some point in this hierarchy the settlement ceases to be a mere village and becomes a town. For the purposes of town, as distinct from regional, Planning it is less important, though still necessary for some purposes, to know the position occupied by a settlement in the service hierarchy than to appreciate its essential structure and internal functioning. Settlements which may, for Planning purposes, be considered to be towns are those which have or which it is intended shall have a physical structure sufficiently large and complex to involve problems concerning the location and spatial relationships between land uses and the form of the road system.

Professor Griffith Taylor, in " Urban Geography", analyses a large number of human settlements and places them within a hierarchy based primarily not upon the central services they render but upon the complexity of their structure. This hierarchy may be summarised as follows, using Professor Taylor's nomenclature :—

Infantile. In this type of settlement there is no separation into zones of different kinds of land use nor of dwellings for different social classes (e.g., the ordinary English village).

Juvenile. Shops are separated from houses into definite groups but few factories exist (e.g., many urban villages).

Mature. Houses are separated into areas of distinct types, commercial and industrial areas are fully formed (e.g., fully-fledged towns).

Senile. Extensive areas of the town are in a state of physical decay and the prosperity of the town has declined (e.g., town in the depressed areas).

These are the main stages, but Taylor distinguishes other minor divisions; thus he describes as *sub-infantile* a settlement with only one street, and that ill-defined, and as *adolescent* one in which the house types have begun to be segregated but the first-class ones have not yet formed a distinct area.

It is important to realise that settlements may not necessarily pass through all, or even any, of the stages enumerated. An ordinary English village may have remained at the infantile stage for many hundreds of years, while, on the other hand, some industrial towns have in little more than 100 years passed through all the stages from infantilism to maturity and already show signs of senility, although an ancient city which has long been mature may bear no marks of senility. Equally, a change from one stage to another does not necessarily denote an *improvement*, even when the change is not to senility. The change from infantilism to juvenility or from juvenility to maturity may mean a change from a convenient and well-balanced arrangement to one which is lop-sided, congested or unbalanced. In the latter case, particularly, a town centre which was perfectly adequate in the juvenile stage is likely to become hopelessly crowded and inconvenient during maturity.

The social structure of a town may be as complicated as or more complicated than its physical structure, and the two have close, though not simple, connections.

Many writers have drawn attention to the process of invasion and succession which occurs in many growing towns and which results in the poorer quarters nearer the centre spreading to more prosperous areas and driving the better-off residents to the outskirts. The first-class houses of one decade become the second-class houses of the next decade. Invasion and succession are enlarged upon by Gist and Halbert in " Urban Society ".

Towns normally grow outward in concentric rings from the centre. Typically, these rings form a series of distinct use and class zones which, starting from the centre, as applied to the larger British towns and cities, are as follows:

(1) *The central area* of the town, in which the principal shops, offices, warehouses, civic buildings and places of amusement are concentrated. Competition for land is very acute and rents, therefore phenomenally high. This leads to very intensive building development, the proportion of the site covered often approaching 100 per cent., and high buildings are prevalent. It becomes unprofitable for private enterprise to provide services such as car parking which are essential for the satisfactory functioning of the area but which give a small financial return per unit of land. Equally, the burden on the public purse if the municipality steps in to purchase sites for the provision of such services becomes unendurably great.

A peculiar feature of the central areas of many towns is that residential use by the very rich in blocks of luxury flats and by the very poor in slums often continue side by side where multiplicity of ownership, or other complicating factors, have prevented full utilisation taking place.

These slums extend outwards into:

(2) An *area of suspended animation and deterioration*, in which, owing to the prospect of expansion of the central area, site values are very high, but, because intensification of land use is not yet practicable, the value of the buildings may be very low. These buildings are frequently allowed to deteriorate because the owners, expecting profit from redevelopment, do not find it worth while to maintain them.

A certain amount of business, industry and storage is commonly found in this area, generally for purposes which need a considerable amount of land, can utilise existing buildings, but do not require a very central position sufficiently urgently to make it worth the promoters' while to pay the much higher rents demanded in the central area. This area of transition normally displays an air of the utmost decrepitude, and it is not uncommon to find within it small areas which, because of their unfavourable situation or detailed physical characteristics, have been left as islands in the outward flow of development, and which remain as weedy patches upon which garbage is dumped and rickety hoardings display advertisements.

The area generally includes a number of buildings which were the mansions of a previous generation, and which have either become occupied as flats without the structural alterations and additional sanitary and cooking facilities necessary for satisfactory conversion or have been put to some non-residential use.

(3) *High-density small houses* which may not have degenerated into slumdom, but which, in the inner part of the area, developed before building by-laws were applied, form a dense and confused mass. Beyond this lie the no less drab but slightly more spacious " by-law " houses and the villadom, at substantially lower density, of the years of the twentieth century before the First World War. Within the whole of this area shopping areas and public buildings occur spasmodically and have often been provided in a makeshift fashion, e.g., by the rough-and-ready conversion of the ground floors of a row of houses into shops to meet a local demand. Usually, however, the great majority of such buildings are placed in long rows along the main radial roads leading from the town centre because of the trade accruing from the large volume of vehicular and pedestrian traffic which uses these roads.

Open spaces within this area are normally either almost completely absent or else in the form of large units on its outskirts, sited without regard to easy accessibility for the inhabitants of the whole area.

(4) *Inter-war housing.* Density is much reduced; the great bulk of this development is in the form of small pairs of houses of stereotyped design, larger pairs and detached houses occupying somewhat segregated positions; provision of shops, public buildings and open spaces is still spasmodic; often development has now reached so far as to engulf former villages, the shops of which are added to, and form local centres. In this area the " council estate " makes its appearance, and occupies sites similar to, but often in some way inferior to, those occupied by speculative development.

(5) On the periphery lie villages and hamlets sufficiently close to the town to provide attractive sites for the homes of the well-to-do in the form of additional houses or by the invasion and conversion of existing cottages. Small groups or ribbons of isolated dwellings fulfil a similar purpose.

The theory of ring growth is correct in general terms. Certainly the general direction of growth is outwards from a centre; certainly the pressure of development also drives the more prosperous outwards to relatively uncrowded surroundings with unpolluted air, leaving their former abodes to be occupied, altered or unaltered, by the less fortunate, but it is rare for the process to be regular. Development follows the lines of least resistance, topographically and economically, and, in addition, the location of industry exercises an influence over urban growth which prevents it being entirely concentric. There is generally a greater weight of development in the quadrant or quadrants of the town in which the majority of the industry is sited.

The sites for industry established during the nineteenth century were usually determined by definite factors—the location of minerals, of transport routes or of power—and the mass of housing required for the workers in the factories which were built had to be close at hand. Before the introduction of public transport or the bicycle it was imperative that this housing should be really close to the factories.

This is probably the main reason for much nineteenth-century housing being sited on steep slopes which few modern developers, public or private, would consider because of the expense and difficulty involved. A second reason is that this development took place at a time when the cost of building labour was very much lower than it is now, so that the developer was not so worried by the expense of developing difficult land.

There is no typical location for industry in relation to other zones except that, as already noted, the bulk of the workers' houses will be found close to it. Industry may be in one, two or more concentrations located in accordance with its economic requirements, but, on the other hand, it may not be in any concentrated mass but may be fragmentarily dispersed (see Fig. 18 (vi)) through zones (2) and (3) with outlying units in zones 1 and 4, or the basic industry may be concentrated, with service industry and industries linked to the basic scattered wholesale.

A clear understanding of the tendency of development to follow lines of least resistance is essential. Though it may often be necessary for Planning action to be taken to curtail the extent to which development would spread in a particular direction in the absence of control, or even to seek to reverse such trends, it is obvious that more effort is needed and more opposition to be expected when this is done than when it is only necessary to guide and mould development which would have taken place spontaneously in much the same way without control. However imperfect the results of uncontrolled development, most of it does at least take place at a high enough level of efficiency to be justified by the rough measure of profit.

It is generally true to say that the value of land for any particular use is the resultant of its position and its physical characteristics, and this is as true of agricultural land as of shops. The agricultural value of land with quick and easy communication to markets may, for example, be as high as that of more fertile land less conveniently situated, and this is reflected in the rents a farmer will be prepared to pay. Similarly, the value of steep and broken land, costly to develop for housing, may nevertheless be as great as that of flat land which is cheap to develop but farther from a town centre or area of employment. This is so because, once developed, people will be willing to pay higher prices for more conveniently located houses, and these higher prices enable a developer to get as good a return for his outlay as that given by the lower prices secured for houses more remotely situated on land less costly to develop.

Example: Remote land easy to develop

Cost per house to developer...			...	...	£2,000
Selling price realised ...		...	...	...	£3,000
Profit ...	...	...	...	...	£1,000

More Central land difficult to develop

Cost per house to developer...			...	...	£2,500
Selling price realised ...		...	...	...	£3,500
Profit ...	...	...	...	...	£1,000

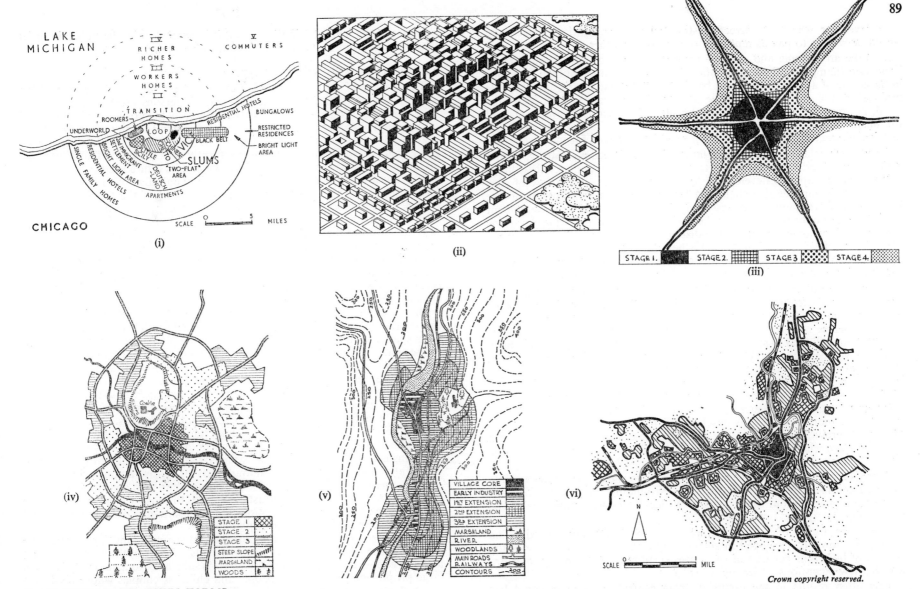

FIG. 18. UNPLANNED TOWN FORMS

(i) Social and racial distribution in Chicago. (After Gist & Halbert.)

(ii) "The Urban Pyramid". Typical progressive increase of site coverage and building heights as the town centre is approached.

(iii) The typical "octopus", "starfish" or "umbrella" form of unplanned town growth where there are no natural or artificial obstacles to development.

(iv) Where obstacles are strong and numerous great distortion of form occurs.

(v) The typical form of development in a narrow valley with steep sides, produced by the tug of war between central but difficult and easily developable but relatively remote sites.

(vi) Burnley. Industry cross-hatched, residential oblique hatched, town centre solid black, open spaces etc. stippled. A somewhat extreme example of industry widely scattered instead of grouped in a particular part of the town.

A developer who had correctly estimated the possibilities of each site would be willing to pay as much for one as for the other.

To take an extreme and obvious example where position is much more important than physical characteristics, the value of a piece of land for shops in the centre of a large town would be high even if it had highly unfavourable physical characteristics. The value of land in the open country for shops is nil, however flat and well drained the site. In general, the value of land for business uses depends much more upon position and much less upon physical characteristics than it does for residental or even for industrial uses.

Despite the relative cheapness of labour in the nineteenth century, during which so much urban development took place, it was of course, other things being equal, cheaper to develop the flatter land. Thus, in the case of sites where there is considerable change of levels, there is a constant tug-of-war between the advantages of flatness and of central situation. Development tends to spread outward, following the easiest gradients and leaving elevations and depressions undeveloped until a distance is reached at which the advantages to the developer of building farther out on level land are balanced by the advantages, in terms of rent or selling price obtainable, of building closer to the centre on sites physically less favourable. (See Fig. 18 (v).)

A similar tug-of-war operates in relation to land close to main radial routes, and that remote from them. This has been intensified by the growth of public transport and of the custom of providing main services in such roads at public expense. In the absence of complicating topographical factors, development will tend to stretch outward along radial roads, leaving the back land undeveloped, until a point is reached at which the disadvantage of the distance of the radial development from the town centre is balanced by the indirectness of communication between the back land and a radial route. (See Fig. 18 (iii).) Once the back land has been developed, radial development may continue to stretch outward for a time until a halt is once more called while more back land is developed. This may happen several times during the growth of a town. At any given time, therefore, the shape of a growing town, where radial roads spread out from the centre, is likely to be that of a star.

There is a very strong tendency for main roads to run as straight as possible to town centres from other towns and surrounding villages, to form an " umbrella " pattern, but roads too follow lines of least resistance, as can be seen in Fig. 18 (iv).

One other aspect of town structure must be briefly investigated. The " normal " town is developed in such a way that the intensity of use—the volume of buildings per unit of site—rises steadily from periphery to centre with but few exceptions. (See Fig. 18 (ii).)

This often results in the exclusion from central areas of essential but not very intense uses which cannot earn sufficient to pay high rents. The private ownership of land involves the investment of capital, which, in turn must be justified by putting the land to a use which secures a rate of return, in the shape of profit or rent, comparable to that obtained from other forms of investment, or, alternatively, the compensation of the owner and/or

occupier of the land at crippling loss if it is purchased by the public in order that it shall be put to its most useful purpose socially.

8-2. TEXTURE AND STREET PATTERN

The texture of a town is roughly expressed by the overall density of the developed area, typically between 10 and 30 persons per acre, but this, of course, only tells one whether density is generally high or low; it conveys no information as to whether, for example, a low overall density contains patches of dense development offset by other patches of exceptionally low density, or is the result of uniformly, or almost uniformly, low density. This may make all the difference to the character of a town and its future needs.

The low overall density, of, for example, Tunbridge Wells, is due to its large common, which penetrates to the very heart of the town, and to the considerable number of houses with very large gardens indeed, between 2 and 5 acres in extent. These, together, give the town an air of pleasant spaciousness delightful to the visitor or to the more favoured of its residents, but the very low residential densities of parts of the town exist at the expense of a very substantial congestion in other residential areas. The total acreage of open space may not in itself be an accurate reflection of its adequacy, though it will certainly affect the visual character of the town. Use and distribution are, socially, much more important.

On the other hand, Sevenoaks, not far away, which also has a remarkably low overall density, has a totally different character. There are no very large open spaces within the built-up area, though Knole Park is close by, and few houses with enormous gardens, but, apart from some old houses along and near to the ancient High Street and a tiny area of industrial housing to the north, there is no really high density housing at all.

Quite sharp differences in density may be admissible and even desirable, indeed, too little variation is likely to induce flatness and boredom; but such variation should be intelligently sought, not fortuitous. Reference has already been made to the almost universal rule of increasing intensity of land use towards the centre of the town, and doubts cast upon its inevitability. Thus, instead of placing high density flats close to the town centre and developing all outer residential neighbourhoods at a low and nearly uniform density, there is much to be said for providing some high density flats in each neighbourhood to provide contrast. We are, to make the point again, too slow to break free of the assumption that the economics of competitive land development should govern town planning.

Nevertheless, within limits, the policy of intensifying land use towards the centre is reasonable. The town centre itself is, of course, the area of greatest activity, and hence of greatest density. It is safe, also, to assume that quite a large proportion of the single people and childless couples whose needs are satisfied by a flat are those who will use the cultural and entertainment facilities of the central area most and who will welcome a location close to it. Equally, the comparatively small number who desire a really big garden—an acre or more—and who have either the time to cultivate it themselves or the money to have it cultivated for them, are, almost without exception, those who least need a central location and can appropriately be housed on the

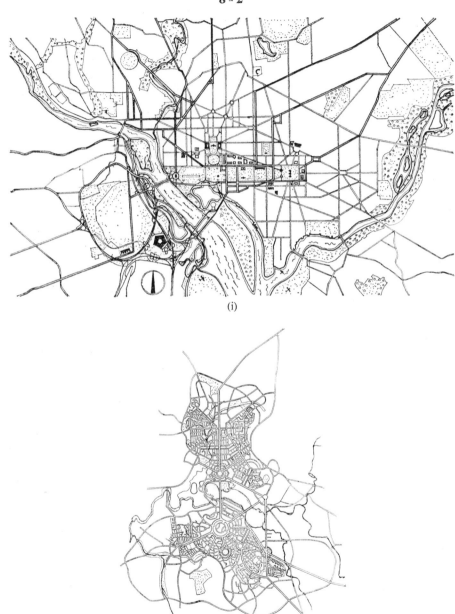

(i)

(ii)

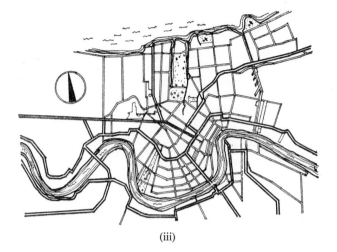

(iii)

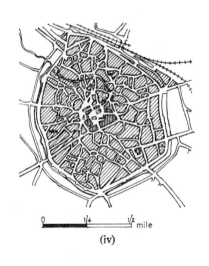

0   ¼   ½ mile

(iv)

(v)

Fig. 19. STREET PATTERNS

    (i) The central part of Washington, an artificially created capital.

    (ii) Canberra.   Another artificially created capital.

    (iii) New Orleans.   A convenient example of a waterfront town which shows the effect of curved and of straight waterfronts upon the road system.

    (iv) Soest.   Extreme formlessness of road system.

    (v) Where gridiron street patterns oriented to converging main roads meet the result is chaotic.

outskirts of the town.   It is obvious that, in a town whose shape approximates to a circle, the total amount of land available at approximately the same distance from the centre increases as the distance from the centre increases.

But, between the extremes of very high and very low density dwellings, it is now fallacious to assume that people possess finely distinguished grades of wealth and leisure, and that their needs are met by providing gardens of gradually increasing size as the distance from the centre increases.   This was always a dubious assumption but between the wars it bore some relation to the truth.   Now it is becoming less and less true, and there seems no probability that the tendency will be reversed.

Towns are classifiable into various types, not only as regards function but as regards physical pattern, as evidenced by the street system.   Here, it should be made clear, we are dealing with the pattern formed by the main streets, exclusive of that of the minor ones, which are discussed in Chapter 17. While the two patterns are frequently similar and complementary, this is by no means always so, and indeed the two may conflict, with consequent distortion and confusion.   (See Fig. 19 (v).)   This distinction between the two patterns needs to be emphasised because, in small communities, including most ancient examples, there is no strong distinction between major and minor roads, and, hence, only one pattern to discuss.

The main difference between street patterns is between those which have grown up naturally and gradually without conscious design and those which have developed rapidly, and which have therefore unavoidably involved a degree of conscious design in order to make sufficient land available quickly.

Of the first kind, by far the commonest is the radial or " umbrella " pattern already mentioned, the regularity of which may vary considerably, but which, in its purest form, consists simply of the most direct routes between the town and other places, all converging toward the town centre.

A variant of the radial pattern is the spider's web, in which one or more ring roads are present as well as the radial roads.   This is a system which is peculiarly well suited to modern traffic conditions, since it enables traffic travelling between different parts of the town to reach its destination without passing through and so increasing congestion at the centre.   It is therefore regrettable that examples of spider's web patterns are comparatively rare. Too often development has proceeded too far before the need for lateral roads has been realised, and this is understandable in the case of unplanned towns, since the *main* stream of traffic and attention is bound to be directed towards the centre.

Sometimes, however, happy accidents or the cessation of need for peripheral fortifications have resulted in the construction of ring roads.   Paris, Vienna and Moscow are Continental examples, while Norwich is perhaps the best example in this country.

A variant of the spider's web plan occurs in the case of water-front towns, where the focus of importance is not a centre of strictly limited size but a length of sea, lake or river frontage.   Where the waterfront curves outwards from the town it is natural for roads to be made parallel to it and others radial to them.   Where, however, the water-front is of irregular shape great

distortion may result and the simplicity of the road pattern be lost. (See Fig. 19 (iii).)

Yet another important type of natural road system is the amorphous, in which no distinct pattern can be discerned.   This may occur where natural or pre-existing artificial features cause a radial pattern to be altered out of recognition.   It may also be seen in towns which have originated as medieval walled cities in which the need for relative self-sufficiency and for a compact, and thus easily defended, site prevented the normal centripetal tendency of the radial pattern from developing, and in which the pattern and orientation of several important parts of the town was carried out quite independently, without consideration of how they were to be linked.   This cannot wholly explain, but gives some clue to the fantastically tangled street plan of many such towns.   It is as if the several units of development flowed towards each other like waves, their meeting-place becoming the site of turbulence.

In the case of towns which have developed comparatively rapidly, either as the result of industrialisation or to meet military needs, the rectangular plan is by far the commonest.   It has persisted from the time of ancient Egypt, through the Greek and Roman Empires to the chief cities of the United States and the British Commonwealth.

The great disadvantage of the grid-iron plan is obvious: a destination which does not lie on the same road as the point of origin cannot be reached without traversing two sides of a triangle.

On the other hand it has the one great merit of simplicity.   No one who knows the address he is aiming for need ever get lost.

This, I emphasise, is said of the grid-iron plan in relation to a major network of roads.   In relation to the minor street pattern its disadvantages are overwhelming.

Some towns have been laid out to elaborate patterns such as Washington, Canberra and New Delhi (see Fig. 19 (i) and (ii)).   These have frequently been artificially selected capitals or court towns, and the designs used bear a striking similarity to each other, non-rectangular geometrical shapes being predominant.   These designs have certain merits; they are comparatively well adapted to modern traffic circulation (though the plan for Washington has caused difficulties in this respect), they are far more flexible than the rectangular pattern, and they have a unity and logic which makes some appeal; but they are often needlessly elaborate, and have a formality which can really only be appreciated from the air.   The functions they perform could generally be more simply and equally well discharged with a less mathematically disposed layout.   When possible, it is well to have a street pattern which can be readily memorised; both spider's web and grid-iron patterns are essentially simple, and it is not so easy to lose one's sense of direction within them as in the case of more elaborate compositions.

8-3.   DISTRIBUTION OF LAND USES

There are five distinct parts of any planned town, and even in unplanned towns they can be seen, although not usually with the same clarity.   These are as follows :

The Town Centre.   This is the area in which the commercial and administrative and some aspects of the social life of the town take place in their highest and most complicated form, and in which the most important central services supplied by the town are made available. The essential constituents of the central area are shops supplying occasional needs, offices, banks, administrative buildings—the town hall, etc.—and important buildings for social and cultural purposes, such as the principal library and museum, the theatre, and the largest churches. A good deal of wholesale and retail storage accommodation is likely to be required.

The industrial Area. As already noted, this may be split into a number of parts and is the area in which the manufacturing industry and the largest service industries are located, together with electricity and gas generators and large-scale warehousing of bulky goods.

The residential Area. This is the area in which people live; although it is principally made up of dwellings and gardens, it includes many other uses: local shopping, primary schools, local open spaces, and the smaller service industries.

Chapter 14 is devoted to discussion of the Residential Neighbourhood Unit idea. This is so important a concept in connection with town structure that it must also be briefly mentioned here. In a town of any substantial size the distance between perimeter and town centre creates a demand for local facilities conveniently situated to serve the inhabitants of the part of the town immediately adjoining each rather than the town as a whole. Shops and primary schools are the most obvious examples of these facilities. The area which each facility serves may be different, but even in an unplanned town there may be sufficient congruence between the service areas of different local facilities—particularly where railways, parks or other dividing features split the town into physically distinct units—for a recognisable system of sub-units, districts or neighbourhood to come into existence, the centre of each acting as a centre for services of a lower order than those provided by the town centre. This may be recognised by them becoming known, informally at least, by particular names, and may be reflected in the system of division of the town into wards.

Where the division into sub-units is particularly distinct, each may bear something of the same relation to the town centre, in terms of the services locally supplied, as do the villages surrounding the town, though I hope that this will not lead anyone into the error of supposing that the neighbourhood idea is a kind of romantic attempt to introduce a village green atmosphere into town life, as has sometimes been suggested. It is in fact simply the rationalisation and completion of an extremely strong tendency based upon real needs, although in unplanned towns the attraction exerted by main radial roads and the effect upon development pattern of land values often distort it almost to the point of meaninglessness.

Open Space. This is a term which is used very loosely but generally refers to all land which is used for purposes which do not require many buildings, and which enable it to be left substantially in its natural state or to be treated so that it has visually pleasant qualities.

Within the category of " open space " one must first include parks, in the

widest meaning of the word, and playing-fields. Cemeteries and allotments are quite often so described and also secondary schools, hospitals and other institutional buildings with extensive grounds. Small areas of allotments, children's play spaces, and small rest parks are, on the other hand, frequently reckoned as part of the residential area along with the curtilages of dwellings.

In my view " open spaces " should properly be applied only to parks, playing-fields and those areas of undeveloped land larger than the purely incidental open spaces within a residential layout to which the public have access. Secondary school sites, hospitals, and other institutional sites should be categorised separately, and allotment land, unless very large in area, included with the residential area, while cemeteries are quite different from any other kind of open space.

The Town Periphery. This includes all the land surrounding the town, the use of which is influenced directly by the town, but which cannot be considered as part of the town itself. Such land would include market gardens and nurseries and golf courses.

Clearly, on a wide interpretation of the term " open space," the only difference between much of the periphery and much of the open space will be its position. In fact, where the principle of running wedges of open space from the circumference of the town to its centre is adopted, they will merge into each other with no definite break.

Another important part of every town, in a different sense, is its transport system and, particularly, its road system, and it is frequently the part most in need of improvement.

8-4. TOWN PLANNING THEORIES

Mumford has coined a series of descriptive titles for the stages through which human civilisations have passed and are passing. The terms he uses are as follows:—

Eotechnic. The beginnings of civilisation founded upon mechanical power, using wind, water and wood for power, and wood as the chief building material. Existing in Europe between the tenth and eighteenth centuries A.D.

Paleotechnic. The age of coal and iron economy, the steam engine, steamship and railway, mass production processes in manufacturing industry. Dominant in Europe during the nineteenth century.

Neotechnic. Emerged towards the end of the nineteenth century and is based upon the use of electricity as power, upon light metals such as aluminium and copper, rubber and plastics. Elaboration and perfection of many kinds of machinery; invention of the internal combustion engine and the aeroplane.

Biotechnic. The civilisation of the future, which Mumford sees as a development from the purely mechanical achievements of the Neotechnic age, will, in his view, involve the co-ordination of the many isolated, and even conflicting, Neotechnic devices and organisations, the application of biological knowledge to technics, and the enlisting of technology in the service of life rather than in the service of rivalry and personal enrichment.

Mumford points out that although Neotechnic inventions and industrial processes are at present generally dominant in Western Europe, the towns in which these processes are carried on are, in the main, relics of the Paleotechnic age. He claims that some essential parts of cities appropriate to the Biotechnic age can only be provided if a pecuniary economy is abandoned.

From this point of view modern Town Planning may be regarded as an attempt to formulate principles for the creation or modification of towns which will be fitted at least for the Neotechnic age, and which may be expected to be capable of further successful adaptation to the Biotechnic age. It is important to realise how wide a gap there is between the motives and assumptions of modern Planning, based upon social requirements, and those of royal, dictatorial, military or merely pictorial Planning, even though there may be resemblances between the end products.

There have been numerous attempts to work out forms which will result in a town becoming a balanced organism rather than a mass of isolated or mutually hampering elements. Theories of town building concern themselves with two main aspects—size and shape.

First place must be given to the teaching and efforts of Ebenezer Howard. Howard's ideas grew from and clarified the tentative gropings towards a civic theory of nineteenth-century philanthropists and reformers. He was appalled by the conditions of life in the Paleotechnic industrial town at the end of the nineteenth century and regarded its very size as a factor severely aggravating to these conditions.

In his book "Garden Cities of Tomorrow" (re-published in 1946 by Faber and Faber) he contrasted the advantages and disadvantages of town and country: the varied social life possible in the town, and the comparatively high wages obtainable there, which were, however, accompanied by squalor, atmospheric pollution and savage inhumanity, as against the beauty of the countryside, its pure air and natural mode of life, but also its lack of social variety and poor wages. The remedy appeared to Howard to lie in a town of limited size which would combine the advantages of both town and country with the disadvantages of neither.

Howard's well-known simile is of town, country and town-country, each acting as a magnet, drawing people towards it because of the attractions it offers, with town-country offering the best bargain, counteracting the stream of new population which was then still flowing to the cities in undiminished volume and adding to their congestion and difficulties.

Howard's idea of town-country was a garden city with a population of about 30,000, each family with its own house built on a plot of an average size of 20ft. by 130ft. The town was to be a satellite of the great city in whose service area it was situated, but was to have its own industries. The site of the garden city, of some 1,000 acres, together with a peripheral belt of 5,000 acres, was to be in the ownership of the town so that its citizens would reap the benefits of appreciation in land values due to development. Growth would not take the form of peripheral accretion but of further satellite towns, each with its own green belt, until eventually the parent city was ringed by satellites.

Howard's ideas have remained fresh and valid for more than half a century.

Without any governmental aid whatever, they have been exemplified with a great measure of success in Letchworth and Welwyn Garden Cities and are basic to the New Towns policy at present being pursued; they have indeed become so thoroughly assimilated into Planning doctrine that they are today frequently expressed and acted upon by people who do not even know their origin.

Like all inventors and reformers, Howard has suffered from misunderstanding and distortion of his theories and by his terms being exploited and applied to forms of development which they do not truly describe. Between the wars many developers found that the term "garden city" had a selling value, and applied it to development which bore no relation to Howard's Garden City. In his preface to the new edition of "Garden Cities of Tomorrow," Sir Frederic Osborn has emphasised this debasement of Howard's coinage.

Howard did, of course, suffer to some extent from the tendency to oversimplify, which is an unavoidable, even perhaps a necessary, trait in the reformer. He ignored the advantages and pleasantness both of the larger village and of the large city which is not yet swollen to inhuman size, and did not sufficiently take into account the immovability of many kinds of industry or the profoundly modifying influences of topography. Perhaps, too, his "magnets" notion is too crude to have much value when the need for a graduated hierarchy of settlements is realised.

Also there is, in present-day conditions an element of question-begging when ideal sizes of town are postulated. What *is* a town? What degree of separation from adjoining communities qualifies a place to be regarded as a separate town rather than part of a large city? It will be realised from what has been said in Chapter 5 that these are not questions to which there are simple, unequivocal answers, and from Chapter 4 that population density in this country is now too high for it to be possible to do without large cities.

Reformers of town structure have mainly opted for small populations—Howard, 30,000; 100 New Towns Association, 50,000; New Towns Report, 30,000—50,000. The reasons for this seem sensible and are threefold.

In a town of this order of size the population is sufficiently large for all kinds of people to find congenial companionship and form associations devoted to special interests. Institutions of most kinds can be supported. But in the very large city a dreadful impersonality emerges; the individual is apt to become an anonymous unit whose death or disappearance is hardly remarked upon; civic leaders represent too large a body of citizens to be effective representatives.

Second, as regards physical size, a town of 50,000 people at an overall density of 20 persons per acre occupies a circular area with a radius of only a mile, which brings every resident within easy reach both of open country and of the town centre.

Third, Lewis Mumford has suggested that, for reasons which are obscure, beyond a size of 40,000 to 50,000 a town becomes incapable of reproducing its own population so that it is continually declining, and must therefore continue to draw immigrants from outside.

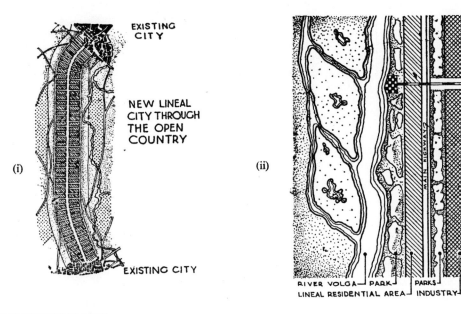

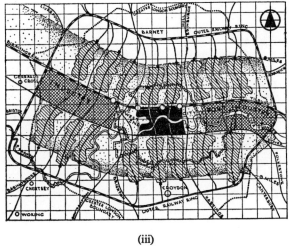

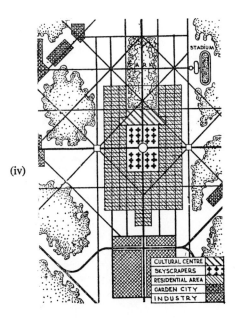

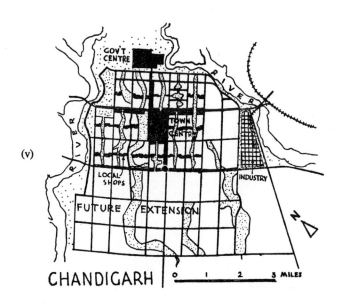

FIG. 20. PLANNING THEORIES

    (i) The original Ciudad Lineal
    (ii) Part of a lineal plan for Stalingrad.
    (iii) M.A.R.S. group Plan for a lineal London.
    (iv) Le Corbusier's " City of Tomorrow ".
    (v) Chandigarh.

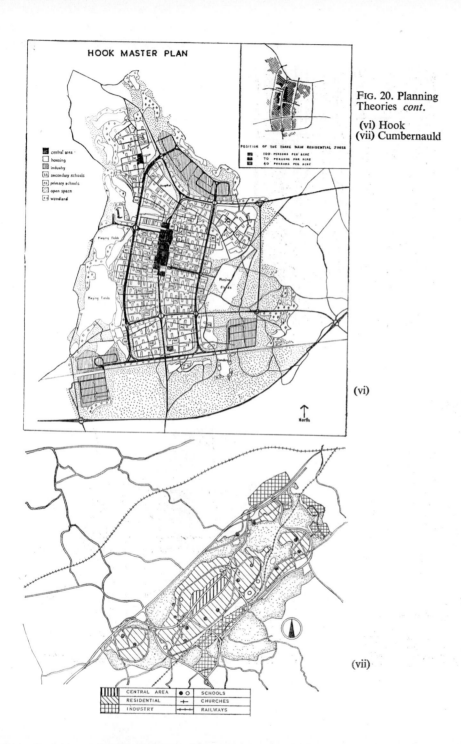

HOOK MASTER PLAN

- central area
- housing
- industry
- ss secondary schools
- ps primary schools
- open space
- woodland

Playing Fields

Playing Fields

Playing Fields

North

(vi)

POSITION OF THE THREE MAIN RESIDENTIAL ZONES
100 PERSONS PER ACRE
70 PERSONS PER ACRE
40 PERSONS PER ACRE

FIG. 20. Planning Theories *cont.*

(vi) Hook
(vii) Cumbernauld

(vii)

CENTRAL AREA	● ○ SCHOOLS
RESIDENTIAL	＋ CHURCHES
INDUSTRY	＋＋＋ RAILWAYS

We must be careful not to arrive at false conclusions by comparing facts which are not truly comparable. The inhumanity, formlessness and apparent comparative infertility of the Paleotechnic large town need not necessarily obtain in a large town developed or redeveloped according to Biotechnic principles.

Various suggestions have been made for the establishment of towns which, by reason of their shape and the relationship of their functions, have been considered by the authors to avoid the faults of the Paleotechnic city, and which are radically different in form from those with which we are familiar.

Among the best known of these is that of Don Arturo Sonia y Mata, who, in 1882, propounded the idea of a lineal city of 30,000 people. He based his proposals on the principle that transport routes should determine city designs and that the city should be designed in advance of development. The form he proposed was a wide and nearly straight spine road down the centre of which ran railways; access to development was obtained by straight roads meeting the spine road at right-angles. Ultimately, Sonia y Mata envisaged the connection of existing cities by series of lineal towns, the land within the triangles so formed to be used for agriculture or industry. Tony Garnier, a French architect, also worked out proposals for an industrial town of 35,000 population on lines somewhat similar to those of the Ciudad Lineal. (See Fig. 20 (i).)

Extensions and modifications of this idea have been carried out in Russia; a plan for Stalingrad on the lineal principle has been prepared, while the M.A.R.S. group of architects worked out in some detail a scheme for the complete redevelopment of London on lineal lines. (See Figs. 20 (ii) and (iii).) In this case a series of lineal units.

The principle of the lineal city is vertebrate; the main transport route is the basis of the whole thing, as compared with the invertebrate form of the ordinary town, which may be compared rather with that of an insect, the whole forming a stable structure with no one member having predominant importance; but it would be a mistake to carry the biological simile too far, and to infer from it that, because the vertebrate is the dominant animal form, similar advantages accrue to this form of city development.

The lineal town has one or two advantages: it is capable of indefinite extension without seriously upsetting the balance of the whole, which is one of the most serious problems in enlarging the normal town; it ensures that the whole population is in close touch with the countryside and it affords opportunities for spectacular architectural and landscape effects.

On the other hand, its defects are far more apparent and serious. The chief and fatal one is that it is quite impossible to arrange that all parts of residential areas shall have equal or reasonably equal access to local centres. Second, as Purdom points out in " The Building of Satellite Towns", all forms of public transport take up and set down passengers at definite stopping points. These stopping points cannot be too frequent or the transport service is unduly slowed down, and consequently it is reasonable for buildings to cluster at the stopping points rather than to spread out uniformly between them. One can readily imagine that houses, shops and offices midway between stopping points in a lineal town would be unpopular! In fact, for it to be successful the invention of a transport system in a series of endless belts which can be boarded at any point seems necessary.

Thomas Sharp in "Town and Country Planning", (Penguin Books) marshals arguments of such weight against the lineal idea as to dispose of it finally:—

"Linear City is a planned form of that unplanned Ribbon Development which has caused such havoc in England that legislation (the feebly ineffectual legislation of the Restriction of Ribbon Development Act) has been directed against it.[1] The planned form certainly avoids many of the grosser faults of the unplanned form, but it still has faults enough to condemn it. Principally, instead of being specially suitable for a 'Transport Age,' it is just about the least suitable form of development that could be devised for such a time. The point about the new transport is that it facilitates swift movement. It is not very reasonable, then, to do the very thing that will impede that characteristic swift movement and so stultify the whole development. And that is precisely what the pure Linear City is bound to do. The 'big arteries of contemporary life' are of all features the ones that should be kept free. Why clutter them up with purely local traffic, as you are bound to do if you build towns along them? Or if on the other hand you keep your local traffic off the arteries and limit it to service roads alongside, where is the point of the Linear City? In any case, wherever you concentrate all your local traffic on one or two parallel streets, you also increase the amount of travel necessary to get about your 'city'—for the thin rectangle (which is what the linear pattern is) offers far less freedom of movement than say the square or the circle, and the thinner it gets, the more restricted does movement in it become, until eventually all movement is going backwards and forwards along the same line."

Nevertheless in the plan of Hook, already referred to in Chapter 1 it is revived, accompanied by a good deal of spurious argument about its merits. Although the plan for Hook is not in fact in lineal form the descriptive matter in the book rather oddly assumes that it is. Some excuse for this lies in the fact that the proposed Town Centre is in lineal form and is adjoined by residential areas which, as regards what is called the "inner town", are in more or less lineal form. (See Fig. 20 (vi).)

The fundamental fallacy, swallowed hook, line and sinker in the Hook book, is that a lineal centre affords greater accessibility then a centre of the same area of compact shape, whereas in terms of accessibility to all parts of the centre, which is the real test, its accessibility is much less. This subject will be pursued further in Chapter 12.

The lineal town, though not at all a satisfactory form of development, has enough merit to be worth consideration. I am not sure that as much can be said for Frank Lloyd Wright's idea for a town in the form of a single building a mile high—an extreme reaction from his earlier " Broadacres " scheme for town development at an exceptionally low density. Nor is it easy to find a great deal of practical advantage in the various ideas for

contemporary Planning advanced by Professor L. Hilberseimer in " The Nature of Cities ". Having reasonably enough said that at the present time cities are " dominated by industry and ruled by interest," and expressed the hope that the time will come when they will be " developed according to the needs of man and ruled by reason " he puts forward ideas for fulfilling this hope which appear to be to determine the shape of communities chiefly by what is needed to avoid air pollution of residential areas by factories (easier to control the source of pollution?) and to arrange the regional pattern of communities and the grouping of units within metropolitan areas so as to reduce the incidence of aerial bombardment.

Hilberseimer's proposals include the complete redevelopment of Chicago in order to attain the latter object by means which would necessitate the imposition on the people of the United States of a code of Planning control far more rigorous than anything attempted in this country. I should not wish to belittle any imaginative Planning experiment, but this is an example of the futility of entirely ignoring the maxim that " Planning is an exercise in the practicable."

Two other striking and original methods of city development must be mentioned: Le Corbusier's " City of Tomorrow ", first described in 1922, and his later " La Ville Radieuse ", the former designed for three million inhabitants, the latter for one and a half million, but capable of expansion. (See Fig. 20 (iv).)

The " City of Tomorrow " had elevated main roads and subways for goods traffic and trains; airfields and railway stations were co-ordinated. The central part of the town consisted of a skyscraper area, the blocks 700ft. high and a quarter of a mile apart and devoted to business and entertainment uses. Surrounding this central area was the residential area, mainly in the form of five- to seven-storey flats, and beyond this isolated settlements which Le Corbusier termed " garden cities," but which were really detached dormitory suburbs. Industries were also concentrated in a large area apart from the rest of the town.

The " Ville Radieuse " is on similar lines to the " City of Tomorrow ", but more densely developed, without detached settlements, and with the skyscrapers on the edge of the town instead of at the centre.

These ideas, however imaginative, and however visually exciting they might be if realised, cast to the winds the central Planning idea of accessibility. They combine the minimum of horizontal compactness with the minimum of vertical compactness

So far as this country is concerned, although we might possibly need to create new great cities, if one among some of the possible alternative regional Planning policies discussed in Chapter 4 were adopted, this is far from being an imminent probability, and the gradual redevelopment of existing cities on sounder lines is a problem sufficiently challenging to need most of our energy. It seems certain that it is not possible to effect a radical change in the basic form of a great city unless it has been virtually destroyed by some disaster, since this would involve an extremely rapid process of redevelopment in order to avoid complete chaos while it was going on. Even technological revolution of the most dramatic kind could hardly do more than bring such

---

[1] Sharp was writing in 1940.

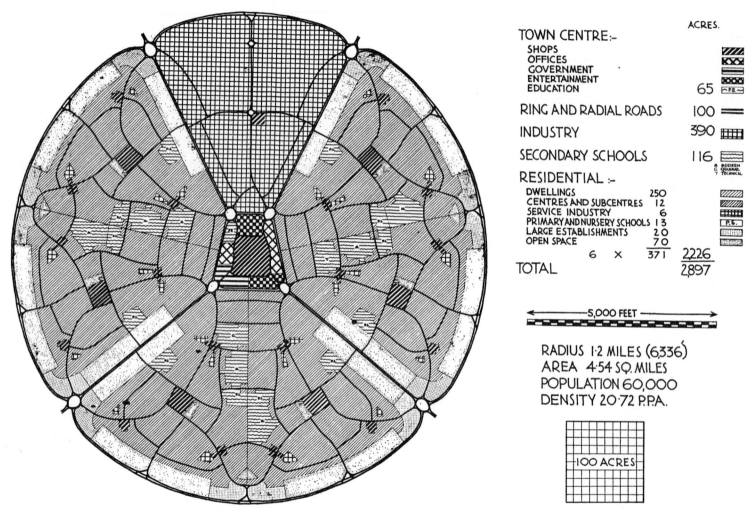

TOWN CENTRE:-
  SHOPS
  OFFICES
  GOVERNMENT
  ENTERTAINMENT
  EDUCATION

RING AND RADIAL ROADS

INDUSTRY

SECONDARY SCHOOLS

RESIDENTIAL :-
  DWELLINGS   250
  CENTRES AND SUBCENTRES   12
  SERVICE INDUSTRY   6
  PRIMARY AND NURSERY SCHOOLS   13
  LARGE ESTABLISHMENTS   20
  OPEN SPACE   70
                        6 ×   371

TOTAL

ACRES.

65

100

390

116

2226

2897

M.G.T. MODERN GRAMMAR TECHNICAL

5,000 FEET

RADIUS 1·2 MILES (6,336')
AREA 4·54 SQ. MILES
POPULATION 60,000
DENSITY 20·72 P.P.A.

100 ACRES

FIG. 21. The theoretical New Town from which examples are taken throughout Parts I and II of this book. This illustration is in the form of a " Town Plan ".

action over the horizon of possibility, and were this to happen it might well seem, nevertheless, hardly worth doing.

We must now return to rather more detailed discussion of the principles which should govern the development of new towns, since apart from the intrinsic interest and importance of the subject, the methods used may serve as a useful guide to the best ways of reshaping existing towns, providing that they do not involve forms of development so completely dissimilar from existing forms that no adaptation is possible.

Of the numerous theoretical town plans which have been produced through the ages, in varying degrees of detail, in order to illustrate their authors' ideas of the most satisfactory way of combining the elements of a town in the absence of disturbing factors, such as topography or existing development, many have assumed a form approximating to a circle. This is true of plans produced by Vitruvius, and of many ideal towns of the Renaissance. There are good reasons for this, which apply whether the dominant motif behind the design is social or military. Of all figures the circle contains the largest area of land for a given perimeter. This, of course, makes for economy in the building and manning of defences, and ensures the greatest possible compactness and degree of convenience of intercommunication between the different parts of the town. A further less obvious advantage is that the smaller the length of frontier between urban area and surrounding agricultural land the less the amount of interference to the prejudice of agriculture. The general proximity of an urban centre is advantageous to agriculture because it provides quick access to a market for produce, but, on the other hand, direct contact with it may be highly detrimental by reason of trespass and vandalism on the part of the urban inhabitants.

Fig. 21 is an example of yet another ideal town. I have prepared this in order to illustrate the effects of carrying out generally accepted contemporary ideas of Planning where there is nothing to hinder their application. No existing town will serve for this purpose, for it is somewhat startling to discover that no single one even of the British New Towns is a complete example of unobstructed Town Planning. In almost every case difficulties of topography, of existing main roads or of existing building development have dictated a pattern which is far indeed from any theoretical norm.

The only exception to this is Harlow, which was practically a virgin site, the only important existing features being a railway line and a canal; these, however, have been allowed to dominate the plan to the extent of forming the diameter of a semi-circular form of development rather than a circular one. Also, it was decided to develop in the form of a comparatively large number of small built-up areas separated by extremely large areas of open space, so that the general effect is rather of a number of villages in the countryside than of a single town. (See Fig. 26.) This arrangement may have considerable merit, but it seems a pity that the opportunity should have been lost of carrying out at least one complete town development on a site which made it possible to exemplify orthodox theories comprehensively.

The town shown in Fig. 21 is in essence typical of many medium-sized English towns, with the vagaries and disadvantages of unplanned growth

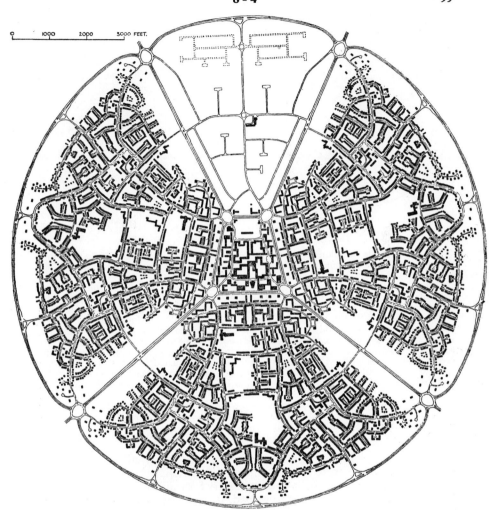

FIG. 22. The same town showing simply buildings and roads. Imaginary buildings have not been shown in the Industrial Area because of the impossibility of forecasting their number, sizes and disposition.

removed. It is assumed to occupy a completely even and featureless site.

Four main roads, assumed to bear approximately equal quantities of traffic, and with no one type of turning traffic predominating over another, enter it from the outside world. So that traffic which has no business to transact in the town shall not require to enter it, an outer ring road is provided.

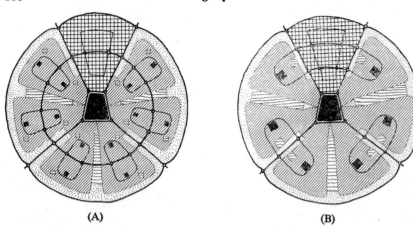

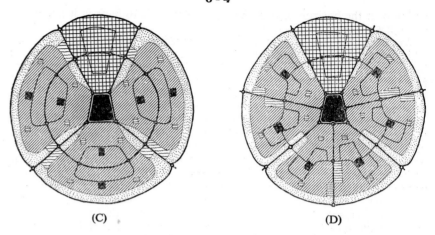

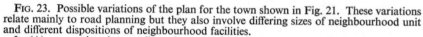

(A)   (B)   (C)   (D)

FIG. 23. Possible variations of the plan for the town shown in Fig. 21. These variations relate mainly to road planning but they also involve differing sizes of neighbourhood unit and different dispositions of neighbourhood facilities.

In (A) a complete intermediate ring road facilitates movement within the town and necessitates neighbourhood units of 5,000 instead of 10,000. (Such a plan would also be very appropriate for a town of 120,000, with neighbourhoods of 10,000.) (B) returns to neighbourhoods of 10,000; the neighbourhood centres are linked by loop roads, and short-cuts between neighbourhoods through minor residential roads are severely discouraged, indeed physically prevented, because no roads other than those shown would give access to ring or radial roads. (C), like (A), has an intermediate ring road but residential units are of 10,000 population, at the cost of having very attenuated form. (D) is much the same as Fig. 21 but there is a radial road on both sides of each neighbourhood in order to provide a more strongly marked distinction between principal roads and local roads. (E) is also similar to Fig. 21 but is based on neighbourhoods of 20,000 instead of 10,000.

Each of these alternatives has advantages and disadvantages, which need to be carefully compared in terms of free flow of traffic, safety and accessibility to local services in order to discover the optimum arrangement.

More drastic variations of form are shown in Fig. 24.

It is perhaps a little difficult to believe that such a road would ever be constructed. Since there is no frontage to the radial roads and access to them is severely limited, and it is not necessary for traffic to enter the centre of the town, because of an inner ring road, it might easily be argued that no sufficient volume of traffic would be likely to use the outer ring road to justify its construction. The distance straight through the town is a little over 2·4 miles; via the outer ring road it is 3·8 miles.

It is, however, also a little difficult to imagine that so obviously convenient a road for the purposes of facilitating movement as between one residential area and another as well as for the purpose of by-passing the town completely, would not be built in connection with such a plan. Fortunately, as we shall see in Chapter 14, when considering the detailed design of one of the residential neighbourhoods which make up this plan, it makes remarkably little difference to the design of the rest of the town whether the outer ring road is constructed or not.

The road surrounding the town centre, as already stated, makes it easy for all traffic to reach destinations within the town without entering the central area, which can therefore be developed in the form of a completely or mainly pedestrian precinct, as will be explained in Chapter 12.

The bulk of the open spaces are placed adjoining radial roads and the outer ring road in order to provide a cushion against noise between these and adjoining residential development, and because in the interests of compactness it is best if the majority of open space is placed on the periphery of built-up areas, thus making accessibility of shops, schools, etc., as great as possible. It is true to say that such an arrangement may reduce to some extent the accessibility to major space, but one cannot have it both ways, and in fact accessibility to open space in this plan is high enough to satisfy the most rigorous requirements.

It should be especially noted that although there is a general tendency, in the interests of compactness, to place open space and schools towards the periphery of residential areas this is not carried to extremes, partly because to do so necessarily diminishes the accessibility of these elements and partly because, visually, successful Town Planning requires a subtle interplay between built-up areas and open areas—in architectural terms, between solids and voids. To fly to the opposite extreme from Harlow and push all public open space and the larger school sites outside the built-up area, as was proposed in Hook and as the plan for Cumbernauld New Town postulates, seems to me to be flying from one disadvantageous extreme to another. In the case of Hook, I am not sure about Cumbernauld, this process went so far as to divorce the playing fields of Secondary Schools from their buildings, which seems to me just about as foolish as cutting off the nose to spite the face. Large continuous built-up areas unrelieved by open space constitute one of the worst features of the unplanned nineteenth century town; it seems at the least very, very doubtful whether a Planned twentieth century

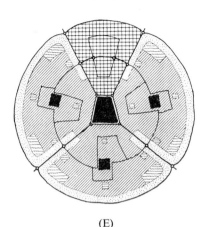

(E)

town can be successfully designed without taking advantage of the relief afforded by the fairly frequent punctuation of open spaces.

Cumbernauld having been mentioned, this may be the appropriate place to mention another feature of its Master Plan which exemp'ifies very well the unfortunate lack of logical rigour in many discussions about Planning principles, and the regrettable ambiguity of many familiar Planning terms. The gifted and intelligent designer of Cumbernauld's Master Plan, Hugh Wilson, claims in its favour that it abandons what he regards as the outmoded and invalid idea of the Neighbourhood Unit. A substantial proportion of the town's population will be grouped around the Central area in a continuous mass. Beyond this will come all major open space and larger school sites and beyond these a number of what Mr. Wilson calls "villages". Since each "village" will contain shops and one or more Primary Schools they seem to me to accord in every way with what I call "neighbourhood units", and I therefore feel justified in describing the plan as one with unduly concentrated inner neighbourhoods and unduly dispersed outer neighbourhoods. Mr. Wilson calls it a plan for a compact town without neighbourhoods. (See Fig. 20 (vii).)

It seems to me that the balance of advantage, both functionally and visually, is decidedly in favour of a relationship between built-up area and open space (very similar to "solid" and "void" in architectural terms) which, while avoiding "bittiness" introduces quite numerous and substantial open areas within the main area of the town, and this principle is followed in all the variations of the Plan shown in Fig 23. Some idea of the relationship sought is given in Fig. 22, though it must be remembered, when looking at it from this point of view, that the industrial segment at the top of the drawing would be virtually fully built up.

The residential areas of the town are divided into six neighbourhoods each with a population of 10,000, which is convenient for the school system. Each neighbourhood has its own primary schools, and adjoining neighbourhoods share secondary schools, which form a break between neighbourhoods, giving visual relief and a sense of identity to each neighbourhood.

Apart from very minor service industry, the entire industry of the town is massed in one area surrounded by main roads for easy access. This has great advantages from the point of view of economy in the provision of services.

From the point of view of accessibility of homes to workplaces, it might from some points of view be better to split the industrial area into two at opposite ends of the town, thus spreading the rush-hour traffic load rather than concentrating it, and probably causing comparatively little loss of economy of trunk services. There is, however, one fairly strong argument against this alternative arrangement: if there were only one industrial worker in each family it would no doubt in the long run be possible for families to find homes in a part of the town closely adjacent to the particular factory or type of industry in which the breadwinner worked, but where, as is so common, there is more than one industrial worker in the family, it is clear that this advantage is cancelled if those concerned work in factories or industries located in different industrial areas. The most convenient location of the home from the point of view of one may be the least convenient for another. The town in any case has a radius of only 1.2 miles, so that nobody can be farther than 2½ miles from his work as the crow flies, and very few will be anything like as far as that. The road system should be easily capable of absorbing without difficulty all that it is likely to be called upon to bear. A second industrial area could not be provided with quite the same high degree of accessibility to main roads without the construction of an additional radial road superfluous for other purposes. Nevertheless, the advantages between one and two main industrial areas are fairly evenly balanced, and an equally satisfactory plan could probably be produced with two as with one.

No railway has been shown, because, assuming that a new line would be constructed to serve the town—and one must assume this in order to maintain the completely untrammelled nature of the exercise—two quite different solutions to the problem could be adopted, depending entirely upon considerations of cost. The cheaper method undoubtedly would be to run a railway line tangential to the town and passing close to the industrial area, with the station immediately adjoining one of the radial roads bounding the industrial area. The only disadvantage of this is that it makes the railway station comparatively inaccessible to a proportion of the town's inhabitants, although it is necessary to stress that, with unobstructed main roads, the time likely to be taken in reaching the station from even the remotest part of the town would be an inconsiderable fraction of that involved in threading one's way through the central area of an existing traditional town to the station.

Alternatively, a railway station could be provided at or near the town centre, and the line could traverse the town either alongside radial roads or between neighbourhoods. Within the central area, however, it would have to be placed either overhead, or preferably underground, in order to avoid interference with road communications. Moreover, the expense of bridges and cuttings where subsidiary roads crossed it to join the radial roads or link neighbourhoods would be very heavy.

It will be interesting to compare the allocations of land use in this theoretical town with allocations in existing towns. R. H. Best and J. T. Coppock, in " The Changing Use of Land in Britain ", analyse the distribution of Land Uses of various grades of settlement in England and Wales. The one of particular interest for our purposes is that dealing with " Large Settlements ", which are Town Map Areas with over ten thousand population in each. They derived average figures from a sample of 160 such areas, and divide land uses into four chief categories: Housing, Industry, Open Space and Education, and find that the total urban area is allocated as follows:

Type of use	% of Urban Land	Acres per 1,000 people
Housing	43·5	31·7
Industry	5·3	3·9
Open Space	21·5	15·7
Education	3·0	2·2
Residual	26·7	19·4
Total	100·0	72·9

These figures relate to existing land use in about 1950 and it is interesting to compare them with the figures for the theoretical town, which are as follows:

Type of use	Percentage	Acres per 1,000 people
Housing	51·8	25
Industry	14·5	7
Open Space	14·5	7
Education	6·2	3
Residual	13·0	6·3
Total	100·0	48·3

The most striking difference between these two sets of figures is the much greater percentage and amount of land given to industry in the theoretical town than in the existing average, which reflects the need for plenty of reserve land for industrial purposes.

The theoretical housing is both at a higher density and yet occupies a larger proportion of the total urban area than does existing housing. The higher density reflects the absence of waste of residential allocation in the theoretical town, and the higher percentage of space which residential land occupies reflects the avoidance of over-provision of open space, which is the other great disparity, the allocation of open space being nearly nine acres per thousand people more in existing towns than in the theoretical one. This

would be slightly reduced if the various large establishments which I have included in the residue of the theoretical town were added to the open space, as has probably been done with the existing towns, but it would not make any significant difference.

In short, my theoretical town, which has been criticised in some quarters as excessively low in density, is, overall, much more sparing with land than the average of existing towns in this country.

These existing towns of over 10,000 population exclude County Boroughs, and in order to get a closer comparison of the theoretical figures with existing conditions it may be as well to quote the comparable figures for County Boroughs, given by Best and Coppock. The sample used is of seventy-nine out of a total of eighty-three.

Type of use	Percentage	Acres per 1,000 people
Housing	43·4	18·8
Industry	8·1	3·5
Open Space	18·7	8·1
Education	2·8	1·2
Residue	27·0	11·7
Total	100·0	43·3

From this we see that the amounts of Land Use allocated in my theoretical town are much closer in most respects to the County Boroughs, including some of the densest development in the country, than to the smaller, more open country towns, despite the comparatively low residential density adopted, which is, oddly enough almost exactly intermediate between that of the County Boroughs and of the smaller towns.

A good deal of space has been devoted to description and analysis of this theoretical town because it demonstrates as thoroughly and simply as I find possible what seem to me the basic principles which should be followed in designs for towns. Many people are repelled and inhibited by the symmetry and inevitably artificial seeming characteristics of diagrammatic representations of this kind. It has to be realised that in practically any real case irregularities of topography and existing artificial features would break down such symmetry however vigorously Planning principles were applied.

The diagrammatic representation of the " round town " will continue to be useful when we turn to consideration of the advantages and disadvantages of various alternative designs. First, what modifications would be desirable if the origins and destinations of through traffic were distributed unevenly around the circle. Fig. 24 (ii) shows the effect where there is simply one main road which, in order to avoid bridging and tunnelling, is to be kept outside the built-up area. The shape is changed from circular to something nearer semi-circular, which in turn alters the shapes of the neighbourhoods and other components.

Fig. 24 (iii) shows the modification involved where two important roads are required to cross each other near the town, but it is desired to keep the junction outside the town. This arrangement avoids the necessity of traffic

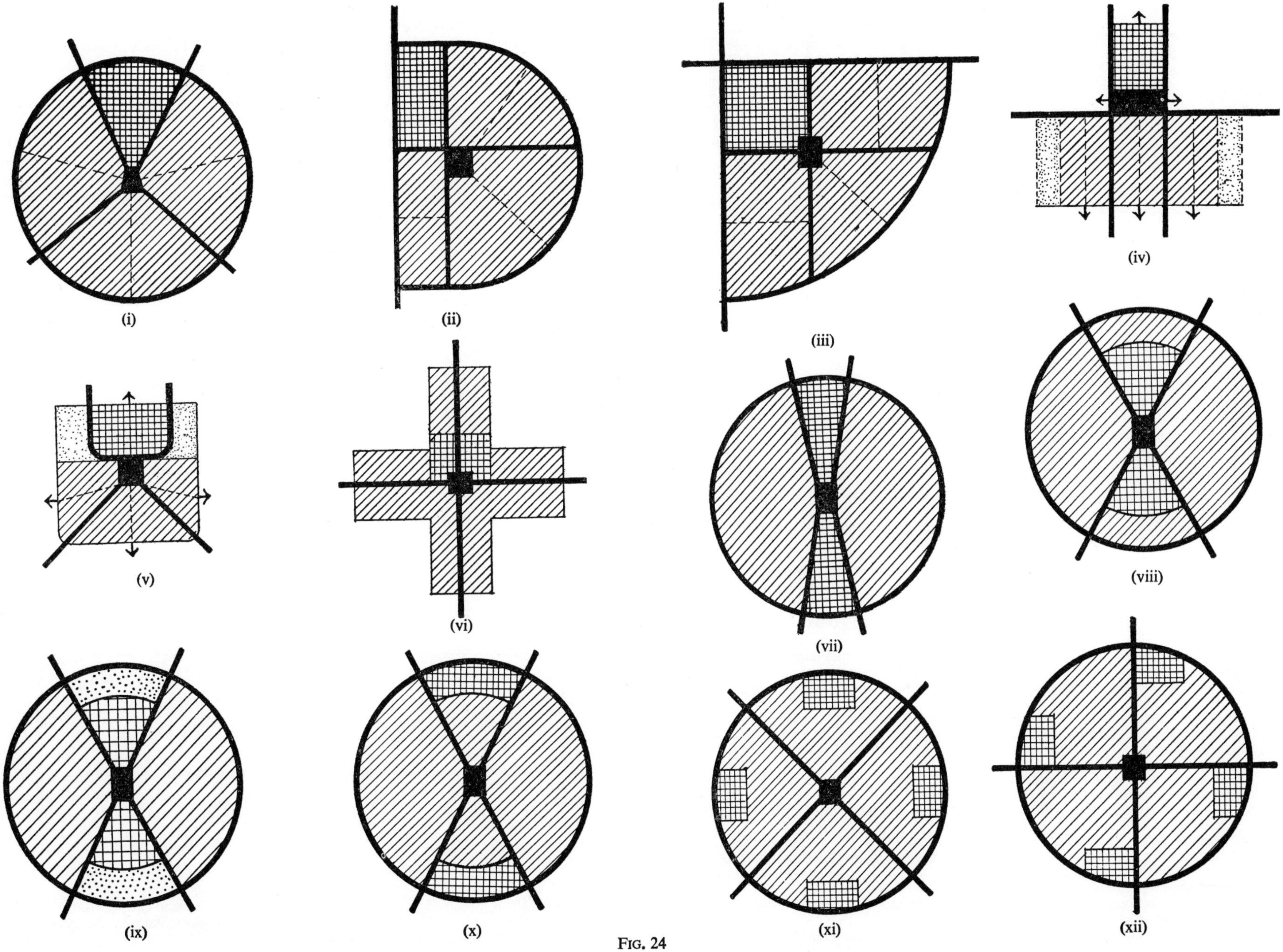

(i)

(ii)

(iii)

(iv)

(v)

(vi)

(vii)

(viii)

(ix)

(x)

(xi)

(xii)

FIG. 24

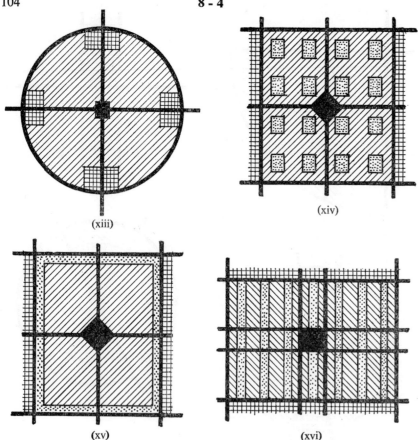

(xiii)

(xiv)

(xv)

(xvi)

FIG. 24. TOWN FORMS. Town Centre, black. Industry, cross hatched. Residential neighbourhoods, oblique hatched. Open space, when shown, stippled.
  (i) The town shown in Figs. 21 and 22 reduced to its essentials for comparison with other forms.
  (ii) A single main through road runs past the town. Industry needs to be close to it and to the town centre, which drags the latter away from the geographical centre.
  (iii) The crossing of two main through roads is kept outside the town. Again, some displacement of the town centre results.
  (iv) Growth of all elements is untrammelled but compactness and accessibility between different parts of the town are much impaired.
  (v) Another device which allows growth for all elements except the town centre, with less sacrifice of compactness.
  (vi) A much larger town arranged to secure accessibility to the countryside for all, but the sacrifice entailed is very great: there is no reasonable accessibility between districts located in adjacent arms of the cross. This is in fact a " multi-lineal " plan somewhat akin to the M.A.R.S. Plan for London.
  (vii)–(xiii) Variations in the disposition of the elements in a circular town. Each has fairly obvious advantages and disadvantages.
  (xiv)–(xvi) Alternative types of " pedestrian " town (see also Fig. 25).

wishing to turn from one main road to another having to make a detour around a section of an outer ring road. Here again the essential structure of the town is not changed, but only the shapes of its constituent parts.

One further matter, which perhaps falls more naturally for full discussion into Chapters 14 and 17, must be mentioned here. The idea of the " super-block ", linked with the cognate idea of providing in a Town Plan for a complete network of pedestrian ways independent of the traffic road system has recently become prominent, and has fallen the victim, like so many other inherently good ideas, to the excessive enthusiasm of its advocates.

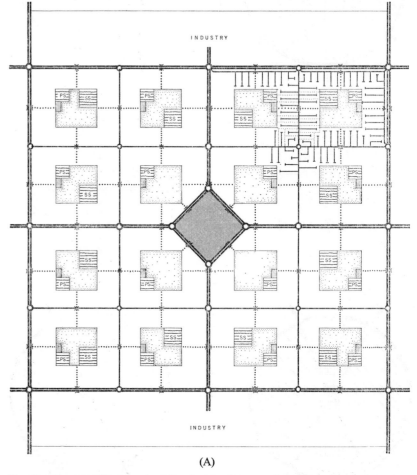

FIG. 25. Three possible layouts of " pedestrian " towns. In each case one unit is shown laid out in some detail. PS = Primary School. SS = Secondary School. Pedestrian ways dotted. Shopping, etc., areas stippled.

There is no doubt that the provision of continuous, or nearly continuous, pedestrian and cycle ways, running for the most part through or alongside open spaces of various kinds is an admirable minor way of enriching the lives of urban dwellers by giving them the opportunity to make journeys within the town right away from either vehicles or buildings. But this is rather different from going to the extreme of insisting that for every vehicular road there must be a corresponding pedestrian way following a separate parallel route. Such insistence, in my opinion, leads to absurdities. Similarly, the provision of open space and schools within the network of major roads to create fully self-contained units is also attractive but leads to extraordinary results if taken to its logical extreme.

Figs. 25 (A), (B) and (C) show three ways, however, in which such a

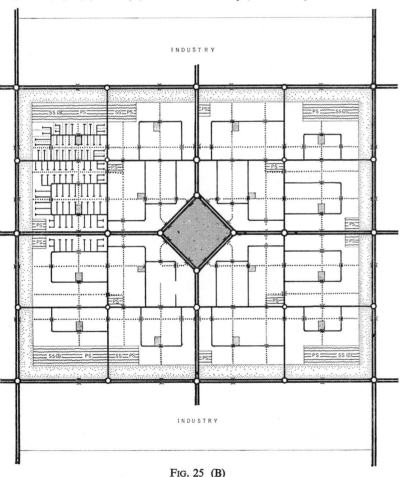

FIG. 25 (B)

town could be laid out; for such purposes a rectangular form is easier to use for demonstration purposes than a circular form. In each of these examples dimensions are based on the assumption that a residential cul-de-sac ought not to be more than about 200 yards long.

(A) is essentially the original "Radburn" idea applied to a complete town of 80,000 people. There are 16 units or neighbourhoods, each containing 5,000 people, a primary school, local shopping and open space. Every other unit contains a secondary school. Footways lead between every cul-de-sac to the interior of the unit, and a number of footways link with adjoining blocks via bridges or tunnels. This does enable all primary school children to walk to and from school without encountering a motor vehicle but, as will be suggested further in Chapter 12, this does not in the least mean that no pedestrian will ever cross a road except by bridge or tunnel.

Reduction of the numbers who do cross roads is dependent upon multiplication of pedestrian bridges or tunnels to a horrifying total, but, however many are built, some will always find it more convenient to cross the road itself.

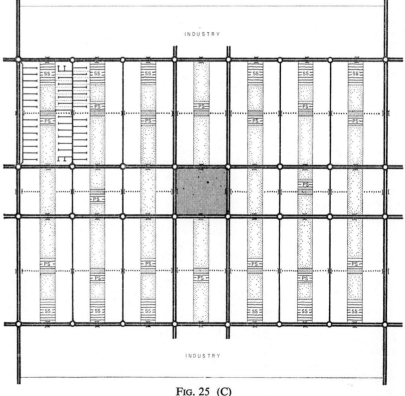

FIG. 25 (C)

In terms of town structure, the total area of the town will be exactly the same as with any other arrangement of components, accessibility to local neighbourhood facilities of all kinds will be excellent, but the town will tend to have a rather monotonous evenness of texture, and local visiting by car and the collection and delivery of goods will be very inconvenient. Evenness of texture could to some extent be avoided by varying the physical size and density of units but only at the expense of complicating the main road network.

(B) is a simplification and rationalisation of the Hook-Cumbernauld idea. Open spaces and secondary schools are pushed to the edges of the town, and even primary schools are placed in the part of each block farthest from the town centre in order to allow for as large an extent as possible of continuously built-up land (on the doubtful assumption that this is a good idea!). Since the interior of each super-block is now used for housing instead of for open space and schools, loop roads can be introduced and local vehicular accessibility somewhat improved. With the simple arrangement shown the numbers of people living in each super-block will obviously vary a good deal though a graduation of super-block size could avoid this.

(C) restores open space and schools to the interior of the super-blocks, in strip form, which is more logical, in relation to a continuous pedestrian system than either (A) or (B). However, because of the limited variations of shape and size possible for school sites and playing pitches, a town laid out on this system would be likely to be a good deal more rigid and monotonous than either (A) or (B).

Naturally, these are simply diagrams, just as Fig. 21 (Town) is; ingenuity and variations of topography would make it possible to relieve somewhat the rigidity of any of them. Nevertheless, these are forms which *require* a good deal of rigidity if they are to work at all, and, in particular, reliance upon a very large number of culs-de-sac of similar length. The only reason for using any of them is the pedestrian way system which they incorporate. Since this cannot come anywhere near eliminating the crossing of roads by pedestrians, and since there is, in any case, no need for such extreme segregation of vehicles and pedestrians there is no sufficient case for using such town forms.

It can never be certain that it will be possible to confine a town to the size for which it is originally planned, and even with a purely theoretical exercise, it is desirable to make provision for the possibility of substantial expansions. Fig. 24 (i) is not ill-suited in this respect. A ring of additional neighbourhoods at the same density as the remainder of the town could be placed around the periphery, and it would not matter whether one or several were added. In this way the size of the town could be increased by 60,000 people with proportionate extra land for industry, and the overall distance from the centre of the circle to the outermost limits of the town would still be only 1·7 miles. Such neighbourhoods would be no more separated from those adjoining them than the existing ones are from each other and would be as accessible to main roads.

The absence of the outer ring road, however, would facilitate expansion if only minor additions were required. With the outer ring road, such small-scale expansion is only possible at the expense of open space, or in the form of isolated small units on the far side of the ring road.

However, it is worth noting that, in practice, such an outer ring road would probably be constructed some distance beyond the limits of planned urban use for this very reason. If the farms in the vicinity were on an average 100 acres in extent and roughly square in shape, the ring road could be moved " one farm out " and still be only about 700 yards farther from the town, (a little less than that required to accommodate an extra ring of neighbourhoods). With the ring road farther out, the extra distance to be traversed by through traffic using it would be about $1\frac{1}{4}$ miles in the case of vehicles going straight on and $\frac{5}{8}$ mile in the case of vehicles switching left or right to another main road.

Figs. 24 (iv) and (v) show possible arrangements for towns which allow growth of all elements (including the town centre which cannot readily be expanded in a circular town) to take place without interference with each other or with the main road system. The loss of compactness and increase in the complexity of the main road system to secure this is, however, obvious.

The effect of variations of residential density and other space standards upon the overall size of a town has obvious relevance here, but it can be much more conveniently dealt with in connection with discussion on space standards, and is accordingly to be found in Chapter 17.

Further attention must now be given to the advantages and disadvantages of varying the number and position of industrial areas, a matter which was dealt with rather cursorily a little earlier.

Figs. 24 (vii) to 24 (xiii) show the fairly numerous different ways in which, within the general context of the design shown in Fig. 21, this can be done.

(vii) shows two industrial zones, each running from centre to outskirts. The advantages of this in terms of possible increased accessibility between homes and work are clear, but the main road pattern becomes less convenient.

(viii) remedies this but at the expense of easy industrial expansion. If ample reserve industrial land is provided there will be a wasteful " hole " in the town.

(ix) gets over this difficulty: industrial expansion would only require the diversion of open space to other areas, whereas with (viii) extensive demolition would be needed.

(x) sacrifices linkage between town centre and industrial areas but allows adequate reserves to be provided with loss of compactness.

(xi), (xii) and (xiii) all have four industrial areas, each arrangement having fairly obvious advantages and disadvantages, though it is probably only with towns larger than about 250,000 that the advantages are likely to lie with such a large number of industrial areas.

As will be emphasised later in this chapter, it is well worth while spending a good deal of time, trouble and money to find out in any given case what the most satisfactory general arrangement of uses is likely to be.

(xiv), (xv) and (xvi) show in outline, for comparison, the " pedestrian " towns illustrated in Fig. 25.

Every Town Plan, especially, needs to be checked, as regards its main road system, by means of traffic forecasts to ensure that it will in fact be able to deal adequately with the traffic produced, and not only adequately but at least as well as any other Plan which would be reasonably appropriate as regards general Planning aims.

Fig. 26 shows the main structure of four English new towns and two old ones which illustrate the tendencies and principles described above.

8-5. THE CURRENT SITUATION

The objectives of Town Planning (excluding the objectives of Regional Planning on the one hand and detailed Planning on the other) may be summarised as the provision of the right amount of land for each use in the right place and on sites physically suitable for each use. This includes the proper spatial relationship of homes and workplaces, of homes and schools, of homes and shopping places of various levels, and of homes with places of entertainment, both indoor and out; success of course depends at least as much upon the successful arrangement of the town's road system as upon the actual selection of land uses.

As we have seen, this is not altogether a simple matter in the case of new towns, but it is enormously more complicated to reshape an existing town so as to bring about satisfactory conditions within it. In fact, so far as I know, it has never been done completely and successfully, if judged by the standards which we should look for in the case of a new town. This does not mean that it will never be done but indicates that we are dealing both with a virtually new and a very difficult subject.

Almost without exception, every town in this country is to some extent a sick town. The defects described below are so common as to be almost universal; so common, too, as to be generally accepted, not as remediable evils, but as normal parts of an urban environment. In fact an appreciable number of present-day architects seem absurdly to regard one of the greatest evils of the contemporary town, namely congestion, as a positive asset, substituting the word " urbanity " for congestion, and referring to examples of development less crowded as " prairie Planning ". It may be safely said that in the field of Town Planning, what we are accustomed to see around us, which the layman regards as normal, is usually very far indeed from even the reasonably desirable, and further still from the attainable ideal.

As has already been seen, the phenomenon of the motor vehicle led to urban sprawl, or octopus growth along main roads, to an extent hitherto undreamed of, and there are few towns indeed which do not suffer seriously, both visually and in loss of compactness and safety, from ribbon develop- ment along the main roads leading to them.

Another evil directly caused by the motor vehicle is the intolerable congestion it brings about in town centres. The typical town centre in the medium-sized town in this country is simply a crossroads, very often the point of origin of the town. Central area uses, shops, offices and public buildings, have disposed themselves along these roads for comparatively short lengths from the actual point of junction. Competition for accom- modation in this area has usually been acute because the geographical advantage of a central location is confined to a very small area of land around the actual point. Demand, and consequently prices, being high, the land has been very intensively developed. The roads are often narrow, and there arises hopeless confusion, for normally these roads have to carry not only traffic whose destination is the town centre, but traffic for which the town itself is merely an incident during a long journey. The roads of the town centre therefore cannot act efficiently either as access roads to the central area uses beside them, nor as through routes.

This, although seen at its worst in and near a town centre, applies also to the entire lengths of main roads within the urban area. It is impossible for a road to function efficiently as both a route for main traffic and a local service road, yet this is what the ordinary town main road has to do. It is inter- sected by innumerable minor roads and fronted by innumerable private properties, each with its own pedestrian and vehicular access to the road. Every single one of these points is a potential source of congestion and danger; this is enhanced by the effect seen in Fig. 67 (i) of uses such as shops which ought to be located on back land to serve housing areas being attracted on to main roads, and thus intensifying the congestion and danger.

It may confidently be stated that, wherever there is a main road with a line of shops on either side of it, proper Planning demands either that the shops shall be removed or that part of the main road diverted.

The last-mentioned item is really one among a large number of examples of displacements of use found in towns where the location of uses has been determined by the free functioning of the market. Fig. 67 (i) also indicates the way in which all non-profit making uses, and, one might add, uses which earn a comparatively small profit per unit area, tend to get forced from the positions in which they could function most usefully towards the periphery of the built-up area.

The fact that industry in the established town is often scattered piecemeal all over the built-up area has already been commented upon. It has grave effects upon the towns in terms of general interference with the quietness and safety of residential roads caused by large quantities of traffic, and very often causes atmospheric pollution and severe visual detriment. In their own way minor industrial and commercial uses—" backyard industry "—cause similar trouble, of less seriousness in each individual case, but because they are scattered in most cases in very small units over a very large area each has an adverse effect over a number of adjoining homes, and it may often be that they exert their influence over the whole at least of the older residential parts of the town.

Worst of all, perhaps, we are at a stage where the problems of massive obsolescence in town buildings seem insuperable. The Victorian speculative builders created deplorable physical environments for those who had to live in the areas they developed but, after the advent of the Public Health Act of 1875, the buildings they erected were very strong and enduring. Now, in the larger towns, square miles of this development are reaching such a condition that, while it may continue to stand indefinitely, it is in other respects almost but not quite unfit for human habitation. Because of its vast bulk, the problem of replacing it with reasonable speed seems insoluble unless a very optimistic view is taken of the possibilities of the second industrial revolution.

108

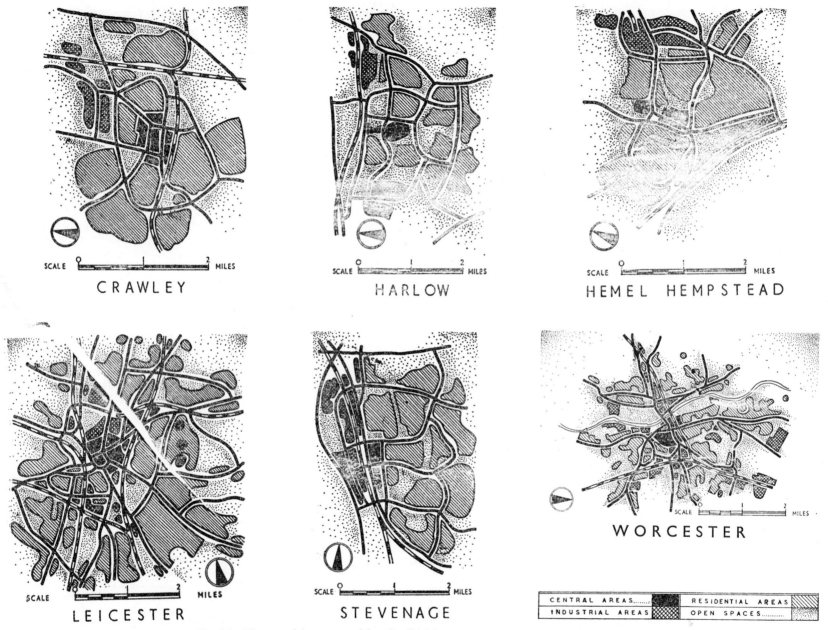

CRAWLEY

HARLOW

HEMEL HEMPSTEAD

SCALE 0 __ 1 __ 2 MILES

SCALE 0 __ 1 __ 2 MILES

SCALE 0 __ 1 __ 2 MILES

LEICESTER

STEVENAGE

WORCESTER

SCALE 0 __ 1 __ 2 MILES

SCALE 0 __ 1 __ 2 MILES

SCALE 0 __ 1 __ 2 MILES

CENTRAL AREAS........ RESIDENTIAL AREAS
INDUSTRIAL AREAS OPEN SPACES........

FIG. 26. The essential structure of four English New Towns and two existing towns.

This raises a peculiarly difficult question. However difficult it may be to plan for the fulfilment of conditions at present regarded as acceptable, including the fully effective use of important machines such as the motor car, which at present tends to dominate urban life, it is at any rate a problem of finite difficulty; but the motor car may vanish, leaving as little trace as the tram car.

The motor car was with us in a fairly highly developed state and in considerable numbers in 1914, and the probability of its increased use reasonably apparent, yet no effective action was taken to modify the pattern of new development in such a way as to enable full advantage to be taken of this increase or to prevent its becoming a menace. The possible rise to importance of methods of transport as yet undreamed of cannot be wholly discounted; it may be that today we stand in the same relation to the helicopter and the hovercraft as the generation of 1900 did to the motor car.

It is apparent that universal use of the helicopter would demand drastic modification of urban layout, yet we do nothing about it. Why? Because such a development may never happen and it would, perhaps, be even more foolish to Plan for such a development if it did not occur than to fail to Plan for it when its occurrence became reasonably certain. There is, unfortunately, no escape from this dilemma: the development of inventions is unpredictable in the Neotechnic age and it would be over-hopeful to assume that prediction can become possible in a future Biotechnic age, though it would be an important aim of biotechnic society. We might, of course, employ clairvoyants in the government service but the results of following their advice would not necessarily be beneficial.

The changes in what are regarded as the minimum standards essential for the population in general are almost equally unpredictable. Compare, for example, the post-war local authority housing estates—or even the pre-war ones for that matter—with the estates built for low-paid workers in the nineteenth and early twentieth centuries. The difference is enormous, and if standards have changed so greatly in the last 50 years, may they not continue as fast in the same direction during the next 50 years? The disparager of the local authority housing estate, who sneers at it as a " modern slum " is generally comparing it with his own more spacious home environment rather than its counterpart of the previous generation.

Government policy since the war has, on the whole, rather tended to shirk the need for long-term planning. Despite an early injunction from the then Minister of Town and Country Planning to " plan boldly ", difficulty and expense have subsequently been emphasised officially, and this attitude is expressed in the Development Plans Regulations under the Town and Country Planning Act, 1947, which require the submission of plans based upon anticipated happenings within a period of 20 years, only the most vital proposals which are likely to take longer to bring about being included.

There is very evident common sense in this policy; it helps to keep the feet of Local Planning Authorities on the ground, to make them work out what really can be done within a limited period, to prevent the Local Planning Authority which really intends to do nothing masking this intention beneath a grandiose and unrealisable plan. Further, it is of assistance in preventing

public interest and optimism being aroused by the publication of long-term Plans, of which only a very small fraction can be implemented quickly, with subsequent disillusionment, cynicism, and even hostility towards Planning. Something of this kind happened in areas for which ambitious preliminary post-war plans were prepared and published.

Nevertheless, there is much to be said on the other side. True Planning must seek to look ahead as far as the complete solution of the problems with which it deals, and in many towns the redevelopment of the mass of dense nineteenth-century housing will probably hardly even have been begun in 20 years' time. Yet it is something which must happen eventually; the houses will sooner or later fall down if they are not pulled down, and no sane person would suggest their replacement at the same density. Hence, the extent and shape of any town after the redevelopment of all excessively dense housing is bound to be very different from what it will be in 20 years' time, and it seems to be absolutely essential that development plans prepared now or in the near future should take account of that eventual size and shape, otherwise it is unlikely that the comparatively short-term plan will fit in with them.

The greatest obstacles to successful Planning, however, are still, since the abandonment of the financial provisions of the 1947 Act, excessive cost in acquiring land for Planning purposes; the failure to create Planning Authorities whose areas reasonably coincide with Planning units; and a general failure to accord Planning its proper place as a major instrument of social advance, with the allocation of the resources and status to Planners which are needed.

It is easy enough to list the results produced by an absence of Planning, but since, as already suggested, there is no example of a town raised to a state of complete effectiveness as the results of Planning action, it is not quite so easy to visualise the results of full and effective replanning.

Nevertheless, since the war Town Planning in this country has achieved a very great deal. The New Towns have been the objects of world-wide interest and acclaim. The legislative code included in the New Towns Act of 1946, the Town and Country Planning Act of 1947 and the National Parks and Access to the Countryside Act, 1949, constitute the most comprehensive yet flexible set of legal tools for the control of land use ever brought into being. Since the exercise of Planning powers necessarily involves limitation upon the freedom of action of individuals, and thus is bound to cause resentment and frustration in some quarters, and since many of the achievements of Planning are necessarily preventive, and thus unseen, the public generally have not appreciated the achievements of Planning. This is aggravated by the fact that the most obvious end result of Planning, the appearance of buildings, poses the most difficult problems and has been dealt with least successfully. This is the more regrettable because, in terms of human welfare, the successes achieved remarkably out-weigh this comparative failure. It is therefore desirable that great and persistent efforts should be made to publicise the achievements of Planning. These include the following:—

The establishment and maintenance of Green Belts around the great cities; the overall success of these is far greater than the detailed local failures which have sometimes occurred.

The growth of towns has been kept relatively compact by refusing permission for excessive peripheral development; in particular the pre-war menace of ribbon development has been virtually eliminated. The full effects of this limitation are not always apparent because of existing sprawl and because even outward growth has for various technical reasons not always been possible, but as the development Planned for in town maps approaches completion the beneficial results will appear.

Similarly, tremendous success has been secured in keeping the growth of villages reasonably compact. But for the exercise of firm control since the war innumerable villages would by now have lost all charm, compactness and even identity. In this respect there has recently been some backsliding but, not yet at least, to such an extent as to nullify seriously the general success achieved.

Very great savings in public money have been secured by reserving and keeping clear of development the routes of future roads and the sites of future important development which it is not yet feasible to carry out.

Many areas of natural beauty have been saved for the nation by refusing permission to development which would have obliterated them.

Substantial success has been secured in preventing intrusive and incompatible uses being introduced into urban areas, which would otherwise have prejudiced convenience, pleasantness, the flow of traffic and safety.

Density control has been generally effective in preventing the exploitation of land by over-intensive use, with all the social and economic disadvantages which this entails, though here again there has been deterioration in the last few years. Also, we may note here, density control has been handicapped by a lack of logic in the methods and standards used to administer it.

In innumerable cases, the amenities of local residents have been protected from the intrusion of minor uses incompatible with residential areas.

Most important of all, the overall control of land use has achieved much in conserving the country's natural resources, in particular by preventing the loss of valuable agricultural land to urban development and in preventing the loss of valuable mineral resources through development above them rendering them inaccessible.

Large-scale improvements in the structure of the existing built-up areas of towns, however, have not yet occurred. Redevelopment, or urban renewal as it has begun to be called, has been carried out in fairly substantial units during the last few years but, generally speaking, without making much contribution to improved urban structure. This, to a large extent, has been because Development Plans with which to shape and guide redevelopment have not been nearly sufficiently detailed to achieve their purpose. As will be stressed later, the Town Map at a scale of six inches to the mile, is quite inadequate for such a purpose. The large-scale redevelopment of outworn residential areas has hardly yet begun, except as regards slum clearance. It will be vital that, when it does begin, as it soon will, Planning Authorities are not caught similarly unprepared.

8-6. THE PLANNING BALANCE SHEET

Mention was made at the end of Chapter 2 of the concept of the " Planning Balance Sheet". For a full explanation of this very important idea the reader is referred to Dr. Lichfield's book, " The Economics of Planned Development," particularly Chapters 18 and 19. The essence of the idea, as applied to the Town Plan, is that it can usually take one of a considerable number of forms. It is seldom that only one solution is possible for a given problem, and the Town Plan may be regarded as the solution not of one, but of many problems, each of which is capable of being solved in several ways. The relative advantages and disadvantages of the different possibilities are by no means always so evident, and the Planning Balance Sheet provides a method of choosing between them, which, though it may not be infallible and though it certainly cannot exhaust the factors which need to be taken into account, can, at least, bring a large proportion of them within the scope of accurate comparison by measuring the private and public benefits and costs accruing from each.

As Lichfield is careful to point out, an increase in public benefit may also entail an increase in private costs, though this is by no means necessarily so, and it is necessary for Planning decisions to be taken with full cognisance of the effects which they will have on private costs. As has already been explained, good Planning must necessarily result in greater efficiency and a reduction of private and social costs overall, but some of the methods used to attain reduction in social costs may increase private costs, not overall, but in relation to particular groups or interests.

Lichfield summarises the policy which should be followed, in these words: " In short, therefore, Land Planning aims at a reduction in costs both private and social, and at an apportionment between private and social costs which is in accord with social conscience." Later, he enlarges somewhat on this: " In avoiding prospective liabilities that can be avoided by the exercise of foresight, planning can be said to pay always, for ' a city must pay for planning or lack of planning.' But since the liability that is avoided would sometimes fall on the individual, and sometimes on a local authority or the National Income, it is relevant to ask ' Whom does it pay? ' "

The main reason underlying this possible conflict is that the approach of private developers is inevitably somewhat different from that of the Planning Authority, which must be concerned with wider effects than those which the private developer considers to be his concern. As the Planning machine is at present constituted this is not the end of the matter, for even Local Planning Authorities may not necessarily take as wide a view of the economic consequences of their decisions as is desirable. The arrangements of local authority finance may well mean that a Planning decision which would be the most truly economical in terms of national finances, would be less economical in terms of Local Planning Authority finances. And, again, a form of development which would be most economical from the point of view of a County Council might not be the most economical for a Borough or District Council.

It may reasonably be said that it is anomalous for this to occur, and that a well-devised machinery for local government would avoid such anomalies.

but they spread beyond the limits of local government. As we shall see later on in considering the economics of different kinds of housing, the artificial devices of subsidies may have a profound effect on local housing policy quite independently of and having results which sharply conflict with real economy.

Lichfield gives interesting examples of the ways in which the economic advantages and disadvantages can be worked out in relation to specific items. He pays special attention, for example, to the loss to the community of agricultural land and its potential produce, and illustrates the use of the " food replacement yardstick " suggested by Dr. G. P. Wibberley, which is intended to assist in arriving at a decision as to whether to use good quality farm land for housing, cheap to develop because of its physical characteristics, or poor quality farm land producing less food, but more costly to develop because of its physical character. The yardstick is whether the loss of food resulting from the use of the better land will be more or less than what could be made up by investing the difference in development costs in the improvement of other agricultural land elsewhere, or in the reclamation of unused land. If the loss is greater then the poorer land should be developed, if less then the better land should be developed and some other land improved agriculturally by spending on it the development costs saved. It is worth pointing out that at present we do not, of course, have any machinery for securing that such money is, in fact, invested in the improvement of other land but this does not invalidate the principle.

The selection of one site rather than another for development should, however, be influenced by many other factors, some of them capable of expression in monetary terms—others not. In discussing the factors involved in deciding between four different schemes of development for the extension of a town Lichfield has the following to say, which makes clear the great range of the subject. " The financial appraisal, not only for the dwellings . . . but also for ancillary development, would tell the authority which scheme would be cheapest in capital and annual cost. . . . In making its decision the authority would also be influenced by the other expenditure that the scheme would cause to fall on the rates. For example, less expenditure by the authority in providing schools, open spaces, community buildings, libraries, etc., would be probably required with the greater concentration because more people could make use of the facilities which existed in the centre, and also less expenditure would be required to run the municipal services of the authorities, the policing, refuse collection, street cleansing, gully emptying. With the greater spread there would be greater cost on new and improved principal traffic roads and also higher costs in maintaining, cleansing and lighting the new roads. It might be, however, that the new mileage justified the use of vehicles and plant which were not previously economical in use, so reducing the average costs of maintenance, etc., throughout the town.

" The authority might or might not take into account also the following implications. The more the town spread the more capital expenditure would be required of the Gas and the Electricity Boards. But even in the most expensive scheme it would not follow that the cost per unit of producing the extra gas or electricity would be more than the cost per unit before

expansion, and that all current consumers in the locality would thereby need to face an increase in charges. It might be that because of the way in which the existing mains were distributed, or because the existing works had latent capacity, the additional consumption would enable the undertaking to reduce its cost per unit for any of the schemes. This could be calculated.

" The bus services on the road would probably cost more per head of the population with the greater spread; but here again the results could only be judged in relation to the economics of the existing services. The additional dwellings in any scheme might, for example, be located where newcomers used the section of the service previously running at a loss. In the high density scheme the occupiers of dwellings on the inner sites, including families with children would have the disadvantage of living in flats on a congested site. In the lower density scheme more of these people would be living on the outskirts where they could if they wished, have family dwellings; and the remainder would have pleasanter living conditions in the inner areas because of the lower density.

" The lower density schemes would spoil the amenities of more open country than would the high density scheme with the greater spread of the town into the country. They would also sterilise more agricultural land but would give rise to more production from houses, gardens and allotments. This could be measured financially."

Among other items examined are the relative advantages and disadvantages of widening an existing Trunk Road or building a by-pass in specific circumstances and the costs and benefits of widening a bridge. Valuable though the economic analysis of a particular project or of alternative policies in general terms may be, what is clearly needed if the Planning Balance Sheet is to become the vital tool for Planning which it should be is a technique for comparing as wholes the costs and benefits of alternative Plans for a Town.

The example from Lichfield's book which has just been summarised might easily be only one out of a dozen or more items involved in preparing a Town Plan, each more or less equally important, each reacting upon every other one, and each perhaps susceptible of half-a-dozen or more different solutions. To be certain of choosing the best possible Plan it would be necessary to work out a Planning Balance Sheet for each possible combination of items—a total of $12^6 = 2,985,984$. Clearly, such a task can only be done by a computer and equally clearly, the economic importance of finding the most economical combination of possibilities justifies its use. Assuming that only acceptable possibilities have been cited and taken into account, the most economical combination will normally be the one to select. One says " normally " because one of the great blessings about help gained from a machine is that its advice can be rejected without hurting its feelings. It might very well be that occasionally the most economical solution might deliberately be rejected in favour of one slightly more expensive because, all in all, the latter "felt" more satisfactory.

A very important item in a Planning Balance Sheet for a Town Plan is the principal road system. So far as it is concerned, aesthetic and social judgments which are not financially measurable and which might, in respect of other items very properly be held to override purely economic assessments of the best Plan hardly affect the issue. If a road system is really safe and efficient in every way, and this includes not splitting up the town in an undesirable way, it is unlikely that there will be significant advantages other than economic ones as between one possible form for it and another. The number of possible combinations of feasible alternatives in respect of items in the road system is likely to be very great and to justify and necessitate the use of computer techniques for this purpose alone.

Very large sums of money indeed depend upon the adoption of an economically sound Plan so that however expensive the employment of computers in the service of Planning may be it can be regarded as certain that they would easily earn their keep.

8-7. CONCLUSION

This chapter has dealt in outline with the shape, size and anatomy of the town as a whole. The two following chapters deal with the technical processes of preparing Plans to remedy and improve the condition of towns. This, strictly speaking, is the scope of Town Planning as such; all the Planning work described in the various chapters of Part II which deal with the different parts of towns has to be undertaken in the light of the Plan decided upon for the town *as a whole*. It is very important to bear this distinction in mind, for, in ordinary conversation, and even in learned discourses, the different levels of Planning are commonly confused. *Town* Planning ought to mean Planning *towns*, not Planning bits of towns.

CHAPTER 9

LOCAL SURVEY

9-1. INTRODUCTORY

Local survey includes a study in greater detail of many of the subjects dealt with under Regional Survey, with the individual town or village as the survey unit, but, whereas the Regional Survey is confined almost entirely to an investigation of the facts needed to ensure the satisfactory location and distribution of new development, a large part of the Local Survey is concerned with the analysis of the present distribution, density and condition of existing development with a view to deciding what changes should be made when redevelopment takes place and the amount of extra land which will be required to reduce the density of building to a satisfactory level if the existing overall density is excessive or what land can be saved if it is lower than necessary. In relation to statutory planning, the Local Survey is that upon which the town map is based, just as the county or joint board map is based upon the Regional Survey.

The Local Survey may deal with a town, a village, an area of sporadic development or a new town site. It is important that the survey area should cover not only existing development but all surrounding land which might possibly be required for its future development. A generous margin should be allowed; it is much better to cover rather more land than is required than to omit the smallest portion needed. Apart from the loss of time involved in making a supplementary survey it will be desirable to have special 6 in. to one mile base maps prepared for each local area, and if these do not, in fact, cover all the land which proves to be needed they will be useless.

9-2. LAND USE SURVEY

(i) Scope

This survey needs to be prepared in the first instance at a scale of 1/2,500 or 1/1,250 and should cover every part of the region in which non-agricultural buildings and uses exist (" agricultural buildings " being taken to mean buildings other than dwellings). Development control problems may arise anywhere; they are not confined to town map areas, and a thoroughly accurate and detailed picture of existing land use is necessary to deal with them. The survey of existing land use is of fundamental importance; all proposals are based upon it, and great care should be taken to ensure its completeness and accuracy. The portions of the survey covered by town map areas can, for convenience, be extracted and shown on the 6 in. to one mile base maps for these areas.

(ii) Survey methods in the field

Much of this section also applies to surveys made in the field in connection with the subjects other than land use, but because of the paramount import-

ance of this survey, its relatively complicated nature, and the fact that it is needed for densely built-up areas as well as rural areas, an account of the appropriate procedure is included here.

Experience suggests that most Planning surveys can best be carried out by people working in pairs, one to record information on the map, the other unencumbered and free to prowl round and tell the first what he discovers; particularly is this the case in land use survey. Some writers have urged the desirability of collecting survey information on all subjects during one visit. While there is much to be said for this point of view, I do not myself believe that it is normally the best procedure; much of the information to be obtained from inspection needs the exercise of judgment if it is to be recorded correctly, and it is difficult to consider a number of diverse subjects on a single occasion. There is, too, a certain rhythm about such work; a land use survey sometimes proceeds at considerable speed, and the sudden intrusion of difficult problems relating to other subjects would be calculated to reduce this seriously. Further, particularly in unfavourable climatic conditions, it is extremely difficult to record a large volume of information on a map in the field sufficiently clearly for it to be able to be plotted afterwards with certainty.

On balance, therefore, I believe that, just as " one subject one map " is a sound rule for presentation, " one subject one visit " is a sound rule for survey, and that what is lost in expenditure of footwear and petrol is likely to be more than repaid in the results achieved.

This is not, of course, a rule to be followed slavishly; the small extent of a particular survey area, its remoteness, or even the personal preference of the surveyor, may suggest some other procedure in a particular case. In a very large town with a severe redevelopment problem, for example, where a small army of surveyors has to be employed, it may be best not to mark any information at all upon maps but to have a card or paper form for each building and to record upon it at one visit all the survey information needed, the necessary maps being prepared afterwards from the information given on the forms. Examples of the forms used for this method are to be found in the Ministry of Town and Country Planning's Handbook on the Redevelopment of Central Areas. It is, however, improbable that this would prove the best method in any except the most densely built-up portions of large towns since, although it is capable of yielding a great deal of precise information, it is inflexible and does not lend itself to short cuts.

There is little doubt that, in residential areas and areas of scattered development it is best to use a car; the surveyor in the passenger seat carries the map, marks it and observes the land on his side, while the driver observes on the other side and supplies the passenger with information at intervals, such as " All houses this side: solidly built up." Whenever anything requiring detailed scrutiny appears, the car must, of course be stopped. As density and diversity of use increase it will become necessary to stop more and more frequently and to make sallies from the car for purposes of detailed investigation, until eventually the stage is reached at which the pattern of development becomes so complicated (and often traffic so congested) that the car ceases to be useful, and the work continues on foot.

It is possible in this way for a pair of fairly experienced surveyors working well together to carry out an accurate and detailed use survey of a town of normal structure with a population of 35,000 in ten to twelve working days of moderate length.   The great advantage of using a car is that in every town there are large areas containing practically nothing but dwelling-houses, and the survey can be done perfectly well by driving through them at about 15 miles an hour, a vast saving compared with the time which would be taken in walking.

It is important to be properly equipped for the work; most people find that it is best to cut the old style 1/2,500 ordnance sheets into four quarters and to fasten them to map boards.   The new style sheets are of convenient size, undivided.   Information is plotted on the map quite roughly in coloured pencil, using colours and notations approximating to a simplified version of those to be used on the final map.   Written notes and inset sketches should be used fairly freely to clarify complicated points which might later cause difficulty.   Great care should be taken to make these legible.   It is surprising how quickly memory can fade and fail to recall the meaning of an illegibly written note.

In many areas the most recently published 1/2,500 ordnance sheets are badly out of date, and the approximate revisions which will often have been carried out and plotted by local authorities should be used whenever they are available.   Where such revision has not been done much work can often be saved by the turning up plans of recent development deposited with the local authority for Planning permission or by-law consent purposes and plotting these on the maps.   Often, however, development has not been carried out in accordance with the plans submitted, and they should be checked against aerial photographs before being plotted.   Plotting from ordinary small-scale aerial photographs is not a rewarding procedure, as the difference in scale is too great.

All too often, however, the difficulty of gaining access to information which should be readily available drives the surveyor to direct site survey; also, there may often be a small amount of development of which no documentary record is available; in particular, areas of shack development which have never received any kind of sanction.   These will have to be plotted by direct survey.   Although, for most Planning purposes it is sufficient to plot such development quite roughly, it is usually worth while to fix it accurately since this may later save a great deal of trouble in identifying the sites of applications for permission for " infilling " development.   This will have to be done with tape and chain, distances to plot boundaries, etc., being measured from existing features clearly identifiable both on map and ground.   The boundaries of land owned by public authorities, where complicated or inaccessible, can best be obtained direct from the owners; much time may be wasted in plotting them on the ground.

It is extremely important that every map used for Planning purposes should be right up to date.   The map is the planner's principal tool, and any defects in it are bound to be reflected sooner or later in his work.   Accordingly, all development added to the 1/2,500 maps in the course of carrying out a use survey should be transferred in the appropriate degree of detail to the 6 in. to one mile, 1/25,000 and 1 in. to one mile maps.   This is an ideal seldom realised but is of great importance, for it is not practicable constantly to refer back to the 1/2,500 map to check the accuracy of others.

(iii)   Subject-matter

A complete use survey should denote the use of every building and every parcel of land within the survey area, but in order to make the map easily comprehensible it is convenient for closely similar uses to be grouped together under a single notation, and for others less similar, but still related, to be shown with only minor differences of notation.   The following suggested notation, which is not complete in every particular, closely resembles that contained in Circular 63 of the Ministry of Town and Country Planning but with some alterations, thought to be improvements, which will be considered later when the Ministry notations are discussed.   Colouring should cover the entire site in every case, not merely the buildings on it.

Any item not referred to here but included in the Circular 63 notation is intended to be coloured in accordance therewith.   The colours named are those in the standard range of Town and Country Planning colours issued with Circular 40.

GROUP I—RESIDENTIAL

Single family dwelling-houses	*Red-brown* (1.3)
Residential buildings, such as holiday hotels and flats, whether built originally as flats or converted from single family dwelling-houses	*Red-brown* (1.1)

GROUP II—BUSINESS

Shops, including banks, public houses, and post offices	*Blue* (1) Banks marked "*B*" Post Offices marked "*P.O.*", Public-houses marked "*Pub,*" all in black.
Petrol-filling stations and repair garages	*Blue* (1) and marked GAR *in black.*
Commercial hotels	*Blue* (1) *and marked HOT.*
Offices	*Edging and fine horizontal Hatching in Blue* (1).
Miscellaneous business uses, such as builders' yards, bus garages, telephone exchanges, etc., not covered by other business categories	*Edging and fine vertical hatching in Blue* (1) *with the particular use shown in black.*
Warehouses (if not ancillary to a shop or other business)	*Edging and fine crosshatching in Blue* (1)

GROUP III—PUBLIC BUILDINGS

Places of Assembly, Public buildings and institutions, including hospitals, clinics, churches, government and local government buildings frequently visited by members of the public, cinemas, swimming-baths, stadia and sports grounds normally making provision for large number of spectators, railway and bus stations, docks and harbour buildings used by passengers	*Red* (2) *with the particular use shown in black.*
Schools, colleges, etc.	*Yellow* (1)

GROUP IV—INDUSTRY

Land used for general industrial purposes, including electricity power stations, gas works and waterworks	Red-purple (1)
Land used for special industry	Red-purple (1) with black edging and horizontal hatching.
Land used for surface mineral working	Edging in Red-purple (1) note of mineral being worked, depth of working, etc., in black.

GROUP V—MISCELLANEOUS URBAN USES OF LAND WITH FEW OR NO BUILDINGS

Street markets ⎫ Auction grounds ⎬ Car parks ⎭	Area used bounded by broken Blue (1) line and use indicated in black.
Unused land	Uncoloured
Railway lines, sidings, engine sheds, etc.	Grey (1.2)

GROUP VI—NON-AGRICULTURAL USES OF OPEN LAND

Open spaces normally open to the public in general without payment	Yellow-green (1)
Private open spaces:— Golf courses ⎫ Private sports clubs' grounds ⎬	Green (1.2)
Grounds of hospitals, institutions and other uses other than schools mentioned in Group III, where the buildings occupy not more than about one-twentieth of the total area	Edged in Red 2, buildings themselves Red 2, remainder Green (1.2) with the particular use marked in black.
Grounds of residential buildings where the buildings occupy not more than about one-twentieth of the total area	Buildings and immediate curtilage Red-brown (1.1), remainder Green (1.2).
Gardens of houses where the gardens are larger than two acres	House and immediate curtilage Red-brown (1.3), remainder Green (1.2)
Allotments	Green-brown (1) Statutory allotments marked " S " in black.
Cemeteries and crematoria	Brown (2)
Sewage disposal works	Yellow Brown (2) marked " SD " in black .
Land used for disposal of refuse	Yellow Brown (2). Note in black as to nature of waste and height of deposit
Areas used by Service Departments for operational or training purposes	Red (2) broken edging. Note in black of use where security permits.
Civil airfields	Edged in Blue (1), buildings in Red 2, remainder in Green (1.2).
Holiday camps, whether or not permanent buildings exist	Edging in Red-brown (1.1).
Land covered by water, including reservoirs	Blue (2.2).

GROUP VII—AGRICULTURAL USES—(if required)

Pasture	Green-brown (1.2)
Arable	Brown (2.3).
Hops	Brown (2.3) fine cross-hatched Green (1)
Woodland	Green (1). Forestry Commission woodlands indicated by black lettering.
Orchards, market gardens and fruit plantations	Yellow-green (1.2)
Rough grazing	Yellow (1.2).
Land entirely unused	Uncoloured.

It may often be difficult to decide whether a particular building should be classed as a dwelling-house or as a residential building. Houses are quite often split up into flats in the most informal fashion without any real adaptation. A house should be shown as such unless there is clear evidence that it has been converted into flats; the presence of several bells by the front door is a definite and readily visible proof of this. Merely suspicious circumstances such as heterogeneous window curtains, or several prams in the front garden should not be accepted. It does not very much matter whether every home in multiple use is so recorded; what is of importance is that the survey should reveal the areas, usually fairly definitely bounded, in which numerous such conversions are taking place.

It will often be found, particularly among buildings in business areas, that several uses occupy a single building—e.g., shops on the ground floor with offices and flats above. Nearly always the ground floor use is the predominant one; the map should be coloured in accordance with this, and the existence of the other uses can be shown by notes written on the maps, such as " 2F " to denote two floors used as flats, or " 1O " to denote one floor used as offices.

Occasionally, there will be a case where the ground floor use is clearly not the predominant use—e.g., a ten-storey block of flats with the ground floor used as shops; this creates an awkward problem, and the method just described, although it would give all the information needed, would be visually misleading. Probably the best method although not altogether satisfactory, is to indicate the predominant use by the appropriate colour and to indicate the ground floor use by means of a note.

Mention has already been made of the need to present the use survey at various scales and for the notation to be consistent throughout. No great difficulty is likely to arise in transferring from one scale to another, the principle being to attempt only the degree of detail which can be shown with clarity at any particular scale. For example, on the 6 in. to one mile scale, occasional isolated shops within residential areas would not be shown and no distinction would be made between houses and flats. Much the same would apply to the 1/25,000 scale, the division between what would be shown and what would not being adjusted slightly. At the 1 in. to one mile all finer detail would necessarily disappear, and nothing but the fundamental use structure of the area would appear.

There is one difficulty, which is likely to arise fairly frequently. Many towns contain areas of mixed uses, in which residential predominates, but shops, pubs., and industrial buildings are so numerous, though the sites are small and scattered, that the area has a special character—usually unpleasant —and it would be quite misleading to show it as residential. In such circumstances it is desirable to show the non-residential uses on the smaller scales, even though each site, individually, would otherwise be considered too small to differentiate. If the mixture of uses is so intimate that this cannot be done it may be necessary to introduce a new notation, probably in the form of hatching, to denote " mixed uses."

9-3. DENSITY SURVEYS

Density, in relation to Planning, means much the same as it does in ordinary language, the number of objects—houses, rooms, persons, etc.—per unit of space. Detailed information about density is of vital importance for Planning purposes, for upon it are based most of the proposals for reducing congestion.

The subject is a difficult one and, as will be seen, no completely adequate technique has yet emerged.

The study of density may be divided into residential and non-residential.

Residential Density. Residential density has at times been expressed in terms of houses per acre, habitable rooms per acre and persons per acre. The land included in the density calculation may be the whole area of the town, in which case the resulting density is usually called " overall density ", the whole of the land in a predominantly residential area, known as " gross neighbourhood density ", or the land included in house plots, residential roads and incidental open spaces only, known as " net residential density ". The sub-areas for this last category may be broken down to very small dimensions to give results in as great detail as may be required; normally, however, the unit used is each continuous area of houses of generally similar type.

Of these, houses per acre, which was generally used for density calculation before the war, has been seen to be unsatisfactory, since houses may vary between the three-room cottage and the thirty-room mansion. Flats, too, are difficult to account for, since, if the flat is taken as the unit, a building identical with neighbouring ones, which may, in fact, house no more than the average number of people living in a single house, will have to be counted as two or more units instead of one, merely because it has been converted into flats. This would be shown in the density maps as an intensification of land use which would be misleading.

The method of calculating density set out in Circulars 40 and 63 of the Ministry of Town and Country Planning abandons the house as the unit and provides for separate surveys of the number of habitable rooms per acre, or *accommodation density,* and of the number of persons per acre, or *population density,* each survey being made in respect of the same units of development, so that the two can be directly compared, and the " *occupancy rate,*" or number of persons per habitable room, found in order to reveal areas of under-utilisation on the one hand or overcrowding on the other.

There is little doubt that this is a generally sound method; its only drawback is that it fails to take account of the sizes of rooms, which may materially affect the number of persons who can live comfortably in a house. A possible alternative would be to calculate accommodation in terms of habitable floor space per acre and to measure the occupancy rate in terms of persons per 1,000 square feet of floor space. This, however, would leave out of account the fact that a comparatively large number of small rooms may be conveniently occupied by more people than a smaller number of large rooms with the same total area, an omission at least as serious as the other. In any case this alternative method would be very much more laborious to carry out than the first, with which, on the whole, the weight of advantage seems to lie.

Carrying out the Accommodation Density Survey. The first step is to obtain 1/2,500 sheets of the whole of the built-up part of the survey area. Street numbers should be marked on them. All predominantly non-residential areas should be blocked out, since no realistic figure can be obtained for the residential density of, for example, the residential accommodation in a shopping area, which, if quantitatively great enough to be relevant can best be separately noted as a total figure rather than as density.

The predominantly residential portions should then be divided up into areas of similar type. This can usually be tentatively done from the map with the assistance of some local knowledge plus, perhaps, an inspection of doubtful areas. The areas should be similar, both as regards the type of house and the size of garden, though even quite substantial variations in the sizes of gardens due to accidental circumstances such as the incorporation of an irregular property boundary into the lay-out as a back fence line can be ignored provided the general character of the area is homogeneous.

Occasionally one may be misled by the presence of blocks of three-storey houses of similar ground area to adjoining two-storey houses, but this is soon detected and corrected. The object of this preliminary sub-division is, in fact, quite tentative, and merely provides a starting point.

It is important that the sub-division should take account of type of house as well as of apparent density, because, as already explained, the same sub-divisions have to be used for the population density survey, and the occupancy rate may vary markedly between houses with similar sized gardens; e.g., an inter-war speculative estate where the number of children may be well below the average, and a post-war local authority estate in which size of family is an important qualification for tenancy.

The land included within each sub-division should be chosen in order to calculate net residential density; i.e., it should include the house plots themselves, the roads giving access to them, and any purely incidental open spaces such as small roadside greens. It is not always easy to decide where to draw the line as regards the last item. Small open spaces in the centre of house blocks used by the inhabitants in common should clearly be included, but, on the other hand, larger areas of allotments are also to be found, which should not be included. Each case must be judged on its merits and the best test is to consider whether a particular open space is in the nature of an extension of the gardens of a few houses which is used in common, or, on the other hand, is used or likely to be used by the inhabitants of a wider area, in which case it approaches the character of an ordinary local open space and should not be included.

The next step is to find the number of habitable rooms in each area and its acreage; the latter divided into the former gives the net accommodation density in habitable rooms per acre. Ministry of Town and Country Planning Circular No. 63 recommends that all habitable rooms in excess of six in a house in occupation by a single family should be ignored. The object of this is to take account of the fact that in many large houses there are rooms which are hardly used at all, and their omission gives a picture which is in some ways more informative. On the other hand, such houses may at any time be converted into flats, and although the extra habitable rooms cannot be fully used until extra kitchens, bathrooms and W.C.s have been created, it is advisable to have a record of them. On balance, my own opinion is that these extra rooms should be included in the survey.

Some difficulty may arise in deciding what can and what cannot be reasonably regarded as a habitable room. Living rooms and bedrooms are, of course, the habitable rooms proper, but it is sometimes reasonable to include a kitchen. If, for example, there is a separate scullery, and particularly if there is also a wash-house, the kitchen is likely to be used for all the purposes of a living room as well as for cooking, and to be perfectly suitable for these purposes. But if the room has to be used for drying clothes, or, still more, for washing up, though it may still perforce be used as a living room its suitability for the purpose is much less, and it should not be treated as such in the survey. In other words, reasonable suitability is a better criterion than actual use for assessing future needs.

Similarly there may often be a doubt whether " box-rooms " used as bedrooms are suitable, which can only be resolved by making a more or less arbitrary decision and following it consistently.

A problem arises regarding the treatment of hotels, nursing homes and institutions. Where these occupy extensive grounds it means nothing, particularly in the case of hotels, to express density per acre in terms of the number of habitable rooms—some of which, such as lounges, may not be rooms in the ordinary sense at all—divided by the area of the grounds. Such buildings should be entirely excluded from the survey. On the other hand, small private hotels, nursing homes, etc., among ordinary residential property should be treated in the same way as their neighbours.

Various methods can be used for obtaining totals of habitable rooms; minute accuracy is not essential, and a house-to-house inquiry is unnecessary. It is frequently possible to obtain information from rating officers and building inspectors and other local authority officers, whose intimate knowledge of the locality, supplemented by reference to record books and house plans submitted for purposes of by-law consent in doubtful cases, normally proves quite adequate. In the rare cases where this is not so a representative sample survey undertaken by making personal inquiry at several houses of each type, the number of inquiries being proportionate to the total number of houses of that type, will give the information needed. If it is decided to do this, information should be obtained at the same time regarding the number of persons normally resident in each house visited for the purpose of the population density survey (see below). However, even a sample survey may well take more days to carry out than it takes hours to obtain information at least as accurate from local officials, so that it should not be undertaken unless this source fails or the survey is going to be undertaken in any case for population density purposes.

Carrying out the Population Density Survey. The demarcation of sub-areas and determination of their acreages will already have been carried out in connection with the accommodation density survey. All that has to be done is to determine the number of people who live in each block. This is by no means easy to do, except by means of direct sample surveys. The electoral registers give the adults living at each house and are conveniently arranged street by street but provide no clue as to the distribution of persons below the age of 21. Multiplying the total number of voters in an area by a factor $\dfrac{\text{total population of town}}{\text{total number of voters in town}}$ will make the grand total right but will mask any variation in the distribution of juvenile population. It may be possible to obtain the distribution of children of school age from school registers, but this leaves out of account all children below school age, all at private schools and all who have left school but not yet reached the age of 21.

Usually a sample survey will be the quickest method of obtaining reasonably accurate information, but even this is likely to prove a formidable task. For example, a town of 60,000 persons would contain perhaps 18,000 households, and it would probably be necessary to visit at least 10 per cent. of these, or 1,800. Allowing for time spent in movement, for a proportion of refusals to answer and for houses with no one at home, it is unlikely that more than 5 visits per hour could be made by each investigator, so that the field work alone would take about 350 man hours. This may not sound a great deal, but, repeated for each town in a county, it represents a serious expenditure of the limited survey labour available.

The information obtained from a population density survey, though immediately valuable, is unlikely to remain accurate for very long, for occupancy rates can change significantly in quite a short time. In towns where it is known that overcrowding is not a problem of serious proportions it may therefore be defensible to use figures based on the electoral rolls, and to accept the inaccuracy known to be entailed.

A simple division of the estimated total population of each area divided by its acreage gives population density in persons per acre.

Occupancy rates. $\dfrac{\text{Population density}}{\text{Accommodation density}}$ gives the occupancy rate in persons per habitable room; this information can be used in the calculation of areas required for the reception of overspill resulting from the reduction of occupancy rates in order to relieve overcrowding, as will be explained in Chapter 10.

Presentation of Residential Density Surveys. The whole of the information obtained from the three surveys just described should be tabulated to facilitate detailed calculations, but a map should also be prepared for each to emphasise visually its most important lessons.   For accommodation and population densities similar broad ranges of density should be differentiated, colours or hatchings becoming stronger as the density increases.

The ranges selected will naturally vary with the type of town concerned, but might typically be as follows:

Up to   20 rooms or persons per acre.
                     21– 40 rooms or persons per acre.
                     41– 60 „   „   „   „   „
                     61– 80 „   „   „   „   „
                     81–100 „   „   „   „   „
                     101–120 „   „   „   „   „
                     121–140 „   „   „   „   „
                     141–160 „   „   „   „   „

Occupancy rates should also be grouped, and suitable ranges might be:
     Less than 0·5 persons per habitable room.
          0·5 –0·75   „   „   „   „
          0·76–1·00   „   „   „   „
          1·01–1·25   „   „   „   „
          1·26–1·50   „   „   „   „
          Over 1·50   „   „   „   „

(See Figs. 30 and 31.)

Non-Residential Density.   In non-residential areas the measurement of density in terms of buildings, rooms or occupants per acre can seldom provide any useful information, yet some comparative measure of the quantity of accommodation on different sites is necessary.

For this purpose a method based upon the floor space index has been devised. This is described in great detail in the Ministry of Town and Country Planning's handbook on the Redevelopment of Central Areas.   The floor space index is the area of the total floor space of the buildings on any particular site divided by the area of the site, including half the area of any roads adjoining it. This gets over the difficulty of comparing directly the greatly differing sizes of buildings and rooms which obtains in non-residential areas. The F.S.I. survey can only usefully be applied to central areas of considerable size in which some redistribution of uses is contemplated.

The theory on which the F.S.I. survey is based is that sites can be developed up to various maxima of intensity according to their use, having regard to the need for a street system adequate to accommodate the traffic, both vehicular and pedestrian, to be expected in various parts of the central area, sufficient parking spaces and access for goods vehicles to buildings and satisfactory daylighting standards for buildings.

There are various practical difficulties which limit the usefulness of the F.S.I. survey. In the first place, if the town plan postulates an increase of population for the town, it by no means follows that accommodation for uses in the central area will need to be increased *pari passu*, for some uses may be able to serve considerable additional population without increased accommodation or the introduction of new firms.

Second, even in terms of existing population, it may often be extraordinarily difficult to find out whether the present central area accommodation is sufficient; it will frequently be the case that some firms are operating under a handicap because of cramped conditions, while others do not make full use of all their floor space. Yet others may have a sufficient area of floor space which is so awkwardly shaped and divided that it cannot be used to the best advantage.

Third, much of the redevelopment necessary in a central area is unlikely to take place for many years, and when it does take place the space requirements of some classes of users may have altered substantially.

Fourth, the maximum floor space indices fixed for the different use zones within the central area can at best only approximate to the optimum; they certainly are not capable of being exactly calculated, and, until a great deal of research has been carried out, whatever standards are fixed can hardly be regarded as more than intelligent guesses.

Fifth, at any given F.S.I., the proportion of site occupied by buildings obviously affects the area available for car parking. A tall building containing a given floor area will occupy less ground area than a lower one with the same floor area and leaves a larger area clear for car parking and pedestrian circulation.   A site developed with tall slim buildings can therefore sustain a higher Floor Space Index than one with low squat buildings, so that, in relation to design a code of control based on Floor Space Index should be in the form of a sliding scale. Development entailing a smaller site coverage than a given standard should be allowed an increase of Floor Space Index, and vice versa.   So far as I am aware no authority has done this, but without some such refinement Floor Space Index is an extremely crude method of control.

As a matter of fact it is doubtful whether, in relation to detailed design and development control, Floor Space Index is now a worthwhile tool.   The combination of daylight and parking standards seems capable of doing as much as the Floor Space Index and rather more efficiently.

Nevertheless, the Floor Space Index Survey is still very necessary as part of the information on which to base a town plan. It will give an estimate of the total floor space and land currently occupied by each central area use and some idea at least as to whether the amount of land for each or any needs to be increased or reduced, but a detailed and meticulously exact survey is hardly justified.

The following method, based on that described in the handbook on the Redevelopment of Central Areas, using as many time-saving approximations as possible, is thought to be satisfactory, providing that those doing the fieldwork are reasonably skilful and experienced. Experiment has shown that, using this method, two men working in a densely developed central area can survey about four acres a day, although in places where the intermixture of uses is exceptionally intimate this would, no doubt, have to be reduced somewhat.

1/2,500 is too small a scale on which to work in densely developed areas. If there are no maps published to a larger scale, photostat enlargements of the 1/2,500 sheets to 1/500 will prove a great help.

The information which the survey seeks to obtain is twofold: first, a statement of the total floor areas devoted to each class of use within the central area, distinguishing only between quite distinct kinds of use, e.g., shop, office, place of assembly, in conformity with the land use survey notation, and, second, a picture of the intensity of use of each street block in the central area in terms of its overall floor space index. A street block is an area entirely surrounded by roads other than secondary means of

the ground floor, they should be shown as proportions of the ground floor area. Normally the land use survey will have been carried out before the F.S.I. survey, and in this case it will be helpful, before setting out, to copy the land use survey colours lightly on to the field sheets, which should be cut to a convenient size to carry on a map board. It is essential to have a large blank margin for notes surrounding each field sheet.

The procedure should be to mark all the information required on the

SUMMARY OF FIELD SHEET

Sub-Division No.	Floor Areas in Square Feet						Total Floor Area	Total Site	F.S.I.
	Shop	Dwelling	Office	Wareh'se	Assembly	Industry			
							sq. ft.	sq. ft.	
1	4,375	1,250					5,625	5,400	1·04
2	1,500	375	750				2,625	3,200	0·82
3	1,450		725				1,875	3,300	0·57
4	4,800	3,120					7,920	2,400	3·30
5		1,280	3,200				4,480	2,100	2·13
6		628	4,406				5.034	2,400	2·10
7					450		450	900	0·50
8	1,280	1,280	1,280				3,840	1,280	3·00
9		2.695	1,925				4,620	1,575	2·93
10	1,690	760	760				3,210	2,800	1·15
11		2,940					2,940	2,450	1·20
12				2,800		1,400	4,200	4.950	0·85
13	6,000	1,500	2,400				9,900	5,500	1·80
14				7,245			7,245	14,000	0·52
15						7,000	7,000	6,300	1·11
16	1,925	577	577				3,079	4,400	0·70
17				2,100			2,100	3,000	0·70
Total	23,020	16,405	16,023	12,145	450	8,400	76,443	65,955	1·16

A sample F.S.I. survey field sheet and the information to be derived from it.

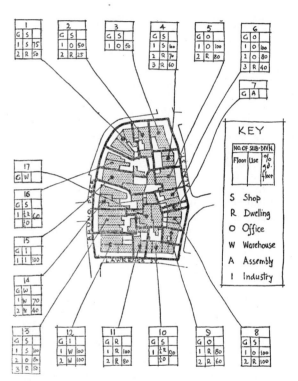

Fig. 27. An example of the kind of field sheet which needs to be prepared for a Floor Space Index Survey.

access to the buildings, but not intersected by any roads. Although the street block will frequently be a satisfactory unit over which to give an average F.S.I., some may be sub-divided into two or more areas of markedly different use or character of buildings, and where this is so each sub-area should form the unit.

No calculation of areas should be attempted in the field, but where, as is often the case, some of the upper floors of a building are of less area than

field sheets so that tables of floor areas and F.S.I. maps can be prepared from them in the office. (See Fig. 27.)

The method used is an approximate one; time should not be wasted in trying to secure a degree of accuracy for any particular site which will not be reflected in the final results as a whole. It should seldom be necessary to enter a building; a great deal of time will be spent in stating one's business and overcoming objections if this is done. External inspection of the windows of upper floors will nearly always enable a fair estimate to be made of the uses to which they are put, but every external wall of every site should be looked at, since some floors may be in multiple use, and inspection of one side only may give misleading information. In such cases the estimate made of the proportion of floor space on any particular floor used for each purpose is likely to be very inexact, but any estimate short of actually entering and measuring up rooms—obviously quite impracticable—would also be inexact.

It may very often be impossible in business areas to tell by visual inspection how much of the unbuilt-on space within a street block belongs to any particular building or part of a building. Where this is so a commonsense division should be made. The survey is for the purpose of estimating future needs, and the recording of illogical distributions of unbuilt-on space, which will often be due to purely fortuitous circumstances, will not help such estimates.

Measurement of the areas of buildings and sites is carried out in the office after the fieldwork has been completed. Although it is possible to do this by planimeter, scaling dimensions and doing the necessary multiplications by slide rule will probably be quicker and nearly as accurate.

If lack of funds or labour, or the relatively small amount of useful information expected from the survey in a particular town precludes even the approximate method just described, it is possible to get some idea of non-residential building quantities by an even more rapid method. The only fieldwork which this involves is to note the number of storeys of each building. The rest of the work would be done from the map and would consist simply of calculating the areas of buildings and sites as before, multiplying each building area by the number of storeys and taking the predominant use of each building, as indicated by the land use map, to be its sole use. Reduction of floor areas on upper floors due to setbacks would be ignored.

Clearly, such a survey would fall a long way short of accuracy, yet it would probably be better than no survey at all. It would assume that all uses of buildings, other than predominant uses, were purely ancillary, and this is often not far from the truth; it would exaggerate the total amount of floor space in the central area, but in many towns the error caused by this would not be dangerously large.

In each area made the subject of a F.S.I. survey note should be made of the existing F.S.I.s of one or more buildings or blocks devoted to each principal use which seem to function satisfactorily in regard to all the functions affected by F.S.I., so that regard may be had to these in fixing suitable maximum F.S.I.s for each use.

It should be noted that in connection with F.S.I. surveys the term " central area " is not necessarily confined to a single area for each town; in some very large towns there may be subsidiary centres where the quantity, variety and congestion of non-residential uses are sufficiently great to necessitate an F.S.I. survey as a preliminary to formulating Plans for redevelopment.

In London the " Plot ratio " is used to measure non-residential density instead of the " Floor Space Index ". The only difference between the

two is that Plot Ratio is measured over the net site, half widths of roads being ignored. As a measure for control of development of individual sites Plot Ratio is probably the better, since it prevents the unduly dense development of a site, such as a corner site, which happens to be adjoined by an exceptionally large area of road. For purposes of comprehensive development or redevelopment, however, Floor Space Index is clearly more useful.

9-4. THE AGE AND CONDITION OF BUILDINGS

History of Growth. This survey which can be mapped at a scale of 6 in. to one mile, or even 1/25,000, is one of those which provides the planner with general background information rather than specific pointers to solutions of problems. It tells him which parts of the town area were most popular for development, at different periods, the main directions of growth and the speed of growth in different directions. It is an easy map to prepare, in fact, many experienced Planners could prepare a fairly accurate one for a town of which they had no knowledge simply from the different types of layout, density, shapes of houses, etc., shown on the 1/2,500 map.

The method used is to colour or otherwise distinguish between areas first developed at different times, ignoring very small patches of development of a different period. Not very many periods should be distinguished and the dates selected should be arranged to coincide as nearly as possible with significant events in general history or the history of housing. Suitable dates would be:

Development before 1875 (The Public Health Act).
      ,,   between 1875 and 1914 (First World War).
      ,,   ,,   1914 and 1939 (Second World War).
      ,,   since 1939.

In addition, the earliest developed portions of the town should be distinguished; these often show very clearly the reasons for the town's origin and the form of its subsequent development. The date selected should be that of the earliest obtainable map of the town which is drawn sufficiently accurately for building sites on it to be positively identified; some very old maps are hopelessly indefinite.

Areas developed during succeeding periods can be identified from maps published at various times. It may not be possible to obtain maps of exactly the right date, but 6 in. to one mile Ordnance maps were published for most areas about 1880, which is near enough to 1875. These can be found in public libraries, museums and local authority offices. In one public library, at least, they are the maps offered for inspection to people who want general, not historical, information about the town!

Similarly, other 6 in. to one mile maps were published for most areas at various times between 1909 and 1914.

Assuming that fully up-to-date maps are available, as they should be (see page 114), it is a simple matter to identify the development between 1914 and 1939, since this only involves subtracting the readily identifiable post-war development.

It should be noted that a history of growth map is not quite the same thing as an age of buildings map. The latter shows the date at which the buildings at present on a site were erected, the former the date at which buildings were first erected on various sites. An age of buildings map will be required for areas in respect of which detailed redevelopment plans are to be prepared, but for the Town Map, which is concerned with areas, not individual buildings, it is unlikely that it will differ sufficiently from the History of Growth Map to justify being separately drawn.

Conditions of Buildings. A careful survey of the condition of buildings within a town is of great importance.

Condition surveys have one special characteristic: they are used to assist in determining programming, or the order in which Planning proposals are intended to be implemented far more than in deciding the actual nature of the proposals, but they do have some effect in this way also.

As a matter of simple economics it is desirable that those buildings most nearly worn out should be replaced before those which are still comparatively serviceable. In the case of urgent projects which involve the demolition of buildings, such as the construction of an inner ring road, detailed knowledge of the relative condition of buildings which lie within the possible limits of deviation of the route will greatly help to secure the optimum efficiency and economy; in many cases the selection of a route which requires a comparatively small expenditure on the acquisition of buildings in its path may be a decisive factor in securing that the project is in fact carried out.

For the general purposes of preparing a Town Map the degree of detail entered into by the Condition Survey need not be nearly as great as for the precise determination of a by-pass route; areas rather than individual buildings should be considered. The principles concerned are the same in either case but it is likely that information readily available from official sources will more often relate to the detailed conditions of small areas than to the relatively broad comparisons required for Town Map purposes. Official information, such as that prepared for slum clearance purposes, apart from covering too small a part of the town, is often, detailed though it may be, ill-adapted for purposes of comparison and is apt to include official wording which cannot be penetrated, and does not describe the real nature of the defects. This is of some importance because the selection and programming of areas for clearance by Local Authorities is not always done solely in the light of the impersonal technical data which are needed for Planning purposes. The personalities of councillors and political promises may well determine the choice of a particular area for early clearance rather than its physical decrepitude as compared with other areas.

Nevertheless, unless inordinate time and expense is to be incurred in carrying out a Condition of Buildings Survey, official information will largely have to be relied upon. Sanitary and Building Inspectors are often able to provide information which can be built up into a reliable estimate of condition although it was not originally collected for the purpose of deciding the relative urgency of redevelopment in different parts of the town.

There is little doubt that the best way of assessing the relative condition of buildings is to select a number of significant factors making for bad condition, to plot the incidence of each, and, by means of a sieve map, to determine the areas affected by many, few or no factors.

It is important that the factors chosen should not only be those which have a marked effect on condition but that they should be selective; if, as is common, hardly any of the houses in a town which were built before 1914 have bathrooms it is very little help to record the fact on the Condition of Buildings Map.

It is also necessary to choose factors which cannot be easily or economically changed. To take as an extreme example a factor which, for all its absurdity, has in fact been used, the existence of overcrowding in a house is no evidence whatever of its bad condition as a building. To take a case which may well cause genuine difficulty, the excessive smallness of rooms in the houses would often be a useful factor but the design of some houses might well be such that they could cheaply be converted into satisfactory dwellings by knocking two rooms into one.

The actual factors chosen and the number used must depend upon the physical circumstances in each individual town and, for the sake of economy of effort, upon what information already exists. It will usually be better to use not more than four important and selective factors than a larger number of less definite ones. Selection must also be affected by the time and money which can reasonably be devoted to the survey.

Conditions vary so much in different towns that no general rules can be given, but the following is a list of factors from which a selection might be made:

> Net density in excess of 120 habitable rooms per acre.
> Daylighting seriously inadequate.
> No bathroom.
> No indoor sanitation.
> No separate sanitary accommodation.
> No piped water supply.
> No main drainage.
> Rooms excessively small.
> Dampness.
> Bad structural condition.
> Inadequate garden or back yard space.
> Proximity of detrimental uses (noxious industry, etc.).

A small amount of fieldwork will probably be necessary in order to check the building inspector's views on structural condition, so that buildings with comparatively minor and remediable defects shall not be included.

Obviously the areas subject to the greatest number of unfitness factors are, *prima facie*, those in most urgent need of redevelopment.

It may be necessary to make separate condition surveys for non-residential areas, such as old industrial areas, where unfitness factors different from those used in the residential condition survey may be the most suitable.

9-5. FACTORS LIMITING DEVELOPMENT

This survey map is little more than a reproduction at a larger scale of the sieve map described in Chapter 6. (Fig. 15.) Any more detailed information which can be obtained for the area surrounding the town should be included. The collection of this for the whole region would frequently entail too much work to be justified but is of great assistance in selecting precise areas for future development. This information would probably not introduce fresh subjects, but would give a greater accuracy of boundary for the areas affected by the various factors. For example, any detailed local levelling operations which had taken place could be utilised to delineate areas of steep slope more precisely than could be done from published information.

It will often be of great importance to determine areas which can be drained by gravity into the existing sewerage system. Assuming that the system, or the particular part of it concerned, is capable of dealing with substantial additional volumes of sewerage, it will be far more economical to develop such areas than to resort to pumping or to create a separate sewerage system draining to a new sewage works. It may even pay to use the existing sewage works, if its capacity is sufficient, even though new main sewers have to be laid to supplement those existing.

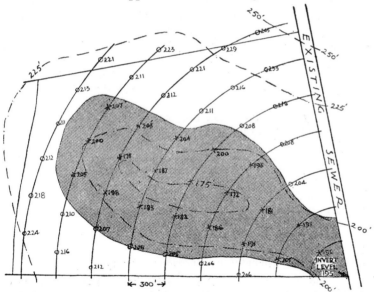

FIG. 28. Land not capable of being sewered by gravity is stippled. An illustration of the method of determination of such areas is described on this page.

The following is a method of determining rapidly and approximately the practicability of draining land by gravity; the work can be done considerably more speedily than would be supposed from the description.

The process is illustrated in Fig. 28.

(1) Obtain a 1/25,000 fully coloured Ordnance sheet covering the land to be examined. Transfer the contours crossing this land to the corresponding 1/2,500 or 6 in. to one mile Ordnance sheet. (The 1/25,000 scale is too small to work on.)

(2) Ascertain the invert level of the lowest accessible point of the nearest existing sewer and plot its position on the map, showing the height above datum of the invert level.

(3) Cover the area to be examined with a series of arcs drawn from this point, at intervals of about 300 feet.

(4) Figure the estimated ground levels along each arc. This can be done with fair accuracy by studying the contours intelligently.

(5) Determine which of these points can be drained into the sewer by gravity by applying the following formula :

$$\text{Level of point} - \left[\left\{ \begin{array}{c} \text{Distance to} \\ \text{selected point} \\ \text{on sewer} \end{array} \times \begin{array}{c} \text{Flattest} \\ \text{acceptable} \\ \text{gradient for} \\ \text{future sewers} \end{array} \right\} + \begin{array}{c} \text{Least} \\ \text{acceptable} \\ \text{depth below} \\ \text{surface for} \\ \text{inverts of} \\ \text{future sewers} \end{array} \right]$$

If the resultant figure is greater than the invert level of the existing sewer the point can be drained into the sewer, if less it cannot.

It will not, of course, be possible to determine accurately the flattest acceptable gradients for future sewers, since this depends upon their sizes, but the whole process is in any case an approximation and since the actual routes of the future sewers are not known and can, within limits, be varied to suit the contours, 1 in 300 is a reasonable figure to take. Five feet and eight feet are reasonable minimum and maximum depths of invert below the surface.

The points which, it appears, can be drained should be ringed and the points which cannot be drained should be marked with a cross. The land which can be satisfactorily drained can then be seen at a glance.

This method does not, of course, take account of land which is so steep that it prevents economical drainage, but skill and ingenuity in designing the routes of sewers will generally enable this difficulty to be overcome, whereas no ingenuity can make up for insufficient fall being available. The approximate nature of the results obtained from this method must be stressed. Much depends upon accurate estimation of the levels of the land.

9-6. CATCHMENT AREAS

In preparing the town plan it is useful to know the catchment areas or areas of influence of various public services, since the formation of satisfactory neighbourhood boundaries can sometimes be based on them.

The process is much the same as that described in Chapter 6 for determining the areas of influence of urban and rural settlements, but over a smaller area of more intense utilisation.

The factors used must be carefully chosen to indicate, so far as possible, the exercise of free choice. Schools, for example, are not a very satisfactory service from this point of view because administrative boundaries have a considerable influence upon their catchment areas. Shops, cinemas, pubs. and churches are better because freedom of choice is untrammelled. But even these are not perfect.

The factors governing choice are not solely related to convenience of location of access, or even the less easily assessable factors of social homogeneity—the tendency of groups of people with similarity of needs and outlook to carry on most of their day-to-day activities within the area inhabited by that group. The fact that a particular kind of shop is missing from one local group of shops but not another, the film circuit to which a cinema belongs, and hence, to some extent, the kind of film shown, the brew provided at a particular pub. and the personality of its landlord, the personality of the minister at one church compared with another, may all exert a substantial influence upon areas of influence. Furthermore, these are all factors liable to sudden change, while Planning is concerned with the much more permanent spatial distribution of general kinds of land use, so that the practical usefulness of mapping such local areas of influence in connection with the preparation of a development plan is necessarily limited.

But the usefulness, though limited, does exist. The coincidence and overlapping of the boundaries of different areas of influence can reveal the existence of common interests and social partnership throughout areas, which could not readily be deduced from inspection of map or ground, and it will usually be desirable to arrange Planning proposals with a view to preserving and enhancing such areas, which can properly be regarded as neighbourhoods in more than a purely physical sense.

The factors selected for mapping areas of influence should not only be free from artificial distortion but should be services used by the community as a whole, not merely by comparatively small sections of it. In the case of the local survey it will probably be quicker and more accurate to go to the suppliers of the services and obtain from them information as to the areas which they serve than to go to the consumers, although this may have to be done in cases of doubt or non-co-operation.

The boundary of the catchment area should be drawn so that it excludes exceptional outlying users who probably have special individual reasons for using that particular centre. To borrow a military term, the effective beaten zone rather than the 100 per cent. beaten zone should be mapped, and to do this it is probably safe to omit the most remote 10 or 15 per cent. of users.

Nursery schools, it is often said, should be sited so that no child needs to travel more than a quarter of a mile to get to one, small groups of shops supplying everyday needs should be sited at similar intervals, and so should some form of public open space, while larger local shopping centres and infant and junior schools might appropriately be provided within half a mile of all dwellings. A comparison of existing and ideal catchment areas will be helpful in indicating the appropriate location of new local service centres intended to serve both existing development and near-by proposed development.

I cautiously advance the view that, if time presses, the mapping of such

accessibility patterns as these in relation to existing facilities may well suffice as a guide to Planning proposals by showing clearly areas already developed which suffer from a lack of accessibility to existing facilities and the location of undeveloped land which is accessible to them, thus indicating in general terms the most satisfactory areas for new residential development from this point of view and the places in which new shops, schools and open spaces can best be located in order to strengthen the pattern of accessibility.

9-7. RELATIONSHIP OF PLACE OF WORK AND HOME

We turn now the the determination of another kind of catchment area of importance in the case of large towns of, say, a quarter of a million population or more, where the developed area is so large that the part of the town in which a worker lives may depend upon the location of his place of work because of the distances involved. Briefly, it is essential that the Planner should know, in general terms, where the bulk of the workers in a particular residential area work, and, conversely, the area from which large centres of employment draw their workers. It is a fundamental aim of Planning to provide most people with the opportunity to live reasonably close to their place of work, primarily in the interests of personal convenience and economy, secondarily in order to relieve urban traffic congestion.

Completeness and exactitude are not possible in this matter. The presence of two or more wage-earners with different employments in numerous households in itself precludes this, and personal considerations other than nearness to work influence the choice of location of homes. Places of employment, too, can be changed with much greater ease and frequency than homes. There will always be cases of people living at A and working at B while others work at similar jobs at A and live at B. These are economic absurdities, but, for various human reasons, are abundantly justifiable.

Nevertheless, it is essential that sufficient information should be available to ensure that development and redevelopment proposals, both of residential and industrial areas, shall not inevitably bring about crazy, general post, cross-town journeys to work for substantial numbers of people.

The method used for collecting the necessary information must necessarily vary according to the degree of co-operation which can be obtained from the Ministry of Labour or from employers. If the Ministry of Labour cannot supply sufficiently detailed information it will be necessary to approach all employers of more than about 100 people. Smaller concerns will not often provide information which is quantitatively significant, although the kinds of industry predominating in a particular town may make it advisable to adjust this datum figure upwards or downwards.

A list of addresses of employees would enable a catchment area for each concern to be mapped. Some firms, though co-operative, might feel that they were not entitled to divulge the private affairs of their employees, even to the extent of providing addresses, since a Local Planning Authority with sinister designs (though what these might be it is difficult to imagine) could readily relate addresses to names by the use of a local directory. In such cases information limited to the names of streets and not to particular numbers would be adequate, since employment catchment areas do not need to be defined as precisely as local supply service catchment areas.

The map prepared from a survey carried out by inquiry from employers should prove sufficient to meet Planning needs; it is, of course, only a one-way survey; it shows where concerns get their workers but does not show where all the workers living in a particular locality work; a sample survey will, however, enable a fair estimate of the latter to be made. A good example of such a survey is shown in Plate VII of " When We Build Again ", the Birmingham Planning Survey. This shows, by means of a series of diagrams, the places of work of the inhabitants of each main residential area.

9-8. TRAFFIC AND PARKING SURVEYS

Brief reference has already been made in Chapter 6-3 to the need for information about traffic volumes on main through routes. At the local level the subject is also of importance, and the information needed more detailed. It is easy enough to see which of a town's streets are frequently seriously congested, but less obvious how to apply remedies, and the cost of road improvements is so great that mistakes cannot be afforded.

It is essential, where the situation is not perfectly straightforward, not merely to know how much traffic uses a road but what kind of traffic it is; whether it is through traffic having an origin and a destination outside the town and using a congested route through the town merely for lack of a better, in which case the appropriate remedy may be a by-pass, or, on the other hand, if it is traffic which either originates in the town or has its destination there, in which case the remedy must necessarily lie in the improvement of the town's internal road system.

To this end an origin and destination census is of great assistance. The technical memorandum issued by the Ministry of Transport with Circular No. 612, provides valuable information about how to conduct such surveys. Four methods are described: (a) by direct interview; (b) by observation of registration numbers; (c) by the use of postcards, and (d) by attaching tags to vehicles.

Of these (b) is the only one which can be carried out without interference with road traffic and which could therefore be done at short notice without elaborate preparation and the co-operation of other authorities; although not the most accurate method, there seems no reason why it should not serve perfectly well for diagnostic purposes in connection with the preparation of a town Plan.

Those carrying out the survey work in pairs, one man to call out numbers, the others to book them. Usually, a pair will be required for traffic moving in each direction at each census point, and a census point must be established at each entrance and exit to the town. In order to facilitate observation they should, obviously, be established at points where traffic necessarily has to travel slowly.

In the case of a large town or one of exceptionally complicated structure, or where for some reason a specially detailed analysis of traffic needs to be made it may be necessary to place a cordon of observers around each of the main functional areas of the town as well as around the town as a whole. Obviously this will increase the cost of the survey very greatly but it may well be a cost which it is essential to accept. It may do more than give a detailed picture of existing traffic patterns; it may provide understanding of the reasons lying behind these, and hence give great help in deciding how to organise the traffic forecast which needs to be done in conjunction with the preparation of the Town Plan in order to check the adequacy of the Plan to deal with the new patterns of traffic which will emerge as a result of changes in the distribution of land uses proposed.

The number of each vehicle, its type, e.g., private car, lorry, tradesman's van, and the time it passes the census point are noted. By comparing the lists of each pair of observers the track of the vehicle through the town can be discovered. Where there are several alternative routes through the town internal census points will be necessary to establish this with certainty. Tests must be made to establish the normal time taken for a vehicle to pass between census points, and any which exceed this by more than twenty minutes are assumed to have made a call in the town—i.e., not to be through traffic.

A day must be chosen for the census when traffic conditions are normal. Where there is more than one traffic problem it may be necessary to do more than one census. For example, a market town which is also situated on a main route between London and South Coast resorts, may suffer severe traffic congestion both at the time of the weekly market and at week-ends in the summer. It is unlikely that the congestion from each cause will be at the same points, and it will be necessary to seek a remedy which will alleviate both.

The office work necessary to analyse the results of an origin and destination survey is great but for a town with any complexity of traffic it is essential.

As with most other surveys a good deal of economy can be secured by the use of short cuts and sampling. For example, a survey carried out over quite a short period at a time chosen because preliminary observation had shown it to be especially suitable might give results as good as and at a fraction of the cost of one carried out over a much longer period.

Parking surveys are also very important. How many vehicles are parked in or near the Central area of the town at different times of the day and week? How many frustrated parkers are there at given times who would have wished to park in the Central area if they could have found a space, but had to park outside it? How many habitually make the journey to the Central area on foot or by public transport because of the difficulties experienced in parking there? How many, for this reason, do not usually use the Central area at all but use the centre of some other town better equipped with parking facilities?

It is clear that answers to all these questions are needed in order to obtain an adequate idea of the parking needs of the Central area and of the capacities necessary for the roads and road intersections leading to it, both in relation to the town as it exists and to any proposed increase of population.

Full answers can only be obtained by sample surveys conducted by means of written or verbal questionnaires, and the subject obviously has a regional as well as a local aspect. This is not the place to elaborate on the exact methods appropriate; broadly, they will be similar to those suggested earlier for other sample surveys for Planning purposes. They are bound to be costly and to take some time to carry out and analyse, but a good starting point is to find out how many vehicles are parked in and near the Central area at significant times. This is difficult to do by ordinary survey methods because, like the sheep in the well-known story, vehicles decline to stay parked long enough to be counted accurately. Though there are ways of partially overcoming this difficulty the best solution is to take a series of aerial photographs at the significant times and from them to count the numbers of parked vehicles.

9-9. RESEARCH AND SOCIAL SURVEY

We need to know many basic facts in relation to Planning which have a more or less universal applicability. Is there a critical gradient above which development of land becomes materially more expensive? How can the degree of flooding which is seriously prejudicial to building be determined in relation to particular sites? Above what intensity of use do grass verges of streets become too trampled to be worth while? What floor area per worker is needed in different kinds of factories? What maximum F.S.I.s are appropriate for different central area uses? How many shops per 1,000 people should be provided in a local shopping centre? What acreages of service industries and large establishments are needed per thousand of the population? What is the ultimate traffic capacity of a road intersection? What distribution of flats and houses and of garden sizes among a normal population will produce the maximum satisfaction?

These, and many more, are questions which need answering, and none of them, so far as I know, can at present be answered with any real confidence. It is the function of *research* to find these answers, to establish authoritative yardsticks, while it is the function of *survey* to establish the facts relating to any particular area by reference to those yardsticks. A great deal of this kind of research needs to be done, yet the responsibility for carrying it out, the co-ordination of programmes, and even the subjects to be tackled have not yet for the most part been clearly stated.

Some of the questions asked above deal with purely objective physical facts, others introduce matters dealing with opinion and social habit. In respect of these latter questions the sociologist, who specialises in the analysis of human needs, desires and habits, has an important contribution to make.

With his entrance we are immediately plunged into consideration of extremely difficult philosophical, political and practical problems, almost inextricably interwoven. Very clear and honest thought is necessary to sort them out and come to valid conclusions. It is solely in the interests of clarity that the following points are stated in somewhat dogmatic fashion; each is susceptible to argument.

First, it can confidently be asserted that, in relation to Town Planning, sociological investigation is useless unless it answers questions in such a way that the answers help to determine the optimum distribution of land uses and building types. It is only by insistence on strict relevance to realisable Planning aims that the danger of getting lost in seas of unassessable information of doubtful relevance can be avoided. It is, of course, true, as with other aspects of Planning, that too harsh an insistence on direct relevance may prevent the emergence of much useful information, but the connection with action which is legally, politically, and economically feasible must not be lost.

It is absolutely essential that Planning should be entirely dissociated from sectional attempts to influence social pattern and behaviour, however enlightened and well meaning. It must be the Planner's aim to produce a physical environment in which rich and varied activities can flourish, in which religious, social and political gatherings, sports, work, education, amusement, lovemaking and trade can all be carried on at their highest pitch, but it is entirely illegitimate for him to seek to influence the particular way in which such of these as involve social organisation are run.

It is clearly impossible to consult all the potential users and occupiers of land and to meet all their conflicting wishes regarding the details of layout. It is the duty of democratically elected representatives to create what they conceive to be the optimum arrangement in the case of public development and to require it (so far as it is in the public interest to do so) in the case of private development. To what extent the wishes of the public generally are met as regards the provision of flats rather than houses, of terrace houses rather than semi-detached, and in architectural style, is extremely doubtful.

It is no part of my design, even if I were competent to do so, to embark on a treatise concerning sociological method, but a few notes regarding the kind of information useful for Planning purposes which point out some elementary pitfalls may be helpful to the Planner who is forced to undertake sociological investigation without expert assistance.

To be helpful, information of this kind, which may be obtained by personal interrogation, the filling in of questionnaires, or partly by both methods, must be relevant, representative and realistic.

As regards the first, at the risk of becoming wearisome, I emphasise that the information obtained must in some way be capable of being translated into terms of the distribution of land uses; as regards the second it is obviously essential that all classes of opinion should be obtained; as regards the third, the form of question must not be of the " Have you stopped beating your wife ? " or even " Would you like a net income of £5,000 a year ? " type. It must be capable of eliciting an unambiguous answer related to practical possibility.

For example, it would be of little use asking the inhabitants of a large town acutely short of land whether they would like quarter-acre gardens and 18-hole golf courses adjoining all residential areas. " Would you like ? " must be accompanied by an indication of the sacrifice which may be involved if the wish is granted.

Again, when it is a matter of choosing between alternatives it is not much use asking the opinions of people who have no knowledge of one of the alternatives. For example, an expression of preference for a semi-detached house rather than a terrace house is of little value if it comes from people who have never seen, let alone occupied, a well-designed modern terrace house. Similarly, preference for a house rather than a flat is of small value from people who have no knowledge of really well-designed flats unless the reasons given for the preference are independent of the kind of flat visualised.

The kind of thing which needs to be brought to light is the proportion of people who really welcome gardens of different sizes, the proportion of people who really prefer a good flat to a good house, the kind of leisure activity in which people indulge, the number of rooms and disposition of functions between the various rooms which are desired, and so on.

The framing of questions demands extraordinary care, for an apparently clear and unbiased question may, through some accidental infelicity of wording, evoke a misleading response. For example, it has been related that when members of a somewhat poverty-stricken coloured community in the United States were asked if they were in favour of taxing profits a surprisingly small number of affirmative answers were given. The people concerned were in the " Bible belt " and most failed to distinguish between " profits " and " prophets ". Again, questionnaires asking people whether they consider that they belong to the upper class, middle class or lower class have been known to bring quite different patterns of response than when the same people were asked whether they considered themselves to be members of the upper class, middle class or *working* class. " Working class " has not the pejorative ring of " lower class ".

Other sociological investigation takes the form of detailed analysis of the structure of communities, their social ranking and social homogeneity. A whole section of Max Lock's Middlesbrough Survey and Plan, written by Ruth Glass, is devoted to this kind of study. With great respect, and fully conscious that the error may well be mine, I am bound to say that much of this seems to me altogether irrelevant to the purpose of preparing a Plan, however great its sociological interest and significance.

Demography, or the study of population is an important branch of sociology. Probable future changes in population due to natural increase and changes in family structure are of vital importance to the Planner, but most decidedly not a suitable subject for investigation for anyone but a qualified statistician. This applies, too, to the study of migration from one area to another, which, in the absence of any counteracting Planning action, may have important effects upon the population of an area.

9-10. DETAILED SURVEY

Detailed survey relates to areas of neighbourhood unit size or less, for which detailed Plans (known as comprehensive development area maps or supplementary town maps) have to be prepared. It will be necessary to take sufficient levels for contours at 5 ft. vertical interval to be interpolated. Information about all natural features, including those such as copses, small quarries, hedges, and individual trees, which are too small to have been considered at earlier stages of survey, are required and the routes, depths and capacities of all public services. Details of any existing buildings, tracks and roads will also have to be obtained. In short, it will be necessary to obtain all the information which a prudent developer would wish to have

before deciding on the form of development to be undertaken. The sieve technique of survey analysis can still be employed here in a modified form; all areas of steep slope and unfavourable aspect should be mapped. The detailed levels obtained will enable this to be done very accurately.

Small areas of special beauty which it would be appropriate to keep as local open space should also be marked. The sieve map should build up to give a picture of all the individual small areas of land which ought not to have buildings actually placed on them (although some of them may form parts of the curtilages of buildings). Detailed analysis of this kind can do a great deal to reduce the labour of formulating satisfactory detailed proposals.

As indicated earlier, where areas of existing development are to be re-developed much additional material will be needed. Detailed information about the floor space devoted to different uses, the household composition of residents who will have to be rehoused, the condition of individual buildings, ownerships and so forth will all have to be obtained and mapped. Not all of this will be strictly relevant to making decisions about the physical form of the Plan to be adopted. Some of it will relate only to the actual process of development, but the two merge into each; they cannot be definitely separated.

9-11. VILLAGE SURVEY

Villages in which substantial development or redevelopment is contemplated will require individual consideration as regards the amount and nature of local survey necessary. There is no point in using a sledge-hammer to crack a nut; normally all that should be needed is a detailed land use survey, a sieve map dealing with physical characteristics, and an investigation of the routes and details of public services. The area dealt with is usually so small that local survey and detailed survey can be combined.

9-12. SURVEY FOR NEW TOWNS

Only a brief word need be said about survey work before the preparation of a Plan for a New Town, which will never exceed the scope of that required in connection with an existing town, and, in the case of a virgin or *demie-vierge* site, will be limited to physical surveys: topography, agricultural value, landscape features, ease of provision of services and the like. Only if the site has a substantial amount of existing development upon it will density and condition surveys be important. It may well be, of course, that very elaborate investigations have to be undertaken in order to determine the practicability of providing water supply or dealing with the disposal of sewage, but upon these depend whether a particular site is in fact selected for a New Town, so that they form part of the process of regional survey.

9-13. CONCLUSION

Survey is a continuing process of very great social and economic importance. Even the most backward authorities will, in the course of their quinquennial revision of survey, have the opportunity of bringing their surveys to a reasonable degree of completeness and satisfactory presentation. Such surveys have uses far wider than the mere preparation of statutory Development Plans; they constitute a record of value to all land users, industrialists, traders and administrators. Lack of space has prevented consideration of the ways in which a Planning survey can appropriately be modified and extended to be of special use to bodies other than the Local Planning Authority, but there is scope for much useful co-operation in this way.

Other countries which have not yet adopted a full land Planning policy will sooner or later begin Planning survey, so that although much of the most important local survey work has already been done in this country, no apology is offered for a fairly thorough treatment of the subject, based on the assumption that a complete programme of fieldwork and map preparation is necessary.

Finally, lengthy though this chapter has been, it contains little regarding the tabulation and written analyses of surveys, which will often be needed.

The essence of survey is presentation in map or diagram form; tabulation presents no considerable problems, and involves merely a somewhat wearisome process of measurement and calculation. This can, I suggest, well be left to the imagination of the reader. The kind of tabulation I refer to is the compilation of tables showing total areas devoted to open spaces of various kinds, total shop frontages, total areas devoted to each kind of land use, calculation of overall town density and so on. This work can be elaborated indefinitely, but the survey maps are the basis for practically all of it; most of it should only be undertaken as and when the need for a particular item becomes apparent, otherwise a great deal of written junk, seldom or never referred to, is likely to be amassed.

" Surveys for Town and Country Planning " by J. N. Jackson (Hutchinson, 1963) gives an admirably full account of the subject, and is especially good on sources of information, sampling methods and questionnaires, which have been dealt with very briefly here.

Figs. 29 to 38 illustrate local surveys and Town Plans based upon them.

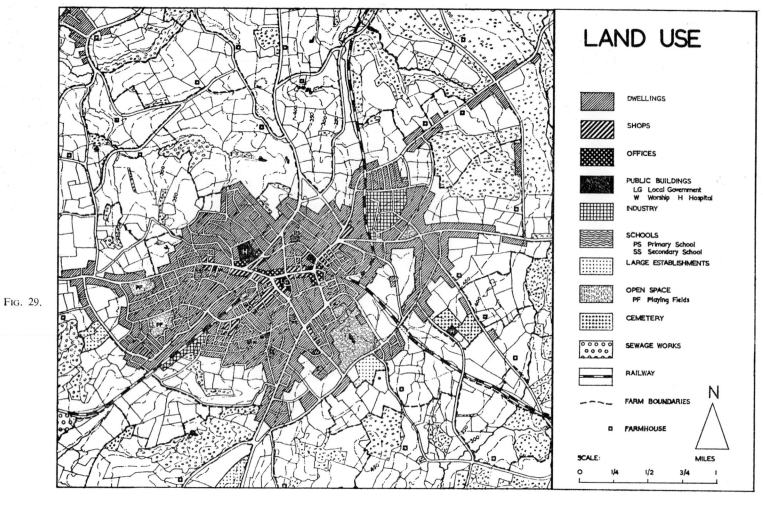

LAND USE

DWELLINGS

SHOPS

OFFICES

PUBLIC BUILDINGS
LG Local Government
W Worship H Hospital
INDUSTRY

SCHOOLS
PS Primary School
SS Secondary School
LARGE ESTABLISHMENTS

OPEN SPACE
PF Playing Fields

CEMETERY

SEWAGE WORKS

RAILWAY

FARM BOUNDARIES

FARMHOUSE

SCALE: MILES

0   1/4   1/2   3/4   1

N

FIG. 29.

FIGS. 29—37. The following illustrations show summaries of surveys carried out for TREMEL and the TOWN MAP and PROGRAMME MAP prepared. The proposals conform with those in the first and second stage Regional Plans shown in Figs. 16 and 17.

The present population of the town is 58,420 and that proposed under the Plan 70,420.

Tremel is to be imagined as a town in a state of serious physical decay but of considerable business and industrial importance. As shown in Fig. 14, it imports considerable numbers of workers. Under the Regional Plan it is proposed to expand Tremel in order to receive 12,000 additional population partly as the result of metropolitan decentralisation, partly in order to accommodate workers who at present have to travel to the town to work. The large increase of land for industrial purposes, however, is needed almost entirely to relieve the very severe congestion under which industry in Tremel at present labours, not to create new places of employment.

The expansion of Tremel also provides the opportunity to regroup the present very

scattered Central Area Uses, a process facilitated by many of the buildings concerned being old and in bad condition.

In other respects the Plan follows fairly conventional lines, but one special point is worth noting. Topographical difficulties prevent even outward growth from the centre and also make it appropriate to provide a quite unusually large amount of parkland, since there are substantial areas of land quite near the centre of the town which it would be uneconomical to build upon, and for which the only reasonable use is as parks.

As explained in Chapter 11, during the processes of redevelopment a great deal of amendment to the layout of roads would naturally occur, but the Town Map is concerned with changes of use and of fundamental structure so that only those road proposals which affect the Town as a whole are shown.

Opportunity is taken to provide for the eventual removal and inclusion in open space or restoration to agriculture of several outlying ribbons of housing.

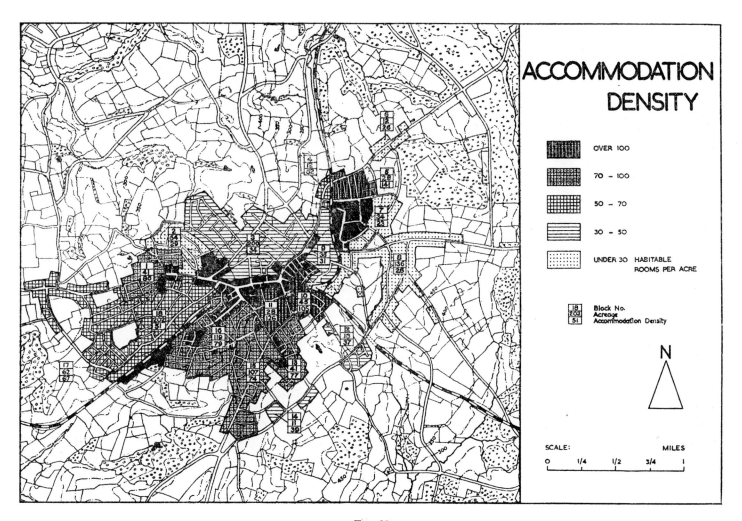

Fig. 30.

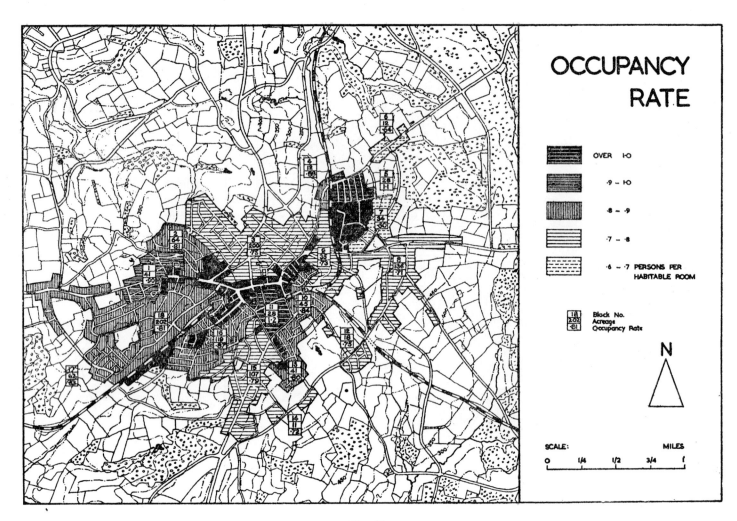

OCCUPANCY
RATE

OVER 1·0

·9 – 1·0

·8 – ·9

·7 – ·8

·6 – ·7 PERSONS PER
HABITABLE ROOM

Block No.
Acreage
Occupancy Rate

N

SCALE: MILES
O   1/4   1/2   3/4   1

Fig. 31.

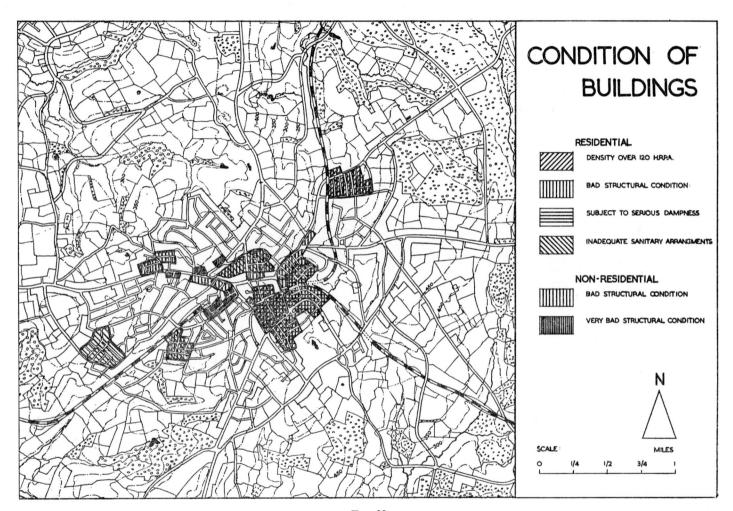

FIG. 32.

132

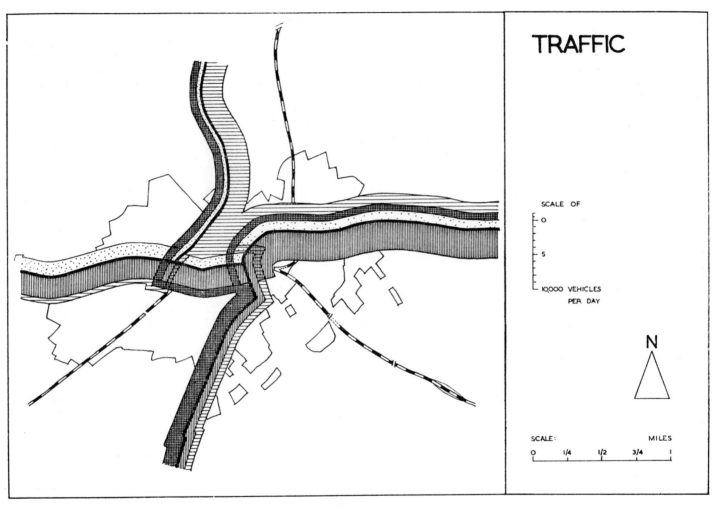

TRAFFIC

SCALE OF
0

5

10,000 VEHICLES
PER DAY

N

SCALE: MILES
0   1/4   1/2   3/4   1

Fɪɢ. 33.

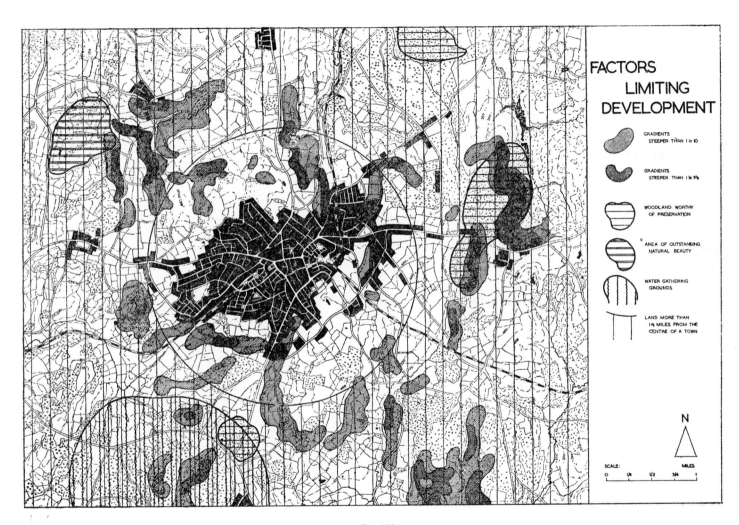

FACTORS
LIMITING
DEVELOPMENT

GRADIENTS
STEEPER THAN 1 in 10

GRADIENTS
STEEPER THAN 1 in 7½

WOODLAND WORTHY
OF PRESERVATION

AREA OF OUTSTANDING
NATURAL BEAUTY

WATER GATHERING
GROUNDS

LAND MORE THAN
1½ MILES FROM THE
CENTRE OF A TOWN

N

SCALE: MILES
0   1/4   1/2   3/4   1

FIG. 34.

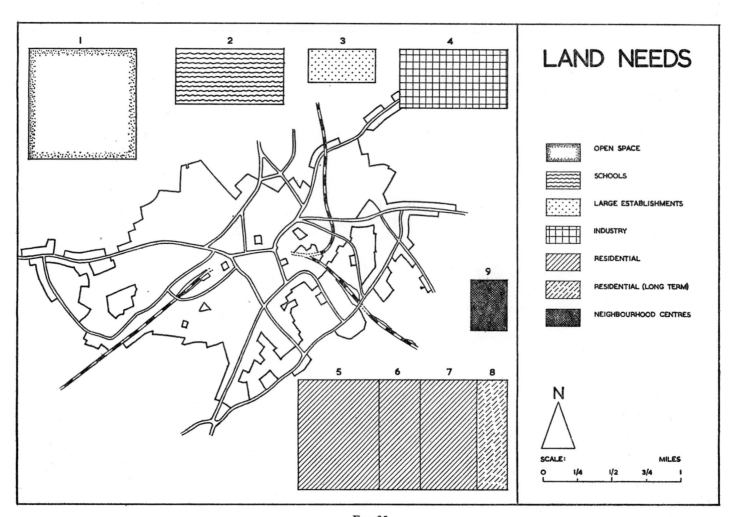

FIG. 35.

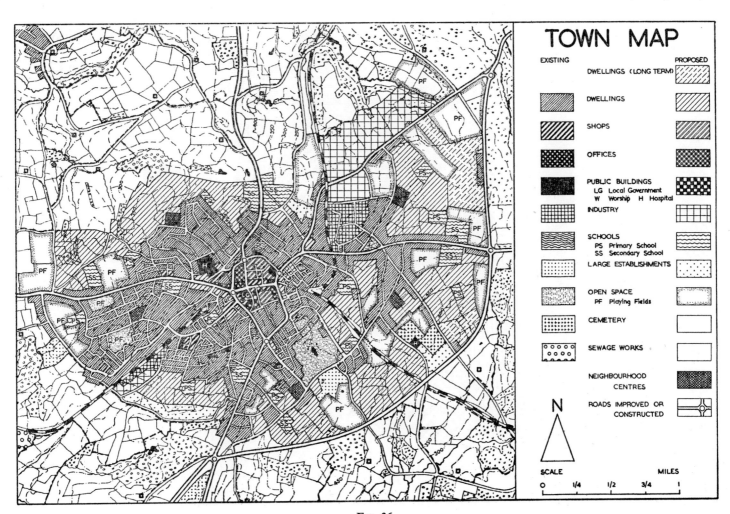

TOWN MAP

EXISTING   PROPOSED

DWELLINGS (LONG TERM)

DWELLINGS

SHOPS

OFFICES

PUBLIC BUILDINGS
  LG Local Government
  W Worship   H Hospital

INDUSTRY

SCHOOLS
  PS Primary School
  SS Secondary School

LARGE ESTABLISHMENTS

OPEN SPACE
  PF Playing Fields

CEMETERY

SEWAGE WORKS

NEIGHBOURHOOD
CENTRES

ROADS IMPROVED OR
CONSTRUCTED

N

SCALE   MILES
0   1/4   1/2   3/4   1

Fig. 36.

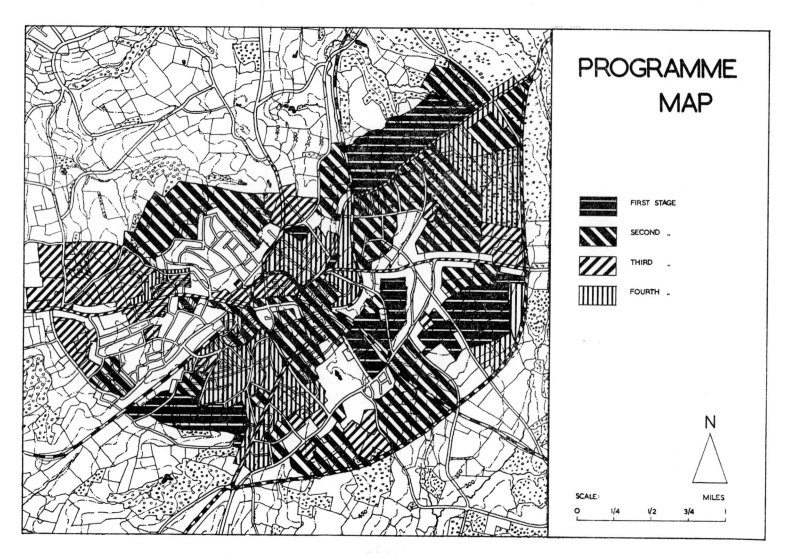

FIG. 37.

SUMMARY OF RESIDENTIAL DENSITY SURVEYS

Cartogram No.	Acres	Acc. Dens.	O.R.	P.P.A.	Total Persons
1	41	86	0·90	77·4	3,173
2	64	29	0·81	24	1,525
3	200	34	0·75	32·50	5,100
4	12	62	0·88	54·56	655
5	28	141	1·1	155	4,340
6	12	26	0·64	16·64	200
7	34	23	0·60	13·80	469
8	136	28	0·71	19·88	2,704
9	35	31	0·73	22·63	792
10	45	105	0·84	88·20	5,654
11	28	126	1·20	151	4,241
12	18	37	0·75	27·75	500
13	41	77	0·80	61·60	2,526
14	11	39	0·72	28·08	309
15	107	74	0·79	58·46	6,255
16	119	79	0·87	68·73	8,179
17	62	67	0·83	55·60	3,447
18	202	51	0·81	41·31	8,344
TOTAL	1,195				58,423

LAND REQUIREMENTS FOR OVERSPILL REVEALED BY RESIDENTIAL DENSITY SURVEYS

Cartogram No.	Persons in Excess of 0.8 O.R.	Rooms in Excess of 50 H.R.P.A.
1	353	1,476
2	19	—
3	—	—
4	60	144
5	1,183	2,548
6	—	—
7	—	—
8	—	—
9	—	—
10	189	2,475
11	1,411	2,128
12	—	—
13	—	1,107
14	—	—
15	—	2,568
16	659	3,451
17	124	1,054
18	103	202
TOTAL	4,101 At 40 P.P.A. = 102·5 Acres	17,153 At 50 H.R.P.A. = 343 Acres

SPACE STANDARDS FOR TOWN MAP

Accommodation Density	50 H.R.P.A.
Occupancy Rate	0·8
Playing Fields	6 Acres per 1,000 people
Parks	1 Acre per 1,000 people
Schools	Ministry of Education Standards
Large Establishments	2 Acres per 1,000 people
Neighbourhood Centres, Sub-centres, etc.	12 Acres per 10,000 people

Industry: 20% of total population in industrial employment, accommodated at 50 workers per gross industrial acre.

The remaining survey maps are much as described in Chapter 9. It will be noticed that condition of non-residential buildings is assessed in relation to structural condition only. This is done because so many of them are so bad structurally that this is the predominant factor.

The sieve map showing factors limiting development is necessarily shown at a smaller scale than the remainder in order to include a wide area of search for developable land.

LAND USE

Use	Existing	Additional needed to fulfil standards	Total
	Acres	Acres	Acres
Railways and Main Roads	181	—	181
Central Area and Public Uses	95	—	95
Cemetery	28	—	28
Open Space:			
Playing Fields	28	394	422
Parks	64	6*	70
Large Establishments	67	73	140
Schools	9	211	220
Industry	61	219	280
Neighbourhood Centres and Sub-centres	19	66	85
Residential:	1,195		
New Population		300	
Reduction of Occupancy Rate to 0·8		102	
Reduction of Accommodation Density to 50 H.R.P.A. ... 343			
Less saving on redevelopment of old low density housing ... 20			
		323	
Add residential land lost by change of use 25			
		348	
1st 20 years (⅔)		232	
Ultimately (⅓)		116	1,945
TOTAL	1,747	1,719	3,466

*Very much more than this is provided.

The PROGRAMME MAP is divided into four stages and indicates the order both of development and redevelopment. As explained in Chapter 10, a Programme Map ought to show both programming and the land uses involved, but this is hardly possible with black and white presentation. Very rapid implementation of the Town Plan is envisaged, since, as will be seen, the new development to take place in the fourth stage consists principally of that shown on the Town Map to take place after 20 years, the first three stages being virtually completed during the first 20 years.

138

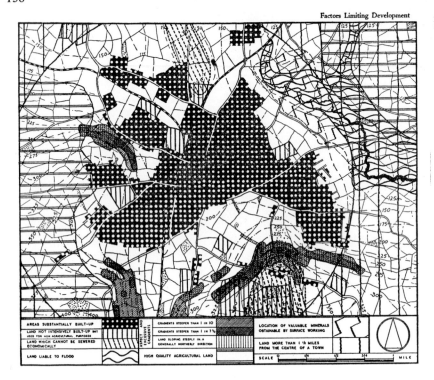

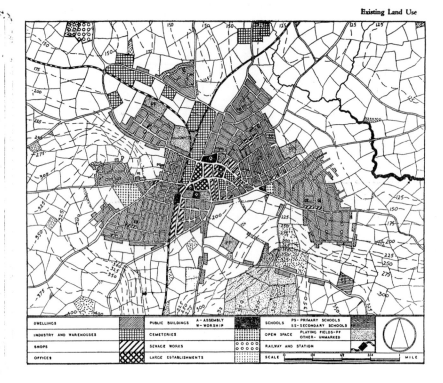

Traffic Flow.

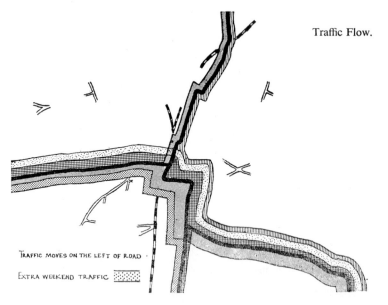

Fig. 38. This is another example showing a Town Plan and some of the principal surveys on which it is based. The maps are placed so that they can be seen together and easily compared. This illustration shows a more conservative Plan than that for the town in Figs. 29-37. One of the main differences is that it is here deemed necessary to arrange for the progressive decrease of occupancy rates, which, it will be seen, considerably complicates the calculations needed.

The town has at present a population of 47,000, which the Regional Plan proposes should increase to 50,000. There is a good deal of industry, some of it on very congested sites, but the town derives much of its importance from the administrative and commercial functions which it performs.

There are valuable minerals in the river valley to the east of the town, working of which is shortly to be begun.

The golf course to the south of the town is in parkland open to the public, so that no very large amount of new public open space other than playing fields needs be provided.

The traffic flow diagram shows the generalised results of an origin and destination survey. It gives only data relating to through traffic, there being no special aspects of importance concerning the distribution of stopping traffic.

It will be noticed that the space standards used are not identical with those in Fig. 36. In particular the standards for schools are more liberal than those now current.

Land Needs

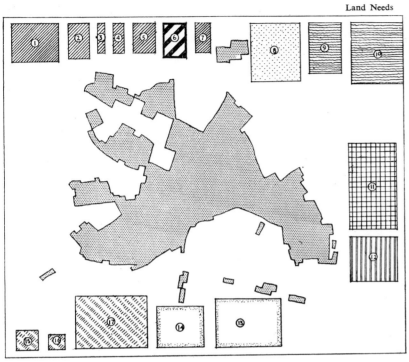

Town Map

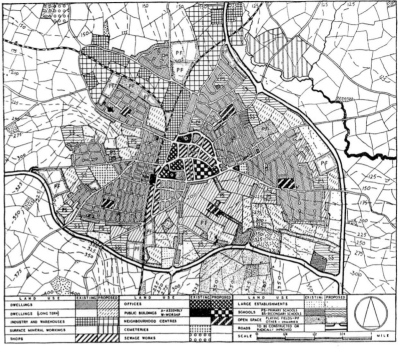

LAND USE	EXISTING	PROPOSED	LAND USE	EXISTING	PROPOSED	LAND USE	EXISTING	PROPOSED
DWELLINGS			OFFICES			LARGE ESTABLISHMENTS		
DWELLINGS (LONG TERM)			PUBLIC BUILDINGS A-ASSEMBLY W-WORSHIP			SCHOOLS PS-PRIMARY SCHOOLS SS-SECONDARY SCHOOLS		
INDUSTRY AND WAREHOUSES			NEIGHBOURHOOD CENTRES			OPEN SPACE PLAYING FIELDS-PF OTHER = UNMARKED		
SURFACE MINERAL WORKINGS			CEMETERIES			ROADS TO BE CONSTRUCTED OR RADICALLY IMPROVED		
SHOPS			SEWAGE WORKS			SCALE		

Existing land uses are as follows :—

	Acres
IN CENTRAL AREA:	
Shops	36
Offices	19
Public Buildings	9
Industry and Wholesale Warehouses ...	9
Open Space	9
Dwellings	15
Total of Central Area	97
ELSEWHERE :	
Industry and Wholesale Warehouses	115
Dwellings	682
Open Space : Playing-fields 44	
Other 11	
Golf Course (part only shown) ... 200	255
Schools : Primary 4	
Secondary 18	22
Large Establishments	31
Shops	30
Public Buildings	7
Allotments	19
Cemeteries	22
Sewage Works (part only shown)	75
Total of all non-agricultural uses	1,355

Land required to implement the proposals of the Town Map.
(Numbers correspond with Land Needs diagram).

REQUIREMENTS DURING FIRST 20 YEARS :   *Acres*

1. Increase of population by 3,000 at 40 persons per acre   75
2. Overspill of 1,800 rooms from the worst areas of existing housing, occupying 25·7 acres with an average accommodation density of 120 habitable rooms per acre, to be redeveloped at 50 habitable rooms per acre... 36
   Less allowance for more intense development of old housing, 8 acres in extent, at present at a density of 12 habitable rooms per acre and to be redeveloped at 50 habitable rooms per acre 6   30
3. Overspill from 1,200 rooms occupying 11 acres, with an average occupancy rate of 1·6, which is to be reduced to 1·3 9
   Less 50 habitable rooms added by conversion of houses into flats 1   8
4. Nursery Schools* 15
5. Service Industry at 6 acres per 10,000 population* 30
6. New Neighbourhood Centre plus allowance for houses displaced by redevelopment in Central Area and by creation of neighbourhood centres in areas already built up 35
7. Sites for neighbourhood sub-centres and isolated public buildings* 20

Total residential and ancillary requirements for first 20 years 213

8. Large establishments at 3 acres per 1,000 people ... 150
   Less existing 31   119

C./f. 332

	Acres B./f. 332
9. Schools : Primary	75
Less existing	4
	71
10. Secondary	158
Less existing	18
	140
11. Industry and Warehouses	280
Less existing to be retained	115
	165
12. Area for extraction and processing of minerals ...	90
13. Playing-fields at 3½ acres per 1,000 people ...	175
Less existing	44
	141
14. Other open space	90
Less existing (other than Golf Course)	11
	79
Total 20-year requirements	1,018

LONG-TERM REQUIREMENTS:

15. Occupancy rates to be reduced from an average of 1·2 to 0·8 within an area of 30 acres with an average accommodation density of 60 habitable rooms per acre   19
16. Occupancy rates to be reduced from an average of 1·0 to 0·8 within an area of 40 acres, with an average accommodation density of 50 habitable rooms per acre   10
17. Overspill, at 50 habitable rooms per acre, arising from reduction to 50 habitable rooms per acre of 187 acres at present at an average of 90 habitable rooms per acre   150

Total long-term requirements   179

*Not separately indicated on the Town Map.

CHAPTER 10

PREPARATION OF THE TOWN PLAN

10-1. INTRODUCTORY

The two previous chapters have paved the way for consideration of the central job of the Town Planner—Planning towns. This stage has been reached without consideration of space standards for the various uses which make up a town or of the requirements for road layout, of town and neighbourhood centre design and so on, all of which necessarily affect the form taken by the Town Plan. As explained in the Introduction, it has seemed better to proceed consistently from the general to the particular, but the reader who feels that he cannot think properly about Town Plans without first getting his mind clear about standards and detailed design is invited to break off here and read Part II before tackling this chapter. The order of chapters is for the benefit of the probably more numerous class of persons who feel unable to understand argument about detail before acquiring some comprehension of the whole.

Chapter 8 examined the characteristics of towns at some length and attempted to suggest criteria for a satisfactory town. Chapter 9 outlined the kind of information which is needed in order to prepare a good Plan, one which will enable the resources likely to be available for development, redevelopment and preservation to be put to the most effective use in order to produce a convenient, safe and sightly town.

We now have to discuss the actual methods by which this may be done.

It will be well to emphasise here that from many points of view the designing of a new town is a very much easier process than the preparation of a Plan for the reshaping of an existing town. In the former case the siting of land uses and the design of the road system is relatively unhindered by existing conditions, and, if the town is genuinely to be a new one, the correction of past errors, which is so important a part of the replanning of existing towns, is hardly involved.

The peculiar problems of most new towns are the creation of a special visual character, the fostering of social cohesion and the correct deployment of capital rather than those of actual Town Planning, so that further separate consideration does not appear to be necessary.

The process of preparing a Town Plan may be divided into the following stages:—

I. *Determination of space standards for all uses.* This will not be considered in this chapter since it is fully dealt with in Chapters 12 to 17. It may be said here that the more this can be a technical rather than a political process the better are the results likely to be.

II. *Determination of the Total Amount of Land Required for the Town*, taking into account any new population and industry postulated by the Regional Plan, any additional land needed in order to bring existing uses up to proper space standards, and on the other hand allowing for land at present developed at an inappropriately low intensity which it is thought practicable to redevelop more intensively. As regards this last item, the assessment of practicability, particularly in relation to time, is likely to be very difficult.

III. *Examination and solution of the town's road problems and the problems of other forms of transport if these arise.*

IV. *The selection of actual sites, at present undeveloped, for urban use in order to accommodate all the additional areas determined by II above.*

V. *The arrangement of all the land uses and transport routes concerned to form as satisfactory a totality as possible*, using as criteria those suggested in Chapter 8, viz. the most effective use of the resources likely to be available to produce a convenient safe and sightly town.

VI. *The determination of the sequence in which future development shall take place*—known as programming—so far as this is within the control of the Planning Authority, in order to avoid undue dislocation of the town during the implementation of the Plan and also to ensure that the capital invested in past development shall not be prematurely lost as a result of demolition or the vacation of properties being brought about before this is necessary.

Although the sequence given above is appropriate in general terms it is likely to be necessary constantly to examine the requirements under one head in the light of those under others, if the final result is to be the best possible.

It would be foolish to determine space standards for a particular town according to some theoretical system if the local topography, the nearness of other towns or the social habits prevalent in that town made it clear that some departures from theoretical norms would be desirable. The town's road problems cannot be finally solved without reference to the actual location and extent of the sites to be used for future development, since the character and availability of land in particular situations is bound to affect the routeing of any new main roads considered desirable. Again, the choice of land for future development must often be substantially affected by the existing pattern of development; it would be highly inappropriate to select land for development in only one quadrant of the town because of its special physical suitability for development, if, in fact, in other quadrants there were incomplete neighbourhoods requiring expansion for their proper functioning. Clearly, therefore, III cannot be considered except in relation to IV, IV cannot be considered except in relation to V, while V cannot be considered except in relation to VI. These are obvious links between the different headings; there are many others.

In the majority of cases, nevertheless, the solution of road problems is likely to be the principal determinant of the form which the plan takes, for in very many towns it is the existing road system which is the most seriously defective part of the town, and which poses the most severe problems for its solution. Very often the solution cannot be obtained without accepting some distortion of other aspects of the Plan.

The use made of survey information in preparing proposals should already have become clear from a reading of Chapters 6 and 9, and will be further explained later on in this chapter. Meanwhile, it may be helpful to point out that, in order to deal with No. II above, land use, density and condition surveys are needed, to deal with No. III traffic surveys are needed, to deal with No. IV all the factors comprised in a factors limiting development map as well as an existing land use map are needed, to deal with No. V the existing land use map is needed, to deal with No. VI a condition of building survey is needed.

10-2. STAGES OF PREPARATION

The steps in the preparation of the Plan briefly listed above will now be more fully discussed, with the exception of No. I.

(II). The amount of land needed for future development

This is basically a straightforward calculation, but it is complicated in several ways by the need to make assumptions regarding future events. The steps in this calculation are as follows; their application is illustrated in Figs. 35 and 37.

(1) *Accommodation for future increase of population.* The present population of the town deducted from its intended future population—assuming that some increase is being planned for—gives the population for which no accommodation, even inadequate, already exists. The net residential density, in habitable rooms per acre, at which these people are to be housed should have been decided. It is best to decide an average net residential density for the town as a whole, leaving any substantial areas of exceptionally high or low density to be dealt with as special cases; they will not greatly affect the town's total space requirements.

The average occupancy rate must also be estimated; this may vary considerably, according to the general economic level of the town's citizens but a reasonable general figure might be somewhere between $0\cdot7$ and $0\cdot8$. The intended increase of population divided by the net residential density and by the occupancy rate gives the total area required for *housing* for these people.

(2) *Accommodation for buildings displaced on redevelopment of areas built up too densely.* The redevelopment of excessively densely built areas means that the same number of habitable rooms cannot be replaced on the site, the remainder, colloquially known as " overspill," must be put elsewhere.

The problem here is to decide which areas are to be regarded as possible subjects for redevelopment within a reasonable time. Although consideration of areas for redevelopment should not, in my view, be limited to those which can be dealt with within twenty years, in order to produce a useful Plan some kind of limit must be observed. For example the redevelopment of soundly built houses dating from the early years of the present century is so remote that, even if they are built at an excessive density, it is hardly realistic to include them.

Here the condition of buildings map described in Chapter 9 is useful. It enables areas to be selected in which, because of excessive density, unhealthiness, bad structural condition, lack of daylight and so on, standards are below not merely the ideal, but the civilised, and redevelopment must be regarded as urgent, even if it cannot, so far as can be seen at present, be carried out within twenty years. When these areas have been selected it is simple to calculate from the accommodation density survey how many habitable rooms can be replaced on the site at the average net residential density which has been decided upon and how many acres are required to rebuild the rest elsewhere at that density. From this number should be deducted the number of extra habitable rooms which could be built in areas of old low-density housing to be redeveloped if these amount to a significantly large total.

Note that persons do not come into these calculations, which deal entirely with building accommodation.

(3) *Accommodation for persons living at an excessive occupancy rate.* From the Population Density Survey, the number of people who must be provided with other accommodation to reduce occupancy rates to whatever figure is decided upon as acceptable can be found. In towns where overcrowding is widespread and severe it may be necessary for purposes of programming to divide the calculations into two or even more stages; to work out first the amount of land needed to reduce occupancy rates to a tolerable level everywhere and then the further amount needed to reduce them to the satisfactory level postulated in fixing space standards, with perhaps, in extreme cases, an interim stage at which they are transferred to a level better than merely tolerable but short of entirely satisfactory. (See (5) below).

From the total obtained should be deducted the approximate additional number of people who could be accommodated in areas with exceptionally low occupancy rates if they were to be more fully utilised. This is difficult to determine. Such areas consist usually of large Victorian houses, no longer attractive as single family residences to the kind of people who can afford them, and suitable for conversion into flats. The need for additional kitchens, bathrooms and lavatories means that, when converted, there will not be as many habitable rooms as previously, though this may be offset by the possibility of dividing some large rooms into two. Three-quarters of the number of existing habitable rooms might be a reasonable proportion to take. This calculation should not be made unless there are enough such houses to make a real difference to the final figures of space requirements.

The acreage required to house the overspill of people can then be calculated in the same way as for additional population, as described in (1) above. *Note that this calculation refers to redistribution of persons, not of buildings.*

(4) *Total area required for new housing and other new uses.* The areas found from 1, 2 and 3 make up the total area of land required for new housing required to accommodate any intended increase of population and to bring about reasonably decent living conditions in the whole town. It is now necessary to determine the total area required for the intended population of the town for public buildings, shops, industry, open spaces, and other non-residential uses, in accordance with whatever standards have been adopted. The existing area devoted to these uses is deducted (less some allowance for "overspill" from existing non-residential development at excessive intensity) from the total needed, and the difference between the two figures is the additional area required for non-residential uses.

It is just possible, though very complicated, to base the calculations of new residential land required upon gross neighbourhood densities rather than net residential densities; indeed, at first sight it seems simpler to do so, but the reader who does not care to take my word for it is invited to try some calculations for himself. In trying to decide how much new residential land can be served by existing neighbourhood facilities and how much requires to be developed in the form of new neighbourhoods he is pretty sure to land himself in a remarkably tangled arithmetical thicket.

(5) *Calculation of long-term requirements.* It is desirable to work out the additional land required for the redevelopment of dense residential areas with a long life and to reduce occupancy rates further from the barely healthy to the satisfactory. However long it may be before this can come about it is necessary to calculate the amount of land involved so that it can be established that there is, in fact, sufficient physically suitable land adjacent to the town for this final step to be carried out. If there is not, it will be desirable to consider slightly increasing average densities in order to leave space for these ultimate operations. There is no need to estimate land requirements for the non-residential neighbourhood uses to be associated with this long-term redevelopment, for the total land requirements for the whole population of the town have already been taken into account at (4) above. This theoretical basis should prove satisfactory in practice, since the overspill from final redevelopment would, for many reasons, almost certainly be in the form of additions to existing neighbourhoods rather than new neighbourhoods.

It may not always be appropriate to divide the reduction of occupancy rates into stages, since it may well be considered feasible to reduce all excessive occupancy to a satisfactory rather than a merely tolerable level during the main period of the Plan, but the splitting of accommodation density reduction into two stages will almost invariably be necessary if the Plan is to be realistic.

It will be well to emphasise once more that Planning cannot be an exact science. One cannot Plan for shopping and open space facilities with precision, so that their quantity is " right." To take shops, as an example, if a group of shops earns a bare living from a service area with 1,000 population, that population may be capable of rising to 5,000 before the existing shopping facilities become seriously inadequate. Planning to standards is an attempt to ensure something near the optimum provision of all uses but considerable flexibility is inevitable. It is for this reason that in (2) and (3) above it was suggested that adjustments to calculations should not be made unless they would result in considerable modification of the total figure of space requirements.

Page 137 gives an example of the calculations required to determine total space requirements for a development plan for a medium-sized town.

Fig. 36 shows the essential features of the Town Map which might be prepared subsequently from these, and Fig. 38 also illustrates the process.

A further warning is necessary if this section is to be fully understood. The processes of decanting surplus accommodation and surplus people from densely developed and densely occupied areas, although *described* separately, in fact, of course, proceed simultaneously. Most, though not all, areas with an excessive occupancy rate also have an excessive density of habitable rooms and, if such an area is redeveloped, new accommodation has to be found at the same time for the people whose accommodation cannot be replaced on the site and for the people who must be housed elsewhere in order to secure satisfactory occupancy rates in the new houses built. Failure to distinguish between these two statistically distinct processes results in hopeless confusion.

Further, the mathematical approach to the problem required for the purpose of estimating space requirements, and the use of the convenient but somewhat repulsive terms " overspill " and " decanting " should not prejudice the reader towards acceptance of the view which enemies of Planning are fond of putting forward, that land Planning involves an inhuman and impersonal treatment of the people involved. To try to estimate land requirements sensibly in no way prevents the people necessarily displaced from receiving the most sympathetic treatment and the utmost consideration in being found acceptable new homes. Indeed, much of the process, particularly in the later stages, is likely to be voluntary and so gradual that no one will be conscious of pressure being exercised by Planning control; it may well come to the eventual demolition and redevelopment of houses in which, for some time, no one has lived or been willing to live.

One additional common source of misunderstanding had better be cleared up. It is, of course, true, that you cannot solve the overcrowding problems of individual families by building more houses, leaving all parents in their old homes and sending all their children of whatever age, to a new Housing Estate in order to reduce occupancy rates! The whole process of clearance, redevelopment and resettlement is a complicated problem of Estate Management. Nevertheless the method which has been described produces correct quantitative results. It does no more and no less than to indicate the amount of elbow room needed to solve the various problems of residential overcrowding.

It is of course perfectly possible to make an estimate of the total amount of land needed for a town without carrying out the elaborate calculations described in this section. If space standards have been decided and the total population to be Planned for is known a simple multiplication— Planned population in thousands × acres per thousand people required by space standards, will give the amount of land needed for urban purposes. If, in a particular case, the relief of residential congestion can reasonably be expected to be completed within a decade or two it may be quite unnecessary to do more than this, but in less favourable cases, where relief is certain to take much longer, the quantitative assessment of land needs at various stages which is made possible by these calculations, makes the preparation of a better Plan possible. It is essential to Plan in such a way that results will be satisfactory if development not to be expected for many years, and therefore by no means certain to take place, never eventuates. In many minor ways a Plan which assumes the certainty of all parts of it being carried out is likely to be different from one which is based on more cautious assumptions.

(III). The solution of road problems

This is a very involved matter. Just as with the formulation of regional road proposals so with the town. It is easy enough to draw lines on paper which will constitute a complete solution of the problems if you are prepared to build enough new roads and enough complicated road intersections, but a useful set of road proposals must take account of the amount of money likely to be available for road construction and also for the acquisition and demolition of buildings which obstruct road improvements.

In the absence of detailed long-term estimates for the allocation of funds for road works this can only be a matter of guesswork. Proposals should be formulated with a view to producing the best possible results for an assumed maximum expenditure. If adequate traffic surveys have been carried out they will provide the basis for the road plan which, important though it is, must, as already indicated, be worked out in conjunction with other aspects of the Plan and pay due regard to them. There must in fact be a prolonged process of mutual adjustment between road proposals and land use proposals until the best balance between the requirements of each is found.

The making of traffic forecasts, already referred to in Chapter 9, is of great importance in deciding upon road proposals. These have two distinct aspects, which should be clearly distinguished. Traffic forecasts should (a) show whether a proposed road system is likely to deal adequately with the traffic patterns it will have to accommodate and (b) whether a given

solution is more or less economical than possible alternatives. The second of these aspects is among the most important items in the Planning Balance Sheet.

It is very difficult to suggest general principles, but one may perhaps distinguish between two distinct problems. Very often the total amount of traffic passing through a town is so excessive for the capacity of the existing roads that serious traffic blocks frequently occur. This can often be solved by a by-pass or a complete or partial outer ring road. The cost of these can be calculated with some precision, and routes chosen and kept clear for ultimate construction however remote they may be. Similarly, traffic within the town may create very serious local congestion, particularly in and near the town centre. Here again a complete or partial inner ring road can be planned for, and may be the means of resolving the difficulty. But even when there is no acute problem, almost every main road within almost every town is, to some extent, unsatisfactory and dangerous because of intersections by minor roads, property accesses and insufficient segregation of pedestrians. In most cases the general line of such a road is satisfactory, subject possibly to minor straightenings, but its improvement to the extent of forming a proper track for motor vehicles is likely to be so costly, involving as it does the demolition of buildings on both sides and the stopping up of innumerable accesses, and there are so many of these roads in existence that improvement is likely to be exceedingly remote in time. It is probably best to ignore such roads in the Town Plan and to assume (and state this in the written part of the Plan) that they will automatically be improved when the general redevelopment of the land on either side of them takes place; when this happens the improvement need be neither difficult nor costly.

On the other hand it is absolutely essential, as I have several times stressed already, that where shopping fronts such radial roads a definite decision should be taken either to remove it or to divert the radial road, and such decisions should be expressed in the Plan so that the route for the new part of the road or the new site for the shops may be protected. Occasionally it may be feasible to do more than divert a radial road around shops, to provide a wholly or substantially new route for it through more or less undeveloped backland, the original road then becoming merely an access road. Where this appears feasible the new route should of course be shown in the Town Plan. (See Fig. 39 (v).)

(IV) Selection of land

Once it is known roughly how much land is required for the development Plan, the actual land to be used can be selected, and here the sieve map described in Chapter 9 is invaluable. The best method is to select all the land which, by reason of position in relation to existing development, configuration, sewerability, and so on, is reasonably suitable for housing development, the physical requirements for which are less stringent than for most other uses, except parks, to divide this land into units whose boundaries are well defined and to measure the area of each.

It will probably be found that the total land first chosen as suitable will not be sufficient to meet all requirements; further selection should be made from the least unsuitable land remaining until the necessary total is reached. The Planner will then have a defined area within which to accommodate his design.

It may be desirable to select further land as a reserve, which, although there are disadvantages attaching to its development, may on balance be found preferable, because of its position, to some of the land originally chosen when the Plan comes to be worked out in detail.

At this stage the economic implications of the choice of land should initially be considered. Is it better to take this area of flat, well-drained fertile land for housing, which can be developed cheaply, rather than a comparable area of steep, broken, heavy clay agriculturally of small value but costly to develop for housing? Will the cost of pumping sewage from this low-lying land, if it is developed, be greater, all told, than the cost of the new length of road required to obtain access to other land suitably located for sewering by gravity?

The extent to which these considerations affect the final form of the Plan depends very much, of course, upon whether the Planning Authority concerned is also a Developing Authority or whether, as in the case of a County Council, it stands comparatively aloof. It depends too, on any arrangements which may be made for encouraging the development of comparatively expensive land by means of differential subsidy or otherwise in order to conserve the more valuable agricultural land. Such arrangements are at present unfortunately lacking in this country.

The need for the drawing up and comparison of Planning Balance Sheets for all promising alternatives, as suggested in Chapter 9, now becomes apparent. At this stage, however, the number of these is not likely to be astronomical and, even without the aid of a computer, the relative costs and benefits can and should be at least roughly calculated.

(V) Designing the Plan

Not very much can be said about this. Clearly it is necessary to design with the various principles already suggested clearly and constantly in mind, but no one can tell a Planner, or any creative designer, how to produce good work; it is a matter of innate skill, training, experience and industry. It may, however, be said that it is a good idea, as in most affairs, to proceed from the general to the particular and thus to concentrate upon producing a Plan which is satisfactory in broad essentials before tackling any details of design in any part of it. At this stage it will be necessary to prepare numerous rough drafts from which the most satisfactory is finally selected.

There are two main methods of working, and it will depend entirely upon the temperament of the Planner which of them is adopted. One is the intuitive, which involves a great deal of doodling without much conscious effort until something promising springs to life; the other is the analytical, where the designer seeks to tabulate mentally and on paper the existing and potential qualities of the site, and postpone the subconscious leap from thinking about the design to actually making it until he has amassed all the information he wants. It is also possible to combine the two methods in any proportion.

If the analytical method be used (obviously one cannot say anything more about the intuitive method) it may be helpful to note on a plan, in order of suitability, all the possible uses for each area to be developed and, by studying these notes, to seek a combination into which each use fits harmoniously in relation to existing and other proposed uses. This could be carried further by making lists of some of the more promising combinations of uses, and drawing these in sketch form.

Certain general considerations independent of the ordinary surveys and their analysis must be dealt with by the designer at the very beginning. One may express these in a series of questions:—

Which existing features of the town are of special merit and so must be preserved however inconvenient it may be to do so in terms of other Planning Requirements?

Which existing features, on the other hand, are so bad that they must somehow be got rid of?

Which bad existing features is it unfortunately quite impracticable to get rid of, and so necessary to incorporate with as little disadvantage as possible?

In some cases these questions may be so important that special and elaborate investigations may be necessary to find the answers to them. Usually, their importance would have been appreciated early on and these investigations would have been carried out as part of the process of survey.

It is hardly possible to particularise about such problems but they may often turn on the economics of moving a large intrusive industrial building or of preserving a beautiful but ill-sited public building in poor condition.

When the main features of the Plan have been settled a tentative division into residential neighbourhoods and a tentative distribution of local shopping and schools should be carried out. Numerous adjustments will have to be made before the best arrangement is found.

Each case must be considered on its merits; where it is decided that change is impracticable the Plan as a whole must obviously be modified from the ideal so as to make the best of a bad job; where change is decided to be possible the future uses of the areas to be changed must be decided upon, and the Plan designed in such a way that things will work reasonably well in the period before the change takes place as well as afterwards. It is no good making a plan in such a way that after the removal of a factory everything will go smoothly, but during the intervening twenty or thirty years there will be severe local confusion and inconvenience.

This is a matter of the greatest importance, for the uncertainty of implementing Planning proposals makes it essential that each interim stage of development and redevelopment envisages an acceptable state of affairs.

Rather similar considerations apply to certain unbuilt-on land so sited that it would produce a better Plan if part at least, were devoted to housing or some other building use, and other land better located in relation to the residential areas of the town generally, put to open space use. Very often local pride, the historical associations of a particular open space or sheer conservatism may conspire to render such proposals impracticable.

A striking example of such land is Wythenshawe Park, which virtually splits in two Manchester's satellite town, providing locally enormous areas of open space, while the remoter residential neighbourhoods have no adequate public open space near at hand. All land Planning considerations would dictate the use of part of Wythenshawe Park for housing, but I find it difficult to think that anyone has ever regarded this as a practical proposition.

The large area of allotments serving as grouped garden space for an area of dense nineteenth century housing is a slightly less hopeless case. In my view, allotments are only needed where garden space is inadequate or wrongly distributed, as will be further explained in Chapter 17, so that when re-development of the housing served by such allotments takes place it ought to be possible to devote the allotments to some other use.

At various stages during the preparation of the Plan the Planning Balance Sheet technique should be applied to reveal the most promising alternatives. The thoroughness with which this is done will depend upon the resources available and also upon the complexity of the problems involved. For similar reasons the actual forms in which the technique is applied at different stages will vary a good deal. Eventually, however, it is likely that two or three alternative draft Town Plans will emerge, each acceptable on general Planning grounds and each, at first sight at least, appearing to have similar cost-benefit characteristics. Each will probably have a markedly different road plan because of differences in the location of its main land use groupings.

It will then be desirable, if Planning is accorded appropriate importance to make a final, thorough Planning Balance Sheet comparison to determine which out of two or three otherwise equally desirable schemes is the most truly economical.

It is hardly feasible to give examples of Planning Balance Sheets in connection with the Town Plan examples in this book. For one thing I have no means of obtaining the use of a computer specially programmed for the purpose, for another, adequate techniques for preparing comprehensive Planning Balance Sheets as distinct from those relating to simple alternatives have not yet been worked out. In addition to these not unimportant difficulties the Town Plan examples given are of imaginary towns, and have been devised to demonstrate clearly and simply the main principles of Planning and survey which I have tried to describe. They would, to be frank, collapse if the large additional weight of numerous Planning Balance Sheet assumptions were placed upon them.

For the same reason it is impracticable to provide an example of a traffic forecast. The compilation of detailed forecasts is, too, a highly skilled technical task which falls outside the range of techniques to be expected of the Town Planner.

On the other hand the elements are fairly simple, and should be understood and used by every Town Planner. Having prepared a draught Plan the probable maximum concentration of traffic which will occur in every principal road and, especially, every intersection of such roads, is calculated in the light of " desire lines ", " work trips ", etc., having regard to the likely number of workers in the Town Centre, each Industrial Area, etc. and to the distribution of population within various residential areas. If it appears that any roads or intersections will have to bear a load which they are incapable of carrying without being constructed in an abnormally costly fashion then consideration needs to be given to modifying the road pattern in order, literally, to spread the load more evenly and/or to modifying the land use pattern to alter the distribution of traffic. This process may have to be repeated a number of times until the best compromise between land use distribution needs and road needs is discerned.

(VI) Programming

When dealing with the programming of the Town Plan one does not of course, as in the case of the Regional Plan, have to take mobility of labour into account.

The prime consideration is the preservation of compactness, so that, if growth is unexpectedly halted, temporarily or permanently, the town will, nevertheless, be a balanced unity. This principle is modified, however, by two considerations: Industrial growth, in a really large town, must be accompanied by residential growth in convenient relationship to it and residential development, where it is in the form of neighbourhood units, must be so arranged that there is no danger of a halt to growth resulting in several neighbourhoods being left incomplete, and consequently unable to support neighbourhood services. This consideration must often prevent outward growth taking place evenly in all directions. (See Fig. 39 (i) and (ii).)

In normal circumstances it is clear that, to ensure that orderly growth provides a satisfactory balance at all stages, residential development should proceed in the following order:

(i) Development of vacant sites within the built-up area.
(ii) Completion of neighbourhoods already partially developed.
(iii) Creation of new neighbourhoods.

Redevelopment of outworn areas should of course proceed at the same time.

In a good many towns, where no substantial growth is contemplated and no large amount of early redevelopment feasible, there are so many vacant sites within the built-up area that no development of new areas ought to be contemplated until they have been filled in.

The case for completing neighbourhood units before beginning to develop new ones is even stronger. If an incomplete neighbourhood is already fully supplied with services its completion will involve the erection of dwellings only, while, if it is not fully supplied, its completion will ensure earlier full provision, as against the probability, if a new neighbourhood is begun, of both the new and the existing having to suffer the disadvantages of inadequate services for a long time. It is, therefore, clear that the programme for the Town Plan should be arranged so that as few residential areas as possible, consistent with the fulfilment of needs for different kinds of development and the relationship of homes to workplaces, are developed simultaneously.

Subject to the need for development to grow outwards as evenly as possible, for proper relationship between homes and work places to be maintained and for as few separate areas as possible to be developed simultaneously, there is, of course, every advantage to be gained from developing first those parts of the available building area which can be built up most economically and which offer the freest scope for design. In order to achieve this, the sieve map already used in selecting the actual areas for future development, is of

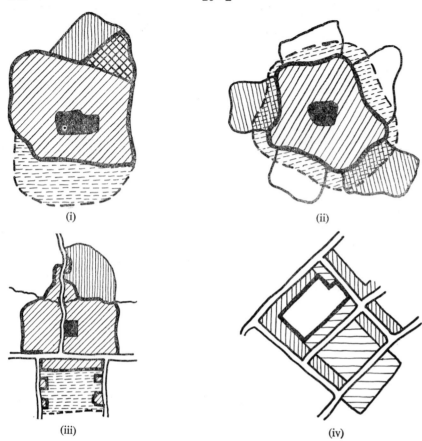

(i)

(ii)

(iii)

(iv)

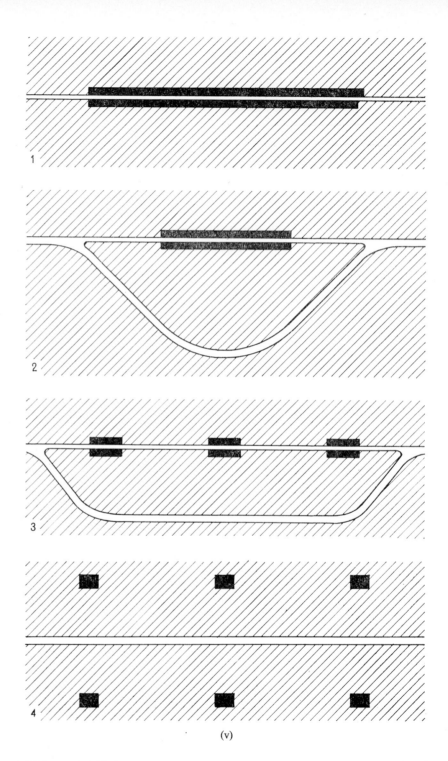

1

2

3

4

(v)

Fig. 39. Problems of programming and redevelopment.

(i) Existing town within black border. Industrial area cross-hatched. In order to secure concentric growth most of the new development ought to be at the bottom of the town but a proportion will have to be in the vertically hatched area at the top in order to relate work places and homes satisfactorily.

(ii) For the reasons given in the text it is necessary for new development to be undertaken neighbourhood by neighbourhood rather than strictly concentrically as would be theoretically desirable in the interests of even growth.

(iii) The construction of a new bridge is necessary if new development is to take place in the right location at the top rather than at the bottom, which will involve loss of good agricultural land and perpetuating the splitting of the town by the trunk road running across.

(iv) Vertical hatching represents medium density housing, horizontal hatching represents low density housing. The black edged area is unbuilt on.

(v) The problem of the overlong shopping frontage astride a main road, and three possible ways of solving it: (1) as existing; (2) the shopping shortened and by-passed; (3) split up and by-passed; (4) shopping moved to back land to serve residential areas, main road retained.

great value. Given two areas of equal centrality and equally suitable in other ways, that which is less affected by adverse physical limiting factors should obviously be developed first.

There may, however, be other factors, apart from those already mentioned, which upset this; it would, for example, usually be necessary, irrespective of the convenience and economy possible in its internal design, to develop an area with satisfactory existing access routes before one which required the expenditure of substantial sums on bridges or other engineering works in order to secure proper communications. Similarly, the need for constructing a long length of unproductive outfall sewer might well prevent the early development of an area entirely suitable in other ways.

The order in which the redevelopment of existing built-up areas shall be undertaken is another important element in the programme for the town Plan. Where no change of use is involved the process merely involves the selection from the blight factors sieve map described in Chapter 9 of the areas in greatest need of redevelopment and providing for work to be done in order of need. Even in this simplest case, however, it will be necessary to take into account the relationship between the location of areas for redevelopment and new housing and of workplaces, so that as little upheaval and wasted travelling as possible may result.

Where the use of land is to be changed from residential after redevelopment great complications are likely to arise; the best order of redevelopment can only be decided after giving due weight to several factors not easily compared with each other. These factors are, briefly:

(i) The continued detriment to residents in the most unsatisfactory dwellings if the order of redevelopment postpones the replacement of some of these until after that of less bad areas.

(ii) The capital loss involved in replacing buildings before it becomes physically necessary to do so. This ought not to have to be taken into account, because no dwellings which are wholly unsatisfactory should be tolerated, but in circumstances which combine housing shortage with economic stringency it cannot be ignored.

(iii) The various losses which are liable to arise from the postponement of provision of essential non-residential uses on suitable sites.

This is a problem which must be faced in preparing almost any programme. The difficulties involved may be illustrated by an example.

Consider the case of a town which urgently requires an inner ring road, the lack of which causes enormous loss of time through congestion and also great danger to life. The construction of the ring road will involve the demolition of some two hundred houses which lie on its route, but most of these are by no means of the very worst type, of which a dense mass unfortunately lies well clear of the route.

Who is to say which should come first; the ring road, which will increase the safety, the efficiency, and hence the prosperity of the whole town, or the clearance of the slum, which will relieve the wretchedness and, no doubt, prolong the lives of many who now live in it? The immediate appeal to human emotions of slum clearance projects is always likely to tip the balance in that direction, but, on a dispassionate assessment of all the facts, it may well be that the construction of the ring road constitutes the greater increase of human welfare. It will be noticed that some of the factors of most importance here cannot be assessed in financial terms.

A special case arises where a " key site " obstructs the proper redevelopment of an area. The widening of an important road or road access to a large area of back land is often blocked by one large, substantial building where all others are ready for redevelopment. In such a case the removal of the obstruction is likely to have beneficial results far exceeding the capital loss involved in demolishing it before its earning power has expired. This is a point not sufficiently realised.

Conversely, the carrying out of a single constructional project may liberate the capacities of a large area. Fig. 39 (iii) shows a smallish town, requiring some increase of population, but with a hopelessly outworn and congested residential core, from the overspill from which the main need for new housing arises. A trunk road runs through the town and there is development on both sides of it, but the town centre and the great majority of the town are to its north; a small river runs parallel to the trunk road, and urban development has crossed it, the only access being a narrow bridge with confused and narrow approach roads. The land to the north of the trunk road is of very poor quality, while that to the south is rich.

Clearly, the maintenance of a properly integrated town structure demands that further development shall be to the north of the trunk road, and this need is reinforced by the demands of agricultural conservation. But if this is to happen a new bridge must be constructed almost immediately, for the traffic demands made on the existing one are already excessive and there are virtually no building sites left on the south of the river. There is, therefore, every reason to provide for the early construction of a bridge, a costly proposal which might well cause prolonged headshaking in the Ministry of Transport.

Yet the long-term effects of failing to authorise the bridge can readily be seen to be very serious. Good agricultural land will have to be built on instead of poor land and the town will be severed by the trunk road, so that the construction of a by-pass will eventually be essential, whereas both these things would have been avoided by the construction of the bridge. On redevelopment of property fronting the trunk road it would eventually have been possible to abolish that on the south side and deny direct access to that on the north, thus improving the road situation without any new road construction.

If ever a time comes when redevelopment is possible on a really grand scale these problems will diminish in intensity because of the shorter waiting periods involved for those who will benefit by redevelopment.

New or extended central services need to be tied into the town programme in such a way that they come into operation as soon as they can be worked economically. This applies particularly to neighbourhood services such as schools and local shops, the inevitable lack of which, during the early stages of new development, cannot but cause considerable inconvenience.

The increased provision of central area services can be much more flexible.

As I have mentioned elsewhere, a central area which has been adequate does not suddenly become grossly inadequate; the pressure on services gradually builds up as population increases until it becomes uncomfortably great. Except, therefore, where very large increases of population are expected within a short period the programming of central area services need not occasion great concern. This, of course, does not apply to the detailed redevelopment of central area building sites, the effective programming of which may well constitute the greatest difficulty of such projects.

10-3. PRESENTATION

Special problems of presentation arise in connection with the town map and its accompanying programme map. I have already outlined in Chapter 3 the general principles which I think should be followed in designing the notation for a town map but some amplification of these is necessary. The principles apply whether one is using colour or monochrome and are exemplified in Figs. 36 and 38. They may be summarised as follows:

Notation used for each use proportionate in intensity to the intensity of that use.

Existing uses to be retained shown more intensely than proposed uses.

Proposed uses likely to be brought about within a fairly definite period. usually taken as twenty years, shown more strongly than uses not likely to be brought about until later. While it is important that the latter should be shown, in order that the intended eventual form of the town may be clear, there cannot be the same degree of certainty about them as for the more immediate proposals, so that they should not be shown as definitely. This is in a sense, applying programming to the town map, but only in a very special way. Generally speaking, it is essential for a separate map to be prepared to show programming; the town map is too complex to allow of this further important item being shown upon it.

Some confusion is caused by doubt about the appropriate scope of the town map. The town map's main job is to show intended changes of use; it therefore does not show redevelopment, however extensive, where this involves no change of use. It does not show the routes of proposed new roads if of a minor kind, or of road improvements, within such areas, since

these have no effect upon the Plan of the town as a whole, and will probably not even have been designed at the time the town map is prepared. On the other hand all important road improvements intended to be carried out independently of riparian redevelopment, whether in the form of new roads or of widenings, should be shown because of their effect on the functioning of the town.

The programme map produces great presentation difficulties. It should show strongly the order in which changes in the town are intended to take place, but to be fully meaningful must also show, though subordinately, what land uses are involved in the areas of change. The Ministry notation shows the land uses concerned with great prominence but reduces the more significant question of sequence to inconspicuousness. In my opinion the best method of resolving this dilemma is to use as a base a copy of the town map in monochrome and to superimpose in varying intensities of a single colour, the sequence of changes, the earliest development being shown most strongly.

It is a matter of some doubt whether, having omitted from the town map redevelopment which does not involve a change of use, one ought to follow suit with the programme map. I do not think one ought, for redevelopment may constitute a considerable proportion of the development contributing to the realisation of the plan, and to omit it is therefore likely to give a misleading impression. The town map should show as clearly as possible the intended eventual form of the town and the kinds of changes needed to bring this about; the programme map should concentrate rather upon the amount of change and the sequence of change.

Fig. 37 is an example of a Programme Map for a Town, somewhat limited by the need to present it in monochrome.

10-4. CONCLUSION

The Town Map is no more than a skeleton based upon approximations, which serves as a guide for more detailed Planning. If properly prepared it ensures that growth and redevelopment shall result in a town with its parts in proper proportion. To judge the town map properly it must be capable of being comprehended *as a whole*. The fact that most of the calculations suggested above as necessary in connection with the preparation of a Town Map are inevitably inexact and to some extent are based upon predictions which may not be fulfilled in detail does not render them superfluous or useless; they are the means by which a proper balance for the town is attained.

PART II

SPACE STANDARDS AND DETAILED PLANNING DESIGN

CHAPTER 11

THE TRANSPORT SYSTEM

11-1. GENERAL

TRANSPORT MAY BE by land, air or water, and land transport is divisible into two great divisions, road and rail. The hovercraft, capable of travelling on a cushion of air just above the surface of either land or water, heralds the possible general introduction of a distinctive new form of transport requiring only an unimpeded but otherwise unprepared strip of territory for its passage. This opens up tremendous possibilities for the creation of communication networks at relatively negligible cost, but we are hardly yet at the stage at which possibilities and limitations can be sufficiently assessed to form a basis for Planning action.

We need not spend very much time considering requirements for air and water transport, since the former resolves itself into discussion of the siting, size and shape of landing grounds, the latter of docks. The number of docks and airfields with the establishment of which the Planner is likely to be intimately concerned is so small that it would be quite inappropriate for him to attempt to master the technical details of their site limitations and requirements. In these affairs he must either remain content to accept the developers' statements of their needs, or, if he suspects its accuracy, to consult an independent expert.

Very much the same sort of thing applies to railways; the number of new railway lines which a Planner in this country is likely to be concerned with is indeed small, but since new spur lines, and, in particular, spur lines to New Towns, are occasionally required, and railway sidings to new industrial areas are frequently needed, it may be well to bear in mind the following data.

On curves a railway line must be canted or tipped up on its outer edge to reduce the upsetting effect of centrifugal force. The maximum amount of cant which can be used is six inches, and it is found that with this the sharpest bend which can be safely negotiated by a train travelling at 60 m.p.h. is one with a radius of $35\frac{1}{2}$ chains. In circumstances where speed need not or cannot be so high the curve can, of course, be sharper, and the following minimum radii apply.

For trains entering and stopping at stations	$21\frac{1}{2}$ chains
For trains leaving stations at which they have stopped ...	$14\frac{1}{2}$ chains
For shunting movements	10 chains

Gradient is another important limiting factor in the design of railways. A heavy train with a good locomotive can keep up a speed of 50 to 60 m.p.h. on a 1 in 200 gradient, but when the gradient becomes as steep as about 1 in 100 the speed is reduced to 30-35 m.p.h.

One in 100 may be regarded as the most severe gradient which should be accepted for main lines, while gradients in the vicinity of stations where trains may have to stop and restart should not be steeper than 1 in 260.

The minimum satisfactory headroom for bridges over railway lines is 18 ft. 6 in.

11-2. ROADS

When we turn to roads it is a very different matter, for they are the very skeleton of any Town Plan, or, to vary the simile, the arteries of the organism, through which the life blood of communications flows. The Planner must necessarily let the road engineer have the last word regarding road materials, gradients, cambers, super-elevation, radii of horizontal and vertical curves, etc. though he should be well aware of the technical factors governing them. He should regard the Traffic Engineer or Traffic Planner as an indispensable colleague without the seal of whose approval no Town Plan should be adopted. This is not to imply that sheer traffic efficiency should be the principal determinant in preparing the Town Plan, for numerous other factors may well be of equal or greater importance, but certainly a Town Plan which does not ensure the efficient flow of traffic is little more useful than an aircraft which will not fly.

Roads are of the greatest antiquity. Beginning in far-off times as pedestrian tracks along which, before the invention of the wheel, loads might be dragged on rough sledges, they became, as human civilisation progressed, routes along which animals were driven, led or ridden, and horse-drawn and, later, mechanically propelled vehicles travelled.

Always, roads have had a dual function: as traffic routes and as means of access to dwellings and other buildings; it is only since the vast growth of transport which has arisen from the invention of the internal combustion engine that these functions have been seriously in conflict with each other. Today this conflict is very grave, and leads to terrible injury and loss of life and to grossly wasteful delay in the transport of workers and goods. In " Technics and Civilisation ", written in 1946, Lewis Mumford suggests that if the question were asked in cold blood whether the advantages of the rise of the motor car are worth the loss of 30,000 American lives a year the answer would probably be in the negative.

In Great Britain today (1964) personal injuries and deaths from road accidents total a third of a million a year, the greater number of casualties occurring in built-up areas.

It is, perhaps, only because road deaths do not occur in a single dramatic disaster, such as a battle, or the loss by delay in one colossal fog, that society has not found and insisted upon a drastic remedy for them.

Sir Alker Tripp, in " Town Planning and Road Traffic " (Edward Arnold & Co., 1942) analyses the defects of our present road system. He puts his finger on the spot when he points out that: " Any town so planned that its citizens are killed and injured in vast numbers is obviously an ill-planned town ", that " . . . the entire layout of all newly developed areas must, if necessary, be made dependent on (the) safety factor; it would be rather futile to plan, by means of layout, for hygiene and amenity, but at the same time to overlook that this same layout is likely, daily and hourly, to cause death or maiming", and that " . . . pedestrians and fast motor traffic will never, and can never, safely mix. . . ." One could, in fact, with both pleasure and profit go on quoting indefinitely from this admirable book, to which every person concerned with physical Planning is enthusiastically referred.

A casual inspection of road traffic is apt to give the impression of a vast number of vehicles moving about the country in random fashion, but this impression is false. Traffic forms definite patterns which vary from day to day and at different times during each day. Nearly all journeys have a purpose, so that careful observation of existing traffic patterns and analysis of the numbers of people likely to visit traffic-attracting uses to be established in the future enable fairly reliable predictions to be made of future road requirements.

It is remarkable that the average length of a vehicle journey in this country is only about 6 miles. In the early hours of the morning there are usually very few vehicles on the road—in the U.S.A. this traffic is termed the "OWL" traffic. Around 6 a.m. however, early manual workers appear on the scene, together with vehicles delivering milk, newspapers, etc. This traffic builds up to a peak, usually before 8 a.m., to be joined by the rest of the office workers and the school traffic. The office traffic may continue until about 10 a.m. but by 9 a.m. it has diminished greatly even on a few special routes, while elsewhere it has virtually disappeared. Traffic then falls to a level well below the daily average, being made up of local delivery traffic, and a limited amount of business traffic, but as the morning progresses flows tend to build up again as the business traffic increases, and a small quantity of shopping traffic joins the stream. By 11.30 a.m. flows are equal to average daily flow and the hour of 11 a.m. to 12 noon is a useful period to assess this figure. Owing to the universal habit of lunching sometime between 12 and 2 p.m. traffic declines again during this period although there may be short bursts of 10 to 15 minutes when flows are considerable. By 2 p.m. flows have returned to average.

In the afternoon of a typical weekday, flows increase again because of commercial traffic and shopping traffic. Shopping traffic has so far not been of great consequence in Great Britain, but owing to the rapid rate of growth of vehicle ownership it may be expected to increase very considerably. By 4 p.m. children are returning home from school, commercial vehicles are returning to their depots, and mothers who have been shopping are returning home to their children; flows tend to increase appreciably at this time. Some manual workers finish work as early as 4.30 p.m., but most do not finish until 5 p.m. or later; office workers tend to finish work between 5 p.m. and 5.45 p.m., and so the evening peak period is much more compressed.

After 6 p.m. much depends on the nature of the road and the time of year as to the amount of traffic which it carries but as a general rule flows tend to decline appreciably as the evening wears on, except for a short peak about 10.30 p.m. when the pubs. close. By midnight, nearly all the evening social travellers are home and flows are once more down to the OWL level.

Although the above is generally true much depends upon the location and nature of the road. A radial road linking extensive dormitory development with a central area will tend to carry only office workers on their journeys to and from work. Conversely, a minor lateral road will carry a more or less uniform flow throughout the day.

As a general rule, a road system which has been designed to carry the work traffic will have a sufficient capacity to accommodate all flows during the remainder of the day, though there are exceptions in the immediate vicinity of shopping centres, football grounds, and roads carrying large volumes of racing or holiday traffic.

The Planner should always ask himself what type and volume of traffic his proposals are likely to generate or attract and should design his road system accordingly rather than basing it upon a preconceived pattern.

Sir Alker Tripp considers that roads fall into three main classes— "arterial", "sub-arterial" and "local"—the first carrying great masses of traffic between different towns or different parts of the same town, the second linking networks of local roads with each other and with the arterial roads, the third having the main function of giving access to premises. This is a convenient nomenclature, although it is not altogether easy to decide which roads should be placed in the intermediate class of "sub-arterial".

In this chapter I use the terms "arterial road" (=Tripp's arterial), "major road" (=Tripp's sub-arterial), and "minor road" (=Tripp's local).

The problems of designing new roads and road systems and of improving existing ones are obviously very different, and it will be convenient to deal with them separately and in that order.

The arterial road is commonly likened to a railway, inasmuch as the criterion of its success is the extent to which it provides a route along which motor vehicles can proceed safely and uninterruptedly, except at infrequent controlled points, at speeds comparable to those of trains. It follows that, except at these infrequent controlled points, there should be no intersections with other roads and that no buildings should have direct access to the road.

These requirements are accepted as absolutely essential for railways but are still sometimes regarded as startling or impracticable in relation to roads; yet, in fact, the dangers of uncontrolled intersections and access points are vastly greater in the case of arterial roads than of railways. Large units (trains) pass along the railway lines at fixed and relatively infrequent intervals at a fairly constant speed, while hordes of vehicles traverse arterial roads in no special order or rhythm and at considerably varying speeds. The dangers of accident bear no comparison; yet, although to build a row of houses fronting directly on to an unfenced railway would be regarded as the act of a lunatic, such a procedure beside an arterial road was common form between the wars. The reason for the difference in viewpoint is, fundamentally, that the railway came to life in a virtually mature form, with everyone alive to its dangers, whereas the long history of the road and its dual function have prevented public opinion from insisting upon similar restrictions to the frontages of arterial roads.

Arterial roads can appropriately be subdivided into the following principal types:—

(i) *National and regional through routes*, which link different parts of the country, avoid towns, and are fed by

(ii) *Main routes*, leading out of towns and joining them to other towns.

(iii) *Intermediate and outer ring roads*, which in the spider's web system, link the radials. An outer ring road may also join, or, for a short distance, merge with a national or regional through route. (The inner ring road can hardly be considered as an arterial, since, because of its comparatively small radius and the number of road junctions along it, high speeds are inappropriate.)

The treatment appropriate to each of these subdivisions varies slightly.

National and regional through routes. Pedestrians and cyclists have no place on national and regional through routes, and there is, therefore, no necessity to provide either cycle tracks or footpaths along them. The sole points at which access should be provided are at junctions with each other and with their feeders and for occasional filling and service stations and places of refreshment. These could appropriately be combined and sited in valley bottoms for the benefit of those who run out of fuel on the road. Such roads should bridge or underpass all roads other than their feeders. They should be planned to allow vehicles to travel safely at the highest speed of which they are capable, and gradients and curves, both horizontal and vertical, should therefore be of the easiest.

The necessary components are simply two unidirectional carriageways of sufficient width to carry the volume of traffic which will use them. The physical separation of fast-moving streams of traffic moving in opposite directions is, of course, essential for the avoidance of head-on collisions, and the removal of this possibility materially relieves the strain and fatigue of driving.

Fatigue may also be reduced by other means which, fortunately, also assist in enhancing the visual attractiveness of the road itself and in reducing its inevitably marked effect upon the landscape. It is undesirable that a road should run dead straight or dead level for any great distance, for the monotony which this causes exerts a marked hypnotic effect on long journeys, and may contribute substantially to a driver falling asleep at the wheel, with hideous results. The route may, therefore, within reasonable limits, follow contours, hedgerows, and the sides of woods, which helps the road to fit in with the landscape rather than violate it, and enables interference with farm units to be minimised. Similarly, it is unnecessary for the two carriageways to run parallel to each other. They may, appropriately, diverge to a considerable distance at some points, and may run at quite different levels in hilly country.

If all existing roads, including farm tracks, are bridged or underpassed, the interference with agriculture will not usually be appreciably increased by the carriageways being widely spaced; indeed, if the route is planned with agricultural requirements well in mind, such interference may even be reduced. On the other hand, the cost of bridging or underpassing is very great, and economy may dictate the closing together of carriageways in agricultural areas.

The divergence of carriageways assists in preventing the very considerable menace of headlight glare, and it is axiomatic that, throughout their length,

the carriageways of a dual carriageway road should be screened from each other by distance, difference in level, embanking the strip of land between them or planting it thickly.

It is not appropriate to treat a national or regional through route as a parkway (which is separately dealt with later) for it runs through the English landscape, which is sufficiently beautiful not to need embellishment; what is requisite is that the road should respect and fit in with the landscape through which it runs.

Ring and radial roads. Pedestrians and cyclists must necessarily be provided for on these, which afford the main communications between different parts of the town. It is, however, essential that motor traffic, cyclists and pedestrians should be effectively segregated on all arterial roads, which means not only that separate tracks must be provided for each, but that each class of user must be physically prevented from straying off his own track on to that of another class. It is, for example, not sufficient to provide a footpath immediately adjoining a carriageway, since pedestrians can, and often do step off and get knocked down by motor vehicles. A good solution is to provide complete physical separation and to combine this with parkway treatment of the road if land availability allows.

This means that the total width of the road is considerable, that each element of it is separated by a substantial strip of land and that the parts of the road not occupied by carriageways, footpaths and cycle tracks are given landscape treatment, not in an attempt to simulate the open countryside, but in a more sophisticated fashion appropriate to an urban area.

As radial roads approach the town centre and converge upon each other, the requirements of the Town Plan may not enable sufficient width to be allocated to them for parkway treatment to be possible, and it will then be necessary for separation of the different elements to be achieved by fences, hedges, walls or embankments. The need for pedestrians to cross the road is also likely to become greater as the centre is approached, and, in order to preserve the safe flow of fast traffic, bridges or subways must be provided for them at suitable points.

Two or three general aspects of radial and ring roads must be considered. First, a ring road must not be understood necessarily to encircle a town, but rather to be an arterial road affording lateral communication between different parts of the town. The absence of radial roads in one or more sectors, or the arrangement of land use, may make it quite unnecessary for the ring to be complete.

Second, the intermediate ring road will seldom be necessary except for towns of very considerable size. Provided each neighbourhood unit can readily be connected with a ring road, communication is perfectly adequate (roads linking adjoining neighbourhoods need not be of arterial type), so that it is possible for a town to have a double ring of neighbourhood units, with a population of 120,000 to 150,000 without an intermediate ring road being required.

Third, rush-hour traffic creates a special problem on radial roads, since most of the traffic travels in one direction in the morning and in the other direction in the evening. This can be solved in two ways. One is to have triple

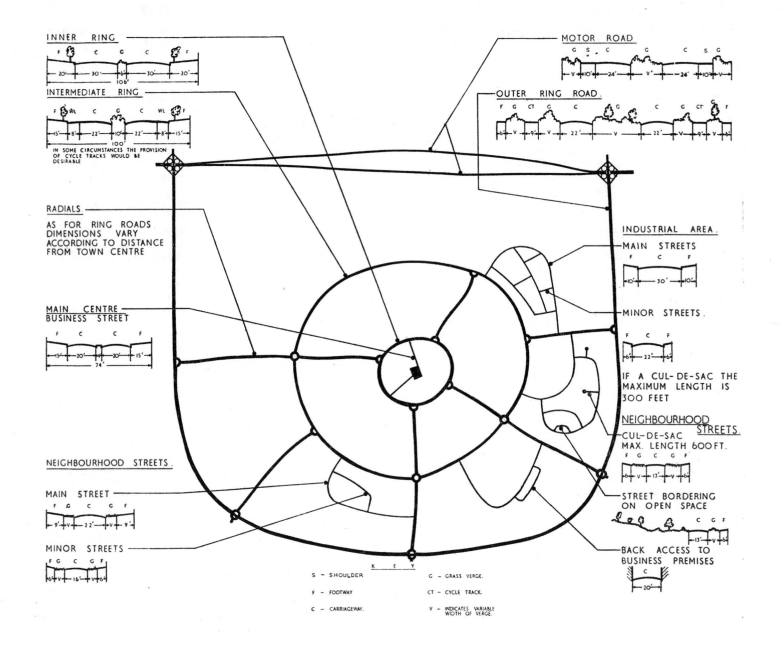

instead of dual carriageways on the radial roads, the direction of traffic along the centre one being changed twice daily to accommodate the excess traffic; the other is to have two rows of dividing kerbway in a single wide carriageway which can be raised or lowered flush with the roadway, and thus to adjust the carriageway width devoted to each direction of traffic flow, in accordance with temporary conditions. Both are, needless to say, extremely expensive solutions.

The inner ring road. This road is of very special character. It will encircle the central area of the town; on its outer side it will be joined by radial roads and on its inner side by roads leading into the central area; the town's bus station must necessarily be located close to it. Traffic will be very heavy and intersections numerous, so that a high average speed of traffic will not be possible. The main objective must be a free and safe flow of traffic.

If 100 acres is accepted as a probable size for the central area and the area is approximately circular in shape, the radius of the road will be in the neighbourhood of 1,176 feet, or 392 yards. This agrees closely with the maximum suggested radius of 300 yards for inner ring roads in the Report on Roads in Built-up Areas previously referred to and is, in itself, a limiting factor in relation to speed.

Segregation of motor traffic and pedestrians is more essential than elsewhere, and since width is likely to have to be restricted, can best be achieved by vertical rather than horizontal barriers. Cyclists become an insuperable problem; it is desirable that they be segregated because of the great density of traffic to be expected, yet the cost of their segregation becomes prohibitive, since, to be effective, cycle tracks must cross intersections either above or below vehicular level, and, as already noted, intersections are numerous.

Although results obtained by methods other than spatial arrangement are really outside our terms of reference it seems reasonable to suggest that

---

Fig. 40. ROAD SYSTEM FOR A TOWN. Diagrammatic representation of a road system suitable for a large town, NOT TO SCALE. The widths, etc., suggested are based upon the recommendations in the Report on the Design and Layout of Roads in Built-up Areas and in Circular 19 of the Ministry of Local Government and Planning. The roads within the main centre, the industrial area and the residential neighbourhoods are, of course, samples only. Circular 19 suggests that no street in a residential or industrial area should be more than half a mile from a street which is " part of the main framework of streets ", and that no street in a principal business area should be more than a quarter of a mile from a street which is part of the main framework.
A street bordering an open space, i.e., with single-sided development, should not be more than 1,000 ft. long.
As regards culs-de-sac in neighbourhoods, Circular 19 suggests the following, too complicated to be shown diagrammatically: Footpaths may be reduced to 4 ft. 6 in., if verges are provided in addition, and there need only be one footpath if there is access to property on one side only; this applies also to minor streets, both residential and industrial. Where the total length of the carriageway is less than 200 ft., only one footpath is required, 4 ft. 6 in. wide, and the carriageway may be reduced to 9 ft. wide along any portion where there is no access to property.
Waiting bays or lanes 8 ft. wide, or 9 ft., if they are to be used by public service vehicles, may be necessary at some points in main and minor neighbourhood streets and in industrial areas, while footpaths on such roads should be 12 ft. wide wherever there are groups of shops.

cyclists should not be permitted to ride in the inner ring road, but be required to wheel their cycles.

The cyclist presents a very special and intractable problem. His vehicle is capable of rapid acceleration and deceleration and of extremely rapid variation in direction, yet it is very unstable, and the rider is unprotected by even the flimsiest envelope. A collision which, between motor vehicles, would mean no more than a dented wing may result in death if a cyclist is involved. In face of all this it is not surprising that motorists, who are well aware of the above facts, are seldom also cyclists but positively staggering that cyclists' associations should violently resent the provision of cycle tracks on roads!

Major roads. These include all those roads to which it is impracticable to restrict access but which inevitably carry a substantial volume of traffic. They comprise roads within the central area, the principal roads within industrial areas, roads linking neighbourhood units and the principal roads within neighbourhood units.

On these roads high speed cannot be permitted because of the multiplicity of road junctions and individual accesses, each of which is a danger point, and it is therefore less necessary to segregate different classes of road use, as well as being impracticable (cycle tracks are obviously futile if they are crossed by carriageways every few hundred yards). Adequate widths of carriageways and footways, and the maintenance of sufficient sight-lines at junctions are of first importance.

The principal roads of residential neighbourhoods, or spine roads, constitute a problem of special difficulty. They are examples of Sir Alker Tripp's " hybrid " roads, and they cannot be entirely avoided.

The whole road system is like a river, with its tributaries, streams and brooks, all bearing water to each other in varying quantities. At some point there necessarily has to be a road which, having gathered the traffic from the minor roads and culs-de-sac which flow into it, becomes of more than purely minor importance but which, because of economy and indeed of convenience of layout, nevertheless has to be treated as a minor road to the extent of having buildings alongside it with individual access to it, as well as a large number of minor roads leading into it. These roads, which will usually carry local bus services, are likely to be very dangerous unless special steps are taken to safeguard them.

The first requirement is not to make them too long or too straight, for this, even though a speed limit is enforced, will encourage dangerously fast speeds. But this is not too easy to contrive without serious disadvantages. It is important for numerous reasons that the spine roads of a neighbourhood should contribute to the coherence of the area, and should lead traffic reasonably directly from all parts of it to its centre. Here, there is clearly a contradiction. In the absence of such directness the structure of the neighbourhood tends to break down into a formless " mediaeval " pattern in which accessibility is severely reduced and the multiplicity of turning movements at road junctions may, quantitatively, create more danger than the dangers of speed on a straight, direct spine road. Examples of the latter are regrettably common in the New Towns. It is necessary to seek a compromise, and I think that the arrangement shown in Fig. 69 is a reasonable one.

Another possibility is to do as the French have sometimes done, and to create artificial " gutters " across spine roads, so that a driver who crosses one at excessive speed will suffer discomfort and perhaps a broken spring. This would be an admirable device were it not that here again it might create more danger than is avoided, for a vehicle sustaining a shock of the kind described may very possibly get out of control. There is a private road near Caterham, however, in which speed is similarly discouraged by building semi-circular raised " humps " across the road. This seems to work very well.

The other essential measure of safety on spine roads is to provide a really wide grass verge between house forecourts and garage entrances and the carriageway, and for these to be unobstructed by obstacles to view. If this is done vehicles on the spine road at least have good visual warning of vehicles or children emerging from the houses fronting them. It will also be desirable for the footpaths of such roads to be set well back from the edge of the carriageway.

An interesting possibility for treating roads in this category in a quite new way has been explored by Leonard Vincent, until recently Chief Planner to the Stevenage Development Corporation. His idea is to form a series of " superblocks " bounded by roads which would give no direct access to buildings. All buildings would be served by culs-de-sac, which would join the road bounding the superblock at frequent intervals. Footpaths would not be provided alongside the bounding roads, and indeed pedestrian traffic along them would be discouraged or prohibited. Instead, pedestrian tunnels or bridges, according to the lie of the land, would cross them fairly frequently, thus enabling pedestrian movement to be entirely independent of through roads over the whole of a neighbourhood, or indeed the whole of a town. If the detailed layout of the housing areas were such that pedestrians and vehicles were separated within them (on the lines discussed in Chapter 17) one would then have a town in which pedestrians and vehicles would never have to meet except at the times and places at which people boarded or left vehicles.

The attractions are obvious, but there remain difficulties in relation to the through roads. It is obviously essential that speeds on these should be kept low because of the numerous junctions with minor roads. This, it is claimed, can be secured by deliberately making them somewhat circuitous, and by building them in switchback form to reduce the cost of pedestrian tunnels. One remains a little sceptical that the level of safety so secured would be satisfactorily high. The costs of bridges and tunnels would be far from small (an average of perhaps £2,500 for each),[1] and, to afford really satisfactory communication there would have to be many. The extra road costs would necessarily be severe because even though at the junctions of culs-de-sac with through roads almost as many houses could be fitted in as with

---

[1] I am informed that at current prices a pedestrian underpass, or tunnel costs about £4,000, or, if combined with a cycleway, £5,000–£8,000, while a footbridge costs about £1,000.

an ordinary layout, at the junctions of through roads considerable duplication of roads is unavoidable (see Fig. 25). Appearance might well be somewhat unsatisfactory. The through road would certainly have to be lined by virtually unclimable barriers in order to prevent pedestrians crossing it. (Even so they might still do so via culs-de-sac.) The effect of these barriers and the absence of any fronting buildings would be likely to produce an arid and forbidding prospect. If, on the other hand, to aid appearance, buildings faced onto the through road and were served from culs-de-sac behind, then costs would mount formidably.

FIG. 41. L. G. Vincent's "snake" spine road idea, to make pedestrian routes more direct than road routes.

One would like to see more work done on this idea. Unfortunately it seems likely that it involves too many temptations to pedestrians to behave in undesired ways to be entirely practicable. Even if deliberate efforts were made to make pedestrian routes direct and attractive and road routes indirect and unattractive, in terms of journeys to shops, schools etc., (see Fig. 41) there would inevitably remain innumerable short personal journeys for which a quick dash across the road would be too advantageous for temptation to be resisted, so that the result might well be that numerous expensive tunnels and bridges had been constructed without succeeding in keeping the through road clear of pedestrians.

Minor roads. The requirements for these are, first, that the system of minor roads should not afford opportunities for the astute motorist to take short cuts through it instead of using the arterial and major roads; deliberate modifications of the layout may be necessary to secure this.

Second, the imposition of a speed limit is, of course, essential, but in addition, long, straight lengths of road should be avoided so that the law-breaker is discouraged.

Third, the capacity of the roads must be sufficient to allow the free passage of vehicles even when other vehicles are parked outside buildings.

Fourth, sight lines at junctions must be adequate, and direct intersections avoided as far as possible. However few the vehicles which use minor roads a collision is always possible at an intersection, and can be just as serious as one on an arterial road.

Fifth, roads are very costly to construct, and the total lengths and widths of minor roads constructed should be kept to the minimum consistent with fulfilment of the foregoing requirements.

The footway and carriageway widths of minor roads must be graduated according to the amount of traffic likely to use them. The residential cul-de-sac will only be used by the people living in it and those who call on them. Several culs-de-sac may open on to the same minor through road, which will be used by people going to and from the culs-de-sac in addition to those using the through road itself. This increase of traffic volume continues progressively until eventually a major road must be provided.

The prescription of suitable widths for minor roads has a long and curious history, starting with the completely illogical requirements of the model by-laws and proceeding by way of the much better, but still peculiar, recommendations of the pre-war Ministry of Health Model Clauses to the recommendations of the Handbook on the Redevelopment of Central Areas, the Housing Manual, 1949, and Circular 19 of the Ministry of Local Government and Planning. These three are all very similar to each other, the last-named being the latest and most satisfactory (but see page 163).

Requirements for components and widths of all the different kinds of road needed in a town, and the relationships of different kinds of roads with each other are shown in Fig. 40.

11-3. TECHNICAL CONSIDERATIONS IN THE DESIGN OF ROADS

We have now seen how a road system designed on ideal lines would graduate from the national through route, on which safe speed would be the governing factor, by several stages through the ring and radial roads, the major roads and the minor roads right down to the footway within the residential area, each type of road being designed to accommodate the traffic using it with the greatest possible degree of safety and convenience. Motor vehicles, cyclists and pedestrians would be physically separated from each other, wherever practicable, and no buildings would have direct access to roads intended for through traffic, but, on the other hand, no convenience would be offered to through traffic within parts of the road system designed to give access to buildings.

Let us now turn to the actual requirements for carriageway widths, curve radii, and so on, necessary to produce the best results. There are two outstanding sources of information of special value, which relate principally to arterial roads: *the Report on the Design and Layout of Roads in Built-up Areas*, already referred to, and *the Ministry of Transport's Memorandum* 780 *on the Design of Roads in Rural Areas* which is a successor of Memorandum 575, published in 1943 and, until recently, the main source for material of this kind.

As regards minor roads, *Circular* 19 *of the Ministry of Local Government and Planning*, also previously referred to, is of importance.

The following observations incorporate technical recommendations made in the documents referred to above.

Design Speed. On a straight, level and empty unrestricted road, drivers may travel sensibly at any speed they choose, being limited only by the performance of their vehicles. In practice, however, roads have vertical and horizontal curves, road junctions, etc., so that there are practical limitations which set an upper limit to what the fastest vehicle will attain.

One may therefore approach the problem from two directions:
- (a) what is a reasonable maximum speed which should satisfy nearly all traffic in rural conditions?
- (b) what maximum speed is desirable for the locality in urban conditions?

In order to limit speeds a speed limit may be imposed, but a tortuous road can impose a speed limit far more effectively than any statutory limitation.

In Memo. 780 of the Ministry of Transport, "Design of Roads in Rural Areas", the following design speeds are suggested:
- (a) Dual carriageways 70 m.p.h.
- (b) All 33 ft. single carriageways and trunk and Class I 24 ft. carriageways 60 m.p.h.
- (c) Other classified roads with 2-lane single carriageways 50 m.p.h.

Urban radial roads will need to be designed for 70 m.p.h., but Inner Ring Roads should be designed for much lower speeds—40 to 50 m.p.h. because there will be much lane-changing, and vehicles will discharge onto slow urban streets.

Sight-lines. There are two criteria for sight-lines over vertical curves:
- (1) At crests safe passing distances.
- (2) At dips the foreshortening of headlight beams.

Crests. The sight-lines should be long enough to allow a driver to ascertain that he has an adequate distance to draw out and pass the vehicle in front, and to return to his own lane or to stop before reaching an obstruction. It is apparent, therefore, that the minimum distance is governed by whether the carriageway is unidirectional or two-way, the speed of the vehicles on the road, and over summits, the height of the driver's eye above the carriageway.

The following are the values given in Memo. 780 (1961) which is based on pre-war data, visibility distances being measured between points 3 ft. 9 in. above the carriageway. In a very large number of modern vehicles, the eye-height of the driver is in fact only about 3 ft. 0 in. It is better, therefore, that the Memo. 790 distances should be applied assuming the height above the carriageway as 3 ft.

	Visibility distances (feet)	
Design Speed (m.p.h.)	*Minimum overtaking (single carriageways)*	*Minimum stopping (single and dual carriageways)*
70	—	950
60	1,400	650
50	1,200	425
40	950	300

Dips. The lowering of the driver eye-height has led to a corresponding lower mounting of headlights; at dips this may result in the very drastic foreshortening of headlight beams, giving the driver only a very few seconds notice of obstruction at night-time. As long a vertical curve as practicable should therefore be inserted to connect gradients at a dip.

Horizontal Curves and Super-elevation. When a vehicle is travelling at speed "v" round a bend of radius "r", it is subjected to an outward radial acceleration of "$K \dfrac{v^2}{r}$" —where K is a dimensional constant dependant upon the units used for "v" and "r".

This outward acceleration tends to throw both occupants and vehicle off the road and to overturn the vehicle.

In order to limit the discomfort to the occupants and to prevent the vehicle from sliding, a limitation must be placed on the minimum radius of curvature of the road; the greater the speed the greater the minimum radius. Further assistance may be given by banking or "super-elevating" the road, but consideration for vehicles travelling at minimal speeds in icy conditions imposes an upper limit of 1 in $14\frac{1}{2}$ to the permissible degree of super-elevation.

In Memo. 780, the recommended super-elevation is one in $\dfrac{37r}{v^2}$ where r is the radius of the curve in feet and v is the design speed of the road in m.p.h. Curves are designed so that the value of $\boxed{\dfrac{V^2}{15.r} - \tan.x}$ does not exceed $0 \cdot 15$, x being the angle of super-elevation.

Design Speed (m.p.h.)	Desirable Minimum Radius (feet)	Absolute Minimum Radius with 1 in $14\frac{1}{2}$ crossfall. (ft.)
70	2,800	1,500
60	2,100	1,100
50	1,450	750
40	900	500

With the typical motor vehicle with steered front wheels only, the rear wheels tend to run out of track on curves sharper than 500 ft. radius (crab-wise movement) so that a widening of the road becomes necessary. Memo. 780 suggests that 12 ft. lanes should be increased by 1 ft. for curves of 500 ft. radius and where lanes are less than 12 ft. wide the 1 ft. increase should be applied at 1,500 ft. radius, increasing to $1\frac{1}{2}$ ft. per lane at 1,000 ft. radius.

In order to prevent the occupants of a vehicle from being suddenly thrown outwards when a vehicle encounters a circular curve at speed, or alternatively the vehicle from wandering from the line of the curve, the road curvature is gradually applied. This gives rise to a transition curve, which may shift the line of the circular curve towards the centre by several feet.

The length of a transition curve may be calculated from the equation $L \text{ (ft.)} = \dfrac{3 \cdot 38 \ V^3}{R}$ and the Shift $S = \dfrac{L^2}{24 \ R}$ where V is in m.p.h., L is the length of the curve in feet and S is the inward shift in feet.

Road Capacities. In rural areas, capacities are based upon p.c.u.'s[2] per

---

[2] p.c.u. is an abbreviation for passenger car units.

16-hour day, taken during a busy week in August. Usually, a 7-day survey is used, otherwise one week-day, one Saturday and one Sunday, in which case, the average daily flow (A.D.F.)

$$= \frac{\text{(Weekday flow)} \times 5 + \text{(Saturday flow)} + \text{(Sunday flow)}}{7}$$

It is usual to assume there will be 150 per cent increase in traffic flow over present day, and it may often be desirable to take account of exceptional circumstances. In particular, if the flow is strongly tidal, the peak-hour flow divided by $1 \cdot 5$ may be taken as the average hourly flow on which to base the A.D.F.

Flow (A.D.F.) P.C.U.'s total flow:	Design Standard
Less than 6,000	Single 24 ft. carriageway (2-lane).
6,000–11,000	Single 33 ft. carriageway (3-lane).
11,000–25,000	Dual 24 ft. carriageways.
Over 25,000	Dual 33 ft. carriageways.

In urban areas, general design should be based upon daily flow (roads) and detailed design (road junctions, etc.) upon peak-hour flow.

All capacities in vehicles/hour (detail), v.p.d. (planning)

Conditions	Constructional Standards	Parking Control			
		Some Stationary Vehicles		No Waiting	
		Detail	Planning	Detail	Planning
Little restriction of access	2-lane single c'way	600 both lanes	6,000	1,500 both lanes	15,000
	2-lane dual c'way	1,250 one c'way heaviest flow	20,625	1,500 one c'way heaviest flow	42,750
Restricted access	Dual 2-lane	—	—	2,500 one c'way heaviest flow	42,750
Little or no traffic crossing at street level	Dual 3-lane	—	—	3,500 one c'way heaviest flow	58,000

The above A.D.F. figures are based on a tidal division of traffic at peak hour in the ratio 60/40. For stronger tidal flows the planning figures should be adjusted accordingly.

Vehicle Equivalents in p.c.u.'s per Vehicle

Traffic Conditions	Cars, light vans, motor cycle comb.	Goods vehicles (medium and heavy)	Buses and Coaches	Solo motor cycles	Pedal Cycles
Rural roads	1·0	3·0	3·0	1·0	0·5
Urban roads	1·0	2·0	3·0	0·75	0·33

Carriageway width. The normal width of a lane for moving traffic should be 11 ft. (12 ft. for Trunk Roads), but where provision is made for more than two lanes of traffic on an undivided carriageway, or more than two lanes in each carriageway of a dual carriageway road, this should be reduced to 10 ft., and where there is not sufficient volume of traffic to calculate on this basis 16 ft. should be regarded as the minimum width of carriageway, except for " . . . subsidiary development roads of relatively short lengths ", the width of which, it is suggested, should conform to " . . . any regulations or provisions made for inclusion in a planning scheme ", a somewhat question-begging statement. The number of lanes provided for a carriageway should obviously depend upon the amount of traffic likely to use it.

Gradient. One in 30 is regarded by Memo. 575 as the maximum desirable gradient, and 1 in 250 as the minimum necessary for effective surface drainage. The former figure can, of course, only be regarded as the maximum for arterial and major roads, gradients of 1 in 10, or even steeper, being sometimes required for minor roads.

Footpaths. Three feet is generally regarded as a suitable unit or lane for footpaths, hence the minimum width suitable for a footpath is 6 ft. where there is any appreciable volume of pedestrian traffic. This allows two perambulators—the widest users of footpaths—to pass each other comfortably. The width needs to be greatly increased where pedestrian traffic is heavy. Portions of footways immediately adjoining carriageways, fences, buildings, etc., are not fully used, and constitute dead width. This may amount to as much as 3 ft., but grass verges adjoining may reduce this to 1 ft. 6 in. The Report suggests that, after deducting dead width, each 2 ft. width of footway can conveniently accommodate up to 20 pedestrians per minute, with serious congestion if the flow becomes greater than 30 per minute.

Cycle tracks. The Report agrees with Memo. 575 that cycle tracks should be unidirectional, with a width of 9 ft., reducible where space is short to 6 ft., and with increases over 9 ft. where volume of traffic demands it, in units of 3 ft.

Verges and other means of segregating traffic. These are really safety margins which protect different classes of traffic travelling in the same direction, or vehicular traffic travelling in opposite directions, from collision. The thoroughness of segregation needed depends partly upon the likeliness of collision and partly upon the probable seriousness of its consequences. For example, the separation between dual carriageways on a motor road ought ideally to be so complete that even a vehicle travelling at high speed out of control cannot find its way on to the other carriageway, though the flimsiest separation is better than nothing, indeed, even white lines along wide single carriageways and at all bends and vertical gradients with poor visibility are

better than nothing, since they serve to show the safe limits of divergence. On the other hand, in many minor residential roads it may be debatable whether any separation between vehicles and pedestrians is necessary at all, since the chances of collision, mainly through a pedestrian absentmindedly stepping off the path at the moment when a vehicle is passing, are not very great, and, because of the slow speeds to be expected from vehicles, they may not be very serious. Generally speaking, the more thorough the method of separation the more expensive will it be either in land or in construction, and also the more inconvenient. To take an extreme example, if absolute road safety were to be provided in residential areas it would be necessary not only to separate motor vehicles from bicycles and pedestrians, and bicycles and pedestrians from each other, but it would be necessary, at every road junction, to provide underpasses for pedestrians and cyclists. Pedestrians could only cross the roads by means of bridges or underpasses at selected points.

It is necessary to find a reasonable compromise between the advantages of safety and the disadvantages of expense and inconvenience. All methods of separation are expensive either in land or in construction. For example, to return to the division of carriageways on a motor road, a very wide grass verge is necessary to secure safety or, on the other hand, a very stout wall.

The choice between width and height is also governed by the need to guard against deliberate as well as accidental passage from one part of the road to another, and by appearance; no verge, however wide, will prevent people crossing a road at undesirable places, but a fence will, and even a flower-bed may do so. Verges, flower-beds and shrubberies are generally more pleasant than fences and walls. It is therefore pointless to attempt to lay down definite widths for means of division.

Where the separation is between pedestrians and vehicles it can, as already said, be very slight on a minor road, if needed at all, but, at places, such as the junction of a ring road and a radial road, where it is essential for traffic safety that pedestrians shall only cross at specially arranged points, it is best to have a fence or other obstacle which can only be surmounted by an act of deliberate defiance.

Where grass verges are used for separation they should not be skimped, and, generally speaking, if it is not possible to have a width of at least 6 ft., shrubs, flower-beds, dwarf walls or setts are more satisfactory. A very narrow grass verge not only looks mean, but is liable to be trampled into mud. If dwarf walls are used it is essential that they are not so low that they can be tripped over, or they will create a worse hazard than the absence of separation.

Road junctions and intersections. A road junction, as the term is generally used, is the point at which one road meets another, an intersection the point at which two or more roads cross each other. Both junctions and intersections are, of course, the worst danger spots in a road system. A large percentage of the accidents which occur at road junctions involve a right-hand turn by one of the vehicles concerned.

The problems of reducing danger at these points are those of cost and space. If junctions and intersections are such that all classes of traffic meet each other at the same level there is danger of collision, not only between members of the same class but between those of different classes. Almost complete segregation of different classes can be achieved, and the need for users of the same class to cross traffic streams, the most dangerous process of all, can be avoided, but only at enormous cost and by using more land than can easily be accepted if compactness of development is to be maintained.

An example of complete segregation of different classes of traffic and of the avoidance of crossing traffic streams is the cloverleaf (see Fig. 42), which occupies about 24 acres and at which no collision can occur between vehicles if the drivers of those leaving the intersection can manage to avoid those already on the road they are approaching—not a very difficult feat. Even so, to illustrate the difficulty of a perfect solution, pedestrians and cyclists cannot be completely segregated from incoming traffic unless their tracks are made to pass over or under the carriageway at each point where there is an entrance or exit.

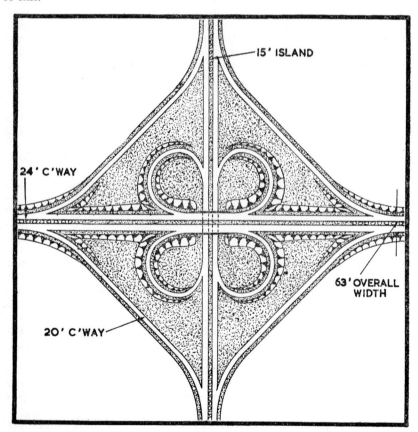

FIG. 42. Design for a cloverleaf junction of two motor roads from " Roads " by R. G. Batson.

At the other extreme there is the plain rectangular cross-roads, without safeguards of any kind, at which motor vehicles, cyclists and pedestrians may indiscriminately collide with each other without let or hindrance. Which of these extremes or of the numerous possible solutions intermediate between them is selected is a matter to be determined separately in each case according to the dictates of cost, space and traffic speed and volume.

All forms of road junctions and intersections come within one of three classes—multi-level junctions, roundabouts and others.

Multi-level intersections. The cloverleaf, an elaborate example of these, has already been mentioned. The Report suggests that there is justification for multi-level intersections where three conditions are fulfilled: (i) The

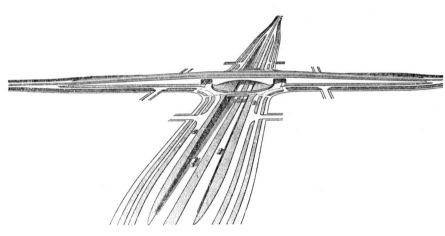

FIG. 43. Another means of securing the same results as that shown in Fig. 42. This three-level intersection is taken from Fig. 34 of " Design and Layout of Roads in Built-Up Areas ". However expensive it may be in construction costs the amount of land needed is negligible in comparison with the cloverleaf.

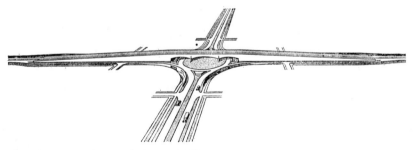

Fig. 44. Less costly and elaborate than Fig. 43, this is a two-level intersection on the same general lines, and taken from the same source.

volume of traffic would otherwise be sufficient to justify the provision of a roundabout; (ii) only a small percentage of the traffic turns to left or right, and (iii) the major volume of traffic is travelling on a fast through route.

A multi-level intersection is likely to cost between ten and fifteen times as much as a single level equivalent, so that it is only feasible to adopt this solution where the need is great.

Maximum gradients admissible at intersections are 1 in 20 for carriageways, for pedestrian ramps 1 in 10 and for unidirectional cycle ramps 1 in 20 uphill and 1 in 15 downhill.

Vertical clearance at bridges and underpasses should conform to the following minima:—

Over railways	...	...	...	...	15 ft. 0 in.
Over roads ...	...	...	...	...	16 ft. 6 in.
Over cyclists	...	...	...	...	7 ft. 6 in.
Over pedestrians	...	...	...	...	7 ft. 0 in.

Fig. 43 shows an equally effective intersection which takes up much less land.

Roundabouts. Unlike multi-level intersections, roundabouts do not enable traffic to cross without slackening speed, but, if properly designed, ensure an uninterrupted flow of traffic provided they do not have to carry more than about 6,000 p.c.u.'s an hour. Pedestrians and cyclists cannot be segregated unless costly over or underpasses are constructed, but otherwise construction is much less expensive than for a multi-level intersection.

The Report suggests that no universally applicable rules can be applied to determine circumstances where the provision of roundabouts is justified but that the factors to be taken into account are the volume, character, direction and periodicity of vehicular traffic, the amount of pedestrian traffic and physical conditions. It suggests that cross-roads on a heavily trafficked route where more than 25 per cent of the traffic using the intersection enters from the minor roads or where there is a heavy right-hand turn, provides a *prima facie* case for a roundabout or fly-over.

The central island of a roundabout should be circular and large enough to enable a vehicle to keep close to the inner kerb. The Report suggests 100 ft. as a minimum diameter, which enables a vehicle to go round it at 15 m.p.h.

The success of a roundabout depends very largely upon the ease with which vehicles using it can " weave " or pass from one traffic lane to another, with overtaking on both sides, in order to reach different exits as directly as possible. The greater the length of road in which the weaving can be carried out and the smaller the angle of approach of converging streams of traffic, the more easily can weaving be performed. The angle should not exceed 30 degrees. The greater the diameter of the island, the smaller the angle of convergence.

The width of the carriageway of the roundabout should be the average of the widths of the carriageways entering it, subject to a minimum of 30 ft. The outer kerb of the carriageway should be straight between the kerbs of

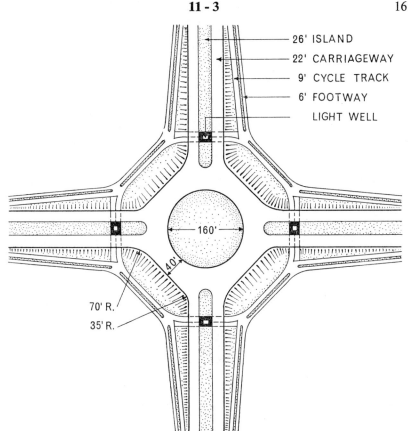

FIG. 45. A roundabout with underpasses for pedestrians and cyclists.

adjacent entering carriageways. The kerb radii at entries should be such that vehicles can keep close to the kerb; 35 ft. will secure this for practically all vehicles, but greater radii enable smoother transitions to be made. The Report suggests that radii should be 60 ft. at entrances and 150 ft. at exits where space is not restricted, but otherwise 35 ft. and 70 ft. respectively.

Fig. 45 shows a roundabout based upon an example in Circular 575. In this case pedestrians and cyclists are conducted below carriageway level, but, where this is not practicable, cyclists have to take their chance with motor vehicles unless making a left-hand turn and pedestrians can be provided with pedestrian crossings at the approaches to the roundabout. Where this is done the outer kerb of the roundabout carriageway should be fenced to prevent pedestrians making promiscuous crossings.

Other intersections and junctions. At an intersection where traffic is not

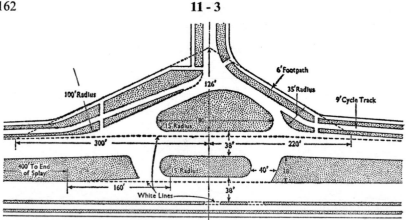

FIG. 46. This junction is illustrated in Fig. 59 of " Roads " by R. G. Batson. Junctions of this kind provide a very safe means of junction between a minor road and a dual carriageway road. They can also be used in pairs opposite each other to form an intersection, but where this is done there is a danger of motorists thinking that they are entering a roundabout and so becoming involved in collisions.

heavy enough or there is not sufficient turning traffic to warrant a roundabout, a solution of the type shown in Fig. 46 is effective.

Much less elaborate arrangements are required within the minor road system. The principal requirements are that there should not be direct crossroads, or, if this is unavoidable, that vehicles from the less important of the two roads should not be able to cross the more important road unchecked, and that there should be adequate sight lines.

The first necessity is that carriageways should meet as nearly as possible at right-angles, since other angles encourage turning at too great a speed in one direction, while in the other, they involve a difficult manoeuvre and prevent vehicles keeping close to the kerb.

At junctions sight lines should be ample. It is most important that the area between sight lines and carriageways should not only be kept clear of buildings, but also of trees, shrubs, hedges and fences which obscure visibility; where the roads are in cutting, grading at the junction will be necessary if the sight lines are to be effective. It is best for the land comprised in " visibility triangles " to form part of the road so that that they can be more readily controlled.

The first costs of intersections and junctions usually vary in inverse proportion to the cost of running them, in much the same way as the relationship between land and cost of construction in the case of means of separation. A multi-level intersection is immensely costly to construct, but once constructed traffic can look after itself. A roundabout is much less expensive, and traffic should usually be able to look after itself there, but at times of exceptional traffic a policeman (who is paid wages) is needed to supplement it.

Traffic lights are much less expensive to install but use current, and need maintenance and repair. At an ordinary crossroads no money has been spent on the junction as such, but if it is a busy one it will take up a great deal of policemen's time.

The practical or design capacity of a roundabout weaving section should be calculated from the formula

$$Q_p = \frac{86.w. (1 + \dfrac{e}{w}). (1 - \dfrac{p}{3})}{(1 + \dfrac{w}{l})} \text{ p.c.u.'s per hour.}$$

where   w is the width of the weaving section in feet. (20–60 ft.)
       e is the average entry width in feet. (0·4 w–1·0 w ft.)
       l is the length of the weaving section. (2·5 w–8 w ft.)
       p is the proportion of traffic weaving. (0·4–1·0 of total traffic)

It is often necessary to work out roughly the area of land likely to be required for a roundabout in relation to the traffic volume it will be required to carry before any detailed design of it is undertaken. R. Brain has worked out a useful table for such purposes. For further details of the method used see his article in the " Surveyor and Municipal Engineer " of 27th July, 1963.

His table assumes that the roundabout will be in approximately square form and the table is as follows. The " square " includes the whole area of the roundabout except for external verges and footpaths:

Side of square (feet)	Practical capacity in Vehicles/Hour (Sum of all approach roads)
*100	3,000
*150	4,500
200	5,500
250	7,500
300	9,000
350	9,500
400	10,000

These dimensions are too small to permit convenient passage of large vehicles.

Signalised intersections. For approach road widths greater than 16 feet, the saturation flow equation for the discharge from traffic signals is approximately $s = 160.w$ p.c.u. per hour. Where s = saturation flow w = width of road in feet.

For a non-tidal junction, the capacity of each road leading into the junction is $c = 65w_q$ p.c.u. per hour, where w_q is the lane width given to the traffic queuing up to the lights. Continuous left-filters will achieve about $120 w_f$ p.c.u. per hour where w_f is the width of the filter lane.

Vehicle Equivalents in p.c.u.'s per Vehicle

Traffic Conditions	Cars, light vans, motor cycle combs.	Goods vehicles (medium and heavy)	Buses and Coaches	Solo motor cycles	Pedal Cycles
Roundabouts	1·0	2·8	2·8	0·75	0·5
Traffic signals	1·0	1·75	2·25	0·33	0·2

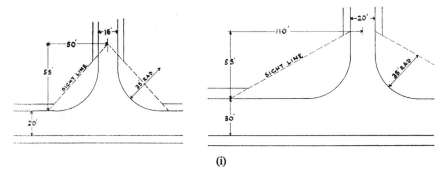

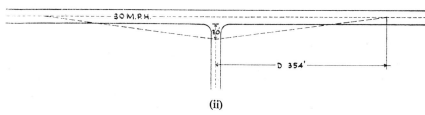

FIG. 47. " Visibility triangles " at the junctions of minor roads.
(i) As recommended in the Report on the Layout of Roads in Built-Up Areas.
(ii) In accordance with more recent ideas.
Both are based on calculations which take into account drivers' reaction times and braking efficiency but in (i) it is assumed that when drivers of approaching vehicles see each other both will stop if necessary, while in (ii) it is assumed that a driver on the through road will not normally stop, leaving it to the driver on the joining road to decide whether he has time to proceed or stop, a more realistic assumption.

The left-hand drawing in (i) is based on the assumption that vehicles on the through road will only be travelling at 20 m.p.h.—applicable obviously only to a very short or winding through road, while that on the right assumes a speed of 30 m.p.h. on the through road. This applies also to (ii), the sight lines in which are based on the formula $D = 11·8 V$ feet, where V = Speed in m.p.h., to be expected on the through road.

It will be seen that the sight lines in the right-hand drawing of (i) are much more restrictive close to the junction than those in (ii) but that the latter operate for a much greater lateral distance.

Widths for minor roads. The recommendations of Circular 19 of the Ministry of Local Government and Planning are indicated in Fig. 40. They appear to be based on the principle of 11 ft. traffic lanes for roads on to which

a considerable amount of local traffic is likely to debouch (the " main street " and " principal shopping street ") 8 ft. lanes for minor roads which are not culs-de-sac (" minor street B ") and 6 ft. 6 in. lanes for culs-de-sac, etc. which cater only for a very few slow-moving vehicles.

In all cases except where there are shops or public vehicles, where additional widths are provided, the fact that a parked vehicle will convert that part of the road temporarily to single traffic lane width is accepted and the widths chosen enable two vehicles of normal width to pass comfortably at speeds which can reasonably be expected. It is to be noted that if a carriageway is to be provided at all it *must* allow two vehicles to pass, or a single parked vehicle can block the street. For this reason the recommendation that the carriageway of a cul-de-sac less than 200 ft. long may be reduced to 9 ft. along any portion where there is no access to property does not seem to me to be wise. I also think that it is much better not to reduce carriageways below a width of 16 ft. even in culs-de-sac. The reduction in first costs may be more than offset by increased maintenance costs due to heavy vehicles, unable to pass parked vehicles, mounting the kerb and travelling along the verge, with damage to both kerb and verge. On the other hand, it would often I believe, be perfectly satisfactory in culs-de-sac, either to omit footpaths altogether or to confine them to a line of flagstones in " stepping-stone " form to allow pedestrians to walk dry-shod when the carriageway was not available.

Although carriageways are expensive it is very important that they should be of adequate width to prevent them being frequently blocked by careless or inconsiderate parking of vehicles. Recent personal observation suggests to me that some increase in carriageway widths even above the modifications of the Circular 19 standards which I have just suggested would be desirable.

The modern motor car or light trade vehicle tends to be a little under 5 ft. 6 in. in overall width. However slowly vehicles move it is desirable for there to be a minimum space of about a foot between them. This leads me to suggest a minimum width for any carriageway, however minor, of 18 ft. With this width, even if two vehicles are parked directly opposite each other it remains possible to pass between them, while if there is a parked vehicle on one side only two slowly moving vehicles can pass each other.

Similarly, a carriageway width of 24 feet rather than 22 feet may well make a crucial difference in the working of a somewhat more important road.

Footpath widths are based upon the minimum necessary to allow two pedestrians or prams to pass comfortably.

Seventy feet is normally regarded as the minimum satisfactory distance apart for two-storey buildings parallel to each other, so that, in the case of a minor street, this leaves 42 ft. not occupied by carriageway or footway, which can appropriately be devoted to two 15 ft. forecourts, either in the form of divided front gardens or undivided grass sward, and two 6 ft. verges between carriageway and footpaths.

Numerous variations in the method of treatment of land between house fronts are possible, and their intelligent use can do much to assist the variety and pleasant appearance of a residential area. (See Fig. 48.)

It cannot be too strongly stressed that the road systems, both major and minor, which we see around us bear little resemblance to the most satisfactory arrangements which could be devised. For the most part they have been constructed with no thought for requirements of the motor vehicle, and even the best examples are carried out over such a limited area that the benefits to be obtained from good design do not attach to them in anything like full measure.

Even in New Towns peculiarities of site, existing development and roads and inadequate money for road construction have prevented model road systems for the towns as a whole being created. Nevertheless, it is remarkable how safe one feels, in the residential areas at least, of a New Town where, simply because direct crossroads have been avoided and reasonable sight lines have been preserved, the situation is much better than in ordinary residential areas. If, with these points in mind, the various illustrations of the theoretical New Town discussed in this book are examined imaginatively, it will be seen how fully the safety and convenience of traffic would be catered for as compared with any existing town in this country.

Assuming the creation of such a town on a completely virgin site, it is worth remarking that this road system would not involve any excessive expenditure, since no multi-level junctions are used and no traffic lights are necessary, nor are single-sided service roads, an extremely expensive interwar expedient to allow houses accessibility to a main road without giving them individual access to it.

It is true that it might be necessary to construct some multi-level intersections in this town if traffic volumes increased substantially. They would probably be those adjacent to the town centre and take the form of two level intersections of the kind shown in Fig. 44. There have been very great divergences in the estimates made of the need for multi-level road intersections in towns. For example the master plan for Cumbernauld and the Hook project (mentioned in Chapter 8) assume the need for numerous multi-level intersections for towns of the order 100,000 population or less, while Frederick Gibberd in his report on the feasibility of expanding Harlow New Town to a population of the order of 130,000 contemplates the need for only one such intersection, and expresses some uncertainty about the need even for this.

So far as long distance arterial routes are concerned the ideal must obviously be to provide roads which make it possible to drive from any part of the country to any other without needing to pass through any towns or villages (except where large cities are encountered, in which case the road would be taken either above or below ground level, independent of the city road system) and without using any except controlled junctions. There should of course be dual carriageways throughout. This may seem a fantastic vision but if we are going to make full use of the motor car it is no more than a simple necessity. If we cannot contemplate the construction of such a road system, towards which the present motor road programme is but a tiny contribution, we should be more sensible to limit the sizes and speeds of motor vehicles to the capacities of the existing road system. This may seem even more fantastic but we may yet come to it.

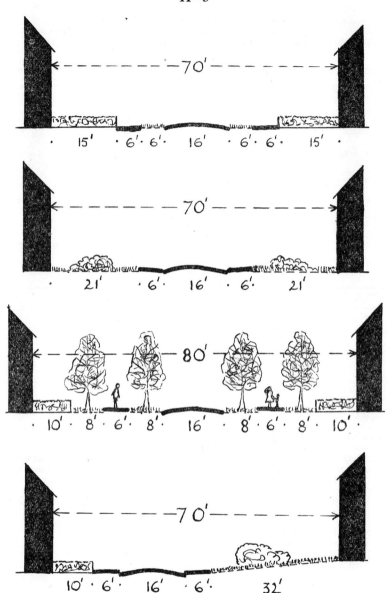

FIG. 48. A selection of the innumerable variations of treatment which are possible for the space between fronts of houses. The trees, bushes, etc., are not to be thought of as extending in rows of indefinite length; there can appropriately be gaps, clumping and complete changes of treatment even in different parts of the same road.

11-4. IMPROVEMENTS TO THE EXISTING ROAD SYSTEM

The foregoing has been confined to consideration of the factors which should govern road design when the designer has a completely free hand, and is unimpeded by existing roads. It is painfully obvious that conditions in existing towns and on existing roads outside towns are very different from those desirable. Improvements are not only costly in themselves but frequently involve the demolition of buildings which have many years of useful life left in them. Nevertheless, as pointed out elsewhere, the remoteness in time of the prospect of carrying out improvements should not prevent plans from being made and, in any case, numerous minor improvements are possible which give results out of all proportion to the amount of labour and materials entailed.

Arterial roads outside towns are mostly very ancient roads which have been improved in piecemeal fashion over a number of years, so that on a single route fairly short lengths of modern dual carriageway road join long stretches of single carriageway three-lane road of excellent surface and engineering design, but inadequate to deal with large volumes of traffic, and these are punctuated by narrow village streets. There are very few routes in this country on which a high speed can safely be maintained continuously for more than a few miles.

Clearly, the villages and towns which lie athwart an arterial road should be by-passed as soon as possible though this must inevitably take many years. It is essential that by-passes should not only provide expeditious routes, but that they should appear to do so. Drivers are in many ways sheep-like

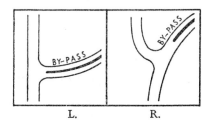

Fig. 49

animals and tend to follow the line of least resistance. If the begining of a by-pass is arranged as in Fig. 49 (L.) for example, it may be little used, while the adoption of Fig. 49 (R.) might appreciably increase the number of vehicles using it.

The Report gives estimates of the proportion of traffic entering places of various sizes which can be induced to use a by-pass; this is as follows:

Population				Percentage of Traffic by-passable
Up to 10,000 ...	...	...	...	80 per cent.
10,000 to 50,000	...	...	...	65 per cent.
50,000 to 100,000	...	...	...	45 per cent.
100,000 to 250,000	...	...	...	20 per cent.
250,000 to 500,000	...	...	...	15 per cent.
500,000 to 1,000,000 ...	...	...	less than 10 per cent.

The volume of traffic by-passable from small towns on a principal arterial route will, of course, be much greater than from the same size on a less important route which serves as the cultural and shopping centre for a large area.

Even when a by-pass has been constructed, this will not remove the need to treat radials as arterial roads even in quite small towns. Every effort should be made to improve them both by giving them dual carriageways and by limiting the number of minor road accesses into them and the number of individual property accesses. As opportunity offers, the most satisfactory method is to remove, and not replace, houses fronting on to such roads. The existing road pattern of such development would be retained if suitable, but the plots adjoining the arterial road should be left open and planted as a screen against noise from the arterial. This would also screen the unsightly views of back gardens, thus opened up to view. There would usually still be too many minor roads opening into the arterial at short intervals, but even this could sometimes be mitigated by means discussed later. As regards ribbon development, that is, development only one plot deep adjoining a main road, it is on all grounds a curse, and the sooner authority is prepared to use egal powers and funds to obliterate as much of it as possible the better.

Various improvements are possible for well-engineered lengths of single three-lane carriageway. Here the great danger occurs when two vehicles moving in opposite directions decide to overtake at the same time, with insufficient width in which to do so. This leads to head-on crashes, desperate last-second cutting in, and the forcing of following vehicles either into collision from behind or into leaving the carriageway. The danger is at its worst on bends and at the summits of convex vertical curves.

The most radical solution is to convert the existing carriageway into a unidirectional one, and to construct another carriageway for traffic in the opposite direction, near, but not necessarily immediately adjoining or exactly parallel. This is, of course, a very costly method, but has the advantage of not disturbing the existing pattern of communications or of radically upsetting the boundaries of farm units. It means some waste, since the existing carriageway would often be much wider than necessary for a unidirectional carriageway.

Second, the existing carriageway could be widened sufficiently to convert it into dual carriageways with a narrow dividing strip. In terms of land taken and disturbance this is eminently satisfactory, but as the widening of a carriageway involves not merely adding a strip but reorganising the existing camber and foundations it is not so economical in labour as might seem to be the case.

Third, where the existing carriageway is wide it might be practicable to convert it into narrow dual carriageways by introducing a kerb down the middle. This would eliminate head-on crashes, except where a vehicle got completely out of control and jumped the kerb but might increase the dangers of other kinds of collision because of inadequate space in which to overtake.

Fourth, though this is a solution of very restricted application, the retention of the existing carriageway as unidirectional and the use of the carriageway of another near-by road running approximately parallel to the arterial road would sometimes be helpful, provided local conditions were not such that hopeless chaos was caused to existing house and farm accesses.

None of these solutions would, of course, convert existing arterial roads into first-class high-speed roads of the kind described earlier. Existing intersections and junctions would still be far too numerous, their number alone would make it financially impossible to treat them all in the elaborate ways described earlier, and this would be aggravated by the fact that levels would often be most unfavourable to such treatment. The advantage of the newly planned arterial road is that it can be routed to avoid many junctions and intersections altogether and to meet existing roads at points where under- or over-passing can be provided without the construction of inordinately long approach ramps. But, even after the construction of great national and regional through routes there will still be large, though reduced, volumes of traffic on the existing main roads, which will need to be better than they are now, and the improvement of many miles of which, in one of the ways suggested, will become feasible long before all national and regional routes can be constructed.

It is of the utmost importance that proposals should be worked out in detail for main road improvements, however far ahead realisation may be, so that no kind of development shall frustrate them, whether it be the erection of a barn or an isolated country house. Sporadic development along such roads is no longer, one hopes, a serious menace.

The great mass of rural secondary and minor roads are of remarkably high standard, probably the finest in the world and, if used for their proper purpose of affording communications between rural communities and farms, are perfectly adequate, apart from detailed improvements to remove the dangers of sharp bends and blind intersections. It is their present use, in the absence of a coherent and adequate main road system, for arterial purposes which makes them unsatisfactory. A first-class arterial system would induce most people who could use it to do so. Where no first-class main road exists many vehicles use secondary roads as short cuts or alternative routes giving greater variety of scene.

In towns the main defects are:

    (i) The presence of what Sir Alker Tripp calls " nondescript " streets which have to combine several distinct functions;

    (ii) hopeless congestion in the town centre;

    (iii) radial roads of inadequate width with buildings fronting on them and innumerable intersections and junctions;

    (iv) absence of convenient lateral routes, and

    (v) Incoherent minor street systems with dangerous intersections.

The nondescript street is at once the worst problem and the most difficult to improve, and the main radials are generally examples of them. Travelling down Oxford Street, Manchester (which continues as Oxford Road and Wilmslow Road), starting from its terminus in St. Peter's Square, in the heart of the city, one traverses first an area of cinemas, theatres and shops, then a long length with shops predominating as frontage, but with dwellings, warehouses, filling stations and pubs. interspersed. This lasts as far as Cheadle, about six miles from St. Peter's Square, but the mixture of fronting uses gradually becomes less intimate, until, at Withington and Didsbury, the non-residential uses are in well-defined groups of limited length. During its progress outwards from the centre the road has also afforded direct frontage access to the University and a group of hospitals, to railway stations and to parks. Nowhere, until Didsbury is reached, about four miles from Albert Square, is any provision made for waiting lanes for vehicles. Except within a few hundred yards of the city centre little restriction is placed upon parking. There are countless road junctions and intersections and several sets of traffic lights.

Yet this is, by existing standards, a remarkably satisfactory radial road. Its generally considerable width of carriageway enables parking to take place on both sides of the road without greatly obstructing the flow of traffic, it is nearly straight and traffic blocks seldom last long, even at rush hours. Although there are innumerable points at which danger of collision and accidents to pedestrians is great conditions are not intolerable.

Oxford Road provides an interesting contrast with the portion of Watling Street which traverses Strood, Rochester and Chatham, and which performs much the same functions. Here the carriageway width is generally much narrower, footpaths are also much narrower and in consequence pedestrians continually encroach on the carriageway. It forms the principal business street of the Medway towns and, although by-passed for part of its length, is chronically in a state of hopeless congestion.

This is an example of an exceptionally bad main radial, as Oxford Street is exceptionally good, yet it seems inconceivable that anything can be done for generations to improve it fundamentally. Apart from anything else, the lie of the land is such that curtilages are unusually shallow and the setting back of buildings on redevelopment presents great problems. The construction of the Medway Towns by-pass will no doubt ease the trouble but will certainly not cure it.

Most radial roads lie somewhere between these two in degrees of unsatisfactoriness. Mostly, the properties fronting on them comprise a large percentage of the most important in the town, and cannot economically be replaced for many years. The ideal solution is that, on redevelopment, all buildings should be made to turn their backs on the main road and obtain access either from an existing minor road or from one introduced as a result of amending the minor street pattern, the number of junctions with the main road being drastically reduced. This is certainly not possible in most cases without revision of ownership boundaries, since, particularly where the main road requires in any case to be widened, there is often enough no room for individual properties to be redeveloped in this fashion.

This can be remedied if the necessary land is included in an area designated for compulsory purchase and if a clear and definite set of proposals is worked out and adhered to, but finance limits the amount of land which can be designated for compulsory purchase, so that there must be a prospect of fairly early redevelopment. Failing this, even if proposals for comprehensive development are worked out, refusal of individual proposals for redevelopment by owners may result in the site being rendered useless, in which case the Local Planning Authority must purchase it if the owner so requires. If the proposed form of redevelopment cannot take place for many years, the Local Planning Authority may have it on their hands quite unproductive of any income.

Individual sites often cannot be redeveloped properly in isolation and it may be a long while before adjoining properties are ready to be cleared away and the sites redeveloped in accordance with a unified scheme, but there is a limit to the number of sites which can be left idle for a long while. Further even if it is physically possible for a single site to be redeveloped in accordance with an ultimate plan, it may not be financially practicable. For example, a large shop housed in a derelict building and, on redevelopment, made to turn about and face on to a minor street, would normally have some difficulty in competing with its neighbours, contained in solid buildings with many years of life ahead, and fronting on to the main street. Such a building might well prove to be unlettable.

These are the difficulties, and they are grave, yet much more might be done to attack them with vigour. Proposals for the re-development of individual sites are being made continually, and, too often, Local Planning Authorities issue permissions which merely require the new building to be pushed back a few feet to permit of some trivial street widening, which may ease traffic congestion a little but cannot possibly effect any radical improvement. There can be little room for doubt that, to secure properly Planned towns, arterial road traffic must be treated as poison to be avoided by buildings at all cost. Although it may not always be possibly in all the prevailing circumstances to realise proposals which seek to divorce the arterial completely from building access, at the very least such setback should be insisted upon as will permit of any necessary road widening being carried out and will provide for a waiting bay in front of the property concerned, though this is a poor substitute for complete divorce.

These proposals are radical; the street fronted by buildings has been regarded as the norm for so long that any other form of development is startling, yet the situation demands such a change.

The architectural problems are not insuperable, nor even especially difficult; they involve merely a new approach. Lest it be imagined that the policy advocated of backing on to roads would produce a corridor effect similar to that now prevailing, but in reverse, I hasten to add that many

buildings could be placed sideways on, but with their access to minor streets.

The reduction of intersections and junctions with arterials is of importance next only to that of preventing access from individual buildings. In the common case where a gridiron layout adjoins an arterial, as in Fig. 50, it should be possible to convert a large proportion of the streets entering it into culs-de-sac by the simple expedient of putting rows of posts across their ends, and thus forcing traffic to use the remainder, which, by traffic lights or, where possible, the provision of roundabouts, could be adequately controlled. The culs-de-sac so created would remain as pedestrian accesses, but pedestrian access to the carriageways of arterials should be further restricted by fencing the footways off, except at pedestrian crossings, which should, where possible, be by underpass or bridge. In such areas sight lines are usually inadequate or even non-existent. Obviously, where houses are built right up to the edges of pavements and there is no sight line at all nothing can be done until redevelopment takes place, but, where there is some forecourt, a safety margin could be provided if steps were taken to ensure that, at corners, no obstruction higher than a driver's eyeline were allowed on it, whether hedge, fence, trees or bushes. This could be secured by simple statutory action backed by vigorous enforcement. It would probably cause resentment, but it would save lives.

These suggestions would certainly cause a good deal of inconvenience, but they would not create an unworkable state of affairs, the cost would be comparatively trifling, they would help reduce traffic congestion, and, more important than all else, they would save lives. If once such a policy were adopted and vigorously prosecuted it would probably quickly be accepted by

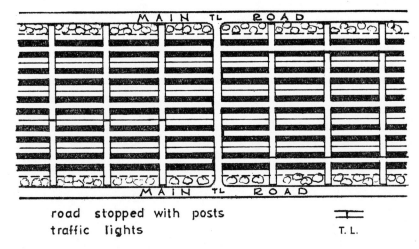

road stopped with posts

traffic lights　　　　　　　　T. L.

Fig. 50. Alleviation of road danger and congestion pending comprehensive development. Plots fronting main roads are cleared and devoted partly to screen planting, partly to increasing depths of plots backing onto them. Road accesses to main roads are drastically limited and direct crossings of minor roads reduced in numbers.

the public, which, to cite Sir Alker Tripp once more, accepts without complaint severe restrictions on the number of points at which it can cross a railway.

Congestion within the town centre can hardly be dealt with, except by the provision of an inner ring road, which, in normal cases, will immediately result in a substantial reduction in the amount of traffic using the central area roads, particularly if, at the same time, a number of roads are converted into culs-de-sac to prevent or render highly inconvenient passage right through the central area. This, coupled with ample car parks within and just outside the central area and such rationalisation of the street pattern as may from time to time become possible, might speedily transform what is at present a picture of hopeless confusion to relative order.

The absence of lateral routes in many towns has already been commented upon. Where they do not exist at all, and vehicles have to thread their way through a maze of minor streets to make lateral movement, it may be difficult to effect much improvement except by planning a long-term new road through existing development, but it will usually be possible to select some route more favourable than the rest, and, by stoppings up, fencing of footpaths and so on, to induce most laterally moving vehicles to use it, and to enable them to do so in safety. Very often lateral routes are nondescript roads of the worst kind, fronted directly by houses and a few shops attracted by the volume of traffic, and not even modified to fulfil their purpose by having a carriageway of greater width than the minor roads in the vicinity. Such roads have been deliberately planned in quite recent years. The remedy for these is the same as for radials.

CHAPTER 12

THE TOWN CENTRE

THE TOWN CENTRE, as already explained in Chapters 4 and 8, is the part of the town in which the central services of the highest order which that particular type of town can support, are found. These are services which are used by the population of the town as a whole and also by the inhabitants of its service area. It is important to remember this, for the scale at which services of various kinds should be provided in the town centre depends more upon the total population of the town's service area than upon that of the town itself. This complicates greatly the determination of standards, which must be calculated specially for every individual town in the light both of the numbers and characteristics of its dependent population.

On the other hand the town centre also acts as a local centre, or neighbourhood centre, for the residential areas immediately surrounding it; in fact the concept of the hierarchy of service centres expounded in Chapter 4 applies to service centres within a town in somewhat the same way as it does to service centres within a region.

The most important requirements for a town centre are geographical centrality, accessibility for vehicles and pedestrians, ample parking spaces and a high measure of compactness.

This last point is of special importance because visitors to the town centre will probably wish to call at a number of different places within it during a single visit. However central and easily approached the centre may be, its efficiency will be greatly diminished if it is so spread out that considerable time has to be spent moving from one destination to another within it. It may reasonably be said that the smaller the area of the town centre is the better, subject to requirements of daylighting, car parking and vehicular and pedestrian circulation being adequately met. Intensive development of land within the town centre is therefore a positive virtue, and high buildings may have a definite functional value.

Nevertheless, the extent to which they should be used in a Plan entirely determined by scientific considerations, and not bedevilled by land value problems, would depend upon balancing the advantages of the additional compactness which their use makes possible against the increased cost of their construction. Ideally, a balance should be struck between these two. In arriving at such a balance it would be necessary also to take into account that the horizontal compactness to be secured by the use of high buildings can only be secured by some degree of loss of vertical compactness. With very tall buildings the time spent within them in waiting for and using a lift may be appreciable, and has to be set against the saving in horizontal movements from one building to another secured by building high. In any case, as will be explained in Chapter 17, the actual amount of land saved by building high is far less than is commonly supposed.

In considering the principles of Planning it is a sound maxim that the patterns of development commonly to be seen in the contemporary world are usually very different from the most satisfactory arrangements that could be devised. This applies with special force to the town centre, which has generally grown in so haphazard and unsatisfactory a fashion that existing forms provide little guide to satisfactory Planning. Historically, many town centres, if not most, have grown around a crossroads forming the point of origin of the town. The positions of greatest centrality, and hence most strongly competed for, are those immediately adjoining the crossing. Relatively unsuccessful competitors have had to content themselves with sites on the roads leading to the crossing but further from it, or, where a geographically central but not especially prominent site is needed, on back land between the arms of the cross. (See Fig. 51.)

Extreme physical centrality is so much of the essence of requirements for central area uses that even where land pressure within the town as a whole is slight it is quite common to find very intensive development of the town centre itself. With the increase of motor traffic such centres have usually become intolerably congested, not only with traffic having a destination within the town centre, but with through traffic, since the roads forming the cross are frequently not only the most important town roads but are regional or even national through routes. Elaborate one-way road systems sometimes relieve this congestion appreciably, but practically invariably the town centre, which should be the area of greatest accessibility in the town,

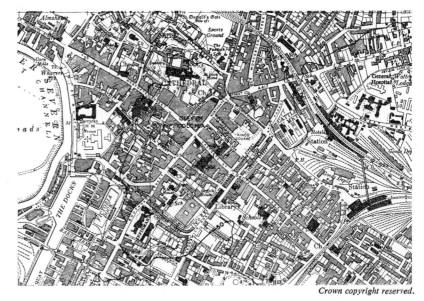

Crown copyright reserved.

FIG. 51. The Cross at Gloucester is a typical example of the traditional town centre. Buildings cluster intensely around the Cross itself but the intensity rapidly falls off.

remains the least accessible part of it, around and within which movement is most difficult and parking space for vehicles hardest to find.

The form of such centres itself suggests a remedy: the construction of an inner ring road surrounding the town centre. All traffic needing to use the roads approaching the centre but not wishing to enter the centre itself can be drained off from it, move more freely on the ring road and lessen the congestion within the centre. If this arrangement can be made it is usually unnecessary to carry out any drastic or premature redevelopment within the valuable sites of the centre itself, the roads of which become local roads only.

It may even be possible to close some of these roads to vehicular traffic, and to create a pedestrian precinct, although it will still be necessary for all properties to have vehicular access for delivery and collection of goods, refuse collection and the like. (See Fig. 52.)

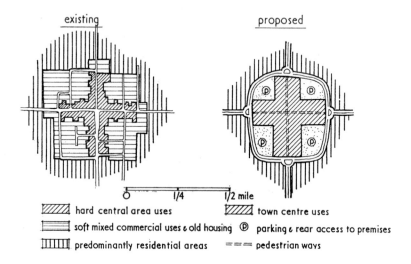

FIG. 52. A typical ENGLISH TOWN CENTRE shown diagrammatically. In such cases the disadvantages which inevitably attach to such an arrangement at the present time can be removed simply, without undue expense and without disrupting the building pattern. From "Town Planning at the Crossroads" by Lewis Keeble, Estates Gazette, 1961.

The creation of an inner ring road must usually involve the acquisition and demolition of costly property, since, to fulfil its purpose properly, it must approach closely to the town centre, and thus pass through areas where land values, although not reaching peaks attained within the town centre, are still extremely high. Such ring roads therefore have not often been constructed in complete form. There can be little doubt that this must be done before very long if many town centres are not to become practically unusable.

In the case of very large towns, as will be mentioned later on, no single simple device such as a ring road can be expected to cure their difficulties, but it is an eminently satisfactory device for towns of moderate size.

Even so, there will usually remain a serious deficiency of parking space, which leads to roads within the town centre which would otherwise be adequate being clogged by parked cars. Car parks are not a highly profitable form of land use in an area where land values are high, so that without drastic public action, possibly involving considerable expenditure out of the public purse, no sufficient remedy is likely to be supplied.

There are good reasons for thinking that by one means or another the costs of providing car parking in town centres ought to be met by the occupiers of premises in it. Every town centre is to some extent in competition with the centres of neighbouring towns, and even slightly sometimes with the local centres of its own town. Any increase in accessibility and convenience for users is likely, therefore, to bring benefits out of all proportion to the cost involved by attracting users from near the edge of the service areas, who, but for the advantage of easy parking, would be just as likely to have used some other centre.

Efforts are, of course, being made today, where sites are redeveloped in town centres, to secure that appropriate parking space is reserved within the curtilage. Useful though this is it is only a partial solution, for the great need is for car parks to be provided in such a form that they serve users of the town centre for different purposes at different times. It is, for example, no use having a car park for shop users if later on in the day it cannot be used by visitors to cinema or theatre. To provide parking space for each individual site would be absurdly wasteful of land. The criterion is that the peak amount of parking at any one time in the centre should be catered for. Unless therefore car parks are provided on a pool basis, rather than as parts of individual sites, wastage of land and/or deficiency of parking space is bound to result.

Apparently it is not at present legally possible to make enforceable arrangements for a developer to pay for the cost of parking instead of physically providing it himself where parking either has to be provided elsewhere than on the site it is to serve, or where it would be better Planning to provide it elsewhere. This is a most hampering limitation.

The difficulties of converting an existing town centre into a pedestrian precinct have already been mentioned, but despite the difficulties it remains a most desirable objective. Many users of the town centre, particularly those on shopping expeditions, want to move about, making numerous short calls at different destinations, and be able to concentrate on their shopping, in particular on the displays in shop windows, without having to avoid traffic and seize opportunities to cross the road. It may in fact be said that the motor car and the shopping area are almost as incompatible as fast-moving motor traffic and the residential area.

Other uses in the central area may not be handicapped as much by vehicles as are shops, but from the point of view of the office worker, especially, freedom from the noise of large volumes of traffic is very beneficial, and within

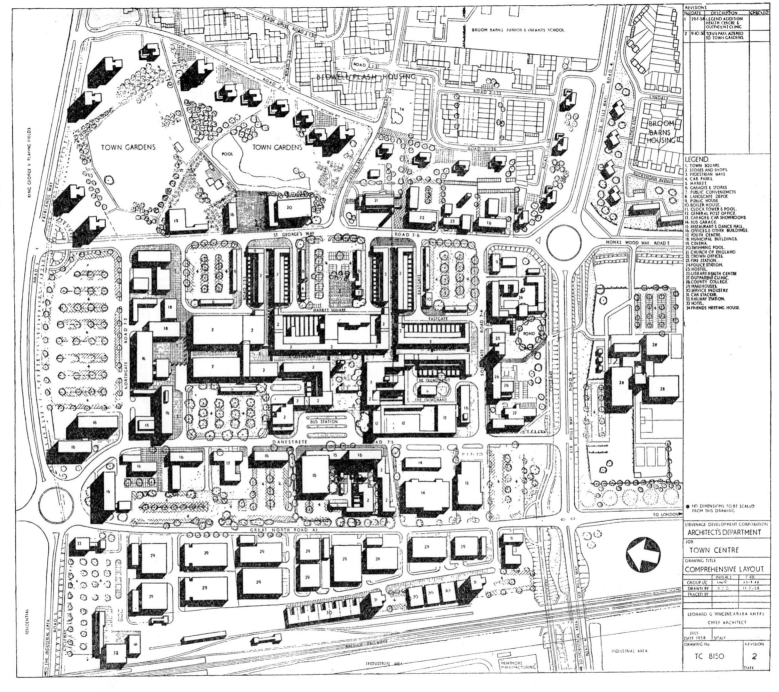

FIG. 53. The Town Centre of Stevenage New Town. The shopping core is entirely pedestrian, and, now nearing completion, affords an impressive example of the successful application of the pedestrian precinct principle.

Scale of feet:

0   100   200

the intensely built-up town centre the reduction of exhaust fumes is of benefit to all.

Each individual town has to be considered individually, and no stock solution is possible. As already suggested, the problems of securing vehicular access for servicing each individual property are great.

In general, the larger the town centre the greater the difficulty in converting it into a pedestrian area, and numerous varieties of compromise are possible. It may, for example, be practicable to convert the shopping area itself into a pedestrian precinct, since it is the part of the town centre in greatest need of this, leaving the remainder with a normal street pattern. Again, the prospect of extensive redevelopment may offer opportunities, if not for complete remodelling on pedestrian lines, to do something quite different, namely to raise the level of shopping and similar uses to the first floor, access being obtained by a system of raised pedestrian ways, leaving the road pattern as it is, with parking, service access and storage at road level. While this does not do anything to mitigate the nuisance of exhaust fumes, in other respects it could be a great improvement.

A New Town affords the opportunity, when it is built on a comparatively clear site, to apply the pedestrian principle much more fully. Regrettably, Stevenage is the only case in which full advantage has been taken of this opportunity; the Master Plan for its Town Centre is shown in Fig. 53.

The history of the Stevenage Town Centre is of interest. The original Master Plan was designed on pedestrian lines, but, owing apparently to the reluctance of some firms to take leases of sites in the town centre because they feared economic disadvantage, the Development Corporation prepared an amended design providing for normal road access in the centre. Local opinion, however, was so enthusiastically in favour of the pedestrian principle that it induced the Corporation to change its mind again and restore the pedestrian Plan.

Despite the need for a town centre to compete successfully with others in relation to its outlying service population, it nevertheless enjoys a monopoly situation in relation to the inhabitants of the town itself because of its proximity. If the form selected for its development is otherwise socially and economically satisfactory, it is not likely to suffer material detriment on account of competitive disadvantage alone.

There are however certain inherent difficulties connected with a pedestrian town centre. Though they can be overcome they are sufficiently intrusive to require special attention:—

(1) Without intimate knowledge of the layout of the centre visitors may park in the most remote part from their destination, and be thereby involved in a walk of some considerable distance.

(2) In wet weather and for invalids it is inconvenient when visits have to be made to different parts of the centre. It is also inconvenient to carry parcels long distances.

(3) It is difficult to arrange the layout so that service roads to buildings do not interfere with pedestrian ways.

There are some fairly obvious methods of overcoming these. Large

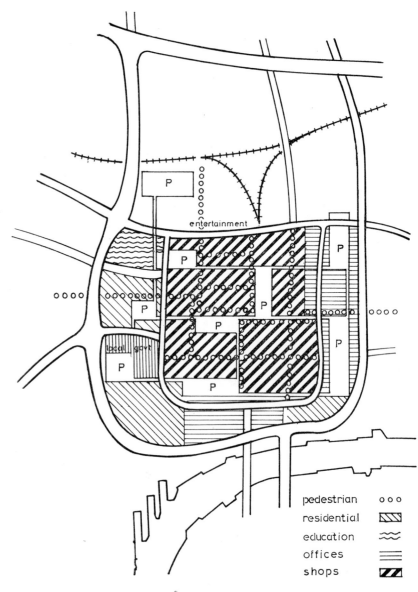

entertainment

P

pedestrian   o o o
residential   ⬙⬙⬙
education   ∼∼∼
offices   ≡≡≡
shops   ▰▰▰

Fig. 54

scale layouts of the centre can be displayed on hoardings; covered pedestrian ways can be provided as protection from the weather to form a network all over the centre, and if costs permit even be walled in with glass and heated. It would also be possible to provide a wheel-chair service for invalids and a supply of trolleys for parcels. A car, when it has been parked, need not necessarily be left in the same place for the whole duration of a visit to the centre, but if it is thought worth while to do so can be moved to another part more immediately accessible to the next destination to be visited. This may be done by travelling round the inner ring road until the entry to the appropriate car park is reached, or the car parks themselves may be linked by access ways within the centre, a method used in the example illustrated in "Town Centres Approach to Renewal". See Fig. 54. This method has considerable advantages but inevitably reduces the degree of separation of motor vehicles from pedestrians. In some cases it is virtually impossible to secure a completely pedestrian precinct within a town centre because the layout simply does not permit this being done without exorbitant expenditure or the unwarranted destruction of beautiful buildings. A main shopping street may, in these circumstances, have to continue to be used by vehicles. Nevertheless the disadvantages of this can be mitigated either by physically blocking through traffic by means of a barrier across the road at about its mid-point or by restricting the use of the road to service vehicles, or both.

Although I have stressed the possible difficulties I do not personally believe that there is the slightest risk of a pedestrian town centre proving unattractive to its users once it is constructed. However lazy the motorist may be he is

not incapable of learning by experience, and is likely after a comparatively short period to appreciate the advantages of quick and easy parking and safe shopping.

There is, of course, a limit to the physical size of a single pedestrian precinct beyond which splitting up into two or more units becomes necessary. If extreme accessibility to the parked car is to be maintained it can even be argued that this is so with a town as small as 60,000 population.

Broadly speaking two main types of layout can be adopted, as shown in Fig. 55. The first has a number of roads running inwards from the inner ring road in the form of culs-de-sac terminating in car parks. The other has what might almost be described as an " inner-inner ring road ", with limited points of access to the inner ring road and with car parks leading directly from it. With the latter arrangement the visitor to the town centre is not completely free from the menace of road traffic as he is with the former, but he *is* free of through traffic, and he *does* enjoy much greater mobility by motor car within the centre.

It should be borne in mind that even within the town centre some uses need greater accessibility and prominence than others, that some are the subject of incidental " impulse " visits among a number of other visits, while others, such as churches, museums, theatres will usually be either the main event or even the sole destination of a visit to the centre. There therefore seems no grave disadvantage in at least these two kinds of use being separated from each other by a vehicular road, since the amount of pedestrian movement back and forth between them is not likely to be serious.

such as churches, museums, theatres will usually be either the main, or During the last few years the idea of building town centres in two-level form has been widely canvassed. The attractive basis for this idea, which has already been briefly mentioned in Chapter 5 is that vehicular circulation, parking and the carrying out of servicing of buildings from vehicles should take place at a lower level, usually ground level, and that all pedestrian movement and pedestrian entrances to buildings should be on a higher level or deck.

Plans for town centres of this kind have been prepared for Fort Worth in America and for Hook and Cumbernauld New Towns, among others, in this country. It is intended to carry out the Cumbernauld plan, though the town has not yet reached the stage at which development of the town centre can begin. Meanwhile, a considerable number of town centre schemes on these lines are in course of or have been prepared.

It is very much to be hoped that Cumbernauld will be used as a pilot scheme and substantially completed before any others are brought to the stage of irrevocable commitment. There are many promising features about the idea, but on the other hand there are many difficulties and drawbacks which need to be examined in detail from a working example to see whether they can be overcome or sufficiently reduced. An idea which is new and interesting is not necessarily sound, and, in this case, technical difficulties apart, cost is an extremely important factor, which is frequently likely to be crucial. It would be extremely unfortunate if a wave of enthusiasm resulted in a large number of two-level centres being started and left incomplete through lack

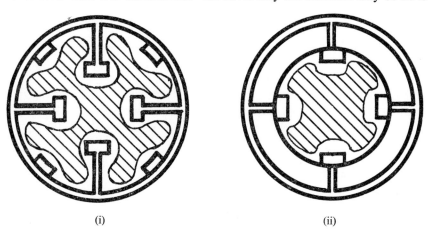

(i)   (ii)

Fig. 55. Two different forms of planned town centre.
(i) Once within the central area the pedestrian visitor need never encounter a motor vehicle.
(ii) Here there is an " inner-inner ring road ". The pedestrian visitor is not completely segregated from the motor vehicle but accessibility and servicing of buildings is greatly facilitated.

of funds or else completed and proving a severe financial handicap to the communities which built them.

The advantages of the two-level centre may be summarised as follows:—

(1) It enables the town centre to be confined to a much smaller area of land than in the case of an ordinary one-level centre.
(2) It produces very complete separation of vehicles and pedestrians.
(3) It removes parked cars and service vehicles from view, so that at the upper or pedestrian level there is a quiet, safe and visually attractive area in which buildings, landscaping and people can mingle harmoniously.

There are, however, disadvantages too:—

(1) Constructional costs are high. A pedestrian deck costs roughly one pound per square foot, or in round figures, £50,000 an acre. In financial terms, therefore, other things being equal, it will not pay to construct such a deck (which is, in effect, artificially created land) unless the cost of acquiring land for the central area for the developing authority or company would have been greater than about £50,000 an acre. Since land acquired for a new town is likely to cost more like £100 an acre, other things would have to be very unequal indeed for there to be economic justification for the building of a New Town centre on two levels.

Such inequalities could conceivably occur. A two-level centre in a New Town might prove so attractive because of the high degree of accessibility within it, freedom from danger from vehicles or visual beauty, that it attracted users from a catchment area much wider than would otherwise have been expected, thus inducing such prosperity in the town centre that rents high enough to provide an adequate return on the extra capital invested could be obtained. But it seems very doubtful indeed whether this would in fact happen.

In the case of an existing town, where land prices might be very high indeed the reverse might easily be the case, but the adoption of a particular form of development simply in order to reduce land costs is as little justified in the case of a central area as it is with residential development. It is a surrender to inadequate compensation-betterment legislation, not a surmounting of technical difficulties.

Furthermore, there are wider economic implications in the case of an existing town. One needs to take account not only of the cost saved by a smaller area of land needing to be acquired for two-level development than for single level development, but also of the costs of putting an end to central area uses which exist outside the future intended town centre area. For example, it might be that in an existing town centre central area uses substantially covered an area of say 100 acres. It might be decided to redevelop the centre by means of a two-level scheme which would require only 50 acres of land, and the developers would be delighted at only having to acquire 50 acres of high priced land instead of 100 acres. But when the two-level centre had been built there would remain outside it in the other 50 acres a host of central area uses. It would be extraordinarily bad Town Planning policy to leave these as a kind of central area fringe to compete with the new town centre; indeed, it would be unthinkable to do so. The essence of a successful town centre is that it should be self-contained and sharply defined. It would be necessary to acquire the remaining 50 acres, either at once or piecemeal when applications were made from owners within it to redevelop their properties. All these acquisitions would have to be at full market value, taking account of existing use rights. It is highly doubtful whether in the end any saving in land costs would have been secured.

(2) However great a degree of horizontal compactness is secured by multi-level development, this is inevitably counter-balanced to some extent by a loss of vertical compactness. The existence of gravity means that, in general, vertical movement is much more laborious than horizontal movement, so that a large increase in horizontal compactness is needed to balance quite a small loss of vertical compactness. It is much easier to carry an armchair from one ground floor room to another than to take it upstairs. This is very relevant when one considers that in a multi-level town centre all goods coming into the town centre will have to be conveyed by one means or another from a lower vehicular level to the upper pedestrian level; not only will this have to be done for goods, it will have to be done for all the people who visit the centre.

Lifts and escalators could and no doubt would be provided to assist, but their provision, running and maintenance represent further heavy expenditure not entailed in single level development.

(3) Artifical ventilation of the vehicular level would be essential to disperse harmlessly the exhaust gases of vehicles.

(4) A two-level town centre would inevitably be somewhat inflexible. Having designed such a centre, it would almost certainly have to be built as designed, once the process of development had begun. It would hardly be feasible to extend or reduce the area of deck. This may not be a fatal objection, but some degree of flexibility is desirable for any Planning project in order to meet changing circumstances with as little loss as possible.

(5) The whole structure would be very complicated. It would be difficult to lay it out in a form sufficiently clear and simple for people to be able to find their way about easily, since on arrival at a car park they would not usually be able to see any of the buildings they wished to visit. Very thorough and efficient sign-posting would no doubt reduce this disadvantage considerably, but it may fairly be said that contemporary life is physically sufficiently complicated for it to be desirable to avoid unnecessary further complications.

(6) Unless the areas needed for vehicular circulation, parking and servicing of buildings and for pedestrian circulation more or less balance, it will be difficult to produce an efficient and reasonably economical scheme.

The disadvantages of two-level development are less obvious and so need more explanation than the advantages, but the greater space devoted to the former in the preceding paragraphs should not suggest to the reader that a two-level town centre is necessarily a hopeless proposition. It may well not be. It is, however, important that its possibilities should be thoroughly and impartially investigated. A burning wave of undiscriminating enthusiasm may do little harm in the spheres of painting or sculpture and relatively little harm even in the costlier sphere of architecture, but extended to a large Town Planning project it would be unforgivable for it to allow economic facts to be obscured.

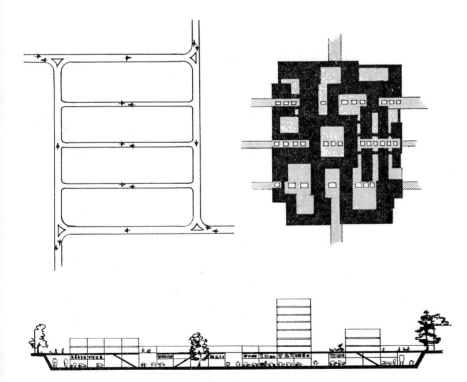

FIG. 56. Vehicular level, pedestrian level and section of a two-level town centre to illustrate the principles of this type of plan.

The natural levels of a site may enable two-level town centre development to be carried out more economically than otherwise. Where the site is the floor of a valley, for example, the pedestrian deck may be arranged so that at its edges it meets the natural ground level, thus reducing the need for ramps, escalators or lifts. Conversely, with a site on the top of a hill it may be possible for the more central part of the pedestrian level to be at natural ground level and for vehicular circulation, servicing and parking to be placed around its edges where the land falls away without the cost of excavation, the deck being cantilevered out above.

It may also, and quite frequently, be possible to take advantage of the characteristics of the site so as to produce a town centre plan which is at two levels over only part of its area. This is something which consists in ingenious seizing of particular opportunities in particular places; one cannot generalise about it.

It will be appropriate to discuss here two ideas which are not in any way necessarily associated with the idea of the two-level town centre, but which have become associated with it in relation to the Hook project. One is the idea that the town centre should "merge" into surrounding residential or other areas, the other is that it should assume an attenuated or lineal rather than a compact "chunky" form.

The idea of "merging", exemplified in the Hook project, seems to me to be fundamentally wrong. Successful Town Planning involves producing simplicity and clarity in the form of the town. This necessarily implies that the different main parts of the town should be physically distinct so that they can be seen for what they are. This principle has both practical and aesthetic aspects. While harmony and skilful cohesion between different parts are extremely desirable, any blurring of their distinct entities is undesirable, and to attempt, as appears to have been done in Hook, to make the town centre blend with its surroundings so that the transition from town centre to residential area is almost imperceptible seems to me quite wrong.

The linear theory has already been discussed in relation to the town as a whole in Chapter 8. The arguments advanced there are equally applicable to the town centre as to the town as a whole. It would hardly be necessary to mention the subject again were it not for the extraordinary fallacy embodied in Fig. 19 on page 29 of "The Planning of a New Town", the L.C.C. publication which describes the Hook project. This is disentangled in Fig. 57 of this book. The argument used in the Hook project is that with a centre of linear form, the number of people living within a ten-minute walk of it is much greater than the number of people living within a ten-minute walk of a circular centre of the same acreage. This would only be relevant if the number of people living within a ten-minute walk of any point on the periphery of the town centre were a valid measure of accessibility. But, of course, it is not. Most users of a town centre wish, during any given visit, to go to a number of places within the centre; it is unlikely that they will have only a single destination at the centre, and even more unlikely that, even if they have, it will be at the point on the edge of the centre nearest to their home. A rough but slightly truer measure is the number of homes within a ten-minute walk of the central point within the centre; on this basis

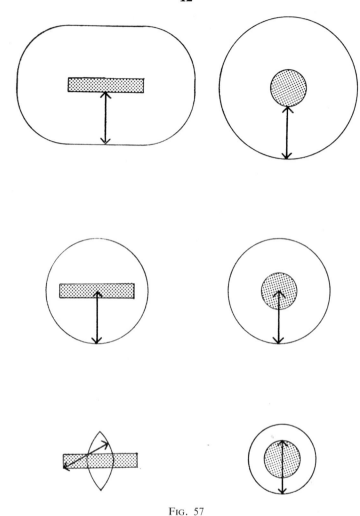

Fig. 57

The relative accessibility of linear and round town centres.

Top: The area within a given distance of the nearest part of the centre is obviously much greater with a linear centre

Middle: The area within a given distance of the central point within the centre is obviously equal in both cases

Bottom: The area within a given distance of the farthest part of the centre is much *less* for the linear than for the round centre

circular and linear centres have exactly the same measure of accessibility. But a much truer measure is the number of people living within a ten-minute walk of the farthest part of the town centre from their homes. On this basis the circular centre has an immensely higher degree of accessibility than the linear centre.

A different application of the idea of the two-level town centre has recently been proposed in a new central area Plan for Bracknell New Town. It is an idea which has not been applied in extreme form, but essentially it consists in providing parking in one or more layers above the pedestrian level instead of below it, on the roofs of buildings. One cannot at present assess the economic validity of this principle, but it has the great merit of introducing flexibility into a two-level method of development, because, provided sufficient strength is incorporated in buildings when they are first erected, additional layers of parking can be added to the tops of buildings as the need for them becomes apparent without any disorganisation of the general form of the centre.

Flexibility of parking space is desirable in any town centre design, since the quantity of parking ultimately needed is impossible to assess accurately, and excessive initial provision is nearly as bad as inadequate provision. Such flexibility can be incorporated in ordinary single level schemes by setting aside sites for multi-storey parking buildings to be erected if they prove necessary. This was done in the case of Stevenage, where town centre parking is at present all at ground level but sites have been earmarked for parking buildings if they are found necessary.

Parking involves serious aesthetic problems. A compact group of central area buildings surrounded by a large sea of parked vehicles which has to be traversed before the centre can be reached from outside is an idea which pleases nobody. On the other hand, multi-storey parking buildings hardly lend themselves to attractive visual treatment. As with many aspects of Planning, it is much wiser to try to determine and adopt the most satisfactory functional and economic solution of a problem and treat it visually as effectively as possible, rather than to adopt a visually admirable solution and then try to arrange it to make economic and functional sense.

In this context it is well to remember again the relative ease of horizontal movement as compared with vertical movement, both for people and vehicles. A very large horizontal spread has to occur before its disadvantages exceed those of multi-level parking. In a multi-level parking building the vehicle has to be driven to its allotted place; its occupants must then descend to ground level to go about their business and ascend again to the car in order to take it away, which must usually involve a substantial waste of time and effort as compared with horizontal movement from and to the vehicle even over quite a considerable distance. It is difficult to define acceptable limits for the horizontal spread of car parks, but up to very large sizes effective ameliorative measures are practicable.

The " sea of cars " effect can be substantially reduced by skilful tree planting within car parks. This has the advantage too of screening vehicles from the sun. Another method is to obscure the view of vehicles by constructing grassed banks of earth between the rows of cars, which can be exceedingly attractive. Further, the splitting of car parks into fairly numerous, fairly small units also has advantages both functionally and visually, particulary if the parks are surrounded partly or entirely by buildings. This method has its limitations, but, within these, great advantages. Fig. 59 is an example of its use.

Uses in town centres

The uses which are needed within a town centre are as follows:—

Shops	Offices—	Cinemas	Civic	Hotels	Churches
Market	Professional	Theatres	Headquarters		
Cafés	and	Dance Halls			
Restaurants	Commercial	Concert Halls			
Public Houses	Municipal	Meeting Halls			
Banks	Offices	Art Galleries			
Post Offices	Departments	Libraries			
Coal Order	of Central	Museums			
Offices	Government				
Dry Cleaners	Offices of				
Building	Statutory				
Society	Undertakers				
Payment	Clinics				
Offices					
House Agents					

The above Table needs some explanation. In the first column are included not only shops, but certain " shop-like " uses, comprising places which make retail sales of all kinds and those which deal with comparatively minor and periodic exchanges of money, all the places, in fact, to which numerous brief visits are made by the public generally.

A distinction is made in column 2 between professional and commercial offices. The former are visited by members of the public, but only occasionally by any particular person, and only for the purpose of obtaining advice over an interview of some length. Commercial offices are not so much used by the public but are the principal places where office workers " get on with the job ". These do not require the same degree of prominent siting as do the other central area uses so far mentioned.

Column 3 includes all uses associated with entertainment and culture. These are not for the most part the objects of " impulse visits ". They occupy comparatively large sites, do not need the same centrality but need to be prominent. Column 4, the civic headquarters, is the place where the Local Authority meets, where election results are announced and where civic ceremonies of various kinds take place. Column 5, hotels, is obviously independent in siting of the other uses. Such hotels will be used almost entirely by visitors to the town. Provided that they are accessible to the town centre, the industrial area and the railway station their detailed siting is not of great importance.

Column 6, churches, obtain advantages from seclusion and are probably less the objects of " impulse " visits than any other buildings.

To these classes must be added petrol filling stations and repair garages which must obviously be provided in the town centre, the most appropriate locations being near the inner ring road.

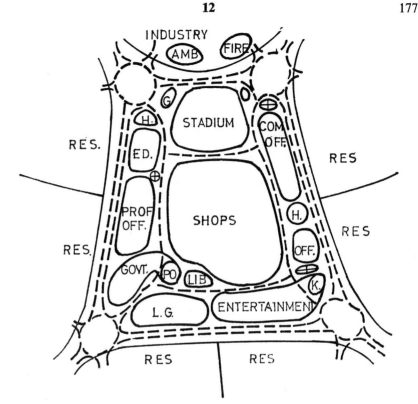

Fig. 58. Schematic diagram of the use zoning for the New Town Centre shown in detail in Fig. 59. This zoning is shown more formally in Fig. 21.

A stadium may sometimes advantageously be provided, as may a town park, though it need not be in conventional park form but comprise no more than pleasant facilities for sitting in the open air within the pedestrian precinct. It may be that establishments providing further education, and not needing playing fields may also appropriately be located in the town centre.

There are obvious linkages between these different classes of use, which need to be reflected to some extent in the physical arrangement of the layout, though it may be difficult, and involve contradictions to do so fully. For example, some of the " shop-like " uses, though they can best be sited within the shopping area for the sake of general convenience, are linked with professional and commercial offices, which may need to be sited elsewhere, while the connection between municipal government offices and the civic headquarters is obvious, as is that between the civic headquarters and art galleries, museums and meeting halls, that between public houses and hotels and that between banks and offices.

No single obviously correct solution exists. Even on a virgin site quite a

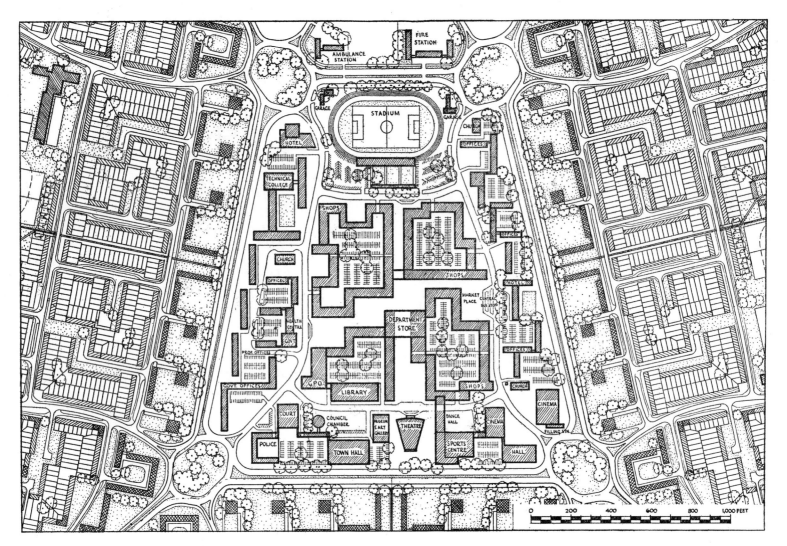

FIG. 59. The Town Centre of the Theoretical New Town. With an area of some 65 acres, it includes both a Stadium and a Technical College. The Ambulance and Fire Stations, however, are placed outside the Centre itself within the Industrial Area, from which are likely to emanate many of the most serious calls on their services.

It will be seen that the design of the Centre follows the " inner-inner ring road " principle, the main shopping core being limited to pedestrians except for car parks.

large number of different relationships between uses could be devised, each having considerable advantages.

In the case of redevelopment of an existing town centre it will almost invariably be the case that the existence of predominating features will dictate the use of zoning adopted to an extent which dominates any theoretical pattern sought. It is, however, important that whatever use of zoning is adopted it should be drawn up with the need for appropriate harmony between spatial relationship and functional relationships fully borne in mind. Fig. 58 shows one arrangement for distribution of uses in a centre for a New Town, which should prove satisfactory in practice, and it is worked out in some detail in Fig. 59.

It will be seen in this example that the fire station and ambulance headquarters are not placed within the town centre proper but within the industrial area. These need to have the greatest accessibility to main roads so that their vehicles can proceed with the least possible delay to any part of the area which they serve. This necessitates them being sited near the inner ring road. At the same time the most urgent and serious calls which both are likely to receive will often be within the industrial area, so that it is appropriate to place them on the part of the inner ring road skirting the industrial area.

A stadium has been placed within the town centre. The provision of this, of course, depends upon there being sufficient demand. A town of 60,000 would often have a club playing in the Football League and depending for its success upon substantial gates. Such a location for a stadium therefore seems appropriate.

As the calculation of land space needs in the town centre is difficult and uncertain, and provision for expansion especially difficult to arrange, it has the special advantage of constituting a reserve of land for the town centre. It is likely that the construction of costly and elaborate buildings in connection with a stadium will happen comparatively late in the development of the town centre, and, until they are constructed, the stadium site can be taken into use if a serious underestimate of space need has been made. The stadium will then have to find a home elsewhere, which will no doubt be regrettable, but is likely to result in less injury to the life and structure of the town than if more urgently needed and less seriously space-consuming uses are denied satisfactory location within the centre.

A main town clinic, which might be combined with consulting rooms for a group medical practice, has also been located in the town centre. Because many of the people visiting it will be infirm and unable to walk any distance conveniently it is desirable to site it as close as possible to the main bus stop and interchange point.

In this connection it will be seen that it has not been thought necessary to provide a bus station as such within the town centre. No doubt, facilities such as waiting rooms and lavatories and a refreshment kiosk would be provided here, but the main bus garage for the town can best be allotted to the industrial area.

Certain uses are either wholly inappropriate in the town centre or have a doubtful claim to a place there. In order to observe the principle of maximum compactness and accessibility in the town centre it is of course necessary to try to confine its uses to those which really need to be there, even though the presence of others may not be harmful.

There seems to me to be no place for residential uses within the town centre. A home which has shops, offices and other central area uses immediately adjoining it, either alongside or below, must inevitably lack a good deal of the components of a really satisfactory home. Noise, traffic and lack of outdoor space are the most obvious drawbacks.

There may of course be some demand for flats actually within the town centre, and if it can be ascertained that there definitely is, it should be met provided this is not at the expense of genuine central area uses or of enlarging the town centre unduly. But of course, if there is no serious limitation on the route of the inner ring road the provision of residential accommodation must always enlarge the physical size of the centre to *some* extent. If a site is suitable for flats it is suitable for offices, which could be placed there rather than elsewhere.

It is fairly frequently the case that site conditions require the inner ring road to be routed so as to embrace a considerably larger area than is needed for real central area uses. If this is the case it will very often be appropriate for the extra area so enclosed to be used for residential purposes.

Manufacturing industry has no place in the town centre, its requirements are accessibility to labour and transport routes for raw material and finished products. No manufacturing industry sells its products entirely locally, or even mainly locally, with the exception of a few small craft industries. There are, of course, certain industrial and quasi-industrial uses which are ancillary to shops, such as the cleaning and repairing of clothes and the preparation of food. These, when ancillary, can perfectly well be provided in the town centre on the same premises as the shops they serve. When they are more than ancillary they should be in the industrial area.

The same considerations apply to warehouses. Large department stores no doubt need to have considerable storage space on the premises for reserve stock, which constitutes a warehouse, but wholesale warehouses have the same site requirements as the industrial area, and should be placed within it.

There is a school of thought, to which a good many architects are attached, which seems to view the problems of town centre design more from the standpoint of drama than of function. Adherents of this school would deplore the exclusion of residential and industrial uses from the town centre on the grounds that without them the centre is likely to appear " dead ".

It is necessary to disentangle the issues involved in this argument. It is perfectly true that the success of certain central area uses, particularly shops, depends upon continuity so that a large number of people visiting the centre for a specific purpose are induced by what they see on their way to expend money on purchases which they had not originally contemplated. A concentration of shopping and quasi-shopping uses within one area ought to be sufficient to secure this, though the shops may, for example, suffer some slight diminution in trade if the entertainment uses are segregated from the shopping rather than being mingled with it because people on their way to the cinemas will not pass by so many shops and be induced to make casual purchases.

But the school of thought referred to goes, as I understand it, far beyond this, and wishes in particular to promote the night-time liveliness of the town centre by providing for a resident population within it. I find it difficult to regard this as much more than romantic nonsense. Some parts of the town centre will be used at night, even late at night, in particular the parts devoted to entertainment, and these late night uses may make it worth while for some restaurant and café proprietors and filling stations to remain open. Equally some parts of the central area, such as the shopping and office areas, will not remain in use late at night. This will be so whether or not there are residents within the central area, although it will no doubt be true that a somewhat wider range of facilities will stay open at night because of them.

The deduction to be drawn, in my opinion, is that there is much to be said for concentrating the entertainment area of the town centre so that it shall constitute one small " bright light " patch rather than a number of isolated points of activity over the whole centre. Such isolated points will certainly not infect their surroundings with similar activity except to a very tiny extent. A solicitor's office will not remain open until ten o'clock at night because it is next to a cinema, although a café admittedly may. Cafés however, are often provided within the cinema premises.

The origin of the " bright light " line of thought, however, is, I believe, a nostalgic yearning for the kind of night life to be found in the centres of continental towns, and is really an example of the kind of attempt stigmatised elsewhere in this book as aimed at altering the pattern of people's lives without taking full account of their desires. Continental urban night-time facilities are indeed in many ways delightful, but their availability springs in part from a different pattern of social life, based less firmly upon the home than that of Britain, and in part on a kindlier climate.

This issue is really a part of a much wider one. The world has not yet seen a town comprehensively and thoroughly Planned in order to provide the maximum efficiency, convenience and safety for its inhabitants. Given such a town, it could, in my view, provided competent architects and landscape architects were available, hardly fail to be staggeringly beautiful, yet beautiful in a totally different way from the accidental beauty of the unplanned town, many aspects of which are hardly more than *fleurs du mal*.

A town centre in which a concentrated, bright and lively entertainment area contrasts at night with the gloomy bulks of closed offices is capable of at least as much beauty as the widely diffused liveliness of the more traditional centre. In any case, in the smaller British town, the total demand for night time activity and amusement in the central area is severely limited as anyone who visits an ordinary English provincial county town at night will notice. The population of Britain does not consist of people with a frustrated hankering after café society, and a reasonable sense of proportion should be observed in considering the matter.

Space allocations in central areas

The assessment of space needs in the central area is a matter of very great difficulty. It involves determining the total population which will regularly use the town centre, and makes a simple comparison of towns of similar size quite unreliable. Demand for various kinds of use may vary widely in different parts of the country. Demands for parking space are growing and there is no foreseeable limit to them. Wide variation is possible between the extent to which uses are divided vertically and horizontally. For example, it might be possible to provide nearly all the office space in a town centre on the upper floors of buildings above shops, though many office users would find this disadvantageous. On the other hand, certain " shop like " office uses may find positive advantage in having ground floor accommodation within the shopping area and other accommodation above it. House agents and building societies are obvious examples of this. Finally, the heights at which buildings are erected affects to some extent the total amount of land needed.

At best, therefore, calculations of space needs for each use are liable to be very inaccurate, but remarkably little research seems to have been done in this field. The final report of the New Towns Committee suggested that about one acre per thousand of town population should be allotted to the Town Centre. Most of the master plans of the New Towns which were first produced exceeded this amount substantially, but in the course of the numerous revisions which have been made to them over the years they have tended to come down to a fairly close approximation to this original rough estimate. The table on the next page shows both the correspondences and the wide divergences of provision between different towns.

The Handbook on the Redevelopment of Central Areas published by the Ministry of Town and Country Planning in 1946 provides a curious confirmation of the overall standard of one acre per thousand population for the town centre. It gave existing and proposed acreages of central area uses in the town of 250,000 population studied (now known to be Leicester) as follows:—

					Existing	*Proposed*
Shops ...	...	...	...	...	95	87
Wholesale business	...	...	...	...	86	100
Offices ...	...	...	...	...	13	20
Light Industry ...	...	...	...	...	13	11
Industry ...	...	...	...	...	28	
Residential	...	...	...	...	47	
Public Buildings ...	...	...	...	...	9	17
Unused Land ...	...	...	...	...	2	
Railway Station ...	...	...	...	...		5
				Total ...	293	240

If one deducts from the latter figure the areas for light industry and railway stations as being generally inappropriate the total acreage is 224 or almost exactly 0·9 of an acre for every thousand of the town's population. One would hardly expect that the central area space provisions appropriate to a town of 250,000 would be equally applicable to a town of 60,000, so that

CRAWLEY NEW TOWN

Nett Acreages

Shops and Banks	20·10
Offices	3·36
Market	·64
Petrol Filling Station	3·67
Warehouses and General Business	3·49
Residential	·19
Special Residential	1·81
Reserve Areas	15·46
Education	6·42
Government Offices	1·70
Local Government Offices	3·45
Places of Worship	5·32
Public Open Space	4·56
Car Parks...	3·65
Bus Station	3·00
Railway Uses	2·82
Service Industry	7·15
Territorial Army H.Q.	2·31
Telephone Exchange	2·00
Existing G.P.O.	·18
Recreation	14·67
New Roads and Verges...	29·15
Old Roads and Verges	6·4
	141·50

STEVENAGE NEW TOWN

	Acres	
Public Library	0·5	includes car park.
Dance Hall	0·85	
Cinema...	0·6	
Swimming Pool	1·2	includes car park.
Youth Centre	0·9	
Church...	1·25	
Town Hall, Council Chamber and administrative offices	2·1	
Health Centre...	0·5	includes car park.
Out-patients Clinic ...	1·2	includes car park.
Town Park	7·25	
Apprentices' hostel	1·1	includes car park.
Shops	16·0	this includes Town Square, Banks. Most shops have offices or living accommodation.
Offices	11·5	These areas are allocated to office blocks, with a proportion of small shops at ground level.
Head Post Office	1·25	includes sorting office.
Police Station	1·2	
Fire Station	0·8	
Bus Station	0·85	
Bus Garage	2·25	
Service and Petrol Filling Station	1·25	
Car Parks	18·2	
	70·75	

HARLOW NEW TOWN

	Acres	*Acres*
(i) *Roads and other Site Works*		
Perimeter Highways and Roundabouts (including verges, footpaths, etc.)	14·12	
Internal roads (including lay-bys)	6·26	
Cycle track	0·36	
Car and cycle parks	5·75	
Paved areas and service yards	9·50	
Bus lay-bys	0·48	36·47
(ii) *Open Spaces*		
Small Landscaped Areas	3·50	
Civic Gardens...	2·88	
Natural Landscaping...	7·35	13·73
(iii) *Commercial Buildings*		
Shopping and Ancillary uses (including Banks and Licensed Premises other than Hotels)	12·03	
Service Courtyards	2·80	
Hotels (including gardens)	0·63	
Entertainment Buildings (including theatre) ...	2·17	
Service and lock-up garages, stores, etc. ...	1·81	
Professional offices	0·75	20·19
(iv) *Public Buildings*		
Church...	0·64	
Civic Group (excluding theatre)	1·61	
Library...	0·30	
College of Further Education	5·24	
Courts ⎱ Police Station ⎰	1·71	
Crown Offices		
General Post Office	0·90	
Waiting and Cloakrooms	0·10	10·50
(v) Balance—(Minor open spaces, verges, etc.) ...		3·58
		84·47

these figures must be treated with reserve, but in the largely unchartered field of central area space provision any correspondence of estimates is to be welcomed!

In dealing with existing towns there is one cardinal factor which I think can be accepted with some confidence. In many towns the amounts of each use, at least in terms of floor space, must approximate very closely to the town's requirements, something which does not occur in other parts of the town. The reason for this is that land values and rents are so high that with rare exceptions uses do not seek to establish themselves nor to acquire more space than is necessary for their purposes. Indeed, they tend to cramp themselves rather than to expand unduly.

It would be an interesting and comparatively simple study to analyse the floor spaces devoted to each of the main uses in a town centre, to assess the adequacy or otherwise of each of the sites in relation to the floor space index, and from this to deduce the total land area needed for each use for efficient functioning. If this process were applied to a number of similar towns, and adjustment made for any variations of the population of their catchment areas, a useful datum of space requirements could be obtained. Unhappily, so far as I am aware, no such study has been made.

Such a study is of importance, not only for the establishment of space standards in the centres of New Towns but in order to provide a basis for redevelopment proposals in existing towns. A floor space index survey if carried out in suitable detail provides a sound basis for such an investigation.

Nevertheless it is extremely difficult to arrive at suitable maximum floor space indices for purposes of development control. Clearly, the higher a building is the more ground area on its site is left available for car parking and pedestrian movement, so that the maximum F.S.I. tolerable is greater with a tall building than with a low one. On the other hand there is a limit to this because, with a tall slab block as opposed to a low block, buildings on neighbouring sites have to be pushed further back in order to enjoy proper daylighting, and so the increase of F.S.I. can only be obtained at the expense of F.S.I. on these adjoining sites. With a tall tower block the situation becomes more complicated. Although adjoining sites will probably have to suffer some reduction of F.S.I., it will not be as much as in the case of slab block because of the light which they can receive around the sides of the tower. It would be very difficult to express these various relationships between height and permissible F.S.I. quantitatively although the effort should probably be made by Planning Authorities because of the increased flexibility of siting which would be secured by applying a sliding scale—the smaller the proportion of site covered the higher the permissible F.S.I.—as compared with the normal method of applying a flat rate of F.S.I. for any given use irrespective of heights of buildings to be erected. (See Fig. 60.)

Here again, remarkably little study seems to have been made of what constitutes a suitable F.S.I. for any given use. Broadly speaking in the provincial counties without great cities the very tentative suggestions made in the Handbook seem to have been uncritically adopted, while in the large cities and London, where land values are so high that it is difficult to force developers to comply with reasonable F.S.I. standards, a compromise has

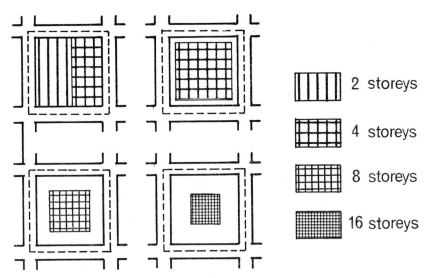

Fig. 60. Four different ways of developing a site at a floor space index of 2·0. The broken lines indicate road centre lines.

‖‖‖	2 storeys
▦	4 storeys
▦	8 storeys
▦	16 storeys

been sought by permitting a comparatively high F.S.I. provided that car parking is provided within the site. In the case of very high land values the developer prefers to provide this in the form of a basement car park rather than use up any of his valuable ground space.

The tentative recommendations of the Central Areas Handbook were as follows:—

Shops	...	...	...	...	...	1·5
Offices	...	...	...	...	...	2·0
Wholesale warehouses	...	...	...	...	2·25
Light industry	...	...	...	...	...	1·5

It will be apparent that these are based on the relative amounts of vehicular and pedestrian visitors to be expected.

Redevelopment of town centres.

The pedestrian town centre principle, as already suggested, cannot be fully applied to the centres of very large towns, which, because of their sheer physical size, need to allow opportunities for complicated vehicular movement within them. The principle in modified form can, nevertheless, be applied by careful segregation of uses into zones and the creation of one or more pedestrian precincts for each, adjoining precincts being linked by pedestrian bridges or tunnels. In the centre of a large town there is likely to be a considerable mixture of existing uses; it is not at all necessary that this mixture shall be entirely done away with—many people would passionately claim that it should not be, and in any event it would be a very costly business.

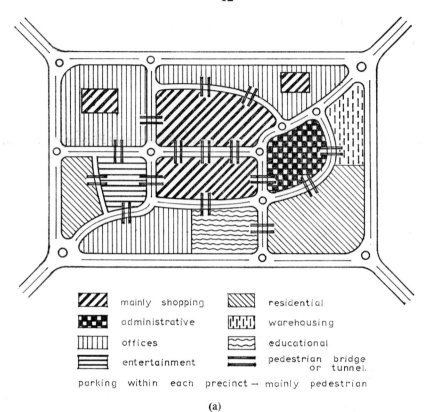

▨	mainly shopping	▧	residential
▩	administrative	▥	warehousing
▥	offices	〜	educational
▤	entertainment	▬	pedestrian bridge or tunnel.

parking within each precinct — mainly pedestrian

(a)

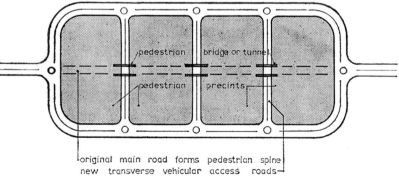

original main road forms pedestrian spine
new transverse vehicular access roads

FIG. 61 (b)

But a *general* grouping of uses to form precincts which are predominantly used for shopping or for offices or for entertainment is both practicable and desirable in order to reduce the total amount of walking within the centre or of movement of vehicles from park to park to a minimum. Fig. 61 (a) illustrates the kind of central area plan on these lines which seems to offer the best chance for the effective but reasonably economical redevelopment of many large town centres. Fig. 61 (b) shows the same principle adapted to a town whose centre has developed in linear form, a special case which is not very uncommon.

It is becoming apparent that the comprehensive redevelopment of town centres in accordance with sensible Planning principles is an almost impossible task where the only mechanism available is the development control exercised upon the piecemeal proposals of individual developers. The larger the centre the more this applies. Given a determined Local Planning Authority and a firm ministerial policy it is no doubt possible to do a good deal by means of rigid zoning, control of F.S.I., the imposition of daylighting standards, requirements on developers to provide parking space and control of external appearance though, as noted on page 170, individual parking space rather than pooled parking space is extremely wasteful. It is technically possible to go even further, and to design what are known as " building envelopes " for the whole of the central area, which fix not only the use, height and proportion of site to be covered by each building but also its size and shape, leaving a developer flexibility of design only as regards external appearance and internal arrangements of the building. The snag about this, as well as with other less drastic weapons of control, is the same as that of taking horses to water. Developers will not undertake development unless they think it will prove sufficiently profitable, and an over-severe control in central areas may result in the slowing down or cessation of much needed redevelopment.

In some cases the only rational method of dealing with a town centre is to bring the whole of it into one ownership so that redevelopment can take place without the crippling handicap of irregular and fragmented ownership boundaries. But at least as often, such drastic treatment is unnecessary. Practically every town centre in the country is in fairly urgent need of drastic redevelopment but the expenditure of the capital, organisation and technical expertise needed to treat all of them as areas for comprehensive acquisition and redevelopment by a single agency within a short time would be quite impracticable. It is also unnecessary. Many town centres will be redeveloped quite slowly over a considerable period because there is no social or economic need or promise for rapid redevelopment. In such cases it is important to produce a plan which will allow for the rapid solution of traffic problems but will also permit most of the redevelopment to take place block by block, almost building by building. All the capital and skill which can be mustered are likely to be needed for the intractable cases in which the only practicable remedy is a drastic one; there is no point in delaying action on these because of unnecessary devotion of resources to the less difficult cases.

Naturally, even where gradual replacement is considered appropriate there will often be cases in which the redevelopment of individual sites must be resisted because of the impossibility of doing so without prejudicing the satisfactory redevelopment of a wider area but this is a very different thing from applying clean sweep methods.

The great financial rewards to be obtained from town centre development have resulted in great activity in this field, and the production of fairly numerous town centre plans of high competence.

In most town centres there are buildings, particularly factories, which have no need to be there and which prevent it from functioning satisfactorily, but which there is no prospect of moving for many years.   Meanwhile, buildings which are urgently needed in the centre may not be represented there at all. If there is no room for them in the existing centre or reasonably close to it, and if they are consequently provided in permanent form elsewhere, the prospect of ever achieving a properly integrated functional centre becomes remote, and when the time comes for removing intrusive uses there may be no uses appropriate to a central area which are not already accommodated elsewhere.

Two solutions are possible: either for some existing buildings within or as near as possible to the centre, which perform no vital central function, to be taken over temporarily to meet an urgent need, or if no reasonably suitable buildings can be found, to construct temporary prefabricated buildings on the nearest possible vacant site; these can be removed when a central site becomes available.

Both these alternatives are likely to cause a good deal of annoyance and inconvenience, yet they are well worth while.   Every permanent building suitable for a central area which is built outside it constitutes a tragic postponement of the achievement of a well-Planned town which can only be condoned in the rare cases where no existing or temporary building can be used or erected and the need is urgent.

The problem is difficult enough when no considerable increase in the size of the town is contemplated.   When the increase is substantial it becomes baffling in the extreme, for it then becomes necessary not merely to find suitable sites for a few additional buildings, but, very often, to change the scale of the entire centre and of the chief buildings in it.   For example, local government offices perfectly adequate for the staff of an urban district with a population of 15,000 would prove to be impossibly cramped for a town of 50,000.   It is, of course, much more difficult to expand the area devoted to each of the individual uses in a centre, leaving the existing building in each case as the core, than to work in extra uses.

Large-scale expansion of a town may be intended to be carried out comparatively quickly in pursuance of a policy of metropolitan decentralisation, so that gradual expansion of the town centre implemented by the judicious redevelopment of individual obsolete sites at fairly long intervals will not be possible.   It will generally be necessary in such cases to accept a complete change round of uses, perhaps letting the town hall as private offices and building a new one on a cleared site, even though great wastage of capital may be entailed.

A better solution where the degree of expansion is so great as virtually to mean the creation of a new town may be to convert the existing town centre into a neighbourhood centre which will probably be somewhat in excess of minimum requirements and to build a completely new town centre on a suitable virgin site, though the suitability of so drastic a remedy obviously depends upon the shape of the town and the position of the existing centre.

The creation or substantial expansion of a town centre is, at best, a complicated process needing much care and patience, and involving an immense amount of negotiation.   The detailed needs of different uses as to position and nature of accommodation are so widely varied, and require so detailed a knowledge of the activities carried on that no preliminary Plan prepared with the object of satisfying the needs of all central area users is likely to bear more than a slight resemblance to the final Plan, hammered out by dint of numerous difficult and painful compromises to come as near as possible to suiting everybody.

Parking

The provision of parking space arises not only in town centres but in neighbourhood centres and industrial areas.   The problem is greatest, however, in the town centre, and, as it can most conveniently be treated as a whole, is briefly dealt with here.

A valuable survey was made by the Middlesex County Planning Department and was described in the Journal of the Town Planning Institute for June, 1958.   Although it was confined to Middlesex, and was not exhaustive it was done in such a way that clear conclusions could be drawn and specific suggestions for parking standards made.   These were as follows:

An increase of 100% over present parking demand is taken as the basis for future provision.

Shopping and Commercial Centres

Type of Centre	No. of car spaces per 100 ft. of Shopping and Commercial frontage
Regional	12
Major	10
Minor	7

Industrial buildings

Industrial floor space (sq. ft.)	No. of parking spaces required
0— 1,250	4
1,250— 2,500	5
2,500— 5,000	6
5,000— 7,500	7
7,500—10,000	8
For each additional 1,250...	1 space

Offices

Office floor space (sq. ft.)					No. of parking spaces required
0— 750	...	...	...	...	4
750—1,500	...	...	...	...	5
1,500—3,000	...	...	...	...	6
3,000—4,000	...	...	...	...	7
4,000—5,000	...	...	...	...	8
5,000—6,000	...	...	...	...	9
For each additional 2,000...		...	...	...	3 spaces

Since the publication of the Middlesex Parking Study many Local Planning Authorities have adopted sets of parking standards, most of them somewhat similar to the Middlesex proposals, although often expressed in rather different form. Although the standards vary a good deal from authority to authority, the following is a reasonably representative sample:—

Use	Parking spaces required
Residential	1 per dwelling.
Shops	1 to every 500 sq. ft. of gross floor space.
Offices	1 to every 500 sq. ft. of gross floor space.
Hotels	1 to every 3 bedrooms.
Hospitals	1 to every 12 beds.
Theatres and Cinemas	1 to every 30 seats.
Restaurants	1 to every 10 seats.
Industrial Buildings	1 to every 500 sq. ft. of floor area.

These figures are averages; for several uses a sliding scale is frequently used which requires a higher level of provision for small buildings than for large ones.

It is important to remember that these suggested standards relate to *cars* of visitors and employees, and not to service vehicles, for which, of course, separate provision should be made. Nor do they take account of the economy to be secured by the use of pooled parking space whereby daytime parking and evening parking can take place on the same piece of land.

For purposes of development control and as a basis for calculating parking requirements in areas of Planned development parking standards are very useful provided that they are applied with commonsense. They cannot be successfully applied to individual small sites, on which the provision of parking to the required standard may be physically impracticable. As noted earlier, it is important that the law should be changed to allow financial contribution to the provision of parking by a developer to be made a condition of Planning permission in suitable cases in place of its actual physical provision.

Programming

No hard and fast rules can be laid down for programming the development or redevelopment of a town centre. Two general principles apply as with other aspects of programming, namely the need to postpone provision of any particular facility until the population who will use it is sufficiently large to enable it to function economically, and secondly the need, though somewhat modified in a town centre, for development to grow outwards from the middle in as orderly a fashion as possible. The problem of catering for unforeseen expansion has already been mentioned, and is severe. It is seldom possible to set aside land in a town centre for problematical future use, for if it is never used there will be a bleak open expanse in the part of the town where the greatest compactness of development should for all reasons occur.

Again, if development is carefully designed to provide the maximum intensity and compactness compatible with other needs, further intensification of development, either by adding storeys to buildings or by building on hitherto unused space can only have bad consequences. The device mentioned on page 179 of providing a stadium as a reserve against contingencies is obviously not one which can universally be applied. Conversely, should development of a town centre cease before it is complete, good programming can do much to ensure that what has been built before cessation will form a satisfactory unit.

As regards the former case, no really satisfactory policy can be suggested, and the choice seems to lie between intensification of building use, with costly provision of underground car parking to make up for that which has been lost and to cater for the greater demand to be expected from increased building, or else to divert the inner ring road so that it embraces a larger area, and to demolish and redevelop existing property lying within the area which, as amended, it will embrace. The costliness and unsatisfactory nature of both these alternatives is obvious.

Presentation

An ordinary single level Plan for a town centre can readily be expressed in the form of a Supplementary Town Map in accordance with the principles suggested in Chapter 3·2.

With a multi-level Plan, which may well provide for different uses at various levels of the same building, and in which roads will run underneath buildings, some more elaborate method of presentation is necessary. An axonometric projection indicating roads and distinguishing uses from each other by means of colour is a satisfactory way of dealing with the problem.

Whatever the kind of Plan, however, it will be necessary to go well beyond the detail which can be shown in a Supplementary Town Map, to indicate future building forms, at least in general terms, as well as land uses, and to show clearly where there will have to be new buildings and where roads or pedestrian ways will necessitate the removal of buildings. A series of plans and models is likely to be needed, and among them there should certainly be a plan of the kind mentioned on page 36 which shows proposals in transparent outline form superimposed upon a detailed base map of existing conditions, so that the full range of changes proposed in the Plan can be readily appreciated.

Fig. 62 goes a little beyond the degree of detail usually shown in a Supplementary Town Map yet stops short of indicating building forms. It is in practice a useful intermediate stage, and one which is especially useful for the purpose of a book illustration since it can be readily shown in simple monochrome form.

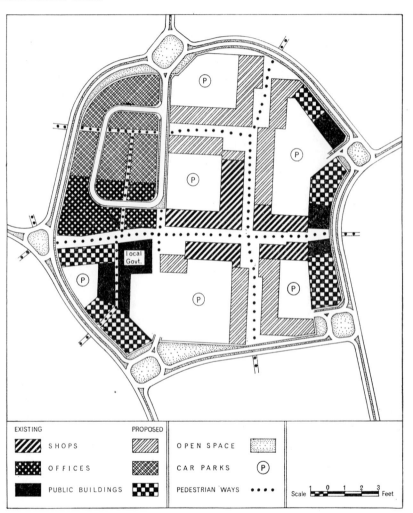

FIG. 62. A supplementary Town Map for the central area of the town shown in Fig. 36.

CHAPTER 13

THE INDUSTRIAL AREA

IT IS NOT EASY to say very much about the Planning requirements for an industrial area. The space requirements of different industries vary enormously in relation to the numbers of workers they employ, and it is of course quite impossible in advance of the development of an industrial area to foretell except in the very broadest terms, what kinds of firms will establish themselves in it.

Nevertheless, certain broad principles regarding the Planning requirements of an industrial area can be affirmed. These relate to the location of the area, site requirements, space needs, division between uses and layout.

Location

In general terms this has already been discussed in Chapter 8. Accessibility of labour, communication routes, ample supplies of power and water and sewage disposal facilities are of prime importance. There is no doubt that some slight separation from residential areas is desirable. This is so not only because even the best arranged industrial area is liable in parts to be somewhat unsightly, but also because it is likely to involve the emission of smoke and fumes and to be noisy.

Site requirements

It is more necessary than for any other use that land for industrial purposes should be flat and even because of the very large areas of building which have to be placed under one roof at one level. In the very lightest industries this does not apply, for the small bulk of raw materials and products enables them to operate in small buildings and on upper floors, but for the great majority of industries it is of the greatest importance.

Space needs

The Ministry of Housing and Local Government's Technical Memorandum No. 2, entitled " The Use of Land for Industry " gives useful information. It gives the allocation of employment between the three main divisions of primary production, manufacturing industry and service employment in June 1954, as respectively 7·6%, 41·7% and 50·7% of the total insured employees in Great Britain. The employed population of England and Wales is about 46% of the total population, so that about 19% of the total population is engaged in manufacturing industry.

But those engaged in primary production constitute about 3½% of the total population, and since there are no agricultural, mining or quarrying workers to speak of actually living in towns, it would be reasonable to find a slightly higher proportion than the national average engaged on manufacturing industry in towns. If one assumes that about half of the national percentage of workers engaged in primary production would be in manufacturing industry in towns and adds a few workers in transport and other non-manufacturing industries who would find their place within the industrial area, 20% of the total population seems a reasonable basis.

The Ministry's Technical Memorandum suggests that between fifty and sixty workers per industrial acre is a reasonable density to assume, and this estimate is closely confirmed by R. H. Best's analyses mentioned on page 102.

With 20% of the population engaged in manufacturing industry at a density of 50 workers per acre, 4 acres of industrial land per 1,000 of total urban population is required. Best found that in Town Map areas of over 10,000 population 3·9 acres was in fact allotted to industry. In county borough areas he found that the amount was 3·5 acres per 1,000 of total population. A survey of industrial use of space in Trafford Park, a very large industrial estate in Salford covering 1,200 acres and accommodating many industries including heavy ones, which was carried out in connection with the "City of Manchester Plan, 1945 " arrived at the following results:—

SURVEY OF INDUSTRIAL USE OF SPACE IN TRAFFORD PARK

Industry	Sub-division	Persons per acre of floor area	Proportion of site built up
Building			
	Saw-milling and general timber	43	0·37
	Joinery and woodworking	101	0·43
	Other building	42	0·33
Engineering			
	General	33	0·74
	Motor	237	0·37
	Electrical	241	0·5
	Constructional	7·5	0·61
	Heating and ventilating	178	0·47
	Casting (ferrous and non-ferrous)	118	0·66
Chemicals			
	General	46	0·53
	Oil-refining	29	0·56
Food			
	Flour-milling	78	0·53
	Edible oils	86	0·46

Analysis of this Table shows that the density per gross industrial area works out at about 45 workers per acre.

So uncertain are industrial land needs that it is essential to allocate a substantial margin over and above anticipated needs as a reserve. Since, wherever possible, it is desirable that the industrial area should occupy its own sector of the town running from the town centre, or at least near it, to the outskirts of the town, this ought not to be hard to arrange with towns of reasonable terrain. If development proceeds outwards from the centre in accordance with a predetermined programme and layout it should not be difficult to bring into use additional industrial land as and when it is required. In the case of the theoretical New Town, for example, with a population of 60,000, on the space standards suggested, 240 acres would be needed for industry, but in fact some 390 have been provided. The balance would amount to a small farm which could remain in agricultural use until it was needed.

Even within the industrial area there needs to be some division of uses. It has already been suggested in Chapter 12 that the town's main fire station and ambulance headquarters can well be provided within the industrial area. Some local shopping will also be needed near the centre of the industrial area in order to meet the immediate day to day needs of workers. The need to provide canteens, restaurants etc., depends very much upon the arrangements made by individual firms in the area. A certain amount of open space is desirable to enable the younger workers to play scratch games of football, cricket etc., during the lunch hour and other breaks.

Although it is not likely to be fully within the control of a Local Planning Authority or Development Corporation, it seems doubtful whether the provision of expensive and elaborate sports facilities within the industrial area is at all desirable. This tends to focus the workers' spare time activities too much upon his work place rather than upon his home, and may upset the balance of neighbourhood provisions.

As regards industrial uses themselves the main division will be between general industry and special, or noxious, industry. A long list of the latter can be found among the classes of permitted use in the General Development Order 1950, and their very names, in many cases, indicate their offensive nature. Although modern preventive methods may do much to reduce the unpleasantness and nuisance caused by smoke, fumes, smell and excessive noise, there must always remain a residue of exceptionally unpleasant uses.

So far as possible residents in the town need to be protected from these, as do other workers in the industrial area, and indeed the surrounding countryside. It is hardly possible to meet all these needs fully, and the general assumption unpalatable though it may be to rural dwellers, is that it is more important to protect the rest of the town than the rural surroundings since the effects of objectionable industry disperse themselves fairly rapidly over the adjoining countryside and the lower density of rural population means an adverse effect upon fewer people.

The traditional siting for offensive industry is to the leeward side of the town in terms of the direction of the prevailing wind, but the Ministry's Technical Memorandum points out that this is not necessarily a sound method since many towns have no clearly prevailing winds, the wind blowing from two or three directions with almost equal frequency. It also points out that winds which blow with greatest frequency are often the strongest, or those associated by marked atmospheric instability, which causes rapid horizontal and vertical dispersal of smoke and dust, in contrast with which slow local flows of air under stable atmospheric conditions may largely determine the area of concentrated pollution.

Layout

Because of the uncertainty of the size of the individual undertakings which will come to an industrial area, it is hardly possible to arrange a subtle layout;

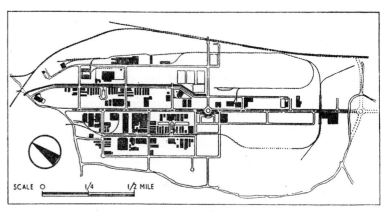

FIG. 63.   The Team Valley Trading Estate, designed by Sir William Holford.

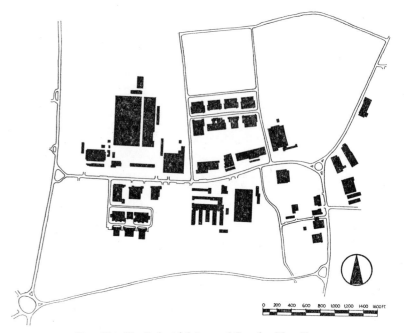

FIG. 64.   The Industrial Area of Crawley New Town.

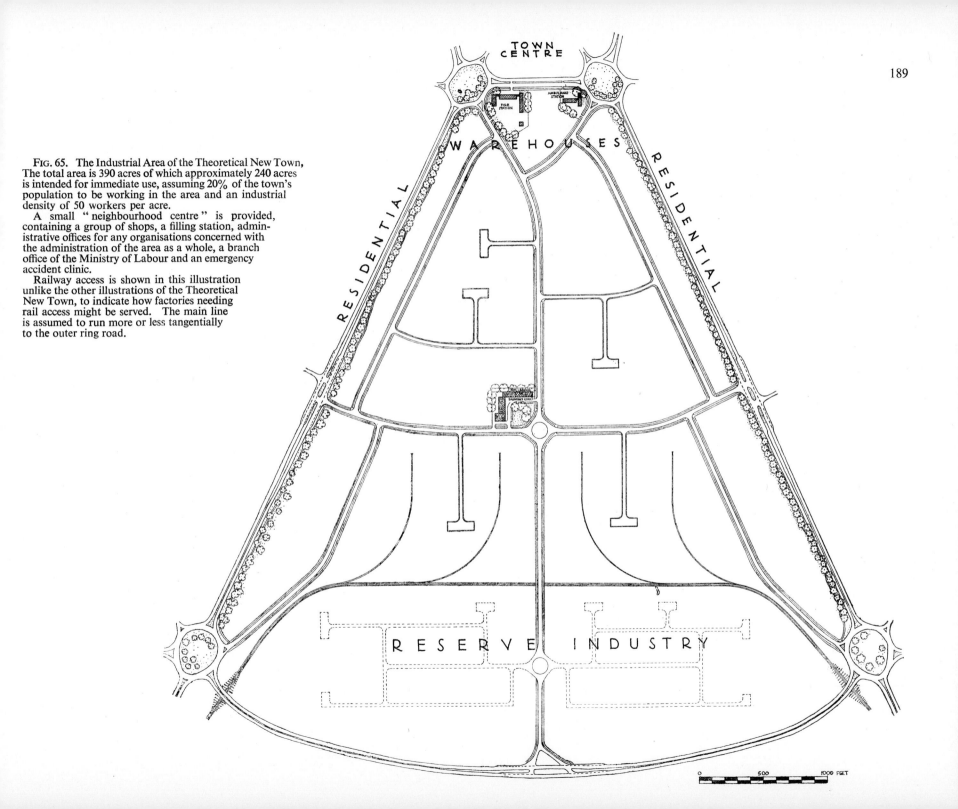

FIG. 65. The Industrial Area of the Theoretical New Town, The total area is 390 acres of which approximately 240 acres is intended for immediate use, assuming 20% of the town's population to be working in the area and an industrial density of 50 workers per acre.

A small "neighbourhood centre" is provided, containing a group of shops, a filling station, administrative offices for any organisations concerned with the administration of the area as a whole, a branch office of the Ministry of Labour and an emergency accident clinic.

Railway access is shown in this illustration unlike the other illustrations of the Theoretical New Town, to indicate how factories needing rail access might be served. The main line is assumed to run more or less tangentially to the outer ring road.

TOWN CENTRE

WAREHOUSES

RESIDENTIAL

RESIDENTIAL

RESERVE INDUSTRY

0   500   1000 FEET

simplicity and flexibility are the most important determinants. These requirements can most easily be met by a grid-iron layout, the major junctions of which have roundabouts and the minor junctions staggered. A proportion of the minor roads can well be culs-de-sac. Just as with a residential cul-de-sac, an industrial cul-de-sac provides opportunities for extra large plots at the closed end. Figs. 63 and 64 show typical Planned industrial layouts, and Fig. 65 that for the theoretical New Town.

Appearance

The variety of sizes and shapes of industrial buildings and of their requirements for fuel and water tanks and large outdoor plant is so great that it is hardly possible to Plan for unified and harmonious appearance. The best that can be hoped for is for each individual building to be of good

design, and for visual effectiveness to be derived from contrast and diversity rather than from harmony.

With firm control something can nevertheless be done to smooth down the harsher contrasts, as can be seen on the Team Valley Trading Estate in Durham designed by Sir William Holford. Here, careful planting schemes, insistence upon uniform facing bricks and the placing of the office portions of factories, which are more capable of unification than the factories themselves, on the parts of the plots adjacent to the road, have created an unusually integrated effect.

It is neither practicable, nor necessary to aim at the kind of quiet and restful beauty in an industrial area which would be appropriate in a residential area, but the avoidance of discord, of untidiness and disorderly site development, together with the application of such unifying elements as can be provided can be of great help.

CHAPTER 14

THE RESIDENTIAL NEIGHBOURHOOD UNIT

14-1. INTRODUCTORY

THE CONCEPT OF the neighbourhood unit has briefly been referred to in Chapter 10 in connection with the preparation of a town Plan, and must now be dealt with more thoroughly.

The neighbourhood unit concept saw its birth in the United States in the inter-war period, at which time it entered little into Planning thought in this country. From 1945 onwards great attention has been paid to it, and the supplement to the Dudley Report on " The Design of Dwellings " published in 1944 contains an exposition of the basic idea which remains valid.

There is an interesting parallel to the idea of the neighbourhood unit in that of the hierarchy of settlements described in Chapter 4. A town centre not only supplies services of a high order to the whole of the town and to the service area of the town, but also supplies services of a lower order to those of the town's inhabitants who live close to it. The neighbourhood unit aims to supply these services of a lower order to its inhabitants; to the whole of them from the neighbourhood centre and to some of them from whatever sub-centres may be established within the neighbourhood.

With a neighbourhood of a population of about ten thousand the services supplied in the neighbourhood centre would be analogous to those of the town centre of a small town of ten thousand population and those supplied by a sub-centre perhaps analogous to those supplied by an urban village.

One says analogous rather than similar because the nearer physically a centre is to a centre of higher importance the less independent can it be. The country town of ten thousand people may be able to support several solicitors but it is very doubtful whether the neighbourhood centre of a neighbourhood of ten thousand people would be able to support any, because the town centre is relatively so close at hand and is certain to house so many solicitors that it would hardly be worth anyone's while to set up practice in a position which, though very close to a limited number of people, is much less accessible to the public generally. Similarly, a neighbourhood sub-centre cannot hope to support services comparable to those supported by an urban village because of the physical closeness of the neighbourhood centre.

One can carry this a stage further. In a very large town it may be desirable to provide centres of a higher order than the neighbourhood centre yet of a lower order than the town centre. Such centres might serve a population of fifty thousand, but could not contain services as extensive as those of the town centre of an independent town of fifty thousand because of the physical nearness of the city centre.

The idea of the neighbourhood unit has attracted a good deal of unearned opprobrium.[1] This is partly because the principles upon which it is based

---

[1] Proposals have even been made that it should be abandoned, though with doubtful success (see page 102).

have been misunderstood and partly because some of its more enthusiastic advocates have claimed more for it than is justified.

In the first place it may confidently be said that the residential neighbourhood unit is not an artificial creation. It can be seen in embryonic form in most towns with a population of more than twenty or thirty thousand.

Wherever physical size renders the town centre inconveniently inaccessible for everyday needs for an appreciable portion of the population minor centres will spring up to meet these needs, although often in a distorted form. The extra trade to be gained from casual passers-by will attract shopkeepers away from the centre of a local service area to such main roads as are adjacent to it. Non-profitable uses such as schools and open spaces will be forced on to relatively remote sites where land values are low, instead of being placed where they are most accessible. The net result is a pattern which is very much inferior to the best obtainable by careful Planning, but which still has a perceptible resemblance to the neighbourhood proper. Fig. 67 (i) illustrates this point.

The following are the principal ways in which the use of the neighbourhood principle can be of advantage. As we shall see, it is a principle which can only be used to full effect where one or more neighbourhoods are being planned *de novo*, but it can, at least in modified form, be used where an area is already partially developed or is to be redeveloped.

(1) Assuming a population for a neighbourhood of the order of 10,000, such a unit can conveniently be fitted within a network of main roads, which facilitates the Planning of a road system with the status of roads sharply divided between main traffic routes and local roads, thus securing safety within the neighbourhood and a physical identity for it.

(2) This physical identity is something which is usually almost entirely lacking in inter-war areas of housing, and can be observed to be an important element in the unsatisfactory feeling that they give. The entire residential area of a town of 30,000 or more is too big to constitute a reasonable unit. It tends to give the feeling of a desert of unbroken masses of houses, spotted with other uses but not punctuated by them. The use of main roads, railways and marked physical features of one kind or another, combined with distinctive visual treatment in architecture and landscape architecture and the rational grouping of elements ancillary to the houses, can transform this, and give a feeling of identity and locality likely to be psychologically, and perhaps socially, beneficial.

(3) Within such an area it is possible to support and to distribute within reasonable reach of the whole population all the services required for day-to-day living except the centres of main employment, which must necessarily be sited in relation to the town as a whole in the form of office and industrial areas.

(4) A neighbourhood of the kind described can conveniently form a ward for local political purposes, and it can hardly be doubted that

such an area, with boundaries which are physically real, is likely to produce greater political interest and awareness than is one whose boundaries are entirely arbitrary, and visible only on a map. Hardly anyone, I think, would question the desirability of strengthening local political interest.

It will be seen from the above that the neighbourhood unit is here conceived simply as a sub-division of the town, seen principally in terms of service centres and service areas, with the requirements of the road system and of political sub-division enhancing its desirability, which is further sustained by the opportunities for visual treatment afforded.

This, in my opinion, is sufficient to establish the neighbourhood as a valuable principle. It is quite unnecessary to reinforce it with theories about the opportunities which it presents to create social homogeneity and to foster social activities. I have already set out in Chapter 1 my reasons for thinking that these are dubious objectives for physical Planning, although it may fairly be said that it is legitimate and even desirable so to dispose development as to facilitate social life, which the neighbourhood principle certainly does.

The social aspects of neighbourhood Planning require very careful consideration. It has often been assumed that each neighbourhood should include, in due proportion, representatives of all the kinds of people to be found in the town, in terms of economic status and employment, or, at least, since Planning action cannot directly secure this, that accommodation suited to all such groups should be provided. In existing development, class segregation in terms of " working-class areas ", " middle-class suburbs ", and so on, has certainly been a deadening influence.

But the fineness of mixture within what has been called " the all-class neighbourhood " is capable of great variation, and the appropriateness of making social mixture an objective of physical Planning is at least doubtful.

The New Towns Committee, in its Final Report, said:

" So far as the issue is an economic one, balance can be attained by giving opportunity for many sorts of employment which will attract men and women up to a high income level. Beyond that point the problem is not economic at all, nor even a vaguely social one; it is, to be frank, one of class distinction. So far as these distinctions are based on income, taxation and high costs of living are reducing them. We realise also that there are some who would have us ignore their existence. But the problem remains and must be faced; if the community is to be truly balanced, so long as social classes exist, all must be represented in it. A contribution is needed from every type and class of person; the community will be the poorer if all are not there, able and willing to make it."

All kinds of views are held about this: at one end of the scale there is the man who says that people one shared a slit trench with during the war ought to be good enough to live in the same street; at the other end there are still people who object, apparently seriously, to the location of a local authority housing site on the grounds that the value of their own houses will be reduced by the tenants of the local authority houses using their road. The matter is complicated by the fact that economic status and " class " or cultural level are no longer nearly so directly related as they were.

In the larger towns there are often areas of Victorian houses which are spacious yet still relatively cheap to buy, in which families with children find the best solution to the housing problem which is available to them. These families include people of very diverse origins and educational attainments whose economic situations have been raised or lowered by post-war conditions to a common level, but it does not appear that severe friction is common. Further, the size of garden required, which is a big factor in differentiating the character of housing areas, no longer varies so markedly with economic and social status as once it did, because of the far smaller number of people who can afford regular paid help with the garden.

Nevertheless, a very fine mixture of different social groups is likely to result in friction through no fault of any of the people concerned, and it is perhaps in dealing with the upbringing of children that the greatest difficulties are encountered. People who think they have enlightened ideas about children often wish to bring them up in accordance with standards very different from those of their neighbours. Rules about bedtime, cleanliness, courtesy and even speech are very difficult to enforce if neighbouring children are not expected to comply with them. It is hard, indeed, to get a child to come in to bed early on a summer evening and go to sleep when the other children in the road go on playing noisily and happily for hours afterwards.

This is simply an illustration of the fact, which should occasion no heart-burning, that, on the whole, people with fairly similar cultural and economic status tend to live together more happily than the very diverse. This is not by any means entirely a matter of class distinction; artists and commercial travellers may get on together less well than artists and navvies.

If one accepts the view that it is, on the whole, better to avoid Planning to promote the highest degree of social mixture, what is the happy medium between indiscriminate mingling and the " one-class " suburb? It must be remembered that only the smallest extent of control is, in any case, capable of being applied—by the choice of sites for the more expensive and slightly larger houses and plots which are likely to attract those with higher incomes.

It would, I think, be wise to consider this matter from the point of view of dwelling requirements and density rather than deliberately to seek to promote a mixture of social classes. Tendencies for class mingling and class segregation are likely to proceed quite independently of neighbourhood Planning. The most that can be said is that visually and functionally a wide variation of dwelling types within the confines of the neighbourhood is desirable.

The appropriate size for a neighbourhood has often been a matter of dispute. It seems, however, fairly clear that it can most appropriately contain a population of about 5,000 or about 10,000. The smaller can support one two-stream primary school, the latter can support two. Below about 5,000 the unit is too small for flexibility and must lack substance; above about 10,000 it becomes too large for its identity to be appreciated, and begins to suffer from the " sea of houses " symptoms of inter-war housing.

There is, however, no need to strive for finicking exactitude. All neighbourhoods services, even schools, have some degree of flexibility, and can cater satisfactorily for fairly wide variations from the population which would fit them best.

In terms of choice, flexibility, suitable size and ease of fitting within a main road framework, however, there seems little doubt that a size of about 10,000 offers the greatest advantages.

Some idea may already have been given of the ways in which the neighbourhood principle can cause misunderstanding and hostility. There are two other reasons.

First, the notion that in an area of existing development which has a strong sense of social homogeneity this can be preserved after redevelopment is somewhat absurd, for, necessarily, redevelopment takes a considerable time. While it is going on the previous inhabitants of the area have to be found homes elsewhere, and it is highly unlikely that, even if it were sensible to provide in the form of redevelopment for the social structure previously obtaining, a recognisably similar community would eventually take the place of the original. Impracticable suggestions that this could be done have sometimes understandably aroused hostility among the practically minded.

Second, the neighbourhood is sometimes treated by unimaginative Local Planning Authorities as merely a statistical device, a " cartogram area " of roughly the right size for a neighbourhood over which density calculations are worked out, but with its boundaries drawn in complete disregard of physical, functional and social boundaries. Clearly this is absurd.

14-2. ELEMENTS IN THE NEIGHBOURHOOD UNIT

On the basis of providing within the neighbourhood unit not only dwellings for the people concerned but all the everyday needs which can be supported by a population less than that of the town as a whole we have to consider what the neighbourhood should contain. The elements other than dwellings which are likely to be required are:

Schools
Open Spaces
Large Establishments
Shops and similar uses
Places of Assembly of modest scope
Service Industry

All these items are dealt with in some detail in Chapters 15 and 16. We are here more concerned to discuss their siting and scale of provision than the form which each should take.

The school needs of a neighbourhood of ten thousand people can be met by six nursery schools, each with about forty pupils, two two-stream primary schools, each with an infants' department and a junior department, and a three-stream secondary modern school for both sexes or alternatively a boys' three-stream secondary modern school and a girls' three-stream secondary modern school, each shared by two adjacent neighbourhoods of ten thousand.

The number of shops which can be supported by a particular population is a matter of uncertainty which is discussed in Chapter 16. These elements are

mentioned first because they represent the essential neighbourhood services, and it is necessary for requirements regarding their siting and service population to be fully met if a satisfactory neighbourhood Plan is evolved. Whatever pattern of siting is decided upon for the shops most, if not all, places of assembly can be appropriately placed in conjunction with them.

The siting of both shops and schools needs to be determined mainly by accessibility, and the following requirements, though somewhat arbitrary, have been widely accepted as reasonable: nursery schools to be within a quarter of a mile of every home, primary schools to be within half a mile of every home, a group of shops to be within a quarter of a mile of every home.

These distances may perhaps more helpfully be thought of as a five-minute walk and a ten-minute walk. Obviously there is nothing precise about them, but a five-minute walk for the toddler, a ten-minute walk for the child between five and eleven and a five-minute walk for a packet of cigarettes represent high standards of convenience.

Secondary schools, which serve a much larger population individually than primary schools, cannot, obviously, be placed with the same high degree of accessibility, and the greater age of the pupils attending them makes this unnecessary.

An additional point about the siting of shops is that, apart from accessibility in " crowfly " distances, they must be sited in such a way as to gather in the maximum of passing trade, and should be at, or very near, to focal points in the neighbourhood. All neighbourhood shopping groups are to some extent in competition with the town centre shopping. To take a simple example, the housewife about to embark on a shopping expedition may well be undecided whether to go to the neighbourhood centre or to go to the town centre, where a wider range of goods is inevitably available, and to take in a film at the same time. If the neighbourhood centre is to thrive it must be so sited that its very convenience induces a fair proportion of housewives to choose it frequently rather than the town centre.

Subsidiary shopping groups within a neighbourhood are in an even less enviable position, for they have as their rivals not only the town centre but also the main neighbourhood centre and each other. They are frail things whose economic viability must always be precarious, and this is borne out by the very limited extent to which they have been provided in the New Towns, although in Wythenshawe they have been provided on a very liberal scale. There, they appear to function successfully, but it is worth noting that so far Wythenshawe is without a town centre. When this is developed it will be interesting to see whether all the subsidiary shopping groups can survive.

It is therefore of prime importance to secure that subsidiary shopping groups shall be sited with the very greatest care so that they do not miss any possible opportunity for trade.

The siting of the remaining elements in the neighbourhood is much more flexible. Open spaces, by which of course are here meant playing fields and parks, not small children's play spaces and minor amenity greens, cannot easily be sited with the same degree of accessibility as shops and primary schools, and indeed there is no need that they should be, although it is desirable that *some* open space accessible to the public should be within a few minutes' walk of every home. The subject is discussed in detail in Chapter 15 but it is worth noting here that open spaces will not necessarily or invariably be based on the neighbourhood unit at all. It may well be that the site characteristics of a particular town require that they be grouped in larger units, each serving more than one neighbourhood. This will especially be so where the existence of a large area of broken land incapable of being built upon suggests its use as a major park and, conversely, where land sufficiently flat for use as playing fields is not distributed over the whole town site but is concentrated, it may be necessary to site a large proportion of the town's playing fields within one area.

The siting of large establishments is even more flexible. Only in the most general sense of the term can they be regarded as service establishments at all, and most will certainly not function on a neighbourhood basis. This being so, although they can conveniently find their place within the residential neighbourhood they can best be sited on the edges of it in the same way as open spaces and secondary schools in order that they shall not dilute the accessibility of residents to shops, places of assembly and primary schools.

Indeed, even primary schools occupy sufficiently large sites for it to be desirable for them to be placed towards the edges of the neighbourhood rather than in the middle.

The design of the neighbourhood must constantly be determined by this paramount need to conserve accessibility, without which its main advantages cannot be fully enjoyed, and some of its services may not be able to remain permanently in being because of the adverse competitive circumstances under which they operate.

Finally, service industry is a very special case. This is not to be confused (as it often is) with light industry, or with any theory of providing within the neighbourhood a proportion of industry to satisfy the needs of part-time employment near their homes for married women, and even less to provide extra visual diversity within the neighbourhood. These, I believe, are mistaken notions. All manufacturing industry involves some disturbance and increase of traffic within its vicinity. To this extent it is incompatible with siting in a residential neighbourhood, whose homes should enjoy all the advantages of not being subjected to disturbance and whose roads should be kept free of all but local traffic. Furthermore, in a town of medium size the greatest accessibility of labour to industry, and vice versa, can only be secured by concentrating industry in as few groups as possible.

These considerations in my opinion far outweigh any advantages which might accrue from introducing industry into the residential neighbourhood. Service industry is rather in the nature of commercial and quasi-industrial undertakings of small scope which can more conveniently be provided on a neighbourhood than on a town basis. The bakery and the laundry are the classic examples of service industry, although there is more and more a tendency for these to be run by large concerns on a town basis. However, where they are still needed on a neighbourhood basis they can very appropriately be sited in or close to the main neighbourhood centre. There is however another class of user needed in any town, and very difficult to cater for. The small builder, the firelog merchant, the sweep, the rag and bone

merchant and many others play a small but essential part in the community. Their activities all require the use of land, and mostly in such a way as inevitably to cause visual detriment. For the most part, although they need to be accessible, they do not need to be central in the neighbourhood. Moreover, a good many of such uses require quite large sites, so that they cannot appropriately be provided adjacent to the main neighbourhood centre even if they could be effectively screened.

The most practical solution, though it is admittedly not an ideal one, is to provide sites for them on back land in housing areas, preferably where the housing plots are deep, so that they can be screened from sight and, so far as possible, from sound. The exact siting will depend upon the road pattern and upon topographical considerations. It is certain that activities of this kind will spring up in a town whether provision is made for them or not, for they represent very small-scale individual enterprise and initiative which springs into being to cater for specific demands. Unless sites are made available for them on which they can operate with the minimum of nuisance they will certainly be started in back gardens and other places where their nuisance is at a maximum. Though enforcement action may stamp out some and harry others from place to place it is obviously neither possible nor desirable to do without them.

14-3. NEIGHBOURHOOD FORM

The conclusions arrived at in Chapters 15, 16 and 17 will show that on the space standards tentatively suggested, about three hundred and seventy acres is needed for a residential neighbourhood of ten thousand persons. However, before considering the form of the neighbourhood on this basis it may be helpful to see how, at even a very low density the accessibility of service facilities in a neighbourhood can be provided. Fig. 66 shows a circle with a radius of half a mile, which therefore has an area of just over five hundred acres, giving a neighbourhood density of twenty persons per acre for a population of ten thousand. This in fact comes close to the density suggested for " open " development in the Dudley Report already referred to, and probably represents a lower gross density than would ordinarily be contemplated nowadays over a complete neighbourhood in a normal town. Nevertheless it will be seen that accessibility requirements can be almost completely met.

In practice, a neighbourhood is seldom likely to approximate to a circle in shape because of the very large blank areas necessarily left between adjoining circles. In a town of approximately circular shape it is much more likely to take a roughly wedge-like form as do the neighbourhoods of the theoretical New Town referred to at intervals throughout this book. Fig. 55 shows one of the neighbourhoods of this town to a degree of detail sufficient to show clearly the disposition of its main elements, and this drawing would, incidentally, with the addition of net residential density provisions, approximate closely to what is required for a Comprehensive Development Area Map or Supplementary Town Map, referred to later. Other shapes to which neighbourhoods may often approximate in new or existing towns, are the

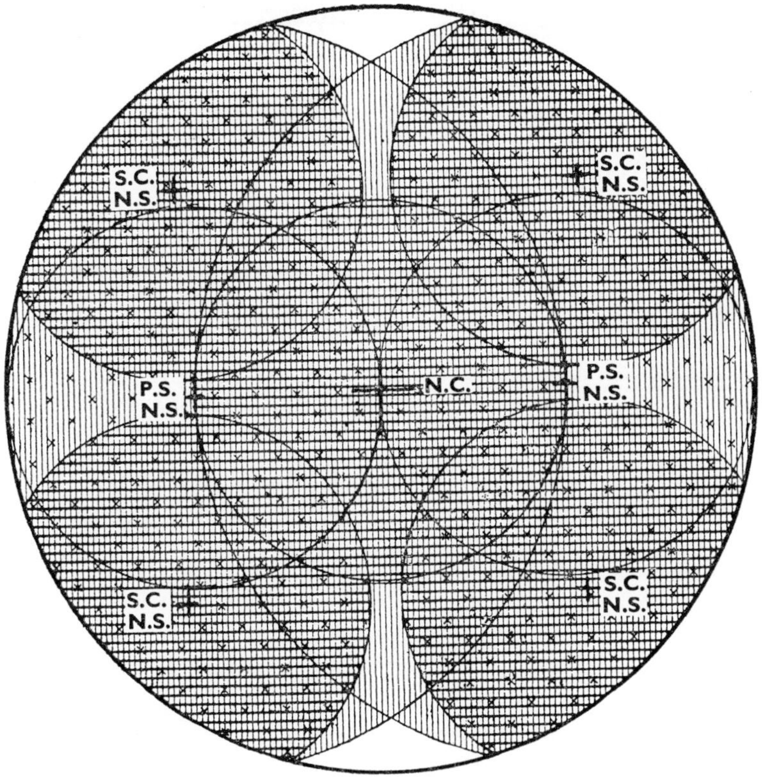

FIG. 66.   This diagram shows the high degree of accessibility to neighbourhood services which can be secured even at a low density.   The neighbourhood has a radius of half a mile and therefore an area of about five hundred acres.   The smaller circles and arcs show distances of half a mile from primary schools and of a quarter of a mile from shopping groups and nursery schools, and the hatchings indicate the degree of accessibility enjoyed by different parts of the neighbourhood.   P.S.=Primary School, N.S.=Nursery School, N.C.=Neighbourhood Centre, S.C.=Sub-centre

oblong and the square, and Figs. 67 (iii) and (iv) show examples of neighbourhood patterns corresponding to these.

Examples of complete neighbourhoods the design of which has not been strongly affected by unusual topography, existing development or exceptional circumstances of one kind or another, are few.   Attention will therefore be concentrated upon the neighbourhood shown in Fig. 69, the detailed design of which is also shown in Fig. 68.   It will be seen that a very high degree of accessibility is secured by placing all land uses without buildings or with a small proportion of buildings on the outskirts.   Three sub-centres are provided, but it will be apparent that the viability of the one nearest the town

centre is bound to be doubtful because of its closeness both to the town centre and the main neighbourhood centre.

The large majority of the population is concentrated in such a way that it is very close indeed to all neighbourhood services, while the lowest density houses and the large establishments, which by their nature are least dependent upon neighbourhood services, are the most remote.

As regards density, it is assumed that the bulk of the high density development will be nearest the town centre and that the majority of the medium density development will be around the neighbourhood centre.   There is therefore a rough grading of density downwards from the town centre outwards, though with a small local increase around the neighbourhood centre.   This corresponds both with the needs of accessibility and compactness and with the requirements of residents.   A more detailed analysis of this aspect is given in Chapter 17.

There is one point of special interest.   It will be obvious that a higher degree of accessibility to primary schools could be secured if they were placed vertically instead of horizontally to the main neighbourhood centre, and it is indeed a moot point whether this would not be preferable.   However, two factors militate against it.

In the first place, if the kinds of dwellings provided are appropriately occupied then the areas least accessible to primary schools are those which would use them least.   In particular it is to be hoped that the high density development nearest the town centre will be occupied almost exclusively by families without young children.

Second, secondary grammar and technical schools have to be located near the town centre since they serve the population of the whole town.   In a neighbourhood within which one of these schools has to be sited it is therefore difficult to place the primary schools vertically without having an undue concentration of schools, and hence virtually of open space, near the town centre, where residential development should be approaching its most intense.   Furthermore, the pushing outwards of primary schools to the edges of the neighbourhood increases the concentration of population possible immediately surrounding the neighbourhood centre and has the additional advantage that residents of adjacent neighbourhoods who for any reason do not like the primary school within their own neighbourhood have an alternative close at hand.

Service industry is distributed in the way suggested earlier in this chapter.

The boundaries of the neighbourhood are carefully arranged to give it the greatest possible measure of identity and unity.   Open spaces and large establishments and schools occupy the greater part of its perimeter, and, as regards the latter, it will be seen from Fig. 21 that the arrangement of schools in adjacent neighbourhoods reinforces physical identity and separateness.

The siting of open space around the edges of the neighbourhood is functionally useful not only for reasons of compactness but because it provides a cushion between main roads and dwellings.   Noise and fumes are inseparable from main roads, and it is desirable that they should be appreciably separated from dwellings.

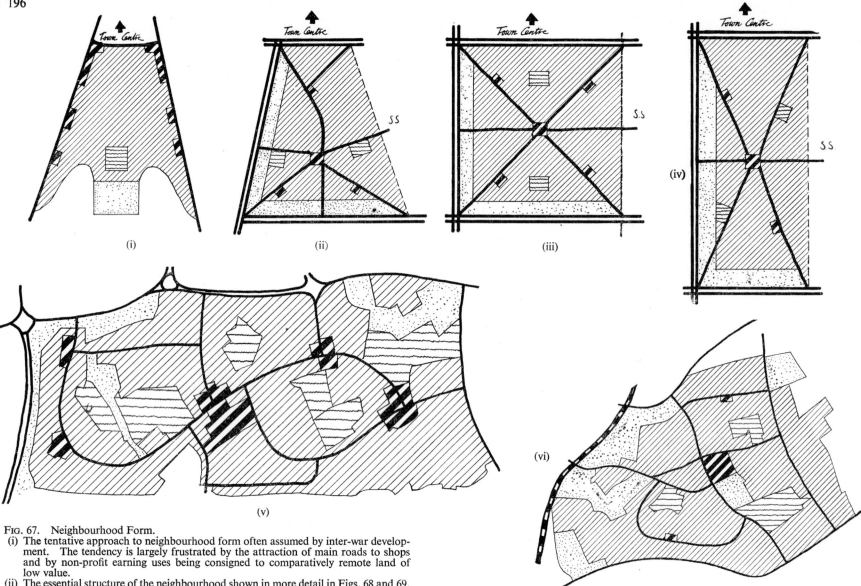

FIG. 67. Neighbourhood Form.
 (i) The tentative approach to neighbourhood form often assumed by inter-war develop-
     ment. The tendency is largely frustrated by the attraction of main roads to shops
     and by non-profit earning uses being consigned to comparatively remote land of
     low value.
 (ii) The essential structure of the neighbourhood shown in more detail in Figs. 68 and 69.
     This is the basic neighbourhood shape demanded in the town of ordinary radial
     structure.
(iii) The same basic idea applied to a town divisible by reason of its road structure into
     roughly square neighbourhoods.
 (iv) The same idea applied to a town whose road structure demands division into oblong
     neighbourhood units.

 (v) Woodhouse Park neighbourhood, Wythenshawe.
 (vi) Adeyfield Neighbourhood, Hemel Hempstead New Town.
   Throughout roads are black, shopping and associated uses heavy diagonal hatching,
primary schools irregular horizontal hatching, secondary schools marked S.S., open space
stippled, residential light diagonal hatching. Roads in (ii)–(iv) are of course purely
diagrammatic.

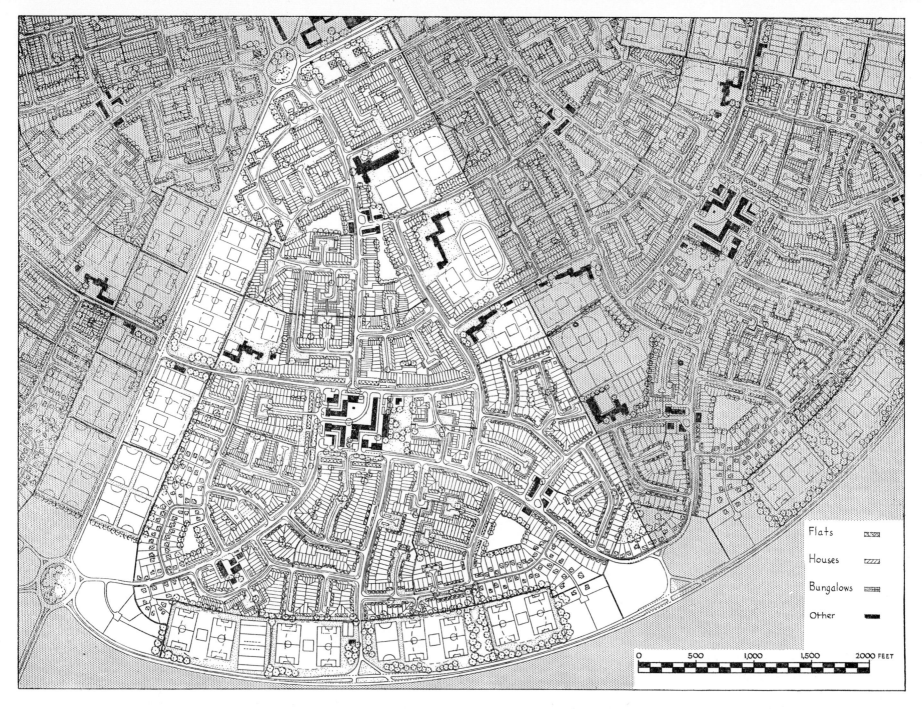

Flats
Houses
Bungalows
Other

| 0 | 500 | 1,000 | 1,500 | 2000 FEET |

FIG. 68. The same neighbourhood as that shown in Fig. 69, together with adjoining development, as it might be built. Space standards etc., are in accordance with the suggestions made in Chapters 14–17.

198

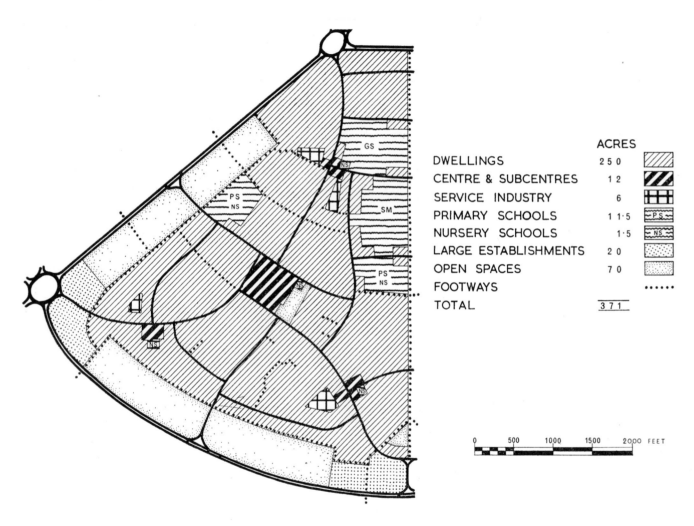

	ACRES	
DWELLINGS	250	
CENTRE & SUBCENTRES	12	
SERVICE INDUSTRY	6	
PRIMARY SCHOOLS	11·5	
NURSERY SCHOOLS	1·5	
LARGE ESTABLISHMENTS	20	
OPEN SPACES	70	
FOOTWAYS		······
TOTAL	371	

0   500   1000   1500   2000 FEET

FIG. 69. One of the Neighbourhoods of the Theoretical New Town, population 10,000, shown as a " zoning diagram " or " Supplementary Town Map " in slightly greater detail than Fig. 21. In order to avoid confusion the residential area has not been divided into zones of different density.

It should be realised that the 250 acres shown for dwellings is an average. Neighbourhoods with two secondary schools within them have rather less than this, those with only one rather more. (See Fig. 21.)

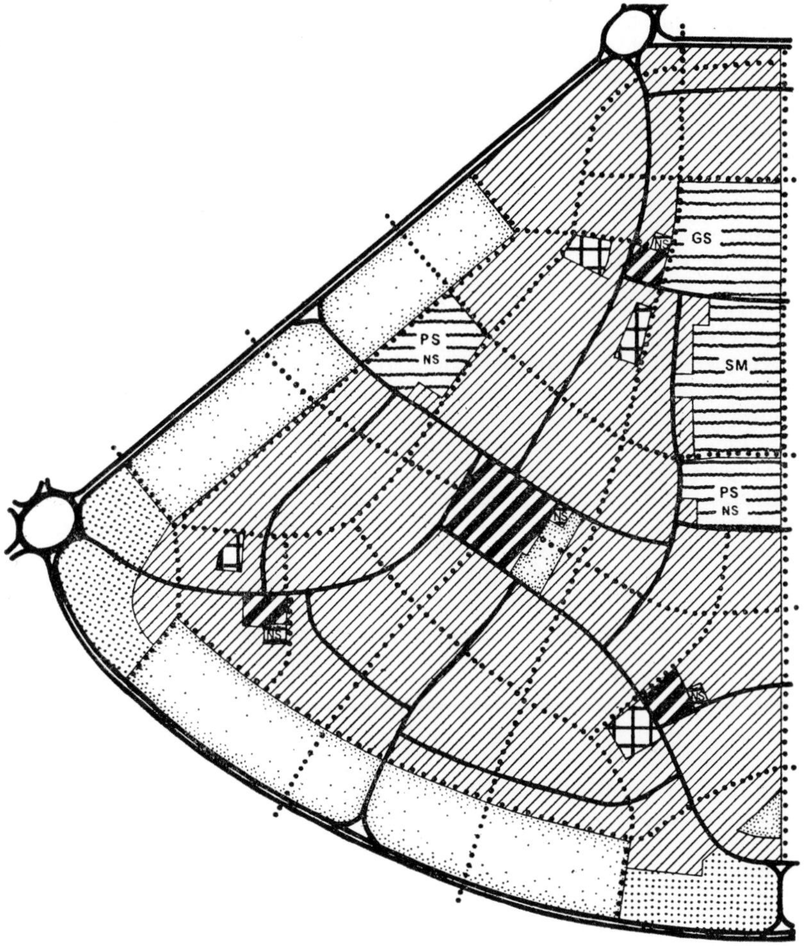

It will be seen that although physical separateness is given to the neighbourhood this in no way implies or involves segregation, an absurd notion which, it may be noted in passing, has sometimes been conceived as an objective of neighbourhood planning. There are several road links between the neighbourhood and its neighbour to the right, and, although the common boundary between them is formed by a continuous footway linking the perimeter and the town centre, there are places where housing is continuous except for this slight interruption.

Because of the featureless nature of the site advantage cannot be taken of natural features to give physical distinctness, but, obviously, where these exist they can appropriately be utilised, as can also artificial features such as railways and embankments.

The communication system of the neighbourhood is designed to secure immediate access both to town centre and bounding main roads yet to avoid giving encouragement to traffic moving between different parts of the town to cut through the neighbourhood road system. In this way the distinction between main roads and local roads, the importance of which is stressed in Chapter 11, is sharply maintained. A further fairly sharp distinction is made between neighbourhood spine roads and minor access roads, a subject which is also dealt with in detail in Chapter 11. All the spine roads lead directly to the neighbourhood centre, thus giving it accessibility in terms of road travel as well as of crowflight. This arrangement also makes it possible to keep the spine roads of moderate length, thus discouraging excessive speed.

A footpath system linking the outskirts of the town with its centre and the neighbourhood with that next to it is also provided. This does not aim at being very elaborate or complete, but one could walk right round the edge of the town by footpath; one could walk from its outskirts to the town centre by footpaths between neighbourhoods; and there are a number of other footpaths of varying length which would enable one to take quite long walks between various parts of the neighbourhood mainly by independent footpath, though occasionally a road would have to be crossed and for parts of these walks the footpath would be alongside a road.

It would be perfectly possible, as Fig. 70 shows, to make the footpath system much more complete and elaborate without making more than trivial alterations to the neighbourhood design. But it seems very doubtful whether this would be worth doing. The cost of surfacing and lighting would be considerable, the cost of making pedestrian bridges or tunnels great—and to provide a comprehensive footpath network entirely independent of roads it would be necessary to have these.

I do not think that, regarded soberly, the balance of advantage would be found to lie in going much further than the degree of footpath provision in Fig. 69 for footpath systems create their own problems. Unless fully and expensively lighted and controlled by the police they tend to be happy hunting grounds for rapists and robbers. I am aware that almost any amenity which it is sought to provide in a town may be criticised because of the consequences flowing from its possible misuse, but the difficulties here involved are somewhat acute, though it may be pointed out that while it is

Fig. 70. The same Plan as in Fig. 69, slightly rearranged to make provision for a more complete system of pedestrian ways.

possible to walk about the footpath system, making little use of roads, it is equally possible for the nervous and vulnerable to avoid the footpaths, and use only the road system.

This comforting alternative hardly applies to " pedestrian towns ", such as those illustrated in Fig. 25, the main object of which is to force pedestrians off the roads and onto the footpath system.

It is, to sum up, *physically* possible to design a neighbourhood so that virtually all pedestrian movement *can* take place on footways independent of the road system, even down to the " Radburn " system of providing the road on one side of a row of houses in a cul-de-sac and the footpath on the other side. It may even be possible to secure that a considerable proportion of pedestrian movement *does* take place along the pedestrian ways (though not all, as we have seen on page 157) but the extent to which it is worth while making such separation is much more debatable. It is, for example, most desirable to design thoroughly safe road systems within a neighbourhood so that pedestrians, especially children, may not be exposed to undue danger; it is, at the very least, open to question whether it is desirable to design a neighbourhood in such a way that children do not have to cross any roads whatever. Sooner or later, as the range of their activities increases, they will have to do so, and it is reasonable that they should have had some previous experience of avoiding vehicles on a safe local road system before being thrown into the perils of the outside world.

It is, finally, worth mentioning that wherever a footpath is provided independently of a road consideration should also be given to running a cycle track parallel to it. The separation of bicycles from motor vehicles is nearly as important as the separation of pedestrians, and, wherever cycle traffic is likely to be considerable, this is a satisfactory method of securing separation.

In Chapter 8, page 100, it was questioned whether, in a town of this kind, the outer ring road would in fact, ever be built because the main radial roads and inner ring road provide routes for through traffic incomparably better than any that exists at present in a British town.

It is interesting to find that the inclusion or omission of the outer ring road in fact makes no difference to the appropriateness of the disposition of land uses within the neighbourhood. It might well be that the town would be built in advance of the construction of the outer ring road but that it was desired to provide for the latter to be made later on if it was found to be necessary. If this were so the only modifications necessary would be to alter the junction of the spine road running downwards from the neighbourhood centre with the southernmost minor road running left and right and to construct a temporary access road to the open space, a road which would, on the construction of the outer ring road, be replaced by a continuation of the spine road previously referred to. The only other modification would be initially to omit the short link road with the outer ring road at the common boundary between the adjoining neighbourhoods. The efficiency of the neighbourhood would be left unimpaired.

Although it is very desirable to arrange the elements in the neighbourhood in accordance with the principles which have been suggested, these principles

have to be modified where exceptional topographical conditions exist. Just as the form of the town may have to be varied to take account of site characteristics to such an extent that a different set of principles has to be evolved, as explained in Chapter 10, so may the same thing happen to the Neighbourhood.

Dwellings cannot suitably be sited on very steep slopes, nor on low-lying and boggy land, but apart from this their site requirements are fairly flexible. Playing fields and schools need very flat sites unless their development is to be inordinately expensive. Satisfactory and attractive parks can be produced from almost any site that is not hopelessly infertile. Neighbourhood centres and sub-centres clearly must be on fairly flat sites, as must areas devoted to service industry. The needs of large establishments are very flexible.

14-4. VISUAL TREATMENT OF NEIGHBOURHOODS

It is generally agreed that there is a tendency to monotony in contemporary housing, and indeed in building generally. The reasons for this are numerous and need not be further discussed here except to say that such monotony may often arise despite the excellence of design of individual buildings. Thorough functional Planning of land uses in a town automatically reduces this tendency since it introduces an orderliness and logic into the urban scene which is in itself refreshing and to some extent satisfying. This can be greatly reinforced by adding to the physical separateness and identity of each neighbourhood visual identity. This is an idea which has been played with tentatively and rather nervously in connection with the New Towns, but virtually abandoned. In effect, what has usually been done has been to avoid monotony within the neighbourhood by splitting it up into several sub-units each designed by an individual architect or group of architects. This has to some extent been successful, but the variety within the individual neighbourhood has usually been accompanied by an absence of any dominant visual motif, and hence an absence of visual identity and of contrast with other neighbourhoods.

In the absence of examples to which to point it is somewhat difficult to explain the possibilities, but they seem to me to be very great. I believe that an able and enthusiastic group of designers in charge of the construction of a New Town could, if they were unhampered, set out to build a series of neighbourhoods which, while they would not lack variety within them, would each be visually distinctive. The elements available to achieve this are architectural style, materials and grouping, plant species, landscaping style, colour and texture of surfacing of all hard surfaces—carriageways, footpaths and forecourts.

I am not suggesting that the changes should be rung on these in any crude way. To have a neighbourhood in which all the buildings had monopitch roofs, all the trees were poplars and all the hard surfaces were pink, in contrast with one in which all the roofs were pitched, all the trees were weeping willows and all the hard surfaces were yellow, would not be likely to produce happy results. I am rather thinking of a contrast between, for example, a neighbourhood in which the shapes, colours and textures of all the elements would be gentle and subdued in contrast with one in which boldness would be the dominant motif. One has, of course, to bear in mind that as regards vegetation certain limitations are imposed on variety because of local soil qualities. Nevertheless, a deliberate policy of this kind seems to me to afford opportunities for creative design on a large scale not hitherto attempted, and having potentialities for the creation of beauty and surprise which are enormous.

Another aspect of visual treatment which is of great importance is the creation of what might naïvely be called " a sense of direction ". It ought to be possible, from most parts of a neighbourhood, to see or to sense in which direction the town centre lies, in which direction the neighbourhood centre and in which direction the edge of the town. The logical disposition of the elements of the neighbourhood and a logical road layout will themselves do much to secure this, but the siting of any tall buildings used and the deliberate creation of glimpses and vistas can supplement the logic of the Plan considerably. These, incidentally, are all factors which contribute far more to that feeling of " urbanity "[1] so prized by some, than the general height or density of buildings. It is awareness of being within a town and of the relative positions of its principal parts rather than being closely surrounded by looming masses of buildings which gives this feeling.

14-5. APPLICATION OF THE NEIGHBOURHOOD PRINCIPLE TO EXISTING TOWNS

It has been noted earlier that the Planned division of the future growth of existing towns into neighbourhood units must be attempted with great caution. In many towns where there are large quantities of inter-war development within which substantial undeveloped pockets remain no such treatment is possible, for the distribution of the services required may, for lack of sites available in the best places, have to be greatly changed from the ideal, and the boundaries of residential units may enclose areas far too large or too small for them to be properly termed neighbourhoods. In such cases arbitrary division on paper into neighbourhoods is likely to be meaningless or even misleading.

Boundaries, if they are to live up to their name, must be marked by physical barriers, or, at least, by the watersheds at which local interest turns towards different foci. For example, all too often a radial road bearing considerable traffic runs through a residential area but does not mark off any division of interest, being treated by the inhabitants as a residential road. The real neighbourhood boundary may be a park two or three hundred yards away from such a road.

In such a case the adoption of an unreal boundary, with the provision of services based upon it, must result in dislocation, some services being over-strained and others not fully used. Study of survey information relating to service catchment areas should prevent errors of this kind being made, and the aim should be, where no coherent neighbourhood system is possible, to site new services where they can best supplement existing ones in relation both to existing and proposed areas of dwellings. (See Fig. 71 (i).)

In towns where a great deal of redevelopment overspill will have to be

---

[1] Inverted commas because the noun which goes with urban is urbaneness, not urbanity, which goes with urbane.

accommodated, or where an increase of population is proposed, it will often be possible to Plan some complete new neighbourhoods for development at later stages, even though existing development and its immediate extensions cannot be so treated.

It must once more be emphasised that there is no such thing as the perfect provision of services, most of which can operate with fair success between fairly widely separated limits of demand. If no services are seriously over-

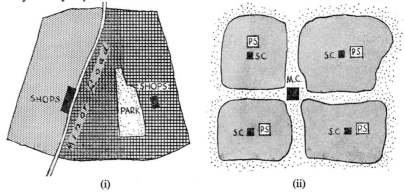

Fig. 71 (i) For a unit to be a real Neighbourhood it must have sensible boundaries. Here the stippled area will clearly form a Neighbourhood. To plan on the assumption that the cross-hatched area would function as a Neighbourhood because a road " ought " to form its boundary would be wrong unless the road was a major road, frontage development was removed from it and the shops were moved to back land.
(ii) The " Cluster " Neighbourhood theory. Main Centre, M.C.; Sub Centres, S.C.; Primary Schools, P.S.

strained and none so little used that they are in danger of perishing, a satisfactory balance will have been struck.

The use of the neighbourhood principle in large areas of redevelopment demands some mention. Some have maintained that existing service institutions in such areas, together with their areas of influence, should be carefully studied, particularly where neighbourhood structure and community spirit is strong, with a view to the re-provision of at least the most important of them as near as possible to their original sites so as to leave the neighbourhood pattern as little altered as possible. This is, at first sight, an attractive idea, and in some special circumstances may be worth serious consideration; on the whole, though, closer examination dispels most of the attractiveness.

In such areas, where buildings are seldom well adapted for their purpose, the personalities of a few prominent local leaders probably contribute far more to successful neighbourhood structure than do any elements of the physical pattern. Any wholesale redevelopment is certain to involve substantial overspill, and a proportion of such people are sure to be among those who depart, with the consequent disappearance, deterioration or transformation of the activities with which they were connected.

In any event the necessarily long-draw-out physical upheaval of redevelopment cannot but disturb, and probably alter permanently, the character of such a delicately adjusted unit as a happy slum neighbourhood.

It is a truism that Planning should be done for the people, not for the Planner, but what is often forgotten or not understood by critics is that Planning is the creation of a physical pattern so designed that personal, family, social and economic life can flourish within it. It should not and cannot provide the optimum environment for a given set of transient persons at a given moment of time.

Rather, as suggested in Chapter 5 (Urban Regions), very large scale redevelopment ought to lead to the creation of neighbourhoods even where none existed before because the extensiveness of the area dealt with enables considerable redistribution of land uses to be brought about.

14-6. ALTERNATIVE NEIGHBOURHOOD THEORIES

I personally consider that what may be called the orthodox neighbourhood theory, set out in the preceding pages, is on the whole the most satisfactory. It is based on fundamental functional requirements, and, as already explained, is no more than a rationalisation of a distribution which already occurs in unplanned towns. Nevertheless, other arrangements have their merits, and need to be considered.

The most important of these is the arrangement adopted in Harlow New Town, see Fig. 71 (ii). The basis of this is that a cluster of small neighbourhoods, each with a population of three or four thousand, is served by one large neighbourhood centre which, because it serves a population of about twenty thousand rather than about ten thousand, can be weightier, and thus more satisfactory. Each of the small neighbourhoods forming the cluster has one minor centre to serve its purely local needs. School provision is based on the large neighbourhood. The great advantage of this idea is that it provides greater flexibility in the provision of local services than does a neighbourhood of ten thousand, and also ensures greater viability for the smaller number of shopping centres provided. Its great weakness is that if, in fact, each of the cluster of small neighbourhoods is to be physically distinct, development becomes very diffused. And this is indeed what has happened in Harlow. There are so many small units that seldom does one come across an unbroken area of development sufficiently large to be visually satisfying or to provide a satisfactory degree of compactness.

The opposite of the Harlow theory is really the abandonment of the neighbourhood principle: by Planning for the maximum compactness to do away with the need for nearly all sub-centres, and thus to concentrate upon a highly equipped town centre, the strength and variety of which are not sapped by a number of sub-centres. This idea can be taken to extremes or used in modified forms. It will be interesting to see what its implications are in the most extreme form, still using the space standards adopted throughout this chapter.

The results are not very impressive. If we push to the outskirts of the town everything except the town centre, the main industrial area and the net residential areas, the radius of the circle containing these will still be 1,738

yards, so that residents on the outer edge of the residential area will be nearly a mile from shops, and, conversely, those on the inner edge nearly a mile from schools.

Confronted with this obviously unacceptable situation one would then, no doubt, re-introduce primary schools and small shopping sub-centres into the residential area, and this would, indeed, improve accessibility without expanding the size of the built-up area appreciably. But even so no dramatic increase in compactness has been secured. The radius of the built-up area is reduced by only about 370 yards, dwellings have to approach closely to all the main radial roads and the old inter-war suburban problem of large masses of uninterrupted housing is reintroduced. I cannot think that the advantages to be secured are appreciable.

14-7. THE SUPPLEMENTARY TOWN MAP AND COMPREHENSIVE DEVELOPMENT AREA MAP

These are virtually identical documents, as explained in Appendix 1. In terms of statutory Planning they represent the stage of detail equivalent to the design of a neighbourhood unit. As suggested in Chapter 20-3, in areas of piecemeal development and redevelopment such maps are indispensable in order to guide development into the right places and into the right form, though not many have yet been prepared.

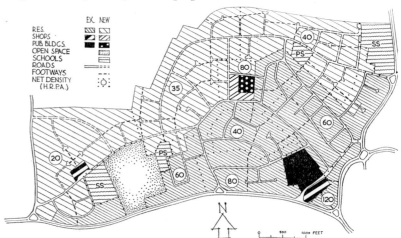

FIG. 72. A Supplementary Town Map covering part of the western portion of the Town Map shown in Fig. 36. It lays down the future road and pedestrian network for new and redeveloped areas and prescribes permitted densities in detail. These additions to the information shown on the Town Map make all the difference; they provide an adequate guide to development control.

The Town Map shows the disposition of main areas and use and the main transport network in the town. The more detailed Plan needs to show the exact use to which every piece of land will be put and the details of the road system which serves the area, stopping short of the design of individual

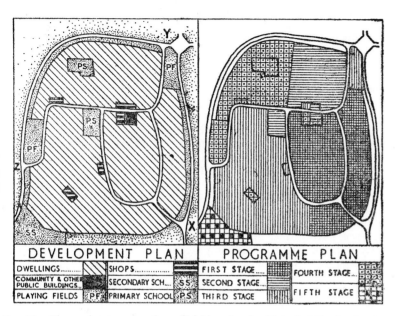

FIG. 73. Plan and programme for a Neighbourhood. Note that the development of each non-residential item is delayed until there are sufficient dwellings within its service area to provide it with sufficient support to enable it to operate at least on a restricted scale.

buildings and of the determination of such detailed matters as, for example, which kinds of shops should be placed within a particular shopping group.

It is especially important to show the distribution of net residential densities to be permitted within the area. For an area of neighbourhood size to be socially and visually satisfactory it is important, as explained in Chapter 17, that a large variety of dwelling types at widely varying densities, should be included, but if, as is the case with the Town Map, only a general indication of average density for the neighbourhood as a whole is available, it would be unsafe to permit individual developers to develop much in excess of this average and correspondingly difficult to persuade others to develop at substantially lower densities.

14-8. PROGRAMMING THE NEIGHBOURHOOD PLAN

Programming of the Neighbourhood Plan naturally needs to be more detailed than for the Town Map. The dual aim should be to stage development in such a way that the provision of services keeps step with the building of dwellings, and that each stage results in the creation of a self-contained unit which can stand by itself if further work has to be suspended indefinitely.

It is also important that roads and other engineering works should be so arranged that they begin to pay their way as soon as possible.

Fig. 73 shows the kind of programme which might be adopted for an entirely new neighbourhood. Work begins with the construction of an access road. The first stage of building development consists exclusively of the construction of dwellings in the part of the neighbourhood nearest to the town centre, which the residents can temporarily use for the services they need without undue inconvenience. Apart from the access road, no roads need be constructed long in advance of development alongside them.

Stage 2 sees development of dwellings extending farther from the town centre, and towards the end of this stage some shops and public buildings, the latter possibly in temporary form, will be required and able to support themselves; a further access to the main road system is made and a primary school can support itself.

Stage 3 sees development extending even farther afield; a subsidiary shopping centre will now be required and the main shopping centre expands; the laying out of some playing-fields becomes justified.

Stage 4 sees the completion of housing development, the establishment of another minor shopping centre, primary school, and block of playing-fields. The main centre is completed and a third access made.

Finally, secondary schools are built.

It has been assumed in this example that main roads adjoining the neighbourhood exist in their final form, but where this is not so their construction would proceed in step with the neighbourhood development so far as possible, or, if it necessarily lagged behind, temporary accesses would be made to existing roads.

Secondary school provision might be begun earlier than indicated, according to distribution of secondary school facilities throughout the town.

14-9. CONCLUSION

It will be convenient to end this chapter with a summary of the space allocations made in the Plan for the theoretical New Town neighbourhood:—

					Acres
Residential ...	...	...	...	...	250
Centres and sub-centres		...	...	...	12
Service Industry ...	...	...	...	...	6
Primary Schools...	...	...	...	...	$11\frac{1}{2}$
Nursery Schools...	...	...	...	...	$1\frac{1}{2}$
Large establishments ...	...	...	...	20
Open Space ...	...	...	...	...	70
				Total	371

CHAPTER 15

OPEN SPACES, LARGE ESTABLISHMENTS AND SCHOOL SITES

15-1. INTRODUCTORY

HAVING IN THE previous chapter discussed the general requirements for the Neighbourhood Plan, we turn, in this and the following chapters, to consideration of the various elements that go to make up the neighbourhood. In this chapter open spaces, large establishments and schools are dealt with together because they are the uses within the neighbourhood which require sites of which only a very small proportion is occupied by buildings. In visual terms, therefore, they have a close affinity with each other, although, of course, the ways in which they are used are very different.

In the case of a New Town it will usually be appropriate for all these uses to be provided more or less on a neighbourhood basis, and, indeed, schools are closely linked to the whole idea of the neighbourhood. But there is no special reason why large establishments should be, and no compulsive need for open spaces to be on a strictly neighbourhood basis. In the case of some New Towns topographical considerations may suggest the reverse, and, as already stated in the previous chapter, the applicability of the neighbourhood idea to existing towns is bound to be limited.

Nevertheless, in the terms in which we are defining the various components of the town, many of these uses fall within the category of neighbourhood uses because they serve parts of the town rather than the town as a whole. This hardly applies to large establishments and to secondary grammar and technical schools, which will usually serve the whole town.

As already emphasised in several parts of this book, it is most desirable that all these elements should be combined into a system which, so far as it is possible to reconcile and fulfil the different aims involved, shall produce a meaningful design in which closely built-up areas and open areas supplement and contrast with each other visually in a relationship somewhat similar to the voids and solids of a building, in which there is a considerable measure of linkage between different items so that many journeys by foot within the town can be through mainly open areas; and in which some open space accessible to the public is within a short distance of every home. The New Town design illustrated in Figs. 21, 68, 70, etc. fulfils these aims reasonably completely, and, as regards the last, provides open space so that very few homes are more than a quarter of a mile from some open space.

15-2. OPEN SPACE

Open space as here referred to comprises only the larger open spaces, and does not include small children's play spaces, amenity greens and so on, which are parts of the net residential area.

Open spaces are divisible in function as between playing fields and parks, although both functions may often appropriately be provided within a single site, in which case, when the playing fields are not being used for games, they form part of the park. Questions of position, distribution, amount and site treatment arise.

Position

A good deal has already been said about this in connection with the Town Plan and the Neighbourhood Plan. We may summarise the most important considerations involved by saying that open space of all kinds may very appropriately be used to cushion the impact of main roads on residential areas and to act as a buffer between residential areas and agricultural land in order to minimise damage to the latter. A very high degree of accessibility is neither necessary nor practicable. No one who wishes to play football, hockey, cricket and the like seriously, minds travelling some distance for a game, and, obviously enough, since roughly half the matches played by any club are away matches some substantial amount of travelling has to be undertaken. Also, since any large open spaces within built-up areas inevitably reduce their compactness, only strong positive reasons should lead to such positioning. This leads us to distribution.

Distribution

From the purely visual point of view it would probably be best to split up playing fields into as many units as possible (the smallest unit possible obviously being the single playing field) and to scatter these widely over the parts of the town in which it was intended that open space should be provided. This, however, is not a practicable proposition. Many groups of playing fields are municipally owned or owned by works sports associations etc., and the provision of changing rooms and other necessary buildings and maintenance is much more economical if a fairly large number of pitches is grouped into one unit. Furthermore, the technical requirements of games commonly played make it suitable to combine the areas devoted to cricket and to football or hockey pitches. It is, however, vital, that the land needed for actual cricket wickets should not be used for other purposes, and, in particular, should not be trampled over in winter by football boots. Except in the case of grounds where the highest class of cricket is to be played this does not apply to the outfield, so that it is a usual and economical method to site a cricket wicket or " table " between two adjoining football or hockey pitches, or at the junction of four of them.

These considerations are so strong that they must inevitably override the disadvantages involved. It is very desirable to split large areas of playing-fields into distinct units. An example of this can be seen in Fig. 68. This can be done by means of groups and rows of trees and bushes or hedges, and has several purposes. A large flat undivided expanse of playing-fields, with various types of goal posts dotted about it and muddy patches in the goal areas of the soccer pitches, is not usually a particularly pleasing sight, and, on this score alone, skilfully designed subdivision of it would be desirable. But, also, large unbroken expanses are likely to be swept by fierce winds, detrimental alike to the comfort of players and spectators and to ball control, and subdivisions can be arranged to form effective wind breaks. Further, it is most helpful to the concentration of players if adjoining pitches, particularly those whose ends are adjacent, are screened from each other's view.

Also, where playing-fields are combined with parkland, it is helpful to the quietness and repose of the latter if the playing-fields are at least partially screened from it.

The screens need not by any means be continuous or impenetrable; frequent breaks are desirable, both for the free passage of mowers, rollers, etc., and for the convenience of casual spectators who like to wander from one game to another.

The combination of playing-fields and parkland can often have the happiest results, as can readily be seen in places such as Didsbury Park, Manchester, and, in its very different way, the L.C.C.'s Hampstead Heath extension. Where playing-fields and parks are mingled in this way there is a greater flexibility in the use of land. For example, in the evenings the playing-fields as well as the park portions can be used for exercising dogs, flying kites, etc. The concentration of playing-fields is somewhat reduced and a much greater feeling of spaciousness is produced. Where the total amount of open space that can be supplied is limited this is of special importance.

Normally it will be desirable, within a neighbourhood, to have at least two separate areas of open space rather than a single one, primarily from the point of view of accessibility, but secondarily, even with the most skilful arrangement, too large a concentration of games spaces is likely to be undesirable because of the visual dreariness produced.

Amount

There are two special problems which make it peculiarly difficult to fix appropriate standards for the provision of open spaces. First, what account is to be taken of private open spaces? The ground of a private cricket, tennis, football or hockey club may well provide exercise for as many people as the equivalent area in public ownership; in many towns a proportion of such clubs play on grounds owned and leased to them annually by the local authority. Clearly, it would be pointless to exclude such grounds from the total of open space.

At the other extreme there are private golf clubs and polo grounds which are used by very few people in proportion to the area they occupy, and some of the country's finest cricket grounds are spacious and played on comparatively infrequently (they often have no winter use). To include any of these in the total would be wrong.

There are, too, awkward intermediate cases. It is quite common for works' sports grounds to occupy land which it is known will eventually be required for extensions to the works; the people who play on it will not be content suddenly to give up playing games when this happens.

Second, the parkland to be provided for a town is hardly capable of accurate estimation. To estimate the greatest number of people likely to use parks simultaneously and the minimum number of square yards each would require in order to enjoy himself is a task for which one would require skill

equal to that of the German officer who is said to have calculated during the First World War, the number of hospital beds which should be set aside for soldiers kicked by mules.

To hazard what can be little more than a guess as to the total required, if one-eighth of the population simultaneously decided to take to the parks and were content with 100 square yards of park each, something very close to $2\frac{1}{2}$ acres per 1,000 persons would be required.

Parks, of course, may range from a formal town garden to an area of country left entirely or almost entirely wild and it is obvious than an intensity of use which would be perfectly acceptable for the first would entirely prevent enjoyment of the second.

This problem must also be looked at from another angle; within a town there may be extensive areas of broken and steeply sloping land, land liable to flood, or other land which cannot satisfactorily be used for building or agricultural purposes. It may be entirely appropriate to devote the whole of such land to parks, and thus produce a very substantial total area of parkland (see Fig. 36). So long as at least a reasonable *minimum* is provided it does not matter much how much parkland there is if it does not unduly reduce the compactness of the town. In a town with difficult topography it may indeed be appropriate to regard parkland as a residual use to which all land is devoted which is unsuitable or unneeded for any other urban purpose.

Any standards for open space which lump together parks and playing-fields, therefore, seem to me to be useless; a town may well possess huge areas of wild heath land and yet be sadly short of playing-fields.

A further minor problem is how to classify parkway strips adjoining roads. In my opinion, if their function is wholly to increase the enjoyment, safety or comfort of the users of the road they adjoin they should be included with the areas of roads, but if they form a genuine park used by people as such they should be included in the area of open space.

Let us now return to consideration of space standards for playing-fields. The aim should be to ensure that all who want to play games should be able to do so at the times they find convenient, but it is by no means easy to translate this into acres per 1,000 persons. There are two main difficulties. First, how can we find out what proportion of the population would like to play games and, second, even if this can be worked out, how do we know the numbers of games players who would choose any particular game? This is particularly important because different games need very different areas per person. Four people can have a game of tennis in a total area of about 780 square yards or 195 square yards per person, but 22 people require about 15,000 square yards for a good game of cricket, about 680 square yards per person. Furthermore, there are many people who enjoy playing games in summer but who have little taste for being hurled into liquid mud on a January afternoon.

It may be as well to explain that by games playing one means the more or less regular and serious pursuit of a game which provides a measure of exercise. One would include bowls, gentle though the exercise is, because it is a real game played by many with skill and assiduity, but one would not include putting courses, which, for most of their users, merely provide an inexpensive method of wasting half an hour, nor need the occasional **tennis** player who sallies forth with a frayed tennis racket only two or three times in a season be included.

No serious attempt seems to have been made to solve the first problem. In order to do so one would have to start by finding out what proportion of the population does at present play games and what further number could be expected to do so if sufficient conveniently located facilities were available. In order to obtain reliable figures upon which to base provision of facilities in a new town, a representative sample survey on a large scale would have to be carried out and the number of people who did not already play games but who said they would like to would have to be substantially written down. Everyone who has tried to start a club or society knows that the gap between the number who evince initial interest and those who actually take part in the enterprise is wide. I am not aware that such a survey has been carried out anywhere, although it would certainly be extremely useful.

Various estimates have been made of open space requirements.

The *National Playing Fields Association* estimated in 1927 that in every 1,000 persons there were 500 between the ages of 10 and 40 years, of whom 200 (20 per cent. of the total population) would need provision for games playing, and that this ought to be provided at the rate of 6 acres per 1,000 population. It was suggested that an additional 1 acre per 1,000 was needed for other kinds of public open space.

The Ministry of Housing and Local Government's Technical Memorandum on Open Space produced in 1956, does not go any further than this. It observes that the N.P.F.A. standards " . . . have been prepared after careful study and as a general guide. No better assessment of need has so far been put forward ".

The National Playing Fields Association's further memorandum on Standards of Playing Space, produced in 1955, is printed as an Appendix to the Ministry's Memorandum.

A six-acre site, it says, provided it is of suitable shape, and reasonably level, will only just accommodate two football or hockey pitches, one cricket table, a three rink bowling green, two tennis courts, a small children's playground of half an acre and a pavilion. Excluding the small children's playground it seems that, on this basis, provision is made for about fifty people to play games simultaneously in winter on five and a half acres, so that if the assumption that two hundred people per thousand need playing space is correct, several uses per week for the football pitches is necessary.

In 1937, the *Juvenile Organisation Committee of the Board of Education* recommended a standard for use by young persons between the ages of 14 and 25, assuming that only one youth in three and one girl in five (i.e., not much more than a quarter of the population between those ages, and about one-twentieth of the total population) would wish to play, that one-tenth of those concerned could play on days other than Saturday, and that $1\frac{1}{2}$ acres were needed for each pitch. This made a total of about $2\frac{1}{2}$ acres per 1,000 persons or 1 acre for every 20 users. Tennis and other games requiring relatively

small areas were not allowed for, which may account for the obvious discrepancy with the 50 persons per acre of the N.P.F.A. estimate.

The Greater London Plan states that " ideally there should be at least 10 acres of open space to every 1,000 residents in a community, including 3 acres attached to schools ", and suggests that the remaining 7 acres should be distributed as to 1 acre parks, 4 acres public playing-fields and 2 acres private playing-fields. This accords with suggestions in a memorandum submitted to Lord Reith by the N.P.F.A. in 1941.

A table in the Greater London Plan (page 117) shows a distribution of the 6 acres per 1,000 for playing-fields in a neighbourhood of 10,000 people, which adds up to 23 " pitches ", a bowling green, 18 hard tennis courts, an unspecified number of grass courts, and 12 courts for netball, etc.

How many people could play simultaneously on this? It is hard to tell. The " pitches " obviously relate to pitches for winter use, when the tennis courts, even hard ones, could not be in regular use; the total number of cricket pitches could not be much more than half of that of the football and hockey pitches. On this basis, in summer, something like 260 people could be playing cricket, 72 could play tennis on the hard courts and, say, another 72 on the grass courts, and about 20 could play bowls, making a total of 424, which is 71 persons per acre of playing-fields, or a little over 4 per cent. of the population. This is comparable to the Board of Education figure of about 5 per cent., but it includes people over as well as under the age of 25. In winter 506 people could play on the 23 " pitches ", more if some of them were Rugby pitches, and 84 on netball pitches, plus a few hardy souls on the hard tennis courts, making the considerable total of about 600, or 6 per cent. of the total population. It is difficult to believe that more people than this would ever want to play games at the same time. With three uses per week, i.e., early closing days, Saturdays and Sundays, 180 per thousand of total population could be provided with games facilities in winter, which comes very close to the N.P.F.A. assumptions about numbers of players.

The City of Manchester Plan allows for $4\frac{1}{2}$ acres per 1,000 for organised games, of which $2\frac{1}{2}$ acres is to be found by part use of school playing-fields. This figure assumes various numbers of uses per week for the various kinds of pitches, ranging from 6 for tennis to 1 for Rugby football and hockey.

One of the great difficulties about assessing playing-field requirements is that it is difficult to express " need " precisely. The amount of land required to ensure that any scratch team which occasionally plays matches can always book a pitch, would obviously be enormously greater than that required to accommodate the needs of established clubs. The Ministry memorandum deals with this point well. It says " it will usually be unwise to rely on disclosed demand (e.g., by clubs for the use of pitches) as the sole basis for making allocations. Frequently, the demand is not publicly expressed but there are none the less many individuals who like to play organised games, and would do so if facilities were provided near enough at hand. Similarly, the absence of a play space means that children are compelled to play in the streets while older people stay at home for the lack of park or garden where they can walk or sit in the sun. Nor will it usually be sufficient to accept the present level of demand. In the majority of cases, the trend of demand is likely to rise; increasing physical education in schools, public interest stimulated by achievement in athletics, the growing number of youth clubs, the increase in leisure time, the lengthening span of active life are all factors which must be taken into account in assessing future needs."

I share the Ministry's inability to improve upon the N.P.F.A. standards but I am extremely surprised that the Ministry have not conducted and published the results of an investigation of the kind desired earlier in this chapter.

Fig. 68 shows 60 acres of playing-field area and 10 acres of park for a neighbourhood of 10,000 people. It includes 20 pitches for football or hockey, most of them full-size or near it, which is probably the reason for the number being less than that given in the Greater London Plan. It still looks to me to be a very large number of pitches to serve a total population of 10,000. On the other hand, the amount of space devoted exclusively to park use seems insufficient unless the existence of a major park close to the town is assumed.

Treatment of Open Spaces

Parks needs to be dealt with according to the functions they are intended to perform. For example, a somewhat formal treatment is generally regarded as suitable for a small park in a town centre or adjoining a neighbourhood centre where it is sought to provide somewhere pleasant to stroll and sit and perhaps for small children to play. At the other extreme, the landscape treatment of a very large park of several hundred acres might well be informal in the extreme, and little more be done than to accentuate the natural features of the site. It is extremely difficult to generalise, for in all kinds of parks special efforts should be made to make the very most of all features, particularly water and trees, which are already there. Furthermore, as has already been pointed out, it will often be appropriate to devote to park use land within the town area which, because of its physical characteristics, cannot readily be used for building purposes, and such land is often extremely interesting landscape without much special treatment being necessary.

It is important not to forget the importance of parks as " courting grounds ". While, to some minds, the idea of encouraging alfresco eroticism is profoundly shocking, and many would even say that every effort should be made to discourage and prevent it, this does not seem to me either an enlightened or even a sensible point of view. Readers are referred to Lewis Mumford's works in which the theme frequently recurs that it is profoundly important for positive efforts to be made to provide an environment both inside and outside the home in which the erotic life can flourish without furtiveness.

It goes without saying that sites for playing-fields should be as level as possible and well drained. Extremely attractive playing-fields can be made by terracing a stretch of sloping ground, but the cost of doing this is great.

The detailed layout of playing-fields is a subject of some intricacy. " The Planning, Construction and Maintenance of Playing-fields," by Percy White Smith, Chief Technical Adviser to the National Playing-fields Association,

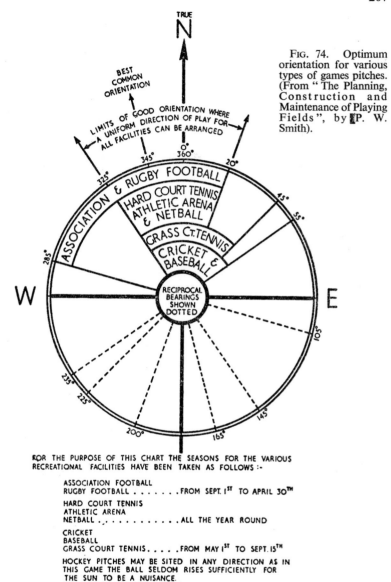

FIG. 74. Optimum orientation for various types of games pitches. (From " The Planning, Construction and Maintenance of Playing Fields ", by P. W. Smith).

FOR THE PURPOSE OF THIS CHART THE SEASONS FOR THE VARIOUS RECREATIONAL FACILITIES HAVE BEEN TAKEN AS FOLLOWS :-

ASSOCIATION FOOTBALL
RUGBY FOOTBALL . . . . .FROM SEPT. 1ST TO APRIL 30TH
HARD COURT TENNIS
ATHLETIC ARENA
NETBALL . . . . .ALL THE YEAR ROUND
CRICKET
BASEBALL
GRASS COURT TENNIS. . . . .FROM MAY 1ST TO SEPT. 15TH

HOCKEY PITCHES MAY BE SITED IN ANY DIRECTION AS IN THIS GAME THE BALL SELDOM RISES SUFFICIENTLY FOR THE SUN TO BE A NUISANCE.

the Oxford University Press, 1950, is an excellent work, which can be thoroughly recommended for detailed study. So far as we are concerned, it is principally necessary to know the dimensions required for the playing areas and surrounds of various games and the orientation most suitable for each, having regard to the need to reduce to a minimum the glare of low sun in players' eyes. This depends chiefly upon the months of the year during which a particular game is played and the positions of the sun at sunset during these months. Fig. 74, based upon that given on page 53 of the book referred to, provides a useful summary of information on this subject.

The following table gives the dimensions required for various popular games, figures for adult players only being given:

AREAS REQUIRED FOR VARIOUS GAMES

ASSOCIATION FOOTBALL
110 yards by 70 yards. 20ft. clearance at each side and 30ft. clearance at each end.

RUGBY FOOTBALL
140 yards by 75 yards, 20ft. clearance at sides and ends.

HOCKEY
100 yards by 60 yards. 10ft. clearance at sides, 15ft. clearance at each end.

LACROSSE
As for Hockey.

NETBALL
100ft. long by 50ft. wide. 5ft. clearance at sides and ends, 10ft. clearance where court adjoins a boundary or another court.

TENNIS
Court 78ft. by 36ft., total size including surround 114ft. by 56ft. Where there are a number of courts side by side within the same enclosure, the distances between them can be 10ft. less than provided for in the above figures.
In the case of grass courts an extra width should be allowed in each enclosure to permit each court to be shifted sideways to reduce wear at the centres of base lines.

CRICKET
Cricket table (i.e., area on which wickets are pitched)—30 yards by 30 yards.
Complete pitch.—This can be varied widely according to the space available, but no part of the boundary should be closer than 50 yards to any of the corners of the table. Cricket pitches, which occupy a large area, are best combined with pitches for other games such as football and hockey, the table being situated in the space between such other pitches.

BOWLS
Bowling greens may vary considerably in size. The larger they are the more can wear at the ends be reduced. The length of the play area is 126ft.

CROWN BOWLS
This game is not played in the South of England. The usual dimensions for Crown are 40 yards by 40 yards.

15-3. LARGE ESTABLISHMENTS

There is not very much to be said about these. The nature of the need for them has already been generally indicated. They constitute uses which mostly demand a certain amount of privacy, seclusion and spaciousness. Some of them, such as private schools, may need to be so large as to include playing-fields, while others such as convalescent homes might appropriately have attached to them a pitch and putt golf course. While some such uses,

particularly the larger ones, find satisfactory homes in country houses too large to be nowadays attractive as family residences, many of them face severe problems of staffing, and prefer positions on the outskirts of towns for this reason. It is hardly possible to anticipate demand, and indeed I have not been able to find any quantitative basis for the allotment of such uses. In the theoretical new town, used for the purposes of illustration in this book, an area of two acres per thousand population has been assigned. Fig. 68 shows how access could be provided for these areas, and gives a rough division into units, a division which could easily be modified if necessary.

15-4. SCHOOL SITES

The siting of schools has already been sufficiently discussed in Chapter 14. Because school buildings are usually low and extensive, and because the majority of the site is occupied by playing-fields, it is important that the sites chosen should be as flat as possible. They must also be of such a shape that games pitches will fit into them satisfactorily.

An assessment of land needs for schools is not at all easy to make for the purposes of a New Town. Where there is an existing town there will no doubt be a detailed educational plan prepared in the light of existing accommodation, population structure and anticipated growth. The drawing up of such a programme is a complicated and expert task.

Nevertheless, the method of calculation can be given in order to show the principles involved, and it would often be necessary in making a preliminary Plan for a New Town to make some such assessment in advance of detailed investigation in order to provide a roughly appropriate basis for site allocations.

The basis of the British educational system set up by the Education Act of 1944, and administered by the local Education Authorities, is as follows:

Nursery Schools for children between the ages of two and five years, attendance at which is voluntary.

Infant Schools for children of five, six and seven years old.

Junior Schools for children between the ages of eight and eleven years inclusive.

The Infant and Junior Schools are jointly known as Primary Schools.

Secondary Schools for children over eleven years old. These are divided into:

Grammar Schools for children of marked academic ability. It is intended that they shall absorb about $12\frac{1}{2}\%$ of the Secondary School population, and that pupils shall remain in them until about the age of eighteen years.

Technical Schools for pupils with a more practical bent. These too are intended to take about $12\frac{1}{2}\%$ of the Secondary School population.

Secondary Modern Schools to take the remainder, i.e., 75%. These provide a general education. Attendance is compulsory up to the age of fifteen, but facilities are available and encouragement given to pupils to remain longer.[1]

---

[1] The whole system is now, of course, in a state of flux; great modifications may be expected before long.

There are also *special schools* for mentally or physically handicapped children, schools linked to the general educational system but *under the aegis of various religious bodies* and *private schools*, which may or may not receive grants from public funds.

While the basis of provision of nursery and primary and secondary modern schools is likely to be fairly uniform, that for the remainder is highly uncertain, and depends upon many variable factors. For example, the location of grammar and technical secondary schools is likely to be dependent upon regional requirements rather than those of an individual town, since the proportion of the population for which they cater is so small that their catchment areas must be large.

The numbers of school children and hence of classes and schools obviously varies with the varying birth rate, but equally obviously has to be made on a long term basis, and there is a good deal of flexibility. Schools are very expensive to build, and it would be absurd to base a school building programme upon a temporarily inflated school population which it could confidently be estimated would decrease in a few years. It is preferable to accept somewhat larger classes than desirable for a short period, rather than to expend a large proportion of the nation's resources on accommodation which will not long be needed. In extreme cases it is always possible to build some additional temporary classrooms, at comparatively small expenditure, which can be dismantled when they are no longer required. This point is emphasised because, as will be seen, the Ministry of Education regulations regarding sizes of school sites are complicated and not entirely free from ambiguity.

Size of site depends upon numbers of classes and numbers of pupils. From the point of view of the town Planner what is needed to be known is the total numbers of school sites of each kind required and the approximate numbers of pupils to attend them, so that sites of about the right size may be tentatively allocated.

The following paragraphs therefore do not aim at an unattainable precision but seek only to provide a reasonable basis of calculation. The birth rate in this country has fluctuated a good deal since the war and a large " bulge " was caused by the very large numbers of children born in 1946, 1947 and 1948. It appears, however, that by about 1967 population structure is likely to be fairly stable and that children of school age will constitute about fourteen per thousand for each year of age, i.e., in a population of normal age composition for every thousand people there will be about fourteen five-year-olds, fourteen-six-year olds and so on. Of these some 12·4 are expected to find their way into the local educational authority system.

Let us now relate this to school demands for a population of 10,000 persons of normal age structure.

Nursery Schools

These cater for two-year-olds, three-year-olds and four-year-olds, so that with a population of ten thousand there will be about $140 \times 3 = 420$ potential nursery school pupils. But attendance at these schools, as has already been said, is voluntary. It might well be that not more than about half this number will have to be catered for.

Forty is the commonly accepted figure for the number of pupils in a nursery school, so that on this basis six nursery schools would be needed in a neighbourhood of ten thousand.

Primary Schools

Taking now the estimated basis of 12·4 per thousand per year coming into the primary schools system, a population of 10,000 persons will produce about 124 primary school children for each year of age. We may here note that throughout primary and secondary school education children normally move up a school by yearly changes of class, and that primary schools are usually of such a size that they either have two classes for each year of age or three, while secondary schools usually have three. These are known respectively as " two-stream " and " three-stream " or " two form entry " and " three form entry " schools.

At present classes of forty are accepted as reasonable for primary schools and classes of thirty for secondary schools, so that the 124 children could be accommodated in a three-stream school with classes of just over forty. But a class of forty is a very large one. As numbers shrink slightly from year to year it will not be possible to reduce the number of classes in the school but each will gradually diminish in size, and it does not seem unreasonable to hope for an eventual average size of class of thirty in primary as well as in secondary schools. On this basis the 124 children per year could be accommodated in two two-stream schools each with classes of just over thirty. This, in terms of accessibility, is a much more satisfactory arrangement. Although infant and junior schools are sometimes on separate sites they are often combined as different departments on a single site, and this has the advantage of conferring administrative economy and flexibility.

Secondary Schools

With a distribution of 75 %, 12½ % and 12½ % as between modern, grammar and technical secondary schools a neighbourhood of 10,000 will produce sufficient children to occupy a three-stream secondary modern school and to supply half a stream for a grammar school and for a technical school. While both sexes nearly always attend the same primary school some secondary schools are for one sex and some for two. Accordingly, a mixed secondary modern school can be provided for each neighbourhood of 10,000 or a boys' modern and a girls' modern school for each pair of such neighbourhoods.

With only half a stream per neighbourhood for each, a town of 60,000 can only support one three-stream grammar school and one three-stream technical school from its own population, or, since technical schools are for boys, 4½ classes per year of grammar school pupils and 1½ classes per year of technical school pupils. It will, however, be very likely that such schools will have to accommodate considerable numbers of pupils from surrounding smaller towns and villages, so that it has been assumed in the theoretical New Town illustrated that two grammar schools will be provided and one technical school.

All these provisions are upset if comprehensive schools are provided instead of the three different types of secondary schools. The appropriateness of doing this is, of course, at present a bitterly controversial issue.

The sizes of sites for various kinds of schools are at present determined by the Standards for School Premises Regulations, 1959 of the Ministry of Education (S.I.No.890 of 1959). The following are the portions of these regulations which are relevant to our purposes.

PART II
PRIMARY SCHOOLS

Sites

3.—(1) *The site of every primary school shall comprise an area not less than the area specified in this paragraph as appropriate to the number of pupils for whom the school is designed:—*

Number of pupils	Appropriate area
Not more than 25	$\frac{1}{2}$ acre
26–50	$\frac{5}{8}$,,
51–80	$\frac{3}{4}$,,

and thereafter for every additional 40 pupils, or part thereof, the appropriate area shall be increased by $\frac{1}{8}$ acre:

Provided that in the case of a school designed for more than 480 pupils, the site area shall be such as may be approved in each case.

Playing Field Accommodation

4. *Every primary school, other than an infant school, shall have appropriated to it playing field accommodation comprising an area not less than that specified in this regulation as appropriate to the number of junior pupils for whom the school is designed:—*

Number of junior pupils	Appropriate area
Not more than 50	$\frac{1}{2}$ acre
51–120	1 ,,
121–200	$1\frac{1}{2}$,,
201–280	$2\frac{1}{4}$,,
More than 280	3 ,,

PART III
SECONDARY SCHOOLS

Sites

15.—(1) *The site of every secondary school shall comprise an area not less than the area specified in this paragraph as appropriate to the number of pupils for whom the school is designed:—*

Number of pupils	Appropriate area
Not more than 150	$1\frac{1}{2}$ acres
151–210	$1\frac{3}{4}$,,
211–300	2 ,,
301–360	$2\frac{1}{4}$,,
361–420	$2\frac{1}{2}$,,
421–450	3 ,,

and thereafter for every additional 50 pupils, or part thereof, the appropriate area shall be increased by $\frac{1}{4}$ acre.

(2) *Where the curriculum of a secondary school includes gardening, horticulture, agriculture, or the keeping of livestock, the appropriate area specified in this regulation shall be increased to such extent as may be approved in each case.*

Playing Field Accommodation

16. *Every secondary school shall have appropriated to it playing field accommodation comprising an area, suitable as to shape, levels, surface and drainage and free from obstructions, not less than the area specified in this regulation as appropriate to the type of the school for which, and the number and age of pupils for whom, such accommodation is intended:—*

		Number of pupils aged 11–15 years inclusive	Appropriate area
(a)	Boys' schools	Not more than 150 ...	$4\frac{1}{2}$ acres
		151–300	$7\frac{1}{2}$,,

and thereafter for every additional 150 pupils or part thereof aged 11–15 years inclusive, the appropriate area shall be increased by ... ... $1\frac{1}{2}$,,

		Number of pupils aged 11–15 years inclusive	Appropriate area
(b)	Girls' schools	Not more than 150 ...	4 acres
		151–300	$6\frac{1}{2}$,,
		301–450	$8\frac{1}{2}$,,

and thereafter for every additional 150 pupils or part thereof aged 11–15 years inclusive, the appropriate area shall be increased by ... ... 1 ,,

		Number of pupils aged 11–15 years inclusive	Appropriate area
(c)	Schools for pupils of both sexes	Not more than 150 ...	$4\frac{1}{2}$ acres
		151–300	7 ,,
		301–600	10 ,,

and thereafter for every additional 300 pupils or part thereof aged 11–15 years inclusive, the appropriate area shall be increased by ... ... 3 ,,

Provided that where playing field accommodation is intended to be used by pupils who have attained the age of 16 years, the appropriate area specified in this regulation shall be increased by 1¼ acres for every 120 such pupils, or part thereof:

Provided also that where playing field accommodation is appropriated jointly to two or more boys' schools the appropriate area shall be calculated as for one boys' school of the total number of boys for whom the accommodation is intended, and where the appropriation is jointly to two or more girls' schools the appropriate area shall be calculated as for one girls' school of the total number of girls for whom the accommodation is intended, and where the appropriation is jointly to two or more schools involving pupils of both sexes the appropriate area shall be calculated as for one mixed school of the total number of boys and girls for whom the accommodation is intended:

Provided also that if a part of the playing field accommodation is provided with a hard porous surface suitable in size for the playing of hockey, Association Football or other appropriate games, that part may be deemed to be three times its actual area, so, however, that at least one half of the appropriate area shall have a grass surface:

Provided also that where approved facilities for regular instruction in swimming are provided, the area of the playing field accommodation may be reduced to such extent as may be approved in each case.

These standards are somewhat less liberal than their predecessors, contained in the Regulations of 1954, and these, in turn, were less liberal than the ones before. There seems little doubt that land values rather than educational need have dictated these changes and that it is time to call a halt to progressive reduction of standards. The following table is therefore based upon the 1954 Regulations:

School requirements per neighbourhood of ten thousand
   Nursery Schools   Six, each of one quarter-acre.   Total 1½ acres.

Primary Schools   Two two-stream, each with infant and junior department, each with site of 5¾ acres.   Total 11½ acres.

Secondary Modern Schools   One mixed school, 13 acres. (Or one boys' school, 12 acres and one girls' school, 11½ acres, shared between two neighbourhoods.)

School requirements for town of 60,000 as a whole
   One boys' grammar school, 14½ acres
   One girls' grammar school, 14 acres
     (Or two mixed grammar schools each of 15½ acres)
   One technical school 12 acres.

One or two additional points must be made about the siting and layout of schools. If six nursery schools are to be provided so that there is one within a quarter of a mile of each house, it seems appropriate to site them in relation to the neighbourhood shown in Fig. 68, at or near the neighbourhood centre, the three sub-centres and the two primary schools. In the case of the last-named it will no doubt be desirable for the site of the nursery school to be separated by a fence or hedge from the primary schools and with a separate entrance, but for administrative reasons and spatial convenience juxtaposition appears sensible.

It is eminently desirable that the importance of schools in the life of the community should be reflected in the quality of design of their buildings and in the prominence with which they are sited. But the latter can be carried too far; schools are sometimes placed on island sites surrounded by roads, which have only single-sided development on the sides remote from the school. This is wildly extravagant in terms of road costs and is quite unnecessary. It is actually more effective to frame the view of school buildings by seeing them through gaps in other development of ample but not unlimited width, as shown in Fig. 68.

CHAPTER 16

NEIGHBOURHOOD CENTRES AND SUB-CENTRES

THE HIERARCHIC NATURE of service centres within the town as well as within the region was stressed in Chapter 14, as was the delicate economic balance of neighbourhood centres and sub-centres. Both of these must not only be suitably located, but laid out to afford the maximum of convenience and attraction if they are to thrive. Perhaps the most important decision which has to be made in connection with the neighbourhood centre is whether an attempt should be made to design it in the form of a pedestrian centre, a miniature version of the kind of pedestrian town centre discussed in Chapter 12.

There are arguments in favour of doing this and also against it. Economically, at least, the most important component of the neighbourhood centre will be its shops, and here one has to balance the undoubted advantages of pedestrian shopping areas in terms of safety and comfort against the convenience of kerbside shopping, the accessibility of which from the motor car may often be a decisive factor in influencing a choice between a shopping visit to the town centre or the neighbourhood centre. In a town centre nowadays it is impossible to provide for kerbside shopping; in a neighbourhood centre it may be difficult but it is not yet impossible to provide, if not for all at peak hours, at least for a considerable proportion of shoppers, and it seems to me that this added convenience may well be an important factor in ensuring the viability of a neighbourhood centre.

Fig. 75 shows some alternatives. (i) is the " natural " form, a centre growing up around a road junction in the traditional way. Since it is essential for the neighbourhood centre to be located at a nodal point in the neighbourhood road system this cannot be regarded as very satisfactory (though it is not nearly as bad as a centre around a cross roads!), because the roads forming the junction are bound to carry an appreciable amount of traffic, making movement within the centre somewhat hazardous. This disadvantage is removed if the whole centre is placed within one of the arms of the junction as in (ii) and the shops set back behind a parking area.

A pedestrian centre is shown in (iii), exactly on the lines of a tiny town centre. There is no doubt that it works satisfactorily but a good deal of doubt about whether enough people would bother to use it rather than the town centre, since in both cases a walk from the parked car to the shops is necessary even though it is a shorter walk in the case of the smaller neighbourhood centre. This is not a subject upon which it is easy to arrive at a decisive conclusion; specifically directed research is necessary to do so. I therefore find myself unable to express a definite preference between (iii), on the one hand and (ii) or (iv) on the other. (iv) is based upon the ingenious

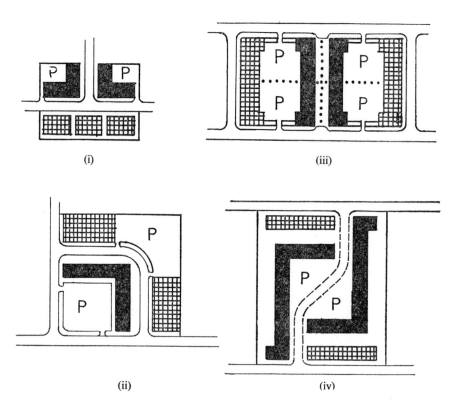

FIG. 75. Basic forms of Neighbourhood Centre. solid black other buildings cross-hatched in all cases.

arrangement used at Adeyfield, Hemel Hempstead and is really a doubling of (ii). Vehicles can drive right through the centre, and can park anywhere within the paved area of the square, the carriageway itself being indicated by colour or texture and a very slight shoulder, and not by a high kerb, so that it can be left at any point in order to park. At the same time this road is so routed that it offers no inducement to anyone to use it unless he wishes to visit the centre, and gives no opportunity for speed.

Components of the Neighbourhood Centre

The services to be provided will depend upon the size, character and prosperity of the town and upon the extent to which services in the town centre can support a branch within neighbourhood centres. Generally speaking we may expect to find the following:

Shops
Sometimes a dairy and bakery
Petrol filling stations
Public houses
A branch library
A branch clinic
One or more halls for meetings and dramatic performances
A public lavatory.

Components of Sub-centres

These in turn will depend upon the ability of offshoots from services in the neighbourhood to support themselves in sub-centres. Often one would expect to find a group of shops, a petrol filling station and a public house.

As has been suggested in Chapter 15, it is appropriate to site nursery schools in close association with neighbourhood centres and sub-centres.

As regards places of worship a very special problem arises. In this country today religious allegiance is widely spread among a large number of religious sects, but most people either adhere to none or have but the scantiest association with a religious body. Although, therefore, it is appropriate to provide places of worship in the town centre for those religious organisations sufficiently strong numerically to support churches in the town centre as well as in neighbourhoods, and, at the other end of the scale, those so small that they can only support one establishment for a whole town, it does not seem to me, on the whole, appropriate to provide places of worship within main neighbourhood centres.

Such a centre, unlike the town centre, is so comparatively small and made up of such small units that a church is likely to dominate it. In a community of strong and homogeneous religious convictions this would not matter, but in a community with weak and scattered convictions it is inappropriate. This is particularly so from the point of view of relationships between religious bodies. It would be fantastic to house more than one church in a neighbourhood centre because there is something slightly grotesque about the close juxtaposition of the headquarters of what may often be rival organisations. Any sect therefore which is successful in occupying a place of worship in a neighbourhood centre will have secured an advantageous position in relation to others, which may well be resented.

These considerations do not apply nearly so strongly to sub-centres, which are not to any great extent centres of interest but merely convenient concentrations of very low-level services. For reasons of accessibility to their adherents, and also in order to give some body and substance to a sub-centre, churches can in my view very appropriately be located in relation to them.

Equally, however, there is no reason at all why places of worship should not occupy sites independently of any centre or sub-centres. If this is done no questions of rivalry can arise, and the buildings can provide additional points of visual interest within the neighbourhood.

Scale of Provision

This is very difficult to assess, and indeed in any particular case can only be worked out as a result of detailed investigation of probable demand. The following paragraphs do no more than suggest approximate scales of provision which might prove suitable.

Shops

Calculations about numbers of shops needed are very specially difficult to make because of two particular points. First, in unplanned areas there are far more shops than could possibly be provided in an area of Planned development. Many of them have been cheaply converted from houses, and are not the main source of income of a family. They may, in fact, be expected to provide no more than pin money for the wife while the husband provides the main family income as a result of some quite different kind of work. It would not be possible to cater for shops on this basis in Planned development.

There is also a good deal of difficulty in deciding what constitutes a shop. For example, chain stores are often virtually a dozen shops under one roof and co-operative shops and supermarkets, half a dozen, so that it is doubtful how they should be counted. The best way is probably to count up " shop units " rather than the number of shops in separate buildings, a " shop unit " being floor area sufficient for the normal small shop.

At the time of writing (late 1963) it appears that the scale of provision of shops in neighbourhoods needs complete reconsideration. Shopping by car has recently become so much more general that the viability of local shopping centres is much less certain than previously. Given a properly Planned Town Centre with sufficient and convenient parking facilities the much greater range of goods available there must necessarily attract a far larger proportion of shopping visits by the mobile, car-borne shopper than previously. At the same time, methods of retail distribution are changing rapidly and radically. It would not be altogether surprising if, in the near future, the typical pattern of local shopping provision largely took the form of a supermarket in the neighbourhood centre and a row of automatic " vending " machines in sub-centres. One cannot yet say that this *will* be so but it seems very likely. Everything that follows concerning neighbourhood shopping provision must therefore be looked at with considerable reserve.

Various estimates of shopping provision have been made, and, for what they are worth, are given below.

The New Towns Committee's Final Report gives the number of shops in old towns as one to forty or fifty people, and on new housing estates as one to 150-325 persons. Without apparently taking into account the different functions performed by central area and neighbourhood shops, it suggests that one shop to 100–150 people is desirable, and abstains from suggesting any allocation of shops between the central area and neighbourhoods.

The Dudley Report says " . . . there should be at least an allowance for shops in a neighbourhood (i.e., local shopping facilities additional to those available in the central areas of a town) at a rate of . . . one shop per 100–150 inhabitants; or somewhere between 100 and, say, 70 shops per neighbourhood of 10,000 people."

A recent study in Stevenage suggests that expenditure in Town Centre shops and in neighbourhood shops is likely to be roughly equal.

The City of Manchester Plan, 1945, allows for 30 shops in a neighbourhood centre, with reserve space for 15 more and two subsidiary groups of four shops each, making a total of 53 shops for 10,000 people, or one shop to about 189 people. (One shop per 263 people, excluding the reserve shops.)

The Manchester estimate is supported by figures indicating the weekly expenditure of working-class families in various kinds of shops. (These already have a quaintly archaic flavour!) An estimate is made of the proportion of this attributable to expenditure within the neighbourhood but one is not told whether this is based on existing or ideal distribution of neighbourhood shopping centres. The annual turnover necessary to support each kind

of shop is given and the number of shops which each neighbourhood can therefore support, together with distribution between main and subsidiary neighbourhood shopping centres. The number does not include the reserve of 15 shops previously mentioned, which, it is thought, could be supported from the greater turnover resulting from a possible generally higher standard of living, and hence greater spending power.

Here is at least some factual foundation, not invalidated, though it might have to be modified, because of changes in the purchasing value of the pound.

The table below is taken from page 250 of the *City of Manchester Plan*, 1945.

Clearly, it is not possible to derive from these any definite and authoritative standard, but it looks as if one shop to about every 170 people, i.e., six shops per 1,000, is a not unreasonable figure to adopt for shops in neighbourhoods, making a total of 60 for 10,000 people, of which about 40 might be in the neighbourhood centre.

The next point to consider is the actual area required for shop sites. *The Dudley Report* suggests an average of 270 square yards (one-eighteenth of an

Trade	Expenditure per household per week	Expenditure per household per year	Total yearly expenditure for neighbourhood unit	Percentage of 2 spent in neighbourhood	Net annual expenditure in neighbourhood	Estimated turnover per shop in main shopping centre	Estimated turnover per shop in subsidiary shopping centre	Number of shops in main shopping centre	Number of shops in subsidiary shopping centre	Total number of shops in neighbourhood unit (minimum)
	s. d.	£	£		£	£	£			
Grocery and provisions	15 3	39·6	113,137	80	90,500	24,000	8,660	4[1]	2	6
Baker and Confectioner	3 11	10·1	28,855	60	17,313	5,000	3,656	2	2	4
Butcher	5 9	14·9	42,569	80	34,000	8,000	4,500	3	2	5
Dairy	3 8	9·5	27,141	15	4,071	4,071	—	1	—	1
Fishmonger	1 0	2·6	7,429	75	5,572	5,572	—	1	—	1
Fish and chips	0 5	1·1	3,143	100	3,143	3,143	—	1	—	1
Greengrocer	3 8	9·5	27,141	80	21,713	6,500	3,250	3[1]	2	5
Café	1 1	2·8	7,999	15	1,200	1,200	—	—	—	{ To be located over confectioner
Newsagent and Stationer	1 3									
Tobacco	2 6	11·0	31,427	75	23,570	7,857	—	3	—	3
Sweets	0 6									
Men's Outfitters	2 10	7·4	21,142	15	3,171	3,171	—	1	—	1
Women's and children's outfitters	4 0	10·4	29,712	30	8,910	4,455	—	2	—	2
Dyers and cleaners	0 2	0·4	1,143	—	—	—	—	—	—	—
Boots and shoes— Sales	1 11	5·0	14,280	33⅓	4,760	4,760	—	1	—	1
Repairs	1 1	2·8	8,000	7	5,600	2,800	—	2	—	2
Hardware	1 2	3·0	8,751	50	4,375	4,375	—	1	—	1
Glass and China	0 2	0·4	1,143	—	—	—	—	—	—	—
Furniture	1 9	4·6	13,142	—	—	—	—	—	—	—
Hairdressing	0 7	1·5	4,285	80	3,428	3,428	—	1	—	1
Chemists	0 6	1·3	3,714	90	3,343	3,343	—	1	—	1
Corn and seed	0 1	0·2	571	—	—	—	—	—	—	—
Post Offices	—	—	—	—	—	—	—	1	—	1
Banks	—	—	—	—	—	—	—	2	—	2
Totals								30	8	38

[1] Two of these may have a smaller turnover than that given.

acre approximately), including service roads and delivery space per shop. It is not clear exactly what is meant by " service roads ", but, applied to a row of shops fronting a road with a 22ft. carriageway, and with an 8ft. lay-by and a 12ft. footpath along the shopping frontage, the half width of fronting road would be 31ft. Add to this 40ft. for the depth of the building, 20ft. for back yard and outside storage space and 21ft. 6in. for rear access road, and the total plot depth from the centre of the road is 112ft. 6in.

This, divided into 270 square yards, gives an average shop frontage of about 21ft. 6in., but access is necessary to the rear access road—two for each block of shops unless the complications of a cul-de-sac are to be encountered, and each, as it happens, exactly the width of a shop—so that for a row of 20 shops the frontage would have to be 21ft. 6in. × 22 = 473ft. With a depth of 112ft. 6in., this would give about 296 square yards per shop, or $16\frac{1}{3}$ shops per acre.

The Cheshire Plan suggests averages of 18ft. frontage (perhaps rather narrow) and 120ft. depth, exclusive of fronting road (perhaps rather long) for shop sites. The densities suggested, inclusive of roads, are one-fourteenth or one-fifteenth per shop in subcentres and one-tenth or one-twelfth in the main neighbourhood centre.

In the *Manchester Plan* the allowance is about one-tenth of an acre for shops in neighbourhood centres and one-fourteenth for those in minor centres, the former being stated to include allowance for car parks and garages.

The need for shops to be of different sizes according to whether they are in the main neighbourhood centre or in sub-centres is, of course, due to the different volume of trade, and hence of service and storage space necessary. The following figures in the Manchester Plan give estimated space needs for various kinds of shops:—

Trade							Shop front floor area sq. ft.	No. of shops
Main shopping centre:								
Grocery and provisions...	...	...	...	...	...		350	1
							450	1
							900	2
Baker and Confectioner	...	...	...	...	...		350	2
Butcher ...	...	...	...	...	...	...	450	3
Dairy ...	...	...	...	...	...	...	350	1
Fishmonger	...	...	...	...	...	...	350	1
Fish and chips	...	...	...	...	...	...	350	1
Greengrocery	...	...	...	...	...	...	350	2
							450	1
Newsagent, stationer, tobacco and sweets	...	...	...		450	3
Gentlemen's outfitter	...	...	...	...	...		350	1
Ladies' outfitter, draper, etc.	...	...	...	...		450	2
Boots and shoes (sales)...	...	...	...	...	...		450	1
Boots and shoes (repairs)	...	...	...	...	...		350	2
Hardware...	...	...	...	...	...	...	350	1
Hairdresser (ladies' and gentlemen's) ...	...	...	...		350	1
Chemist ...	...	...	...	...	...	...	350	1
Banks ...	...	...	...	...	...	...	900	2
Post office	...	...	...	...	...	...	450	1

Trade							Shop front floor area sq. ft.	No. of shops
Subsidiary shopping centre:								
Grocery and provisions...	...	...	...	...	...		350	2
Baker and confectioner...	...	...	...	...	...		350	2
Butcher ...	...	...	...	...	...	...	350	2
Greengrocery	...	...	...	...	...	...	350	2

" Shop front floor area " is presumably the area within which customers move about and are served and does not include internal storage space, lavatory, etc.

It is possible to vary the widths and depths of the shops themselves and the amount of outdoor storage space attaching to them as may be required, with consequent alterations to density and depth of site; the figures given above are merely what are thought to be reasonable to meet average requirements.

A rather firmer estimate is possible for public houses. *The City of Manchester Plan*, 1945, gave national beer consumption as being about half a barrel per head of population per year, or 100 barrels in a 10,000 population neighbourhood per week, and stated (page 251) that large houses have a weekly turnover of 50 barrels a week, and can conveniently occupy a site of $1\frac{3}{4}$ acres; medium houses have a turnover of 20–25 barrels per week, with 1 acre as a suitable site, and small houses have a weekly turnover of 12 to 15 barrels, with half an acre as a suitable site. Appropriate provision in a 10,000 neighbourhood would therefore seem to be one large house in the main neighbourhood centre, and one medium and two small in the sub-centres, occupying a total acreage of $3\frac{3}{4}$ acres.

The site areas suggested above are quite misleading; a mere fraction of each would be quite sufficient. All that is needed for a public house is the actual site of the building plus sufficient space for parking, which may well be pooled with parking for other uses. In the theoretical neighbourhood shown in Fig. 68 sites are allocated for five public houses. Two of these are sited in the main neighbourhood centre in order to provide choice. They might both be medium-sized or one might be medium, and the other small.

It is one of the more difficult problems in connection with neighbourhood centre development to avoid giving a monopoly to a shop or similar use selling a particular range of goods without providing more facilities of that kind than the neighbourhood can support. Sometimes, it may be sufficient to provide a choice between two shops of the same kind, one in the neighbourhood centre, one in a sub-centre, if it is not feasible to have both in the centre.

These remarks, of course, apply only to shopping centres in public ownership, in which lettings can be controlled. Elsewhere, the types of shops which may choose to establish themselves are outside the scope of Planning Control.

Among the shops in the neighbourhood centre one might reasonably expect to find several branch banks, a branch post-office, a branch library and a branch clinic. These can probably be economically run, and certainly will be of great convenience to the inhabitants of the neighbourhood. A petrol filling station should certainly be provided but it is probably better to have only one in the centre and another in each of the sub-centres rather than to try to provide choice within the centre itself, which, with the mobility of the motor car, is unnecessary. A few modest workshops for constructional and repair work of a minor kind, not directly linked to individual shops and not requiring the substantial area of land associated with the ordinary kind of service industry described on page 194 will be useful.

The usefulness of a public lavatory needs no explanation. It can even contribute visually to the appearance of the centre. Anyone who doubts this should look at the public lavatory in Adeyfield Neighbourhood Centre, Hemel Hempstead.

I have left until last consideration of any public halls which may be located in the neighbourhood centre, for at the present time they constitute a serious problem. The combined effect of very high building costs, of political and religious apathy and of the enormous popularity of television have resulted in a far smaller effective demand for such buildings than used to be the case. Any or all of these trends may change, and make the position more favourable, but it seems unlikely that public halls can ever again be provided on the scale common in the inter-war and pre-1914 periods. Many buildings erected fifty or more years ago for these purposes are still in use, and when at last they come to the end of their lives it is doubtful whether more than a small proportion will be replaced. A partial solution is perhaps to be found in making available at low rents accommodation for clubs and societies on upper floors of buildings, above shops.

I do not think that there is a place for dwellings within the neighbourhood centre, any more than there is for them in the town centre, and although the provision of flats or maisonettes above shops is often regarded as desirable if not essential, in order to introduce some bulk and height into the centre on visual grounds, I do not think that it is justified. Having lived for some time in a flat above a fishmonger's shop, and at another time next door to a green-grocer who stored his stock in the cellar, I have personal experiences of the disadvantages entailed, which incidentally are likely to be even greater with small shops in a neighbourhood centre than with larger establishments in a town centre.

There is no reason why the skilful interplay of heights and spacing between low buildings of varying heights should not be as effective as between high buildings of different heights. The neighbourhood centre is certainly not an area in which monumentality is required, it is rather an adjunct to the domestic scheme.

Nevertheless, theatrical societies, chess clubs and groups of animal fanciers, as well as political and philosophical societies, may well wish to have perm-anent accommodation without the desire or the financial ability to erect or lease separate premises of their own. For them modest accommodation above shops is eminently satisfactory.

Relationship of different uses in the neighbourhood centre

Most of the uses in the neighbourhood centre should be placed slightly away from dwellings. Drinkers in public houses tend to sing and shout and worshippers in churches sing. However much those taking part in these activities may enjoy them they tend to be disapproved of by people trying to go to sleep next door. As already suggested, smell and noise make shops undesirable neighbours if they are very close. The first need, therefore, is to ensure a slight insulation of the neighbourhood centre from adjoining residential development, even if the insulation is on some sides no more than the width of a spine road. In the case of the theoretical neighbourhood centre shown in Fig. 76 this is slightly augmented by parking space on most of three sides, and on the fourth side by a small neighbourhood park, an attractive ancillary to any neighbourhood centre, where in fine weather shoppers may care to sit for a while before returning home and children can play.

The uses are also on the whole grouped in such a way that those who visit the centre for purposes other than shopping do not need to penetrate to its interior but find their destination on the periphery. The library and clinic are placed on what is likely to be the quietest part of the site; the shops are concentrated into one mass in order to facilitate moving from one to another. A few of them are directly accessible to kerbside parking without going into the interior of the centre.

Some New Town neighbourhood centres are shown in Fig. 77.

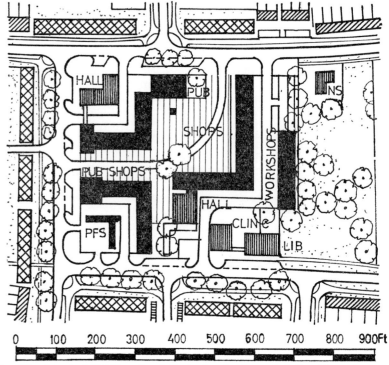

FIG. 76. A typical Neighbourhood Centre for the theoretical New Town shown to a larger scale than in Fig. 68.

Disposition of uses in sub-centres

It has already been suggested that a typical sub-centre is likely to consist of a group of shops, a filling station, a nursery school, a public house and a church, though of course there may be other elements. For example, there would be no reason whatever not to locate a public hall in a sub-centre if the fortunate position were achieved in which more were required in the neighbourhood as a whole than could conveniently be accommodated within the neighbourhood centre. The relationship, spatially, between these elements constitutes an interesting little problem.

As already suggested, neighbourhood sub-centres will not survive unless well-located and extremely convenient. For this reason they must usually be placed at the junctions of spine roads. They will not however, generate any appreciable amount of traffic, and visitors to them will by no means always, during a single visit, use more than one of their elements, in fact it will probably be the exception for them to do so. There therefore does not seem to be any objection to placing them around the junction of two spine roads. Because of their very small size they are inevitably very close to adjoining dwellings, and the main problem is so to dispose them that they cause the least possible nuisance. Various alternative arrangements are shown in the theoretical neighbourhood illustrated in Fig. 68 and are reproduced at a larger scale in Fig. 78.

Of the uses involved, the nursery school and the petrol filling stations are probably those least likely to cause annoyance to close neighbours, though some noise is associated with each. This can be got over if it can be arranged that the house adjoining either can be occupied by a teacher in the case of the nursery school, or the proprietor in the case of the filling station, which may be useful for other reasons. The same applies to churches. If the houses nearest them are occupied by vicar, or churchwardens, so that the church is insulated from the general public by its own officers, who can hardly complain in their official capacity, much friction can be saved.

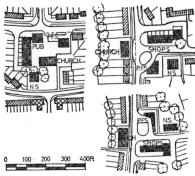

FIG. 78.   Typical neighbourhood sub-centres for the Theoretical New Town shown in Fig. 68.

Unfortunately the problem does not end here because friction may also be caused by the juxtaposition of uses thought to be inappropriate. For example, many people will hold up their hands in horror at the idea of a nursery school and a public house being immediate neighbours, while others would do the same at the idea of a church and a public house adjoining each other. Yet others, perhaps with more reason, would deplore the juxtaposition of a petrol filling station and a public house. A vociferous minority may be equally indignant at the idea of nursery schools and churches being next to each other.

It may well be impossible to avoid all conceivable sources of friction, and it would be foolish to overstress the importance of these points, but they are worth bearing in mind. In any case the degree of separation of these uses from dwellings need not be at all great in terms of distance, and the break provided by the entry of a rear service road for shops to a public road may often be sufficient for this purpose.

The Table on the next page summarises the scale of provision, in terms of areas, which might be appropriate in a neighbourhood of 10,000 population and which has been used in the theoretical neighbourhood illustrated.

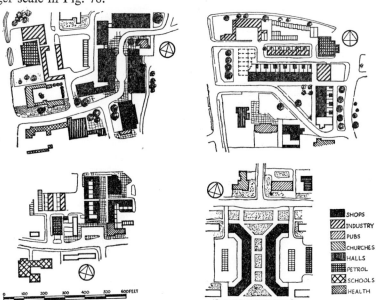

■	SHOPS
▨	INDUSTRY
▧	PUBS
▨	CHURCHES
▦	HALLS
▦	PETROL
▧	SCHOOLS
▨	HEALTH

FIG. 77.   Four Neighbourhood Centres of varying design.
U.L.   The Stow, Harlow.
U.R.   Adeyfield, Hemel Hempstead.
L.L.   Gadebridge, Hemel Hempstead.
L.R.   Woodhouse Park, Wythenshawe.

Neighbourhood centres and sub-centres in areas of existing development

Just as the neighbourhood principle itself is of limited applicability in existing towns, so is that of neighbourhood centres and sub-centres. It may, however, often be possible over a period to promote the establishment of

such centres, and this is greatly facilitated if suitably located uses of the kind
needed in such centres can form nuclei.   In fact, it is usually better to accept
such nuclei, even if not ideally located, rather than to seek to proceed de novo
on a perfectly situated site.

THEORETICAL NEIGHBOURHOOD CENTRE AND SUB-CENTRES

Approximate areas devoted to each use.
(The provision of car parks common to several uses precludes precise determination)

Use	N'hood Centre Acres	Sub-centre No. 1 Acres	Sub-centre No. 2 Acres	Sub-centre No. 3 Acres	Total Acres
Shops	3·50	0·45	0·60	0·45	5·00
Public Houses	1·00	0·26	0·25	0·21	1·72
Petrol Filling Stations	0·25	0·42	0·25	0·49	·41
Workshops	0·25	—	—	—	0·25
Halls	0·75	—	—	—	0·75
Library	0·5	—	—	—	0·50
Clinic	0·5	—	—	—	0·50
Places of Worship	—	0·39	0·40	0·475	1·265
Lavatory and unallocated parking space	0·75	—	—	—	0·75
Total ...	7·5	1·52	1·50	1·625	12·145

CHAPTER 17

RESIDENTIAL ACCOMMODATION, DENSITY AND LAYOUT

THE ARRANGEMENT of the various items which go to make up a residential neighbourhood having been dealt with in Chapter 14 we now turn to consideration of the arrangement of dwellings, the roads which serve them, and the grouped or individual space which they enjoy, and shall not be concerned with the spatial relationship of residential areas in relation to shops, public buildings or open spaces. We are, in other words, about to deal with the land comprised in net residential density calculations.

17-1. BASIC TYPES OF ACCOMMODATION

Housing accommodation is divisible into two broad classes, houses and flats, the fundamental differences between which are that houses always have ground floor accommodation, usually have individual outdoor space associated with them, and never have other dwellings above or below them, while flats unless they happen to be on the ground floor do not have ground floor accommodation, usually do not have individual outdoor space allocated to each flat, and may have dwellings above and below them as well as on either side. It will be seen that on this definition houses include bungalows and flats include maisonettes.

Houses and flats are further divisible into important types. Houses may be one, two or three storeys (in the past they have sometimes been built with more than three storeys but, according to modern ideas, with more than three storeys a lift is required, which is impossibly expensive for a single house). They also may be divided into detached, semi-detached and terrace houses. Flats are divisible into low blocks without lifts, high blocks with lifts, long blocks and point blocks, with compromises between these two. Sometimes they form part of a block which is wholly flats each occupying a part of a single floor; in other cases the lower part of the block may consist of ordinary dwelling houses with flats above, or the flatted accommodation may consist of units each with accommodation on two floors, known as maisonettes. These too may be combined with ordinary flats with accommodation on one floor only. One might distinguish between blocks of flats which stand on their own and those, usually corner blocks, which are joined on either side with ordinary dwelling houses.

All dwellings need storage space, which may be within the main structure of the house or form an ancillary building. Some dwellings require garages, which may form part of the main structure of the house, be placed adjoining it or form part of a group of garages placed in some convenient place.

The accommodation in dwellings is divisible into habitable rooms, that is rooms in which sleeping, eating, work and recreation go on, and ancillary rooms such as W.C.s, bathrooms and kitchens. The distinction between all of these is not entirely clear-cut; for example, as already mentioned in Chapter 8, a kitchen may also be used for habitable purposes, and rank as a habitable room in some circumstances. A third category is circulating space comprising halls, landings and staircases.

All these elements may be combined in different ways, for example W.C. and bathrooms may be combined, a stairway may lead directly out of a habitable room, and, as already mentioned, a kitchen may be used for habitable purposes. Generally speaking the aim is likely to be to reduce circulation space and functional space to the minimum, leaving as much as possible for living purposes. A good deal of the architect's skill lies in achieving this.

The Housing Manual, 1949, gives examples of typical designs for most kinds of dwellings likely to be built by Local Housing Authorities in accordance with the standards adopted by the post-war Labour Government. Its successors, " Houses, 1952 " and " Houses, 1953," perform similar functions in respect of the standards adopted by the succeeding Conservative Government. It is no part of my purpose to discuss here in detail the respective merits of the two policies but they must be mentioned because of the considerable effect which house type has upon density and layout. Generally speaking the earlier standard included two W.C.s for each house while the later required only one. The amount of space for living purposes is more generous in the first than in the second, and this applies also to storage. Most types of terrace house conforming to the earlier standard have individual passageways providing access to the rear of the house, while those of the more recent type often necessitate going through habitable or working rooms to reach the back, although there are some of the earlier types, particularly three-storey houses, which have the same arrangement. The principal effect of this, so far as layout design is concerned, is that with the newer type of house it is possible to economise considerably in the width of plot per house—eighteen or nineteen feet as compared with about twenty-four feet being possible. It must be remembered, however, that this saving is not effected without considerable sacrifice.

It may be well to list the principal variations of dwelling design commonly used. To take the kitchen first, there is the working kitchen, which includes all the necessary appliances for cooking, eating, and washing-up, the latter possibly being in a separate compartment known as the scullery. Then there is the dining-kitchen type, in which the kitchen is enlarged to accommodate a dining table, so that meals may be taken in the same room as they are cooked. Commonly, here, the scullery forms a separate compartment. Third, there is the living-kitchen type, in which a large kitchen combines all the functions of a kitchen, dining-room and sitting-room. Here a separate scullery is essential.

Whatever may be the kitchen arrangement, the living room accommodation may be in the form of one large all-purpose living room or two smaller rooms, one serving the purpose of dining room, and the other as sitting room.

Hallways and staircases may either be separated from rooms or may, as is common in America, lead out of rooms without separation.

Stores for garden implements, fuel etc., may either be placed in separate buildings behind the house, be at the side of the house separated from it by a passage or may be within the main walls of the house.

This affects the question of secondary access. The most convenient arrangement is for it to be possible to pass from the front side of the house to the back garden and return without actually entering the house, and for it to be possible to enter the house from the garden without going into a habitable room, in order that dirty shoes may be removed before carpets are encountered. It is also convenient to be able to do this if farmyard manure is obtained.

I am personally lucky enough to live in a house where the scullery is separate from the kitchen, the bathroom is separate from the W.C.s and the dining room and sitting room are also separate. There is access from front to back of the house without going inside it, and separate storage space is provided at the side of the house. While I might be willing to accept one or more of the amalgamations or economies of space mentioned above, provided this resulted in substantial economy, the comfort of the family's life would necessarily be reduced.

Having now summarised very briefly some of the variable factors involved in the actual dwelling, together with some which may be grouped separately from it, it will be convenient to list the total components of the net residential area, that is to say, the area of dwellings with their purely ancillary uses, omitting all non-residential areas. These components are as follows. Dwellings, out-houses, garages, forecourts, back gardens, incidental open space, such as, for example, small children's play space used communally by the children from a number of houses, carriageways, including local parking space, and footpaths.

17-2. RESIDENTIAL DENSITY

A good deal has already been said on this subject in Chapters 9 and 10. First, there is density of persons within the buildings, usually known as occupancy rate. As explained in Chapter 9 a rough measure of adequacy of accommodation available is gained by measuring this and expressing it in terms of persons per habitable room.

The occupancy rate is important in two quite different ways. First, it is a rough measure of overcrowding. Experience suggests that living conditions are comfortable up to an occupancy rate of about 1·0 and become distinctly crowded at 1·3; somewhere between 1·5 and 2·0, overcrowding, as defined by the Housing Act, 1936, sets in. These Housing Act standards cannot be compared directly with occupancy rate measured in accordance with ordinary Planning survey methods for the latter merely give a generalised standard suitable for measuring overcrowding over a number of dwellings. They ignore age and sex as factors in utilisation of living space, assuming that the number of people who can share bedrooms cancels the living rooms, whereas the Housing Act standards are intended to measure utilisation within an individual dwelling. The Housing Act standards are as follows:

Legally a dwelling is deemed to be overcrowded " when the number of persons sleeping in the house either (a) is such that any two of those persons,

being persons ten years old or more of opposite sexes and not being persons living together as husband and wife, must sleep in the same room; or (b) is, in relation to the number and floor area of the rooms of which the house consists, in excess of the permitted number of persons as defined in the tables below. In determining for the purposes of this section the number of persons sleeping in a house, no account shall be taken of a child under one year old, and a child who has attained one year and is under ten years old shall be recorded as one-half of a unit.

The number of persons permitted to use a house for sleeping is the least of the values given in Tables I and II of the Fifth Schedule of the 1936 Housing Act. In calculating the number of rooms, those with floor areas of less than 50 ft. super are ignored.

TABLE I

Where a house consists of:				
(a) One room..	..	..	..	2
(b) Two rooms	..	..	..	3
(c) Three rooms	..	..	..	5
(d) Four rooms	..	..	..	7.5
(e) Five rooms or more	..	..	..	10, with an additional two in respect of each room in excess of five.

TABLE II

Where the floor area of a room is:			
(a) 110 sq. ft. or more	..	..	2
(b) 90 sq. ft. or more, but less than 110 sq. ft. ..	..	..	1.5
(c) 70 sq. ft. or more, but less than 90 sq. ft.	..	..	1
(d) 50 sq. ft. or more, but less than 70 sq. ft. ..	..	..	0.5
(e) Under 50 sq. ft. ..	..	..	Nil

Obviously no comprehensive survey could apply and map intelligibly such complicated standards; nor would it be useful to attempt to do so, since detailed changes in occupancy rate are a matter of daily occurrence; a marriage, a birth, a death, or getting a job which entails leaving home all alter it.

In any area, however poor and congested, there is sure to be a proportion of dwellings substantially less densely occupied than at the average occupancy rate; the lonely widow, the couple whose children have all left home and many others continue to occupy, at least for a time, dwellings suited to accommodate considerably larger families.

In fairly prosperous areas the spare room reserved for occasional visitors, perhaps used as a study at other times, becomes a factor to reckon with. It is an important and pleasant element in the lives of many whose economic level is not so close to bare subsistence that they cannot afford the extra rent or its equivalent attaching to a house large enough to include this amenity. In calculating amounts of accommodation required it would be quite unrealistic to ignore the demand for spare rooms.

It is worth while at this point to try to clothe the cold figures of occupancy rates with some human warmth by giving examples of what various occupancy rates mean in terms of individual living family conditions. A married couple with two children living in the conventional house with two living rooms and three bedrooms live at an occupancy rate of 0·8 and can do so in quite reasonable comfort. According to ages, sexes and dispositions they can either let the children share a bedroom and maintain a spare bedroom, or occupy all the bedrooms, and there is a living room in which meals need not be taken and in which homework and so forth can be undertaken. Such a family with three children instead of two goes up to an occupancy rate of unity, and while it still lives in perfectly reasonable and tolerable conditions, it is likely to be a little short of space. A single person in a two-room dwelling lives at an occupancy rate of 0·5, in a bed-sitting room at an occupancy rate of unity. A family consisting of a married couple and five children living in the three bedroomed house previously described lives at an occupancy rate of 1·4 and is likely to be very crowded indeed.

Dr. N. Lichfield has suggested (See "The Chartered Surveyor", Sept. 1960) a method of measuring density of a simple kind, namely the " design density " based upon the number of single and double bedrooms. This is exactly what Local Authority and New Town housing designers use. They assume a desirable density, expressed in persons per acre and provide, in terms of bedrooms, total accommodation to accord with it. This is very satisfactory if the bedrooms kept as spare roughly balance those into which an extra person is squeezed, and it may well be the simplest and best method of controlling private development. Nevertheless, in an area of growing prosperity it may be necessary to allow for, and to attempt to assess, a substantially greater number of spare bedrooms than of over-used ones, which, in effect, comes back to the need to estimate probable occupancy rate.

Next comes density of residential buildings or building bulk per unit area, usually now expressed in habitable rooms per acre and known as **net residential density.** This does no more, when a survey is carried out, than state an existing state of affairs, which may imply over- or under-intensity of development, though this depends very much upon the actual form of development existing. So far as proposals are concerned a statement of net densities indicates the amount of development intended for a given area but has nothing to say about the form which it shall take, which obviously affects very much whether future development will be satisfactory when it takes place. From another point of view, net residential density is also a statement of the amount of garden space per acre existing or intended. This garden space is not necessarily all in the form of individual house plots; some of it may be in the form of common gardens to blocks of flats, some in undivided forecourts and roadside greens, some in children's play space, small groups of allotments and tennis courts. The common characteristic of all these is that they comprise space for family use in connection with and physically close to the home occupied. The proportions in single family use and in grouped use should be determined in relation to local needs, wishes, topography and economics, and not by density standards. It is important to understand that such small common open spaces as have been mentioned above are counted as house plot allocation, not as part of the open space allocation.

Although net residential density is a measure of garden space per dwelling,

yet it is expressed in habitable rooms per acre. There is a difficulty to be resolved here. The amount of garden space required by a household does not depend directly upon the number of persons in it. True, a very large family, including several young children, will, on the average, need a bigger garden than the very small family, irrespective of interest in gardening, for the sake of the play space provided, but this is the only link between size of household and size of garden. The large and energetic family, with social, political or sporting interests, may well be content with a much smaller plot than the quiet couple who grow roses. Size of house, then, is little guide to size of garden required, and the latter should be related to the number of dwellings per acre rather than the number of habitable rooms or persons per acre.

The form of development affects, to some extent, the amount of garden space per acre available, irrespective of density figures, but the difference is not really very great since for given daylight standards, every time the height of a group of buildings is doubled all that is added to available garden space is half the actual ground area of the buildings erected at the previous height. In other words, two-storey houses, at twelve houses to the acre, provide more garden space than twenty-four bungalows to the acre each with half the number of habitable rooms that the houses have, only to the total extent of the ground areas of twelve bungalows, which may be no more than about 530 sq. yds., over an acre, or barely a tenth of an acre which, split among twelve houses, is 1/120th of an acre—or only about 40 sq. yds. Even less dramatic results are obtained by building say, six-storey flats instead of three-storey houses. This simple fact is really the fallacy at the root of the frequently heard statement that " building high saves space".

Net population density is simply another method of expressing net residential density; it is in fact net residential density multiplied by the average occupancy rate which it is assumed will prevail in the area in question. Having arrived at net population density we can next determine the number of dwellings per acre by dividing by the probable average household size, and, from a knowledge of probable household structure, assess the relative numbers of small, medium and large dwellings which should be built and the distribution of single and double bedrooms.

Gross population density measured over the whole of a residential neighbourhood is important only because, unless the information is conveyed by other means, it tells us how many people live or are intended to live within a given residential unit, and thus enables us to make an estimate of the number of shops, school places, etc., which will be needed.

Density, usually in persons per acre, measured over the whole of a town is a useful figure for comparison of different towns, although it needs scrutiny and analysis if any detailed information is to be drawn from it.

The essential difficulty in determining the appropriate residential density for a given area and in trying to control development so that it shall conform to the chosen density is that control of density has to fulfil two quite different purposes and is concerned with two quite different units: buildings, which are easily controlled, and people, who cannot be controlled except if gross overcrowding occurs.

This can best be illustrated by taking the simplest possible case, a substantial area of undeveloped land allocated in a Town Plan for residential use and stated to be intended to be occupied by say, 5,000 people. We can readily come to reasonable decisions about the amounts of land which will be needed for open space, shops, schools, etc., for these 5,000 people, and the land remaining after these have been provided for will be available for net residential use. Let us assume it is 125 acres, which will give an average density of 40 persons per acre for the intended population. It will be essential to ensure that, in fact, something fairly close to 5,000 people will live in the area when it is fully developed. If the number should be substantially exceeded, provision for shopping, schools, etc., will be inadequate, and the planning of the area will have been unsuccessful, while if the number is substantially less than 5,000, schools will be under-used and shops will not prosper.

If similar errors are made all over the Town Plan then, unless they are in opposite directions, and cancel each other out, the eventual population of the town may be much larger or smaller than that Planned for, and central area services, sewage disposal arrangements, industrial areas and so on will all be thrown out of gear, with either severe congestion or under-utilisation. Ultimately, therefore, the success of Town Planning depends upon making a reasonably accurate assessment of the number of households which the Planned population will comprise and upon ensuring, not only that the right number of dwellings is erected for them but that these are in appropriate proportions as to size.

The simplest starting point, where development is to be carried out by a large number of different developers is to estimate the probable average occupancy rate and operate control on the basis of habitable rooms per acre. If, in the example we have taken, the occupancy rate is estimated as 0·7, a net density of 40 persons per acre will mean about 57 habitable rooms per acre. But this is only a starting point; unless the occupancy rate assumed is close to being correct the results will not be successful, and, unless a watch is also kept upon the average number of dwellings per acre, and hence the total number of dwellings, too few or too many households will be provided for. Further, if too many small dwellings or large dwellings are built this will also distort the population, because the families attracted to them will be those of sizes to fit the dwellings rather than of sizes to suit the Planned population, unless a housing list or some other " captive " population is involved, in which case they may be fitted somehow into the dwellings built but in an uncomfortable and inefficient manner.

What it really comes to is that there are three items involved: dwellings, rooms and people. We can control the first two as much as we like but unless we make accurate forecasts about the third this control will not be very effective. If we only control one of the first two it can be entirely ineffective.

The following table demonstrates these points.

Within a single net residential density we might fairly easily get the following variations:—

Net residential density 60 habitable rooms per acre

Average number of habitable rooms per dwelling	Average number of dwellings per acre	Average number of people per dwelling	Average occupancy rate	Average number of people per acre
3	20	3	1·00	60
3	20	2	0·66	40
3	20	4	1·33	80
4	15	3	0·75	45
4	15	4	1·00	60
4	15	5	1·25	75
5	12	3	0·60	36
5	12	4	0·80	48
5	12	5	1·00	60
5	12	6	1·20	72
6	10	4	0·66	40
6	10	5	0·83	50
6	10	6	1·00	60
6	10	7	1·17	70

A possible variation in population density from 36 persons per acre to 80 persons per acre might obviously be disastrous for shop and school provision.

The foregoing has dealt mainly with the quantitative aspects of residential density and methods of controlling it. The qualitative or amenity aspect is of at least equal importance, but with this, too, density control tends to be a clumsy and inadequate control, indeed even harmful unless operated with full understanding. Although it is the quantitative aspect which is the important one for the purposes of Town Plan design, the qualitative is the one with which local authorities are most concerned in their day-to-day operations; many of them display no understanding at all of what they are trying to do.

So far as the individual is concerned it is obvious that, other things being equal, the lower the density of the area in which he lives the greater will be the spaciousness and privacy which he enjoys. A residential area with a density of 4 houses to the acre gives much more garden space and much less interference from the activities and overlooking of neighbours than one with a density of 12 houses to the acre.

In these stark terms, therefore, the lower the density the better the living conditions; but other factors come into play. The cost of land, the extra costs of roads and services, the reduction of accessibility to other parts of the town, the labour involved in maintaining a very big garden, all operate to suggest the desirability of densities somewhat higher than those at which the maximum privacy and spaciousness could be obtained. Also, even at a given density, the form in which development is carried out generally affects its acceptability in terms of spaciousness and privacy.

In terms of the table given a little earlier, a density of 60 habitable rooms per acre would be congested if development were in the form of 20 small bungalows to the acre, perfectly acceptable if in the form of 12 houses to the acre and extremely spacious (even though lacking individual outdoor space) if in the form of a 5-storey block of flats, 4 flats to each storey and 3 rooms in each flat, per acre.

It is therefore very misleading to judge the pleasantness of an area simply by the net density assigned to it in terms of habitable rooms or persons per acre, without taking account of both the number of dwellings per acre and of whether these will be all dispersed horizontally or will be wholly or partly stacked vertically.

Similarly, the greater the building bulk per acre the greater will be the amount of overlooking, and the less wide the view and the less the amount of sunlight and daylight enjoyed, even though the latter may still be much above minimum requirements.

Nevertheless it remains generally true that privacy and quietness increase as density falls. The more people there are living in a given area the more noise they will make in terms of children's noise, radios and gramophones and motor car engines and the more visitors and tradesmen, with vehicles, will visit the area.

Another source of confusion when considering residential density arises from the very different density figures which may be obtained by choosing different unit areas for measurement.

A gross population density of 40 persons per acre might represent a very low net residential density if the neighbourhood concerned contained an exceptional number of schools sites and an exceptionally large amount of open space, and vice versa. As regards net residential density, mere figures may be even more misleading. A density of 50 habitable rooms per acre measured over the whole net residential area of a neighbourhood may well include substantial areas at a density of 4 houses, or about 20 habitable rooms to the acre and others in multi-storey flats at 120 or more habitable rooms to the acre. To give anything like a useful measure, density must be expressed over units within which the dwelling types are fairly similar and the plot sizes within not too wide a range of sizes.

For example, suppose there is an area of high density bungalows, extending over 3 acres at 20 dwellings to the acre and 4 habitable rooms to the dwelling. The density will of course be 80 habitable rooms or 20 dwellings to the acre. If we include in the unit over which density is measured two adjoining houses each occupying an acre of land and each with 5 habitable rooms, the overall density will be as follows:—

$$\frac{\text{Total number of habitable rooms: 250}}{\text{Total area of site 5 acres}} = 50 \text{ habitable rooms per acre.}$$

But this will mean very little in terms of amenity. The overwhelming majority of the inhabitants will be living in conditions to be associated with a density of 80 habitable rooms per acre, rendered more spacious and enjoyable to only a minute extent by virtue of the open areas around the two houses with large gardens.

If to this development we add a further acre occupied by a tall block of flats containing 120 habitable rooms we have a total site of 6 acres with 370 habitable rooms on it, giving an average density of 62 habitable rooms per acre, though no one on the site lives in conditions which approach to those to be associated with such a density.

Needs of different households. The needs of different households for dwelling accommodation may vary as regards the type of dwelling, the amount and kind of accommodation in it, and the amount and kind of outdoor space associated with it. The determining factors are the number and ages of people in the household, their income level and their living habits. One of the main objectives of an enlightened public housing policy must be to secure that as large as possible a proportion of the people to be housed have the kind of dwelling which they want and are able and willing to pay for. Once built, dwellings last for a long time, while the make-up and needs of the population which they serve are continually changing, so that at the very best only a rough approximation to the best possible provision can be hoped for. This need cause no great concern. Many families can live perfectly happily for many years in accommodation which is, theoretically, not well suited to their needs. Some dwellings, moreover, are suitable for more than one kind of household; bungalows for old persons can almost as well be occupied by young couples who have not yet got children. Nevertheless, good use of the resources available for housing demands that a serious attempt should be made to meet household demands for different forms of accommodation as closely as possible.

It has already been suggested that the position is complicated by the considerable changes of the composition of the population to be housed over the life of a dwelling. It is further complicated, and, in fact, becomes an almost impossible task in areas of housing built by private enterprise. Private enterprise is concerned to build at the highest profit which can be obtained with reasonable security. It therefore tends to build " average " dwellings likely to be tolerable, if not ideal for a wide range of household types; hence the prevalence, particularly between the wars, of the three-bedroom, two living-room house. No mechanism has yet been found to induce private enterprise to carry out development in close accordance with the needs of household structure. Where large units are developed by single developers it may, in future, be possible to improve the situation, but where development takes place piecemeal over small units it is almost inconceivable that this can be done, since such a policy would involve the imposition upon individual developers of relatively risky, or low-profit earning forms of development; you could not possibly arrange for each small developer to carry out a representative cross-section of all the different forms of development required.

Throughout this book the aim has been to seek reasonable datum lines to suit average conditions, so that it now becomes of importance to try to formulate an average net residential density which would be applicable to a substantial area of development, for example, a neighbourhood of ten thousand people, assuming that all types of households were represented therein in proportion to the national average distribution of households, and that all income groups were catered for, again in rough proportion to the national average.

Distribution of Dwellings for a Hypothetical Stationary Population of 10,000

Size of Household (Persons)		Number of Dwellings containing the Following Numbers of Habitable Rooms								Totals	
		1 room	2 rooms	3 rooms	4 rooms	5 rooms	6 rooms	7 rooms	8 or more rooms	Number	%
1		521	306							827	23·6
2			509	416						925	26·4
3				445	296					741	21·2
4					357	167				524	15·0
5						148	76			224	6·4
6							79	46		125	3·6
7 or more								67	67	134	3·8
Totals	Dwellings	521	815	861	653	315	155	113	67	3,500	
	Dwellings as % ..	14·9	23·1	24·8	18·6	9·0	4·4	3·3	1·9		100
	Rooms	521	1,630	2,586	2,612	1,580	930	796	603	11,258	
	Rooms as %	4·6	14·4	23·0	23·2	14·0	8·3	7·1	5·4		100

While it may be that no existing town and no new town would have a population which exactly accorded with this, such a density would represent a very useful average from which departures upwards or downwards could be decided upon in the light of local circumstances.

There is a good deal of material available to assist in arriving at such a datum. A paper entitled " Residential Density " read at the Town and Country Planning Summer School of 1950 provided useful information, and much that it contained was subsequently published in the Ministry Handbook on the Density of Residential Areas. Two papers by S. P. Brown, and by Ruth Glass and S. G. Davidson published in Population Studies, Vol. IV No. 4, March 1951, are also invaluable. The following paragraphs owe much to the facts set out in all these documents to which further detailed individual references will not be made. The reader in search of further detail should refer to the originals.

The 1951 Census gives information about distribution of households of various sizes, which is set out in the following Table (reduced to the nearest whole number).

No. in Household	% of People	% of Households
1	4½	14
2	20¾	30
3	25¾	24
4	24	18
5	12¾	8
6	6¼	3
7+	6	3
	100	100

It is well known that a " household " is not, at least potentially, the same thing as a family. A household is a group of people living together in structurally separate accommodation, but many households include lodgers and also people such as mothers-in-law who, if they could obtain suitable separate accommodation, would set up households to the benefit of all concerned. The Tables on pages 224 and 225, which take account of these

Distribution by Type and Size of Dwellings required for a Hypothetical Stationary Population of 10,000

Size of Dwelling in Rooms	Absolute Numbers and Percentage Distribution of Houses and Flats within each Dwelling Size						Total
	Houses		Flats		Old People's Dwellings		
	No.	%	No.	%	No.	%	
1	—		332	63·6	189	36·4	521
2	—		555	68·1	260	31·9	815
3	610	70·8	251	29·2	—		861
4	644	98·7	9	1·3	—		653
5	315	100	—		—		315
6	155	100	—		—		155
7	113	100	—		—		113
8 or more	67	100	—		—		67
Total Dwellings	1,904		1,147		449		3,500
Total Rooms	8,318		2,231		709		11,258
Rooms as % of all rooms ..		73·6		20·0		6·4	

$$\text{Average Occupancy Rate} = \frac{10,000}{11,258} = \cdot 89$$

" concealed " households, do not conform to the existing distribution of households.

The most important conclusions to be drawn from these Tables are that, to provide a more or less ideal mixture of types of dwelling, about 73% of rooms would need to be in the form of houses, 7% in the form of old persons' dwellings, and 20% in the form of flats. However, when one looks at the matter from the point of view of percentages not of rooms, but of dwellings, these percentages become, houses 54%, old persons' dwellings 13%, flats 33%. This paints a very different picture and emphasises the enormous importance, when talking about " the percentages of flats," of being absolutely clear whether percentages of rooms, or percentages of dwellings is being talked about. Failure to do this leads to the worst kind of misunderstanding. Whether considered from the point of view of proportion of accommodation or proportion of households, the figures given above for

flats are startlingly high. They exceed enormously any known demands for flats, though it might be that in an area of development excellently carried out, where all the flats built were arranged to perfection in order to provide privacy and freedom from noise, and where rents were arranged so as to make flat tenancy attractive, such known demands might be greatly exceeded, particularly after a lapse of some years to allow for the advantages of living in well-designed flats to become well known. There is of course a prejudice against flat dwelling, because so many flat dwellers either live in households which are not suited to flat life (and we may positively say that no family which contains children of school ages is well fitted to flat life), or else have had experience of badly arranged flats, particularly flats which are rough and ready carvings up of large houses originally designed as single family dwellings.

Nevertheless, it would be rash to underestimate the desire for a house and garden, not merely by those who live in households which positively need one, but by others who like such a dwelling for its own sake. The elderly couple, whose children have grown up and left home are not guilty of any kind of impropriety if they prefer to stay on in their old house, enjoying a garden which may have been cultivated and been their main hobby for a generation or more, and having available the space in which to accommodate visiting children and grandchildren.

There must, on the other hand, be many thousands of families who occupy houses much larger than their needs, with consequent extra expenditure on rates, Schedule A, heating, lighting and repairs, simply because no suitable flat is available to them at a price they can afford. No one I think, can say with certainty what the ultimate demand for flats might be if constructional, layout and economic conditions for their occupation were thoroughly favourable, but I think that 33% would still be on the high side.

Estimation is further bedevilled because it is probably true to say that at present in this country a majority of households who would like and be suited by a flat have to live in houses, while the majority of existing flat dwellers consist of households who would prefer and be better suited by a house!

The foregoing Tables were based upon intricate statistical and demographic data beyond the scope of this book, but it is useful to know that the conclusions arrived at are based upon the following assumptions: (1) Married couples would share bedrooms, (2) each additional person in a household, irrespective of age or sex would have a separate bedroom, (3) every growing household would have a spare bedroom, as well as every middle-aged and old married couple without children. Each household would have one living room, with some exceptions. Households with children up to the age of twenty-five would all be accommodated in houses as would all growing households, that is to say young couples without children. Stationary households requiring not more than four rooms would be accommodated in flats, while those requiring five rooms or more would be accommodated in houses. Declining households requiring one or two rooms would be accommodated as to half in old people's dwellings, and as to half in flats. Those requiring three rooms would be accommodated in flats, and those requiring four or more rooms would be accommodated in houses.

Growing households are those which may expect children or further children, based upon the age of the housewife and the duration of the marriage.

Stationary households are those which have reached their maximum size and are likely to remain at this size for some time, and include married couples without children of under twenty-five, with marriage durations of over ten years or with housewives aged between forty-five and fifty-four years, married couples with children and with housewives who are over forty-five years or with marriage durations which are of such length that no further children can be expected, single or widowed persons of under forty-five years of age with children, and single or widowed persons under fifty-five years of age without children under twenty-five, but with other adults, and finally one person households with single or widowed persons under fifty-five years of age.

Declining households are those which are likely to decrease in size. In this group are all the households which are estimated to contain sons and daughters over school age as well as all those households, including one person households, which consist of adults over twenty-five years only, and in which the housewife or single or widowed householder is over fifty-five years of age.

The average occupancy rate of 0·89 which is derived is so much higher than in fact occurs in existing areas of development where there is a reasonably high level of prosperity that one views it with some suspicions, although it may be that a scientific matching of household types and sizes to household structure would bring about a considerable increase in average occupancy rates. The average occupancy rate for England and Wales given in the 1951 census is, nevertheless, only 0·74.

Making allowances for rising standards of living which call forth greater demands for living space, and also making due allowance for the appreciable amount of accommodation bound to be empty at any given time as a result of movement of families, an occupancy rate of 0.80 (also arithmetically much more convenient!) seems a sensible one to adopt. This of course increases the number of habitable rooms required to accommodate a given population and accounts for discrepancies between the Tables and calculations given later in this chapter.

No Table setting out the types and proportions of dwelling accommodation required can carry with it precision. Income levels, tastes and habits and the family structure of a population inevitably change, and bring with them changing needs of accommodation. All that we need hope to do is to try to build in such a way that requirements are reasonably met, without, on the one hand, waste of accommodation, or on the other hand undue cramping and overcrowding. It is important that a reasonable basis be assumed, for the proportions of various kinds of dwellings selected have a considerable effect upon residential density, as will appear later.

In order to translate a Table of accommodation requirements into terms which will allow an average net residential density to be arrived at, a number of rather intricate calculations have to be done which it is necessary to set out here step by step, at rather tedious length, if they are to be properly understood.

Throughout, it has to be borne in mind that great precision of calculation is not necessary since in the field of Planning we are concerned more with space requirements than with the division of buildings into rooms, and with the effect upon density of different arrangements of dwellings. It thus becomes permissible and sensible to coarsen the calculations to a considerable extent.

Space Requirements for Dwellings
Houses. It is important to remember that a good deal of variation in the numbers of rooms per house, and hence in occupancy rate, is possible without materially affecting net residential density in terms of houses or building bulk per acre. Also, a larger number of small rooms can be placed on the same area of building as a smaller number of large rooms, and a three-storeyed

house of six rooms may take up no more ground area than a two-storey house of four rooms.

Let us first decide what is the very smallest plot which will give a garden which can be so described rather than as a back yard and the largest house which can be used in conjunction with it. These will give us the maximum density practicable for single family dwellings.

Seventy feet between the backs and fronts of parallel rows of houses has long been accepted as a minimum desirable to ensure privacy and for back gardens. It is also adequate for daylighting for most types of houses. Fig. 1 in " The Density of Residential Areas " makes it clear that, from the point of view of daylighting alone, ordinary two-storey houses with pitched roofs can be placed 46′ 6″ apart and three-storey houses 68′ apart.

The Housing Manual, 1949 gives some types of three-storey houses with six habitable rooms each, house frontages averaging about 18 ft. and house depths about 25 ft. The three-storey house is, from the housewife's point of view, distinctly less convenient than the two-storey house, but with good internal arrangements, not so much so as to make it unacceptable. Allowing an increase in average frontage of 20 per cent, to take account of breaks in blocks of houses and frontage lost at road junctions, the minimum plot will be 95 ft. deep from middle of road to back fence, by about 22 ft. wide, an area of roughly 2,100 sq. ft., which comes to 20·7 dwellings per acre, 124 habitable rooms per acre, and with an occupancy rate of 0·8, 99 persons per acre. If we call this 120 habitable rooms per acre and 100 persons per acre it will be near enough for all practical purposes. This *minimum* would be hopelessly inadequate as an *average* but at least gives us a point of departure.

The subject of density is much confused by emotional and wishful thinking. On the one hand many architects sincerely believe that it it only by a substantial increase of density that good modern housing development, comparable in quality with the best housing of former times can be achieved. In particular, they tend to argue that fairly continuously built up frontages are essential in order to give a feeling of urbanity, and that, on the other hand distances substantially smaller than 70 ft. between facing fronts of houses are necessary in order to give a proper proportion between the horizontal and vertical elements of the street picture, particularly where the houses are no more than two storeys high.

There is, of course, a good deal to be said for this point of view. Many of the most admired examples of housing development of previous generations are quite deficient in space standards according to modern ideas, yet one must always remember that the object of housing development is not solely, nor even primarily, to create a beautiful environment, but an environment which shall be, in all ways, satisfactory to its inhabitants. Most of the narrow-fronted terraced housing, with parallel rows facing each other across a narrow street was built for people who could make no effective demands for the housing conditions they would like. In a country where it is the avowed aim to raise the standard of living for all, and where the criterion for provision of accommodation must, if democracy is to mean anything, be provision, as far as possible, of the kinds of homes desired by the majority of people, it is impossible to believe that such housing would be carried out.

A rising standard of living seems bound to be reflected in a demand for more spacious living accommodation both inside the building and outside, and unless there are overriding economic reasons for resisting such demand, it should be met.

Some assessment of demand can be made by examining the kinds of houses provided by speculative builders for purchase between the wars. This material must be regarded with great caution, for the majority of purchasers did not really have a free choice. They were able only to choose between a number of very slightly varying kinds of houses, all of them architecturally bad, and practically all incompetent from the point of view of layout. It is also true that in many areas the curious density zoning of inter-war planning schemes artificially forced down the density of housing development, and made the speculative builder provide far larger plots than he would have done of his own accord. Nevertheless it seems safe to say that in this country a very large majority of people would choose a detached house, with a fairly large garden, if they were able to afford it, regard a semi-detached house, with a somewhat smaller garden as a second-best, and are only prepared to live in a terrace house if lack of income or choice force them to do so.

There is, no doubt, an element of snobbery here. The doctrine of " conspicuous consumption " is applicable not only at the highest income levels, but almost everywhere, and the size of a man's house and garden is one of the most obvious ways of demonstrating his prestige. Nevertheless, it would be foolish to suggest that these preferences are not based on real advantages.

Take first, the question of the distance between facing fronts of houses. I personally believe from observation that 70 ft. is a reasonable minimum. This is not something that one can prove by demonstration. An attempt to discredit the 70 ft. standard was made by Walter Manthorpe in the "Architectural Review" of December, 1956. By photographing a figure standing in a room from varying distances he sought to show that it did not become invisible until a distance of nearly a hundred yards was reached and that " common-sense privacy i.e., privacy at the back of the room is obtainable at a minimum distance of about fifty feet as thousands of Londoners know". This experiment seems to be based upon various fallacies. Most people do not seek complete visual privacy in an uncurtained room, but like to feel that they are not under detailed observation from the opposite side of the street and there is a tremendous difference between fifty feet and seventy feet. But visual privacy is not the only kind of privacy; privacy from noise is another important one and even olfactory privacy may be an important issue if one dislikes the smell of highly savoury cooking. I feel confident in saying that to a person of normal sensitiveness a distance from facing windows of 70 ft. provides a general feeling of comfort, while a distance appreciably smaller than this gives a general feeling of discomfort. The climate of the British Isles is such that the enjoyment of as much sunshine as possible is important. Observation will show that in streets where the houses are much less than 70 ft. apart, most of the inhabitants feel it necessary to safeguard their privacy by the use of net curtains, not merely in bedrooms but in living rooms, whereas at 70 ft. or more this tendency diminishes sharply.

It is often said that even if 70 ft. is a desirable minimum where habitable rooms face each other this distance can be reduced without detriment if there are not habitable rooms on both sides of the street. This is at least partly true as regards visual privacy, though one can be stared at from a kitchen as readily as from a living room. As regards noise and smell there is no difference. It would, I think, be foolish to be too dogmatic about this matter. Occasional reductions of distance below 70 ft. need not be unduly objectionable, particularly where habitable rooms do not face each other, and where reductions may help greatly in creating interesting street pictures. It is where the general distance is substantially less, involving overlooking from a number of houses, that it is really detrimental.

Let us turn now to consideration of width and house type. This is a much more complicated matter. The advantages of the detached house are clear, it has no party walls so that there is absolutely no noise transmitted directly from neighbouring houses through the walls. The wider the plot is, the greater the degree of separation from neighbours, and consequently freedom from the noise they may make in their garden, and the more spacious can one's own back garden be. With the terrace house, on the other hand, one has, unless one is fortunate to occupy a house at the end of the terrace, neighbours on the other side of party walls on either side, and the width of one's plot is usually limited to the width of the house, which means that, where the house is a narrow one, a back garden of reasonable length is quite out of proportion and tends to give the feeling of a strip of land reserved for a railway line which has never been built. The semi-detached house is essentially a compromise between the detached house and the terrace. There is a party wall one side, but not on the other, and the width of the garden is not limited to the width of the house.

The situation is further complicated by the possible presence or absence at the side of the house itself of outbuildings and/or garage. Every foot of width of the house plot costs something like four or five pounds in terms of the road and services fronting upon it (houses do not necessarily have to front on to roads but this is a point discussed later). This is no small item in considering plot width and suggests that it is wise to select as narrow a plot as is compatible with the needs and wishes of the occupier. Yet, as I have already suggested, a rising standard of living ought reasonably to be accompanied by a rising standard of living accommodation, and whatever ingenious economies may be achieved by skilful arrangement of the elements of the home there is no denying the fundamental fact that a narrow plot affords less opportunity for comfortable living than does a comparatively wide one. It is much more pleasant, if one is going to have a garage, to have it beside one's house than some distance away among a group of others. It is much pleasanter to have outbuildings at the side of the house rather than at the back where they intrude upon garden space, and may interfere with daylight. It is much pleasanter to have a reasonably wide garden than a strip of railway line. Many people are able and willing to varying extents to pay something extra for these advantages.

In fixing an average net residential density one has to try to estimate the effective demand for something more than the bare minimum width of plot. This can only be done very roughly. It may help in deciding this to suggest certain basic minimum plot widths for the various common arrangements of houses.

We may reasonably take twenty feet as the minimum width for the house itself; it is true that houses of considerably smaller frontage can be designed but they all in one way or another suffer from the limitations mentioned near the beginning of this chapter, with a house twenty feet wide these can be avoided. If therefore, you wanted a detached house with the bare minimum of plot you could have a house twenty feet wide with a four-foot gap on either side giving a total foot frontage of twenty-eight feet. This would be cramped and meagre, and a street of such houses would look unutterably horrible. They are not very common in this country but can be seen in profusion in the United States. If you added a garage to the side of this house you would need another nine feet but, on the other hand, provided the local byelaws allowed you to do so you could, with careful arrangement of the house plan, omit the four-foot strip on the garage side, giving a total plot width of thirty-three feet. Probably most people would not think it worth while to have a detached house of this kind, and would settle for a semi-detached house; it would then be unnecessary to have the four-foot gap on the other side, and the plot width would be twenty-nine feet.

If you wanted to have not only a garage on one side but decent outbuildings on the other, then it would probably be necessary to add about ten feet to the total width, as there would have to be a four-foot gap between the side of the house and the outbuildings themselves in order to afford proper access to the rear of the house. This would give a total plot width of thirty-nine feet. Such an arrangement is not, of course, possible with a semi-detached house, and either garage or outbuildings have to be sacrificed or the outbuildings placed at the rear.

In practice, people do not generally find it worth while to build a detached house on a plot less than about forty or fifty feet wide, and semi-detached houses are seldom built with a frontage of less than thirty feet.

Terrace houses can be built which are only 15 feet wide, or less, but most designs which provide what I would regard as satisfactory secondary access and space standards have a frontage of twenty-five feet or more, and personally I think that this is about the minimum plot width if a decent garden is to be provided. I should consider that the extra road costs involved in increasing frontage to this extent, were worth while. The three-storey house, in any case, is principally of use in providing for the larger family, though it is also possible to have three-storey houses with a comparatively small number of habitable rooms and a garage incorporated in the ground floor of the house. The main disadvantage of incorporating a garage in any house, as compared with setting it alongside the house, is the additional cost involved in carrying out the necessary fireproofing.

It is important to bear in mind that whatever average frontages may be decided upon for particular types of houses, a percentage has to be added in order to arrive at an average frontage in order to allow for the inevitable

PLOT SIZE (ACRES)	PLOT DIMENSIONS (FEET)		
½	60 × 363	80 × 272	100 × 217
¼	40 × 270	60 × 182	80 × 137
⅙	30 × 240	40 × 180	50 × 146
⅛	30 × 180	40 × 136	50 × 110
1/10	25 × 171	30 × 145	35 × 126
1/12	25 × 143	30 × 122	35 × 105
1/14	25 × 124	30 × 105	35 × 90
1/16	20 × 132	25 × 110	30 × 92
1/18	20 × 120	25 × 96	30 × 80
1/20	20 × 107	25 × 86	30 × 70

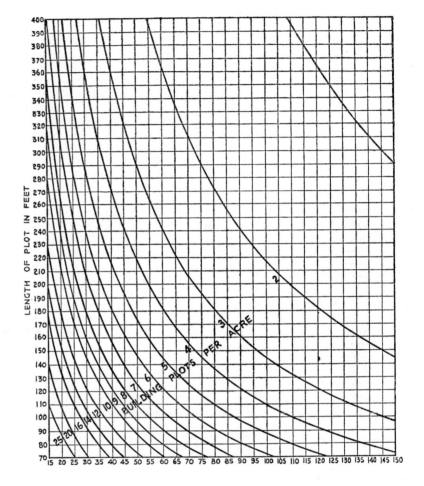

FIGS. 79 AND 80. Fig. 79 gives examples of plots at various densities showing alternative widths and depths of plot in each case. The stippled area represents half width of road of normal width. All the houses are thirty-five feet back from road centre lines. In order to secure at least 70 ft. between backs of houses back fence lines must project at least to the 95 ft. line while to secure a back garden of 60 ft. they must project beyond the 120 ft. line. Note that the plot areas are " net " areas, i.e., a proportion has not been added to frontages to allow for loss at junctions etc. Fig. 80 supplies a convenient method of finding the density which will be produced by development of plots at various sizes and shapes, or conversely, where required density and frontage are known, the average plot depth necessary. Here again a proportion must necessarily be added to take account of waste frontage.

increased frontages at road junctions and where there is a break in terrace housing. Experience shows that 20% is about the right amount to add in most normal layouts.

Finally, we turn to the third element in assessing density, namely length of back garden. Here one is in rather the same difficulty as in discussing the reasonable minimum distances between fronts of houses. It is hardly possible to determine scientifically what constitutes a good depth of back garden, but again experience shows that for the ordinary householder a back garden sixty feet long is satisfactory, although there are plenty of people who want to live in a house rather than a flat but want no more than a tiny garden. As will be seen later in this chapter their needs can very conveniently be met by providing quite small gardens at road junctions; the sixty feet I am suggesting as a normal minimum is for gardens where corner site problems do not arise.

A suggested minimum of sixty feet is apt to cause eyebrows to be raised, and voices to be heard talking about the common neglect of large gardens, the terrible burden which an overlarge garden is upon a householder not over-keen upon gardening, and the " waste of land " involved. There is not much in any of this. A garden may be very thoroughly utilised for play and recreation even though few flowers or vegetables are grown in it, and in any case it is much better to provide for likely requirements than to be too parsimonious in this respect for, with a normal layout, once the size of plots has been determined no human power can increase the back gardens if they are found to be inadequate, whereas if they are found to be too large there is no disadvantage, and indeed positive advantage, in planting unwanted portions of them with trees and shrubs. Alternatively, it is comparatively easy to lay out any part of a garden which it is not desired to cultivate intensively as a lawn for it is not so much the area of lawn to be mown but the turning of the mower at the ends which is laborious. It is clear that the larger the lawn is the smaller is the proportion of the total labour involved in this tiresome exercise.

Very roughly, it is probably true to say that if one excludes the garden so large that it virtually constitutes a small estate, and the demand for these at the present time is so slight that it can hardly have any appreciable effect on density calculations, and, on the other hand, excludes tiny gardens, of which mention has already been made, there are three main sizes of garden demanded. First the really large garden which requires quite exceptional keenness on the part of the owner or some paid help for its proper maintenance. This could suitably be provided on a plot with a total area of about a quarter of an acre. Second, the sizeable garden which can adequately be maintained by a reasonably keen gardener on his own, or by a less keen gardener with a small amount of paid help, which can be provided on plots of between a sixth and an eight of an acre. Third, the ordinary garden easily maintainable by the owner without help. This can appropriately be provided on a plot about one-twelfth of an acre. The word " plot " here refers to the total area of house and garden stretching from the middle of the road at the front to the back fence. The Table on this page sets out the dimensions and densities of a number of typical kinds of house plot.

The figures given in the Tables of Distribution of Dwellings suggested that

Type of House	Extras at sides	Plot width (ft.)	Plot width + 20% (ft.)	Plot depth (ft.)	Approx. Density in houses per acre	Remarks
Detached	—	28	33½	120	11	Bare minimum
Detached	Garage and Outhouses	43	51½	140	6	4' way on each side
Detached	As desired	50	60	180	4	
Detached	As desired	100	—	215	2	Addition of 20% to frontage not applicable at this density. Room for tennis court in back garden
Semi-detached or Terrace	—	25	30	120	12	Minimum for semi-detached.
Semi-detached	Garage or Outbuildings	30	36	150	8	Linked garages, no way at side.
Semi-detached	Garage and Outhouses	39	47	120	7¾	

Plot boundaries are from centre of road to back fence. Front wall of house assumed to be at least 35' back from centre of road. Houses at least 25' deep. With a 60' back garden the minimum plot depth which satisfies these requirements is 120'. Densities are based on plot widths plus 20%. Garages assumed to be 9' wide, ways at side 4' wide. Outbuildings 6' wide.

1,904 dwellings in the form of houses would be required to accommodate about 7,300 people. At an occupancy rate of 0·8 this would mean a total of 9,125 rooms making an average of about 4·8 habitable rooms per house.

The next step is to try to determine in what proportions houses at these various ranges of density should be provided. Very little research has been done into this and it is hardly possible to proceed by anything better than intelligent guesswork. I think it would be reasonable to assume demand as follows:

65% of houses averaging 12 houses to the acre
15% at 8 houses to the acre
15% at 6 houses to the acre
 5% at 4 houses to the acre

On this basis we can arrive at the following result. Out of a hundred houses:

65 at twelve to the acre occupy	5·4 acres	
15 at 8 to the acre occupy	1·9	,,
15 at 6 to the acre	2·50	,,
5 at 4 to the acre occupy	1·25	,,

100   11·05

        =9·05 houses per acre

            = at 4·8 habitable rooms per house 43·44 habitable rooms per acre

            at 0·8 occupancy rate = 34·75 persons per acre.

In round figures we may call this an average density for houses of 44 habitable rooms per acre, or 35 persons per acre.

The only estimate of a similar kind of which I know, is contained in the Hertfordshire County Council " Report on Living Standards for Hertfordshire with special reference to the Housing Density " by E. H. Doubleday, published in 1951. In this Report 60% of houses were assumed to be required at an average density of 15·3 houses per acre, 25% at 8 to the acre, and 15% at 6 to the acre, giving 9·9 houses to the acre as against my 9·05. In view of the numerous unassessable factors involved this is quite a close correspondence.

Flats. The determination of suitable densities for flats is even more difficult and complex than for houses, for although considerations of daylight

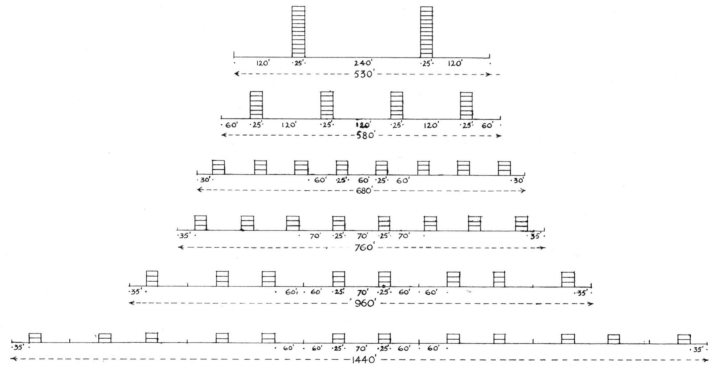

FIG. 81. The three upper drawings, with dwellings spaced for daylighting with an angle 25°, show the principle that, by doubling the heights of parallel rows the amount of land saved is half the area occupied by the actual buildings at the lower height. In practice, tall flats show a greater saving than this, for, although an angle of 25° provides satisfactory daylighting, lower dwellings need to be spaced further apart in order to give a satisfactory amount of privacy and, in the case of houses, adequate gardens.

Reading downwards, the fourth drawing shows the additional spacing required for privacy, while the fifth and sixth show, respectively, three- and two-storey houses with back gardens 60 feet long.

Each of the drawings has the same total number of habitable rooms. Lengths of blocks are of course assumed to be equal. Taking the density of the lowest drawing as unity, the densities of the others are, reading upwards, 1·5, 1·9, 2·12, 2·48, and 2·72; e.g., if the density of the two-storey houses is 60 habitable rooms per acre, that of the twelve-storey blocks will be about 163.

and privacy are somewhat the same as for houses, variations in height and layout are much greater. Buchanan and Crompton put the matter very pithily in their paper referred to earlier:

" Turning now to the ranges of density appropriate to areas developed with flats only, it is evident that the controlling factors are the way flats are arranged inside the blocks, the number of storeys and the length and depth of the blocks. These in turn are governed by the spacing of blocks required to give daylighting, sunlighting, noise and fire insulation and good access. A further need, and a difficult one to analyse, is for outdoor living space and semi-private gardens. Our investigation of these aspects has given us some idea of the densities appropriate for areas consisting of blocks of flats only.

" For simple rectangular-shaped blocks laid out in parallel rows the spacing required for adequate daylighting will limit densities to about 120 rooms per acre for low blocks, up to about 180 rooms per acre for taller, longer blocks. Other layout arrangements, encouraged by the use of daylight indicators and being in the main varieties of the broken cruciform, would make higher maximum densities possible, depending on a number of variables, sometimes as high as 200 to 300 rooms per acre.

"We feel on fairly safe ground in saying that the spacing of blocks to ensure daylighting will in general automatically ensure space to meet the minimum needs of access, privacy and insulation. The great imponderable, however, is the amount of space needed for what we call outdoor living. We think more investigation is needed on this point, particularly from the angle of the use flat dwellers make, or could make, of the space between blocks. We venture the generalisation, however, that when medium and tall blocks are spaced for daylighting there will be enough usable amenity space between the blocks to meet most outdoor living needs, provided only that there is not a high proportion of children living in the flats. As a very rough basis of comparison we find that the usable outdoor living space per person for flats spaced to ensure daylighting is equivalent to the total garden space per person for high density terrace housing.

" We are prepared to say that at these densities it is possible to secure daylighting, sunlighting (except in special circumstances), insulation and access. These are straightforward, assessable factors; the doubtful one is the amount of space required around blocks for outdoor living."

This suggests two comments. First, Buchanan and Crompton are dealing with the redevelopment at high densities of congested areas as well as with new development, hence the reference to cases where there is a high proportion of children. Second, some amplification of the factors governing flat density is desirable.

As compared with development in the form of two-storey houses, flat development at any given density provides a greater proportion of open space as heights of building increase. This proportion is equal to half the previous site area of the buildings each time height is doubled (see Fig. 81), less a certain amount of wastage due to the space taken up by lifts, which are necessary above three storeys, corridor access, and so on. The exact amount depends upon the detailed design of the buildings. It is therefore possible

for high blocks of flats to be built, in conformity with reasonable standards of daylighting, privacy and open space at a substantially greater density than houses. The higher the blocks the greater the distance which they must be set apart from each other and from other near-by buildings. With a daylight angle of 25 degrees, ten-storey flats in parallel rows must be placed about 195 ft. apart (see Fig. 81), which limits density to about 174 habitable rooms per acre, unless very long blocks are used; other arrangements of blocks enable this figure to be substantially raised without reducing daylight below an acceptable standard.

In order to provide the opportunity for variety and drama in the urban scene, high density flats in tall blocks are admirable. If a flat is a suitable dwelling for a household, then, subject to the limiting factors already mentioned, it does not matter how great the density is. Unfortunately, building costs rise sharply with height, and Buchanan and Crompton suggest that, per household unit, high flats may cost $2\frac{1}{2}$ times as much as two-storey houses, which puts them pretty well out of court for most sites during our present economic difficulties. Near the centre of large towns the cost of *land* may be so high that development at a very high density is cheaper in total cost, but I am here concerned to formulate acceptable human standards related to needs and resources rather than to the artificial difficulties imposed by a Paleotechnic economic system.

The Handbook on the Density of Residential Areas gives on page 51 the following Table of Cost Factors for a dwelling of fixed size in various structure forms.

Type of Structure	Cost Factor
Houses semi-detached	1.0
Houses terrace, two-storey	1.0
Houses terrace, three-storey	1.1
Flats, three-storey	1.2
Flats, five- to six-storey with load bearing walls	1.5
Flats six- to ten-storey with frame structure	1.7

Figure 25 on page 52 of the same publication shows that:
(1) Total cost per room decreases irrespective of land costs with increase of density, until it becomes necessary to start using flats.

The increased cost of structure then causes the total cost per room to rise sharply. At still higher densities it starts to fall again, but unless land is very expensive the cost per room does not recover sufficiently to drop below the first minimum, even if the density is increased to 200 rooms per acre. In brief, high densities only pay in the narrow sense when land is very expensive, though this is not to say that the cost of high density in other circumstances may not, on occasions, be justified. The Handbook suggests that, although the cost factor for tall flats is 1.7, in practice the cost of laundries, playrooms etc., and other items associated with flats but yet too variable to be included in basic cost factor would tend to increase the factor for flats, in some instances raising the factor for high flats to as much as 2.5. This agrees with Buchanan and Crompton's estimate.

Effects on net Residential Density and Town Size of variations in density of different types of dwelling.   Occupancy Rate 0·80 throughout

Type of Dwelling	% of total accommodation	Density in H.R.P.A.	Average density in H.R.P.A.	Average density in P.P.A.	Total residential acreage of town	Total acreage of town	Radius of town in miles	Remarks
Houses O.P.D. Flats	73, 3½, 3½ 20	44, 18, 120 120	50	40	1,500	2,900	1·2	Density suggested in text brought to round figures
Houses O.P.D. Flats	73 27	44 200	56	44·8	1,340	2,740	1·17	
Houses O.P.D. Flats	73 27	60 200	74	59	1,017	2,417	1·10	
Houses O.P.D. Flats	50 50	100 200	133	106·4	564	1,964	0·99	
Houses O.P.D. Flats	— 100	 200	200	160	375	1,775	0·94	
Houses O.P.D. Flats	100 —	44	44	35	1,714	3,114	1·24	

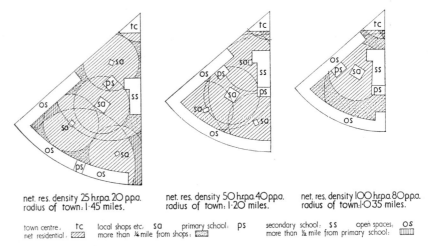

net. res. density 25 h.r.p.a. 20 p.p.a.   net. res. density 50 h.r.p.a. 40 p.p.a.   net. res. density 100 h.r.p.a. 80 p.p.a.
radius of town: 1·45 miles.   radius of town: 1·20 miles.   radius of town: 1·035 miles.

town centre: tc   local shops etc: sa   primary school: ps   secondary school: ss   open spaces: os
net residential: ▨   more than ¼ mile from shops: ▨   more than ½ mile from primary school: ▥

FIG. 82.   The effect of residential density on town size.   A "slice" of 10,000 population is shown.   All elements other than net residential remain constant.

In practice, it is only the inducement of special Government subsidies which makes it feasible for local authorities to build high flats, where the great cost of land allows them to qualify for these special grants.   In basic economic terms, dealing with human effort rather than with the artificialities of high finance, it seems perfectly clear that it is hardly worth while to build such structures, since, as will presently be shown, the increase in compactness of the urban area which it is often suggested can be secured by their use is largely illusory, and the only advantages which thus attach to them are the dramatic contrast which they may afford with other lower buildings in the urban scene, and, conversely the fine and spacious views obtainable from their upper storeys.

For the purposes of these calculations it seems reasonable to assume an average density of 120 habitable rooms per acre for flats.   The number of tall blocks at a higher density likely to be built outside the central areas of large cities is hardly great enough to justify a significantly higher average density.

Much valuable information about the design, layout, densities and costs of flats is given in " Flats and Houses 1958 " published by H.M.S.O.   It greatly amplifies but does not in any material way contradict what has been written above.

Old persons' dwellings.   These are generally regarded as dwellings to be provided for old people who, while not so frail as to require institutional care, require specially arranged dwellings in order to live comfortably and happily.   These special arrangements include internal fittings designed to avoid the need for stooping and stretching. So far as the type and arrangement of buildings is concerned the principal needs may be summarised as :

1. The avoidance of the need to climb stairs.

2. A pleasant outlook, not segregated, but reasonably quiet, since the inhabitants of old persons' dwellings are likely to spend a larger proportion of time in their homes than younger people.

3. No large gardens which need to be individually maintained.

There is, of course, no intention that old people when they reach a certain age should automatically go into old persons' dwellings which are, as already explained, primarily for those who tend to be somewhat frail or in doubtful health.

Accommodation may be either in the form of bungalows or in ground floor flats according to the desires of the potential residents. Bungalows have the advantage that they provide, for the most part, the kind of home more similar to the kind of home that occupants have previously known than do flats. On the other hand in flats it is easier to provide centralised heating, etc., which makes life easier. In tall blocks, with lifts, special old persons' flats could, of course, be provided on any floor without the necessity for climbing stairs, but two factors militate against this: (1) there is always a chance of lifts breaking down, and an elderly person, perhaps with a weak heart, living on a top floor, might find great difficulty in reaching home, and, (2) many old people dislike the idea of living high up, complaining of vertigo when looking out of a window from a height.

In the nature of things old people's dwellings are for small households, a great majority of which will be occupied either by one or two people. It is desirable that they should be mixed with ordinary housing accommodation in fairly small units, for a large colony inhabited solely by old people is likely to be somewhat depressing in atmosphere. There is the advantage too that, not only does the nearby presence of younger people provide some stimulus to the old, but in the event of some emergency help can quickly reach them. On the other hand they should not, if possible, be placed cheek by jowl with ordinary residences with children, as the noise, inseparable from assemblies of children is likely to be tiresome to the old.

The actual siting of old persons' dwellings in detail is therefore likely to present problems. It seems reasonable to suggest that the accommodation required for old persons' dwellings should be split equally as between bungalows and flats. As mentioned earlier any old persons' dwellings temporarily not required for old people can very appropriately be used for households without children, which introduces a welcome flexibility. So far as bungalows are concerned, a common and sensible arrangement is to group them around a communally arranged quadrangle, which may perhaps include a bowling green with small individual gardens behind.

Old persons' dwellings will probably average one and a half habitable rooms each. When in the form of flats their density will, of course, be no different from ordinary flats. When in the form of bungalows they can well be developed at twelve to the acre, the common green in front tending to lower the density, the small garden at the rear tending to raise it. Twelve bungalows to the acre averaging one and a half habitable rooms each gives a density of eighteen habitable rooms to the acre, and at an occupancy rate of 0·8, 14½ persons to the acre.

We are now in a position to suggest an overall net combined density for all types of dwelling in the proportion originally arrived at of 73% of rooms in houses, 20% in flats and 7% in old persons' dwellings. This may be expressed in the following Table.

Combined Density per 100 Rooms

Houses:	73 rooms at 44 habitable rooms per acre	=	1·66 acres
Flats:	20 rooms at 120 habitable rooms per acre	=	0·17 ,,
Old Persons' Dwellings—			
Flats:	3½ rooms at 120 habitable rooms per acre	=	0·03 ,,
Bungalows:	3½ rooms at 18 habitable rooms per acre	=	0·20 ,,
		Total	2·06 ,,

Rooms per acre   48·5
Persons per acre, at O.R. 0·8, 38·80

It will be convenient to reduce these somewhat awkward figures, based upon many approximations, to round figures, 50 habitable rooms per acre, and 40 persons per acre.   If justification is needed for this slight upward adjustment it can be found in the fact that if some blocks of tall flats are introduced the flat density will rise a little above 120 habitable rooms per acre, while, on the other hand, old persons' dwellings in the form of bungalows could perfectly satisfactorily be developed at a somewhat higher density than 12 to the acre.

The preceding discussions and calculations frankly assume a rising standard of living of which an appropriate proportion will be utilised in raising accommodation standards and a general spread of " bourgeois " dwelling standards among the " working classes ."   Many, both of the extreme right and of the extreme left would attack this latter assumption as unjustifiable, and, for very different reasons, would urge the adoption of much higher densities in the interests either of a supposed economy of expenditure on dwellings or on the other hand of a collectivist conception of society in which a high degree of communal living is facilitated by dense flat development. It is bound to be a matter of personal preference and political opinion where one's view on this matter lies.

It will be well to emphasise once more that these figures of density do no more than suggest a reasonable norm for areas of comprehensive development in this country when the habits and income levels of the inhabitants also represent a fair cross-section of the population. They can certainly be varied upwards or downwards to a substantial extent without living conditions suffering material detriment.   For example, in an extremely prosperous surburban town it is probable that a much lower average density would be advisable, since the demand for large houses with large gardens would be much greater than the average. On the other hand, in a northern industrial town, bleak climatic conditions and the virtual absence of members of the highest income groups is likely to lead to a considerable reduction below the average demand for houses with large gardens, and it would be foolish to set aside land for residential purposes which would not, in fact, be needed.

It is of the utmost importance to realise that any sensible housing policy should aim at providing houses with gardens for the households which desire them, and flats for the households which desire them. At present, Government policy forces local authorities to concentrate flats in areas where land values are highest, and to provide them for families with children, while on the other hand, in outlying areas, the supply of flats may be well below the demand. In any case, as pointed out earlier, as far as private enterprise development is concerned, many households which would be well suited to flat life are quite unable to live in a flat because they cannot afford the rent charged for any flatted accommodation comparable in quality to the house in which they already live.

Though it may be difficult to believe this, the whole question of location of flats is determined at present by quite artificial and fallacious economics. It costs no more in terms of material and human effort to build tower blocks ten storeys high in country towns than in the heart of London. It can confidently be said that a good many country towns would benefit by the erection of a few tower blocks, while London would benefit from the cessation of all flat building and the erection of many more single family houses. Additional arguments about the saving in land effected by high density flats and the increase in journeys to work caused by the spread of comparatively low densities are, as we shall shortly see, quite fallacious, and as we have already seen in broad outline, in discussing in Chapter 4 the effect on the size of London of adopting different residential densities.

The Table on page 233, as well as showing the effects on combined density of varying house density and flat density is also related to the New Town illustrated in Fig. 68, the densities in which are based upon those I have suggested earlier in the chapter. It is assumed that, for the purposes of the Table whatever may be done to vary net residential density the other elements in the Town remain constant. The Town, as designed, has a total acreage of 2,900 made up of 1,500 acres devoted to net residential use, and the remaining 1,400 acres to non-residential uses of various kinds. The Table shows quite clearly that no variations of net density within the range of the practicable and probable have any appreciable effect on the overall size of the town, and that even improbable and impracticable variations have surprisingly little effect.

Anyone who has carefully followed the preceding pages can easily see that the notion that net residential density appreciably affects the spread of towns is completely fallacious, but before being satisfied that any particular density standard is the optimum we must consider the effect of density upon food production, cost and appearance.

17-3. DENSITY OF RESIDENTIAL DEVELOPMENT IN RELATION TO FOOD PRODUCTION

The history of the investigations into the productivity of farmland and of gardens undertaken over the last ten years or so in order to try to determine the effect upon national food production of developing at various densities is a quite remarkable one. It is extremely well summarised in a booklet entitled " The Garden Controversy " by R. H. Best and J. T. Ward, published in 1956 by the Department of Agricultural Economics of Wye College. The subject is very complicated, and although somewhat remote from Planning it has an important bearing on Planning policy. There is no space to do more here than summarise very briefly the contents of the pamphlet referred to which readers who wish to understand the subject thoroughly should consult.

There is no exact information about how gardens were used or what they produced before the 1939-45 war, but clearly they were treated partly as a place for leisure and partly for the production of vegetables and fruit. After the beginning of the war the need for food production from domestic sources became great. In 1944 a Parliamentary reply produced the information that produce from gardens, allotments and similar plots of land represented 10% of home-produced food.

After the war the large amounts of land required for new housing and schools caused great alarm in agricultural circles, and there was increasing pressure for urban Planning standards to be tightened. It was generally assumed that the more agricultural land that was taken for urban uses the greater would be the loss for food production. The Ministry of Housing and Local Government, itself appeared to accept this view unreservedly for both in the " Handbook on Residential Density " and " Houses, 1953 " the need for increasing net residential densities in order to minimise the loss of agricultural land was stressed.

In the pursuit of the campaign for higher densities there were some curious alliances. A considerable body of architectural thought is, as already mentioned, in favour of higher densities for aesthetic reasons; on the other hand, the farmers, whose point of view has often been vociferously expressed by the National Farmers' Union, very much disliked the idea of losing land which, after a long period of agricultural depression, was now earning good dividends. Their dislike was intensified by the financially unfavourable terms they could secure for land compulsorily acquired from them under the Town and Country Planning Act of 1947. These two lobbies produced a strong impression.

However, a series of surveys was carried out, which is described at some length in the pamphlet under discussion. The most important facts to be derived from these surveys appear to be as follows. In 1944 in England and Wales about 66% of all houses had gardens and 45% of houses grew some vegetables and fruit. The proportion of houses with cultivated gardens varies very much in different parts of the country, generally decreasing from south to north. For example, in the south-east region some 75% of households had cultivated ground in 1944, in the north-east only 25% and in the north-west only 11%. Clearly climate has something to do with this, but social habit, the varying incidence of hard manual work by day, and even, probably, economic status have something to do with it.

A survey of gardens in suburban London showed that on the average about 14% of the total net garden plot (i.e., ignoring access roads etc.), was devoted to food crops, and it is very interesting to note that this figure is divisible into 21% on Council estates and only 9% on private estates. It has become clear that as the net density of housing decreases and gardens become correspondingly larger, there is a reduction in the proportion of occupiers who grow no food crops at all, and for the proportion of the plot cultivated to rise. This alone is sufficient to cast doubt upon the assumption that the national interest in relation to food production demands higher rather than lower net densities for housing.

It is necessary to go into some detail and make careful comparisons in order to arrive at a reliable conclusion. Gardens and allotments are almost entirely limited to the production of vegetables and fruit, with a little production of livestock. On agricultural land only market gardeners grow a similar selection of products, while farms generally produce the more basic commodities, such as cereals, milk, meat and larger livestock. It is therefore sometimes suggested that the output from market gardens should be used in this form of comparison, but this is not sound, for only in a limited number of cases does new development take place on land devoted to market gardens. On the whole it is likely to occur on better than average farm land, and for this reason it is this kind of land which is used for the purposes of general comparison. Since, on the average, only about 14% of an area formerly used for farm land and now used for housing, produces food, and since only about half the land taken for major urban uses will go to housing development, the remainder, such as industry, open space and education, being virtually unproductive for food purposes, this means that when farm land is taken for urban development only about 7% of the land is likely to remain in cultivation.

The next question is to consider the category of prices used for comparison. If one were only concerned with the direct comparison of physical productivity of gardens and farmland then the same categories should be used, but this comparison would be misleading from the economic point of view, for production is only completed when the product has reached the consumer. Vegetables produced in a garden are available for immediate consumption, and a household growing its own vegetables is clearly saving the retail price of food which would otherwise have to be bought at a shop, so that it is logical to value garden output at retail prices. In the case of food produced on the farm a highly organised and costly process has to be gone through before the food can actually reach the consumer. The cost of this may easily amount to as much of the cost of production on the farm. To get a proper comparison, therefore, the retail price of garden produce should be compared with the " Farm Gate " price of farm food.

Strictly speaking, not only the cost of marketing the food but also the costs of producing it should be compared, but while there can be little doubt that

costs of production are much lower in gardens than on farms, and the work and skill of the food producer in the garden is given for nothing and represents an effort which, if there were no garden, would not be put to any other productive use the difficulties of true comparison are said to be so great that this has been ignored.

The gross output of better than average farmland has been put at about £45 per cultivated acre at Farm Gate prices, while the retail value, of domestically grown food, excluding livestock products, amounts to about £300 per cultivated acre per year. On this basis, gardens and allotments seems to be considerably more productive than general farmland, or even specialised market garden land, which has an average net output of £110 per cultivated acre.

On this basis, with only 14% of the housing estate cultivated for food crops, the value of production per house plot acre is about £42, only a little less than that of the equivalent area of farmland taken out of use by housing development. If one considers the effect of urban development generally, i.e., that only about half the land taken is for housing purposes, the remainder being agriculturally productive, then the final result is an average of about £21 of foodstuff for each developed acre, which is about half the value of output from better than average farmland (£45 per acre) and a good deal below the average output from all types of farmland, which is £36 per acre.

Best and Ward conclude that there appears no reason to doubt that the value of food produced per house plot acre is probably as much as that produced from the type of farmland likely to be taken for housing development, and that if costs of production are taken into account, and productivity assessed in terms of net output the comparison is even more favourable to gardens, while if the price subsidies at present given for major farm crops and livestock products, but not for fruit and vegetables were allowed for the comparison would be more favourable still. They further draw attention to the fact that while the figures used to measure garden output are based on the fact that only 14% of the average houseplot is used for growing crops, one survey indicates that 66% of the average houseplot was potentially capable of cultivation, so that in a national emergency it would be possible to increase output through gardens considerably, and that the major urban uses other than housing contain a large proportion of open space which could also be used for food production in an emergency. If we were in danger of starving many football pitches would be brought into food production. The very great expansion of domestic production during the 1939-45 war shows that this is not, by any means, a theoretical concept.

It is sometimes argued that even if gardens are more productive than farmland, they can grow only a very limited range of crops, mainly food and vegetables, which cannot replace the basic commodities of meat, milk and cereals which are lost through the development of agricultural land, but such an argument overlooks the high vitamin content of garden produce, and makes no allowance for the nutritional value of an adequate supply of fresh vegetables. But what is most important, it ignores the scale of the problem, for the probable loss of land to urban uses would only lead to a very small fall in the output of livestock products and cereals, which could, in fact be more than replaced by a higher production elsewhere, whereas the provision of adequate gardens could lead to a relatively large increase in the consumption of vegetables and fruit.

We now consider the effect of varying density upon the proportion of house plot devoted to food production. The information available here is not very precise or comprehensive, but samples show that in Southampton the proportion of total house plot area under fruit and vegetables declines from 33% at a density of 8 houses to the acre to 24% at 12 to the acre. In Bristol the corresponding decline was from 23% to 14%, in Doncaster from 12% at 9 to the acre to 3% at 13 to the acre, and in Hull from 25% at 7 to the acre to 15% at 11 to the acre. The average percentage for the higher densities quoted was 14%, which was the same as that found in a previous survey, and for the lower densities 23%. It thus at least seems clear that domestic food production tends to increase as housing development becomes more open.

Taking the Southampton case for purposes of illustration, assuming that a local authority estate of 96 houses were to be built, then at a density of 8 houses to the acre 12 acres would be needed, while at 12 houses to the acre 8 acres would be needed. At the higher density four acres of agricultural land would be saved which, with an average output of £45 per acre, represents a gross saving of £180 worth of food, but by decreasing the size of house plots only 24% of the 8 acres (about 2 acres) would be cultivated for fruit and vegetables, which, with an average output of £300 per cultivated acre gives a total production of £600. At the lower density 33% of the area (about 4 acres) would probably be cultivated, giving a total production of £1,200. In this case, therefore, building at the higher density would result in an actual loss of food to the extent of £420 per annum.

Such conclusions might begin to lose their point if the additional loss of farmland due to building at open rather than high densities were so large that it formed a significant proportion of the total area of agricultural land. At a building rate of 300,000 houses a year a saving of approximately 6,000 acres is to be obtained by building at the density of 15 to 16 houses per acre recommended by the Ministry of Housing and Local Government instead of 11 or 12 which was the average net density of 48 postwar housing schemes examined by the Ministry of Housing and Local Government. As this rate of house construction is unlikely to continue over the whole of the next twenty years, the actual area of land saved in that period might not be much more than 100,000 acres.

It has been estimated that half a million acres will be needed for development purposes in the foreseeable future. Of this about one half will be taken for housing, so that the tightening of density recommended would only represent an area of 50 to 60,000 acres over the next 20 years, which constitutes between one half and one quarter of 1% of the total acreage of crops and grass ($24\frac{1}{2}$ million acres) in England and Wales. It is therefore obvious that the saving of land which could be achieved by increasing house densities is negligible.

One would hope that no more would now be heard of propaganda for raising food production by increasing densities. Yet it has probably bitten too deep to be eradicated by any kind of reasoned refutation, and in lay circles, as well as semi-informed circles, the old cry still goes up. It is a great pity that the Ministry of Housing and Local Government which, as already mentioned, did so much to preach the doctrine of increasing housing densities in the interests of food production, has done nothing in the light of the evidence which has been produced to recant. It is perhaps difficult for any Government Department publicly to eat its own words, yet it is very much in the public interest in this case that it should be done.

It is important to remember that the food production aspect of density is after all only a subsidiary one. On this one can hardly do better than quote the words of Derek Senior who, writing in " Town and Country Planning " in March 1955, said: " I would add that for myself I do not regard these findings as an argument for covering farmland with semi-detached cottages at 8 to the acre. I have never considered a house to be primarily a machine for maximising food production. I still prefer mixed development, averaging ten or twelve to the acre, with single persons' flats in tall blocks, detached cottages, and a predominance of short terraces and linked semis forming ' towney ' street pictures but concealing long back gardens. I am unmoved by the knowledge that so high a density must entail some degree of avoidable dependence upon food imports. The only people who are now obliged to insist that no new dwellings shall be built at densities higher than 8 to the acre (or stand self-convicted of hypocrisy) are those who for years have insisted that the over-riding consideration of density policy must be the interests of food production. When they have extricated themselves by quietly dropping the subject we may hope to get this density business discussed in rational terms."

17-4. DENSITY OF RESIDENTIAL DEVELOPMENT IN RELATION TO COST AND APPEARANCE

The initial difficulty with this subject is that one is brought face to face with the unsatisfactory nature of statements such as " the greatest good for the greatest number ", which contain two independent variables. So with residential density and economy: should one seek to discover the density which shall provide the cheapest possible accommodation or, on the other hand, that which will provide the best possible living conditions? It would be possible to find people willing to advocate something very close to each of these extremes as the most truly economical method of development.

My own preference is to postulate certain minimum requirements for reasonable comfort which ought not to be infringed except under quite extraordinary pressure, and then to see what extra cost may be involved by raising these standards from the tolerable to the desirable.

I should regard the following as a reasonable minimum: no family with young children having to live in a flat, 70 feet between the fronts and backs of dwellings facing or backing onto each other, individual back gardens for all houses, lay-out designed so as to ensure reasonable accessibility for vehicles, and seemliness in architecture and landscape.   And as desirable: no family having to be accommodated in a flat unless it would positively prefer this to living in a house, back gardens 50 feet to 60 feet deep except for corner plots, with a proportion of considerably larger gardens, a proportion of detached and semi-detached houses for those able and willing to pay for them, and a high standard of architectural and landscape treatment.

There are a number of factors to be taken into account.   There is the cost of development to the developer; the appearance of residential areas; the cost of repairs and maintenance to the local authority; the blending of dwelling types and sizes to produce the highest occupancy rate consistent with comfortable living; finally, and crucially, there is the general comfort and well-being of the residents.   To me it is axiomatic that one should cater for their actual needs and desires, so far as these can be ascertained, rather than what, for the justification of particular theories of design, one would like these needs and desires to be.   Of course any able and conscientious developer ought to be bold enough to introduce good ideas which, because of the inherent conservatism of mankind, may at first arouse some dislike in the residents.   But he should not go too far.

The question of appearance should be considered from at least two standpoints: (i) the extent to which, as " consumers," contemporary notions of residential design as regards its " street picture " aspect, satisfy the public; and (ii) the extent to which these notions can be made to agree with sound principles of estate management, valuation and land use.

So far as I understand the position, an important section of the architectural profession deplores the lack of " urbanity " in housing carried out in this country over the last half-century, would like to remedy this, not only by building more flats but by building houses at a higher density, and prays in aid of this policy the saving of land and, more recently, the saving in road costs which can be achieved.

In fact it is plot frontage rather than density as such which determines road costs and affects appearance.

If one regards the street side of a row of houses as the public side and the back garden side as the private side, which seems to me an unassailably correct way of looking at the matter, then for the sake of avoiding unsightly views of washing, etc., from the public side—and of preserving the privacy of the private side, one will seek to block the view between all gaps in buildings with screen walls, trellises or hedges.   This will produce an effect of continuity from the public side and one will not from that side be aware of whether the density is high or low, for the only clue to this will be the size of the house block, which determines the frequency of road junctions.   Such a policy is perfectly consistent with the use of all kinds of variation of building line and of orientation of buildings in relation to the line of the carriageway. The only limitation on the architect is that he cannot display the rear elevations of his buildings.

It has sometimes been represented to me by very uncompromising architects that the objection remains that, even with this arrangement, if back gardens are made very deep the visual effect from the interior of the house block is ruined because the proportion between vertical and horizontal

elements is wrong.   I cannot take this very seriously.   The interior of a house block with flourishing gardens is so punctuated with trees and bushes that there are few points within it from which enough of it can be seen for this rather special point to be important.

It seems desirable to emphasise further the very wide variations in density which can occur without any appreciable difference in general appearance from the public side.   For example, in Fig. 84 densities vary from 8·21 houses per acre to 16·43 houses per acre (excluding layout No. 1, the appearance of which *would* be different) yet, from the point of view of someone walking through the area each would look virtually identical.

Back garden width and plot depth can be varied indefinitely yet not affect appearance if buildings are more or less continuous. If one takes as a norm a plot 30 feet wide by 120 feet deep, giving a density of 12 houses to the acre, then reduction of the plot width to 20 feet will increase the density to 18 houses to the acre.   If, further, the back garden depth is reduced from 60 feet to 40 feet the density goes up to nearly 22 houses to the acre.   Many architects would regard the last named as a very satisfactory density and the first named as very unsatisfactory yet so far as anything within an architects' range of interest and competence is concerned the results could be identical.

A matter about which many architects feel strongly is the Englishman's preference for a semi-detached house over a terrace house if he cannot afford a detached house.   This, I am afraid, is a habit which is unlikely to change for a very long time.   Here cost, density and appearance all come into the picture.   Terrace houses are cheaper since, for example, in a terrace of six houses there are only seven side walls as against nine with three pairs of semi-detached, and numerous other small economies are possible.   A terrace of six need only occupy the width of the houses plus two four-foot strips at the ends as against six such strips for three pairs of houses.   This makes a very considerable difference both to density and to road costs.

The cost of small detached and semi-detached houses is high in cash and high in loss of appearance, yet we are bound to accept the cash cost at least as regards that part of the population which directly chooses its own houses; and we could, I am sure, greatly reduce the aesthetic cost if local planning authorities, supported by the Minister, exercised a rigorous control over the layout and external appearance of private enterprise housing.

We now come to the actual relative cost in any given circumstances of building at different densities.   To put the matter in its simplest terms, the wider the house plots, the greater the amount of land and the length of road needed per house, so that lowering density by this means inevitably entails increased costs.   Also, the greater the depth of house plots, the greater the amount of land per house which will be required; but the length of road needed per house, given sensible layout, may actually diminish as plot depths increase, so that with house plots of constant width, the most economical density depends upon the relative level of costs as between land and roads.

This best can be illustrated by some drawings.   For the sake of simplicity I have assumed standard plots of 30-feet width, and houses 25 feet deep.   The argument is valid whatever the width of the plots and whether the houses are detached, semi-detached or terrace.

In all these diagrams, a distance of 70 feet between the front walls of facing houses is assumed.

It has been assumed that there must be a carriage-way reasonably accessible to every house, generally within 35 feet; advantage has not been taken of the savings in first cost which can be obtained by the use of long lengths of footpath access.

An average depth of 35 feet is adopted for back gardens of corner plots with sloping rear boundaries. This is much greater than the permitted bye-law minimum, but constitutes a standard below which congestion and squalor are liable to arise. Corner plots have also been so arranged that no building shall be nearer than 35 feet to the centre line of a road. (See Fig. 84.)

Any system of building up corner sites completely with houses, while it effects economy in road construction, must inevitably entail very bad arrangement of back gardens and increased building costs. This difficulty is overcome where corners are closed by flats, as shown, for example, on pages 13–16 of " Houses, 1953 ", and in Fig. 83, but this device has not been used in Fig. 84 in order to avoid tiresome arithmetical complications.

There is no simple mathematical rule which will relate density to road and land costs, so one must proceed empirically. A price of £750 an acre for land and £8 a foot run for roads has been assumed. The former of course, now bears no relation to land costs in an area in this country within metropolitan influence but a substantial area of unimproved land elsewhere might still cost about this figure, and in the case of a New Town, where land can be acquired at agricultural value, the price would of course be much lower. It would take too much space to demonstrate the effect on cost in relation to density resulting from changes in the relative costs of land and roads but the information in the table incorporated in the diagram makes it easy for anyone interested to experiment.

Obviously, the higher the cost of roads relative to land, the more it pays to keep down the amount of road per house and, if the contrary obtains, to reduce the amount of land per house.

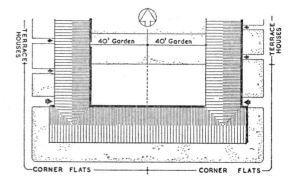

FIG. 83. The use of flats to close the view at road junctions as illustrated in " Houses, 1953 ". Eighty feet is a very short distance between backs of houses but this does not affect the principle.

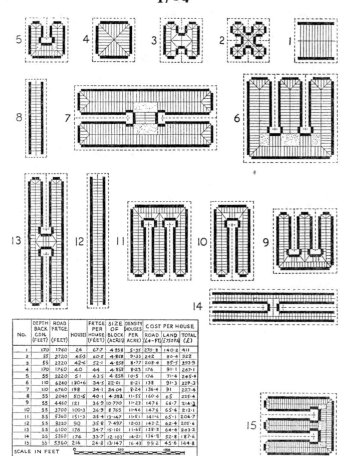

No.	DEPTH BACK GDN. (FEET)	ROAD FRTGE. (FEET)	HOUSES	FRTGE PER HOUSE (FEET)	SIZE OF BLOCK (ACRES)	DENSITY HOUSES PER ACRE	COST PER HOUSE		
							ROAD (£4-FT)	LAND (£750PA)	TOTAL (£)
1	170	1760	26	67·7	4·858	5·35	270·8	140·2	411
2	55	2720	45·3	60·5	4·858	9·33	242	80·4	322
3	55	2220	42·6	52·1	4·858	8·77	208·4	85·5	293·9
4	170	1760	40	44	4·858	8·23	176	91·1	267·1
5	55	2220	51	43·5	4·858	10·5	174	71·4	245·4
6	110	6240	180·6	34·5	22·01	8·21	138	91·3	229·3
7	110	6760	198	34·1	24·04	8·24	136·4	91	227·4
8	55	2040	50·6	40·1	4·382	11·55	160·4	65	225·4
9	55	4460	121	36·9	10·770	11·23	147·6	66·7	214·3
10	55	3700	100·3	36·9	8·765	11·44	147·6	65·6	213·1
11	55	5360	151·3	35·4	13·147	11·51	141·6	65·1	206·7
12	55	3220	90	35·8	7·497	12·03	143·2	62·4	205·6
13	55	6100	176	34·7	15·101	11·65	138·3	64·4	203·2
14	55	5860	174	33·7	12·103	14·21	134·8	52·8	187·6
15	55	5360	216	24·8	13·147	16·43	99·2	45·6	144·8
SCALE IN FEET									

FIG. 84. An illustration of the ways in which the amounts of land and roads involved interact surprisingly to affect the total cost of site development.

The drawings in Fig. 84 are numbered in descending order of the combined cost of land and roads. A glance at the table will show, however, that the separated amounts for land and roads do not descend in the same order. For example, in the case of No. 8, the cost of road per house is higher than for Nos. 6 and 7, though the total cost is lower because the density is much higher. Conversely the cost of land in No. 9 is higher than in No. 8, though the latter's total cost is higher.

It is also interesting to find that road costs do not fall as densities rise in any regular way. Leaving out of account No. 15, which is not comparable with the remainder, it is true that No. 1 has the lowest density and the highest road costs and No. 14 has the lowest road costs and the highest density, but

No. 7 costs only £136 per house for roads, with a density of 8·24 houses per acre, while Nos. 2, 3, 5, 8, 9, 10, 11, 12, 13 and 14 all have both higher densities and higher road costs. This is surprising, and it is important, because although legislation can do all kinds of things to reduce the amount paid for land by the developer or occupier, it is powerless to do much about the cost of roads.

Starting with No. 1, we see the effect of a quite unintelligent layout. Very low density and the complete waste of long return frontages combine to produce extremely costly development. No. 2 is not quite so bad because some economy of road frontage is achieved by the arrangement of plots at corners, thus raising the density considerably, but this is nullified by the use of four culs-de-sac so short that little advantage is gained from them. No. 3 is an improvement on No. 2, because although land costs are increased, road costs are more than comparably decreased. No. 4 is better still because although density is even lower than for Nos. 2 and 3, road costs per house are very low. However, at the given cost levels of land and roads, it pays to increase density by inserting a single longer cul-de-sac which, as in No. 5, results in lowering the cost both of land and roads compared with No. 4. From this we can deduce some elementary principles. Every road junction involves a waste of frontage—some 320 feet. The fewer road junctions there are, therefore, the lower the cost of road per house. The cheapest possible form of development is to use the shallowest possible plots and the fewest possible through roads, as in No. 14. This produces a thoroughly bad layout from all points of view except road costs.

If a more compact block is used, road costs per house decrease as the size of the block increases, because the longer the sides of the block, the greater the proportion of economical plots of normal frontage compared with the necessarily wide-fronted corner plots. This is true if no culs-de-sac are used but applies more fully if they are, for the longer the cul-de-sac the greater the benefit derived from it.

The insertion of a cul-de-sac involves the loss of 320 feet of frontage at its entrance, but this loss is partly compensated for at the closed end because it is possible to gain 190 feet of frontage provided the block is large enough to allow the grouping of houses shown in No. 5 and in the subsequent examples which include culs-de-sac, leaving a net loss of 130 feet compared with the net net loss of 640 feet every time a through road is used. The other plots fronting on the cul-de-sac will be of normal frontage, and obviously the longer it is the more of them there will be and the greater the proportion of normal frontage plots in the layout as a whole. It is because of this that No. 11 is cheaper than No. 9, though in other ways they are exactly similar.

We see from Nos. 6 and 7 and 11 and 13 that a block with two culs-de-sac placed vertically opposite is cheaper than one with two culs-de-sac parallel to each other. This is because the ratio of perimeter to area is greater with a long narrow block than with a more compact one. But the difference is not very great, and the advantage of greater ease of intercommunication is so substantial that it could seldom be justifiable to use a layout as shown in No. 13 in preference to one as shown in No. 11. A compromise would be to use a layout with two shorter culs-de-sac, vertically opposite. If these were

450 feet long, with back gardens 55 feet long, the combined cost of land and roads per house would be intermediate between Nos. 10 and 11, and would be £210·6. The density would be 11·4 houses per acre; there would be 36·2 feet of road frontage per house and the block would measure 1,130 feet by 460 feet, quite an acceptable shape if it were bisected by a footpath to improve pedestrian communication. This applies to any layout with culs-de-sac, but particularly to the longer, narrow blocks.

I think we can conclude that layouts on the lines of Nos. 9, 10, 11, and the extra one just described, all separated by a difference of less than £8 per house in combined cost of road and land, are all acceptable as regards ease of communication, potentialities for attractive appearance, and development costs. If we increase depths of back gardens greatly above the 55 feet common to all these, land costs rise unduly. If we reduce them markedly their general usefulness and amenity is greatly diminished, and so is their food-producing capacity.

If we substitute plots 21 feet wide (the kind of development used in the "Houses, 1953" examples) for 30 feet wide plots and apply the results to the layout of No. 11, we get No. 15—216 houses; 24·8 feet of road per house; density 16·43; and total cost £144·8, a dramatic reduction in costs obtained quite simply, at considerable sacrifice to the resident but having little to do with the interaction of costs and density since like is not being compared with like.

We must now consider the question of the cost of repairs and maintenance of carriageways, footpaths and verges. This is a subject very fully and ably dealt with by Mr. J. Mercer in his paper published in the January, 1955, issue of "The Chartered Surveyor" (see also "The Chartered Surveyor" for February, 1955, page 679). One of Mr. Mercer's main conclusions was that the initial savings in cost secured by reducing widths of carriageways to the bare minimum and so arranging the layout as to give long distance pedestrian access only to a substantial proportion of houses, is considerably outweighed because of the greatly increased wear and tear on verges, kerbs and footpaths through improper use of vehicles and, less directly, by the increased cost of refuse collection, postal deliveries and other social services occasioned by long pedestrian access-ways. I agree with Mr. Mercer, and for that reason have not mentioned the ways in which the extra land costs involved in decreasing density may be balanced by the larger proportion of narrow culs-de-sac and pedestrian access-ways which can be used.

The difficulty of entirely separating aesthetic and economic considerations when dealing with residential layout will now, I hope, be apparent. It is clearly desirable to make the most economical use of available resources by not using more land or more roads and piped and wired services per house than is necessary to secure a given result, provided always that this is not done at the expense of the reasonable design needs for securing good appearance, or of the needs of the inhabitants in terms of convenience of intercommunication and safety. Conversely, no design, however aesthetically admirable is, in my view, justifiable if it sacrifices reasonable economy and convenience.

17-5. THE DESIGN OF RESIDENTIAL LAYOUTS

Residential layout is here taken to mean the design of any area smaller in extent than a neighbourhood and devoted principally to dwellings, including the arrangement of the road system, the division of land into plots and the approximate positioning of buildings, but not the design of the buildings themselves.   Here the Planner, as such, should make a great contribution, for neither the architect, the landscape architect the engineer, nor the chartered surveyor singly embraces all the skills which have to be exercised.

The wide range of the Planner's training should enable him to prepare a design which, though the specialists concerned may need to have minor amendments made to it, does not violate any of the fundamental principles of their respective skills.   Designs by engineers *qua* engineers often emphasise to the exclusion of all else the drainage requirements of the area, and those of chartered surveyors *qua* surveyors the maximum utilisation of every foot of road frontage, while the design of the architect *qua* architect is often extremely uneconomical, fails to provde a satifactory system of communications and does not effectively relate thie various elements in the design as regards their functions, however well it does so visually.

Of these four, however, the architect is clearly the one who is entitled to feel the gravest doubts about the wisdom of the layout plan being prepared by someone else; he can claim with some force that to work successfully he must be able to control the lines of roads and the precise shapes and sizes of open spaces, as well as designing the actual buildings and their precise positions, and that to do all this within the framework of an existing design is unduly hampering.   One cannot but feel sympathy with this, but the fact remains that the buildings and visual treatment generally are only one part, though an extremely important part, of residential layout, and that economy and convenience, in its broadest sense must also be secured.   It would be good if more architects could be trained to understand something about the general requirements for a good residential layout.

Roads must be arranged so that they provide adequate access to every building for vehicles and pedestrians and form an efficient systcm of inter-communication between all parts of the site and its surroundings.   In order to secure this their gradients must not be excessive, their widths must be adequate and their junctions be safe. (See Chapter 11).   The cost of constructing roads is very great, so that it is essential that the minimum length of road consistent with the satisfactory fulfilment of its functions shall be planned.   It is generally most convenient for gas, water and electricity supply lines and sewers to follow the routes of roads, at least for the greater part of their lengths, which reinforces the need for an economical road system.   In the case of sewers it is essential, except in quite exceptional circumstances, that all should be laid at levels which allow the drainage of buildings to flow into them by gravity and at gradients which enable the whole sewerage system also to operate by gravity.   This requirement often exercises a strong effect upon the road layout.

The amount and distribution of open space, by which is here meant all land not covered by roads and buildings, depends chiefly upon the density of buildings, which affects garden size; their height, which affects the distances required between buildings; and their architectural qualities and grouping, which affects the dimensions of open spaces adjoining them.   The proportion of open space to be devoted to common use and that to be reserved for individual households is also a factor.

The density and height of buildings also affect the spacing of the road pattern.

A residential layout must be prepared with all these factors under consideration; the human mind cannot consciously think about several factors simultaneously in any degree of detail, and it therefore follows that the preparation of the Plan must proceed from the general to the particular.   However, the first rough sketch, which is necessary as a point of departure, must be prepared so that it does not prevent any of the requirements just mentioned being fulfilled.   In order to do this successfully, therefore, they must all be simultaneously present in the designer's mind in general terms, a feat which practice makes possible.

Before even a rough draft can be prepared some decisions must be made.   Assuming that the site forms part of a comprehensive development area, some of these decisions will already have been taken; the overall density will have been determined, the areas of land to be devoted to purposes other than residential will have been selected and the routes of all roads which have a function greater than providing access to buildings will have been laid down.

It remains to decide in general terms the approximate sizes of individual buildings and the distribution of open space between private and public or semi-public use, for both of these will have a fundamental effect on the design.

At a given density the average depth of house plots depends upon their average width.   This, in turn, depends upon the widths of the houses and the proportion of detached, semi-detached and terrace houses, for the proportion of frontage occupied by spaces between houses is, evidently, roughly in inverse proportion to the average number of houses in a group, i.e., with party walls.   The depth of house plots also depends upon the proportion of public and semi-public open space, other than comparatively narrow strips situated at the front and rear of houses (which can be counted as part of the house plots) for, at any particular density, this can be found out of the land which would otherwise be included in house plots.

It is improbable that at so early a stage full details of house types and sizes, and the numbers of each required, will be available, and, so far as the distribution of detached, semi-detached and terrace houses is concerned, the exact determination of this depends to some extent upon the details of the site.   However, precision is not required for the purposes of a rough draft Plan; sufficient information only is needed to secure that the average plot depths used, which determine the total road frontage created, will result in that frontage being neither greatly more nor greatly less than that required for the number and types of houses to be provided.   This information can be secured by determining roughly the number of houses needed of four, five, six, etc., habitable rooms, in accordance with the household structure assumed and averaging out the frontage required for standard types of each size, allowance being made for extra frontage for individual garages, for whatever proportion of houses with exceptionally large gardens is thought to be needed, and for the loss of effective frontage which inevitably occurs at corners and bends of roads.   This last item is very substantial and as much as 20 per cent. may need to be added to the total previously arrived at .

The average plot frontage, in feet multiplied by the number of houses to be provided and divided into the total area of the site in square feet (less areas to be devoted to purposes other than house plots) gives the average plot depth, from the centre of the road fronting the plot to the back fence.   This average may, of course, and generally should, be departed from quite widely in both directions, but such departures must be arranged so that they cancel each other out.

For example suppose that one was going to develop at a density of 12 houses to the acre with houses having a plot frontage of 25 feet, then assuming a 20% loss at road junctions, etc., average plot frontage=30 ft.

$$\text{Depth of plot} = \frac{43560}{30 \times 12}$$

$$= \ 121 \text{ feet.}$$

The average plot of road centre depth to back fence for this development must therefore be about 121 feet.

Use of the Density Chart shown in Fig. 80 eliminates the need for such calculations.

The amount of land to be devoted to open space, apart from house plots, is a matter of policy.   At one extreme, it may not be necessary on some sites to provide any at all, while, at the other, local habits and wishes may suggest that individual gardens be cut down to mere " outdoor rooms ", and that the remaining space available be divided between roadside greens, groups of allotments, children's play spaces and communal parkland, tennis courts, etc.

The necessary decisions having been taken, the actual preparation of a draft can be begun; the processes involved can be described in general terms, although, in detail, each designer is likely to work somewhat differently in accordance with his individual approach to the problem.

Most will probably begin by sketching out the road pattern, because this is the dominant component in the design and because the requirements for road routes are so stringent that compliance with them inevitably dictates to a large extent the arrangement of the other components.   Some people disagree with this method, and prefer to begin by deciding the positions of the buildings in relation to each other, afterwards fitting the road pattern to suit the buildings.   This is perfectly logical, for it is the purpose of the roads to provide access to the buildings, not of the buildings to provide a frame for the roads.   Nevertheless, it is hardly possible to follow this course without at least having constantly in mind the probable positions of the roads and all the conditions which must be fulfilled for them; for the comparatively in-experienced, at least, the first-mentioned method is to be preferred.

The road pattern must be so arranged that roads running approximately parallel do not approach more closely to each other than the minimum depth required for two plots, or frontage will be wasted to no purpose.   *On the*

average, the distance between such roads must, of course, be twice the average plot depth decided upon.

It is very important, in the case of large areas, that the size of each " insula " or house-block—a unit of land surrounded by through-roads—should be of appropriate dimensions.   Design is easier and more flexible if it is approximately a multiple of two house plots in both directions, but it *must* be so in one direction, otherwise waste of land is inevitable.

The routes of minor through-roads should first be fixed tentatively and the land for house plots created by them indicated by drawing in their back fence lines.   This will show up the remaining land for which road frontage has to be created, and facilitate decisions regarding the positions of the remaining roads, including culs-de-sac, quadrangles, plots to be provided with footpath access only, etc., to which, both in relation to each other and to the minor through roads, the same rule regarding minimum distances apart applies.

When this has been done the results are checked approximately for suit-ability of gradients and plot depths, ability to drain by gravity, etc.   A rough calculation should then be made to make sure that the road frontage created is approximately correct, for the flexibility of most of the relevant factors makes it easy for serious errors to have been made.   It is, in fact, desirable to prepare several different road layouts and to estimate their relative merit as regards economy in road costs, convenience for residents and potentialities for visual effect, before selecting one for completion.

Next, the buildings can be shown diagrammatically by rectangles of appropriate size, particular attention being paid to arrangement at road junctions, termination of vistas, suitable grouping and variation of building line.   This is best done by first drawing the buildings whose precise position is important in relation to features such as road junctions, and filling in the gaps afterwards.   By first drawing the buildings at one end of a road and working progressively along it, one soon reaches a stage at which groups at key points cannot be fitted in without either crowding or waste of frontage, and the work has to be done again.

When the buildings have been drawn in it is well to add tentative plot boundaries, for it is all too easy to arrange buildings in a way which looks most attractive but which makes it impossible for the garden space to be divided so as to give each a plot of reasonable size and shape.

As the buildings are drawn in it is desirable to keep a running check of their number so that the allocation of frontage may constantly be slightly adjusted to secure that the total number required can be accommodated.   If this is not done the last few which are drawn may have to be either crowded or given unnecessarily wide frontages.

The importance of economy in road design can hardly be overstressed and only the most compelling reasons should lead to the selection of a design which entails the construction of a length appreciably greater than the minimum necessary to fulfil all essential requirements.

When the design has been taken to the stage of representing buildings diagrammatically and showing tentative plot divisions, it is time to consult any specialists employed on the job, to make any alterations which they require and to resolve conflicts between their requirements, after which the architect, the landscape architect and the engineer can proceed to the more detailed aspects of the design in their respective fields, limited only by the need not to make alterations to the outline as agreed without further discussion.

Types of layout.   The design of the road pattern is directly linked with the kind of buildings which it serves, and the subject can only be satisfactorily considered in relation to its history in this country over the last hundred years or so, for present-day practice is derived from many habits, traditions and prejudices which have changed in accordance with social and economic changes, though generally after a considerable time lag.   The housing provided for the mass of the people will first be considered, followed by a brief mention of that occupied by those better off.

In the middle of the nineteenth century, before the advent of effective public health legislation and administration, there were virtually no enforceable standards by which to measure the adequacy of housing accommodation. The limit of ruthless economy was achieved in the back-to-back houses erected for factory workers, which not only had party walls at the sides but at the back, so that the total land required per house was no more than the site of the tiny dwelling itself plus a strip of access way along its front.   The appalling story of death, misery and degradation associated with this development and its accompanying lack of proper water supply and drainage has been told too often to need repeating here.

Other houses of this period were little better and differed from the back-to-backs only to the extent that a narrow strip was left between the back walls of adjoining rows, this was often partly occupied by earth closets and other outhouses, while the width of each house was kept to the irreducible minimum.

Road layout was often confused and opportunist, houses being crammed pell-mell into gaps left between earlier development, but on a clear site, it generally assumed a close chequer-board pattern.

The provisions of the Public Health Act, 1875, apart from the numerous other improvements which they brought about, forced parallel rows of houses a little further apart to secure rock-bottom minima of daylighting;   the standard imposed was, generally speaking, a *width* of 24 feet between fronts of buildings, and, at the back, an *area* of 150 square feet per house, and a minimum *average width* of back yard of 15 feet per house.

House widths remained extremely narrow and any accommodation beyond the minimum, where there was effective demand for it, usually took the form of long " back additions ", stretching out behind the main parts of the houses or, more rarely, by building the houses three-storeys high instead of two.

The chequer-board road pattern, spaced a little more widely than before, remained universal;   indeed, this is the only pattern possible if very high densities are to be secured to accord with even the least exacting of space standards, since any other involves wastages of land insignificant at lower densities.

It is remarkable how high a level in the economic scale people had to reach before they could secure a better type of house, and there was hardly any-where an intermediate stage between the tunnel-back terrace houses, with their dismal back yards, and the substantial semi-detached house of the prosperous Victorian middle class, complete with garden, basement and slavey, although by-law houses with quite deep, although of course very narrow, back gardens were not uncommon.

About the turn of the century this gap began to be bridged as the result of wealth gradually becoming more widely distributed.   This was accompanied in some places by a realisation that reduction of density did not mean a correspondingly great increase in road costs, as demonstrated by Sir Raymond Unwin.   Small terrace and semi-detached houses were built, still very narrow-fronted, but a little less constricted and with back gardens of varying depth, together with a pocket handkerchief of front lawn.   Layout, though still predominantly chequer-board, could, through relaxation of density, be made to accommodate the routes of roads to topography.

This situation prevailed until the end of the first world war.   From then on the further evening out of the distribution of wealth, the rise of the building societies and the entry on the scene of local authorities in the role of large-scale developers produced a complicated interaction of motives and methods. The local authority and the speculative builder, most of his clients assisted by building societies, co-existed in an uneasy relationship, midway between partnership and rivalry, each catering for a distinct clientele which overlapped but slightly.

Both had to build as cheaply as possible to secure a profit or to minimise the burden on the rates.   The local authority, which had to employ someone to prepare the necessary designs, generally secured the assistance of men with at least some smattering of technical competence, while the speculative builder usually saw no reason to supplement his native wit and ignorance, but kept an eye on, and after a time imitated, the technical improvements developed by the local authority, while making his houses look as unlike theirs as possible in detail.

Motives of economy led the local authorities to build at first mostly in terrace form;   standardised plans and sheer indifference combined to produce a mean and dreary appearance accentuated by a chequer-board road plan, although a density of twelve houses per acre, allowing a decent-sized garden, became an officially accepted standard.

Thus the stage was set for a reaction of a fantastic kind.   The clients of the speculative builder were, as a whole, on their way up.   Rising from the proletariat by diligence, intelligence or good fortune, they saw in the services made available by the building societies a dazzling and hitherto undreamed of opportunity of acquiring their own homes.   And who could fail to understand and sympathise with their desire (particularly since, for the most part, their economic betterment had not been accompanied by the acquisition of aesthetic judgment) that house ownership should be demonstrated to the world by the house itself being made to look as different as possible from the dreary old Victorian terrace or the dreary new local authority terrace, both of them the homes of the economically unsuccessful?

The speculative builder was not slow to appreciate the market value of distinctive appearance and abandonment of the terrace, dislike of which was not wholly attributable to social ambition but partly to well-founded dis-satisfaction with the inconvenience of the methods of securing secondary access then prevalent, quickly followed.

The Victorian terrace, though almost always grim in appearance and frequently of debased design, did, at least, because of its standardised elevations and the very closeness of the development, produce a unified street picture. Even this unity was now abandoned by the speculative builder. Using semi-detached houses almost exclusively, and unable, because of the limitations imposed by the similarity of accommodation which was demanded and by his own lack of taste and skill to achieve subtle variations in appearance, he resorted to the wildest devices to make each pair of houses in some way different from its neighbours. Ornamental tiling, strange-shaped bay windows, imitation half-timbering and tortured mixtures of colour and material were used to differentiate neighbouring buildings of identical size, shape and function. The growth of the cheap car made matters worse; garages were tacked on to the sides of the houses or spaces were left for their erection if required. This resulted in the discordant masses being separated from each other by a space wide enough to destroy the last vestige of con-tinuity, yet not enough to enable each to be viewed in isolation. The last touch of horror was added by the popularisation of front fences and gates and front doors constructed in or decorated with jazz shapes.

Meanwhile, many local authorities had learnt from the example of the garden cities and the most capable and enterprising among them had evolved an architectural style which, although generally somewhat pinched and frugal, did not lack humanity and dignity, the achievement of which was assisted by the use of a more varied road pattern.

Increased concern for the welfare of tenants led to the abandonment of long terraces and the general use of semi-detached houses combined with a smaller number of blocks of four houses, in an effort to secure an " open " effect which many think misconceived.

The use of culs-de-sac to open up land behind through-roads, as we have seen earlier, reduces the length of road required per house by making it possible to build houses which occupy no extra road frontage across the closed ends. It has the visual advantage of automatically adding depth and variety to the street picture and of creating closed vistas.

Realisation of these facts, combined with the greater flexibility in road lay-out made possible by a density as low as twelve houses per acre, led to the establishment of a distinctive pattern of layout sometimes called " English informal " and distinguished by a respect for topography combined with freedom, limited only by the requirements for minimum plot depths and safe road junctions.

We must note, in passing, the curious perversion of this method often seen in large estates on flat sites, where, for lack of positive need for variation, an unimaginative designer builds up a repetitive pattern of through-roads, sub-divided into equally repetitive patterns of culs-de-sac, sometimes elab-orated into a complex geometrical pattern of meaningless symmetry. When this happens the monotony of the chequer-board layout is not usually approached but is replaced by a restlessness induced by the constant change of orientation in the buildings required by the number and short lengths of the many culs-de-sac.

The speculative builder, although his antagonism to elevational consistency prevented him from imitating the local authorities in this respect, gradually learnt the economies which resulted from the use of the cul-de-sac and started to use it freely a few years before the Second World War. The results were often grotesque because the discordance of the unrestrained variation of elevational details was emphasised by the inherent symmetry and unity of form of the cul-de-sac but where some restraint was exercised in this direction a certain odd charm emerged. The intimacy and restricted prospects of cul-de-sac development were much kinder to undistinguished little houses than the effect produced when a large number were exposed to view sim-ultaneously by stringing them along a long, straight road.

Towards the end of the Second World War the prospect of resuming building after long abstention, the urgency of creating large numbers of new homes and the idealism fostered by a war of ideas, stimulated imaginative thought about house design and community design to an unusual degree.

The reconstruction of blitzed towns, the decentralisation of congested populations and the development of the neighbourhood theory were themes which suggested unprecedented opportunities for large-scale unified development.

The two dominant ideas which have emerged may be summarised as follows :

(1) The need to introduce visual interest by replacing the almost universal two-storey house with buildings of different heights, carefully related to each other, the heights being determined by the functions of the buildings.
The desired effect is achieved, considering only dwellings, by seeking suitable combination and relationship between :
Two-storey houses to meet the needs of the ordinary family.
Three-storey houses to provide for large families without in-creasing frontage or trespassing on garden space by increasing the depth of the buildings.
Flats of varying heights, to cater for families which do not need ground floor accommodation or individual garden space.
(2) The desirability of restoring variety and urban character to resi-dential areas by drastically reducing the proportion of semi-detached houses and short terraces and re-introducing the long terrace, which can be made acceptable by using improved method of sound-proofing party walls and by designing secondary means of access which do not interfere with privacy and permit passage from front garden to back garden without entering the main part of the house.

The merit of these ideas is considerable, but that of some of the forms of layout designed to give effect to them and the theories which have been advanced regarding the allocation of garden and other space are highly debatable. These are so closely related that they can conveniently be discussed together.

Front gardens and back gardens have quite different functions. Essentially, front gardens are that part of the space between the fronts of houses required to secure adequate daylight and privacy which is not occupied by the carriageway and footpaths of the road.

This space may be treated in numerous ways; the whole of it may be shared between houses opposite each other and each front garden be enclosed by hedges or fences; part may be so allocated and part utilised as verges between footpaths and carriageway and/or between footpath and front fences; the whole may be utilised as unenclosed front gardens or utilisation may be divided between unenclosed front gardens and verges between footpath and carriageway; finally, the allocation may also be symmetrical or asymmetrical (i.e., in the latter case the carriageway and the footpath on one side are closer to the houses on that side of the road than to those on the other, the footpath being set slightly forward from the fronts of the houses to preserve their privacy). All these combinations, and variants of them, can be used to secure interest, variety, surprise, or safety; the last-named being increased by segregating the footpaths and carriageway. (See Fig. 48.)

In my view, there is no doubt that front gardens should normally only be divided and enclosed as a very occasional contrast, or, in an area of detached houses, to frame each house and so help to secure the visual isolation of contrasting neighbours. Ordinarily, the enclosure and cultivation of front gardens by individual tenants is very apt both to obscure the view of the houses and to weaken the unity of the street picture. In short, they are a semi-public part of the street and should be treated from the standpoint of the public. One tenant who refuses to cultivate his individual front garden can spoil the appearance of a whole road.

Back gardens are in a very different category; they should be wholly private and capable of being used exactly as their tenants wish, short of downright unneighbourly behaviour.

This freedom of use is much increased if the gardens are enclosed very completely, ideally by a tall, thick hedge. For the sake of the tenants' further privacy, and to prevent the untidiness of some of the gardens spoiling the appearance of the street, houses, outbuildings and flank walls should be disposed so as to screen the back garden from the road.

Certain special considerations apply to each of the various kinds of open spaces other than gardens which may form parts of the site plan, while one obvious general requirement is that each kind should be distributed so that it is as accessible as possible to those it serves.

Groups of allotments are generally unsightly and so should be screened from the public view. Children's play spaces need not be unsightly, but should be arranged so that children cannot run out of them into a carriageway. Purely ornamental open spaces, such as greens in front of crescents or quadrangles of houses, should be of the minimum size necessary to secure the desired appearance. If they are too large they encourage children to play football and cricket unsuitably close to windows and, although this can be prevented by obstructive planting, the visual effect is likely to be marred. Another important consideration in connection with such greens is road costs; unless the area of a green is so small that access to the houses can conveniently

be secured without constructing a carriageway around it the cost is very high, since only one side of the road frontage can be developed. It may sometimes be worth while doing this to secure an exceptionally spacious effect or to afford prominence to a specially fine group of trees, but the increased cost involved should always be fully borne in mind and the advantage to be secured weighed against it. Normally it will be well to restrict such greens to a size which enables the houses to be served by a footpath or by a cul-de-sac running up the middle of the green.

Many post-war systems of layout have been inspired by the desire to escape from the conception of the street as a corridor lined by buildings and to substitute for it a grouping of buildings and open spaces governed by orientation for sunlight and by the aesthetic relations of building height and width of open space, roadways providing access as unobtrusively as possible and following routes which are not related at all closely to the lines of the buildings. These systems vary considerably in the relative emphasis placed on the several factors mentioned.

The use of parallel rows of houses facing in the same direction and set at right-angles to the adjacent road has frequently been contemplated, and even to some extent carried out. It seems to me to have inescapable drawbacks which far outweigh any advantages it possesses. Some economy in road frontage is secured. If 150 feet is accepted as the maximum distance which a house door should be from a carriageway there is a saving in road construction equal to the difference between 150 feet and the total length of the plot, including the access way along the front. The net saving is less than this, for the flank wall of the row must be set back some distance from the boundary of the road, and this is a loss of effective building frontage which does not occur in the case of houses built parallel to the road

But, if one accepts the view that back gardens should not be exposed to the public gaze—and I should find it very difficult to agree with a contrary opinion—the flanks of the plots next to the road must be protected by a continuous barrier, broken only where access ways begin, at which point the full lengths of barriers protecting the back boundaries of the plots would be exposed to view. If all these barriers were sufficiently tall and opaque to perform their function properly the effect could hardly fail to be most depressing.

As already suggested on page 240 the economies in first costs of footpath access are likely to be more than outweighed by heavy maintenance costs. Also it is unrealistic to ignore the fact that the motor car is an extremely useful aid to comfortable living at the present time. Full advantage can only be taken of it if it can be brought to a reasonable distance from its owner's dwelling. From the point of view of public services too, although the occasional house or two set a long way back from the carriageway is not objectionable, a layout which involves having such a substantial proportion of the houses in such a situation (see Fig. 87), very materially increases the costs of services such as refuse collection, and cannot on practical grounds be justified. My own view is that housing layouts should be so designed that the great majority of houses are separated from a carriageway by no more than the normal depth of a front garden and footpath.

The juxtaposition of front elevations and back fences also reduces privacy as between tenants. With the normal arrangement of houses facing each other the fronts of the houses are at least 70 feet apart and no appreciable amount of activity flows outwards from either row towards the other. At the back, the houses are the depth of two back gardens apart, and although activities in the back gardens may extend until they virtually meet at the back fence, no activity carried on by one family approaches the house of another more closely than the depth of a back garden.

But, with rows of houses facing in the same direction, the back garden activities of one family reach nearly to the fronts of the corresponding house in the row behind and the houses adjacent to it. This is no nearer, in fact not so near, it may be said, than the activities of neighbours on either side, but these reach one at an angle and may often be screened from sight and hearing by outbuildings. The attacks made by the activities under discussion are frontal.

In practice these " single aspect " layouts do not usually have even the advantages of that shown in Fig. 87 (d). The large common strips in front of the houses tend to be reduced to a vestigial front garden, immediately beyond which is the footpath, which, in turn is immediately adjoined by the brick wall or fence of the gardens of the next row of houses. This reduces the maintenance costs of looking after large common strips but is done at the cost of producing a mean, congested effect. The area in the well-known L.C.C. Roehampton estate, in many ways admirable, which is devoted to single aspect houses is an excellent example of this.

Modern theories of layout often involve more or less complete substitution of communal for individual back garden space. This seems to be intended to overcome the difficulties involved in screening gardens by managing them as a single unit and cultivating them in such a way as to render them suitable for public view, and also, by pooling space, to overcome the unavoidable provision of individual gardens which are too large for some tenants and too small for others. The most usual arrangement proposed is to provide a small back yard or " outdoor room " for each house, with the remainder of the space between the backs of the houses available for common use.

I must confess to grave doubts about the probable effectiveness of such proposals. In a group of houses occupied exclusively by childless non-gardeners of serene temperament I can conceive that an arrangement of this kind might prove wholly delightful or, more seriously, that, in a group with a highly developed sense of neighbourliness in which the keen gardeners combined to cultivate the land enjoyed in common instead of leaving the work to outside persons, the results might be quite remarkably good, but such conditions, which can be upset by the arrival of a single jarring personality, do not exist sufficiently often to justify a generally applied policy being based upon their assumed existence.

In a group of houses with plots of normal depth the " outdoor room " cannot be large enough to satisfy the enthusiastic gardener unless the land enjoyed in common is reduced to a mere corridor. This would be disastrous, for the temptation to use it as a dumping ground for rubbish would be strong and the confinement to such a corridor of the large groups of children who might be expected to play there would concentrate the noise they made to a very serious extent.

The problem of the non-gardener is not really very formidable. Given the public control of front gardens and the adequate enclosure of back gardens the nuisance he causes is confined to the unsightly view seen from the upper windows of neighbouring houses, which is not a very serious matter, and the airborne distribution of weeds. The tactful approaches of neighbours may induce him to stop this being allowed to happen, however little he cares for gardening.

Even the man who pulls no weed and sows no seed from one year's end to another may enjoy his garden and benefit from it. He may practise his golf shots there and play with the dog and the children to an extent which makes it a valuable possession; the children by themselves are likely to find it an admirable place for personal play, which is as important in its own way as group play.

It is common in America to see houses with quite large plots which are not cultivated at all and are no more than patches of mown grass, yet the visual effect of these if often pleasant.

There are, of course, circumstances in which the provision of common garden space is abundantly justified. Where, for some reason, roads have to be spaced further apart than the depth of two normal plots or where a pond, quarry or other feature not suitable for incorporation in individual gardens suggests that this be done, common garden space can be a most valuable amenity, and in order to make it large enough to serve its purpose the depths of individual gardens can be reduced.

Where densities are fairly low there is often opportunity for utilising spare space for a variety of purposes, though this can hardly be done in a systematic fashion, but depends upon the exigencies of detailed site shape and characteristics.

It is worth emphasising that the lower the density the easier it is to introduce pleasant features of this kind, such as tennis courts, copses, and children's play spaces. One of the penalties of high density housing is that in order to develop at the density decided upon every available square yard has to be taken into account. This results inevitably in rigid layouts of generally rectangular character and in the total omission of incidental features, since their inclusion would take up more land than could be spared without reducing some individual plots below an acceptable size.

The four alternative layouts for a single site included in " Houses, 1953 " provide useful comparisons of layout method. They have already been referred to in this chapter, and although from the point of view of cost comparison, which is somewhat emphasised, they are valueless since the invalid assumption is made that footpaths cost nothing, the costs of pipes and wires underneath them being ignored, they are from other points of view worth examining in some detail. (See Fig. 87.)

All the four layouts provide for a net residential density of 62 habitable rooms per acre and the proportion of each type of dwelling to be provided corresponds broadly with national average requirements. Not more than 12% of the accommodation is in maisonettes or flats. The average spacing between blocks is not less than 70 feet except that for blocks at right angles this may be 50 feet, or less where windows do not directly face another block.

It is most unfortunate from the point of view of exemplification that the site chosen should have a cycle track running across it which approaches very closely to the spine road, for the result is that this distorts all the sample layouts, and prevents them being true representatives of their types.

Scheme A known as the " Conventional Layout " is really " English Informal Layout " tidied up and disciplined a little. The fairly high density of 62 rooms per acre has not been allowed to prevent the provision of sizeable closes at the end of culs-de-sac, and the substantial amount of land occupied by these has meant that, in order to maintain the density, back garden depths tend to be rather small. Most of the houses are reasonably close to carriage-ways. The spacing of buildings around road junctions is rather loose and formless, but otherwise the layout is pleasant.

Scheme B known as the " Service Cul-de-sac " layout, a good many examples of which have now been built, is an adaptation of the principles of layout used by Clarence Stein in Radburn, New Jersey, which have exercised a great deal of influence on contemporary ideas. The great majority of the houses are intended to be served by culs-de-sac to which the cars of individual owners debouch, from which tradesmen visit the houses, refuse is collected, and so on, leaving the fronts of the houses to be served by a footpath set in a green strip leading inwards to parklands or schools. This idea was originally linked with the " super block " the idea of which was that development of this kind should embrace a whole neighbourhood, and that no child going to school should have to cross a traffic road, but should be able to use the foot-path leading to the interior of the neighbourhood and running between the fronts of houses.

The Radburn principle is attractive and ingenious, and it is with great regret that one feels compelled to cast a good deal of cold water upon it. Generally speaking, family requirements demand, as has already been suggested, that one should be able to drive the family car fairly close to the house particularly where children and luggage need to be transported. If the road access to the house is to be at the bottom of the back garden then the depth of the back garden has to be fairly severely restricted if the carries involved, not only for family purposes but by tradesmen and others, are not to be unduly long. Furthermore, quite apart from length of carry, the back garden of the ordinary family house is liable to be obstructed by the branches of fruit trees, washing, children's tricycles and so on, which makes it a perilous pathway. If the back gardens are short enough for the service cul-de-sac to be able to be used effectively then they are likely to be too short to perform the proper functions of gardens. If, on the other hand, they are long, then the " clean " and " dirty " concept is likely to break down, and tiresome pedestrian journeys are likely to be involved along the front access paths from the nearest point on the through carriageway. Attention should be concentrated in the " Houses, 1953 " layout on the two culs-de-sac to the west of the spine road and to the south of the Hall and shops, and to those on the extreme east side of the layout, for these exemplify the service cul-de-sac principle while the remainder of the layout does not do so to the same extent.

The provision of a continuous system of footpaths over a whole neighbour-hood or more has already been considered in Chapters 11 and 14, and need not be dealt with further here.

Scheme C " Single Footpath " access layout is a curiosity, for, in essence it consists of a normal layout as regards " Front " and " Back " accesses, by means of a large number of short culs-de-sac, which however, have no carriageway but consist merely of a footpath. The proportion of the houses which are an inconvenient and laborious distance from any carriageway in this layout is appalling, and one very much doubts whether anyone would get to the stage of seriously contemplating large-scale development on these lines.

Scheme D " Double Footpath Access " layout has already, in general, been commented upon in some detail on page 245. It is extremely popular among a number of architects, and is common in Scandinavia. It seems to me to have little to recommend it. Its one definite advantage is that it enables housing over a considerable area to be sited so that all have practically the same orientation and so can be of identical design. This is no doubt an excellent thing if an emergency requires extremely rapid development to be undertaken but it hardly conduces to variety and pleasantness.

The " Houses, 1953 " layouts rely to a large extent upon very narrow-fronted terrace houses, so that it is all the more surprising that on the whole, the depths of back gardens provided are inadequate. Nevertheless, the first scheme, " the conventional layout " comes very close to fulfilling the re-quirements suggested earlier in this chapter as desirable (see page 237). A small reduction of density, the elimination of the curious and special site conditions already mentioned, and of the rather excessive amount of incidental open space in closes, would produce living conditions which I should myself regard as excellent, and I do not think that carefully designed development on these lines would be likely to prove unsatisfactory in aesthetic terms, so that it appears to me that a great deal of current archi-tectural ferment is without foundation. If indeed the requirements of privacy and garden space generally demanded are nevertheless inimical to the production of satisfactory aesthetic effects then it is surely up to present day architects to evolve a new aesthetic capable of giving satisfaction without violating standards, for, as already suggested, although the appearance of a residential area is an important element it is by no means the only one.

To produce good housing it is absolutely essential to remember this. It is most desirable, both for the sake of those who live in an area and for the general public who pass through it, that housing should look as pleasant as possible, but this aspect is at the very most no more important than adequate space, privacy, safety or convenience. It ought not be to necessary to say this, but it is; a remarkable proportion of the discussion and criticism which one hears about housing seems to be directed solely towards visual considera-tions.

This fallacy indeed seems very largely to have inspired some of the recent ideas about housing layout which have emerged. Most of these are probably only passing fads which will leave little or no impression upon the future pattern of housing, but they are sufficiently talked about and illustrated to merit some brief discussion. Most are based upon or vaguely related to a misunderstood or imperfectly understood enthusiasm for the " Radburn " idea. " Radburn " is indeed an O.K. word; any housing layout which is described, however mistakenly, as " Radburn " is sure of praise.

As has already been said, the basic idea partially exemplified at Radburn, New Jersey, was the creation of superblocks—units surrounded by a through road from which culs-de-sac projected inwards. Between each of these culs-de-sac ran footways leading to the interior of the superblock, which was occupied by a school or park or both, and adjacent superblocks were linked by pedestrian ways which passed over or under the surrounding road. This general concept has already been extensively discussed in Chapters 8, 11 and 14.

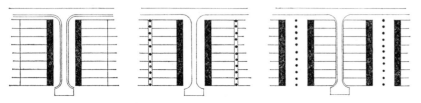

FIG. 85. Left. A cul-de-sac laid out in "orthodox" fashion. Centre. The true "Radburn" type of layout. Right. "Psuedo-Radburn" layout of the type being carried out in this country.

In detail, however, the layout actually used at Radburn was perfectly ordinary. Houses were fairly close to the culs-de-sac serving them, and the footways ran between the ends of back gardens. (See Fig. 85). The so-called " Radburn " layouts used in this country are really exactly the opposite of this; the houses face onto and are close to the footways, while the service culs-de-sac run between the back gardens. The advantages of this are substantial and definite. The whole of the area between fronts of houses is free of vehicles and can be treated as a landscaped unit in continuous form over the whole of a superblock, the fingers of landscape between the houses widening out into major open space, etc., in the interior. No extra road frontage is taken up by garages since they do not have to be placed beside the houses but are at the bottom of the garden. This has the additional advantage that, if necessary, garages can be let independently of houses quite easily.

But the disadvantages are equally definite. Unless back gardens are kept very short the distance between houses and vehicles which are used with them or which visit them, is excessive. Everyone who visits a house in a layout of this kind either has to plod through a back garden or has to leave his vehicle parked in a service cul-de-sac and walk round to the front of the house to make a formal entry through the front door. In many such layouts it is quite difficult to find one's way; a stranger has first to identify the house which he wishes to visit, must then find the nearest point to it where he can park and then find his way back to the house, which can be quite a formidable operation.

The general advantage of this kind of layout, namely, continuous pedestrian ways independent of vehicular roads, can be secured just as well with the real Radburn layout, and the special advantages of this pseudo-Radburn layout, namely, economy in garage frontage and continuous landscaping of fronts of houses, do not on the whole seem sufficient to make its general use worthwhile. This is not to say that an occasional small group of houses laid out on this principle may not be perfectly justifiable; if the back gardens are very short the disadvantages mostly disappear, but this is very different from carrying it out over a whole neighbourhood or a substantial part of one.

In terms of safety, it makes no difference whether the footpath runs along the front of the house or along the back, if indeed the separation of the footpaths and the carriageway of minor roads makes any contribution whatever to safety, which, as I have already said, seems to me exceedingly doubtful.

The next thread in the rather confusing set of ideas which we are discussing which needs to be identified and detached relates to the relative amounts of outdoor space within a housing area which it is appropriate to allocate to private use as individual gardens attached to houses and to open areas enjoyed by the inhabitants of the locality generally.

Each has its uses and advantages. The private garden is private. One can sit out in it without the company of neighbours, which is certain to be unwelcome at times. (At the very least, the company of some neighbours is bound to be unwelcome at times.) It provides an enclosure within which children and animals can be securely confined under the eye of their parents and owners. It is, however, necessarily somewhat inflexible; if an individual family has too much garden or too little garden, not very much can be done about it.

The advantages and disadvantages of common outdoor space are the exact opposite. It provides no privacy; one cannot escape from the friendly but boring neighbour. One cannot confine children and animals; they may wander away to an indefinite distance, and in doing so will, incidentally, inevitably sooner or later be liable to meet motor vehicles. On the other hand, it is flexible; it provides without waste both for those who want to use outdoor space a great deal and also for those who want to use it little or not at all. It can also be comprehensively landscaped and maintained.

It would be very pleasant indeed to lay out housing areas so as to provide both forms of open space in adequate quantity, somewhat in the way originally suggested by Walter Segal in " Home and Environment ", but this necessarily entails very low densities. This would not worry me very much were it not for the ease with which, as we have seen in Chapter 15, major open space can be provided within a short walk of all homes even at quite moderate densities, which suggests that, on balance, much common open space with housing is, as a general rule, rather too much of a luxury to be justified.

The opposite solution seems to me to be even less justified, namely, to make all garden space common except for a vestigial sun porch attached to each house, but layouts which do exactly this have recently been produced, apparently with serious intent. An example of one such is shown in Fig. 86 (a). It would be tedious to detail all the disadvantages of such an arrangement; they will certainly be obvious to all parents of children who keep animals and who have one or more tiresome neighbours. One wonders whether those who design layouts like this are people; one feels fairly confident that they are not parents.

A variation on this kind of layout consists of a mixture of tightly grouped houses around small courts and blocks of tall flats dispersed over a generally open park-like area. The impression which this gives me is that it would provide a unique opportunity for inhabitants of the cluster houses to suffer from claustrophobia and agoraphobia simultaneously. (See Fig. 86 (b).) But it is only fair to say that if the clusters were grouped around rather larger courts and accompanied by individual gardens, however small, on the other side, they might provide quite a pleasant environment for some people.

Mention of very small gardens brings us to consideration of the patio house, enthusiasm for which seems just now to have reached the dimensions of a religious cult among architects.

Essentially, the patio house is a dwelling surrounding a courtyard towards which most of the windows face. Contemporary proposals for patio houses in fact mostly take the form of L-shaped detached houses on very small plots, shut in by boundary walls and the elevations of adjoining houses, (see Fig. 86 (c)). This again is well enough for a group of a dozen houses or so. If carried out over an area of 12 acres or more, as is now being suggested in come cases, it is likely to be unpleasantly claustrophobic and visually deadly monotonous.

An even worse variant is that shown in Fig. 86 (d), in which extremely closely spaced parallel rows of houses are crossed at intervals by two-storey blocks of flats raised one storey above ground level. This arrangement really has nothing to do with the patio idea, although it has been described as such; it can more correctly be described as being akin to extremely dense 19th century by-law development, except that the houses are separated only by a footpath, and that the lateral blocks of flats add a measure of congestion not found even in 19th century by-law housing. These fearsome examples of perverted ingenuity obviously spring from several fallacies which have become muddles together in their designers' minds.

There is first of all the notion that privacy between dwellings can be secured by vertical screens just as well as by horizontal separation. This is absolutely true, if one takes account only of visual privacy. Ingenious house design and the erection of screen walls can, as in Fig. 86 (c), provide complete visual privacy, even though the houses are squashed very closely together, though it is doubtful whether, when the houses are to be two-storey houses, as in this case, they would receive sufficient daylight if the dividing walls were high enough, as they would have to be, to screen the view from facing first floor windows. But privacy is not only visual; one needs privacy from noise and privacy from smells. Only a small effort of imagination is needed to realise the widespread discomfort which would result from just one radio turned on too loudly or just one burnt saucepan in a house within the layout shown in

Fig. 86 (c). One wonders, too, whether most people would be able to live long in such an environment without becoming extremely depressed by looking out in all directions on blank walls.

Other fallacies which must have been present in the designers' minds are the notions that huddling houses closely together somehow promotes neighbourliness, a simple-minded notion if ever there was one, and that squashing them together produces "urbanity", an idea which we have already discussed and which need not be pursued further.

A common characteristic of all these forms of layout is the grouping of garages into large courts and the acceptance of extremely long distances between road to house.

The very high density layout of houses—that shown in Fig. 86 (c) has a density of nearly 90 habitable rooms per acre—is an architects' reaction from the groups of point blocks which all architects seemed keen to build until recently. It now having been found (see "Flats and Houses, 1958") that these are devastatingly expensive dwellings to build, the architect now has to content himself for the most part with being romantic near ground level instead of in the air. He should not be permitted to do it; town planners should be clear minded and strong minded enough to stop him. Unfortunately,

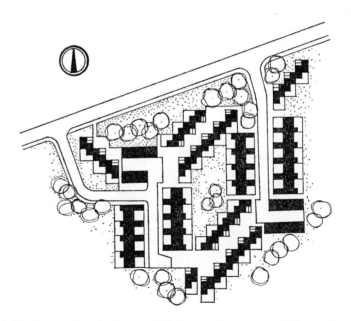

FIG. 86 (a). A type of housing layout which has recently attracted architectural acclaim. It has the "novel" advantage of providing close access to a carriageway for most houses. The great majority of out-door space is commonly rather than individually owned and used.

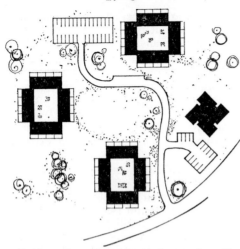

FIG. 86 (b). Claustrophobia and agoraphobia simultaneously. Claustrophobia looking inwards to the courts surrounded by houses, agoraphobia when looking outwards to the " amenity open space ". Clusters of " patio " houses are mixed with tall blocks of flats. Everyone is living in a pack but the distinction between the families who need substantial out-door space and those who do not is ignored.

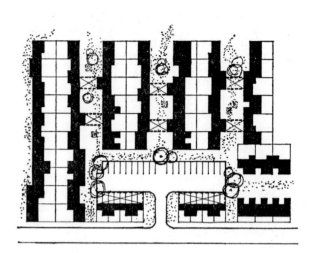

FIG. 86 (d). Another type of " patio " layout. In this case the areas bounded by dotted lines and containing crossed lines represent flats, pierced at ground level to allow for continuous pedestrian ways.

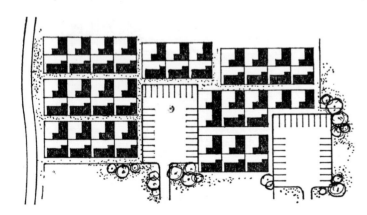

FIG. 86 (c). Plain claustrophobia. Very ingenious design affords complete visual privacy and at least marginally adequate daylighting at a high density and with a little personal out-door space for each house. But, as suggested in the text, the psychological effect and the visual effect hardly seem likely to be good.

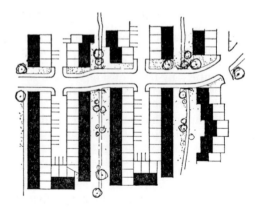

FIG. 86 (e). A very curious example of testing an idea to destruction. In order to allow pedestrian ways to be continous, " Radburn " culs-de-sac are placed directly opposite each other, instead of being staggered, thus providing opportunities for cross-roads collisions to an extent liable greatly to outweight any increases in safety secured by other aspects of Radburn type layout. Pedestrian ways cross through roads by tunnel or bridge.

To meet the objection that many short journeys can still be made more conveniently by road than by pedestrian way it is sometimes argued that all footpaths running beside through-roads should be separated from the roads by fences, and that the same should be done wherever they join a cul-de-sac in order to force people to cross through-roads only by bridge or tunnel. If this were done the probable result would be that many pedestrians would in fact walk along and across the carriageways of through-roads and along service culs-de-sac for short journeys, and that the general level of safety secured would be lower than with a less fanatical attempt to segregate pedestrians from vehicles.

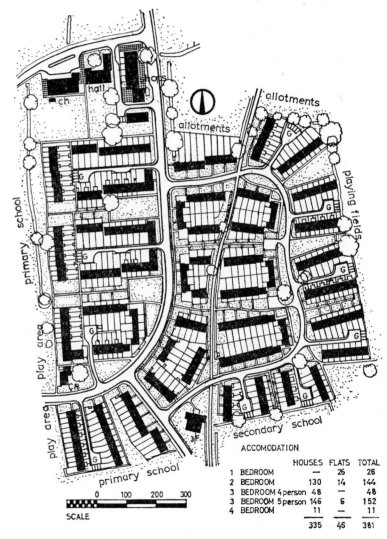

ACCOMMODATION

	HOUSES	FLATS	TOTAL
1 BEDROOM	—	27	27
2 BEDROOM	121	22	143
3 BEDROOM 4 person	48	—	48
3 BEDROOM 5 person	153	—	153
4 BEDROOM	11	—	11
	333	49	382

FIG. 87 (a). The conventional layout.

ACCOMODATION

	HOUSES	FLATS	TOTAL
1 BEDROOM	—	26	26
2 BEDROOM	130	14	144
3 BEDROOM 4 person	48	—	48
3 BEDROOM 5 person	146	6	152
4 BEDROOM	11	—	11
	335	46	381

FIG. 87 (b). The "Radburn" or " Service " cul-de-sac layout.

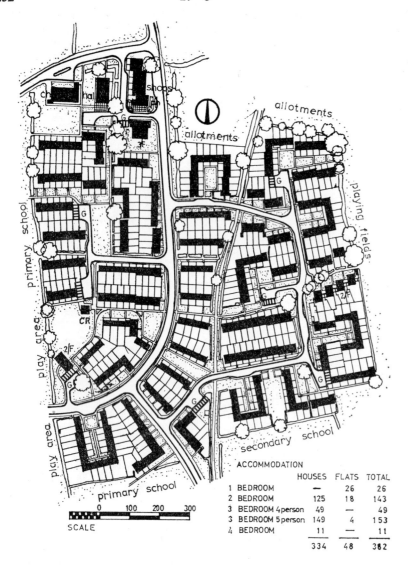

ACCOMMODATION

	HOUSES	FLATS	TOTAL
1 BEDROOM	—	26	26
2 BEDROOM	125	18	143
3 BEDROOM 4 person	49	—	49
3 BEDROOM 5 person	149	4	153
4 BEDROOM	11	—	11
	334	48	382

SCALE   0   100   200   300

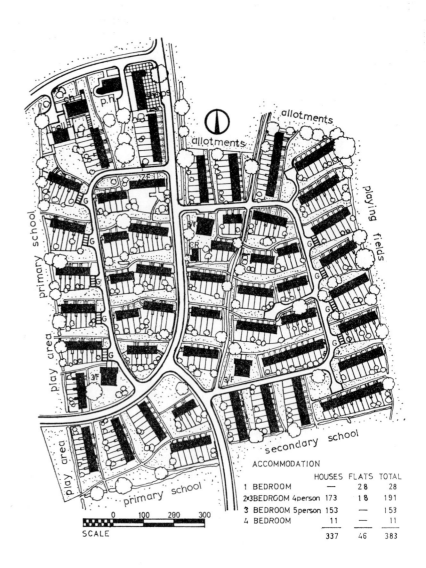

ACCOMMODATION

	HOUSES	FLATS	TOTAL
1 BEDROOM	—	28	28
2 & 3 BEDROOM 4 person	173	18	191
3 BEDROOM 5 person	153	—	153
4 BEDROOM	11	—	11
	337	46	383

SCALE   0   100   200   300

FIG. 87 (c). Single footpath access layout.   FIG. 87 (d). Double footpath access.

Four alternative methods of laying out the same site taken from " Houses, 1953 ".

of course, it is very difficult for them to stop him when the uncontrolled inflation of land values makes it profitable to develop at very high densities, and when the Ministry encourage this to be done.

Turning now to developments in houses for the comparatively well-to-do since the time of Victorian semi-detached houses we find that variations in the sizes, both of such houses and their gardens, have multiplied. Smaller families, increased taxation, and rises in the cost of domestic labour progressively increased the demand for smaller and smaller houses by people quite high in the economic scale, until the smallest differed from the houses of the new inter-war lower middle-class only to the extent that they were generally built of better materials and better designed, were more often detached than semi-detached, had somewhat larger gardens, and were located on choicer sites. A comparatively small proportion were designed by architects, though quite a number were imitations, in whole or in part, of designs illustrated in the architectural press or in magazines which included features about houses. Some of those which were designed by architects were of great merit, but a difficult problem arose in connection with the smallest of them.

People who were sufficiently interested in house design to employ an architect were usually also concerned to get a house which would be distinctive as well as pleasing in appearance and suited to their special needs. Although the skill of the architect could do something to reconcile these requirements with the need to secure harmony with adjoining houses the extent to which he could do so was limited and even the smallest detached houses require a plot frontage not much less than 100 feet, allowing for the most skilful use of trees and shrubs, to form self-contained units rather than elements in a street picture. The provision of plots of this width is seldom economically possible for such houses in view of the high road costs entailed. On narrower plots, furthermore, it is most difficult to build a number of detached houses in such a way as to secure a sense of unity even if wide differences in form and elevational treatment are not desired, because of the numerous narrow gaps between the buildings.

Many people with some margin of income above that required to provide essentials will choose to spend it on a home which is both more spacious and more lavishly equipped and finished than the ordinary run of houses, and the advantages of a detached house, provided its detachment is something more than nominal, are great enough to ensure that it will be the form of house almost exclusively demanded by such people. We cannot hope to provide all such houses with wide fronted plots, yet it would be deplorable if their individual excellence were not to be accompanied by collective excellence.

These houses are certain to form no more than a very small proportion of the total in any balanced community and, from the visual aspect alone, it would be satisfactory to locate them singly and in small groups in inconspicuous positions throughout the residential area; but this may not be acceptable socially.

It is certainly almost impossible to create a satisfactory design for any very large area composed of small detached houses. As with "patio"

FIG. 88 (a). Willenhall Wood, Coventry. An exceptionally interesting example of service cul-de-sac layout. In terms, however, of the living conditions provided, it hardly compares favourably with the older type of layout shown in Fig. 88 (b), which is reproduced to the same scale.

houses and "Radburn" layouts, what is acceptable in small units becomes unacceptable when widely extended.

Where it is possible to control the layout of small detached houses stringently—and it ought to be possible everywhere, various mitigating devices may be employed which are likely to be quite effective provided, once more, the total layout is not too large. Examples of such devices are shown in Fig. 93.

Flats. Something must be said of the development of multi-family dwellings. The forerunner of the modern block of flats was the grim nineteenth-century tenement found in some large towns, which had all the drawbacks of the single family dwelling of the same period as well as weary flights of stairs and impaired privacy.

Advances were made via the tenements erected by the Peabody Trust and others in the late nineteenth century to the inter-war blocks of flats erected by the larger municipalities in and near the city centres. Privacy, accessibility by means of lifts in multi-storey blocks of flats, garden space and architectural design were all vastly improved, but even today, the block of flats is far more often built because the high cost of land precludes single family dwellings than specifically in order to house people whose needs and desires can best be met in that form. Forms of layouts for blocks of flats have been developed principally in relation to two requirements: economy in the quantity of land taken up and economy in the number of flats served by each lift shaft and/or staircase. Unless considerable ingenuity is used daylighting requirements

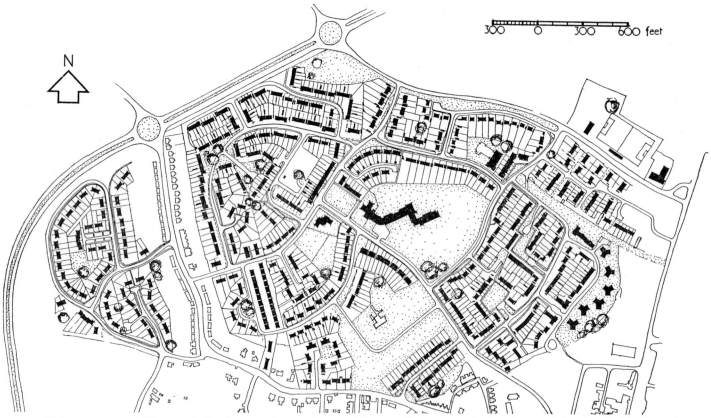

FIG. 88 (b). West Green neighbourhood, Crawley New Town. To many this may well appear old-fashioned; nevertheless it probably gives a higher degree of satisfaction to its residents than does Willenhall Wood.

absorb an undue proportion of the land saved by building high since the amount of communal garden space required is likely to be a good deal less than that made available by the spacing of buildings needed to secure adequate daylighting.

Accordingly, we now find many interesting and curious shapes being used in areas intensely developed with high flats, of which Fig. 89 gives some examples.

The geometry of daylighting requirements means that where blocks of high flats are grouped into considerable numbers they inevitably assume a regular pattern if the density at which they are developed is to be fairly high.

It seems to me doubtful whether these designs are capable of being assimilated satisfactorily to the total urban picture if they make up a large proportion of any particular neighbourhood, for the intricacy of their geometry seems essentially out of harmony with the flexibility which is demanded by the conditions governing areas of single family dwellings. On the other hand, where the proportion of flats is no more than that required to accommodate flat-dwellers who are so by choice rather than necessity it should be possible to make the occasional tall block of flats a focus of dramatic interest and variety contrasting with and dominating the lower buildings without dwarfing or conflicting with them.

The layout of the roads required to serve a group of high blocks of flats resolves itself into providing convenient vehicular and pedestrian access to each entrance and exit used by residents and for service purposes. Daylighting requirements impose by far the most stringent limitations on the siting of such blocks in relation to each other, so that here it is appropriate to fix the positions of the buildings before designing the road pattern, which is likely to take the form of a loop road passing close to as many blocks as possible, with cul-de-sac spurs running from it to take in the remainder.

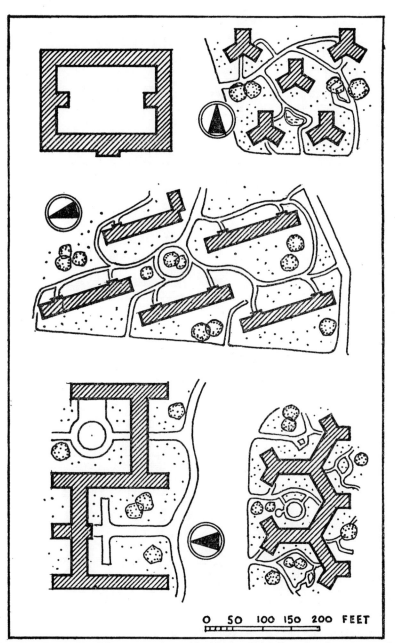

FIG. 89. Examples of the patterns formed by blocks of high flats of various shapes when sited for daylighting.

Appendix III contains a description of the method of determining the spacing and maximum heights of buildings recommended in the Handbook on the Redevelopment of Central Areas.

Redevelopment. A distinction needs to be drawn between " clean sweep " redevelopment and rehabilitation. Where a large area of dense obsolete housing is to be cleared and redeveloped as a single operation, then, subject to making use of a reasonable proportion of the unexpended capital in the area in the form of roads, sewers, water mains, etc., the new development can take virtually any form suggested by the general requirements of the Town Plan. But in many cases outworn buildings and others comparatively new or in good condition are so intermingled that large-scale demolition followed by rebuilding to a totally different layout is not feasible. In areas of this kind great skill is necessary to preserve as many as possible of the buildings worth keeping, and yet to ensure that a satisfactory layout is produced.

There is a danger of prejudicing the permanent success of the whole if a large proportion of existing buildings, streets and services are preserved because insufficient opportunity is then given to improve what is often a fundamentally unsatisfactory existing layout. Also, buildings may in themselves be in good condition, and capable of continuing to be good homes, either as they are or adapted, yet be lacking in daylight, privacy or outdoor space. Nevertheless, economy demands a fair measure of conservation in these areas, generally known as areas of rehabilitation to distinguish

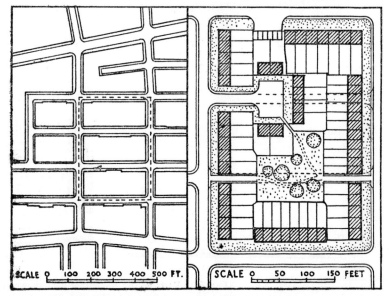

FIG. 90. The drawing on the right shows the method of redevelopment adopted for the area within the broken line on the left-hand drawing.

256

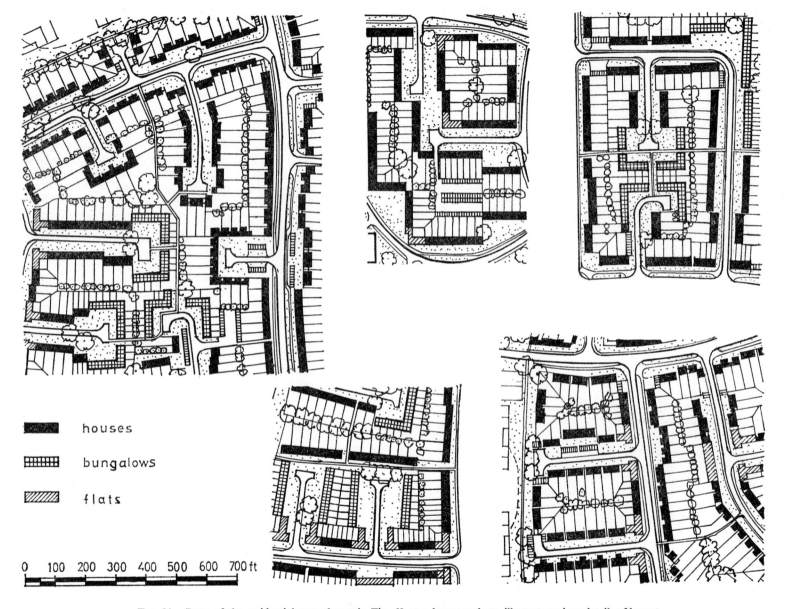

houses

bungalows

flats

0 100 200 300 400 500 600 700 ft

Fig. 91. Parts of the residential area shown in Fig. 68 at a larger scale to illustrate various details of layout.

them from areas of wholesale redevelopment. Judicious stoppings up of streets on the lines discussed in Chapter 11, the conversion of surplus areas of carriageways to pedestrian areas, with planting, the insertion of groups of garages on small vacant sites and the removal of some buildings (even if they are in good condition) which are obstructive to proper redevelopment, can all contribute to the creation of a vastly improved environment at a smaller cost, though with the expenditure of much more effort on the design, than in the case of wholesale redevelopment. It goes without saying that reasonably large areas need to be dealt with by a single developer in order to achieve success.

Garages

Recently the problem of providing garage space for cars has come to the fore, and has presented itself in a very formidable way. In order to provide an individual garage alongside a dwelling-house it has to be accepted that an extra cost in road length occasioned by the extra width of plot of between £40 and £50 is involved. This can be reduced if grouped garages, placed at fairly frequent intervals so that they are accessible to the houses of car owners are accepted, but with a higher standard of living and more widely distributed prosperity, together with the great expansion of the motor car industry, the provision of garages begins to assume major importance. The day may not be very far distant when something approaching one car per dwelling will have to be catered for. In many areas, particularly the larger towns and cities of this country, a large proportion of car owners now do without garages for sheer lack of land on which to build them, and park their cars constantly out of doors, beside the kerb, outside their houses. This does not seem to have as great a detrimental effect upon motor cars as might have been expected, but it is unsatisfactory in all kinds of ways, particularly where local conditions require cars to be illuminated at night. There seems to be scope for a great deal of experiment with covered accommodation for cars, not necessarily in the form of a separate garage for each car, but possible merely in the form of covered space to protect cars from the worst effects of the elements.

If residential roads are almost permanently lined on both sides with cars because of lack of garages or standing space in forecourts, not only is the street scene considerably impaired but carriageways have to be made some twelve feet wider than they would otherwise have to be or the road may be blocked. The actual cost of the area of roadway occupied by a parked car (exclusive of the cost of the land) is about £75, a considerable sum, which could be expended more usefully in other ways. Residential roads will always, of course, have to accommodate a good many parked vehicles, brought by tradesmen and visitors, and for this reason minimum carriageway widths of 18 feet and 24 feet seem advisable in place of the customary 16 feet and 22 feet for minor and major residential roads to ensure that, even with a continuous line of vehicles parked on each side, passage is still possible for a single vehicle or passing vehicles respectively, but this is different from providing what is in effect uncovered garaging for the cars of residents alongside the road.

There are many possible ways of arranging for garages other than the conventional method of placing them alongside houses. Some of these are illustrated in Figs. 91 and 92. All are capable of being used in such a way as to make the garages specific and attractive minor features in the layout rather than embarrassing afterthoughts.

The principal different methods may be summarised as follows:—

   (i) A row of garages acting as a flank screen to back gardens at a junction.
  (ii) Garages projecting from the front elevations of the houses. These may be merely roofs to give some protection from the weather without obstructing daylight very much or they may be ordinary solid garages, in which case they may be used as strong punctuating features in the street picture.
 (iii) A row of garages parallel to the road with houses set back behind them.
 (iv) Garages incorporated in the ground floor of three-storey terrace houses.
  (v) Garages at the ends of back gardens in " pseudo-Radburn " layouts.
 (vi) Separate garage " courts " set in the interior of house blocks.

" Flats and Houses 1958 " contemplates the provision of multi-storey garages in areas of very high density residential development. In view of the considerable inconvenience of such an arrangement to users, its substantial expense and its probable unsightliness it seems safe to suggest that, except in quite extreme conditions, densities should be kept below the level (difficult to calculate in the abstract) at which such provision will become necessary.

Miscellaneous details

The basis of good residential layout is to divide the area concerned into suitable units or house blocks for size and shape of easy communication, both vehicular and pedestrian, so that house plots of the desired size will easily fit in. It is important that the different kinds of roads involved shall be clearly differentiated: spine roads needed for more than purely access purposes, minor through roads, and those giving access to the interior of house blocks. Skilful handling of the last-named can do much to secure an interesting and lively appearance to the residential area, and indeed they may form one of the decisive elements in its character. Among the devices frequently found, one may list the ordinary cul-de-sac with houses built across its blind end, the cul-de-sac widened out to form a close, with space between house fronts treated as a green, the open ended cul-de-sac, with houses projecting somewhat beyond the end of the carriageway in order to mitigate the loss of frontage occasioned by not building across the end, and with the visual point of interest at the end of the cul-de-sac being formed by a group of trees or some other object rather than a group of houses. A variant of this is the pair of vertically opposite culs-de-sac with their closed ends linked by a footpath, which if subtly curved may provide the opportunity for a delightfully interesting siting of houses. Where, for some special site reason, two roads have to approach each other very closely, economy may be effected and a pleasant variation introduced by placing houses at right angles to the roads and fronting on to a footpath rather than on to a road provided that the distance from the farthest house on the carriageway is not excessive. Layout C in the " Houses, 1953 " layouts already described offers a good example of this.

Interest in the residential layout as regards smaller details is of course supplied, primarily, by interesting architecture, in terms of the design, not only of the house, but of garages, outbuildings, screen walls and the like, as well as by the subtle interplay of buildings of varying height. Although nothing can make up for a lack of good architecture the skilful treatment of such minor details makes a tremendous difference to a housing area and so does the landscape treatment of roads and forecourts. It will readily be appreciated how much interest can be created by a really imaginative use of the variations of treatment of the space between carriageway and buildings shown in Fig. 48.

The actual siting of buildings is of enormous importance, particularly as regards their grouping at crucial points of the layout, such as road junctions. It would be beyond the scope of this book to go into the subject in detail, and the reader is referred to Chapter 10 of Frederick Gibberd's admirable " Town Design ". Nevertheless it will be appropriate to mention a few general principles. Road layout and the siting of buildings should march together, and at a road junction, for example, it ought to appear that the road has to be where it is because of the siting of the houses rather than that the houses are strung alongside the road blindly without following any plan of their own. Variations of building lines are extremely helpful provided that they are well considered and give an effect of interest and repose rather than of mere restless variety for its own sake. One very interesting device is to set houses at an angle to the roadway in echelon form and, as already suggested earlier, the careful arrangement of small detached houses can result in them being an asset rather than a drawback to an area provided that they are not built in excesive numbers. If they are made to touch each other at adjacent corners or are placed so as to form some definite rhythm, as shown in Fig. 93, success can fairly easily be achieved.

It has recently become common to site houses in a rectangular pattern, that is to say with blocks at right angles to each other, even though the road layout may not be in the form of a rigid gridiron. The only justification advanced for this (except ease of setting out on the drawing board!) is that it enables the most favourable orientations to be obtained for the houses. I cannot see the force of this, since in most such layouts, there are houses facing in four different directions, and it is difficult to see how the maintenance of a strictly rectangular siting can secure any advantages in the enjoyment of sunlight. In any case, in this country, the proportion of hours of sunlight enjoyed to total hours of daylight is so small that it is extremely doubtful whether siting houses in order to allow as many habitable rooms as possible to secure a full measure of sunlight is worth while. It can reasonably be argued that when the sun does shine the best place to enjoy it is out of doors.

Furthermore, a good many house types involve the use of sitting-rooms running right through the house, with windows at each end, in which case a north or south orientation will equally secure sunshine for the room in which its enjoyment is most important. Finally, even if it were decided that a generally north and south, or east and west relation of orientations were desirable, a change in direction of a few degrees either way could make no appreciable difference to the enjoyment of sunshine, and since the " Housing Manual " and other documents include house types for north, south, east and west aspects, there seems no good reason for failing on this account to take advantage of the much more substantial advantages of interest and variety obtained by the use of curved roads and subtle changes in the orientation of buildings. On a site of varied topography it is preferable, for functional reasons alone, to depart from any regular pattern of layout.

It seems appropriate to end with a description of the residential parts of the neighbourhood shown in Fig. 68, parts of which are shown to a larger scale in Fig. 91, in order to summarise some of the points dealt with in this chapter.

The layout has been prepared in accordance with the general suggestions for desirable space standards for individual dwellings set out on page 237, and the residential density is that suggested on pages 230, 231 and 234, as is the distribution of dwelling types.

Mention has already been made in Chapter 11 of the reasons for the arrangement of spine roads in this neighbourhood, which need not be enlarged on further except to say that they have been so arranged that they have a much more dominant character than any of the other roads, so that it is unlikely that any of the relative functions of different roads in the neighbourhood can be confused. All the other roads are truly minor in character and sufficiently short for it to be unlikely that any vehicles, except those driven by maniacs, will attain speeds likely to be dangerous in a residential area. Culs-de-sac have been kept reasonably short since the visual treatment of the cul-de-sac becomes more and more difficult as the length increases; there is a strong feeling of anti-climax when one reaches the end of a very long

---

FIG. 92. Top: Three ways of dealing with the closed ends of residential culs-de-sac. Each gives a visual effect quite distinct from the others. At the corners substantial areas are left which can be used for children's play spaces or garage courts or can be incorporated in house plots to provide a proportion of exceptionally large gardens. If none of these alternatives is needed or denied (where, for example the maximum practicable density has to be obtained) the closed ends of culs-de-sac can be made to interlock in some such way as is shown in the small scale inset so that all the land is used for house plots but they are all of normal size. The culs-de-sac are linked by footways.

Below: Six ways of dealing with the junction of two residential roads. Again, the different groupings of buildings in themselves give considerable visual variety.

The left-hand upper example gives a closed in effect which may effectively be used to contrast with an opened out cul-de-sac head. The right-hand upper example uses flats to " turn the corner ". The remaining examples contrast less sharply with each other but allow for considerable variation of garden size and shape and in the disposition of garages, or, where these are not placed within the plots, of outbuildings and screen walls. The spaces shown for garages might of course merely be areas for vehicles to stand on.

Note that in all cases, sight lines, shown by thin broken lines, are complied with.

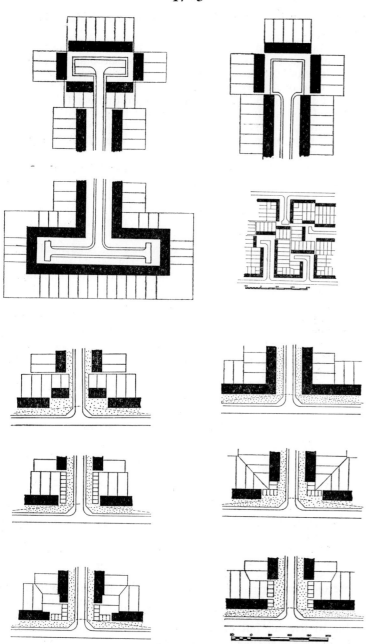

cul-de-sac. In my opinion, although this is going into a matter of fine detail rather beyond the scope of this work, there would be much to be said for treating the carriageways of different kinds of roads differently as regards material, texture or colour, dividing them between spine roads, minor through-roads, and culs-de-sac. Once the system were established and understood it would avoid the need for " No Through Road " signs, for the motorist would immediately recognise a cul-de-sac, from its appearance, even if he could not see the closed end from the entrance.

It has been assumed that it will be possible to build a number of tall blocks of flats. The location of these immediately raises a difficult problem. Broadly speaking, three alternatives are possible: (i) to site all the tall blocks near the town centre on the assumption that this is the part of the neighbourhood where the greatest emphasis is needed in order to direct visual attention towards the focus of the town's life, and also because this is the part of the neighbourhood where it may reasonably be assumed that the households likely to live in the tall blocks will find their social and recreational activities in the facilities provided in the town centre rather than in the more family type facilities likely to be associated with the neighbourhood; (ii) to site the tall blocks around the edge of each neighbourhood in order to provide strong emphasis to the approaches to the town; (iii) to concentrate the tall blocks at the centres and sub-centres in order to provide visual foci which these important parts of the neighbourhood are unlikely to have incorporated in themselves.

The first of these has been selected as, on the whole, the soundest where a comparatively small number of tall blocks can be built. If a large number of tall blocks were needed then one might combine all three alternatives, mass tall blocks near the town centre, site them also around the periphery of the neighbourhood and also place a few at points of special importance in the neighbourhood. This would mean a very large expenditure of money on tall blocks which we are unlikely to see. Contrast of height can be secured just as much between one, two, three and four storey buildings, as between four, six and ten storey buildings.

For the reasons already suggested there is a marked concentration of high density dwellings of all types at the upper end of the neighbourhood adjacent to the town centre. These, in fact, are dwelling types suitable for occupation by households without children, which are more likely to look mainly to the Town Centre for their social life rather than to the neighbourhood centre. Apart from this general grouping there is a substantial weight of flats around the neighbourhood centre, partly for visual reasons but partly also because, just as the dweller in the tall block will look to the town centre for his entertainment, so may also other flat dwellers look towards the neighbourhood centre more than the families with children, and their immediate juxtaposition to it may help towards its success materially. Other flats are placed evenly throughout the neighbourhood, except in the very low density areas, and advantage has been taken of the opportunity to use groups of flats at road junctions in an effective manner. The lowest density housing has naturally been placed on the outskirts of the neighbourhood, partly because it is the inhabitants of this kind of housing who are most likely to possess motor cars in large numbers, and to whom therefore great centrality is relatively un-important, partly, too, because, for obvious reasons, the compactness of the neighbourhood is facilitated by this arrangement. A fair number of houses have been sited so as to front on open spaces, but no very great efforts have been made to carry this to extremes since it presents problems in terms of economy of road layout, and there are advantages in backing onto an open space, in terms of privacy and pleasant outlook, as well as in fronting upon one.

Old persons' dwellings in the form of bungalows are very difficult to site in the most effective manner, for reasons mentioned on page 233. An attempt has been made here to give them seclusion, yet to associate them closely with other forms of dwelling, to avoid too large a concentration of old persons' dwellings on one site, and to place them close to shops and community buildings in order to avoid long walks for the occupants.

The aim has been to provide the very high standard of one garage per house, and this is done partly with the lower density houses by the obvious method of placing a garage alongside the house, partly by the ordinary system of group garages behind road frontage and partly, as already briefly referred to, by the unorthodox method of placing them in front of houses and closely adjoining carriageways. Such garages might not be true garages but merely covered parking bays. There are, no doubt, many objections to such a procedure, but there seems little doubt that garage space of this order of magnitude will, before long, be demanded, and will have to be met in one way or another. It seems inconceivable that we shall ever be able to affordt o build houses of such generous frontage that all shall have space beside them for garages, and it is difficult to work too many groups of garages effectively into a layout without creating awkwardness and indeed even nuisance to residents. Placing garages in front of houses where there is an adequate building line can, if done effectively, provide privacy as regards overlooking from the other side of the road, can afford opportunities for very interesting contrast of building heights (as already noted there is just as much interest of contrast to be obtained from one, two and three storey buildings as between taller buildings of differing heights), and it is also possible on the houseward side of such groups of garages to carry out interesting and effective planting, mainly no doubt in trellis form. Free use has also been made of garages at road junctions, using garages in the place of screen walls.

The siting of buildings and plot boundaries at road junctions has been designed to secure adequate sight lines, effective grouping and back gardens of reasonable size and shape. Not very many odd pieces of ground at the rear of the houses have been left for purposes of children's play spaces, tennis courts and so on, partly because of the fairly tight nature of the layout, but mainly because of the high provision of garages. If it were found desirable to do so it would probably be possible to site more garages in front of houses, and to allocate some of the land thereby saved to these purposes. It might also be possible to use some of the larger house gardens at external corners of culs-de-sac etc.

This is rather a fine point of policy. Children's play spaces etc., need a good deal of maintenance, and are liable to be abused by the dumping of

refuse; not all housing authorities would wish to provide and maintain a large number.

It is quite important to remember that the use of land is not irrevocably fixed for a long period unless a building is actually placed upon it, but that the use of odd pieces of land can be switched between the use of parking spaces, allotments and so on, as need arises. It will be noticed that no allotments whatever have been provided, on the assumption that careful estimation of garden demand and skilful estate management by getting tenants into the houses with gardens of a size which they require obviates the need for these. This no doubt is an optimistic estimate but it is one, which in my opinion, ought to be attempted.

It will be observed that in all essentials the general form of the layout is extremely similar to the first alternative from " Houses, 1953 " and also to the layout of West Green, Crawley, but applied to a considerably larger area than either of these, and I think that one can draw certain useful conclusions from its application. Whatever its faults I do not think that the layout can possibly be described as dull. In any case the actual shapes formed by a road layout really have little effect upon the general appearance of a residential area unless it is quite intolerably dull. Good layout merely assists variety, which is principally achieved by architecture, treatment of details and planting.

The layout is certainly safe for reasons already mentioned in considering the different types of road comprised in it. It is socially reasonable in so far as, although it provides for all kinds of people and for their free association, it does, to some small extent, provide slight separation for different kinds of living patterns—for the very well-to-do and for the old, particularly.

In spite of its informality and variety of shapes the layout is coherent and has a sense of direction. The roads do not wander about aimlessly as in some extremely informal kinds of layout but lead either to the Town Centre, the Neighbourhood Centre, or to a sub-centre. There is a certain logic in the pattern.

Naturally in a work on Planning the houses shown have been drawn without any special thought as to their architectural style. I am quite prepared to be told that in one or two cases it would be difficult or impossible to design an entirely satisfactory house in the position shown, and in relation to plot boundaries, orientation, and neighbouring development. This would not abash me at all, for a layout of this kind is no more, and can be no more, than a firm statement of the disposition of land uses and principal roads, a general statement of disposition of dwelling types and a tentative suggestion about detailed arrangement, which can well be modified in detail, and at a later stage of design. At the same time, the ideas behind this neighbourhood could only be fully expressed by drawing it up in full detail. I am prepared to assert with some confidence that, given competent craftmanship in terms of architecture and landscape architecture, and proper attention to the design of details, development could take place on the lines shown with no more than trivial amendment, and would produce a living area, not only convenient and comfortable to live in, but of high visual attractiveness, and moreover, economical in the employment of resources.

One further point is worth especial notice. The design for the town of which this neighbourhood is a part sprang entirely from a desire to state the functional requirements for a designed town on a regular site unimpeded by existing development or other obstacles, as explained in Chapter 8. No aesthetic considerations entered into the design of the town nor into the disposition of the main elements within the neighbourhood or the design of the road system. They were only considered when the siting of buildings and the routeing of minor roads was undertaken, yet I would claim that the overall interest of the design is probably a good deal greater than in many similar designs where aesthetics were much more prominent in the mind of the designer. There may be more in functionalism than many people would admit.

17-6. SUPPLEMENTARY TOWN MAPS

If a first rate residential area is to be created it seems fairly obvious that it needs to be designed in full detail before the first brick is ever laid. Ideally, no residential development ought to be carried out except in conformity with a detailed plan relating not only to that particular development but to that adjoining it on all sides. But this is an ideal which lies, if anywhere, in the fairly remote future. A multiplicity of ownerships, the vagaries of capital investment and the preferences of individual designers all make quite uncertain the form, timing and extent of proposals for residential development or redevelopment which will be put forward where development is being carried out by private enterprise. Even so, it would, at least theoretically, be possible to prepare detailed designs for all these areas to the degree of detail shown in Fig. 68 and to require compliance with such designs by all developers. This would entail a strength and rigidity of development control of a quite different order from that which is now exercised by Local Planning Authorities (still less by delegate authorities) or which would be supported by the Minister on appeal.

In any case, it would not at present be justifiable to deploy the limited national supply of Planners in such a way as to commit them to preparing innumerable detailed Plans, many of which, or many parts of which, would not be acted upon for a number of years.

In these circumstances a compromise is necessary, and this is to be found in the Supplementary Town Map or Comprehensive Development Area Map. We will concentrate upon the former, because although the two are

practically identical in form, it is procedurally the Supplementary Town Map which is applicable to areas in which a number of different private developers may be operating.

The essential thing for the Supplementary Town Map to achieve is a logical and coherent pattern of uses, roads, pedestrian ways and densities. It should, therefore, normally cover an area which is at least roughly equivalent to a residential neighbourhood. Reference to this subject has already been made in Chapter 14–7.

The point to be emphasised here is that if a Supplementary Town Map is to produce, when implemented, results not too inferior to those which might be expected from development carried out by a single agency, it must have been prepared with the intended future form of development as a whole clearly in mind as regards function, appearance and population. It must, therefore, be, in effect a generalisation or abstraction of a design, not merely a pattern of roads and footpaths and a collection of sub-divisions into varying densities. Such a design need not have been prepared in detail, but can have been quite rough, perhaps even so rough as to have little meaning except to its author, so that this statement is not in contradiction to the earlier suggestion that the universal preparation of detailed designs is impracticable. There is a gap of many scores or hundreds of man-hours between the production of a rough design sufficient to test the general validity of a conception for the development of a residential area and the time needed to draw out a design in full detail.

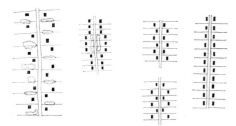

FIG. 93. The problem of layout for detached houses. On the right is shown the fearful monotony which results from regular spacing and regular building lines. The other drawings show, very broadly, the ways in which the introduction of grouping or rhythm, aided by planting, can mitigate the situation.

CHAPTER 18

THE VILLAGE PLAN

No ONE who wants to inform himself about the physical characteristics of the English village can do better than read Thomas Sharp's " The Anatomy of the Village " which analyses the ways in which the village has evolved into the very special thing it is, and the kind of development which is required to maintain and enhance its beauty and general pleasantness. The same author's contribution to " Design in Town and Village " (H.M.S.O.), is equally to be commended.

Attention has already been drawn to the Ministry's policy of not including in a development plan proposals relating to the location of development in communities unless there is likely to be substantial development. So far as one can gather, the reasons for this policy are that in many villages very little development is to be expected over the course of a large number of years and that the setting aside of any area of land specifically for new development is unrealistic, and may encourage unnecessary development which, because of an area having been zoned for development, cannot be refused permission. That, on the other hand, such growth as does occur can better take place, in order to accord with the traditions of village development, in a more or less haphazard way than in the form of a " housing estate ", each application for Planning permission being determined on its merits in relation to the character of the village.

This policy has serious weaknesses. The zoning of an area for development will not usually attract applications unless there is already a demand for development in that locality. If there is such a demand, the existence of an area within which it is known that permission will be readily given will help to confine applications to a limited area, and will largely prevent applications being made in respect of various sites around the village, any one of which could be developed without harm, but development of all of which would result in a most undesirable loss of compactness.

Undoubtedly the fear that the preparation of a village Plan with specific areas for development will attract developers and therefore result in a rapid gobbling up of sites in that particular village because of the ease of obtaining planning permission has some justification. The demand for houses in villages, particularly those near a large town, is to a large extent a floating demand. People who wish to live in a village may not have a strong preference for any particular village, and may well be content to take a house which is available in any village within quite a wide area. The results of this may well be to concentrate development in a village for which a Plan has been prepared to an extent which does not reflect any economic or social reality, and which may cast undue burdens on the various publicly provided services in and around that village.

This evil can be avoided fairly easily, however. One remedy is to prepare and make public Plans for *all* the larger villages in a Local Planning Authority's area *simultaneously*. Another is to apply fairly rigid programming to the Village Plan so as to ensure that development takes place gradually instead of in response to an artificially stimulated demand.

In the absence of a plan, developers naturally select any site which is readily available, and meets their requirements, irrespective of the effect on the development of the village as a whole. The effects of this can clearly be seen in almost any village which has some attractions for non-agricultural residents, the clearly defined core of the old village being surrounded by strings of new houses on all approach roads (see Fig. 94 (i)).

Even since the coming into operation of the Town and Country Planning Act, 1947, the same tendency has been discernible. In the absence of Ministerial encouragement to prepare plans for villages, Local Planning Authorities have tended to permit applications for individual houses anywhere near the built-up area of a village, without any idea of the eventual shape which development should take, and, even where they have dug their heels in, the Minister has not always supported them on appeal.

Fig. 94 (i) shows the site of an application for the erection of a house which was refused by the Local Planning Authority, but allowed on appeal. One can readily imagine the result if applications were made and permitted in respect of every gap in the approach ribbons to this village, yet this, in the absence of a strong policy to force necessary new development on to back land, is exactly what is likely to happen. (Note the word *necessary*. If development is needed in a particular locality, the developer will face the additional cost of back land; casual developers probably will not, but there is no reason why they should not look elsewhere for a site which is cheap to develop and free from Planning objection.)

Permission to develop the kind of site shown is not only the result of the absence of a policy in villages but also part of the policy of permitting " reasonable infilling ", the harmfulness of which is seen particularly clearly on sites near villages.

What is very clearly needed is a plan for every village in which any development beyond one or two houses is expected or intended, the area for development being so arranged that compactness and unity are achieved, peripheral growth being incorporated where this is possible, but otherwise ignored, infilling of it being prevented, and left until the happy day when it can be swept away.

This Plan need not take any elaborate form; indeed, as suggested in Chapter 7, Plans adequate for many villages could be incorporated in the Regional Plan at 1/25,000 for the sole purpose of concentrating development, details being left until greater leisure or an application enabled or necessitated them to be worked out.

Action on these lines is contemplated in Circular No. 50/57 of the Ministry of Housing and Local Government. (See Chapter 7, page 84).

Disregarding current Ministerial policy, the reasonable way of going about village planning seems to be somewhat as follows (see Fig. 94 (xi)):

(1) Prepare a tentative development area for each village in which more than one or two new houses are expected to be needed or demanded. This area should be limited to the space needed for the houses and other buildings which may reasonably be expected to be built, having regard to agricultural demands and the redevelopment, both of existing houses on cramped sites within the village and of scattered houses outside the village but within its service area. The development area should be selected with the greatest possible degree of compactness as its aim, and it should not be treated as an area within which there is automatic free entry for development, but as an area within which any development which may be permitted must take place; the grant of permissions for development should, in some cases, be subjected to strict programming.

One very great benefit of selecting such an area is that it enables access to it to be kept clear. Without a predetermined area for development every gap in existing development may become filled in without anyone noticing what is happening, so that, without demolition, development of back land becomes impossible. This has, in fact, often occurred.

(2) As opportunity or need arises prepare miniature comprehensive development area and programme maps showing in some detail a suitable pattern of development and, subject to the need for keeping accesses to back land open, providing for the filling of existing gaps before any back land is developed. Clearly, development of back land can normally take place only as the result of a fairly large operation and not merely by the efforts of developers of individual houses, so that where it is considered that there is likely to be a demand for individual houses it will be well to leave some vacant frontage for them and to encourage some of the local authority development to take place on back land. But caution is needed here, for two prime requirements are that village development should be fairly continuous and that local authority housing should not be segregated; obviously, too great an allowance for individual houses will jeopardise both these.

The requirements for schools, village halls and shops must be kept in mind so that appropriate sites may be set aside for them. Again, in the absence of a plan for the village, gradual piecemeal development may occupy or block the access to all suitable sites. (See Fig. 73 (vi).)

Apart from reservation of individual sites for specific purposes it is only in the very largest villages that any use zoning will be practicable or desired, for one of the strongest characteristics of the village is its intimate mixture of uses; only in the detailed design of development is it necessary to ensure that uses are so related that sightliness, privacy and freedom from nuisance are ensured. This involves some slight segregation, perhaps no more than a screen of trees, of some non-residential uses from dwellings.

This is a subject further discussed in Chapter 20.

In selecting land for future village development the views of the Ministry of Agriculture will have to be obtained, preferably as soon as a tentative selection has been made, but in any case before giving any permissions for development. A good deal of firmness may be required; the Ministry of Agriculture is sometimes guilty of extraordinary narrowness of outlook and seeks to preserve in agricultural use one field rather than another because of its slight, and even temporary, agricultural superiority.

The site selected for a village extension will probably influence the physical shape and character of the village for centuries, and while, in the case of two sites with little to choose between them as regards suitability for development, it may be perfectly proper to develop the one which is less valuable agriculturally, this should never be done to the detriment of the physical compactness and visual character of the village; to do so is to lack a sense of proportion. Tragic errors of this kind have been made since the war.

The policy which ought to be followed in permitting houses for " adventitious " population in villages has already been discussed in Chapter 4, page 50. As was suggested there it is essential that fundamental decisions should be made about the optimum distribution of population between towns and villages and the extent to which, in the ought of such decisions, any particular village ought to be allowed to grow. It is unnecessary to repeat this discussion here, but, in reading the following pages, it ought to be borne in mind all the time that a rational regional policy is an indispensible background to good village development.

We must now turn to the specific problems of village design. There are, as Thomas Sharp explains clearly in " The Anatomy of the Village ", two basic forms of village pattern, although numerous combinations and modifications of each are possible. These are the **roadside village** and the **squared village.** (See Fig. 94 (i)–(v).)

The roadside village is usually in the form of buildings stretching along the approaches to a crossroads, though quite often it is simply a length of development along a single road. It is, in fact, ribbon development, but of a very different kind from fortuitous modern ribbon development, and for two reasons.

First, the traditional village was based upon an agricultural economy and the population which could be supported by the surrounding countryside limited it to a reasonable size; second, the sites of roadside villages are never arbitrary but are given a sense of enclosure and unity in all kinds of ways.

The limit of development may be at a bend in a road, a crest or a depression, with some natural or artificial feature closing the vista, so that the village is not a collection of buildings which happen to be placed alongside a road or roads, but a *place* with well-marked entrances and exists. The punctuation may be obvious, as where a road makes a sharp bend, or subtle, as where a slight curve with a rise in the ground beyond closes the vista, but it is almost invariably present.

It is for this reason that lineal extensions of roadside villages are hardly

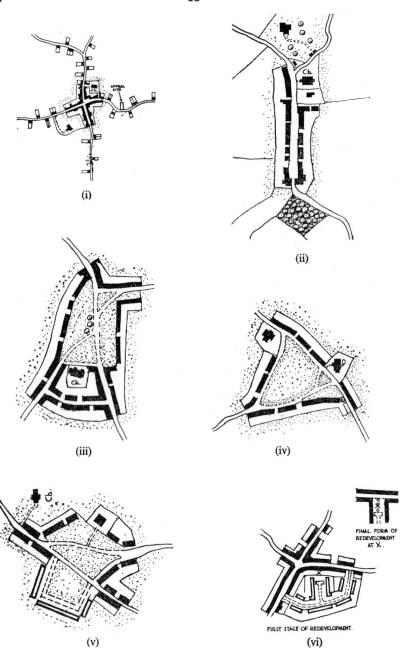

(i)

(ii)

(iii)

(iv)

(v)

(vi)

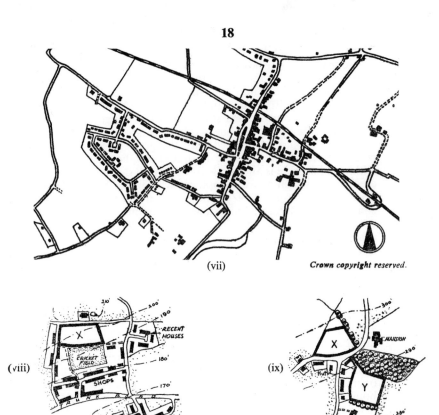

(vii)

Crown copyright reserved.

(viii)

(ix)

FIG. 94. Village forms and village problems. Where proposed development is shown the new development is in outline, the old in solid black.
  (i) The typical English crossroads village with typical sporadic development on its outskirts.
  (ii) The single street village. Note the sense of enclosure given by bends in the road and dominant features beyond.
  (iii) A typical village green village of roughly square form. Note how views out of the village are blocked by buildings.
  (iv) A very common variant of (iii) essentially a road junction rather than a crossroads.
  (v) A village with a green can often be extended without detriment to unity, which may even be enhanced.
  (vi) The kind of solution which should be adopted where existing development does not permit immediate linkage of old and new.
  (vii) A flagrant example of failure to link modern development with old. West Malling, Kent.
  (viii) If new housing is sited at Y the village will be permanently and unpleasantly severed by the trunk road. If it is sited at X this will be avoided and church and village will be more closely linked.
  (ix) A tiny village. If its proposed school is sited at Y it will make no visual contribution. If at X it will give the whole village substance.

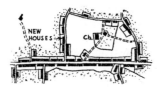

(x)

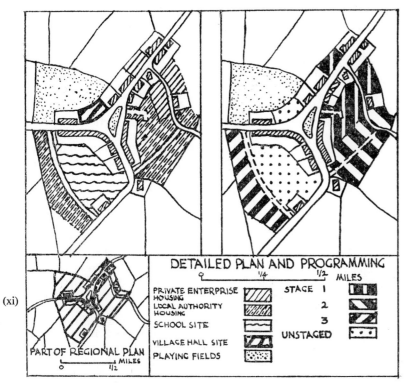

(xi)

ever satisfactory; the extensions lie outside the *place* and appear as intruders. Only when some further point of punctuation exists or can readily be devised can lineal extension be justified at all, and even so it is hardly possible to avoid destroying the original unity, creating duality, with a sense of anti-climax when approaching or leaving the village.

Extension in depth is therefore preferable. In the case of the crossroad village this may be easy to secure by developing the spaces between the arms of the cross, but the danger here is that, even though the unity of the original village will not be impaired, the new development will be shut off from the existing.

This can only be avoided by linking old with new, visually and by opening up communication through existing gaps in development, or, where no such exist, by so arranging the new development that, in redevelopment of existing buildings, a linkage can be created in a natural way. For example, in Fig. 94 (vi) the new development may temporarily have to be shut off from the existing, but redevelopment at X, with buildings set end on to the road, will bring it within the community enclosure.

The extension of a village built along a single road may be very difficult to link with existing development if only a small extension is required, and there are no gaps to afford access. In such a case the only thing to do is to construct a temporary access road to the back land with its access to the existing road just outside the developed area, with a view to integrating the old and new development in a similar fashion to Fig. 94 (vi), when redevelopment provides the opportunity. Much the same thing will be necessary when there are no gaps in the frontage of a crossroad village, but is less likely to occur.

The squared village usually has a more flexible plan, and quite often there is more than one distinct group of development, so that its unity is less delicately balanced than in the case of the roadside village. It is therefore often easier to work new development into the village pattern. Frequently it can be grouped around an open space which reflects the original square. (See Fig. 94 (v).)

The " square " of a squared village may be of almost any shape; oblong, roughly circular or triangular; it may be surrounded by roads or intersected by one or more roads, in fact any really substantial widening out of the building lines at the village centre brings the village into the squared class, even though there may be no village green as such.

It is also common for there to be a good deal of development on the approach roads leading to the greens; where these are not straight but wind about it is usually possible to arrange new development so that it links development around the green with that on the approach road so as actually to enhance the unity of the village and to make the new development appear an essential and established part of the village by reason of being in the very midst of it. This applies also to roadside villages of irregular shape; pages 21 and 22 of the Housing Manual give illustrations of a small and a large village the new development of which has been carried out in this way.

It is absolutely essential that new development should not be set apart from existing development, whatever difficulties may be encountered; still less should this be done deliberately for any reason at all. Pre-war local authority

(x) A large decaying village alongside a trunk road. The ruthless observance of planning principles can give it a new lease of life and a better form without interference to, or from, the trunk road, as shown in the lower drawing.

(xi) Detailed plan and programme for the limited expansion of a village. *Inset*. Proposal for the village included in the Regional Plan. This consists merely in allocating a tentative area for future development (in this case confirmed at the later stage) without differentiation of uses or stages of development.

housing often offended in this respect. Sometimes it was placed right outside the village because no single site of sufficient size existed within the built-up area, and development of two or more smaller sites was not thought desirable because of the greater complications involved in acquiring the land and the real or supposed difficulties and additional cost in carrying out the development; sometimes the contours of available sites within the village were awkward.

The effect of doing this is invariably deplorable, both visually and in the psychological effect produced, which may be summed up in the phrase: " There's the village and there are the council houses." This habit has persisted since the war, though not so commonly as previously, and even though the standard of architectural design is generally vastly improved, the effect of apartness remains. Fig. 94 (vii) shows an example of a large village in which this is apparent from plan shapes alone.

It is, in fact, almost impossible for any very large single mass of development to combine happily with the existing development of a village, whether set apart from or joined on to it, for nearly all villages have developed slowly over a very long period and contain no large number of houses built at the same time. Thus, although consistency and harmony of architectural style are generally present, *identity* of style is usually confined to quite a few buildings. Twenty or thirty houses built at the same time on one site, a common result of present-day concentration on rural housing, which must inevitably be in the same idiom unless insincere and strained variety is sought, overwhelm and clash with the old. If several small sites are developed simultaneously and separated by older development this effect is dispelled, or at least much diminished.

Development has not always been set apart from the village for merely utilitarian reasons; quite often it has been done for social and aesthetic reasons, and the grievously mistaken views which led to this being done have not yet been entirely abandoned by all those concerned with village development, so that some examination of them is necessary.

There has been a kind of stigma attaching to " council houses " almost since they first began to be built; a feeling that their inhabitants are somehow inferior to those of other houses, and best set apart. No doubt there was once some kind of rational basis for this attitude because of the social strata from which tenants were recruited, though it was always a grossly inhumane and pharisaical one, but it bears no relation to fact nowadays, particularly in rural areas where decent housing is generally scarce and council houses eagerly sought.

Nevertheless, it is still quite common for sites for local authority housing to be opposed because they are close to or overlooked by large houses. Not infrequently the argument is used that the construction of local authority houses on such sites will lead to depreciation in the value of the larger houses and hence to successful applications for their rateable values to be reduced, with consequent detriment to the local authority's rate income. There is often, too, an assumption, express or implied, that the view from large houses ought not to be spoiled and that their seclusion from the *hoi polloi* should be maintained as a matter of social justice.

Most of this is quite indefensible. It is no proper aim of land Planning to maintain the value of individual properties, though it is certain that wise Planning will result in overall economy for many reasons. Purchasers of houses do not also buy the view from the windows, and if the requirements of sound community development demand the blocking of that view, this will earn them sympathy but is no source of legitimate grievance.

The maintenance of the peculiar beauty and virtues of the English village is of such incomparably greater importance than some slight loss of rate revenue that no local authority at all worthy of its responsibilities should even take it into account. The reason for the existence of the normal village is its function as a home and service centre for workers in the agricultural industry, and this aspect must be predominant if complete distortion is to be avoided. Further, as was shown in Chapter 8, one of the basic characteristics of the village—the infantile community—is that differentiation of classes of houses does not exist. The village contains a complex interweaving of personal and functional relationships which is expressed in the intimate mixture of uses and social classes commonly seen, and people who are not prepared to take their part in these should live elsewhere. In very many villages large houses and humble cottages stand and have stood side by side for centuries, and there is no very clear reason why this practice should be abandoned.

There is, of course, no doubt that many villages benefit greatly from the presence of a number of comparatively well-to-do people living in the larger houses, but their value to the village is in direct proportion to the extent to which they are of it as well as in it, and those who enter most fully into its life are the least likely to demand apartheid. This in no way conflicts with the views expressed in the previous chapter about mixed development in neighbourhood units, for social and functional relationship in towns are at once more complicated and less intimate than in a village.

Forgetfulness of the primary function of a village can lead to grotesque results; for example, in one village the establishment of a depot for repairing agricultural machinery on a highly suitable site on its outskirts was successfully opposed because of the presence nearby of several large houses sited in sporadic fashion and wholly unrelated to the needs of the village, it being feared that the depot would be " injurious to their amenities ".

Aesthetic reasons for segregating new development are generally as bogus as social reasons. The underlying thought nearly always seems to be that " architecture " stopped rather more than a hundred years ago and that anything new is bound to conflict with and " spoil " the old. If this were true it would be the clearest possible proof of the decadence of our civilisation; most fine towns and villages contain buildings of various styles, each of which was " modern " when it was employed. Failure to adjust the design of new buildings so that they harmonise with the old is merely incompetence, and is not due to the operation of some natural law.

There is, in fact, no reason to think that modern architects are incapable of designing buildings worthy to stand beside the finest of former times, but of course in order to show their worth, they must be employed. To pursue this subject further would be to trespass upon the contents of Chapter 20·5; for the purposes of this chapter it will be sufficient to give two examples of the effect upon the whole structure of a community which can result from efforts to preserve the old from contamination by the new.

Fig. 94 (viii) shows a large village through which passes a trunk road carrying very heavy weekend traffic. The portion to the north of the trunk road is many times larger than that to the south and contains the school, nearly all the shops, some post-war local authority housing, as well as most of the earlier housing, and a fine cricket ground. The ancient church is also to the north and, for obvious historical and geographical but not aesthetic reasons, is somewhat removed from the original village.

Sporadic inter-war development and early post-war housing has reached out towards the church. A substantial further number of new houses was required and the only suitable site for it was X, a large level field between the cricket ground and the church. There was violent, though sectional, local opposition to this site being used on the grounds both that modern houses would be unworthy neighbours for the church and that the view of the church from the village would be obscured by them. It was therefore proposed that Y, on the south of the trunk road, should be used. This would have resulted in a substantial proportion of the village having to cross the main road for practically all local services and the swamping of the existing development to the south, which is practically a self-contained hamlet, by new housing.

After prolonged argument X was eventually selected, it having been pointed out that its development would link the church more closely with the village, from which it had hitherto been inappropriately remote, but also that the layout of the new housing could readily be designed so that not only would the view of the church from the south be preserved, but would actually be enhanced and lent dramatic emphasis by being framed with buildings.

The second example (see Fig. 94 (ix)) concerns a much smaller village, little more than a hamlet, which contained only about a dozen houses, a large mansion of fine appearance, and a decrepit hut used as a clubroom.

For geographical reasons a new primary school was to be located in the village and X was chosen as the site. Not only would this site have been conveniently accessible, but the erection of a school in so dominant a position would have given the village a focus and visual expression of community which it completely lacked.

Again, there was violent local opposition on the grounds that the erection of a school building would spoil the appearance of the mansion. Unhappily this opposition, which quite clearly was not genuinely representative of local opinion, was successful, and the school was consigned to Y, on back land, and so screened by trees that it will be invisible from any part of the village. It can readily be admitted that it might be difficult to make a modern primary school harmonise successfully with a mansion of some antiquity if the two were placed cheek by jowl, but it so happened that existing trees on the east of X would have softened the juxtaposition in a wholly appropriate fashion.

In ways such as this those who, ironically enough, proclaim themselves the staunchest defenders of tradition seek to prevent the village having a live and continuing tradition, the only kind worth having.

So much for the form of the normal village. We next need to consider to what extent an existing pattern of rural development in scattered form with few of any substantial nucleated settlements should be accepted for the future. This matter is discussed in Chapters 4 and 7, and need only be dealt with here in relation to general principles. The pattern of rural development, ignoring recent buildings not based on agricultural requirements, varies greatly in this country. There are areas where fairly large closely knit villages with hardly any buildings outside them are the rule and those where sporadic development is very widespread, condensing only occasionally into something continuous enough to be called a village, and with every imaginable intermediate form between these extremes. The pattern prevailing in any particular area can usually be shown to derive from geological characteristics: the location of sources of water and the types of soil The former fairly strictly limited the location of dwellings while the latter had its effect upon types of farming and shapes and sizes of farms, thus affecting the numbers of dwellings built at each of the sites suitable from the point of view of water supply.

Modern conditions present us with a paradox. The bicycle, the motor car, and the motor bus render compactness of village growth less essential since rural dwellers have become more mobile. On the other hand, universal primary education and the need to have schools within easy walking distance for small children, together with the recognition of piped sewerage and water and electricity supply as essentials rather than luxuries makes compactness more important than ever before, since the economic possibility of providing these services depends upon a reasonably short length of main for each consumer.

It is true that it is hoped eventually to provide every farm in the country with water and electricity for agricultural reasons alone and that if this were done the network of service lines would be sufficiently close to allow practically every community to tap them with comparative ease, but this ideal is a long way from realisation, and, meanwhile, the more compact development of villages would be an important factor to enable the villages themselves to be supplied.

Although collective water-borne sewage disposal is not essential in all rural communities it certainly is so on some subsoils, and once population density arises above the intensity prevailing in any except very dispersed villages it becomes extremely desirable, to say the least of it. It is important to realise that, while many rural communities are too dispersed for services to be provided economically, it is a comparative rarity for them to be so widely dispersed that each dwelling can be regarded as an entirely isolated house.

It is necessary to consider the disposal both of human wastes and of waste water. In a scattered rural community without piped water the earth closet, necessarily outside the main building, may be adequate provided its contents can be disposed of where they will not contaminate whatever source of water is available. It is unlikely that, in such conditions, enough water will be used for its disposal to create a problem. Nevertheless, those inclined to idealise primitive rural conditions might well find it an educative experience to use an earth closet on a wet winter night.

Once piped water is supplied the situation changes rapidly, for W.C.s and baths are likely to follow very shortly, and a simple arithmetical calculation shows that the watertight cesspool regularly emptied before it overflows is a rare object.

If rural dwellers are to have W.C.s and baths (and does anyone suggest that this is not a fairly modest ambition?), sewers also have to be provided to avoid nuisance and danger to health. Sewerage is extremely expensive and can only be supplied when development is reasonably compact. Of course, many houses with large gardens located on a suitable subsoil will continue to use cesspools and septic tanks, as will such isolated houses as are erected in the future, but the above remarks apply to nucleated settlements.

All too often, even now, one sees groups of rural local authority houses erected with their own small sewage disposal plant, admirable in its way, but not designed so as eventually to serve the whole village, the existing development in which is presumably expected to put up with existing conditions permanently.

The case for compact village development is unanswerable, and it seems to be actively opposed only by those who mistakenly think that dispersal is a basic ingredient of rural charm and thus dislike compactness *per se*, those who, equally mistakenly, believe that the mixture of old and new houses is necessarily visually unsatisfactory and who therefore oppose infilling within villages and those who possess a house in a village with undeveloped land opposite it, and understandably, but for no socially valid reason, dislike the idea of having their view blocked by houses.

In the past the advantages of closely nucleated rural settlements were fewer than is now the case because piped and wired services were non-existent. For many people there was no such thing as daily shopping because the farm labourer's wages were to a great extent in kind, and low at that; the only places frequently visited were the church and the pub. Most cottages were tied, the property of the farmer who employed the labourer, and who usually preferred to have him living under his eye. In the absence of strong reasons for living in a village, the labourer himself might well prefer to live as close as possible to his work. Since the farmer provided the houses for his labourers, he naturally preferred to build them on his own land, and this might all be well away from the village.

Today these factors have either disappeared or have become greatly weakened. The importance of compactness for the provision of piped and wired services has already been discussed, and this importance is likely to increase rather than to diminish. District heating, rediffusion and other facilities not yet imagined may all be attainable for the compact village before very long. Although this is the kind of suggestion which tends to raise the blood pressure of the more conservative country lover, who seems to find something unseemly about the idea of rural dwellers enjoying urban conveniences, it is fairly certain that the maintenance of a sufficiently numerous rural population depends to a large extent upon the convenience of rural life not falling too far behind that of urban life. Even though the real joy and glory of living in the country may make it well worth while to forgo many artificial amenities, the gap between town and country must not be too great.

Daily shopping has become an increasingly necessary and varied activity as dependence on local produce for sustenance has declined, and the food products of the whole world have become available to all.

Universal primary education has made the grouping of homes within reasonable walking distance of a primary school a matter of importance, since there is little doubt that, despite the growlings of veterans who recall their seven-mile walk to and from school, sustained only by a chunk of bread and cheese, arduous daily journeys are harmful to small children.

The tied cottage is still with us, although the increasing supply of houses built by local authorities is gradually making it less necessary. The farmer still likes to have his employees on or close to the farm because of their greater availability, which is helpful because agricultural operations cannot be neatly confined to office hours. He still likes some at least of his employees to live in houses which he owns, because they do not enjoy the protection against eviction afforded by the Rent Restrictions Acts; indeed, the present shortage of skilled agricultural workers and of houses makes it almost indispensable for the farmer to be able to offer a house when one of the key jobs on the farm falls vacant.

This last consideration is related to temporary difficulties and passing circumstances, some of which could be easily remedied. It would be a simple matter, for instance, to make it remunerative for farmers to build in villages rather than on their own land. As a permanent policy there seems to be little justification for building agricultural workers' houses outside nucleated settlements, except in the case of those to be occupied by stockmen, shepherds and others whose arduous and intermittent duties make it an overriding necessity for them to live close to the scene of their work. For the others the convenience of the wife and children for access to shops and school respectively, apart from the economic provision of services, seems to be a far stronger factor than for the male workers of the family to live on the site of their work. In country of normal topography a bicycle ride to work of even two miles is a bagatelle for a healthy man, even in bad weather, compared with a journey to school of similar length for a small child.

Economically, socially and visually the regrouping of scattered rural development into compact villages of fair size has everything to recommend it, but if such a policy is successfully pursued it will still be necessary for stringent selection to be made among all the villages which exist to determine in which of them new houses are to be built in order to create a rural pattern which consists principally of villages which are capable of supporting at least a few shops, a village hall and a primary school.

The countryside can only be the home of a limited population for economic reasons, so that in order to secure substantial increases in size of any significant number of villages it is essential to confine new development almost entirely to those which are best located to form part of a well-balanced social and economic pattern. Buildings, even agricultural workers' cottages, do not last for ever, and the logical extension of such a policy is to refuse permission for the re-erection of worn-out houses in such of the smaller villages and hamlets as do not find a place in such a pattern. This means the ultimate extinction of such places, a happening which for many reasons may be extremely regrettable, but which should not be resisted if it can be clearly demonstrated that it is in the interest of the majority of rural dwellers.

An excellent example of the results of trying to carry out this policy occurred in Berkshire. The village of Letcombe Bassett had, in 1948, 51 houses of less than £21 rateable value; of these 12 were subject to demolition or clearance orders under the Housing Acts and 21 were earmarked for such treatment, leaving only 20 in somewhat better condition. There were eight cesspools in the village and the remaining houses had dry closets and sink soakaways. There is extensive watercress cultivation in the district and a comprehensive drainage scheme for the village would probably entail laying a length of a mile or more of main sewer to connect with an existing sewage works at the larger village of Letcombe Regis, $1\frac{1}{4}$ miles away. The Wantage Rural District Council had insisted that proper drainage must be provided before undertaking a reconditioning scheme for unfit houses.

Of the total population of 150, about 26, eight of them self-employed, worked in Letcombe Bassett and the other workers, about 19 in number, worked elsewhere. There were 23 children of school age, of whom the younger went to school in Letcombe Regis and the older in Wantage. Clubs and other social activity were not flourishing.

The Berkshire County Planning Committee took the view, and so advised the Wantage Rural District Council, that, as a matter of general Planning policy, the immediate housing required for Letcombe Bassett and Letcombe Regis should be sited in Letcombe Regis, and that when the demolition of unfit houses became practicable the respective needs of the two villages should be reviewed. This opinion had been arrived at after consideration of all the difficulties and disadvantages, physical, social and aesthetic, of continuing to build houses in Letcombe Bassett or on a site outside it. It was assumed that, if new development were sited in Letcombe Regis, Letcombe Bassett would revert to a group of farms with associated dwellings for stock-men and other key workers, together with a few sizeable houses and houses occupied by retired people and others not associated with agriculture.

In spite of the moderation and reasonableness of these views they aroused a storm of vehement opposition from the Letcombe Bassett Parish Council and others. Questions were asked in the House, and in reply to them the Minister of Town and Country Planning stated that it was wrong to suggest that small villages were to be planned off the map, that it was not the Government's policy to regard agricultural villages as in a state of disintegration and that he did not consider that " there should be any bar to the replacement of outworn houses and the improvement of services in the majority of smaller villages ". Apparently hardly anyone was prepared to look facts squarely in the face and weigh the economic and social needs of rural communities against the supposed desirability of trying to keep life in villages not capable of meeting current needs.

Attention must now be turned to the actual layout of buildings and roads in the village. The layout of an existing village is almost always very simple and this simplicity should be continued in new development. Anything elaborate inevitably conflicts, and even planting schemes should be less varied than might be permissible in urban development.

The need for simplicity, combined with the small extent of most village housing areas, will often entail a more expensive form of layout than would be justified in a town, not in order to *copy* ancient methods of layout but to harmonise agreeably with them. The frequent need to construct road accesses through comparatively narrow gaps in existing development results in lengths of necessarily unproductive frontage which, because of the small extent of the development, comprise a high proportion of the total length. Odd-shaped pieces of back land which could otherwise be opened up for development by means of a number of culs-de-sac may have to be left un-developed because of the need to avoid a complicated street pattern; where the existing pattern is open it will usually be desirable to continue in similar fashion, and if this entails the development of road frontage on one side only costs become very high.

This consistency of pattern is very important; to carry out new development in a conventional close pattern of through-street and cul-de-sac when the existing pattern is quite different is to introduce an element almost as markedly alien as a site outside the village. Conversely, an existing village of some size developed in very close form may require the introduction of one or more greens with single-sided development as relief.

Nevertheless, the layout should not be unnecessarily costly; modern forms of layout designed to avoid waste can often be appropriately used with little or no adaptation. For example, the green with a cul-de-sac running up the middle is a particularly pleasant and economical form of development for both urban and rural purposes. Cross-access development adjoining a footpath can also be used to advantage.

High expenditure in the creation of new road frontage can often be partially offset by full use of existing road frontage. Characteristically, a village is an intensively developed area, and although charming villages exist which have a very loose texture they are the exception rather than the rule and could indeed often be improved rather than the reverse by being more closely built up.

Every chance should therefore be taken of filling up gaps in frontage development so that the contrast between open countryside and close, enclosed village may be emphasised; considerable thoroughness is desirable though it should not be carried to absurd lengths. The wall of a large garden, with trees behind it, may contribute as much to the sense of enclosure of a village as any buildings, and need not be disturbed; a space between buildings may give an entrancing glimpse of country beyond and partake more of the nature of a window out of the village than of a gap in development, and as such should be cherished, but, subject to these exceptions, continuous development is desirable; the vicarage tennis court, the allotment on frontage land and the field bought to preserve the seclusion of a house should all be sacrificed when the future pattern of development would clearly be improved by doing so. Furious opposition may often be encountered and there may be reluctance on the part of the Ministry to confirm a compulsory purchase order in respect of such sites if any other land remotely suitable for housing exists, but they are, in fact, the sites which should be developed first because they positively contribute to village character instead of being an extension requiring special effort if it is to be satisfactorily assimilated. It is a good rule, when considering this kind of problem, to ask oneself whether a private *application* to develop a particular site could be refused; if not there cannot be a very strong case against public acquisition and development.

These suggestions, which many readers will probably feel to be unduly ruthless, constitute the most direct and simple method possible of conserving traditional forms of village development. The original village enclosure is the area within which new development can make its strongest contribution and cannot impair unity, provided it is competently designed; any non-intensive land use which need not occupy frontage within this area should be transferred elsewhere.

It ought not to be necessary to point out that, apart from considerations of light, air, privacy and garden space, the density of development in a village is quite unimportant. The open countryside in unlimited quantities lies close at hand and although in many ways the village is comparable to a small urban neighbourhood its gross density is irrelevant. In the typical village a large proportion of house plots back on to agricultural land and the density could be drastically altered merely by moving the position of the back fence backwards or forwards

Finally, the problem of main roads passing through villages must be discussed Many villages are sited directly on main through roads because, before motor traffic began, this was the logical place for them. The result is that in scores of villages the village street, which quite appropriately provides access to shops, dwellings and public buildings, also resounds to the continuous roar of traffic rushing from London to the coast at weekends, or of heavy industrial traffic every day and night of the week. This is a terrible situation; the noise and danger wellnigh destroy every attribute which should make village life pleasant and should not be tolerated a moment longer than can be helped; most certainly they should not be regarded as normal and inevitable.

A by-pass route should be selected and safeguarded for every village on a main road (and this includes every road carrying a steady volume of through-traffic, not merely trunk roads), however remote the possibility of its construction may be. The by-pass may take the form of an individual loop for each village, or a single new length of road by-passing several villages. Alternatively, a completely new route not passing near any villages may successfully draw off the bulk of traffic from the original main road.

Investigations have shown that the proportion of traffic which can be induced to use a by-pass is roughly in inverse proportion to the size of the place by-passed, so that the construction of a village by-pass is likely to give satisfactory results. But it is important that every inducement should be given to traffic to use it, particularly by facilitating entrance to it. For example, the kind of junction shown in Fig. 49 (R.) would be likely to increase markedly the proportion of traffic using the by-pass as compared with the junction shown in Fig. 49 (L.).

Obviously it is likely to be many years before a substantial proportion of the villages which need it are effectively by-passed, and although little or nothing can be done in most cases, where, as is not uncommon, a village is in a state of physical decay but is of importance sufficient to justify redevelopment, the best plan may well be to redevelop it clear of the main road, as shown in Fig. 94 (x). This would, of course, be an operation of great delicacy and magnitude and would inevitably result in virtual extinction of the existing character of the village. It is therefore a remedy which requires deep thought before it is applied.

CHAPTER 19

COUNTRY PLANNING

THE TITLES OF Acts of Parliament relating to Planning in this country since 1932 have always included the words "Town and Country" and it is probably this which has led a good many people to think of Country Planning as a specific and separate activity. It cannot really properly be regarded in this light. Most of the Planning work which might be regarded as Country Planning falls under the heading of Regional Planning and of the detailed implementation of Regional Planning proposals. For example, the choice of major and minor rural centres and of routes of main roads through the countryside forms an important part of Regional Planning, while Village Planning consists of drawing up details of proposals in respect of the former, and the detailed routeing and landscaping of roads follows from the latter.

Other activities which affect the pattern of life in the countryside or its appearance or both are the control of buildings in rural areas, tree preservation, the setting up of national and regional parks, the selection of sites for service training land, reservoirs, mineral working etc.

There are no legal powers available for undertaking positive landscape design over large areas of privately owned rural land in the eighteenth century manner, nor indeed is it easy to see how such powers could be framed and operated, even if it were thought desirable to do so, though the activities of the Forestry Commission, Statutory Undertakers and the Ministry of Transport and its agent authorities when designing trunk roads have a tremendous effect on the landscape, sometimes for ill, sometimes for good. Again, no powers are available to bring about the regrouping of farm units or to control the kind of agricultural activity carried on in different areas.

Almost the only activities classifiable as Country Planning which do not derive from Regional Planning are control of appearance and the reclamation of derelict land such as mineral spoil heaps, a good deal of work on which is now being undertaken. The control of various kinds of development in the countryside is dealt with in Chapter 20, while the Regional aspects have been dealt with in previous chapters.

There remains the Green Belt policy, the operation of which occupies such a large proportion of the time and energy of the staffs of Local Planning Authorities and the Ministry. Except for the simple purpose of a general statement of policy about areas which ought not in any circumstances to be developed, in order to prevent the undue extension of a city or to prevent adjoining towns from merging, I cannot myself see much virtue in Green Belts. I consider their current use to be a clumsy administrator's substitute for genuine Town Planning; I certainly do not think that they are in general a useful tool for the Town Planner working in an enlightened atmosphere. Their use has certainly plunged Planning Authorities and the Ministry into morasses of illogical thought from which none seem likely to emerge without looking extraordinarily foolish.

I shall not therefore consider them further in a book concerned with Planning Principles and desirable Planning Practice. Those interested can find a full account of Green Belts in Chapters 5 and 10 of my "Town Planning at the Crossroads", Estates Gazette, 1961, and in D. S. Mandelker's "Green Belts and Urban Growth".

PART III

DEVELOPMENT CONTROL AND PLANNING ORGANISATION

CHAPTER 20

DEVELOPMENT CONTROL

20-1. INTRODUCTORY

NO PLAN is of much use unless its proposals are put into practice, even though the march of events may require substantial amendments to be made to the original Plan before it is fully implemented.   The implementation of a Plan depends upon the development carried out by many agencies, both public and private, complying with its proposals.   The process by which this is secured is called development control.   Besides this, development control involves regulation of the detailed aspects of development, about which no guidance is given by the Development Plan, so as to ensure convenient and sightly results.

Broadly speaking, in this country, we have a system of development *control*, rather than a set of *controls*, such as we had before 1943 and as is still the case in most countries which have Planning legislation.   In other words, within extremely wide limits, Planning Authorities are empowered to determine applications for Planning permission on their merits.   They may find it convenient to use certain sets of standards such as, for example, the Day-lighting code or Parking standards, but they are not obliged to do so, as would be the case if such standards were enshrined in sets of by-laws, nor will it be certain that the Minister, on appeal, will uphold a refusal merely because the proposed development violates some set of standards.   There may often be special circumstances which make compliance with them needless.

Such a system is, on the whole, greatly preferable to a code of controls; it is much more flexible and it avoids the considerable likelihood of good development being refused permission solely because it happens to conflict harmlessly with a set of rules.   It has the single disadvantage that it needs a much higher level of competence for its successful operation.

An extremely able and interesting comparison of the two systems is contained in " Land-use Controls in the United States " by John Delafons (Harvard University Press, 1962).

Development control is nevertheless affected by many legislative provisions, both principal and delegated, and it will be necessary, in order to make this chapter fully comprehensible, to review them in some detail; this is done in the next section.

Meanwhile, certain general principles which must always be borne in mind can be suggested.

Powers of development control are so wide, and, as regards some subjects, so vague, that the framing of a clear policy based upon definite principles is essential if control is not to degenerate into either, on the one hand, an irritating petty tyranny, or, on the other, into an ineffective and formless confusion unlit by either principle or precedent.

First and foremost, as already emphasised in Chapter 1, a Local Planning Authority should clearly understand that the sole object of Planning and Planning control is to secure the right use of land, and that Planning powers must not be made to subserve other ends.

It is also important not to attempt to make Planning control do things which, though they may be proper and desirable, are outside the scope of Planning.   There are many examples of this, perhaps the most typical being cases where members of the public or of a Local Planning Authority urge that preventive action should be taken against activities which do not involve controllable development of land or change of its use.   An amusing instance of this occurred when a farmer, wishing to convert one of his buildings into a fruit store, mistakenly thought that Planning permission was necessary, and made application for it.   The Planning committee which considered it decided that such a use, near a public road, was undesirable because of the untidiness likely to result from packing cases, paper, etc., left lying about, and, despite the advice of its officers that it had no power to do so, was within an ace of refusing permission.

Again, the Ministry has taken the view that, normally, the lack of proper drainage facilities is not relevant to refusal of Planning permission because this is a matter that can be dealt with under another set of legal powers. (This does not of course in the least imply that practicability of sewering should not be taken into account in *selecting* land for development in the course of preparing a Plan.)

Yet another perversion of Planning powers occurs when an applicant wishing to do something which requires permission under an Act unconnected with Planning, the establishment of a nursery school, for example, under the Nurseries and Child-Minders Regulation Act, 1948, is told by the authority concerned first to get Planning permission and is refused determination of his application until this has been obtained even though he may rightly believe that, in the circumstances, no Planning permission is necessary.

None of these points, of course, arises in connection with the vast majority of applications, which clearly require Planning permission.   Nevertheless, confusion still commonly occurs, most frequently in cases where there is objection to a proposal on several grounds.   Where this is so it is essential to deal with the most fundamental aspects of the matter first, leaving detail until later.   For example, it is asking for trouble to refuse permission for the erection of a number of dwellings on the sole grounds that their proposed external appearance is unsatisfactory if it is undesirable to have any dwellings at all on the site proposed.

It is prudent and salutary when considering development applications to ask such of the following questions as may be applicable, always in the same order, and not to proceed to the next question until an answer has been found:

(1) **Ought the use of the site in question to be changed ?**
(2) **If so, is the proposed use suitable for the site ?**
(3) **If so, is there some other site MORE suitable for the proposed use ?**

(4) **If not, is the disposition of roads, buildings, open spaces, etc., including the building density, shown in the proposal satisfactory ?**
(5) **If so, are the details of design of the buildings and any landscaping satisfactory ?**
(6) **If none of the above questions apply, will the proposal do any foreseeable harm?**

These questions must, of course, be answered in relation not only to the actual site involved, but to surrounding land.   If the answer to (1), (2) or (4) is in the negative, or to (3) in the affirmative, the answers to succeeding questions should not be sought until it has been decided whether the objection which has been discovered should be considered decisive.   Consideration of less fundamental aspects will subsequently be necessary in framing the decision if refusal or conditional permission is decided upon, in order that any minor objections may be dealt with in the event of an appeal, but it is obviously unnecessary to examine a road layout in minute detail if the site which it is proposed to develop is included in the Development Plan as a public open space.

Question (6) might alternatively be worded:
"What public interest or what private interest which ought to be protected by means of Planning powers will be served by refusal?"

An important issue is at stake here.   It is an entirely mistaken idea to suppose that because proposed development will injuriously affect the enjoyment of people living or working nearby, this is necessarily a reason for refusing permission.   Any development on hitherto open land adjoining existing development is likely to spoil the view from some people's houses and to diminish to some extent the quiet and privacy to which they are used; the same applies to almost any intensification of the use of developed land.   Clearly, if this *were* to be regarded as grounds for refusal very little development or redevelopment would take place anywhere, yet Local Planning Authorities and third party objectors both frequently behave as if the mere fact of some loss of amenity was indeed a reason for refusal (and inspectors sometimes seem to agree with them).

The proper test is whether proposed development or redevelopment is in itself satisfactory in relation to its surroundings either as they are or as they are likely to be after redevelopment and will form an area of well-planned development.   Naturally, one of the criteria for determining this is whether the occupants of surrounding land will continue to have a *reasonable* level of amenity.   Derek Senior in "The Lapse of Richmond Hill ",[1] argues in effect that Planning control should be concerned solely with public welfare and not at all with private welfare but I cannot fully agree with him because the two are not clearly distinguishable.

It is essential that decisions should be clear, definite and comprehensive, and this applies particularly to any conditions imposed upon permission.   Unless an applicant knows what he must do in order to fulfil the Local Planning Authority's requirements he obviously cannot comply with the terms of the decision.   Also, no conditions can subsequently be enforced unless they are stated in the written decision.

It is also important to frame refusals comprehensively, including reference to all aspects of the proposal which are considered unsatisfactory.   Unless

[1] "The Architects' Journal", December 27th, 1961.

this is done, failure on appeal to substantiate a major ground for objection may result in many minor defects slipping through the net.   True, the Minister is entitled to take into account *all* aspects of an application upon which he has to adjudicate, but there is no guarantee that he *will* do so unless they are specifically mentioned in the written decision.

The great difficulty for a Local Planning Authority is to frame decisions in such a way that they are clear and comprehensive and fulfil the obligation to give reasons for a refusal or conditions attaching to a permission and yet are not impossibly lengthy.   An applicant who proposes some quite minor development and receives a decision containing two or three pages of conditions and the reasons for them can be pardoned for feeling himself the victim of bureaucracy;   yet to cover all relevant points such lengthy statements may be necessary.   It is, I think, to avoid this affront to public opinion rather than from negligence that many Local Planning Authorities tend to fall into the habit, in giving reasons, of using vague, comprehensive, almost meaningless phrases like " in order to safeguard amenity " and " contrary to sound Planning principles ".

As regards the wording of refusals, the position is now much improved, since, in implementation of the Franks Committee report, Local Planning Authorities are now required to provide applicants who appeal with a full statement of their reasons.

The degree of strictness with which Planning control should be exercised is a matter requiring very careful thought.   I have constantly emphasised in earlier chapters that, in working out a Plan, any space standards adopted must be regarded as a guide and not as rigid rules; but, once a Plan has been formulated and adopted, it is fatal to permit any serious departures from it unless the reasons for doing so are so strong that they justify deliberate amendment of the Plan to take account of them.   Nothing is harder than to resist proposals which do not comply with a Plan yet which seem harmless.   Every imaginable term of abuse is hurled at those who do seek to maintain the Plan in such circumstances, and it is all too easy to yield to pressure.   But such surrenders, frequently made in deference to the blessed word " compromise ", have a snowball effect;   the first concession leads easily to another, and very soon the orginal Plan is incapable of being carried out because a large part of the uses which it proposed should take place on specific sites have been crowded out by other uses, intrinsically harmless but irrelevant to the fulfilment of the Plan.   A proposed playing-field has become a housing site, a neighbourhood sub-centre has become a private school, a repair garage occupies the site of a clinic, and the final result is that essential uses have to be fitted in on odd vacant sites, if at all, instead of being placed in the optimum positions.

It must never be forgotten that anyone can at any time apply for permission to use any land for any purpose, and such applications may be made in complete disregard of all proposals in the Plan.   A mere negative policy of refusing permission to definitely harmful proposals is not, therefore, sufficient.   The maintenance of the objectives of the Plan by the rejection of proposals which do not contribute to its implementation is essential in many cases.

All professional Planners know this is a bitter truth, but no one else seems to appreciate it. The public do not, because they have not had the opportunity of learning and accepting the necessary restraints upon land use which proper land Planning requires; it is only in the prevention of manifest evils that their support is available. Members of Planning committees do not realise it either; too often their knowledge and wisdom is no further advanced than that of the general public.

It is an extraordinary thing how completely the preparation of a Plan and its implementation are divorced in the minds of many, one might also say most, members. It is often possible to secure the adoption of a sound Plan if the reasons for its provisions are explained fully and clearly and trouble is taken to expose the unsoundness of objections springing from prejudice and vested interests, but it is infinitely harder to get members to take strong decisions on development applications in order to realise it.

One example will suffice to demonstrate this and also the destructive consequences to a Plan which a single wrong decision may bring in its wake. A Regional Plan included the usual proposals for increasing the services and population of a number of selected villages. Among these villages was a quite small one (X), only about 1½ miles from which was another (Y), even smaller and naturally not selected for upgrading. There was no real doubt that X was the better suited to be a rural centre, and no one ever disputed it.

However, the rural district council wished to build a substantial number of houses at X, principally for the occupation of agricultural workers, and selected an admirable site within the developed area of the village. There was some agricultural objection to this site, which could almost certainly have been readily and properly overcome, but, worse, an influential local landowner disliked the proposal for undisclosed reasons. The rural district council, which was in a hurry to build, dropped the site at X like a hot potato and selected one at Y. Both villages were so small that the accretion of even one housing site of the size intended to one of them was bound to have a marked effect upon their relative importance and the services each could support, yet the Local Planning Authority had no difficulty in agreeing to the site at Y without even considering it necessary to examine the reasons which had led to X rather than Y being selected for expansion in the Regional Plan, which some of them had only very recently approved.

Another vexatious problem arising from laxity of control is the creation of unbreakable precedents. A road has partly developed frontages, mainly in the form of houses; the Plan provides for a group of a dozen shops at a convenient point; the site selected is not at the moment in the market and a proposal comes in for a pair of shops on a vacant site in another part of the road. The Planning officer points out that the road should be used mainly for dwellings, and that the limited number of shops required ought, for many reasons, to be concentrated in a single group, but the committee disagrees.

" We need shops along there, Mr. Chairman; it's dreadful the distance mothers have to go to the shops. I can't see that they'll do any harm." Permission is given, and since the site in question has no special advantages, there is no reason for refusing permission for other applications on similar sites. Since there is a local demand for shops, other applications probably come in fairly soon, and before long the shopping requirements of the area are met by a number of shops, isolated and in pairs, the site originally selected for shops remaining vacant.

The Minister has, of course, been at pains to point out that Local Planning Authorities should not be unduly bound by precedent, and that each individual application should be determined on its merits. So far so good, but if a permission is given to an application with no Planning merit there is no earthly reason for refusing other similar ones in the vicinity.

But though it is vital that development control should be so administered that the fulfilment of the Development Plan is not prevented or hampered, it is also important that it should not be repressive or merely fussy. Apart from anything else, Planning is not so deeply rooted in public esteem that it can afford to earn any justified opprobrium. The irritation caused by unimaginative handling of minor matters could yet cause public opinion to force the abandonment of Planning control, oblivious of the irreparable damage which this would do to national well-being but conscious only of the vexation caused by restrictions which do not appear to the man in the street to serve any useful purpose.

Some futile and very silly decisions are certainly made. For example, the proprietor of an existing repair garage sited at the junction of a fairly busy road with a minor residential road was refused permission to install an extra pump (he already had one) on the grounds that it would increase traffic in the residential road; something which, in the circumstances, simply could not happen. Quite often ridiculous requirements are imposed, particularly by district councils acting under delegated powers, in relation to pettifogging details. Generally these arise from the recommendations of officers who know nothing of Planning and care less, who seek to impose what should be freely adaptable standards of density, building line or use as rigid by-laws, a tendency encouraged by memories of the 1932 Act Model Clauses which tried to enable this to be done.

The following are examples of the misuse of the powers of development control on the part of authorities acting under delegated powers.

An applicant in an area of low density housing, wishing to make the best use of his plot, submitted an application which showed the house set well back from the road. The application was refused on the grounds that it did not comply with the building line, being set some thirty or forty feet behind it. There was no question of a unified street picture being disrupted and indeed, on appeal, the Local Authority concerned failed to advance any plausible reason for having refused permission. Needless to say the Minister allowed the appeal.

An industrial firm in a northern town were short of storage accommodation for their raw material, and sought permission to erect a temporary building within their own premises for this purpose. The site was within a proposed town centre business area but was programmed in the twenty years plus period. The applicants were perfectly prepared to accept a temporary permission for twenty years. Every possible attempt was made by the Surveyor of the District Council concerned to prevent Planning permission being given, and, the applicants being unversed in Planning procedure, he was able to avoid the matter being brought to an issue for nearly a year. Upon the applicants seeking Planning advice the Local Authority were told that unless a permission was issued immediately after the next meeting of their Committee an appeal would be lodged forthwith. They were most unwilling to do this but, a conference being called, the County Council backed up the applicants by pointing out that their proposals were in fact in accordance with the proposals of the Development Plan, and that there were no valid grounds for refusing permission.

A District Council in the London area refused permission to the erection of flats in the large back gardens of some Victorian houses on the grounds that the development would result in a density greater than that permitted under the Development Plan. Even when it was pointed out to them, detailed figures being given in support, that in fact the proposal was in accordance with the density provisions of the Plan they persisted in their refusal. Needless to say the Ministry again supported the appellants on appeal.

These are a few examples of the foolish and incompetent exercise of development control by Local Authorities under delegated powers. Some of them verge on the scandalous. No doubt decisions of this kind are made every week throughout the year somewhere in the country. The harm which is done to Planning in this way is incalculable, and tends to impress firmly upon the public mind a feeling that Planning is nothing but a set of tiresome bureaucratic controls.[1]

It is also important to remember that the well-known legal maxim that if a thing cannot be done without causing a nuisance it cannot be done at all ought not to be translated exactly into Planning terms.

If a thing cannot be done without violating Planning principles it must be sited in a place and made subject to conditions which ensure the least possible harm being done. All needs must be catered for, and if the necessary permissions for such uses on the best available site or sites are not forthcoming the demand is likely to be met by unauthorised uses under highly unfavourable conditions, which it will probably take a great deal of time and trouble to get rid of.

It is unfortunate that Local Planning Authorities do not form the habit of making publicly known their detailed intentions, and the reasons for them, regarding the development of areas where difficult problems exist; by so doing they would not only save themselves the trouble of dealing with many unacceptable proposals but would better discharge their duties to the public they serve.

This in fact ought only to be part of a general system by which a Local Authority seeks to cultivate positively good public relations in connection with its Planning duties. Only by constantly placing before the public in the clearest and most emphatic possible way the benefits which it is trying to

---

[1] Further examples, more fully analysed than is possible here, are given in Chapter 10 of my " Town Planning at the Crossroads " (Estates Gazette, 1961). In that chapter and elsewhere in the book Planning practice generally, and development control in particular, are discussed more fully from a political and administrative point of view in relation to the contemporary situation in this country than would be appropriate here. For example, appeal decisions in Green Belts are discussed extensively there but not here because I do not think that Green Belts are good Planning tools and that they have little place in a book on Planning principles.

bring about by Planning action, can there be much hope of bringing Planning to that place in public esteem which it deserves.

Two excellent papers about public relations in Planning by Derek Senior and Sir Sidney Littlewood are to be found in the Report of Proceedings of the Town and Country Planning Summer School of 1956 and in the Journal of the Town Planning Institute for June 1957 respectively.

20-2. DEVELOPMENT CONTROL LEGISLATION

There is no intention in this section of providing a legal guide; its sole purpose is to explain in general terms the statutory framework within which powers of development control have to be exercised. Advice on legal points should always be obtained from persons with legal qualifications.

Between 1953 and 1962 the law concerning Development Control became more and more complex. Gone were the days when a sound knowledge of the Town and Country Planning Act, 1947, and the more important delegated legislation flowing from it was sufficient for most ordinary purposes. Town and Country Planning Acts in 1951, 1953, 1954 and 1959, the Caravan Sites and Control of Development Act, 1960, and the Land Compensation Act, 1961, not to mention the Town Development Act, 1952, the Local Employment Act, 1960, and various other enactments having at least some bearing on Development Control built up an interlaced structure of law of such complexity that Town Planners, for the most part, were saved from despair only by the beneficent activities of Messrs. Sweet & Maxwell, whose constantly revised " Encyclopaedia of Planning Law and Practice ", diligently cross-referenced, made it possible, if still not easy, to discover the law on any given Planning subject.

The passing of the Town and Country Planning Act, 1962, a general consolidating measure, restores the situation considerably for it repeals and re-enacts those parts of the Town and Country Planning Acts of 1944, 1947, 1951, 1953, 1954 and 1959 which had not previously been repealed. It does the same for Part II of the Caravan Sites and Control of Development Act, 1960—thus bringing the part of that Act relating to Development Control within the main legislative code dealing with that subject, but leaves the Land Compensation Act, 1961, untouched as a separate code.

Unhappily the Government's proposals to amend the basis of " Third Schedule " rights were not produced early enough to be brought beneath the umbrella of the 1962 Act, so that, already, there is " overspill " from that Act in the shape of the Town and Country Planning Act, 1963.

Section 13 of the Town and Country Planning Act, 1962, states that, subject to other provisions of the Act, " permission shall be required . . . in respect of any development of land which is carried out after the appointed day " (1st July, 1948).

Section 12 then defines " development " as " . . . the carrying out of building, engineering, mining or other operations in, on, over or under land, or the making of any material change in the use of any buildings or other land ".

The use of the word *material* is to be particularly noted, since whether a particular change of use is material is a matter of fact to be determined by all the circumstances of the case, and is a common cause of dispute.

In Section 221, the interpretation section of the Act, it is stated that " use " does not include the erection of buildings. Thus an application cannot be made to change the use of land if such change of use would involve building operations. This is a point not very generally appreciated and is of some practical importance as the Minister has sometimes refused to accept an appeal made against the decision of a Local Planning Authority because the application had been for change of use instead of for development and therefore ought not to have been accepted as a valid application.

The apparent simplicity of the part of Section 12 quoted is deceptive, for its meaning is qualified in many ways. A clear understanding of the effect of these qualifications is indispensable for the administration of development control.

Section 12 itself goes on to qualify its first statement and lists six kinds of operation which are deemed not to involve development and hence do not require application for permission to be made in respect of them. These are:

(a) Works of maintenance or alteration to a building which do not materially affect its external appearance. (Painting materially affects the external appearance if a new colour is used, but is exempted in Class II of the First Schedule to the G.D.O., 1963).

(b) Road maintenance or improvement carried out by a highway authority within the boundaries of the road.

(c) Work on sewers, mains and cables by the appropriate authority.

(d) The use of buildings or land within the curtilage of a dwelling-house for any purpose incidental to the enjoyment of the house as such. (This is an important provision, and attempts are often made to stretch its meaning; the words " as such " limit it.)

(e) The use of any land for agriculture or forestry, and of any building occupied together with land so used. (Note that this does not include the *erection* of such buildings. The G.D.O., 1963, deals with this.)

(f) The change of use of buildings or land from one use to another if both uses are within the same class in an Order made by the Minister under this section of the Act.

But this does not prevent a Local Planning Authority from imposing conditions upon the grant of Planning permission which prevent changes of use even within the same class being made without Planning permission first being obtained.

The current Order so made is the **Town and Country Planning (Use Classes) Order, 1963 (S.I. 1963, No. 708),** which contains eighteen classes, summarised below. Within the limits of any particular class a use may, to use Desmond Heap's immortal words, " leap about and change itself to its heart's content ".

The classes are:

I. All kinds of shops, except those likely to be offensive because of the trade carried on. Those listed are shops for the sale of fried fish, tripe, pet animals or birds, cats' meat. Also, shops for the sale of motor vehicles. This use, more usually referred to as " car showrooms ", was made a use separate from shops because of the disruptive effect on a shopping area which an accumulation of such businesses may bring about, particularly where large quantities of vehicles for sale are displayed in the open air.

II. All kinds of offices.

III. All kinds of Light Industry. This creates awful difficulties. The definition of light industrial building in the order is " an industrial building (not being a special industrial building) in which the processes carried on, or the machinery installed, are such as could be carried on or installed in any residential area without detriment to the amenity of that area by reason of noise, vibration, smell, fumes, smoke, soot, ash, dust or grit ". There are very few industrial uses of which it can unequivocally be said that they are light industry in the sense of the order. Almost any industrial use is liable to cause nuisance in some residential area for one of the reasons given, and it should be noted that the words in the order are " any residential area ". Accordingly, almost any application for the establishment of industry, or the change of use from one industry to another can be contested by the Local Planning Authority on the grounds that, whatever the applicants may care to call it, it is not, in all the circumstances, light industry. The Lands Tribunal has held, in *Brain and Drive Yourself Hire Co., London v. London County Council*, that a garage is a place where motor-cars are bought, sold, stored, repaired and maintained, and is a place used for light industrial purposes. This seems an odd decision. Could it be maintained that a garage could be carried on in *any* residential area without detriment to amenity by reason of noise, etc.?

IV. General industry of all kinds. (" General industry " is defined as industry other than light or special. " Special industry " is, generally speaking, offensive industry.)

V.
VI.
VII. } Various groups of special industries not readily capable of being summarised.
VIII.
IX.

X. All kinds of wholesale warehouses and repositories.

XI. Boarding or guest houses, residential clubs, hotels providing sleeping accommodation.

XII. Residential or boarding schools, residential colleges.

XIII. Buildings used for public worship, religious instruction and social and recreational activities *of the religious body using the building*.

XIV. Homes and institutions for children, old people and the disabled, convalescent homes, nursing homes, sanatoria, hospitals other than those for persons of unsound mind, epileptics and the mentally deficient.

XV. Health centres, school treatment centres, clinics, crèches, day nurseries; dispensaries, consulting rooms and surgeries unattached to the home of the practitioner.

XVI. Hospitals excepted from Class XIV, homes in which people may be detained by order of a court or as a condition of probation.

XVII. Non-commercial art galleries, museums, public libraries or reading-rooms, public halls, concert halls, exhibition halls, social centres, community centres, non-residential clubs.

XVIII. Theatres, cinemas, music-halls, dance halls, skating rinks, swimming-baths, Turkish or other vapour or foam baths, gymnasia, use for indoor games.

These classes make humorous as well as sad reading, but of course they perform a very useful purpose in removing the necessity for many minor changes of use to receive Planning permission. They are a simplification of the classes contained in the earlier, 1948, Order, and it has been widely suggested that further simplification would be desirable, but critics generally overlook the important point that, while many other changes would be quite harmless in themselves, to leave them uncontrolled might seriously upset the Development Plan. For example, to permit general and light industry to enter freely areas of special industry might well mean that insufficient land would be left to meet the needs of the latter. Planning is not merely a matter of preventing intrinsically harmful development, but also of providing sufficient land in the right places for each use. This means that other uses must often be excluded.

Some of the definitions in the Use Classes Order are very important.

" *Shop* " means a building used for the carrying on of any retail trade or retail business wherein the primary purpose is the selling of goods by retail, and includes a building used for the purposes of a *hairdresser, undertaker* or *ticket agency* or for the *reception of goods to be washed, cleaned or repaired,* or *for any other purpose appropriate to a shopping area,* but *does not include a building used as a funfair, garage, petrol filling station, office, betting office, or hotel or premises (other than a restaurant) licensed for the sale of intoxicating liquors for consumption on the premises.*

" *Office* " includes a bank, but does not include a *post office* or *betting office.*

" *Industrial Building* " means a building (other than a building associated with a quarry and other than a shop) used for:—

(a) the making of any article or of part of any article, or

(b) altering, repairing, ornamenting, furnishing, cleaning, washing, packing or canning, or adapting for sale, or breaking up or demolition of any article, or

(c) the getting, mining or treatment of minerals.

All these exclude processes carried on in the course of agriculture.

It will be observed that, but for the words included in the definition of "shop" a dry-cleaner's would be an industrial building, while, but for the saving words " or for any other purpose appropriate to a shopping area ", this would also be true of a tailor's shop. These saving words, like the definition of " light industry ", which has already been commented upon,

create a great field of uncertainty; it is time that they were reconsidered. Definitions are useful in administering Planning control, but not if they include words which themselves promote arguments about Planning technique, as these do.

We must now return to the Act itself. Section 12 (3) (a) expressly states that the use as two or more separate dwelling-houses of any building previously used as a single dwelling-house involves a material change in the use of the building, and 12 (3) (b) that the deposit of refuse or waste materials on land involves a material change in the use thereof, even if it is part of a site already used for that purpose, if the superficial area or height of the deposit is extended. People sometimes wonder how you can deposit things without extending the superficial area or height of the deposit, but deposited material may become compressed.

There is also a proviso that a site already used for a tip may continue to be used without permission if its area is not extended and the level of the tip does not rise above that of adjoining land.

Section 13 contains some complicated provisions which, broadly, mean that occasional uses of land which took place before the appointed day may continue on the same basis without permission being required.

Section 14 instructs the Minister to provide by order for the grant of permission for development, and the order so made may itself grant certain permissions and authorise Local Planning Authorities to grant others. The current order made under this section is the **Town and Country Planning General Development Order, 1963 (S.I. 1963, No. 709).** This re-enacts, with the incorporation of various subsequent amendments, the General Development Order of 1950.

This was much more lavish in the exemptions from obligation to obtain permission which it granted than its predecessor of 1948.

The First Schedule to the General Development Order lists 23 classes of permitted development. This is development which is not exempted by the Act itself from control but specifically exempted by the Order, and a fresh Order may be made at any time if the need for one is disclosed.

The fact that development is permitted by the Order does not prevent it from being controlled by the inclusion of conditions in a permission if it forms part of other development. For example, Class I gives a wide freedom to carry out minor development within the curtilage of an existing dwelling, or of a future one if no conditions are attached to the grant of permission. But a Local Planning Authority could, if it thought fit, give permission for the erection of a dwelling subject to development of the kind mentioned in Class I not being carried out without permission. The effect of this is to throw existing development to the dogs but to enable new development to be strictly controlled in relation to ancillary structures, which can do much to harm its appearance.

The 23 classes of permitted development are described at length in the Order, and the following is no more than a summary. The Order itself should be consulted for details. Class I, however, is so important that it is quoted in full. The words " *shall not* " do not, of course, *prohibit* anything being done, but only provide that it must be the subject of a Planning permission.

PERMITTED DEVELOPMENT

I. Development within the curtilage of a dwelling-house.

    1. The enlargement, improvement or other alteration of a dwelling-house so long as the cubic content of the original dwelling-house (as ascertained by external measurement) is not exceeded by more than 1,750 cubic feet or one-tenth, whichever is the greater, subject to a maximum of 4,000 cubic feet; provided that the erection of a garage, stable, loose box or coach-house within the curtilage of the dwelling-house shall be treated as the enlargement of the dwelling-house for the purposes of this permission.

    2. The erection, construction or placing, and the maintenance, improvement or other alteration, within the curtilage of a dwelling-house, of any building or enclosure (other than a dwelling, garage, stable, loose box or coach-house) required for a purpose incidental to the enjoyment of the dwelling-house as such, including the keeping of poultry, bees, pet animals, birds or other livestock for the domestic needs or personal enjoyment of the occupants of the dwelling-house.

II. Sundry minor operations.

    1. The erection or construction of gates, fences, walls, or other means of enclosure not exceeding 4 ft. in height where abutting on a road used by vehicular traffic or 7 ft. in height in any other case, and the maintenance, improvement or other alteration of any gates, fences, walls or other means of enclosure.

    2. The painting of the exterior of any building or work otherwise than for purposes of advertisement, announcement or direction.

III. Change of use from general industry to light industry, from a shop for fried fish, pet animals, etc., (see Use Classes Order) to an ordinary shop, and from use as a restaurant to one of these special kinds of shop. (One would have expected this to be included in the Use Classes Order; it is placed here, one suspects, as a result of some slight confusion during the framing of the Orders.)

IV. Temporary buildings, etc., used in connection with building operations and the use of land, other than for building purposes, for any purpose for not more than a total of 28 days in any calendar year, including the erection of moveable structures in connection with such use. (This gives campers the opportunity to use land for short periods without getting Planning permission.)

V. Gives *carte blanche* to members of recognised recreational organisations to camp on land without time restriction.

VI. Agricultural buildings, works and uses.

    1. The carrying out on agricultural land having an area of more than one acre and comprised in an agricultural unit of building or engineering operations requisite for the use of that land for the purposes of agriculture, other than the placing on land of structures not designed for those purposes or the provision and alteration of dwellings.

(The exclusion of structures not designed for the purposes for which they are used excludes the use of bus bodies, glider fusilages, etc., without permission.)

    2. The erection or construction and the maintenance, improvement or other alteration of roadside stands for milk churns, except where they would abut on any trunk or classified road.

    3. The winning and working, on land held or occupied with land used for the purposes of agriculture, of any minerals reasonably required for the purposes of that use, including the fertilisation of the land so used, and the maintenance, improvement or alteration of building works thereon, which are occupied or used for the purposes aforesaid.

This class of permitted development is subject to special conditions, the first of which brings back under Planning control large structures which might be very unsightly if they were not specially designed and sited. It is worded as follows:—

> " The ground area covered by any building erected pursuant to this permission shall not, either by itself or after the addition thereto of the ground area covered by any existing building or buildings (other than a dwelling house) within the same unit erected or in course of erection within the preceding two years and wholly or partly within 100 yards of the nearest part of the said building, exceed 5,000 square feet " (Phew!)

Two other conditions limit the exemption, within two miles of an aerodrome, to buildings not exceeding 10 feet in height and to buildings more than 80 feet from the metalled part of a trunk or classified road.

VII. Extends to forestry privileges similar to those accorded to agriculture. There is no limitation placed on the size of such buildings.

VIII. Industrial development of various kinds, such as the provision and alteration of apparatus, railways, etc. Buildings, too, may be altered or extended up to one-tenth extra volume and 5,000 square feet extra floor space. New buildings within the same curtilage as such buildings are to be treated as extensions.

IX. Repairs to unadopted streets and private ways.

X. Repairs to sewers, mains, cables, etc. (N.B.—Not limited to work by statutory undertakers as in Section 12 (2) (c).)

XI. The rebuilding or replacement of buildings, works or plant which have sustained war damage.

XII. Development authorised by local or private Acts or Orders but means of access, siting and external appearance can be controlled in respect of such development.

XIII. Ancillary buildings required by local authorities on land owned by them in connection with their functions; the erection of street furniture and the tipping of waste material by local authorities.

XIV. Work by a highway authority or the L.C.C. on land outside the boundary of a road, but abutting on it.

XV. Development by river boards and drainage authorities in connection with watercourse and drainage works.

XVI. Development by sewerage authorities if not above ground level.

XVII. Various kinds of development by statutory authorities.

XVIII. Various kinds of development by mineral undertakers.

XIX. Similar concessions to the National Coal Board.

XX. Continuation of development by a local authority or statutory undertaker sanctioned by a Government Department before May 1, 1945, and begun before July 1, 1948.

XXI. Use of buildings on an aerodrome under the control of the Minister of Civil Aviation for purposes connected with flying.

XXII. The use of land as a caravan site in any of the circumstances specified in paragraphs 2–9 of the first Schedule to the Caravan Sites and Control of Development Act, 1960, or specified in paragraph 10 except so far as this relates to winter quarters.

This relates to various temporary and exceptional uses of sites such as use for up to 28 days of any site forming part of a holding of at least five acres, use by specially exempted organisations, by a person travelling with a caravan, for one or two nights only, use by agricultural and forestry workers, and so on. This exemption is in step with the exemptions given by the 1960 Act from the need to obtain a Caravan site licence.

XXIII. Development required by the conditions of a Caravan Site licence.

Most of the 23 classes are subject to one or both of two standard conditions, which are as follows:—

1. This permission shall not authorise any development which involves the formation, laying out or material widening of a means of access to a trunk or classified road.

2. No development shall be carried out which creates an obstruction to the view of persons using any road used by vehicular traffic at or near any bend, corner, junction or intersection so as to be likely to cause danger to such persons.

Some of the development listed in the 23 classes consists of collectors' specimens rather than things encountered every day of the week.

Section 27 of the Act enables a Local Planning Authority to revoke or vary a planning permission given provided the Minister confirms the order, and compensation is paid, while Section 28 enables it to take amending action by requiring the removal of any development carried out, even with Planning permission, express or permitted by order, provided compensation is paid. This is known as a " discontinuance order ".

The relaxations of control provided for by the General Development Order may be restored or varied in two ways.

Permission given by the General Development Order in respect of any of the permitted classes may be withdrawn in respect of any particular area by direction of the Local Planning Authority with the Minister's consent or by direction of the Minister himself. The Minister naturally has to be satisfied that there are special circumstances which justify the making of such a direction. Such a direction is known as an " Article 4 direction ".

The second power is contained in Section 14, which enables a Special Development Order to be made by the Minister in relation to a particular area in order to meet its individual needs.

This does not exhaust the ways in which subsequent sections of the Act modify the definition of development given in Section 12. **Section 199** relates to **Crown land** and provides, *inter alia*, that although proposals relating to Crown land may be included in a Development Plan, including designation for compulsory purchase, powers of development control cannot be exercised in respect of it except in relation to " . . . any interest therein for the time being held otherwise than by or on behalf of the Crown ".

If Crown land comprised only places like Buckingham Palace, Windsor Castle and so on, this would not, of course, occasion any concern, but Crown land also includes all land held by Government Departments, and their exemption from development control was strongly criticised during the passage of the Act through Parliament. Assurances were then given that Local Planning Authorities would be given the opportunity to comment on all proposals for development by Government Departments, and that full weight would be given to their views. The machinery for securing this is described in Circular 100 of the Ministry of Town and Country Planning.

Development by local authorities and statutory undertakers requires permission (unless it is of a kind permitted by a Development Order), just as does development by a private person. (See Circular 63 of 1951 of the Ministry of Housing and Local Government.)

In the case of a Local Planning Authority's own development the Minister relies on it to tell him about important and controversial development before beginning work.

The Development Plans Direction of 1954 requires Local Planning Authorities whose Development Plans have been approved to inform the Minister of any development which they propose to permit which is not in accord with the Development Plan. However, they need not do this if no substantial departure from the Plan is involved and no damage to the amenity of adjoining land is likely.

If nothing is heard from the Minister for 21 days after he has been informed of the intention to permit the proposed development permission may be given. The Minister may, where he decides to take action, either direct that permission shall not be given or may decide to hold a local inquiry.

Financial and other limitation on the exercise of development control.
Even though a Local Planning Authority may consider that something proposed to be done constitutes development and ought to be prevented there are several ways in which their desire to do this may be restrained, even if no protection is afforded to the intending developer by any of the sections or orders already dealt with. Ordinarily the exercise of development control powers does not involve the Local Planning Authority in payment of any compensation; but there are certain exceptions to this.

Section 28 of the Act, already briefly mentioned, enables a Local Planning Authority to make an order to require the discontinuance of use of any land or to impose conditions on the continuance of that use, or to require any buildings or works to be altered or removed if it is considered expedient in the interests of the proper Planning of the area to do so.

If the Local Planning Authority does any of these things in respect of development which is an " existing use " it must pay compensation for any depreciation in the value of the land caused, and if what is required renders the land " incapable of reasonably beneficial use," it may be required to purchase the land. Such an Order can only be made with the consent of the Minister, and, as in the case of practically anything done under Planning powers, objection to it may be made to the Minister by interested parties.

We must turn aside for a moment to consider what it meant by " existing use," and by " reasonably beneficial use ". Roughly, any use is protected against discontinuance without compensation if it was begun in accordance with a Planning permission, express or implied, or before Planning powers had been taken by the local authority in whose area it lies. (Before 1943 Planning powers were adoptive and had not been applied to the whole country.) Even if Planning permission was legally necessary and was not obtained, the use or development is protected after it has been in existence for four years, this period beginning on 1st July, 1948, in the case of development carried out before that date.

This is not the kind of definition a lawyer would approve of, but will suffice as a rough working guide.

" Reasonably beneficial use " is harder to define. It is, as we shall see, an important term because, apart from Section 28, the owner may always require the Local Planning Authority to purchase land, if refusal of permission to develop it or conditions placed upon a permission render it incapable of reasonably beneficial use, by serving a **Purchase Notice** under Section 129, which has to be confirmed by the Minister before it is effective.

That land is incapable of reasonably beneficial use does not mean merely that the value of the land has been reduced, nor even that no profit can be made out of it, but, in effect, that the restriction placed on it has made it of little use to anyone. For example, refusal to permit building to take place on small vacant plot in the midst of a built-up area might well mean that it was rendered incapable of beneficial use, but, on the other hand, refusal to permit development of a strip of frontage land which had been fenced off for housing, but which was backed by agricultural land, would not necessarily involve this, since the land could readily be returned to agricultural use, even though the owner might suffer considerable loss as a result of the refusal.

It would be fatal if this were not so, for otherwise anyone could apply for permission to develop any unusable piece of ground and, on refusal, compel the Local Planning Authority to buy it. In one case the Minister refused to confirm a purchase notice served by the owner of a plot forming part of a large area of scrub woodland who had been refused permission to build a house, because, however little use the plot might be to him without a house on it, the refusal had not rendered it any less useful than the remainder of the woodland.

It will be appropriate here to mention that, under Section 27, a Local Planning Authority may revoke or modify a permission already given if it is " expedient having regard to the development plan and to any other material conditions . . ." to do so. This enables changing circumstances which could not have been foreseen when the permission was originally given to be taken into account, so that future development shall not be hampered. The powers of this section are only available in respect of a permission which has not been acted upon, otherwise Section 28 must be invoked. Compensation must be paid in respect of any expenditure incurred by the owner in respect of the permission and rendered abortive by revocation or modification. For example, if, on the strength of an outline permission to develop land, a developer had incurred expense in having detailed drawings made in anticipation of development, he would be able to recover this sum if his permission were revoked.

Section 123 of the Act provides that refusal of or conditions attached to permission for development mentioned in Part II of the Third Schedule to the Act carries compensation in respect of any reduction of value in the property caused thereby. (It is to be noted that the Minister must confirm this decision either on appeal or by the matter being referred to him for decision in the first instance.)

The kinds of development mentioned in the Third Schedule which are at all relevant to the provisions of Section 123 (the Schedule is compiled for the purposes of a number of sections relating to compensation, betterment and compulsory purchase, and by no means all of them can be applied to Section 123), are as follows:

The enlargement or alteration of any buildings in existence on 1st July, 1948, or destroyed since 7th January, 1937, and later replaced; the carrying out of building operations on agricultural land required for the purposes of agriculture; the working on agricultural land of minerals required for agricultural purposes; where a building or land was used for more than one purpose on the appointed day an increase of not more than one-tenth of the volume or area, as applicable, of any of the uses; the deposit of mineral waste on land which was so used on the appointed day in connection with the working of minerals.

The Minister may direct that any conditions attached to a permission which regulate the design or external appearance of buildings or the size or height of buildings shall be disregarded in assessing compensation.

It is to be noted that Section 123 does not apply to the rebuilding of existing buildings, which can be controlled without payment of compensation. Rebuilding is included in Part I of the Third Schedule, which specifically does not apply to Section 123. However, this does not work out in practice.

A developer faced with a refusal of permission to rebuild an existing building is likely to say, in effect, to the Local Planning Authority, " Well, you may be able to stop me doing this without paying compensation, but you can't stop me altering and enlarging without paying. Since I don't suppose that you are prepared to pay compensation to stop me, surely you'd rather have a good new building here than a tatty, old, enlarged building ".

It is to be noted that the Town and Country Planning Act, 1963, prescribes that the 10% " tolerance " shall henceforward relate to floor areas, not to cubic content. This is quite an important change. Previously, the exercise of Third Schedule rights in respect of old buildings with lofty ceilings meant that a very large increase of floor area could be secured on rebuilding: ten floors could perhaps be built within the volume of a building which had previously had only seven floors.

We now pass to the obstacles which may be set up by intending developers by means of technical arguments.

Section 43 of the Act enables anyone who wishes to carry out any operations on land or make any change in the use of land to apply to the Local Planning Authority for a determination as to whether his proposals constitute development which requires permission under the Act. If he does not like the answer he gets he can appeal to the Minister, who may give a ruling as to the need for permission to be obtained and on the Planning merits of the matter. Section 43 determinations raise all kinds of complicated questions of fact.

Instead of applying under Section 43, the prospective developer may decide for himself that his activities do not involve development or Section 43 determination, and carry on with them without seeking either Planning permission or Section 43 determination. If the Local Planning Authority think that what he is doing is in fact development under the Act, they may serve him with an **Enforcement Notice** under Section 45 of the Act at any time within four years of the work being carried out or the use having been begun. (They may also do this if permission with conditions attached to it has been given for development and the conditions have not been complied with, or if development has taken place in defiance of a refusal of permission.)

Section 45 says that the Local Planning Authority may serve an enforcement notice, " if they consider it expedient to do so, having regard to the provisions of the development plan and to any other material considerations "; a fairly clear hint that action should not be taken unless there is Planning objection to the development.

On receipt of an enforcement notice the developer can either comply with it or appeal to the Minister. The enforcement notice is of no effect until an appeal has been finally determined.

Appeals. An appeal or an objection may be made to the Minister against almost any decision made by a Local Planning Authority. Sections 22, 23, 27, 28, 29, 43, 124 and 129 all contain references to the right of aggrieved persons to be heard by the Minister. The procedure followed is virtually the same however the appeal or objection arises. The normal thing is for a local public inquiry to be held, although, in relation to development control matters, the Minister is not obliged to hold a public inquiry. Where the matter is very simple the Minister may settle it on the written representation

of the parties concerned, without a hearing; but he always sends an inspector to view the site, so that not much time is saved.

Section 22 enables the Minister to require any application to be referred to him for determination by the Local Planning Authority, and, where this is done, he is not obliged to follow any particular procedure but may seek any information he thinks necessary from either or both parties. He may also hold an informal meeting with them to discuss the whole matter. The only limitation is that, if either party wishes it, he must give each an opportunity of " appearing and being heard by a person appointed by the Minister for the purpose ".

Appeals and other hearings are dealt with in Chapter 21.

It is only in cases of great complexity or importance that the Minister exercises the powers contained in Section 22; more often, a Local Planning Authority, to divest themselves of responsibility for problems which they see no hope of being solved without an appeal eventually being made to the Minister, will ask him to determine it in the first instance in order to save time. The Minister may or may not agree to do this; generally he is reluctant to allow a Local Planning Authority to divest themselves of responsibility for a decision.

The Local Planning Authority can, of course, even if the Minister refuses to determine in the first instance, throw the matter upon him by failing to determine or by refusing the application without full investigation, upon some formal pretext, knowing that an appeal will follow, but in so doing they risk incurring considerable odium and may even, if the Minister considers the refusal entirely unreasonable, be charged with the costs of the appeal This is a sanction which can also be levied by the Minister against the appellant in an appeal. It is very rarely used, but has the merit of discouraging entirely frivolous appeals.

The test is that for an appeal to be proper the appellant must be *aggrieved*, he must suffer some disadvantage from refusal of permission or attachment of conditions. Thus, a man who appealed against a refusal of permission for something which, it could be shown, he had in any case no prospect of being able to do might well be charged with the cost of an appeal; if, for example, he was not the owner of the land in question and the owner had no intention of selling. But all genuine appellants are able to appeal without incurring the risk of having to pay costs.

Applications for Planning permission or Section 43 determination. Something must now be said about applications themselves, the vast majority of which do not lead to any of the complications we have been discussing.

Applications for Planning permission are governed by the **General Development Order, 1963,** Article 5 of which states that an application shall be made on a form issued by the Local Planning Authority, shall include the particulars required by the form and be accompanied by a Plan sufficient to identify the land to which it relates and whatever other drawings are necessary to describe the development proposed.

A model application form was included with Ministry of Town and Country Planning Circular No. 45, 28th May, 1948. The notes accompanying the model form state that a site plan should be attached to all applications except:—

   (a) An application relating to a site included in a layout plan for which permission has already been granted by a Local Planning Authority, in which case a copy of this layout, showing the land to which the application relates coloured pink, will suffice, and

   (b) an application relating to the extension or alteration of a building in a built-up area for which the full postal address is given in the application form, in which case the Local Planning Authority may dispense with the plan.

As many additional copies of the form and drawings as the Local Planning Authority may require, up to a maximum of three, must also be supplied. After receipt of the application the Local Planning Authority may require any further information to be supplied which is necessary for them to be able to determine the application. In other words they are entitled to have all the relevant facts before making up their minds.

An application for Planning permission may be made either once and for all or in stages. Article 5 (2) of the Order says that an **outline application** may be made for permission for the erection of any buildings subject to subsequent approval with respect to any matters relating to the siting, design or external appearance of the buildings or means of access to them.

An outline application can be made the subject of permission, conditions, refusal and appeal just as can an ordinary application; it is a convenient device for enabling the more fundamental aspects of a proposal to be dealt with before details are considered.

Where a permission is given in respect of an outline application it must be stated to be such and subsequent approval will be required for all matters expressly reserved by the permission *but only those*, before any development is started.

The Local Planning Authority may feel that they cannot determine an application without taking into account the siting, etc., of buildings. This may well be the case on a site of restricted size or peculiar shape which does not appear suitable for the kind of development proposed, and the Local Planning Authority wish to be satisfied that satisfactory development is, in fact, possible before committing themselves to a change of use. Where this is so they may tell the applicant within one month of receiving the application that they require further information and must specify what they require. If the applicant thinks this is unreasonable he can appeal to the Minister, though he would be causing himself a great deal of delay if he did so.

A complicated application might be in at least four stages; for example, permission for the development of a large area of land for housing and ancillary purposes could probably be most conveniently obtained as follows :

   (1) Outline permission for the development. This is really permission for change of use, but, as we have already seen (page 279), must not be expressed in this form.

   (2) Approval to road layout.
   (3) Approval to plotting and siting of buildings.
   (4) Approval of design and external appearance of buildings.

In this way abortive work is avoided since no detailed work need be done until it has been approved in principle.

Approvals subsequent to an outline permission are obtained by making application in the same way as for an ordinary permission, but no special form is prescribed.

An application for determination under Section 43 must be in writing; there is no prescribed form, but it must contain a description of the operation or change of use proposed and of the land concerned.

Applications for Planning permission are sent to county borough and district councils, *not* to county councils, and the district councils have the duty of dealing with them in accordance with any delegation arrangements made with the county council. The Local Planning Authority, or district council, under delegated powers, must acknowledge receipt of the application in substantially the following terms :

   " Your application dated (insert date) has been received and, if on (insert date of expiry of the appropriate period under Article 5 (8)) you have not been given notice by the Local Planning Authority of their decision, you are entitled, unless the application has already been referred by the Authority to the Minister of Housing and Local Government, to appeal to the Minister in accordance with Section 16 of the Town and Country Planning Act, 1947, by notice served within one month from that date. You may, however, by agreement in writing with the Local Planning Authority, extend the period within which the decision of the Authority is to be given."

Article 5 (7) of the General Development Order authorises a Local Planning Authority to direct an applicant to produce evidence to verify any particulars given by him.

An application must normally be determined within two months of being made (three months where a trunk road is affected). If the Local Planning Authority see that it will be impossible for them to determine an application within the time allowed they may ask the applicant to agree to an extension of time; if he agrees, his right of appeal cannot be exercised until this further period has expired. It is widely held that a permission given after the time allowed for the determination of the application has expired is, in the absence of an extension of time previously granted by the applicant, invalid.

If an application is incomplete, in that it omits some essential piece or information without which it *could not* be determined, it is null and void, the period within which it must be determined does not begin until the omission is repaired, and the applicant must be informed that his application is incomplete, and in what ways. This does not apply to information which would be helpful in determining an application, but is not of its essence; the Local Planning Authority may call for this, as already described, but without extending the period within which the application has to be determined.

A special case arises in relation to applications for permission for industrial development. Section 38 of the Town and Country Planning Act, 1962, provides that such an application shall be *of no effect* unless accompanied by a certificate issued by the Board of Trade to the effect that the development in question can be carried out consistently with the proper distribution of industry. But, by Section 39, this provision does not apply to buildings with a total floor space which does not, together with any other industrial floor space created or to be created by " related development " exceed 5,000 square feet, excluding related development in respect of which an industrial development certificate has been issued. (I have not yet met anybody who confidently claims fully to understand this provision.)

The Board may by regulation extend this exemption if it chooses. The effect is that an industrial application unaccompanied by the appropriate certificate is not a valid application and cannot be considered by the Local Planning Authority. However, Section 40 of the Town and Country Planning Act, 1962, modifies this to the extent that if a Local Planning Authority decides that it would in any case have refused permission it may do so in respect of an application for permission for industrial development even if this is not accompanied by the necessary certificate.

The Town and Country Planning Act, 1959, introduced complications into the system of development control by requiring all applications for planning permission to be accompanied by a certificate stating either that the applicant is the estate owner in respect of the fee simple of the land concerned or is entitled to a tenancy thereof **or** that the applicant has given 21 days' notice to all owners of the land **or** that he does not know the names and addresses of such owners. Where the applicant is not the owner and cannot identify the owner of any of the land to which the application relates he must also certify that he has advertised the application in a local newspaper circulating in the locality in which the land in question is situated.

Furthermore, every certificate must contain a statement that either none of the land to which the application relates is part of an agricultural holding **or** that notice of the application has been given to any tenant of an agricultural holding forming any part of the land to which the application relates.

The Local Planning Authority must allow at least 21 days after the service of any notice required before determining an application. (See Town and Country Planning Act, 1962, Section 16 and Schedule 4 of the General Development Order, 1963.)

A further innovation of the 1959 Act, now embodied in Section 15 of the 1962 Act, empowers the Minister to designate, by means of a development order, certain classes of application which may not be entertained by a Local Planning Authority unless they have previously been advertised in a local newspaper. A 21-day interval has, here also, to elapse between such advertisement and the determination of an application to which an Order made under Section 15 applies. The advertisement must also specify where and when the application and the plans and documents accompanying it can be inspected.

The classes of development to which Section 15 at present applies are listed in Article 6 of the General Development Order, 1963. They are:—

(*a*) Public conveniences.
(*b*) Buildings, operations or use of land for the disposal of refuse or waste materials.
(*c*) Buildings or operations for the purpose of sewage disposal (other than sewers themselves or septic tanks serving single dwellings).
(*d*) Buildings or use of land for slaughter-houses or knackers' yards.
(*e*) Theatres, cinemas, music halls, dance halls, skating rinks, swimming baths, gymnasia except those forming part of schools, colleges or universities, Turkish etc. baths, buildings for indoor games.

The objects of this legislation are clear:—

(i) to ensure that owners and occupiers of land are not prejudiced by the grant or refusal of Planning permission affecting that land without their knowledge and
(ii) to ensure that people likely to be affected by development in a seriously prejudicial way are made aware of and given an opportunity to object to proposals to carry out such development.

The first of these is no doubt a reasonable object, though since it merely ensures knowledge of a third party application without any means of preventing the application being made, its principal effect must be to promote lobbying of Local Authority's members on the part of owners and occupiers. As regards the second, it clearly encourages third party intervention in a matter which it is the duty of the Local Planning Authority to determine objectively. It is true that many of the items listed are likely to be the subject of Local Authority development rather than of private development, and that since, in a County Borough, the Local Authority and the Local Planning Authority are the same body, the powers taken under Section 15 may well prevent something undesirable in relation to surrounding development being quietly slipped through. Nevertheless it is the job of the Local Planning Authority to do the Planning not to carry out development control in response to pressure exercised by neighbours of proposed development.

A man likely to be injuriously affected by development nearby is the last person in the world (except for the intending developer) likely to be capable of exercising unbiased judgment about its merits, and therefore quite unlikely to be able to provide useful data to a Local Planning Authority to help them determine an application.

As already noted on page 276, the fact that proposed development will injure someone's amenities is not necessarily a reason for refusing permission.

When a complete application has been received the Local Planning Authority may do one of five things with it:

(i) Give an unconditional permission.
(ii) Attach conditions to permission.
(iii) Refuse permission.
(iv) Report the matter to the Minister and ask him to decide it (as already noted, he may refuse to do so).
(v) Fail to give a determination.

The applicant can appeal to the Minister within 28 days against conditions, refusal or failure to determine within the statutory period. Conditional permission or refusal must be accompanied by a notice in substantially the following terms informing the applicant of his rights. (G.D.O., 2nd Schedule Part II.)

(1) If the applicant is aggrieved by the decision of the local planning authority to refuse permission or approval for the proposed development, or to grant permission or approval subject to conditions, he may, by notice served within one month of receipt of this notice, appeal to the Minister of Housing and Local Government in accordance with Section 23 of the Town and Country Planning Act, 1962, The Minister has power to allow a longer period for the giving of a notice of appeal and he will exercise his power in cases where he is satisfied that the applicant has deferred the giving of notice because negotiations with the local planning authority in regard to the proposed development are in progress. The Minister is not, however, required to entertain such an appeal if it appears to him that permission for the proposed development could not have been granted by the local planning authority or could not have been so granted otherwise than subject to the conditions imposed by them, having regard to the provisions of the Development Order and to any directions given under the Order.

(2) If permission to develop land is refused, or granted subject to conditions, whether by the local planning authority or by the Minister of Housing and Local Government, and the owner of the land claims that the land has become incapable of reasonably beneficial use in its existing state and cannot be rendered capable of reasonably beneficial use by the carrying out of any development which has been or would be permitted, he may serve (on the council of the county borough or county district in which the land is situated) a purchase notice requiring that council to purchase his interest in the land in accordance with the provisions of Part VIII of the Town and Country Planning Act, 1962.

(3) In certain circumstances a claim may be made against the local planning authority for compensation, where permission is refused, or granted subject to conditions by the Minister on appeal or on a reference of that application to him. The circumstances in which such compensation is payable are set out in Section 123 of the Town and Country Planning Act, 1962.

Article 8 of the General Development Order provides that a Local Planning Authority may grant permission to development which does not accord with the Development Plan so far as the Minister may by direction allow. Clearly some flexibility must be allowed or it would not be possible to accommodate minor circumstances not foreseen by the Development Plan or which had arisen since its approval. The provisions of the Development Plans Direction in this connection have already been noted.

This will be the best place to mention two subjects which are not strictly Development Control but are very closely allied to it. The Town and Country Planning Act, 1959 (see, now, The Land Compensation Act, 1961) introduced the principle of compensation at full market value for land acquired compulsorily for public purposes. "'Full market value" was subject to a number of complicated reservations; the important one for our purpose being that, in assessing compensation regard had to be paid to the provisions of the current relevant Development Plan. This, as explained in Chapter 1–3, frequently means that an answer has to be found to the question: " For what would planning permission be given if this land were not required for a public purpose?"

When, therefore, land is proposed to be acquired by compulsory purchase *either* of the parties directly concerned may apply to the Local Planning Authority for a Certificate of Alternative Development. Such an application must specify one or more classes of development which the applicant considers would be appropriate for the land in question if it were not proposed to be acquired by *any* authority possessing compulsory purchase powers.

It is to be noted that such an application can only be made if the land in question is neither in an area of comprehensive development nor allocated in a Development Plan as an area primarily for residential, commercial or industrial use.

The Local Planning Authority must issue a Certificate in response to such an application stating either that development of one or more specified classes might reasonably have been expected to be granted *or* that Planning permission could not reasonably have been expected to be granted for any development other than the development which is proposed to be carried out by the acquiring authority. Where they think it appropriate, the Local Planning Authority may, in the former case say that permission would only have been given subject to conditions or at some future time, and must specify the conditions or the future time.

If either of the parties directly concerned does not like what is said in the Certificate issued by the Local Planning Authority an appeal lies to the Minister in much the same way as against a refusal of Planning Permission. For a discussion of certificates of alternative development see my article Alternative Development Certificates in the Estates Gazette of June 4th, 1960.

Finally, yet another innovation of the 1959 Act (and in my own opinion one of its few good features) was the introduction of measures to alleviate the distress caused by what is colloquially called " Planning Blight ". Where a Development Plan shows the route of a new road cutting through buildings or their curtilages, or allocates, say, an area of existing housing for a school, the properties affected may become virtually unsaleable, even though full compensation would become payable on acquisition, and even though acquisition is unlikely to take place for many years, because people are generally reluctant to acquire property if they think their possession of it is likely to be disturbed provided that other similar property with no such disadvantage attaching to it is obtainable.

Before 1959 such people had no remedy. If their plight was sympathetically viewed by Local Planning Authorities it was likely to lead to the suppression of long-term proposals and to "secret" Planning on drawings which formed the basis of detailed Planning policy but which were not made public in advance and exposed to general comment and criticism. These were, obviously, most unsatisfactory circumstances for the production of sound, detailed long-term Plans.

The 1959 Act therefore made provision for people suffering from "Planning Blight" to be enabled under certain circumstances, to serve a Purchase Notice on the appropriate authority and require it to buy them out.

These provisions are now contained in Sections 138–151 of the Town and Country Planning Act, 1962. Very briefly, they apply to land designated by a Development Plan as subject to compulsory acquisition, land allocated in a Development Plan for the purpose of a government department, a local authority, a statutory undertaker or the National Coal Board and land for a new road or road improvement and so shown in a Development Plan.

The persons who can take advantage of these provisions are limited to resident owner-occupiers of dwelling-houses and owner-occupiers of farms and small businesses. Hereditaments, to qualify as small businesses, must not exceed an annual value of £750. (See the Town and Country Planning (Limit of Annual Value) Order, 1963).

These powers afford a very modest measure of relief. For my part I can see no objection to allowing almost anyone who *wants* his land to be acquired because he thinks himself injuriously affected by Planning proposals to require it to be purchased. If the authority concerned do not want the land for some considerable time there is no reason why they should not let it remuneratively meanwhile.

I have tried in this section to strike a balance between a full lawyer's account of the framework of development control and the kind of brief popular exposition contained on pages 27-35 of the Progress Report of the Ministry of Town and Country Planning. Brief accounts are misleading in that they necessarily omit many special cases which may be of great importance; full accounts are inevitably so complex that it is difficult in reading them to distinguish the wood from the trees and to get a comprehensive picture of the situation. I do not know whether the above account has succeeded in avoiding either or both of these faults, but, in any event, the reader is warned not to rely upon it as a guide to action in any particular development control problem with which he may be faced. For this purpose recourse to the original documents, if not to a lawyer, is essential. I have entirely omitted reference to many twists and turns which, in a particular case, may be of decisive importance.

It is perhaps, something of a condemnation of a system of development control that it cannot be dealt with, even in outline, in fewer than eleven large pages. The system itself is sound enough; powerful yet flexible, firm yet affording every opportunity for the redressing of wrongs; but the form in which it is couched, which requires reference, cross-references and back references to a large number of documents, is decidedly paleotechnic and adheres far too closely to traditional legislative forms to meet the requirements of so comprehensive a system.

This book, however, is no place in which to discuss reform of statutory

means of expression, to which there are many serious obstacles not immediately obvious to the layman; not least of these is the impossibility of stating anything briefly without leaving loopholes for evasion. But the need for such reform is abundantly clear. The idea of including some items within the Act itself and some, more likely to need periodical amendment, in Orders more easily made than an Act of Parliament is passed, is admirable, but it is at least questionable whether the resulting confusion does not outweigh this advantage. A comprehensive code of development control contained in one document as a piece of delegated legislation and revised when necessary by means of special Parliamentary procedure would have much to recommend it.

Problems relating to the control of various important kinds of Development are now considered.

20-3. DEVELOPMENT WITHIN COMMUNITIES

This may appropriately be discussed under the following heads :

(i) Proposals affecting the eventual boundaries of the community

It is vital that the boundary between the built-up area of a community and the surrounding countryside should be kept sharp and clear. Though some uses, such as schools, hospitals and golf courses, which do not involve a considerable amount of building, may appropriately be placed on the periphery of the town, and though much of the countryside surrounding the town may have a special character because of the direct association of its use with the town, the edge of the built-up area should on no account be allowed to straggle; a sharp division emphasises dramatically the contrast between town and country, enhances the visual qualities of each, keeps communications compact and services economical and reduces the amount of agricultural land injuriously affected by development. (See Fig. 95 (i).) The traffic requirements of a new or radically replanned town will, of course, prevent buildings having direct access on to main radial roads. They will either be set behind service roads or back on to the main roads. In either case functional efficiency must result in some loss of dramatic contrast, but the principle still holds. There are few admissible modifications to it. Areas of low density development can best be placed on the outskirts of a community, but if adjacent to radial roads they inevitably reduce the contrast just referred to. They should, therefore, if at all possible, be sited between radials to prevent this. (See Fig. 95 (ii).)

In the case of a large community it will almost certainly be impossible to forecast with certainty whether development will ever reach, in all directions, the boundary of land zoned for it. It is therefore essential that staging shall be arranged so that the result is satisfactory at whatever stage development ceases, whether permanently or for a considerable time. To this end development should, as far as possible, proceed outwards from the centre successively without islands of undeveloped land being left in its wake. This should be insisted on with greater stringency as development approaches the point at which there is some likelihood of its ceasing.

Applications to carry out development beyond the boundary of the area for development or the stage in course of construction should therefore be resisted, even if small in extent or in distance beyond the boundary. It is difficult to convince Planning Committees of the necessity for this. They tend to assume that small encroachments beyond a boundary are unimportant, whereas to stick rigidly to a line, wherever it may be drawn, is usually more important than its precise position. The special importance of this in the case of village development has already been emphasised in Chapter 18.

Events may, of course, show that the boundaries of development areas have been wrongly drawn because some of the circumstances affecting the optimum rate and direction of growth of the community have been wrongly appreciated. Where this is so the error must be accepted and the Plan revised, but fortuitous circumstances not fundamental to conditions of growth should never be allowed to bring this about. In particular, the fact that an owner of land just outside the development area is anxious to develop while one just inside is not should have no effect; it was in order to secure that land should be put to its best use in the public interest that the 1947 Act was passed.

Again, it will often be found that, because of easier gradients or other physical factors, developers would prefer to develop land outside the development area than land within it, and that they will urge the economic advantages of so doing. These arguments are usually meretricious; the smaller cost of developing one particular site rather than another is likely to be offset, from the point of view of national economic conservation, by greater compactness in the system of services of all kinds, including the postman's round as well as sewers and other mains, conservation of farm units, and in other ways. It is only in the case of sites which are very costly indeed to develop that overall economy will be secured by the sacrifice of compactness.

(ii) Proposals affecting the main areas of use

Many of the remarks made about boundaries of the community as a whole obviously apply to these, too. Accidents of ownership or individual whim should never be allowed to lead to changes in the distribution of the main use zones, although major factors which newly arise may properly do so; for example, a phenomenal increase in the space requirements of a particular industry because of a rapid and unexpected change in its national or world importance might justify the expansion of the industrial zone, leading in turn to alteration, perhaps, of the location of a neighbourhood centre and of a residential area. Happenings of this order are always liable to occur, and the most careful Planning fails to foresee them. Their effect is likely to be serious enough without adding avoidable changes.

(iii) Proposals affecting the central area, industrial area and neighbourhood pattern

It is unlikely that any neighbourhood Plan for an area to be developed by several agencies will please all of them. It is possible to admit many more changes in the detailed Plan of a neighbourhood than in the main provisions of a town Plan, though they should never be made without good reason.

There are always many applications made for the piecemeal development of land, for developers do not direct their actions by the provisions of a Plan or always even consult the Local Planning Authority before making application. It may often be possible to make fairly numerous minor amendments to the detailed Plan for a neighbourhood without causing harm, even where Planning requirements do not necessitate them. There is never one detailed design which is better than any other (in contrast to a town Plan, where the limiting conditions may well dictate a particular pattern of development), and variations of the official Plan to suit the requirements of individual developers of sites may be not merely harmless but positively beneficial if they are prepared by competent designers who genuinely try to fit in with the Development Plan for the whole neighbourhood.

Development by private enterprise must obviously pay for itself and leave a margin of profit, otherwise no one would undertake it. But a neighbourhood design which is, as a whole, eminently economical may not split up into a number of sites which can each be developed independently at a profit, because of the physical characteristics of the site or of the distribution of uses within it provided for in the Plan. It is disastrous if private enterprise is allowed to develop only such sites, or portions of sites, as present attractive financial possibilities, leaving the remainder to be developed, if at all, at the public expense; it is essential that private enterprise development should take some of the rough with the smooth.

The order of release of land for development should therefore be so arranged that, as far as is consistent with orderly centrifugal growth, a proportion of relatively profitable land is included at each stage. Planning permissions for individual sites within areas released for development should carry this process on by including fairly stringent conditions regarding the order in which development is carried out, designed to prevent the developer concentrating on the portions easy and profitable to develop and moving on elsewhere without tackling the more difficult parts. It is useless to include an area of moderately steep slope as land for residential development if it is left as a vacant site for fifty years, surrounded by development on flatter land. Fig. 95 (iii) shows an example of something similar which has been permitted to happen on a municipal housing site; the " public open space " provided is unnecessary and practically unused; much of it could have been built on with consequent saving of land elsewhere, but this cannot now be done without new houses being demolished because no break sufficient for road access to the back land has been left in the frontage development.

An example of quite a different kind is afforded by the case of a private developer who undertook to provide grouped garages at the rear of a row of houses in order to avoid individual garage crossings destroying a fine hedge and hedgerow trees and to reduce the number of accesses to an unsuitable road. Having erected and sold the houses, he did nothing about providing garages, and the Local Planning Authority was subsequently unable to resist the demands of residents to build their own garages, with all the consequences which it had been sought to avoid. (See Fig. 95 (iv).) Stringent conditions as to order of development would have prevented this. Examples of inter-war housing estates in which a site was reserved for shops but never developed are numerous.

Some problems have nothing to do with lack of sincerity on the part of the developer. He may be involved in difficulties for a variety of reasons because of the distribution of uses proposed within his site. The road layout may be such that compliance with it involves a crippling burden in the construction of unproductive lengths of roads and services; the density provisions may not allow him to build a sufficient number of the kind of house in which he specialises; he may feel that there is at present an insufficient demand for the number of houses at the density prescribed over the site. He may doubt the suitability of the site chosen for, say, a minor shopping centre, but think that an alternative site within the area he owns offers a good

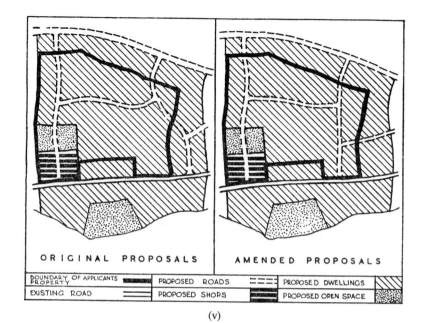

(v)

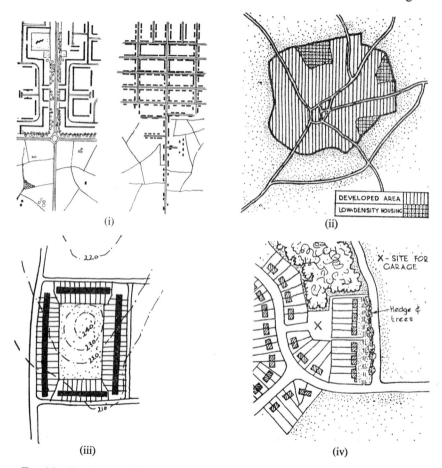

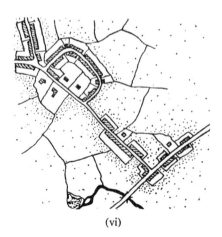

(vi)

FIG. 95.   Development Control.
(i) On the right the typical edge of the unplanned town straggling out into the country-side.   On the left a sharp break between town and country.
(ii) Appropriate locations for low density housing.
(iii) A useless open space.
(iv) Failure to provide grouped garages frustrates an attempt at thoughtful **planning control**. (See page 289.)

(v) Detailed planning proposals amended to enable the owner of part of the land to develop profitably without violating any planning requirements.
(vi) The most central undeveloped land in a straggling village wasted by having only two houses built on it.   (The two buildings in solid black.)

prospect of successful development. These are representative examples of the kind of problem likely to arise which may justify modification of the neighbourhood Plan if this can be done without disorganising the development of adjoining land.

Let us consider first the question of road layout. Fig. 95 (v) shows a case in which the provisions of a neighbourhood Plan absolutely cripple the unfortunate owner of the site whose boundary is marked. He is prevented from getting full advantage from his existing road frontage, for it may readily be supposed that he will not be able to build any shops until a substantial number of houses has been erected and occupied, yet in order to develop his land at all he must build a long stretch of road before he can make any of it productive. The proposed road intersecting his site at the north-east corner mocks him because he cannot link the portion of it within his site to an existing road. In these circumstances it is possible for the route of this road to be varied, thus allowing the developer to use it as his outlet, even though there will not be connection to the north for some time, and to develop the majority of his land by subsidiary roads leading from it, leaving the road on the west side to be made when the shop site is ripe for development, and full use can be made of it. There will be many cases where no simple solution is to be found, but this example at least indicates the kind of approach which should be made to such a problem.

Density may raise very serious difficulties. The whole functioning of a Plan may well be upset unless the net residential density decided on for a neighbourhood is kept to fairly closely, yet developers may quite legitimately feel it necessary to depart widely from it either upwards or downwards, and it is a matter for earnest consideration how far this can be permitted on a particular site if reasonable prospects of adjusting the balance by corresponding variations in an opposite direction elsewhere are not to be lost.

For example, if 8 acres are allowed to be developed at 4 dwellings to the acre instead of 12 to the acre, $10\frac{1}{2}$ acres of land will have to be developed at 12 to the acre instead of 6 to the acre to redress the balance, while if 8 acres are allowed to be developed at 12 dwellings per acre instead of 4, $10\frac{1}{2}$ will have to be developed at 6 instead of 12 to restore the balance. To permit an individual developer to cash in on a strong demand for development of a particular kind may make it impossible to allow his competitors to carry out any development at all on similar lines. It may also have the effect of preventing a satisfactory blending of development. Conservatism in permitting departures from net density provisions is therefore necessary.

Even if the developer does not wish to depart from average net density, taking his site as a whole, it is necessary to prevent too wide a variation within it. If net residential densities have been fixed in accordance with the principles suggested in Chapter 17, the objects of the Plan will not be secured if, on a site zoned at a density of, say 50 habitable rooms per acre, half the dwellings are provided at 4 dwellings (say 24 habitable rooms) per acre and the other half at 15 dwellings or 76 habitable rooms per acre, though variations between 8 and 12 dwellings to the acre would probably be entirely suitable. If garden requirements have been correctly assessed, compliance with prescribed net residential densities must result in the long run in supply meeting demand, and departures from the overall density decided upon should only be permitted if there is irrefutable evidence that a wrong assessment of requirements has been made. Again, permissions should be so framed that the developer is not able to build only the houses at the density he favours, leaving vacant the land set aside in his layout plan for other types.

Attempts to introduce large establishments beyond the degree of provision made for them in the Plan can be absolutely fatal to its implementation and must be resisted unless a case can be made out for the special suitability of a particular site for the purpose proposed and suitable additional land for dwellings is available.

Control of the density of private enterprise residential development presents very great difficulty at the present time. In most areas, the most detailed Plan approved, and in many cases even prepared, is the Town Map, which prescribes maximum gross residential densities over cartogram areas equivalent in size roughly to neighbourhood units. These densities, furthermore, are expressed in persons per acre, so that, in order to judge whether a particular proposal complies with density requirements it is necessary first to decide what occupancy rate is to be expected in the area under discussion, next to deduct all non-residential uses from the cartogram area, then to calculate the net residential density and finally to decide whether, in the probable event of the development not coming near to this figure, it is reasonable to permit deviation from it to the extent proposed. All this tends to become farcical. In practice it is extremely difficult to force developers to adopt a density appreciably below that permitted already in another part of the same cartogram area, so that very desirable variations of density within a cartogram area may be extremely difficult to bring about.

It is also difficult to persuade developers to carry out development at a higher density than they wish if the proposals they submit are for houses larger, and with larger plots, than those envisaged in the Development Plan. On the whole, though, the opposite problem is rather more general.

The net result must often be that, in order to avoid over-population within a cartogram area, with subsequent dislocation of local services, developers must all be forced to develop at something close to the average residential density for the whole cartogram area, or else that, in fact, over population will occur.

The main remedy for this problem is clear. It is for Local Planning Authorities to press forward with the work of preparing Comprehensive Development Area Maps, and Supplementary Town Maps for all those parts of their areas in which development and redevelopment is taking place. On these maps density is expressed as net residential density, in habitable rooms per acre, and there is no reason why a fairly fine subdivision of densities within a cartogram area should not be provided for, so long as this is done in accordance with demand and reasonable possibilities.

In order to do this it is necessary for a number of definite and hard decisions to be taken. For example, there are a good many areas of low density Victorian housing which could quite appropriately be redeveloped at a considerably higher density because there is no longer sufficient demand for gardens of the size which exist. Local residents, who do not yet wish to redevelop may, however, bitterly resist redevelopment at a higher density on the ground that it "lowers the tone of the locality". They may have powerful allies on the Local Council. This is an issue which is becoming increasingly important as the years go by, and more satisfactory results are likely to be secured by definite zoning, even though it may be open to critic-ism, than by leaving things in their present state of vagueness.

In villages, under-utilisation of sites is likely to be a commoner problem than over-utilisation. The limited area of the land which ought to be made available for development in order to maintain compactness and character reduces flexibility and the extent to which any one use can be allowed to take up space. Fig. 95 (vi) shows a straggling village in which permission to take up the whole of a site of an acre or more with two houses (shown in solid black) greatly reduced the extent to which visual unity and physical com-pactness could be enhanced. Mention has already been made, in Chapter 18, of the difficulty in making the most suitable land available for development. This ought not to be aggravated by failing to make full use of any which can be developed.

I once persuaded a Local Authority to refuse permission for some houses in a village development area on the grounds that the density of the proposed development was too low, and so did not make proper use of the limited amount of land zoned for development. Unfortunately, the applicant did not appeal, so that I do not know whether the decision would have been up-held by the Minister on appeal. It seems unlikely that it would have been, but it is very important that all land zoned for development should in fact be developed at something like the intended density, or compactness will be lost. Recently (1963) the Minister has himself, in appeal decisions, begun to specify *minimum* rather than maximum densities at which land may be developed.

The control of redevelopment in central areas is likely to involve appalling difficulties. Unless the whole site is acquired by the local authority and redeveloped under their management, it is almost certain that the need to compromise, the restrictions placed on development by the limited sizes of sites in single ownership, and the difficulty of remodelling the street system without sterilising much land for a long time will produce a result far below the ideal. It is essential that all uses not appropriate to the central area should be kept out, for competition for sites in it is usually so acute that failure to exercise strong control will result in sites going to the highest bidder irrespective of whether it is essential for his activities to be located in the centre. Similarly, the maintenance of zones within the central area—public buildings, shops, offices and warehouses—will require great determina-tion. Weakness is almost certain to result in a mass of new development as incoherent as the old, even though the standards of architecture and daylight may be raised substantially.

It is unlikely that development control within industrial areas will cause any very serious difficulties, since the convenience of the manufacturer is of paramount importance and he is almost always the developer. All that is required of the Local Planning Authority is to hold the ring and ensure that

development is co-ordinated in respect of the transport system, external appearance of buildings, and daylighting. It is necessary to *make* the private developer of dwellings proceed in the best interests of future residents because it is not always to his financial advantage to do so. This does not apply so much to industrial development.

(iv) Minor proposals

In my opinion it is essential for Development Plans to be clear, definite, comprehensive and detailed, and that they should be revised as soon as a need for revision becomes apparent, without awaiting the end of a quinquennium. If this policy were followed much of what has been said in the immediately preceding pages would be dealt with as a result of alert response by the Local Planning Authority. Disputes and appeals over major issues would thereby be much reduced. It would be reasonable for the Minister to support on appeal the provisions of well prepared up-to-date detailed Development Plans except in very exceptional circumstances. This would discourage appeals as well as avoiding altogether many disputes which now lead to appeals. Nevertheless many changes of use and much development of a kind too minor to be clearly in or out of accordance with even the most detailed Development Plan would still occur; the following pages deal with such matters, which are the real concern of development control proper rather than the formulation of Planning proposals.

These include all proposals which do not involve changing the Plan to erect buildings or change uses in respect of single sites of limited size. The aspects from which these need to be considered are, first, whether they will prevent the eventual full implementation of the Plan, and, second, what their effect will be upon neighbouring uses and roads. As things stand as present it is unrealistic to adopt a policy which prevents the full utilisation of any building in sound condition, and this causes complications. The granting of temporary permission is helpful in dealing with many kinds of application for minor development in built-up areas, so it will be well to begin by examining the nature of this device and its uses and abuses.

Section 18 of the 1962 Act enables a Local Planning Authority to grant temporary permission for development which ought not to remain per-manently, but is relatively unobjectionable until redevelopment takes place or more suitable accommodation for the proposed use may be expected to be available. When the period has come to an end the owner must remove the building and make good, or cease the use without compensation, although he can, of course, renew his application and appeal against refusal.

An applicant who receives permission for a limited period must, of course, consider whether he can afford to accept it; whether the cost of the proposed development in relation to the benefit he will derive from it makes it worth his while to carry it out and lose it at the end of the specified period. Ob-viously the length of time fixed has the greatest bearing on this.

A building of considerable size to be used in connection with a factory might not be capable of writing itself off in less than 20 years, while a small extension to a builder's store might be well worth having for only two or three years. There are five purposes for which Local Planning Authorities are in the habit of using temporary permissions, two legitimate, three illegitimate. The legitimate purposes are, first, to secure that an area which requires redevelopment but which cannot be tackled for some time does not, on the one hand, meanwhile become cluttered up with new buildings which would greatly increase the cost of redevelopment or further postpone it, or, on the other, decay through the various enterprises within it being prevented from meeting their needs for expansion and adaption, and, second, to provide temporary homes in existing buildings, or in temporary buildings on odd unbuilt-on sites, for uses which are inappropriate, but which cannot yet meet their needs by means of new permanent construction because sites for them are not available.

The illegitimate purposes are, first, when the Local Planning Authority has formulated no definite Plans for the redevelopment of an area, as a device to avoid coming to a firm decision about a proposed use which takes them by surprise and which might or might not fit in with the eventual Planning of the area. A temporary permission gives the Local Planning Authority the best of both worlds. Eventual redevelopment is not impeded, but, unless the applicant shows fight and appeals, no definite proposals need be formulated. The Minister has come down heavily on Local Planning Authorities who have tried this dodge and whose bluff has been called. Such action is only admissible when the proposed utilisation of a site is obviously unsuitable, whatever the future of the area, but in the circumstances unobjectionable as an interim measure.

Second, a Local Planning Authority may often be in some perplexity as to whether a proposed use is likely to prove harmful in a particular situation and may wish to " put it on probation " by granting a permission for a limited period with a view either to extending it indefinitely when it comes up for renewal, or doing away with it. This does not lack common sense but it is inadmissible; an applicant is entitled to a final determination of his application, and the Local Planning Authority must make up its mind at once, rightly or wrongly. The Minister has not always been as firm as he should have been about this.

Third, temporary permissions are sometimes given in order to control the appearance of structures made of flimsy materials whose appearance is likely to deteriorate in a comparatively short time. This is an example of trying to make one Act do the work which is intended to be done by another, for by-laws relating to short-lived materials which cover this aspect can be made. Planning permission should either be refused on the grounds of unsatisfactory appearance, or given subject to the structure being kept and maintained in a satisfactory state of repair and painted annually in a colour to be approved by the County Planning Officer, or some similar formula.

The main disadvantage attaching to the use of temporary permissions is the shortness of both public and private memory. An applicant with full knowledge of its implications may receive permission for a limited period, and yet fight tooth and nail against bringing it to an end, even though he has no valid reason to seek renewal, and members of a Local Planning Authority are apt to be unwilling to support recommendations made to them to take enforcement action or refuse renewal. Possession is indeed nine points of the law and Planning officers have a well-justified dislike of most temporary permissions.

Where large-scale redevelopment is too remote to be a serious consideration and temporary permissions, except for the purpose of providing temporary homes for uses which will move as soon as possible are thus no help, each proposal has to be considered on its merits. Will it cause congestion or danger to the road system generally or in the immediate vicinity; will it be detrimental in other ways to neighbouring uses? These considerations, of course, apply also to an area of prospective redevelopment when considering whether even a temporary permission should be given. It is undesirable, however remote the prospects of redevelopment may be, freely to admit uses which could have no place in the area after redevelopment; they will be hard to shift when the time comes.

It has to be faced that most non-residential uses are in some way objectionable as immediate neighbours to dwellings, and it is usually more a matter of deciding whether this is enough to justify refusal than of discovering positive merit in an application.

The redevelopment of isolated sites or development of small unbuilt-up areas should be made to comply with the Development Plan, but, in order to secure full utilisation of existing buildings some latitude is necessary in considering changes in their use.

Applications for this are commonest in respect of large houses no longer suitable as single family dwellings. When these are suitable for conversion into flats and are in the midst of houses, one should be chary of agreeing to any non-residential use, for conversion to flats is the normal and appropriate change to be expected; but where they cannot readily be converted, or their curtilage, without being so extensive as to be suitable for the erection of further dwellings, is large enough to provide some seclusion, it is a different matter. One should be quite adamant against conversion to factories, warehouses, or open-air storage in a generally residential area, but schools, hotels, clubs, nursing homes, hostels, remand homes, or even offices whose business is conducted mainly by letter and telephone, may cause little trouble, and find the only practicable home in such houses.

The greater the amount of traffic likely to be attracted to a use the greater must be the insistence on satisfactory road access being available, and any really considerable amount demands seclusion from residential streets. One would not, for example, care to allow an office employing 60 or 70 people to establish itself in an ordinary residential road. This applies to traffic in transit, and parking also needs consideration; visitors at a nursing home and members of a club, for example, may be a great nuisance to adjoining residents by leaving a number of cars parked at the roadside, and, particularly near bends and junctions, danger is often caused. The possibility or otherwise of providing adequate parking space for cars within the curtilage and off the road is therefore a very material consideration.

The other principal factor is noise. Children at play yell and scream; newly-born babies cry, but the sound does not penetrate far; clubmen snore, but the sound does not reach beyond the building. The distance separating a building from dwellings is therefore of the greatest importance in considering such uses. Maternity homes need a little clear space on all sides or the crying can be a real trouble to neighbours; nursing homes not taking maternity cases are unexceptionable in almost any house, but schools really do need quite a lot of room round them or they can be a curse. You cannot keep healthy children quiet at play, nor should you try to do so. The actual amount of space needed depends a good deal on the school A school catering only for a dozen children in the mornings up to the age of five could be accommodated on a much smaller site without being a nuisance than one catering for the full-time education of forty up to the age of eleven.

It would be very difficult to attempt to give dimensions; each case must be judged on its merits, with reference also to contours and the screening of noise by foliage. Nevertheless, some attempt to formulate standards of acceptable distance from neighbours for uses such as schools and similar uses in residential areas should certainly be made in order to introduce a measure of objective assessment. At present evidence at appeals concerned with matters of this kind is generally at the nursery level of " It's alright ", " It isn't ", " It is ". Appendix 1 to the Buchanan Report, which attempts to establish what intensity of traffic is acceptable in various kinds of roads used by pedestrians shows what can be done by the use of ingenuity to work out standards of this kind.

Clubs vary a great deal; they may be so quiet and staid that you would hardly know they were there, or so gay and noisy that they may rival dance halls or pubs., neither of which are suitable very close to dwellings. The kind of activities undertaken by a club must be taken into account before permission is given, and, if necessary, drastic conditions imposed.

Many non-residential uses of existing houses would be entirely un-objectionable if it were not for the excessively large, ill-designed and badly maintained signs that disfigure them. Every permission for such a use should contain a stringent condition limiting signs to the barest minimum necessary to afford identification.

It should be remembered that the grant of Planning permission does not override the law relating to nuisances, and any use of a site which amounts to a legal nuisance can be acted against in the courts by those aggrieved. Nevertheless, the public is entitled to expect the Local Planning Authority to follow a policy which will reduce the need for such action, and to give protection against many things which, although unpleasant, do not amount to legal nuisance. However, in order to avoid trying to make one law do the work of another, it seems that a Local Planning Authority should give decisions on the assumption that any use it authorises will be conducted in a reasonable manner, should limit conditions to those which guard against happenings which, in the absence of such conditions, might reasonably be expected to occur and should leave excesses to be dealt with under the law relating to nuisance.

Applications in areas of mixed use pose some difficult problems. Frequently the existing intermixture is so confused that no definite pattern of uses can be made out from examination of the land use map and no early redevelopment is possible. It is easiest to consider each application separately and to grant permission if it appears improbable that matters will

thereby be worsened; but this is a sterile policy which can bring about no improvement during the many years that may elapse before comprehensive redevelopment can begin, makes it progressively harder to resist any kind of application in the area concerned and complicates the eventual problem of redevelopment. Certainly no new building or drastic remodelling of an existing one should be permitted except where, and in such a way that, it will accord with Plans for the area as redeveloped, nor should changes of use unaccompanied by substantial building operations be permitted at all freely if they do not so comply. The aim should be gradually to steer uses into the areas they will occupy after redevelopment, so that the latter process involves the replacement of buildings only, not uses as well.

A good many exceptions to this are inevitable. The use of surviving large houses for warehouses may, for example, be necessary in the static area surrounding the town centre, even though the eventual use envisaged conflicts with this, but these exceptions should be kept to the minimum. The familiar example of sporadic shopping frontage is a good one; every effort should be made to confine new shops, whether created by new building or conversion to the areas they will occupy after redevelopment.

Complete success in pursuing this policy is unlikely, but it should, if determination is shown, produce results markedly superior to what would have happened if the area had been left to its own devices.

Finally, we come to a difficult class of applications—those which relate to changes of use which are barely material; the kind of case, in fact, which might well be started off by an application for a Section 43 determination. The majority of these relate not to the sole use of a building but to uses different in kind from but subsidiary to the main use, and most of them involve business use of a dwelling. The Progress Report of the Ministry of Town and Country Planning gives an excellent example of this sort of thing on page 30. Speaking of the difficulty of deciding what constitutes a material change of use and of the impracticability of making lists of changes which are deemed to be material, it says: " Dressmaking for profit—to take one example—can, when conducted on a small scale as an ancillary to a shop, be regarded as merged in the shop use, while within limits it can be carried on in a dwelling-house without affecting its residential character; but in any classification of uses it would have to be ranked as a light industry."

Another very relevant passage occurs on page 140 : " . . . it is sometimes held that people should not be permitted to carry on an occupation in a private house, not because it is noisy or intrusive, but simply because it is an occupation, and the mere fact of it may affect the " high-class " character of the neighbourhood. This is a very dubious argument." It is indeed; there are innumerable activities which give an outlet for spare time and surplus energy and bring in a welcome additional income, but which would not be worth while undertaking except in the home, and cause no kind of annoyance to neighbours.

There are also whole-time activities, of which a small tailoring business is a good example, which need so little space and equipment that there is no need to use special premises for them. It is, indeed, always a question of degree; the line is often difficult to draw, but there are various rough and ready yardsticks which are useful in establishing whether any particular use is material. No use in connection with a dwelling can reasonably be considered a material change if it fulfils the following conditions :

(1) No visible alteration in the house or curtilage inconsistent with its use as such.
(2) No noise, smell, etc., attributable to the use which is perceptible to neighbours.
(3) No outdoor storage of materials.
(4) No material increase in number of vehicles calling at the premises.
(5) No material increase in number of persons calling at the premises.
(6) No material increase in number of persons living in or spending most of their time at the premises.

Unfortunately, even in describing these yardsticks, it is not possible to eliminate the element of judgment implied by the use of the word " material ".

Discussion of this subject could be endlessly elaborated, but two pairs of examples must suffice to illustrate the degrees of intensity of use which may be encountered and the extent to which they may be material.

I sit at home writing this book, which I hope will be a remunerative undertaking, but no one outside the house could possibly tell that this was going on except by looking through the window and making deductions from the impedimenta scattered about the floor; no sensible person would suggest that such an activity constituted a material change of use, though I know of one case where a local authority tried to bring something very similar under control and to stop it!

But suppose now that I decided in this same house to start furniture making on a substantial scale. I engage 20 employees and distribute them about the house, keeping only two rooms for living purposes; I install woodworking machinery and stack my stock of timber in the back garden. As well as making the furniture, I sell some of it from the house, and, to this end, remove the window of the front living room and replace it with a shop window. I find it necessary for the purposes of the undertaking to keep two lorries permanently on the premises. Clearly this is a very material change of use. These represent something like the extremes of what can go on in a dwelling.

Now consider two similar uses the differing conditions of which make it fairly evident that one involves a material change and the other does not.

First, an importer of goldfish operates from an ordinary suburban semi-detached house with quite a small garden. Most of the garden is taken up by concrete pools in which the stock is kept; an octopus array of pipes supplies water to each, and a portable pump is available to empty them. Tanks, cans, iron frames and other apparatus are scattered about in haphazard fashion. The whole place is deplorably untidy, but, however well arranged, it would look more like a reservoir than a garden. A large shed houses tropical fish and reptiles from which snakes sometimes escape. Part of the house is used as an office. Callers are frequent, some with lorries. The neighbours must be extremely tolerant not to have invoked the law relating to nuisance.

Second, a horticulturist, interested in fish breeding, has devoted a large proportion of his garden to it, and probably makes a fair income from it, but there is no evidence whatever of commercial use. All the pools, greenhouses and other buildings used are such as might be expected in a garden. No extraordinary numbers of people call. Obviously no material change has taken place.

Numerous problems also arise in connection with uses ancillary to non-residential buildings. For example, a workshop, bakery or other building ancillary to a shop is obviously part of the shop use, but the manufacturing activity may grow at the expense of the shop, and other shops may be supplied by it. It may be very difficult to determine at what point a material change of use occurs, and, when this has happened, how much it can be permitted to extend without becoming detrimental. Common sense is the only sound guide, and a consistent policy which aims at ensuring clear distinctions between use zones without being repressive towards praiseworthy enterprise should be followed.

Special problems arise in villages. Here no definite division into use zones is usually possible or desirable. The shop, the house and the builder's yard may have to be cheek by jowl with each other, and this mingling is an important element in the character of the English village. Nevertheless, so far as possible, it is desirable that uses which are intrinsically unsightly should not be visually prominent, and this can often be satisfactorily achieved by keeping them off road frontage. Even in a village it is a good thing to arrange for uses which do not make pleasant neighbours to dwellings to be placed slightly apart from them; the butcher's shop, for example, is not happily placed in the middle of a terrace of houses. No general principles can be laid down, but careful attention to each case may enable marked improvements to be made without the introduction of any stereotyped arrangement of uses.

In conclusion it may be said that it is in general a fairly sound rule to determine Section 43 applications in a liberal way. If there is any real doubt as to whether permission is required, it is best to determine that no application need be made. Then if the proposed use grows markedly beyond what was originally contemplated it can be coped with by means of enforcement order should it prove objectionable. On the other hand, if, in a borderline case, application is insisted upon and permission granted it may create an unwelcome precedent and extensions and intensifications prove much more difficult to resist than if the original activity had been ignored.

20-4. DEVELOPMENT OUTSIDE COMMUNITIES

This section includes consideration of hamlets and of groups of houses too small to be considered communities as well as of development in the open countryside. The question of appearance vitally affects almost all such development, so that it is impossible to avoid some overlap with later sections of this chapter, but no details concerning the external appearance of buildings or of advertisements are considered here.

Britain has a lovely and varied landscape, but most of it has been greatly changed by man. Contact with wild nature is something which I would go so far as to describe as a basic human need, even though it goes unrecognised by many, and a landscape plentifully sprinkled with human dwellings does not meet this need. Over large parts of the Home Counties, particularly, it is difficult, except in the depths of a wood or a quarry, to get out of sight of a building, and from this consequence of dense population and intensive agricultural use springs the need to pay particular attention to the amount and the disposition of building and other development allowed in the open country.

British landscape may be divided approximately into four main types: Wild moorland, forest and mountain; normal agricultural country; country house areas, and ruined countryside.

Each of these except the first is humanised to a marked degree; the hand of man has altered the species of vegetation and animals which are found, has placed buildings and other objects on the surface, and has even, in many places, altered the natural contours of the land. Unfortunately, the most satisfying and least humanised country is the least accessible, while country house areas and ruined countryside stretch out so far from many towns that few of their inhabitants get much opportunity of visiting even normal agricultural country, let alone wild country.

It has often been remarked that once the number of isolated houses and groups of houses rises above a certain intensity, which is difficult to describe but easy to recognise on the ground, there is no longer genuine countryside but a very low density residential area. This is not to say that in country house areas the visual effect may not be very pleasant; well-designed houses, spacious and beautifully maintained gardens, well-kept golf courses, with now and again an ancient mansion and park, can make a delightful whole. But it is not countryside; it does not make one conscious either of the wild majesty of nature or of the patient struggle of man with nature expressed in the mosaic of farmland. Rather, it reminds one of inequality in the distribution of wealth.

Spoiled countryside is even worse; the location of mines and quarries has there resulted in a desolation of pitheads and areas of surface working combined with a scattering of industrial villages and hamlets whose sites are not based on logic, and within which no one with a surplus of wealth sufficient for the purchase of a large house and the upkeep of extensive gardens would wish to live.

There is little we can do to bring wild country nearer to our dwellings, but a great deal which we can do to prevent the growth of existing country house areas and areas of spoiled country, and to prevent new ones from springing up, so that as large a proportion of country as possible shall at least remain as normal agricultural landscape.

There follows now a discussion of seven important forms of development and preservation of the countryside.

(i) Isolated country houses

People with rural tastes and reasonably high income often prefer to build a house in the open countryside rather than within a village, and this may be for one or more of the following reasons, among others: Possession of means of transport, which reduces dependence upon physical closeness of services;

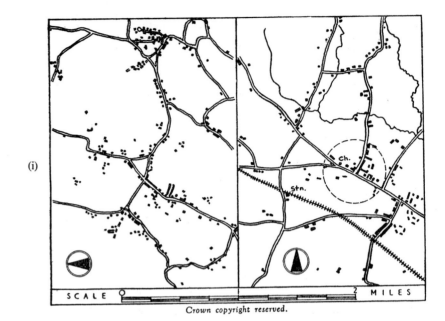

(i)

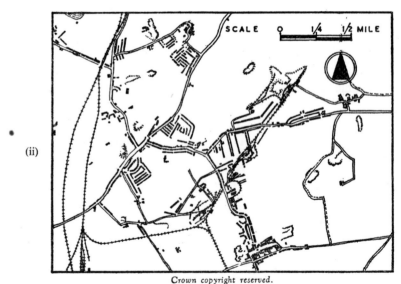

(ii)

FIG. 96 (i) Two rural areas containing large numbers of scattered houses. The inhabitants have the advantages neither of living in a community nor of isolation, and the disadvantages of both.
(ii) An area of spoiled country in County Durham.

dislike of or indifference to human society; desire to enjoy a fine view; inability to obtain a site within a village.

The problem of the isolated country house is one which has never been satisfactorily solved. If suitable sites within villages were freely available the problem, though still difficult, would be reduced to quite small dimensions, for the total number of people who would specifically prefer to live in the open countryside than within or on the edge of a village must be small, though many people would like to have the best of both worlds by living on an approach to a village, a quarter of a mile from the built-up area, thus enjoying seclusion combined with accessibility. We have already seen in the previous section that to allow this is incompatible with the maintenance of satisfactory boundaries for built-up areas.

However, there are those who really want to live in isolation, whose needs will still have to be met.

There are four aspects from which the question must be looked at. In the first place, houses are a national asset, and it is essential that they should be sited where they can reasonably be expected to be useful all their lives. An isolated house may never find another occupier after the departure of the original owner because it does not meet anyone else's requirements; at best, in a period of housing scarcity and high prices, it may be bought cheap and occupied at some sacrifice by someone desperate for a house. This factor alone is enough to condemn the sanctioning of large numbers of such houses.

Second, the necessarily limited size of rural communities makes it desirable that all rural dwellers except resolute hermits should be able to take part in common activities.

Third, for reasons already given, a large number of isolated houses greatly increases the cost of providing services, and even hermits receive mail.

Fourth, the landscape aspect. Every proposal to erect an isolated house should be considered from the point of view of whether it will result in excessive humanisation of the landscape. There are numerous areas in which no new houses at all should be permitted because they have already reached or are approaching the state of low density residential areas rather than the countryside.

For these reasons no simple formula can possibly meet the case. Suggestions have sometimes been made that, as an improvement upon 1932 Act devices, country houses at the rate of one to so many acres should be permitted. But there are some areas where even one house to a thousand acres would be too many and others where, because, for example, of the existence of a small pocket of broken and barren land surrounded by fertile country, 1 to 100 acres would not be excessive.

A promising method would seem to be for Local Planning Authorities, after carrying out the necessary survey, to prepare a map showing areas of land within which isolated houses could be sited because each area fulfilled the following conditions :—

(a) Agricultural value negligible.
(b) Nature of subsoil permits individual drainage system to be used without danger or nuisance.

(c) Contours such that unobtrusive siting is possible.
(d) Distribution of existing buildings (including farmhouses and farm-workers' cottages) such that an additional house or houses would not excessively humanise the landscape.

Within each such area, provided a thoroughly unobtrusive site was chosen and the road access and approach roads were such that danger was unlikely, one or more houses would be permitted, depending on the size of the area and the existing distribution of buildings. If the number of suitable sites, measured by these standards, was greater than required, all but a few of the most suitable and attractive could be omitted. One such house site for every 20,000 of the population of the Planning area would probably be a reasonable total for existing and future requirements combined.

Places such as roadhouses with dancing and swimming facilities are apt to be nuisances within communities because of the noise and general disturbance which they create. They can often be sited appropriately in open countryside and their attractiveness thereby increased, provided the road approaches are satisfactory. They could well be allowed to have a claim on the country house site " ration ".

The old inter-war concept of the Green Belt has re-emerged in recent years. Readers are referred to Circulars 42/55 and 50/57 of the Ministry of Housing and Local Government for details of the Ministry's current attitude and the way in which Green Belt proposals are worked. The fundamental idea of the Green Belt is that the open country surrounding a town is an area of special vulnerability and of special importance. It is vulnerable because it provides extremely pleasant sites for houses, and there is likely to be a great demand for land within it for the more well-to-do members of the population. It is also likely to attract a large number of institutional and quasi-institutional uses. It is especially important because it is the part of the countryside most readily accessible to and enjoyable by the inhabitants of the town concerned.

It is mere common sense to scrutinise with particular care all applications for development within the important and vulnerable areas, and to adopt toward them a more severe policy than elsewhere. Nevertheless, there is a danger that, by defining specific Green Belt areas around towns and cities, other countryside may, by implication, be regarded as less worthy of stringent protection. Planning control over the countryside ought everywhere to be strict, and the proximity of proposed development to a town or city ought merely to provide additional grounds for refusal, grounds which are in any case sufficient.

There is also the danger that a Green Belt may be regarded as an area into which all urban uses which do not involve intensive building up of sites, such as schools and playing fields may overspill instead of being provided within the urban area proper. This would be quite wrong. Although such uses can, for all the reasons mentioned in Chapter 14-3, be very appropriately placed at or near the edge of the urban area, they should be provided for as part of it, and the countryside proper left almost entirely to agriculture.

These remarks apply not only to isolated country houses but to some of the other kinds of development about to be discussed.

(ii) Sporadic development

This consists of groups of houses whether in a row or spaced out, sited in isolation rather than within a community. Sometimes, though rarely, they are in the deep country, but usually they are within a mile of a village, and reach towards or even meet houses which have violated what should have been the boundary of the village development area. The menace of the latter has already been stressed, and it is severely increased when nearby sporadic development has run riot until there is more of it than of the village proper.

In nearly all circumstances, it seems to me, additions to sporadic development are equivalent to throwing good money after bad or reinforcing failure.

Sometimes a patch of sporadic development may happen to have been sited where the creation of a genuine community is appropriate in the interests of establishing a sound pattern of service centres; but this is rare. Much more often they are merely detached bits of suburbia placed where access to bus or train facilities, with or without a preliminary car journey, provides a motive. More rarely still, a patch has become so large that it becomes imperative to permit some expansion of it so that some service facilities can be provided.

I hope it is unnecessary at this point to reiterate the arguments against allowing new areas of sporadic development; my present argument is against the currently accepted policy of " infilling ", or allowing houses to be erected to fill the gaps in uncompleted rows of houses. There may be occasions when this is permissible solely on visual grounds. For example, Fig. 97 (i) shows a length of sporadic development hideously placed on a skyline; to refuse to permit the two gaps to be filled would be as unkind as to deny the making good of gaps in a set of teeth; occasionally, too, a row may end so abruptly that to permit it to extend a little to some natural punctuation may be sensible, as in Fig. 97 (ii).

But these are exceptions; to allow " infilling " wherever there are two or more houses fronting on a road with gaps of not more than about 100 yards between them, is quite wrong. In many cases the frontage in this category would be sufficient to accommodate the entire future housing needs of the rural population, and since these strips of frontage are often in the market at reasonable prices because they have no possible alternative use the demand for the more conveniently situated of them is considerable.

Such infilling often blocks up views to the passer-by which have not been completely spoiled by previous development, and adds appreciably to the traffic, and, hence, to the dangers of narrow and winding country roads.

It is sometimes argued that infilling should be allowed because the gaps between houses are virtually useless for agricultural purposes, and to use them for building enables useful agricultural land to be saved elsewhere. This is a most short-sighted policy; of what use is the saving of a few acres if, as a consequence, the social and economic balance of a wide area is upset and lack of proper distribution of services results in a flight from the land? The pursuit of such a policy might in the long run have precisely these results.

Another argument used in favour of infilling is that it is better to allow additional development in an area already spoiled than to run the risk of fresh areas being devastated. This is a counsel of despair; the need for houses to be sited where they are *needed* completely overrides it.

New houses in hamlets are a sort of half-way house between isolated houses and sporadic development. They can provide delightful homes for those who want quiet and seclusion yet do not want to be entirely out of sight and sound of their fellows, but anything more than the smallest addition is likely to upset the delicately poised visual character of the place. I should like to see Local Planning Authorities make surveys of vacant sites within hamlets and to select and make public lists of those on which it seems that a house could be erected without detriment, never allotting more than a very few sites to any one hamlet, and leaving many without any at all, so that any replenishment of the life of the place would come from the replacement of worn out buildings on the same site. Even this ought not to be a *sine qua non* if the whole hamlet is in decay and the reasons for its original formation no longer apply.

(iii) Houses for agricultural workers and other agricultural buildings

The Notes on the Siting of Houses in Country Districts, issued by the Ministry of Town and Country Planning in 1950, sum the position up very neatly:—

" Many farmers are understandably anxious that as many as possible of their workers shall live near their work, on the farms. Equally understandably, many farm labourers prefer to live in, or close to, a village where they can enjoy community life, where their wives can shop and their children go to school, even if they themselves must walk, cycle or be transported to work. Naturally, neither farmers nor workers are invariable in their views; there are farmers who prefer their workers to live in a village and there are workers who prefer a house on a farm. Views differ, in fact, very largely according to the physical features, the farming pattern and traditions of the particular district, the accessibility of a town and the huddle or straggle of the local communities.

" The Minister believes that, in general and allowing for the variety of local circumstances, it is better to house farmworkers in villages. It must be recognised, however, that where farms, especially those devoted to stock-rearing, are necessarily a distance from the villages or towns, as in the hill farm districts, many farmers must always have their key workers, in particular stockmen and shepherds, on the spot. Authorities will no doubt take into account, so far as they properly can, the preferences both of farmworkers and of their wives."

But this evades discussion of the " tied house " quarrel. A farmworker who occupies a house owned by his employer is not a protected tenant and he can be given notice to quit at any time, which naturally does not make such houses, known as tied houses, popular with the farmworker. On the other hand, the farmer can argue, reasonably enough, that if the house does not go with the job a tenant can go elsewhere to work and continue to occupy a house which the farmer needs to be able to offer in order to secure another employee to take the place of the first. This is particularly important in the case of key workers, such as skilled cowmen, who are in any case limited in numbers; a farmer who quarrels with his cowman can hardly hope to get another unless there is a house available. This problem cannot, of course, be solved by Planning action, but its existence needs to be realised in order that the reasons for the emotions and prejudices aroused by discussion of the siting of farmworkers' houses may be understood. Its final solution, no doubt, depends upon legislative action and/or the achievement of an agreed policy between the National Farmers' Union and the National Farmworkers' Union.

There is no doubt that farmworkers' houses outside villages should be as few as possible. Where the demands of a particular job require that an agricultural worker's house be sited on the farm the landscape aspect can be safeguarded by siting it so as to form a group with other farm buildings, thus keeping increased humanisation of the landscape to a minimum. The farmer may kick against this and insist that he and his employee do not want to live in each other's pockets, but this is usually an empty argument; it is nearly always possible to secure some slight degree of separation and privacy without taking the new house out of the group. Fig. 97 (iii) shows a typical case. Either X or Y would be an acceptable site, but Z would be highly objectionable.

In no case should permission be lightly given for dwellings on a farm.

It seems probable that a little ingenuity and determination might work wonders in reducing the need for key men to live on the farm when there is a village not too far distant. If farmers were given a substantial grant for every

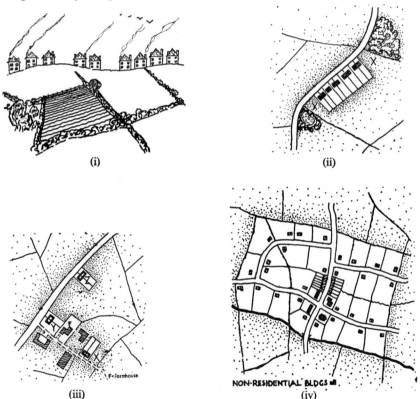

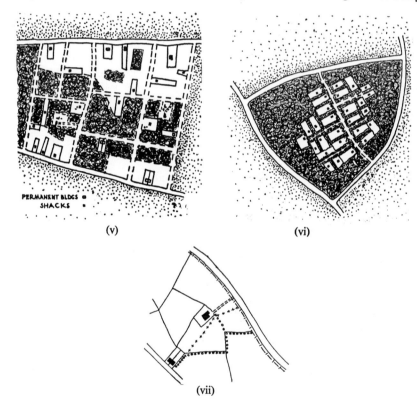

FIG. 97. Problems of Rural Development Control.
(i) This deplorable scene would at least be improved by filling in the gaps.
(ii) Here again additional houses at X would tidy up the scene.
(iii) Three possible sites for keyworkers' houses on a farm. Both X and Y would allow the new buildings to form part of the farm headquarters group, and X would allow farmer and farmworker to keep out of each other's way to a reasonable extent. The use of Z would also allow this but visually would constitute an intrusion in the landscape.
(iv) A reasonably compact group of smallholdings with a dwelling for each and modest provision of social facilities and supply services at a central point.
(v) A typical sprawling shack colony.
(vi) A shack colony brought sufficiently under control to make it inoffensive yet without destroying its purpose.
(vii) Two ways of routeing an overhead electricity line. That represented by the row of circles fits as unobtrusively as possible into the landscape pattern but that shown by crosses is unnecessarily assertive.

house they built in a village, shakedowns at headquarters for cowmen when an animal was sick or expected to calve, and other aids, might suddenly be found to be very easy to devise.

The need for the farmhouse itself to be on the farm is not, of course, to be disputed, but Local Planning Authorities should make it clear that they will not be parties to assisting a very ugly racket which is sometimes worked. The farmer sells the farmhouse as an ordinary dwelling at a high price and then screams for Planning permission for a new farmhouse on the grounds that the holding cannot be properly worked without a house at the head-quarters. The circumstances are usually a little more involved than this, some kind of protective smoke screen being put out to hide the nakedness of the transaction, and the Local Planning Authority may be in a quandary because, however disgracefully the situation has come about, the holding has, in fact, been left without a house as headquarters, and does indeed need one.

When a new farmhouse *has* to be built its detailed siting may often be important. A site in a slight fold in the ground, at the corner of a field, near a copse, can be much more pleasing than one which ignores existing patterns. This seems an appropriate place to point out that buildings and other structures in the landscape should be sited in accordance with one of two principles. The erection of a house in the countryside is not a particularly clever feat, and a touch of humility and acknowledgment of man's dependence upon nature can fittingly be expressed by making the building, in its siting, shape, texture and colour, comply with rather than challenge the patterns formed by nature.

On the other hand, a great dam, a power station or a viaduct cannot be made to merge into the natural pattern except by means of self-conscious attempts at camouflage. Such things demonstrate that man, the tool-using animal, has his passing triumphs and it is preferable, providing vulgarity and braggadocio are avoided, to allow their inherent monumentality to be fully displayed.

Farm buildings other than houses decidedly do not come in this category. Present policy, of course, frees them from control in all except areas of special scenic beauty, but it is to be hoped that this injudicious relaxation may eventually be abandoned. Quite small variations of siting and the use of the right paint may make all the difference between the creation of a monstrosity and something which is perfectly innocuous. Functional requirements usually govern siting strictly, but even twenty feet one way or the other can make all the difference. The use of " rural green " for painting the exterior of farm buildings has caused unfavourable comment, but many other colours, including, particularly, buff, give far better effects than the maroon or natural rust which so often cover corrugated iron buildings. There is little evidence even that most farmers think about this kind of thing, so that " the pledges of co-operation offered by the National Farmers' Union and the Country Landowners' Association, who recommended their members voluntarily to consult the Local Planning Authority before embarking on any development which would *obviously* (my italics) be of interest to the authority " (Ministry Progress Report, page 28) seem unlikely to be worth very much.

The asbestos and corrugated iron which the farmer uses nowadays need exceptionally careful treatment if the effect they create is not to be downright hideous, and this, over and above the need to site all farm buildings carefully, is an additional reason for increasing rather than relaxing control.

Houses in connection with smallholdings constitute a difficult problem. In the first place it is difficult to define a smallholding; it may roughly be said to be a family affair, worked without outside labour being employed, but it is loosely used to include gardens sufficiently productive for a fair amount of produce to be sold from them.

There is no doubt that a smallholder needs to live on his land, so that he can guard it against marauders and work extra hours without missing meals. And here, unfortunately, is the making of another racket. When Planning control began to be seriously exercised after the war the word soon went round that the best way to get Planning permission for an isolated rural house and at the same time to speed up the acquisition of a building licence was to buy a fairly large site, and claim that a house was needed on it in connection with a smallholding. In other cases perfectly genuine people bought chunks of scrub woodland cheaply and persuaded themselves, or were persuaded, that their honest toil would soon convert them to a Garden of Eden.

The County Agricultural Executive Committees did their best to help by supplying the Local Planning Authorities with information about the agri-cultural capabilities of the applicant and the suitability of the site for intensive cultivation. Unfortunately this did not go to the root of the matter. The capabilities of the applicant hardly concern the Local Planning Authority, for Planning permission is normally given for a use or a building, not to a particular person, and the applicant can move on at any time. Theoretically, a permission can be expressly limited to an individual, but such a condition, requiring demolition of a house on vacation by the first owner, would never succeed.

The only complete remedy is drastic; it consists in the Local Planning Authority selecting certain areas which, because of their agricultural charac-teristics, are particularly suitable for smallholdings and which are either close to an existing village or offer the prospect of a community being created. (See Fig. 97 (iv).) If this were done, the land made available, by compulsory purchase, if necessary, and permission refused for smallholding dwellings everywhere else, a great deal of honest but misplaced toil would be avoided and the social, economic and visual evils of this special kind of sporadic development arrested.

But clearly the difficulties of applying such a policy whole-heartedly are formidable. There are many circumstances in which the creation of a single smallholding in a particular area is perfectly reasonable, and could not be refused permission without serious injustice being done. The stage at which action needs to be taken is when several such applications are made within a short time in respect of sites within a short distance of each other; very prompt action has to be taken or it will be found that precedents will make it difficult, if not impossible, to refuse permission for further applications.

(iv) Makeshift dwellings

In Chapter 4-3 some mention was made of the rash of ramshackle buildings to be found on the outskirts of many towns. In their existing form most of them are intolerable eyesores, and many are dangers to health. Most of the buildings in them have been erected without Planning permission or by-law consent, and vigorous enforcement action can appropriately be taken to do away with them. Where, as is often the case, the land they occupy will be needed for future urban extensions this is doubly necessary. Fig. 97 (v) shows a typical area of makeshift dwellings.

But areas of this kind are needed to satisfy a strong human urge and it is a matter of some difficulty to find ways of meeting it adequately without causing public mischief. We are concerned here with urban dwellers who want somewhere to play a sort of Robinson Crusoe game; to lead a primitive life for quite short periods at a time, and perhaps to combine this with the growing of a few vegetables to make the game more realistic. This is not camping; very often nights will not be spent away from home, and a camping site does not meet this sort of need.

We are not dealing with *Planned* development in any ordinary sense of the term, but with something which is utterly unplanned, and most of the requirements for it are the reverse of those for Planned development. Diffusion rather than compactness, primitiveness rather than convenience, inaccessibility rather than centrality are required, with the reservation that the site must not be too far from the homes of those using it. Most of them will have some kind of mechanical transport or the trip will hardly be worth the effort.

The requirements for such a site are:

(1) Negligible agricultural value.
(2) Seclusion; areas of scrub woodland will fulfil both these.
(3) Permeable subsoil with no risk of effluent entering water supply.
(4) Size. Some spoliation is bound to result; the area will not remain genuine countryside, and it should be limited to the smallest size which will suffice.

Fig. 97 (vi) shows such an area. The only public expenditure needed would be the provision of a fairly firm track to provide access to the plots, for they should be kept right away from public roads, and the only condition which would need to be imposed on tenants would be one forbidding the felling of trees within, say, 15 ft. of any boundary of the plot and of the trees between the plots, so that the structures which might be expected to be erected would be screened from each other and from the public gaze. No control whatever over the materials and appearance of these would be exercised.

This sort of arrangement, it seems to me, would enable a lot of fun to be had without raising any serious difficulties. It may be suggested that a main water supply should be provided, but this is undesirable; a couple of jerricans can hold all the water likely to be required for a family visit to the snuggery, and the provision of a supply would be likely to increase the only real disadvantage attaching to the provision of such sites, viz., that unfortunate people unable to secure homes might, as trespassers or with the connivance of tenants, use the buildings as all-the-year-round dwellings. This would be so dangerous to health that every possible step should be taken to prevent its happening.

There may be a tendency for shops to spring up in connection with these legalised shack areas; they should be resisted. The idea is to give people who want it as close an approach as possible to primitive conditions. They cannot have it both ways, and the provision of any ancillary buildings both reduces the primitiveness and the unobtrusiveness of the development and increases the area required.

(v) Camp and caravan sites

These take three distinctly different forms:—

    Sites used for holidays in tents;
    Sites used for holidays in caravans;
    Sites used for residential caravans, i.e., caravans which are permanent, all-the-year-round homes.

In practice there is, as regards the first two, a difference between what may be called casual use and commercial use.

The use of caravans, both for holiday and for residential purposes is now governed by the Caravan Sites and Control of Development Act, 1960, of which Part I, dealing with caravan sites, is still operative.

We have already noted that anyone can use a site for camping for up to 28 days in a year without getting Planning permission, which looks after the casual campers, and that members of approved organisations may do so without a time limit. These comprise organisations granted a certificate of exemption by the Minister of Health under Section 269 of the Public Health Act, 1936, and include bodies such as the Boy Scouts' Association, the Boys' Brigade, the Camping Club of Great Britain and Ireland, and the Caravan Club of Great Britain and Ireland. (See G.D.O., Classes IV and V.) This exemption does not now apply to caravans.

In practice, of course, no one cares whether a site is occupied for 28 days in the year or 32 days; the object is to control constant use, yet to allow complete freedom for the longest period for which any individual holidaymaker is likely to want to use a site.

So far as the casual use of caravans is concerned the position is covered by the G.D.O., Class XXII, which is interwoven with the Caravan Sites and Control of Development Act.

So much for non-commercial sites. Commercial sites range from the field which a seaside farmer lets to relays of holiday-makers throughout the summer to full-scale holiday camps with chalets and dance bands. The same principles apply to all; the objects of control are to prevent eyesores and danger to health, and to confine such uses to compact areas so that excessive quantities of countryside are not taken up. The greatest demand for camping sites naturally arises in the most attractive and accessible areas, principally by the sea, so that there is little chance to steer camp sites right away from the public gaze.   Nevertheless, much can be gained by encouraging development of sites in hollows or surrounded by trees rather than on bare crests.

The total quantity of camp sites which any particular locality can absorb without detriment is, of course, a matter for special judgment in each individual case.   Certainly, a firm line should be taken, when saturation point is judged to have been reached, by deciding to give no more permissions.   This is unlikely to be popular with farmers who find the overflow from properly organised sites a source of profit or who decide to cash in on the established demand in the vicinity by converting fields into permanent and equipped sites.

Appearance and health demand that permissions for camp sites should be very carefully limited by conditions regarding the position and number of tents, caravans, or chalets (the caravans and tents may either be provided by the proprietor or brought by holiday-makers), sanitary and ablution blocks offices, canteens, etc.   An orderly arrangement can do much to render the appearance of the site acceptable.   Any structures erected on the site should be neat and seemly, and bus bodies, glider fusilages and other makeshift affairs should not be tolerated.

Considerations of health demand that piped water, adequate sanitary facilities and sewage disposal—including disposal of refuse—should be available.   Compliance with conditions limiting the extent of the site will be easier to enforce if the provision of proper tracks made of cinder or other suitable materials is insisted upon.   It is desirable to insert a condition prohibiting any use of the site during the winter months, in order to prevent buildings being used as makeshift homes.

These camp sites do not cater for people seeking a back-to-nature holiday, but for concentrations of people taking a cheap but highly artificial holiday. These facts preclude toleration of the free and easy conditions desirable for a site for makeshift buildings.

A different kind of problem is posed by those who, by choice, live in a caravan permanently or who buy one as a home in despair of finding a house or flat.   The reasonable way to deal with these is to regard the caravans as houses and to determine applications as for isolated houses or as a housing site, as the case may be.   The fact that even well-designed modern caravans are unlikely to be so visually satisfactory as well-designed buildings justifies specially strict control over siting.

This is a desperately difficult subject about which to arrive at a useful set of guiding principles.   To most people the prospect of living permanently in a caravan would be repellent, yet to some it is apparently highly attractive, and to others a good caravan seems to present itself as a better alternative than the poor house to which their financial resources or their position on the local authority housing list appear to destine them for an indefinitely long period.   It is therefore necessary to permit the establishment of sites for residential caravans, and to assume that their inhabitants will require the normal degree of access to shops and other services.   Yet to regard caravans as interchangeable with houses would be to accept into the urban or village scene a visually disruptive factor of a very serious kind.   The best one can suggest is that sites accessible to public service and facilities yet unobtrusively situated, should be permitted.   It would be over-optimistic to

suggest that the strange phenomenon of the residential caravan site can be satisfactorily assimilated into any reasonable theory of land use Planning.

The Caravan Sites Act, as we will now for the sake of brevity refer to it, introduced a new legal code in the form of a system of licensing additional to the more general system of Planning control, which is left unaltered.   The grant of Planning permission, express or by virtue of the provisions of a General Development Order, is necessary before a licence, known as a site licence, can be obtained.   If Planning permission has been obtained a site licence *must* be given.   If the Planning permission is for a limited period the site licence must be similarly limited but must otherwise be permanent.

Site licences may be limited by conditions but a condition prescribing the materials of which a caravan is to be constructed is not valid.   Section 5 sets out six kinds of conditions which may be attached to a licence.   They are conditions which:—

> (*a*) restrict the occasions on which caravans may be stationed or the total numbers of caravans which may be stationed at any one time.
> (*b*) control the state of repair or types of caravans.
> (*c*) regulate the positions in which caravans are placed or of any other structures and tents.
> (*d*) secure measures for preserving or enhancing the amenity of land, including planting and replanting.
> (*e*) ensure measures for preventing, detecting and fighting fires.
> (*f*) secure adequate sanitary facilities.

Breaches of conditions and appeals against conditions are dealt with by magistrates' courts.   Conditions may be varied at any time by a Local Authority after giving notice and an opportunity for making representations.

There are various complicated provisions for dealing with sites established before the coming into operation of the Act, with which we need not be concerned.

The First Schedule to the Act sets out the circumstances (which correspond with the exemptions from Planning permission given by Class XXII of the G.D.O.) in which a caravan site licence is not required.

Under Section 5 (6) of the Act the Minister has produced Model Standards, normally to be expected on sites.

The Caravan Sites Act is, despite its complexity, a very useful measure which has codified the law and practice relating to caravans, an aspect of Planning which had previously caused inordinate dispute and litigation.   It divides control effectively if not precisely between general Planning control and detailed, by-law type control.

Finally, there are sites on which caravans are displayed for hire or sale. These are difficult to cope with.   The large area required makes it difficult to find sites in urban areas which are not required for more essential urban uses, even if the proprietors were prepared to pay the high rents involved.   Anywhere else they are likely to be an unwarrantable consumption of agricultural land, and to be visually unacceptable.   Ideally, they should be treated like motor cars, a small number being kept on display in urban showrooms and the remainder stored as close as possible in industrial areas, whence they could be delivered to or picked up by purchasers and hirers. As things stand at present there seems to be an assumption that such sites should be permitted in the countryside because caravans are used in the countryside. This hardly seems reasonable, because caravans can surely best be distributed at service centres conveniently situated in relation to the majority of purchasers and hirers, and urban dwellers want caravans as much as rural dwellers.

(vi) Rural industry and mineral working

Rural industry other than mineral working may be dealt with quite briefly: it should be sited close to a village where possible. Villages do not have "industrial zones", so that protection of residents from offensive sights, sounds and smells can generally best be secured by siting the works a little outside the built-up area of the village, but not so far that it is inconvenient for workers to get to it or sited in such a way that it constitutes an invasion of open countryside. There are a few rural industries, such as fence-making, which can best be carried on at the source of the raw material in order to save transport costs; seclusion from view and safe road access are the most important factors.

Mineral working is a vast subject and it is quite impossible to deal with it at all comprehensively here. A very great deal of highly technical knowledge is necessary in order to cover all facets of even a single application. The Planner's role is principally to decide what the land should be used for after the minerals have been extracted, to secure that they are worked in such a way that the land is left in a suitable state for such use and to safeguard appearance during and after the extraction process. He may also be concerned with the stages by which the working is carried out.

In order to frame conditions which will not only bring about these results, but with which it is economically and technically possible for the mineral undertakers to comply, it may be necessary to obtain much expert advice and to undertake prolonged negotiation. Outright refusal of permission to work minerals in any particular case, however desirable it may be from every point of view other than that of the national economy, may be quite out of the question because of the limited supplies of the mineral which can be economically quarried and marketed.

Excellent official accounts of the problems of mineral workings are available. Chapter VIII of the Progress Report of the Ministry of Town and Country Planning deals principally with the wider aspects of the matter, while the same Ministry's Memorandum on the Control of Mineral Working, issued in January, 1951, goes into great detail concerning technical aspects. Technical Memorandum No. 3 of the Ministry of Housing and Local Government and the supplement thereto are also useful.

In view of the availability of these documents and the special nature of the subject, the following account is confined to generalities.

Planning control over mineral working was gradually extended after the war in such a way as to avoid disrupting production. After 1st February, 1949 all new surface working required Planning permission, but existing workings were not prevented from extending, provided application for Planning permission was made before 1st November, 1948.

There are numerous enactments governing various aspects of mineral working, and the principle that one Act of Parliament should not be made to do the work of another is difficult to apply fully, since there are many subjects dealt with, but only partially covered by, other enactments. For example, the Quarries Act, 1894, deals with the protection of men working in quarries from the effects of blasting but does nothing to protect the public in general or residents in the vicinity from danger, annoyance or damage to property.

The Minister has made far more extensive use of his powers to call in and decide applications for permission to work minerals than in other types of case in order that decisions may be properly related to national need for the mineral concerned and the total amounts available in the country, and because the Minister can more easily call upon expert opinion regarding the numerous technical matters that may be involved than any individual Local Planning Authority. Where he does call in a case, the Local Planning Authority is, of course, able to make full representations regarding its land Planning aspects.

The method of working minerals and the kind of use to which the land can be put after they have been extracted depend principally upon the depth below the surface at which the upper surface of the mineral-bearing deposit is found and the thickness of the deposit. The material lying between the deposit and the surface is called the "overburden".

If both overburden and deposit are thin, as in the case of brick-earth in some areas, where the overburden is little more than the topsoil and the brick-earth may be only 8 or 10 feet thick, it is often possible to work the mineral and restore the land to something very like its original condition so that it can be used for agriculture or building purposes. This also applies where the overburden is thick and the deposit thin, but various complications are introduced. The large quantity of overburden which has to be removed may mean that it cannot be replaced for a long time, and even when it has been replaced it may be some years before it has become sufficiently consolidated to be built on.

There is often a considerable amount of spoil left after initial screening of extracted material at the site and it is essential that every possible means should be used to distribute this within the workings, otherwise not only is an unsightly, barren, unnatural feature, in the form of a slag heap, added to the landscape, but also additional land, over and above that occupied by the workings themselves, is taken up.

Where the overburden is comparatively thin and the mineral deposit very thick, as with chalk, sand and gravel, a large hole is made with no material left over with which to fill it, and although it may sometimes be possible to bring refuse of various kinds from a distance to use as filling, in which case there is the additional advantage that land which would otherwise be needed for refuse disposal elsewhere is saved, the cost may well be prohibitive. In the Progress Report of the Ministry of Town and Country Planning it is stated (page 104) that haulage costs are about 4s. 6d. per cubic yard per mile, so that the filling of a pit fifteen acres in area, with an average depth of 30ft., with a haul of 20 miles, might cost well over £250,000. An additional problem is that many deep workings go below the level of the underground water table and serious results may follow from filling with putrescible household refuse.

The respreading and planting of topsoil is a specially important element in the restoration of most workings, but this, too, has its difficulties. It is thought that if topsoil is stored for very long it loses some of its humus content and thus its fertility. Topsoil is precious stuff; nowhere is it more than a foot or so thick; it cannot be created, though the use of fertilisers can increase the fertility of subsoil, and untreated subsoil will often grow only the rankest weeds. Another trouble is that even if topsoil is respread over a site the surface upon which it is laid may be of much coarser texture than the mineral which has been removed, with the result that the topsoil gets washed down into the subsoil by rain and is lost.

These are but some of the methods used and of the difficulties likely to be encountered in pursuing a policy of restoration after mineral working; some further mention of the application of these principles will be made presently; meanwhile it is necessary to consider the ways in which the siting and extent of mineral workings is likely to conflict with Planning aims.

The three most likely conflicts are where mineral working is proposed in an area required for housing or some other specific purpose, where it crosses the line of a proposed road and where it is within an area of exceptional natural beauty or a nature reserve. It is to be hoped that many of these conflicts, particularly those of the first type, will already have been resolved in the course of the preparation and approval of the Development Plan, but there is, of course, no guarantee that mineral undertakers will not at any time, in view of changed circumstances in the industry, put forward applications which would upset the provisions of the Development Plan, when the whole question will have to be considered *de novo*.

National supply of and demand for the mineral in question is bound to be the most important consideration in arriving at a decision, and this may mean permitting things which, in the interests of purely local land use are undesirable; but it would be a poor sort of Planning which subordinated the former to the latter.

The first thing to be remembered by a Planning Officer advising a Local Planning Authority is that things are not always what they seem; he must beware of tendering advice which seems on the face of things to be sensible but which, in the light of the economics and technics of the industry concerned, is not practical.

To take a single example: it may appear that deposits of a particular mineral are so widespread that there is no justification for selecting a particular area of land, which conflicts with Local Planning needs, rather than another, but one or more of the following factors may overrule mere width of distribution:

(i) The quality of a mineral may vary widely; deposits of the quality requisite for a particular purpose may be extremely rare, so that the presence over a wide area of deposits of a general description— " sand ", " brick-earth ", " gravel "—may be entirely misleading.

(ii) The *purity* may also vary greatly. In one area the deposit may be so mixed with dirt or other useless matter that its extraction is quite unprofitable, while in another it occurs in large volumes in a state of almost complete purity.

(iii) The situation of deposits in relation to the works where they are processed is likely to be of decisive importance. Minerals in the raw state can be carried by conveyor or truck or pumped in a liquid state, but technical considerations and cost limit the feasibility of this fairly sharply. It may therefore often be necessary to permit the workings in a particular area so that the production of an existing works, in which large amounts of capital have been sunk, can continue.

Nevertheless, these factors usually operate relatively rather than absolutely, and it will often be reasonable to insist upon preventing the working of minerals in the way most favourable to the undertakers in order to avoid detriment to local Planning far more serious than mere reduction of profit or even of production. For example, in one case, a Local Planning Authority successfully urged the necessity of limiting the extent, order of working, and depth of excavation of a mineral-bearing site so that the redevelopment of a physically decayed but important village should not be prejudiced.

Clearly, the Local Planning Authority should listen with attention and humility to what mineral undertakers may have to say about the conditions under which they can operate successfully but should have available the services of experts to check the accuracy of what is said. Conversely, the mineral undertakers should listen with equal humility to what the Local Planning Authority has to say about local land Planning requirements; they are equally able to employ a Planning consultant to check for them the soundness of these requirements.

Such humility is not always met with on either side. A local authority which would be the first to complain if materials necessary for house-building ceased to be available is capable of doing its best to prevent the production of these materials within its area. On the other hand, mineral undertakers are inclined to behave arrogantly, to press their technical and economic demands with the full weight of expert evidence, but to try to brush aside Planning requirements, or even to suggest quite ignorantly alternative Planning proposals which fit in better with their requirements but are entirely unsound.

It may often be possible, where suitable building land is abundant, to modify the boundaries of development areas so as to allow greater freedom for mineral working, to provide for playing-fields or parkland to be sited on mineral-bearing areas when these have been worked out, or, where no great depth of mineral is present, to rephase housing and other building programmes so that development can take place after extraction. (See Fig. 98.)

The limitation of depth of working so that sewerage by gravity will still be possible, the working of the floor of the excavation so that it is sufficiently level for the contemplated eventual development to take place, the elimination of dangerous precipices and the screening of unsightly areas are all necessary conditions in order to render mineral extraction tolerable close to a built-up

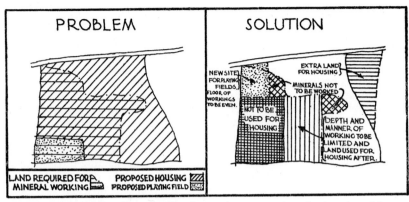

FIG. 98. An example of the modification and programming of mineral working proposals so as to enable the site to be used afterwards for residential and ancillary purposes without sterilising the minerals.

area. It is also essential that satisfactory means of access should be left to workings which are eventually to be used for specific purposes, and that the working of such areas should be completed in sufficient time not to hold up the development intended to take place afterwards, which it may be vital should take place at a particular stage in the development of the community as a whole. Concessions which would have the effect of seriously distorting or cramping urban growth should not be agreed to except in the face of overwhelming evidence.

On the other hand, it may be possible in reasonably level country to divert the route of a proposed road without detriment so that it skirts a working instead of intersecting it; but, where this is not possible, reservation of the route with a sufficient strip on either side to provide for support and screening will have to be resorted to, communication between the severed parts of the working being achieved by tunnel.

Fortunately the need to locate mineral workings close to built-up areas is the exception rather than the rule; far more often the problem is to reduce landscape spoliation to the minimum. In these circumstances the main needs are to secure that as much land as possible is restored to agricultural use after working and that the workings themselves, together with any buildings and apparatus, intrude as little as possible into the landscape both during and after working.

In wild, mountainous and moorland areas appearance is the only consideration, and it is often possible to arrange that workings do not alter a familar profile or, at least, do not contort the silhouette of a range of hills, seen afar, into harsh and unnatural shapes. In wild areas mineral working may, indeed, create few Planning difficulties. The weathered face of a quarry may harmonise quite fittingly with the landscape, and the quarry floor may be left until natural growth clothes it and makes it indistinguishable from the climatic climax which the undisturbed processes leading to a balanced plant and animal ecology have brought about all around. Nevertheless, some

encouragement by initial planting of suitable species and the provision of growing medium may be necessary if rank growing weeds are not to be the principal inhabitants for a long time. The removal of buildings and apparatus when they are no longer required is essential, for the chaos and barrenness of a worked-out quarry are greatly increased by masses of rusting iron and crumbling masonry. If certain items, such as the foundations of buildings, are too bulky or indestructible to be removed they should at least be covered with earth.

The worst problems arise where a large number or area of quarries is necessary in one area. One chalk pit may be a tolerable addition to the landscape where a dozen will not. For example, long stretches of the North Downs have had their visual quality entirely altered by extensive chalk working. This may be unavoidable, but efforts should be made to keep the obtrusiveness of quarrying to a minimum in such circumstances by masking quarry faces by means of planting, and by siting as many pits as possible so that the shape of the hill range itself masks them from distant view from some angles at least.

In an agricultural area more is likely to be necessary, even if restoration to agricultural use is impracticable. A small area which has reached a natural climatic climax superimposed on an area of intensively cultivated agricultural land, can look as out of place as a plantain growing on the Centre Court at Wimbledon. Here a deliberate planting policy designed to shut off the view of the workings by the use of large numbers of trees which fit in with the pattern of the landscape will usually be necessary. In the case of wet workings, planting of the shores with trees and bushes, and of suitable marginal and aquatic plants in the water itself will help to minimise the dreariness of a stretch of artificially introduced lake. Indeed, proper ecological balance of water life is essential if the risk of a scummy, stagnant expanse is to be avoided.

Needless to say, mineral undertakers required to undertake restoration measures as a condition of operation should employ a landscape architect so that these shall bear fruit. The Local Planning Authority should phrase their permission so that a proper scheme can be enforced and the undertakers cannot escape their obligations by making casual gestures towards restoration which can have no substantial permanent effect.

Occasionally a worked-out quarry which cannot be restored to agriculture is so situated that it can very appropriately be used for some special activity, a cycle-racing track or an open-air theatre, for example, but these are fortunate exceptions, and it is highly improbable that the number of sites required for such activities will ever equal the number of quarries available.

(vii) Petrol Filling Stations

The location of petrol filling stations is a problem which arises both in urban and in rural areas, and is one of rather special difficulty. To begin with, what do we mean by a petrol filling station? It may be no more than a concrete apron by the side of a road on which are a row of petrol pumps at which petrol, oil, air and water can be obtained. Or, in addition to these facilities, servicing and minor repairs may be undertaken as well as the sale of motor car accessories. Or the maintenance and repair aspect of the business may be the predominant one and be combined with the sale, on a large or small scale, of motor cars, the provision of fuel being quite a minor activity.

At any rate, we are concerned in this connection only with undertakings which include the provision of fuel, whatever proportion of the business this comprehends. The prime requirement for the location of such undertakings is that they should be placed where they are readily accessible to vehicles. Subsidiary but important requirements are that there should be enough of them to cater for all needs, that they should be placed not only where they are in fact accessible, but where they are easily located by strangers, and that, in detail, they should be placed where they will cause as little traffic danger and congestion as possible. It is regrettable that Local Planning Authorities often seem to be interested only in the last point.

Each of these aspects needs to be analysed. What do we mean by " enough " filling stations? This has to be looked at both from the consumer's and from the producer's point of view. To take the latter first, every petrol company feels entitled to a fair share of filling station sites in a given locality, and, since there are hardly ever as many sites for which the Local Planning Authority is prepared to give permission as there are sites on which the petrol companies would be prepared to open stations, this creates considerable difficulty. Frequently, a filling station on a particular site would be quite unobjectionable, but to allow each of the major petrol companies to open a station next or near to it would produce visually deplorable results. The simple answer is that effective Planning control and unrestricted competition between petrol companies are incompatible. Some sharing out of sites between companies is the only rational solution.

Apart from this the question of quantity is still perplexing. I suppose one could state the desirable state of affairs as being a situation in which no motorist seeking fuel or first-aid for his car shall find himself unduly far from help—however unduly may be interpreted.

In pursuit of this aim it becomes clear that filling stations fall into several loosely definable categories. There must be filling stations within a town centre. These can often appropriately be associated with car parks and with car sales rooms. There also need to be filling stations to supply the immediate needs of residential areas; these can best be associated with neighbourhood shopping centres or sub-centres. Obviously there have to be filling stations alongside main roads also in order to cater for the needs of through traffic. But each of these latter is certain to cater to some extent for casual trade as well as for the type of trade for which it was designed.

We need hardly say more about filling stations in town centres and neighbourhood centres. As regards those on main roads, it is clear that in the open country these should be sited at strategic points, preferably in valleys so that vehicles which run out of fuel between filling stations can coast part of the distance at least towards fuel, and preferably combined with any other facilities such as restaurants which need to be associated with the main road, in order to afford a grouping of necessary buildings rather than a scattering along the road. The Ministry of Housing and Local Govern-

ment in Circular 25 of 1958 quotes the Minister of Transport as taking the view that normally a petrol station should be unnecessary on new by-passes and other new roads on a stretch of road less than 12 miles long. No reason is given to justify the particular distance of 12 miles, and in view of the general unreliability of the Ministry of Transport in providing useful technical guidance it is perhaps best forgotten. It would indeed be extremely difficult to suggest any particular distance as having special merit. Most motor cars have a fuel tank capacity which enables them to travel about 200 miles without refuelling, but human nature and forgetfulness being what they are we should be in a bad way if filling stations were placed 200 miles apart.

There is at all events one special type of location especially suitable for main road filling stations, and that is on main roads leading into towns just at the edge of the built-up area. Stations located here do not, on the one hand, intrude into the countryside, nor on the other hand are they surrounded by development with which they might conflict. They provide a logical and prominent place at which the motorist entering town and short of fuel can replenish his tank and thereby be relieved of the embarrassing possibility of running out of fuel in the midst of dense town traffic. On the other hand, they are equally useful to the motorist leaving town who, through forgetfulness, indolence or failure to find an urban filling station, is setting out on his journey with a low tank. I would go so far as to say that filling stations should be sited on every main road entering a town at the edge of the built-up area.

In larger towns the junctions of major roads, particularly of radial and ring roads, provide sites of special accessibility and visibility, and again I would go so far as to say that every such junction should be provided with at least one filling station designed with the roundabout or other intersection.

The views of the Ministry of Housing and Local Government as expressed in Circular 25/58 agree with mine to the extent that in paragraph 6 the circular says " . . . the fringe of a built-up area may well be the place where petrol stations to serve through traffic will prove least open to objection . . . ",[1] but in paragraph 7 the circular says that a station should not be too close to a " . . . roundabout ", though without saying why it should not be " too close " nor what " too close " means.

We now come to the question of interference with traffic. It is perfectly clear that every motor vehicle which stops, slows down, turns off a road or enters a road, creates a traffic hazard, and that the only way in which motor vehicles can be driven with a full measure of safety is at an even speed with no change of direction at any time; in other words, for safety, we have to turn motorists into a race of Flying Dutchmen who never start or finish a journey and who never turn off their straight predestined course. This is not a possible solution of the problem. It is therefore foolish for Local Planning Authorities in refusing permission for filling stations merely to say that the proposed station would constitute a danger to traffic; all filling stations do. The question is whether in any given place the hazard or interference with traffic is so great as to justify insistence upon the station being moved

---

[1] Note the negative form: " least open to objection " rather than " most suitable "!

elsewhere or not built at all. The simplest and probably the most satisfactory test is to regard a filling station as a road junction and to consider whether a road junction could be tolerated in the proposed position, and if so how it ought to be designed.

Where a filling station is placed beside a dual carriageway road it can of course only serve traffic using that carriageway, and any vehicles travelling on the other carriageway who wish to use it will have to go on to the nearest break in the central reservation and then return to it. All main roads ought, of course, to be dual carriageway roads, but, where they are not, what is known as the " pairing " of filling stations becomes important for safety. It is obvious that less danger and congestion is caused if vehicles use a filling station on their own side of the road instead of crossing to the other side, and this is facilitated if filling stations are placed in pairs on each side of the road, for the inducement to cross over is then reduced to the minimum. The normal method is to stagger stations so that motorists encounter the one on their own side of the road before the one on the opposite side of the road, but there is a school of thought which suggests that, provided both stations can be seen together as they are approached, better results are secured if they are staggered in the opposite direction, since if that is done vehicles pulling away after refuelling are not so likely to come into conflict with vehicles passing those about to pull into the station on the opposite side which have slowed down but have not yet drawn off the road.

Development control in relation to filling stations is very difficult to carry out well, and it is in fact usually carried out very badly, unreasonable permission and unreasonable refusals both being extremely common. The only solution is to tackle the problem in a positive rather than a negative way. This entails every Local Planning Authority selecting, outside central areas and neighbourhood centres, as many sites as it considers necessary for filling stations, having regard to accessibility and prominence as well as to mere numbers, to publicise this information and to give permisssion for filling stations on any such sites but on no others, leaving the petrol companies to arrive at a *modus vivendi*. I can see no suitable alternative to this, because there are innumerable sites in towns where there is no very strong objection to a filling station being sited, but if a proportion of these are in fact used for this purpose without a positive planned policy, there is no reason to refuse permission for the remainder to be so developed as and when applications are received. This produces disorderly and unsightly results.

(viii) Miscellaneous

There remain to be mentioned such diverse forms of development as dams, reservoirs, and other great engineering works, overhead electricity lines and service department development. There is little to say about any of these which has not already been mentioned in connection with other kinds of development, and a few comments on each will suffice.

Major engineering works nearly always arouse bellows of rage from preservationist bodies and individuals, who regard them as vandalism. The hard fact is that you cannot maintain a population at an extremely high density and at a high standard of living without using up for specific purposes a large amount of land which it would be far nicer to keep open and undisturbed.

Once more the Progress Report of the Ministry of Town and Country Planning contains well-phrased wisdom on the subject:

" *Amenity and the work of the Ministry.* Unfortunately the preservation of amenity is not always a matter of ensuring that planning authorities have adequate powers and use them wisely. It is often linked with the much more deeply rooted problem—already stressed in previous chapters of this Report —that in a small, thickly populated and highly industrialised country, whose future depends on its ability to use its material resources to the full, there must often be a clash of interest over the use of the land. When this happens the Ministry's part is often an ungrateful one. Because the Ministry is responsible, among other things, for protecting natural beauty, too many people have the impression that this is its chief—or indeed only—function. This view is clearly at variance with the Minister's duty to secure the right use of land in the national interest. In a larger country, with fewer people to the square mile and less exercised by problems of defence and increased industrial and agricultural output, it might be possible for most conflicts over the use of land to be decided without loss of natural beauty; in England and Wales, at the present time, that is unhappily not possible. This is not always clearly enough understood, partly because planning developed historically from the desire to secure greater amenity in urban development, and partly because amenity, unlike other interests in land, has no other department to champion its cause. As a result, it is often suggested that a decision to allow development which will be unpleasant is a ' defeat for Planning ', whereas all that it in fact represents is a decision that, in the particular case, the amenity interest is not the strongest in the field. Well-known examples are decisions to allow power stations or oil-refining plants in pleasant localities which some people want to see either left clear or developed for other purposes; mineral working in the country; reservoirs in rural valleys; Service training over moors or on the coast; gasholders within general view; industry in residential areas. Opinions will always differ whether, in such cases, the need for the particular development in the particular position is in fact greater than the need for amenity; but while anyone may disagree with a particular planning decision it ought to be recognised that these are planning decisions taken on the view that the development in question represents the right use of the land.

" The attitude that such decisions are ' defeats for planning ' is due mainly to the fact that amenity and convenience are both matters which closely concern the individual, and which he is able to appreciate as he cannot always appreciate the needs of, for example, industry or Service training. He may well feel that these needs could be met somewhere else; sometimes he may be right, but, where the development is needed urgently, investigation of possible alternatives may be a very difficult and protracted business, and the Ministry, in trying to determine what seems the right use of the land, cannot ignore the urgency. This has been particularly so in the last few years, when economic and strategic considerations have been of exceptional importance. It is also true that many of the largest projects, which by their nature are the most likely to be unpleasant, are either carried out by the Government or by one of the socialised industries, or sponsored by the Government; and the individual is apt to assume that if these developments are allowed to override considerations of amenity it is because some other department has been able to override the Ministry. In fact, such large and intrusive development as power stations, training grounds and reservoirs are almost bound, in a crowded island, to 'injure amenity'; and the question must often resolve itself into reducing the injury as much as possible. The best hope lies in trying to foresee what major development is likely to give offence unless very carefully sited, so that possible alternatives can be investigated in time. The Ministry has arrangements for consulting the various departments concerned in an effort to secure this . . . "

It is certainly better for major engineering works to proclaim themselves frankly for what they are than to attempt to be self-effacing, an attempt which will usually be hopeless in any case. This applies, too, to main electricity distribution lines. Rows of pylons cannot be made to melt into the background, and although most people would not regret it if they could be dispensed with, they have a certain grandeur. But low pressure distribution lines are a different matter; they have no grandeur; the poles on which they are carried are often repellent in appearance, though, no doubt, their use is financially essential. Here *is* an opportunity for making something melt into the background. Lines which follow roads without constantly crossing them and which follow hedgerows instead of crossing fields diagonally, can generally be arranged so that they make little impact on the beholder. (See Fig. 97 (vii).) Practically everyone who has been in the Army knows the game of making objects disappear by putting them where they do not break natural patterns, and something of the kind can be done with overhead lines at little extra cost. The Electricity Board seems reasonably willing to comply with representations made with this object.

The establishment of Service departments, far from representing human achievement, are symptoms of man's disastrous inability to behave sensibly. Strenuous efforts were made in the Government White Paper on the Needs of the Armed Forces for Land for Training and Other Purposes (Cmd. 7278) to demonstrate that artillery and tank ranges, etc., cannot be banished to the remoter parts of the Welsh and Scottish mountains, but were not particularly convincing. The Local Planning Authority can hardly hope to override national policy in this respect, and must generally content themselves with trying to secure acceptance of minimum Service requirements rather than maximum Service desires. It must always be remembered that Service people are brought up to demand, on principle, twice as much as they want in the hope that they will then get the correct amount, and initial demands should be regarded with intense scepticism.

Further, the Army, particularly, however proficient it may be in polishing objects which do not need to be polished in order to function efficiently, seems quite unable to erect buildings or use land without making a shocking mess, a fact which casts fascinating light on the military character. This, coupled with the common military attitude of contempt towards civilian control, makes it desirable that any requirements which the Local Planning Authority can get accepted should be directed more towards securing the

segregation of military uses than the observance of conditions regarding modes of use.

20-5. THE CONTROL OF APPEARANCE

It would be perfectly possible to design a town with a very high degree of functional efficiency, thus attaining the fundamental Planning objectives of economy and convenience, but to build it without any regard for its appearance. If this were done, a perfectly balanced allocation of land for various purposes and a road system superbly adjusted to the safety and free flow of all forms of traffic would do little to mitigate intrinsically bad or badly related building elevations, unsightly advertisements, ill-considered landscape treatment, unco-ordinated street furniture and other details. Conversely, we are all familiar with towns and villages of delightful appearance but hopelessly ill-adapted to their functions. Appearance, although it is an important part of most Planning problems, is thus separable from other aspects of Planning. Various powers are available to Local Planning Authorities to control the appearance of proposed buildings and to preserve existing features of the urban and rural scene, but the use of all of them is made extremely difficult by the very fact that they deal with aesthetic values, about which informed and uninformed opinions can be given but only posterity can make the final judgment.

We have no means of foretelling the verdict of posterity, but, in exercising control of appearance, can only try to secure results acceptable to contemporary public opinion or to the persons to whom the public delegates the task. Even this involves great difficulties, among which the most formidable are to encourage bold experiment without destroying continuity, to preserve the old without frustrating the new, and to maintain a firm control without developing a tiresome fussiness. The subject can conveniently be divided into four parts.

(i) The external appearance of buildings

No one, I trust, will expect here an exposition, however brief, of the principles of architectural design. Two books of value to those without architectural training who wish to acquire some knowledge of its fundamentals must be mentioned; the author describes them as dealing with the " grammar " of architectural design. They are " Good and Bad Manners in Architecture ", and " Style and Composition in Architecture ", both by A. Trystan Edwards, and published by Tiranti.

" Notes for the Guidance of Intending Developers ", by James W. R. Adams and E. W. Berridge, published by the Kent County Council, is a most instructive booklet which demonstrates the ways in which some of the worst architectural solecisms can be avoided by observing a comparatively small number of precepts, and is a good example of the guidance given by a number of Local Planning Authorities.

The object of this section is to discuss methods and limits of control, not architectural canons, and to do this it is desirable first to consider the architect's attitude to such control and the public's opinion of it.

Power to control the external appearance of buildings is by no means new, in fact it was contained in all British Planning Acts from 1909 onwards. The fact that a large number of Planning Authorities, until 1943, took no Planning powers at all, and that a much larger number have never applied powers relating to the control of appearance of buildings to any noticeable degree kept most laymen in ignorance of the existence of such powers. The only innovation of the 1947 Act is that it is no longer necessary to relate control of appearance to the level of merit of surrounding development, a limitation in previous Acts which operated to make it impossible to secure improved standards in areas which were being redeveloped in piecemeal fashion.

It is a regrettable but undeniable fact that the general public has for so long been used to being surrounded by masses of buildings which lack any architectural merit at all, which, in fact, are not architectural designs but mere haphazard enclosures of space, that, for very lack of familiar examples, it has failed to develop appreciation of architecture, and, indeed, judges buildings more by their antiquity or impressive size than by their design, mentally excluding modern dwellings from its conception of " architecture " because they are neither venerable nor large. There must, I imagine, be at least a dozen people who enjoy good music and four or five who have at least some appreciation of non-representational painting for every one who enjoys good architecture.

The copious supply of good music on the radio has, no doubt, helped to spread musical appreciation, which an unbroken tradition of music-making in many homes had already founded, while the violent controversies which rage around modern painting have stimulated interest in it. Such controversies have, indeed, arisen in relation to some important modern buildings, but the subject-matter of architecture is less conducive to emotional explosions than that of modern painting, in which the sexual motifs have so often been responsible for the violence of the feelings aroused. In this connection, it is interesting to note that the nude sculptured figures on Broadcasting House and St. James's Park Underground Station caused much more popular excitement and argument than the buildings themselves. It is thus clear that public control of architectural design is carried out, at best, with the consent of the general public, sometimes without their knowledge and certainly not at their behest.

This may dismay but should not deter; public abhorence of architectural control, or dislike for the buildings which it permitted, could speedily end or change such control. In the absence of such a happening, effectively exercised control and the multiplication of good new buildings is the best, and perhaps the only, possible way of developing public taste and demand for satisfactory architecture. I would go further; it is the duty of democratic leaders to be some distance in advance of public opinion. Any popular demand for abolition of control should be resisted and should be acceded to only as the result of a clear demonstration that it is, in fact, the demand of the majority and not of an articulate minority.

Most architects seem to be opposed to public control of the appearance of buildings for reasons which, though valid and sincere, seem to me insufficient. These reasons, as I understand them, are as follows:

(1) Official bodies tend to play safe and a disastrous consequence of official control is likely to be the encouragement, by the readiness with which permission is given to them, of staid, conservative designs which cannot conflict gravely with anything, and the discouragement of the bold and the experimental. The characteristics of " official " architecture—post offices, Government offices, and so on—are cited in support of this view.

(2) A Local Planning Authority is not bound to obtain competent advice or to accept advice given it. Philistines among the members may be able to secure the rejection of distinguished designs.

(3) In any case the advisers of Local Planning Authorities on architectural matters are often less eminent than the applicants whose designs they presume to judge.

There is a comprehensive reply to these. *Appeal against any refusal or conditions thought to be unreasonable.* Appeals exclusively concerned with architectural design are comparatively rare, though it is an issue frequently included with others, but I am not aware that there is any reason for thinking that the result of such an appeal, if well-founded, would be disappointing. The Minister, incidentally, may appoint a special tribunal to hear appeals concerning architectural design.

Architects reasonably point out that the delay and cost of an appeal are likely to deter clients, who, unless they have an exceptional interest in architecture, often prefer to have designs amended to meet a Local Planning Authority's requirements, and may collectively, in the long run, prefer to to employ a " safe " architect rather than one whose designs provoke controversy.

This is all very well, but, though he can do nothing about the delay, there seems no reason why an architect concerned for the maintenance of architectural enterprise and vigour should not make the small sacrifices of time and money required to undertake the conduct of an appeal without charge to his client, nor why local associations of architects should not attend and make representations collectively at appeals where a design of merit is involved.

One resounding defeat inflicted upon a Philistine Local Planning Authority is likely to do a great deal to smooth the path for later applications of merit.

Some Local Planning Authorities have established advisory panels of architects to whom are referred applications involving external appearance which are of special importance or difficulty, or about which, although they are the work of eminent architects, the authority feels uneasy. There seems to be large variations in different places in the effectiveness with which these work but they have the obvious disadvantage that, frequently, the work they do involves the assessment of the architectural designs of colleagues of the members. This may lead to undue severity or undue lenience in the judgments made; it can hardly conduce to impartiality.

But by far the most important aspect of the control of external appearance, and one which, to my mind, virtually sweeps aside the objections of architects, is that *its primary purpose is not to control the designs of architects but those of non-architects.*

It is comparatively seldom that the design of a properly qualified architect, given a reasonably free hand by his client, and made fully aware of proposals for the development or redevelopment of neighbouring sites (to supply this knowledge is an important duty of the Local Planning Authority), will produce a result which can unhesitatingly be described as bad.   It may often provoke controversy, but that is all to the good, and, personally, I should be content to see but the slightest control exercised over such designs.

Drawings submitted by persons who clearly have no competence are quite a different matter, whether they are on behalf of private persons or local authorities.   It seems to me to be the duty of Local Planning Authorities to be absolutely obdurate in refusing permission to a proposal which has not in any real sense been designed; there is a clear difference between a design, whether one likes it or dislikes it, and something which is not a design at all.

Too often the policy is to use the architectural specialist employed by the Local Planning Authority to negotiate with incompetent applicants to secure agreement to amendments which will give the development some semblance of architectural decency.   But you cannot make a silk purse out of a sow's ear; a fundamentally poor set of proposals cannot be made into a good design, however much it is titivated, even if the applicant is co-operative, which cannot be guaranteed.

In my view, the task of the architectural specialist should be to suggest minor alterations, where appropriate, to proposals which contain no fundamental error and can thereby be made acceptable and to confine himself to pointing out the worst faults of those which are hopeless, at the same time indicating general approaches to the problem which should give satisfactory results.   Since there is no statutory power to oblige an applicant to employ an architect, he can do no more than point out the need for a qualified adviser.   The preparation of detailed suggestions is beyond the resources of a Local Planning Authority, raises awkward questions of professional etiquette and is, indeed, a financial burden which they should not have to bear, although, in the absence of sufficient support from his members, the officer concerned may feel compelled to give a good deal of detailed advice for the sake of results which could not otherwise be obtained.

If the Local Planning Authority consistently throw out unsatisfactory proposals, however often these are amended, the applicant concerned will, in the long run, employ an architect in order to get a permission, and thus the eminently desirable end of securing the more widespread use of architects will be brought nearer.   Such a policy also leaves the architectural specialist on the Planning staff free to concentrate on his important and indispensable task of liaising between adjoining developers in order to secure harmony between their proposals, a task which calls for much tact, skill and energy, but is far from hopeless when the applicants concerned are competently advised.

I can see no valid objection in principle to the enforcement of control over the external appearance of buildings provided it is limited to securing competence of individual design and harmony between neighbouring buildings and does not degenerate into architectural censorship, against which

architects themselves can use powerful weapons.   The plea of cost cannot be accepted as valid, for the cost of competent advice is a negligible proportion of that incurred in carrying out any but the most trifling development, and it will often more than pay for itself in the economies effected and the more satisfactory functioning secured by good design.

Perhaps the most difficult aspect of architectural control is to secure reasonable harmony in an area, such as the central area of a market town, where fairly continuous piecemeal redevelopment of comparatively small sites by numerous different developers takes place, yet comprehensive re-planning is unnecessary.   Obviously it will be impossible to secure a completely unified effect, and although splendid results can be achieved by unity through similarity, English market towns are often fine examples of harmony achieved by restrained diversity.   The greatly increased range of materials which are available today, some of them new, others merely made more widely available by the development of transport, makes it much less likely that any such harmony can be achieved without a measure of centralised control.   No comprehensive Plan can be prepared in advance in such cases, save in the loosest and most tentative form, for the individual requirements of developers cannot be foretold in detail.   Each application must be considered as it arises, yet unless there is some general guidance available beforehand, much time and energy may be wasted when proposals for adjoining sites are submitted more or less simultaneously and conflict hopelessly with each other.

Control could be made effective when granting permission to an application consisting only of a layout for roads and building plots by imposing a condition that house designs should be submitted for the whole of a specified part of the layout before applying for permission to erect any houses on it, and that the existence of that condition should be brought to the notice of any purchasers of plots.

Even without this last clause prospective purchasers would be warned, when investigating local land charges, of the restriction, and, in the event of a breach of faith by the estate developer, would have only themselves to blame if individual applications for permission were refused on the grounds that no comprehensive submission of house designs had been made.

It has long seemed to me that there is a way out of many of the difficulties and embarrassments caused by control over the external appearance of buildings.   It would require a simple piece of legislation.   I should like to see an Act passed making it obligatory for applications for permission for all buildings, except perhaps a few specified classes of minor buildings, to bear the signature of an architect, who would be assumed to be responsible for the design.

No application which did not bear such a signature, would be considered by a Local Planning Authority, as it would not constitute a valid application. It would then, in my opinion, be reasonable for the intrinsic architectural merits of buildings to cease to be the subject of public control.   One could be assured that non-design and gross architectural indecency would shrink to small proportions, and the temptation to act as censors of art would be removed from members of Local Authorities.

Attempts to act in this way cannot, in my view, possibly be justified. The revolutionary young architect is as much entitled to have his designs built as is the most conservative past-president of the R.I.B.A. And the censorship of architectural design is something which it is neither proper for Local Authorities to undertake, nor possible for them to do efficiently.

Public control of external appearance would then be confined to securing harmony between proposed buildings and existing or proposed buildings seen in juxtaposition with them, and with any important landscape features. No doubt the exercise even of this control would lead to a good deal of controversy and friction, but it could, at least, be based upon reasonably objective principles. It may not be possible to find any general consensus of opinion, even among architects, as to whether a particular building is a good one or a bad one, but it ought to be possible to secure a fair measure of agreement as to whether a proposed building grossly violates the harmony of its surroundings. Errors made in this field would, I believe, have a less serious effect than having no control at all, whereas it is arguable that the present set-up is worse than having no control at all.

The last word on this subject may appropriately be left to the Ministry of Housing and Local Government. Volume I of the Second Series of Selected Planning Appeals, issued in 1959 is divided into a number of sections, each prefaced by a short sermon on policy statement; that at the beginning of the section on Design, which I commend, reads as follows:—

"One of the objects of planning is to prevent bad design and to encourage good. But unfortunately it is not possible to lay down rules defining what is good and what is bad; and much may in any event turn on the site. Moreover, opinions, even expert opinions, can often differ.

It is therefore difficult to offer useful advice to intending developers other than the obvious advice that they should take trouble to ensure that the designs submitted are good. If they are in doubt how to ensure this, the authority may be able to help them, if they ask for advice before starting on plans.

Two questions can arise on design. The first is whether the design is bad in itself: fussy, or ill-proportioned, or downright ugly. The second is whether, even if the design is not bad in itself, it would be bad on the particular site: right out of scale with close neighbours (which does not mean that it need be similar to neighbouring designs), an urban design in a rural setting, or a jarring design or the wrong materials in a harmonious scene.

It is obviously desirable that in operating control over designs authorities should be guided by the advice of a qualified architect; and if a district council have not got this, the county council may be able to assist them. Authorities should always be prepared to arrange for this architectural adviser to discuss proposals with developers, whether at the outset on a request for advice or when plans have been submitted about which they are doubtful.

Planning control should not be used to stifle initiative and experiment in design; a design is not bad because it is new and different—it may be very good. Designs should be rejected only if the objection is clear and definite and can be explained. It is not enough to say that a design will 'injure the amenities' or 'conflict with adjoining development'; it must be explained why it will do so.

In general, planning control of design should be exercised with great restraint. But where a design is plainly shoddy or badly proportioned or out of place, the authority should not hesitate to ask for something better."

(ii) Tree planting and preservation

The conservation of trees is an activity in which Local Planning Authorities have an important part to play. Trees are at once beautiful, an important crop as raw material for paper, building materials and many other purposes, indispensable agents for the conservation of moisture in the soil, the prevention of soil erosion and the sheltering of crops, and the homes of wild life. Their conservation, replenishment and increase is therefore a vital part of land Planning.

The Forestry Commission exercises powers of conservation to maintain supplies of timber and also undertakes schemes of afforestation to increase them; it is not concerned with appearance *per se*. Under Section 29 of the Town and Country Planning Act, 1962, a Local Planning Authority may make orders for the preservation of trees, groups of trees or woodland in its area if it is expedient to do so *in the interests of amenity*. This makes it clear that timber conservation is not, in this connection, the concern of the Local Planning Authority.

Such an order, known as a tree preservation order, may provide that trees shall not be cut down, lopped, topped or wilfully destroyed without permission, and may provide that any area in which trees have been felled by permission shall be replanted. Compensation is not payable in respect of the making of a preservation order but is payable for any loss suffered as the result of a refusal of permission to fell.

The felling of trees, not ordinarily development, in effect becomes so in any area in respect of which a tree preservation order is made. Orders may not be made in respect of woodland which has been dedicated under the Forestry Act, 1947, woodland owned by the Crown, or Forestry Commission woodlands.

Any preservation order made must be confirmed by the Minister, and there are the usual rights for objectors to be heard, but in cases of urgency, where there is imminent danger of felling, an order may be provisionally confirmed without investigation of objections or compliance with formalities. Such an order lapses two months after being provisionally confirmed unless all statutory requirements have meanwhile been complied with and the confirmation subsequently renewed.

So far as the Forestry Commission is concerned, a licence is necessary in order to fell more than 825 cubic feet of timber in any quarter, the equivalent of about 27 sizeable trees, and this is in itself a check upon wanton destruction. It is said that too many applications for felling licences are made for the Forestry Commission to consult the Local Planning Authority in every case, but where it is known to the Forestry Commission that an estate is being sold or broken up, where 25,000 cubic feet of timber or more is involved, or where the Forestry Commission knows that an important question of amenity is involved, the Commission consults the Local Planning Authority before issuing a licence, so that the latter may take steps to make a preservation order before it is too late, It is difficult to understand why a copy of each application could not be sent to the Local Planning Authority on the understanding that any representation must be made within three days, just as in urgent cases representations regarding Service land requirements must be made promptly.

Despite this apparent defect in liaison, it will be seen that the powers available are reasonably strong. It is sometimes suggested that the felling of a tree ought everywhere to be regarded as development, so that the danger of trees being felled without warning might be averted, but this seems to be going rather far. If Planning permission had to be obtained for cutting down a dead holly tree in the back garden, the position would be absurd, enforcement would be quite impossible and the net result might well be worse than with the existing system, under which the penalties for contravening a preservation order at least make preservation effective in certain defined areas. Obviously, too, there would have to be some downward limit to the size of tree controlled or people would become afraid to clip a hedge without permission![1]

The true solution is for Local Planning Authorities to decide as early as possible the trees which are worthy of preservation, and to make preservation orders in respect of them.

In January, 1949, the Ministry of Town and Country Planning issued a Memorandum on the Preservation of Trees and Woodlands which, both in style and content, was a model of clarity and helpfulness. It is difficult to think that it could be much improved upon, and it should certainly be read by all concerned with the subject. It includes a Model Form upon which to base tree preservation orders.

The following remarks, although not based upon the Memorandum, are in close accord with the statements made therein.

The reasons which make it desirable to preserve trees under the Act are varied and have nothing to do with the value of the trees as a crop, nor, necessarily, with their beauty as individual trees. In the first place, prominence is of importance; there is little point in applying a preservation order unless the trees are where they will be seen by a large number of people, either because they form a feature in some stretch of landscape or because they are close to a road, footpath or river.

There are woodlands which should be preserved because of their sheer mass, which forms an important constituent of the landscape, small woods which are familiar landmarks or give relief to otherwise featureless country, stretches of country in which, although there may be no trees of outstanding size or beauty, small copses and hedgerow trees give the scene most of its character, areas of woodland through which roads pass, and where the intimate patterning of bough and leaf, light and shade are extraordinarily beautiful, trees which lend special charm to a stretch of water, the deliberately grouped trees of a park, planted in the eighteenth century and now reaching their full glory, clumps of trees which hide an eyesore, individual trees of special intrinsic beauty or interest, such as the spreading chestnut tree at the smithy, avenues, and many more, the loss or mutilation of which, as masses, groups or individuals, would cause irreparable harm; any fool can cut down a tree, but no one can put it back quickly.

Obviously, there is no need to duplicate control by making an order in respect of trees controlled by the National Trust, but the Memorandum states that trees or woodland owned by Local Authorities should not normally be included in an order, nor those owned by statutory undertakers and other public bodies. In view of the ghastly things that some Local Authorities do to the trees planted in their roads this seems a dubious doctrine, although many have an admirable record in respect of their roadside trees, their parkland trees and areas of woodland in water-gathering grounds, etc., owned by them.

Trees grow to maturity and thereafter decline and eventually die, though the whole process may take many hundreds of years. Preservation does not imply that trees are to be kept standing until their natural death; in the case of large areas of woodland the preservation of any individual tree is entirely unimportant; what matters is that permission for felling and requirements for replanting should be so arranged that the bulk, density and silhouette of the mass is maintained. In the case of individual trees and groups of trees, and sometimes of particular parts of woodland masses which screen eyesores, and which owe their effect to density of foliage, it may be desirable to insist upon preservation far beyond maturity, and, so far as individual trees and small groups are concerned, until advancing age robs them of their attractiveness. Even so, in the interests of posterity, felling and replanting comparatively early may be the better policy.

Generally speaking, no compensation ought to be payable in respect of restraints on felling imposed in woodland masses, since such restraints need seldom be incompatible with sound forestry practice and the earning of full profits from the crop; only in the special circumstances outlined in the previous paragraph will any question of compensation arise. In the case of trees originally planted for ornament, and usually without timber value, compensation can rarely arise at all. The preservation of trees is, therefore, not likely to lay heavy financial burdens on any Local Planning Authority.

It may sometimes be necessary to abandon a tree preservation order; agricultural requirements may demand the felling of hedgerow and scattered trees in order that the land may more readily be ploughed or a decision may even be taken to convert woodland areas to agricultural use. Where this sort of thing occurs it is but common sense for the Local Planning Authority to give way and revoke the order unless some quite exceptional loss is involved.

The activities of the Forestry Commission sometimes cause problems of an opposite kind to those dealt with by tree preservation orders. The afforestation of a large area of wild country is likely to change its visual character

---

[1] What *is* a tree, anyway? This is important in relation to a " blanket " preservation order covering a defined area of woodland. A seedling four inches high is presumably not a tree, nor one two feet high, otherwise one would hardly be able to walk through an area subject to such an order without violating it through destroying " trees " which one crushed underfoot. There must be some limit of size below which a plant cannot be regarded as a tree, but I cannot discover any pronouncement on the subject.

completely, and this is the more so since the species used are generally conifers not indigenous to the area in question. This policy has been fiercely attacked and the Commission has even been accused of creating sylvan slums. I could not personally find it easy to condemn any policy which resulted in the production of crops from hitherto barren land, and, indeed, it may well be that people will become accustomed and reconciled to such changes quite rapidly.

Nevertheless, it would be regrettable if too large a proportion of the characteristic moorland scenery of Britain were lost, and this may happen not only by actually covering the surface with vegetation but through obscuring views by planting near the crests of hills. The Forestry Commission consults the Ministry of Housing and Local Government on its afforestation proposals and the Ministry, in turn, usually consults Local Planning Authorities. The Progress Report of the Ministry of Town and Country Planning well sums up the situation regarding afforestation on page 145:

" *Afforestation.* The Forestry Commission consults the Ministry on all proposals to acquire land for afforestation. The Ministry is concerned with the probable effect of a planting programme on the appearance of the land-scape, and on access which the public have enjoyed, or are entitled to enjoy. Proposals to afforest land to which the public have had some kind of access for generations, or to change the familiar face of the countryside by planting, are generally unpopular, as, for instance, the proposal to afforest part of the Quantocks, which was still under discussion when this Report went to press. Although the Forestry Commission is primarily concerned with the economic aspects of forestry and the supply of timber for commerce and industry, it does all it can to accommodate the claims of scenery and natural beauty, and of public access. In most cases a satisfactory compromise has been achieved, as, for instance, on Freshwater Downs in the Isle of Wight, where the Commission modified its proposals to plant along the ridge and part of the southern slopes, in order to preserve unimpaired for the public both the access and the magnificent views from the top of the Downs.

" New plantations of conifers, which, from the economic point of view, are most important, often arouse popular disapproval, especially south of the Scottish border. But, as these woods grow, and, with successive thinnings, acquire the variety and beauty of maturity, this disapproval tends to dis-appear. Moreover, as the trees grow and the risk of fire diminishes these new National Forests will be increasingly thrown open to the public. The Forestry Commission has also, on its own initiative, which the Ministry warmly welcomes, created a number of National Forest Parks to which the public have full access."

(iii) The control of details

This heading covers items such as fences or other means of enclosure, ancillary buildings, such as private garages and garden sheds, roadside verges and greens, and items such as lamp-posts, pillar-boxes, telephone lines, and so on, collectively known as street furniture.

The design aspects of many of these are extremely well described in a paper by Frederick Gibberd entitled " Details in Civic Design ", which was read to the Town Planning Institute in March, 1951, and was published in the March issue of the Journal of the Town Planning Institute.

It is hardly possible to give any brief general summary of the principles which should be followed in designing and siting street furniture because of the extremely varied size, height and texture of its components but the sub-ject has an importance in attaining a satisfactory visual effect far in excess of the apparent prominence of any of them.

The design and relationship between these items can make or mar the appearance of a street. Unfortunately, the muliplicity of authorities responsible for those supplied by the public, their complete or partial exemption from Planning control, and the limitations imposed by cost and the materials available makes any collective control all but impossible, except where the main development is carried out by a public agency which, by patient consultation and by giving a strong lead to all bodies concerned with the provision of street furniture, may secure some degree of co-ordination.

Attention must, therefore, be confined to such minor items as are erected by housing authorities themselves or by private developers. The General Development Order, 1950 removed from Planning control a wide range of such development occurring within the curtilages of dwelling-houses, with the declared object of relieving both the private individual and Planning staff of vexatious detailed work not likely to secure commensurate benefits. This was a part of what is popularly known as " Dalton's Experiment in Freedom ".

There can be no doubt that attempts to control development in very great detail are likely to be inordinately time-consuming and to cause great public irritation. For example, a certain local authority, for reasons which may, for all I know, have been aesthetically admirable, once attempted, if Press reports are to be believed, to limit the heights of flowers grown by tenants in the front gardens of the houses it has built. Universal execration rightly compelled the abandonment of this policy because it was one which could not be *imposed* without arousing anger and contempt.

But some of the minor development released from control by the General Development Order was not only of a type likely to have a very marked effect upon appearance but had also been subject to by-law control for three-quarters of a century. The burden of making and determining any applica-tion is little increased by making it subject to Planning as well as by-law control, and it should have been possible in one way or another to retain this control without sacrificing the improvement sought. One way would be to require delegation by Local Planning Authorities to district councils of control over minor development within the curtilage of a dwelling-house and to relieve applicants of the obligation to make specific application for Planning permission, with the additional plans and forms entailed. This would leave district councils with a reserve power to stop harmful develop-ment which might seldom have to be exercised, but which would be a most valuable safeguard.

As regards development which does not require a by-law submission there is much to be said for leaving it to the discretion of developers whether to apply for Planning permission, it being understood that they proceed at their peril and that, subject to the usual right of appeal, enforcement action will be taken against seriously unsightly erections.   There is some objection to this on the grounds that it introduces an element of arbitrariness into public adminis-

Description of Development	Conditions
CLASS I—Development within the curtilage of a dwelling-house.	
1. The enlargement, improvement or other alteration of a dwelling-house so long as the cubic content of the original dwelling-house (as ascertained by external measurement) is not exceeded by more than 1,750 cubic feet or one-tenth, whichever is the greater, subject to a maximum of 4,000 cubic feet; provided that the erection of a garage, stable, loose box or coach-house within the curtilage of the dwelling-house shall be treated as the enlargement of the dwelling-house for the purposes of this permission.	1. The height of such building shall not exceed the height of the original dwelling-house. 2. No part of such building shall project beyond the forward-most part of the front of the original dwelling-house. 3. Standard conditions 1 and 2.
2. The erection, construction or placing, and the maintenance, improvement or other alteration, within the curtilage of a dwelling-house, of any building or enclosure (other than a dwelling, garage, stable, loose box or coach-house) required for a purpose incidental to the enjoyment of the dwelling-house as such, including the keeping of poultry, bees, pet animals, birds or other livestock for the domestic needs or personal enjoyment of the occupants of the dwelling-house.	1. The height shall not exceed, in the case of a building with a ridged roof, 12 feet, or in any other case, 10 feet. 2. Standard conditions. 1 and 2.
CLASS II—Sundry minor operations.	
1. The erection or construction of gates, fences, walls or other means of enclosure not exceeding 4 feet in height where abutting on a road used by vehicular traffic or 7 feet in height in any other case, and the maintenance, improvement or other alteration of any gates, fences, walls or other means of enclosure.	1. No improvement or alteration shall increase the height above the height appropriate for a new means of enclosure.
2. The painting of the exterior of any building or work otherwise than for the purposes of advertisement, announcement or direction.	2. Standard conditions 1 and 2.

Standard Conditions.
1. This permission shall not authorise any development which involves the formation, laying out or material widening of a means of access to a trunk or classified road.
2. No development shall be carried out which creates an obstruction to the view of persons using any road used by vehicular traffic at or near any bend, corner, junction or intersection so as to be likely to cause danger to such persons.

tration, but I cannot see that this is of great weight, provided that the means exist for prior application to be made if a developer is in any doubt whether his proposed development is likely to be challenged, and the position is made clear and effectively publicised.   In fact, this system already operates in practice in respect of some development.   The erection of gates, fences, walls, etc., abutting on a highway and exceeding four feet in height requires Planning permission although I feel sure that application is very seldom made, while control of advertisements is, in part, on the same basis.

The present position is that the General Development Order excludes from control certain operations, some if they are within the curtilage of a dwelling-house and others wherever they are carried out.   For convenience of reference Classes I and II of permitted development are again printed opposite.

It is to be noted that the Order does not preclude conditions prohibiting such operations from being carried out without permission being attached to Planning permissions; in other words, when something is proposed which is sufficiently important to require Planning permission, associated details are brought under control.   This power is of great importance; it may have been justifiable to free such operations from control in areas already developed, though I do not personally think so, but it is essential that they should be effectively regulated in areas of new development.   Intrinsically ugly and excessively variegated front fences and gates, garages and outhouses can speedily ruin the appearance of even the best-designed houses, while uncontrolled alterations to the houses themselves may be even worse.

Accordingly, every permission for the erection of houses should be subject to a condition that such operations shall not be carried out without permission having been obtained.   There is a place for diversity and a place for uniformity.   Front fences, etc., are decidedly objects which should be uniformly treated, or at least designed as a whole, throughout each unbroken length of residential frontage, because of the strong influence they exert on the front elevations of the houses.   Garages and outhouses, although some latitude may have to be permitted when they are added by individual tenants after the completion of the houses, because of the costliness of permanent buildings and the limited range of design of temporary prefabricated structures, should certainly be related as satisfactorily as possible to each other and to adjoining houses.   " Outhouses ", in this connection, should be taken as referring to those visible from the fronts of the houses; there is no reason why garden sheds and greenhouses not so visible should be subject to control unless of excessive size or height.

The extent to which painting the exterior of a building should be controlled is more doubtful.   Certainly one sees many horrible examples of entire fronts of buildings having been newly coloured in utter disregard of their neighbours, and this should certainly be made the subject of a condition requiring permission, but the painting of window-frames, doors, barge-boards, etc., although it may have considerable effect on appearance, is something which is rather too small (and in any case easily changed) to be a suitable subject for control.

Although, as I understand it, it is legally possible, by means of conditions, to retain control over these matters where application is made to carry out development, it is extremely doubtful whether the Minister, on appeal, would support such conditions.

Reference must be made to the difficult problem of controlling roadside verges and open spaces and undivided front gardens in areas of privately built houses. Clearly, undivided front gardens cannot be effective unless they are kept unenclosed and their surface treatment is at least reasonably appropriate. It is, therefore, necessary to impose conditions, where they are proposed, requiring that they shall not be enclosed in any way without permission and that they shall be planted with grass and kept so.

As regards roadside greens and verges the position is more difficult. It is comparatively simple to require their inclusion in the layout and to require them to be appropriately planted, but maintenance is another matter. Where the applicant intends to sell the freehold of all the building plots he cannot reasonably be required to maintain roadside greens indefinitely, for private development will not take place if excessively onerous conditions are imposed. On the other hand, it is not a valid condition to require him to dedicate land to the district council concerned, and the district council may baulk at purchase, or even at maintenance, should the developer be willing to dedicate.

Verges and greens are an essential of good residential development and, even if the Local Planning Authority cannot induce the district council concerned to accept its responsibilities, the permission given should stipulate their provision. If space is not left for them no power can put them there after development has been carried out, but, if they are provided, a change of membership on the district council or the interest of residents may eventually enable them to be satisfactorily maintained, however bedraggled they may become meanwhile.

The relaxations of control given by the General Development Order, 1950 can be further modified by a Local Planning Authority making an order, which must be confirmed by the Minister, requiring permission to be obtained for specified classes of permitted development within certain parts of its area. This enables areas of particularly fine development or areas where detailed control has hitherto been exceptionally effective to be safeguarded and is a valuable weapon, but it appears to me to admit an unsound principle. Such a direction may also be made in respect of agricultural buildings, and the Advertisement Regulations provide for stricter control to be applied to selected areas.

These powers, together with those relating to the preservation of buildings of historic or special architectural value, are too easily used to give effect to a policy of sterile preservationism, a policy aimed at protecting past beauty or exceptional beauty instead of insisting upon a generally high standard of development everywhere. It could convincingly be argued that areas, both urban and rural, which are undistinguished or already damaged by unsightliness are in at least as great need of protection against the loss of their scanty charms or against further deterioration as outstandingly fine areas. Such an argument cannot be pushed too far, for there are some gems whose preservation is more important than that of any more ordinary areas, but, on the whole, I believe it to be sound. Further, the establishment of dual standards

of control carrying different obligations to apply for permission can hardly fail to confuse the minds of laymen who have to comply with them.

The sweeping permission given by the General Development Order to agricultural and forestry buildings and works is little less than tragic. Subject to the standard conditions relating to access to trunk and classified roads, the avoidance of obstructions to visibility at corners, bends, junctions and intersections, and to a limitation of height to 10 feet within two miles of an aerodrome, any such building (which does not, of course, include a dwelling), if it is not nearer than 80 feet to a trunk road or classified road, may be erected without permission on agricultural land forming part of a holding larger than one acre. This permission is not extended to structures not designed for agricultural purposes, which mercifully excludes bus bodies and the like, but includes roadside stands for milk churns (!!) and the working of minerals to be used as fertilsers or for other agricultural purposes on land held with that on which the minerals are worked.

The technical requirements of farming automatically limit narrowly the choice of site for many agricultural buildings, and shortage of materials limits the variety of external appearance possible, while the general use of asbestos and other prefabricated components even determines the shapes of buildings, but this is all the more reason for exercising such degree of control as is possible to reduce harsh intrusions into the landscape, by means of careful choice of the best site possible within the limits imposed by operational necessity, selection of suitable colours and modification of shape.

The bringing back under control of very large agricultural buildings, noted earlier in this chapter, is a welcome step towards a return to more thorough control.

(iii) The preservation of buildings

This is a subject on the edge of land Planning proper, and is of direct importance to it mainly as far as the preservation of buildings of merit requires redevelopment proposals to be modified to secure their continued existence. It can therefore be dealt with here quite briefly.

Section 30 of the Town and Country Planning Act, 1962, enables a Local Planning Authority to make a *Building Preservation Order* in respect of a building of special architectural or historic interest. Such an order may require the consent of the Local Planning Authority to be obtained before the building is altered in any way which would seriously affect its character or before it is demolished. The order must be confirmed by the Minister, before which the owner and occupier may object. In an emergency the Minister may, as in the case of tree preservation, make an immediate provisional order to take effect for not more than two months. A right of compensation is attached to any loss caused by the imposition of a Building Preservation Order.

An order may not be made in respect of an ecclesiastical building in use as such, a building subject to a scheme or order relating to ancient monuments or a building included in a list of monuments published by the Minister of Works.

Section 30 of the 1947 Act required the Minister of Town and Country Planning to compile lists of buildings of special architectural or historic interest. Copies of the relevant portions of these lists have to be sent to each Local Planning and other local authority when they have been prepared, and registered in the Register of Local Land Charges. Every owner or occupier of a building included must be notified. Thereafter owners and occupiers must give the Local Planning Authority two months' notice of any intention to alter or demolish listed buildings, and the Local Planning Authority must, in turn, inform the Minister, so that the desirability of making a Building Preservation Order may be considered.

The process of listing involved a great deal of work, but the chance of buildings of distinction vanishing without warning is now greatly reduced. Nevertheless, the problem remains of trying to ensure that buildings which are preserved are put to some useful purpose. There is something a little futile in preserving any but the most outstandingly beautiful buildings merely as museum pieces, and the burden of compensation involved in doing this is heavy. Yet many fine buildings are quite unsuited to present-day use, the cost of adapting them would be greater than demolishing them and replacing them by new buildings, and their structural condition is often such that to maintain them in a usable and sightly state would be very costly. In this connection it should be noted that a Preservation Order cannot impose any requirements as to maintenance.

It is therefore frequently extremely difficult to decide whether to impose a Preservation Order, and this is especially so in areas which require redevelopment but which nevertheless contain a number of fine buildings, because of the importance of not prejudicing the future for the sake of the past. Although skilful variation of design can often avoid the demolition of a fine building, it would be folly, except in the most exceptional cases, to allow an existing building awkwardly situated to ruin the satisfactory redevelopment of a whole area.

The Ministry lists are sub-divided to take account of this difficulty. They comprise two classes:

(i) Buildings of such importance that only the greatest necessity would justify their removal, and

(ii) Buildings which have a good claim to survival but appreciably less strong than those in Class (i).

In addition, supplementary lists are prepared, the inclusion of a building in which does not involve the statutory obligations imposed by listing. These supplementary lists include a large number of buildings which have charm and merit without being outstanding, and the object is mainly to draw the attention of local authorities to them so that they may be saved whenever the requirements of redevelopment do not preclude it.

(iv) Advertisements

The system of control of outdoor advertisements created by the Town and Country Planning (Control of Advertisements) Regulations, 1948 (S.I. No. 1613), and, after various amendments, consolidated in the Regulations of 1960 (S.I. No. 695), is at once surprising, complicated and somewhat ineffective. The original Regulations run to 31 pages, a good deal more than the space taken up by many Acts of Parliament. They are surprising because they were made by a Government not notorious for its sympathy towards competitive private undertakings, and yet, despite a far greater measure of public support for the control of outdoor advertising than was accorded to many of its policies, they are extraordinarily lenient. They are complicated because they seek to apply a subtly graded strictness of control to different kinds of advertisements, exempt some from the obligation to obtain permission, but not from subsequent challenge, and provide for implied as well as for explicit conditions to be imposed. They are ineffective because of their leniency and because it is not subtle gradations which are needed, but broad, comprehensive principles of control.

Advertisements fall into two main categories: Those the object of which is to give information, direction or advice, whether disinterested—e.g., " GENTLEMEN ", " KEEP TO THE RIGHT ", or in the hope of gain e.g. " GARAGE 100 YARDS ", " TO-NIGHT AT 8.30 ", " FITTO ON SALE HERE ", and those which disseminate propaganda—e.g., " BEER IS BEST ", " REPENT, FOR THE KINGDOM OF HEAVEN IS AT HAND ", " 99 OUT OF 100 SWICKLEFITTERS SWEAR BY SLYDE ".

It seems evident that informative advertisements need to be placed and designed so that they can give their message clearly and unmistakably, are not mixed up with and so obscured by other signs and are reasonably pleasant in appearance.

The position of most informative advertisements is determined, within narrow limits, by their subject-matter, but note that the example referring to FITTO is a hybrid. Placed in a grocer's window, it gives a direct and immediate message of hope and a call to action to the housewife who is wondering what on earth to get for supper, but, in the middle of a field, although less immediately useful, it has not the same irrelevance which " KEEP TO THE RIGHT " would have if transferred there. In short, although FITTO is informative, it also has propaganda value.

There are, of course, many kinds of advertisements which are informative to the extent that they give detailed particulars of the prices and characteristics of the products advertised, but these are hardly ever the subject of outdoor display, with which we are solely concerned.

The most striking thing about purely propaganda advertisements is that it really makes little difference where they are displayed, for they seek not so much to stimulate to immediate action as to inculcate a belief by persuasive repetition. If it does not make much difference to their effectiveness where they are displayed, then why not confine them to the newspapers and magazines, the cinema and television screens, the underground stations and the shop windows, and keep them off the façades of buildings, railway bridges and hoardings, and, above all, out of the fields?

It would be easy to enlarge upon the parasitical, economically wasteful and insulting nature of propaganda advertising, and even upon its immorality, for the greater its effectiveness the more it has succeeded in replacing independent judgment by susceptibility to suggestion, but none of this is central to our theme. All that need be said further is to emphasise that propaganda advertisements do not stimulate trade or lower prices or promote prosperity or anything else of that kind; all they do is to absorb labour and talent which could be better used. There is no conceivable reason for treating them gently when their display is visually offensive.

My own strongly held opinion is that genuinely informative advertisements should be freely allowed, subject to good appearance, the minimum size and number of separate signs necessary being used, and appropriate location, but that the outdoor display of propaganda advertisements should be almost completely prohibited.

It is often said that Times Square, Piccadilly Circus, Blackpool and other big centres of amusement gain in liveliness and interest from the display of large lighted signs but it is a poor philosophy which defends them when other means of achieving the same end are equally possible.

It is entirely justifiable to permit comparatively large, high, lighted signs in centres of amusement in order to identify the various theatres, cinemas, restaurants, etc., from street level, in the dark, and among crowds but this can be done so as to enhance the beauty of the urban scene at night and need not include the vulgarity, chaos and distraction of commercial lighted signs. The effectiveness of lighting buildings, open spaces and water by flood-lighting and other means can be very great, but there is no reason why it should not be subject to the same standards of taste as the buildings and other objects themselves.

Limitation of the sizes of advertisements is of the greatest importance. Lack of restriction leads to competition so that signs get bigger and bigger, each advertiser trying to make his sign stand out from the rest. Since these attempts will always, in the long run, be vain, no hardship is caused by insisting on a quite small maximum size at which competition for attention can remain keen, the rules are the same for all and appearance is saved.

The specially objectionable nature of outdoor advertisements is that their audience is truly "captive". There are few occasions when it is safe or practicable to shut one's eyes while out of doors.

We must now turn to the Advertisement Regulations themselves. It is tempting to refrain from doing so, but contemporary control of advertisements in this country is so drastically conditioned by them that this would be unjustifiable. It is extremely difficult to get a general idea of the Regulations as a whole by reading through them but the Explanatory Memorandum accompanying them is admirably concise and clear; it is, however, inevitably incomplete, and cannot be fully understood without concurrent reference to the Regulations themselves. The following account does no more than give the bare gist of the Regulations, while the accompanying table gives in convenient form a summary of the conditions which an advertisement must fulfil in order to come within one of the specified classes for which express consent is not required.

The Regulations relate to advertisements displayed on *land*.

Regulation 1 defines "advertisement" as "any word, letter, model, sign, placard, board, notice, device or representation, whether illuminated or not, in the nature of and employed wholly or in part for the purposes of advertisement, announcement or direction (excluding any such thing employed wholly as a memorial or as a railway signal) and . . . includes any hoarding or similar structure used or adapted for use for the display of advertisements . . ."

This is very wide, but the Regulations subsequently narrow it. They do not apply to advertisements inside buildings unless the advertisements are illuminated and visible from the outside or the building is used principally for the display of advertisements, nor to advertisements on enclosed land unless they are readily visible from outside it or from any part of the enclosed land to which the public have access.

The control of advertisements is limited to control in the interests of amenity and public safety. Regulation 4 (4) expressly prevents a Local Planning Authority from controlling the subject-matter of advertising material to be displayed. Most applications will be for a sign in some permanent material, with specific words and devices, and the matter does not arise in this connection, but in giving consent for the use of, e.g., a hoarding for advertisements, the Local Planning Authority automatically gives consent to whatever may be put on the hoarding.

All advertisements are subject to two standard conditions requiring them to be safe and reasonably clean and tidy.

Advertisements for which consent is deemed to be given must not endanger traffic in any way, e.g., by resembling or conflicting with a traffic sign.

The permission of the owner of the land or anyone else entitled to give it is an implied, though it may also be an express, condition of any consent to display an advertisement.

Advertisements which were being displayed on 1st August, 1948, the date on which the Advertisement Regulations came into operation, were exempted from control for one year after that date, while, if they had been displayed upon the 7th January, 1947, the date on which the Town and Country Planning Bill was published, the exemption was for three years after 1st August, 1948. Since then they can be "challenged", i.e., a Local Planning Authority may require an application for express consent to be made for their retention, and this application may be refused, upon which, subject to a right of appeal to the Minister, the advertisement must be removed.

Most other advertisements, unless within one of the specified classes, which are dealt with later, require express consent for their display. This consent must be for a definite period not exceeding five years. After the expiry of such period no further application for consent need be made, but the Local Planning Authority may challenge the advertisement. It may, however, in giving express consent, require an advertisement to be removed at the expiry of the period of the consent.

Election posters, notices statutorily required to be displayed and traffic

ADVERTISEMENTS OF THE SPECIFIED CLASSES

No.	Class	Area	Maximum size of letters, figures, etc.		Maximum height of top of sign above ground		Illumination permitted	Number	Other requirements
			In area of special control	Elsewhere	In area of special control	Elsewhere			
I	Advertisements in relation to the functions of Local Authorities, Statutory Undertakers and Public Transport Undertakers	May be displayed in any manner reasonably necessary for the purpose of the authority							
II	Miscellaneous advertisements relating to premises on which they are displayed:—								
	(a) For the purposes of identification, direction or warning	Not exceeding 2 sq. ft. each	1ft.	2½ft.	12ft.	15ft.	Only as reasonably required to indicate that medical or similar services or supplies are available on the premises	As required	
	(b) Relating to a person, partnership or company carrying on a profession, business or trade	Not exceeding 3 sq. ft. each	1ft.	2½ft.	12ft.	15ft.	ditto	One for each person, etc., or two if there are entrances on different frontages	
	(c) Relating to an institution of a religious, educational, cultural, recreational, etc. character or to a residential hotel, block of flats, club, etc.	Not exceeding 12 sq. ft.	1ft.	2½ft.	12ft.	15ft.	ditto	ditto	
III	Temporary advertisements:—								
	(a) Relating to the sale or letting of the land on which they are displayed	Not exceeding 20 sq. ft. or a total of 24 sq. ft. for two conjoined boards. No sign to project more than 3ft. from face if displayed on a building	1ft.	2½ft.	12ft.	15ft.	None	One for each sale or letting	If part of building referred to is above height limit sign must infringe it as little as practicable. Not to be displayed earlier than 28 days before and to be removed within 14 days after a sale or other event due to start on a specified date.
	(b) Advertising a sale of goods or livestock and displayed where these are situated, or where the sale is to be held, not being land normally used for such purposes	Not exceeding 12 sq. ft.	1ft.	2½ft.	12ft.	15ft.	None	One for each place at which such an advertisement may be displayed	Not to be displayed earlier than 28 days and to be removed within 14 days after a sale due to start on a specified date.
	(c) Relating to the carrying out of building or similar work on the land on which they are displayed, not being land normally used for such work	Not exceeding 20 sq. ft.	1ft.	2½ft.	12ft.	15ft.	None	One on each road frontage for each contractor or sub-contractor	Only to be displayed while work is in progress.
	(d) Announcing any local event of a religious, educational, cultural, political, etc. character not carried on for commercial purposes	Not exceeding 6 sq. ft.	1ft.	2½ft.	12ft.	15ft.	None	No limit, but total area not to exceed 6 sq. ft. on any particular premises	Not to be displayed earlier than 28 days before, and to be removed within 14 days after the event.
IV	Advertisements on business premises referring to the business, the goods sold or the services provided and the name and qualifications of the person carrying on such activity. Buildings designed as dwellings are excluded. — In areas of special control	Not to exceed one-twelfth of area of each frontage up to a height of 12ft. Area to be computed as if advertisement were flat against face of building	1ft.	—	12ft.		Only as reasonably required to indicate that medical or similar services or supplies are available on premises	No limit, but total must not exceed area specified	
	— Elsewhere	Unlimited	—	2½ft.		15ft.	ditto	Unlimited	
V	Flag advertisements:— Any advertisement in the form of a flag attached to a single upright flagstaff on the roof of a building and bearing no inscription or emblem other than the name or device of the occupant of the building.								

signs do not require express consent, but, as well as complying with the standard conditions, election posters must be removed within fourteen days after the election to which they relate. This is not a condition which one has often seen observed.

There are three other special cases:

(i) Local Planning Authorities may themselves display in their own areas any advertisements except, in areas of special control, those which they would have no power to grant if application therefor were made by someone else.

(ii) Posters advertising travelling circuses and fairs can be given consent in bulk for posting on unspecified sites, provided that they observe the standard conditions, are not larger than six square feet or placed higher than 12 feet above the ground, are not displayed more than 14 days before the first performance to which they relate, and are removed within seven days after the last performance. In granting consent the Local Planning Authority must specifically inform the applicant that permission must be obtained from the owners or occupiers of sites on which the posters are to be displayed. There is in this case no appeal from the decision of a Local Planning Authority, since the delay involved would render control ineffective.

(iii) Advertisements within buildings which are controllable (i.e., illuminated or in a building used principally for the display of advertisements) are given deemed consent, provided they comply with the standard conditions as to traffic safety, but they may be challenged.

Regulation 12 specifies five classes of advertisement which, subject to limitations as to number, height, overall size and size of lettering (see the table on page 318), may be displayed without express consent. The stringency of these limitations varies according to whether an advertisement is displayed in an area of special control or elsewhere. However, the Minister has power to direct, under Regulation 13, that, in certain areas or circumstances, express consent must be applied for, even though an advertisement falls within one of the specified classes, and, apart from this, a Local Planning Authority can challenge an advertisement within one of the specified classes which is being displayed, just as it can challenge an existing advertisement or one for which the time limit imposed by an express consent has lapsed.

It must always be remembered (though in the course of threading one's way through the Regulations it is easy to lose sight of the fact) that the limitations defined in the Specified Classes are not requirements to which all advertisements must conform, but limits which must be exceeded before express consent can be required. There is a very big difference between the two. It is always much easier to prevent a thing being done than to get it undone, particularly if the doing constitutes no offence.

It is the duty of Local Planning Authorities to consider in which parts of their areas advertisements should be made subject to special control. It appears that the countryside and rural areas generally may be regarded as suitable for such special control, together with parts of urban areas which possess some distinction.

The Local Planning Authority makes an order defining an area of special control, which must be confirmed by the Minister, and may previously have been the subject of a public inquiry.

In an area of special control advertisements are prohibited, and the Local Planning Authority has no power to permit them, unless they are within the following categories:—

(i) Advertisements in the Specified Classes in accordance with the more drastic limitations imposed in areas of Special Control and election posters, etc. (Express consent not required.)

(ii) Advertisements relating to travelling circuses and fairs, and advertisements displayed within buildings.

(iii) Notices relating to local events, roadside advertisements indicating the presence in the vicinity of hotels, garages, etc., advertisements required in the interests of public safety.

In addition, a Local Planning Authority may give consent to an advertisement which would fall within one of the Specified Classes, but for some failure to conform with a requirement as to size, height, number or lighting, *if, and only if*, they are satisfied that there is some special reason why conformity should not be required.

Existing advertisements are protected after an order defining an area of Special Control has come into force until the period for which consent was given, or six months, has expired, whichever is the longer. Advertisements of the specified classes which do not satisfy the stricter requirements for an area of Special Control may remain until challenged.

Two things immediately strike one about this table: first, what appreciable difference is there between an advertisement the top of which is 15 feet above the ground and one which is 12 feet above the ground? And, second, if it is reasonable to limit the height of letters, etc., to be displayed without permission to one foot in areas of Special Control, why should they be permitted to go to the really enormous size of 2 feet 6 inches elsewhere?

The main object of the Regulations is clear; to relieve advertisers of the obligation to make application for trivial displays, yet to safeguard the right of the Local Planning Authority to remove anything unsightly, but it is exceedingly difficult to justify the verbiage used to achieve this. There seems every reason to believe that the universal application of the Regulations for areas of Special Control, and even these in somewhat simplified form, would be more satisfactory in every way.

As in the case of development permitted by the General Development Order, conditions may be imposed which override the exemptions conferred by the Advertisement Regulations where application is made for Planning permission for development of which the display of advertisements is only a part, subject to the right of the applicant to appeal against onerous conditions, though application may later be made for express consent to the display of advertisements excluded by the condition.

This power can be used in various ways to ensure freedom from unsightly advertisements in areas of new development and in connection with changes of use. Perhaps its most important use is to keep the fascias of new shops within bounds.　Detailed control of fascias is niggling and cumbrous, and, providing the total dimensions of letters, etc., are kept to a maximum of about one foot, it is unnecessary.　Although insistence upon a uniform size and style of fascia, as at Wythenshawe, for example, produces a quiet and neat effect it is too lifeless for a row of shops, in which the variety of the merchandise can appropriately be reflected in the fascias.　If, therefore, a condition is made limiting size, time and annoyance are spared by leaving each shopkeeper free to use whatever fascia appeals to him; the effect is likely to be interesting and variegated, and even the occasional tasteless sign in poor lettering will not be unduly obtrusive.

It is difficult to give any specific guidance about advertisement control generally.　The work involved limits the application of challenges to the more flagrant examples.

Circular 52/51 of the Ministry of Local Government and Planning urges Local Planning Authorities " to use their powers with energy, but also with discrimination ", and points out the danger of a sudden flood of appeals resulting from excessively drastic actions.　The fact that the right of challenge does not lapse by effluxion of time is stressed and it is suggested that a policy of cleaning up selected areas of limited extent one by one would be suitable.

As regards the determination of applications for express consent, the best policy would be only to give consent in altogether exceptional circumstances, but this has little chance of success at appeal.　The Minister seems to make his decision principally in relation to the general character of the area concerned, being disposed to grant consent more liberally in areas where visual amenity is low than where it is high.　Although this has the merit for immediate purposes of a certain rough common sense the absence of accepted principles makes the result of an appeal relating to the display of advertisements even more difficult to forecast than in other cases.

20-6.　SUMMARY

It is now time to try to make some assessment of the efficiency of the extraordinarily complicated yet ingenious system of law, policy, pronouncement and precedent which has been described and discussed in this chapter. Complicated though it is, it is very flexible, need not inhibit good development and is a great deal less intricate than would be any code of comparable comprehensiveness produced in the form of a set of " by-laws ".　But how is it used?　What benefits flow from this enormous structure and the many hundreds of thousands of man-hours spent in operating it?

One depressing conclusion that it is difficult to resist is that an intelligent visitor from Mars would not be likely to deduce from an inspection of Britain that there existed there a system of land use control more comprehensive, stringent and thoroughly applied than almost anywhere else in the world. It requires a considerable imaginative effort to visualize the extent to which we should all be worse off if this system did not exist.　Nevertheless, we should be much worse off; because of our high degree of industrialisation and very high population density the demands on land are both more intense and more varied than in most places, and an absence of control would by now have produced not only widespread destruction of the countryside but much

excessively intensive development and innumerable intermixtures of incompatible uses.　This ought never to be forgotten.

Parts I and II of this book have suggested the principles which should be followed in designing development of many different types, while earlier in this chapter principles have been suggested as guides for the appropriate location and design of those kinds of development which do not fall readily within specific categories of planned development.　The reader may or may not have agreed with most of what was said; what he can hardly disagree with is the proposition that applications for permission to develop should be judged in the light of consistent principles and that the nearer one can get to adherence to such principles in development control, the better are the results likely to be.　One is, of course, constantly faced by the awkward fact that the desires of a multitude of people who use land and buildings are hardly capable of being resolved into the kind of fully integrated Plan which might be expected in, for example, a really well designed New Town.　In the case of a New Town one is or ought to be trying to meet the land and building requirements of a population not yet in occupation, and in so doing is dealing with an area not split up into innumerable small separately owned parcels.　With development control the reverse is true; one is dealing with a host of people who are already there and who own or have some interest in innumerable tiny patches of land, buildings and even parts of buildings.　In these circumstances principles of design are impossible to apply fully, but they need not disappear.　Unfortunately one often gets the impression that Planning authorities view the task of development control as so hopelessly difficult that they do not bother to formulate principles because they fear that, even if they did, they could not stick to them consistently or closely enough for this to be worth while.

This is simply not true; the job is a difficult one but it is not an impossible one, given a sound and sufficiently detailed Development Plan, sound principles of development control and a determination on the part of all concerned to do their best.

The most important principle of all is probably to determine that permission must never be refused unless a definite, strong and legitimate reason can be seen for doing so.　If this rule were never broken a great many refusals of applications for permission for minor development would not occur.

Major development ought not, except as regards its details, need to be considered generally as an exercise in development control; whether it is permissible or not ought to be shown by the Development Plan, but this obviously does not apply to minor development.　With regard to this, determined thought and hard work need to be devoted to working out principles and standards reliable as a general guide.

As regards principles, the Ministry's bulletins of selected appeal decisions contain the germ of a set of principles.　The doctrines that can be deduced from them are mostly sensible, and although it is true that they are constantly contradicted in innumerable individual appeal decisions, this is to some extent unavoidable.　In particular, Volume I of the Second Series of Bulletins issued in June, 1959, contained statements of principle on the control of external appearance (referred to in fact as " design "), development in Green Belts, development in rural areas other than Green Belts, non-residential development in residential areas and petrol filling stations.

Even more valuable is the monumental " Digest of Planning Decisions " by Harold J. J. Brown in the second volume of the Encyclopaedia of Planning Law and Practice. This runs to more than 150 pages and is methodically divided and sub-divided to give information about Ministerial policy as deduced from appeal decisions on almost every conceivable type of application. What it lacks, as do the bulletins of selected appeal decisions, is site plans to indicate the precise physical circumstances of the cases discussed. It would have been impossible for Mr. Brown to supply such plans in compiling his digest, but it is far from impossible for the Ministry to do so in issuing their bulletins, and the value of these would be enormously increased by such an addition, for it is very often the precise site circumstances which determine whether permission ought to be given or refused. A further weakness is that, except in the broadest way, the statements of opinion ascribed to the Minister are no more than that; they do not constitute reasoned judgment based on connected technical data.

It has sometimes been suggested that the collation and classification of appeal decisions ought to be carried much further so as to provide a series of formulae. The idea is that one would, by examining all the characteristics of a given application determine which formula it fitted, and one would then be able to give absolutely consistent decisions because the collective wisdom

of some high-level body of Town Planners would have determined what the proper decision was in respect of every formula. This beguiling idea is not, in my view, in the least practicable. Although it is not quite true, as is often asserted, that every Planning application is different from every other, variations of sites and surroundings are so great that at least one can say that it is rare to find two applications to which exactly the same Planning considerations apply. If this is so, and I think it is, the number of formulae required to cover all possible cases would approach uncomfortably close to infinity, and the task of deciding which formula was most appropriate to any particular application would be a good deal greater than the task of deciding what, on its merits, the decision on it should be.

This idea is really an attempt to get back to " planning by by-law " which we have already discussed and rejected. Planning on merits is much more difficult because it requires a much higher level of skill and experience on the part of the people who advise planning committees, but it is capable of producing almost infinitely more satisfactory results.

My final word on the subject of development control is that it is very important, is not on the one hand so difficult as to be almost impossible, nor on the other, as some people suppose, so easy as not to need the employment of expert advice, that the success or non-success of nearly all Planning depends eventually mainly upon the skill with which development control is carried out, and that a great deal more skill and thought at all levels needs to be devoted to it than is so at present.

CHAPTER 21

PLANNING INQUIRIES

General. Many inquiries are held by inspectors of the Ministry of Housing and Local Government. Inquiries have to be held regarding Development Plans, Preservation Orders, etc., but by far the most numerous are appeals against Local Planning Authorities' determinations of applications for Planning permission. Except for the order in which the parties are heard the procedure at all of these is very similar, as it is also at inquiries into objections to Compulsory Purchase Orders.

Circular 95 of the Ministry of Town and Country Planning, issued in September, 1950, set out the procedure to be followed at public local inquiries into Development Plans; this is largely applicable to all public inquiries into Planning matters except appeals.

The Circular states that the procedure adopted at inquiries held under the provisions of the First Schedule to the Town and Country Planning Act, 1944, is thought to be suitable. This procedure is divisible into three main stages:—

(1) Opening statement by the Local Planning Authority and the hearing of general supporting evidence.
(2) Presentation of the objectors' cases.
(3) Summing up or review by the Local Planning Authority of matters raised at the inquiry.

Throughout this chapter references to the " appellant ", " the Local Planning Authority ", etc., should be understood to include reference to their professional representatives unless the context indicates otherwise.

The object of the first stage is to enable the Local Planning Authority to explain the general nature of the proposals, and to clarify any issues which have been the subject of considerable misunderstanding or objection, so that all matters arising later in the proceedings can be related to a coherent and generally understood framework, and time need not be wasted by objectors on points about which there is, in fact, no disagreement.

The procedure during the second stage is flexible. By arrangement with the inspector objections may either be dealt with individually, or, where there are several objections of a similar kind, and the objectors concerned are represented by the same legal and technical advisers, which is commonly the case, they may be dealt with in a group.

Each single objection or group may be dealt with as a small, self-contained inquiry, the objector presenting his case, calling witnesses, and offering them for cross-examination, and the Local Planning Authority responding. Alternatively, the Local Planning Authority may prefer, with the inspector's

agreement, to answer objections *en bloc* at the end of the inquiry in the form of an omnibus statement, which avoids the necessity of repeating remarks appropriate to several objections, but if this is done every objector must nevertheless be given the opportunity of cross-examining the Local Planning Authority's witnesses during the presentation of his case. Yet another variant is for objectors to present their cases in turn, except for the closing statements, which they make in the same order one after the other immediately before the Local Planning Authority's omnibus closing statement. The exact procedure decided upon must depend on the number, nature and complexity of objections; it is desirable that closing statements should not be too widely separated in time from the relevant evidence being heard, or memory is likely to fade, and their effectiveness be correspondingly reduced.

The procedure regarding planning appeals is now governed by the Town and Country Planning Appeals (Inquiries Procedure) Rules, 1962, made by the Lord Chancellor, as a result of the recommendation of the Franks Committee Report on Administrative Tribunals. For the most part they do little more than crystallize a procedure already well-established. The rules are contained in the Town and Country Planning Appeals (Inquiries Procedure) Rules, 1962 (Statutory Instrument No. 1425 of 1962), and Ministry of Housing and Local Government Circular No. 38, 1962 provides a commentary upon them and guidance to Local Planning Authorities as to how the Minister proposes to interpret and work them.

The rules provide that the Minister shall give not less than 42 days' notice of an inquiry to the appellant, to the Local Planning Authority and to all persons (referred to as " Section 37 Parties ") who have made representations on the application which is the subject of the appeal, except that the appellant and the Local Planning Authority may agree to a lesser period of notice.

" Section 37 Parties " is an expression which refers to the provisions of Section 37 of the Town and Country Planning Act, 1959, now re-enacted as Section 16 of the Town and Country Planning Act, 1962. They are, broadly speaking, owners of the fee simple or of a lease having more than ten years to run of any part of the appeal site and tenants of any agricultural holding any part of which falls within the appeal site.

At least 28 days before the day fixed for the inquiry, the Local Planning Authority must furnish the appellant and Section 37 Parties with a written statement of their case, normally referred to as an " Amplification Statement ". This statement must indicate the case which the Local Planning Authority propose to put forward at the inquiry, it must include a list of all the documents, including maps and plans, to which they intend to refer at the inquiry, and must indicate where and when they can be inspected and, if practicable, copied. It must also mention any direction given by the Minister or the Minister of Transport which may be relevant to the inquiry and any expression of view given by any Government Department upon which the authority propose to rely.

The rules enable but do not compel the Minister to require the Local Planning Authority to publish in local papers notices of the inquiry, to serve notice of the inquiry on persons likely to be interested or affected or to post notices in conspicuous places near the site. In practice, the Minister merely asks the authorities to inform the press of arrangements for inquiries without requiring formal advertisements and to notify owners and occupiers of properties near the site, while the burden of posting notices is cast upon the appellant.

The persons entitled to appear at an inquiry are the appellant, the Local Planning Authority, Section 37 Parties and any persons on whom the Minister may have *required* notice to be served of the inquiry. There are, in addition, certain other classes of persons who may have a right to appear in exceptional circumstances such as the Council of the Isles of Scilly, but we need not be concerned with these. Any other person may appear at the inquiry at the discretion of the Inspector. In practice, this is a privilege which is never refused, and the granting of it frequently involves much waste of time when misinformed or malicious neighbours appear to oppose an application.

There is no restriction whatever upon the representation of anyone who appears at the inquiry; he may be represented by leading counsel, by an estate agent or may choose to conduct his own case.

Where the Minister has given a direction restricting the grant of permission for the development for which the application was made, the appellant may, giving at least 14 days' notice, require the Minister to make a representative of his Department available to answer questions in elucidation of the statement of the reasons given for the Minister's objection, but he need not answer questions which, in the opinion of the Inspector, are directed to the merits of Government policy. (A prudent reservation this; what opportunities for torturing civil servants would otherwise be afforded!).

Where the Minister of Transport has given a direction restricting the grant of permission for the development for which application was made, or a Government Department has expressed in writing to the Local Planning Authority the view that the application should not be granted and the Local Planning Authority have referred to this view in their amplification statement, the appellant may similarly require attendance by a representative of the Ministry or Ministries concerned, who has to be called as a witness by the Local Planning Authority and is subject to cross-examination to the same extent.

The procedure at the inquiry is at the discretion of the inspector, but except with the consent of the appellant, the appellant has the right to begin and a right of final reply. Any evidence may be admitted at the discretion of the inspector, except evidence the production of which would be contrary to the public interest. (The location of regional seats of government?).

The Local Planning Authority may, at the discretion of the inspector, alter or add to the submissions contained in their amplification statement or the list of documents which accompanied it so far as may be necessary to determine questions in dispute between the parties, but if necessary the inquiry must be adjourned to give the appellant and other parties an adequate opportunity of considering any new material brought forward. The inspector is specifically empowered to make a recommendation in his report as to the payment of any additional costs occasioned by such an adjournment.

If anyone entitled to appear at the inquiry fails to do so, the inspector may proceed at his discretion. The inspector may take into account any written representation made before the inquiry by anyone entitled to appear but who does not do so, and he may adjourn the inquiry as may be necessary; provided he announces the date, time and place of the resumption no further notice is needed.

The inspector may make an unaccompanied inspection of the site before or during the inquiry without giving notice of his intention, but he must, if requested by the appellant or the Local Planning Authority, do so after the close of the inquiry, and in such cases must announce during the inquiry when he intends to do so. The appellant, the Local Planning Authority and Section 37 Parties are entitled to accompany him on his inspection.

After the inquiry the inspector must make a report in writing to the Minister which shall include his findings of fact and his recommendations, or his reason for not making recommendations.

Where the Minister disagrees with the Inspector on a finding of fact, or receives any new evidence after the close of the inquiry or takes into consideration any new issue of fact other than a matter of government policy which was not raised at the inquiry and therefore is disposed to disagree with the inspector's recommendation, he must not do so without first notifying the appellant, the Local Planning Authority and Section 37 parties of his disagreement and the reasons for it and giving them an opportunity of making representations in writing within 21 days or in the case of his having received new evidence or taken into consideration any new issue of fact, of asking within 21 days for the re-opening of the inquiry.

The Minister must notify his decision and the reason for it in writing to the appellant and the other parties, and to anyone else who appeared at the inquiry and asked to be notified of it, and the decision must be accompanied by a copy of the Inspector's report or a summary.

These rules are a welcome codification of existing practice, but they are not very drastic; they still allow a great deal of useless evidence to be submitted and a great deal of time to be wasted by people who have only a slender interest in the matter being inquired into. They spring from the recommendations of the Franks Committee in its report on administrative tribunals and a good deal in them is designed to prevent a repetition of the events following the famous Chalkpit inquiry, in which it was established that the Minister had listened to the advice of the Ministry of Agriculture after the conclusion of the inquiry in respect of matters which had not been raised thereat.

Under Section 23 (5) of the Town and Country Planning Act, 1962 (previously Section 16 of the Town and Country Planning Act, 1947) the Minister must hold a local inquiry if either the Local Planning Authority or the appellant so desires, but with the consent of both parties he may determine an appeal by means of written representations—a device to which he only resorts in very trivial cases.

Local inquiries are governed by Section 290 of the Local Government Act, 1933, which enables the inspector to compel the attendance of people and to take evidence on oath—powers which he seldom, if ever, exercises. It appears that these rules do not apply to a " hearing ", which is not regarded by the Minister as a public inquiry. These hearings, otherwise indistinguishable from ordinary public inquiries into appeals, are held in relation to appeals against refusal to permit the exhibition of outdoor advertisements and appeals against the granting of certificates of alternative development under Section 17 of the Land Compensation Act, 1961.

Under Regulation 20 of the Control of Advertisement Regulations of 1960, the Minister may settle an appeal relating to advertisements without holding a local inquiry.

The Minister's decision on an appeal is normally final, except that an appeal lies to the high court on matters of law only.

The actual procedure at appeals is that the inspector opens the inquiry by stating its subject-matter, and asks for the names and status of the representatives of the parties to the appeal and the witnesses they propose to call, and of any other interested persons who wish to be heard.

The appellant opens his case, usually in the form of a statement in which he seeks to show that the decision against which he is appealing is a bad one and that the development he proposes is unobjectionable. He then calls his witnesses, who, one by one, give their evidence, either in the form of a statement or by question and answer, are cross-examined by the Local Planning Authority and by any other interested parties present, and, if necessary, are re-examined by the appellant. Next, the Local Planning Authority (and this of course includes a district council acting under delegated powers) presents its case, which may be done in exactly the same way as by the appellant, or, alternatively, and often more effectively, by omitting the opening statement and putting all the punch into the closing statement. The appellant, finally, has the opportunity of making a closing statement, and the inquiry is then closed. The inspector then visits the site accompanied by a representative of each of the parties to the appeal and of any other parties who wish to attend.

At the site the inspector asks any questions about the site and its surroundings which occur to him and the representatives present may point out to him any physical features to which they wish to call his attention. Most inspectors, once the hearing has been closed, will not listen to further arguments about the merits of the case as distinct from physical facts. This is a wise precaution to take, for, otherwise, one provocative remark leading to another, the whole case may be fought out all over again in much less orderly fashion, and without any new information emerging.

On the whole, the procedure which has been described in quite a good one subject to one rather important defect. When submitting his appeal to the Minister an appellant has to fill in a form on which one of the headings is " Precise grounds of appeal ". Since an appeal is supposed to be made within 28 days of receiving the Local Planning Authority's decision, which does not give much time for briefing counsel, retaining an expert witness or witnesses and conferring in order to draft grounds of appeal, and since, naturally enough, the Local Planning Authority's original grounds of refusal are hardly ever sufficiently detailed to explain their case fully, it is quite usual to fill this section in with purely formal words, such as " We contest each and all of the grounds of refusal, which are unreasonable and un-

realistic ". It is extremely rare for a Local Planning Authority to try to tie an appellant down at an inquiry to the terms of this preliminary gambit, for it would be manifestly unreasonable to do so. But 28 days before the inquiry the appellant will have been supplied with a full statement of the Local Planning Authority's case whereas up to the opening of the inquiry they may well have no idea at all of *his* case. It would be very much better to make rules requiring the Authority's statement to be furnished considerable earlier than 28 days before the inquiry and requiring the appellant to furnish a similarly detailed rebuttal of it before the inquiry. If this were done both sides would know what they were up against and the technical witnesses on each side could prepare considered evidence, putting forward their own technical case and an answer to the opposition's case. This would unquestionably shorten proceedings, reveal unmistakably the real areas of dispute and assist the Inspector in reaching a wise recommendation. Too often, under present procedure, both sides blaze furiously away without hitting each other.

Attempts may be made to avert the necessity for an appeal to be heard. Such attempts may save much money and time, both public and private, for the preparation of a case for an appeal involves a considerable amount of work unless the subject-matter is exceptionally trivial, and the number of highly paid people who have to attend the hearing is usually rather frightening if one estimates the total fees and salaries payable in respect of the time spent there.

The Planning department will often approach the applicant, and ask him to hold a discussion with them, before even arriving at a decision in any difficult case, and, on his part, the applicant will be well advised to discuss the matter with the Planning department in such a case before he ever submits an application. Differences of opinion which are not fundamental can often be resolved without much difficulty in this way.

Even if such a discussion is not held (and it may often be necessary, because of dates of committee meetings falling awkwardly, to issue a decision before a meeting with the applicant can be arranged) efforts can appropriately be made to reach a settlement after an appeal has been lodged, but before the hearing takes place. Some Local Planning Authorities have taken the view that once an appeal is lodged, the matter is, in effect, *sub judice*, and negotiations cannot properly be undertaken with the appellant, but there seems to be no substance in this view.

Useful as these activities may be, it is necessary to preserve a sense of proportion about them. All consume the time of Planning staff and thus affect adversely the all-important objective of cutting down as much as possible the average time taken to determine applications. Unless, therefore, a distinct possibility of reaching an acceptable compromise can be seen, extensive negotiations are best avoided, although tentative inquiries by either side to discover such possibilities should not be omitted. Inquiry may sometimes produce results in the most unpromising cases; for example, an applicant who has submitted development which is quite unacceptable because of its location may be found also to own an entirely suitable site, and to be perfectly willing to use it instead of the original. But the parties to an appeal should not ask the Minister to postpone the date of the inquiry because they hope to reach agreement unless the prospects of this are very bright indeed; a subsequent breakdown will inflict grave delay on the applicant.

Representation. The selection of representatives and witnesses at an inquiry needs some thought. Except where one side has clearly been guilty of complete irresponsibility, and the Minister charges it with the costs of the inquiry, each side has to pay its own costs, win or lose, the costs of the Ministry being paid by the public out of central funds and the hire of premises, where this is involved, being borne by the Local Planning Authority.

The private appellant with modest means therefore has to consider carefully what advice he can afford. He may elect to be his own advocate and witness, but this is seldom really in his interests. Although he can be reasonably certain that the Local Planning Authority will behave with courtesy, moderation, and even helpfulness towards a lay advocate, and although the inspector may be relied upon to watch his interests, and elicit all possible information favourable to him, his complete lack of technical knowledge and sheer inarticulateness may easily result in important facts in his favour never emerging at all, since the inspector cannot be expected to be a mind reader.

In relatively simple cases he may be best served by employing an architect or surveyor as both advocate and expert witness; if this person has a Planning qualification and experience, whether or not practising specifically as a Planning consultant, it will be very greatly to his advantage.

Probably the professional man with whom such an appellant has the most regular dealings will be his solicitor, who will generally be a most able advocate for the purposes of a Planning inquiry.

In complicated cases the advice and evidence of an experienced Planning consultant is likely to be of the utmost value.

The briefing of counsel in very simple cases is seldom justified. The particular ability of counsel lies in being able to marshal and present understandably and persuasively a mass of complicated facts; neither this nor his special learnedness in the law can be used to full effect at a very simple Planning inquiry.

The question of cost obviously does not affect a Local Planning Authority so much as it does a private appellant. But, in straightforward cases, and particularly when judicious inquiry shows that the appellant is not likely to be legally represented, the whole conduct of the case can safely be left to a Planning officer. If this is done no impression is conveyed of overbearing the appellant by force of arms, and the combination of inspector, private professional practitioner and Planning officer often produces a brief and well argued hearing, particularly if the subject-matter is highly technical.

In more important and complicated cases it will be necessary for a member of the clerk's staff to conduct the case. So far as a county council is concerned it is eminently suitable if Planning officers in local offices regularly work at appeals in conjunction with the member of the clerk's staff who is allocated to deal with the work of that office. A very high degree of understanding, and consequently of effectiveness, can be attained if this is done. Much the same considerations apply to briefing counsel as in the case of the appellant, but the great advantage of detailed knowledge of all relevant circumstances which is likely to be possessed by the appropriate member of the clerk's staff makes the briefing of counsel for the Local Planning Authority less often necessary than for the appellant.

Conduct of the inquiry. The following account is written chiefly from the standpoint of the Planning officer, but applies, with suitable modification, to other technical witnesses; it also relates especially to the hearing of appeals.

It should, throughout, be borne in mind that the hearing is to a technical tribunal, that specific arguments, therefore, count most, and that general principles to which reference is made need not be enunciated with very great elaboration.

The procedure at a Planning inquiry is based upon that in a court of law, but is very much more lax and flexible. There is no obligation on the inspector to follow any particular procedure, the rules of evidence are only sketchily observed, and it is unusual for an inspector to exclude or sustain an objection in respect of any relevant statement by a witness which is not mere hearsay. The formality with which the hearing is conducted depends upon the lead given by the inspector and upon the persons conducting the case on each side; leading counsel, for example, do not readily abandon all traces of their courtroom manner or settle comfortably into a chatty free-for-all.

On the whole, a fairly strict observance of formality seems to work best; unless some restraint is put on them, appellants and lay witnesses tend to get excited, and interrupt, make statements instead of asking questions, argue instead of answering them, and generally bring about a lengthy and irritating hearing at which all the relevant facts may not emerge clearly because of the general confusion.

The Local Planning Authority's opening statement, if one is made, should be extremely brief, and no more than an indication of the general arguments to be used. It should certainly not include a detailed resumé of the Planning officer's evidence, which will in any case have to be repeated *as* evidence, and which will sound stale and unimpressive if it has already been given by the advocate.

It is very usual for the Planning officer's evidence to be prepared as a written statement, copies of which are given to the inspector and the appellant, and which he then reads aloud. It is obviously advantageous if this closely follows the wording of the Amplification Statement.

The Planning officer must be at his most alert and cautious during cross-examination. He may be asked anything about any aspect of the case, and it is essential that he should weigh his words to guard against the possibility of being tricked into having to eat them later on. This is not the place to discuss the ethics of courtroom tactics, fascinating though the subject is; all I want to do is mention some of the wiles which are commonly employed, and how they can best be overcome, without considering whether such tactics should be allowed.

In withstanding cross-examination the expert witness should be quite clear about certain things. Although not on oath, he has an absolute duty to speak the truth; although not legally bound to do so, he must answer any proper and reasonably relevant question if any weight is to be given to his evidence; he should treat his antagonist with appropriate courtesy; as an expert witness he cannot be expected to confine his answers to " yes " or " no ", but is entitled to reply at whatever length is necessary to give a complete answer to a question; a witness should not be asked and cannot properly answer any question relating to happenings at a committee meeting which have not been made public (for example, it is not proper to ask him whether the voting on some subject was close or even what advice he gave, but only what decision was made or what his professional *opinion* is.)

The Planning officer's manner towards his adversary should be friendly; his answers should be given freely and not appear to be dragged out of him. The greater the confidence and promptness with which he can make his replies, the better the impression likely to be made on the mind of the inspector, which is what matters. Especially should any damaging admissions which have to be made be given frankly and cheerfully. No resentment should be felt or shown concerning questions, however outrageous their implications, if there is no personal discourtesy contained in them. A witness who loses his temper is sunk, but righteous indignation is another matter and we will mention it later on.

The tactics which are likely to be tried on a witness, other than reasoned attempts to refute his evidence, are attempts to bully him, to make him lose his temper, to confuse him, to stifle replies unfavourable to the opposition, and to rush him into giving an opinion on a complicated point without sufficient time for consideration. Any or all of these may be combined. A witness subjected to attacks of this kind can appeal to the inspector or to his own advocate to protect him, and may, indeed, be given such protection without asking for it, but he will make a much better impression if he weathers the storm unaided.

Bullying, in its subtler forms, is no more than " lifemanship ", a manner which draws attention to the prestige and formidable knowledge of the opposing advocate and the undistinguished lowliness of the witness; it is best dealt with by ignoring it altogether, and this also applies to attempts to make the witness lose his temper. It is not a good idea to counter by being clever or funny, which gives the opposition a fine opportunity to assume a manner of great earnestness and say: " Quite, Mr. . . . , but you see this isn't a laughing matter to my client; it's a very serious matter to him; now, if you don't mind, Mr. . . . , don't you think, speaking seriously . . . ? "

There is, however, no reason at all why a witness should submit to real discourtesy and, if ignoring it does not work, a forthright statement, expressed indignantly but controlledly, that if the opposing advocate wants his questions answered he had better look to his manners will generally have its effect, and will draw no rebuke from the inspector.

Attempts to confuse and to stifle unhelpful replies commonly go together. The usual thing is for an advocate to ask several loosely framed questions one after the other and, if the witness's reply seems to be tending in a direction unhelpful to or positively harmful to the opposition, to butt in with another question before the reply has been completed. It is very easy to fall victim to this one, but there is really no excuse for doing so; the witness is on un-

assailable ground if he insists upon questions being put into precise form, upon having them put to him one by one, the answer to the first being given before the next one is put, and upon his right to give a full answer. No inspector could possibly fail to support him in these demands; he should stick like a rock and refuse to proceed on any other terms. This may sometimes produce a blazing row and may even, with luck, make the opposing advocate lose his temper, a highly satisfactory outcome; but the witness should be very careful not to give the impression that he is trying to avoid answering a question, which a skilled advocate will almost certainly try to suggest.

On no account must one be pushed into giving a snap answer on some complicated point, especially if mental arithmetic is involved; a wrong answer, under witness-box conditions, is very probable, and even if this does not help the opposition it can generally be used to create confusion and undermine the confidence in the witness. When such a question is put, sometimes in all good faith and without ulterior motive, it is advisable to reply that to answer it would involve somewhat lengthy calculation which can, of course, be carried out if the information is essential. Very often this will end the matter, but attempts may be made to get the witness to give " a rough idea ". This is sometimes perfectly reasonable and should be given, but often initial calculations far too complicated to be done in the head are required as the basis of even an approximation, in which case it would be folly to be drawn.

Having said all this about cross-examination it may seem an anti-climax to mention that it is rare indeed for an inspector's report to contain any reference whatever to what was said in cross-examination! Nevertheless, it may still have had its effect upon the inspector's mind.

Re-examination of a witness by his advocate must properly be confined to the clarification of matters raised in cross-examination, and it is most useful in order to minimize the effect of any damaging admissions and to pursue to their conclusion any trails followed by the opposition and abandoned, on it becoming apparent that they led to uncomfortable rather than comfortable destinations. The advocate should give the witness the opportunity of making any point which he himself has missed by asking, in conclusion: " Is there anything else arising from your cross-examination which you would like to say ? "

The inspector very often questions witnesses after the advocates have finished with them, not only to clarify any points which may still be obscure, but also in fulfilment of the Minister's duty to consider all relevant aspects of an application, whether or not they have been mentioned by the parties. A witness who feels that he has escaped lightly under cross-examination should not relax too much until the inspector has questioned him or indicated that he has no questions to ask. Though he may be sure that any such questions will be put with the greatest courtesy and correctness they often prove by far the hardest to answer satisfactorily. It is becoming normal for an inspector to put his own questions after cross-examination but before re-examination so that any new hares which he starts may be dealt with by the witness's advocate.

Throughout the presentation of the opposition's case the Planning officer should feed his advocate with material for cross-examination; he will often be able to suggest useful questions which it would not have occurred to the advocate to put to witnesses. This should be done by written notes pushed across the table rather than in whispers; the notes must be *legible*!

Preparation for an inquiry. The first need is for the room in which the inquiry is to be held to be of suitable size for the number of representatives of parties and members of the public likely to attend, which can generally be estimated with fair accuracy. Tables and chairs should be arranged so that the opposing parties are somewhat segregated and can confer conveniently without being overheard, and ample space should be provided for spreading out maps and documents. The inspector is, of course, provided with a table and chair in a dominating position facing those of the parties involved, while a chair and table for witnesses should be placed where they can see and be seen, and consequently heard, by all concerned. Screens for the display of drawings should be placed in full view of all. These arrangements are the responsibility of the Local Planning Authority.

The Planning officer and the appellant's technical witness are principally concerned with preparing their proofs of evidence, or written statements, if these are to be used, and any necessary drawings. It is a good rule to make the former as brief, and the latter as few, as possible, consistent with reasonable completeness. It is better to be slightly under-equipped than slightly over-equipped with ammunition because of the confusion which excessive quantities of paper engender.

The Planning officer's statement should begin by stating the decision given and the grounds therefor, and should proceed to build up reasons justifying them with reference to the existing and proposed character of the area concerned. This process should not be carried too far; common sense must decide the point at which considerations become too remote to exercise any real influence.

Special care must be taken when the Planning proposals upon which the decision is based have not been formally embodied in a Development Plan but are no more than tentative, particularly if they have not even been adopted in principle by the Local Planning Authority. This should, of course, always have been done, but pressure of time and administrative complexity may quite often prevent it. When this happens the appellant is likely to make great play with it, and point out the iniquity of relying upon proposals which have no sanction, so that it is best to refer to such proposals as mere indications of a possible future pattern of development, thought to be appropriate, with which the appellant's proposed development conflicts.

Nearly all decisions must, in fact, be based upon assumptions regarding the future development of a wider area, and it is open to the appellant—indeed, if he has any sort of a case it is his best chance—not only to attack the assumptions put forward on behalf of the Local Planning Authority but to state other assumptions which do not conflict with the development he wishes to carry out, and to show, if possible, that they are at least as sound as those of the Local Planning Authority. It has been suggested earlier in this chapter that appellants do not take this line often enough. A Local Planning Authority's proposals, however carefully considered, are seldom the only satisfactory ones possible, and with skill and ingenuity it may be possible to prepare alternatives which not only suit the appellant but are genuinely as acceptable as the originals in every way. The all-too-common line of attack: " This is what I want to do and I don't see why I shouldn't ", unsupported by positive arguments, does not hold much prospect of success.

To return to the Planning officer's statement or proof of evidence: having set out his main argument he must next consider whether to include rebuttals of any arguments which the appellant may have expressed in making preliminary observations to the Ministry (he will have seen these), or which, it is fairly clear from the facts of the case, may be advanced. To attack arguments which have not been made at the time the statement is prepared may be very dangerous; it may reveal to the appellant lines of attack which he had not thought of. On the whole, the best thing is not to include rebuttals of anticipated arguments in the statement handed in, but to prepare them separately and for the advocate to bring them out by question and answer, if the circumstances warrant it.

The advocate and the witnesses must, of course, confer before the inquiry to arrange the plan of campaign and make sure that there are no misunderstandings. It is especially necessary to ensure that the proofs of evidence of different witnesses do not contain too much similar material; they should confirm each other by similar conclusions arrived at from different premises, not by repetition. It can hardly be necessary to mention that any contradictions must somehow be eliminated.

The drawings used to reinforce evidence at an inquiry are of great importance. Every use should be made of the various devices to secure effective presentation which were described in Chapter 3 but in a matter of any complexity an awkward dilemma arises. The most effective presentation demands severe limitation of the variety of subject-matter shown on any one drawing, yet it is absolutely vital that the number of drawings used should be kept to a minimum. The necessity for providing each party with a copy of every drawing multiplies the number of pieces of paper in the room, and, if both sides produce several, particularly if some of them are large, scenes of wild confusion generally follow. However generous the table space provided, it is almost impossible constantly to refer back and forth between several large plans, which will probably have been rolled up for some time, and have a strong tendency to coil themselves up unless held down at every corner. Multiplicity of plans, in fact, generally proves self-defeating: in the end, by mutual consent, all except one are discarded and this one is made to serve all purposes.

If some one map, such as a Comprehensive Development Area Map, is central to the subject of the inquiry, it will be well worth the trouble to prepare one copy of a very large-scale cartoon of it, omitting unnecessary details, which can be displayed so that everyone can see it sufficiently clearly to follow arguments relating to it. If very close examination is necessary, it is quite convenient for the people concerned to leave their seats and gather round it for a short while. The inspector is almost certain to ask for the loan, if not the permanent retention, of such a cartoon to illustrate his report.

Smaller drawings for individual distribution can be prepared to supplement the cartoon if necessary. Not more than two should be used if it can possibly be avoided; their size should be reduced to the uttermost for convenient handling, and the information given in them should be shown in the starkest simplicity.

At inquiries into development plans, multiplicity of drawings may be unavoidable and it is desirable to prepare special cartoons of all the most important for display, so that tables shall not be excessively obstructed.

In some circumstances it may be very well worth-while to make slides of

the drawings to be used, and to project them on to a screen at appropriate times during an inquiry.

Looking impartially at the situation at the present time (early 1964) it may reasonably be complained that it is far too common for Planning officers to give evidence in accordance with their employing authority's views other than with their own personal opinions and for inspectors to give unmistakable evidence in their reports of insufficient competence. Both these matters are discussed at some length in Chapter 10 of my " Town Planning at the Crossroads " (Estate Gazette, 1961).

CHAPTER 22

THE PLANNING MACHINE IN BRITAIN

22-1. INTRODUCTORY

THIS CHAPTER deals with the system set up to deal with Town and Country Planning in Britain. Although, in accordance with the general purpose of this book, emphasis is principally laid upon the technical aspects of this machinery, a fairly thorough understanding of the administrative and legal background is necessary.

Town and Country Planning in England and Wales is, in the first instance, the concern of the Minister of Housing and Local Government, and in Scotland of the Secretary of State; for the sake of simplicity, separate reference will not again be made to the latter.

The Minister of Town and Country Planning Act, 1943, charges the Minister (until the beginning of 1951 called the Minister of Town and Country Planning, and from then until after the General Election of October, 1951, the Minister of Local Government and Planning) with securing consistency and continuity in the framing and execution of a national policy with respect to the use and development of land throughout England and Wales. In the attainment of this general objective he is now assisted by county councils, county borough councils, and by combinations of these in the form of Joint Boards, New Towns corporations, and the National Parks Commission. All except the last have the duty of formulating and implementing Planning proposals for the areas they administer. In the case of county councils, county borough councils and Joint Boards (the Local Planning Authorities proper) this involves preparing Development Plans in several progressively more detailed stages, and fitting into them the many developments sponsored by themselves and by other bodies and persons. County councils must consult the borough and district councils in their areas regarding the contents of the Development Plan and may delegate, or may be ordered by the Minister to delegate, powers of development control to them.

The Minister has the duty of adjudicating on the merits of Development Plans in the light of national Planning policy; he may " call in " any application for Planning permission and determine it himself, a right which is usually exercised only in particularly important cases; he may also revoke a permission already given. He has to decide whether to approve development sponsored by Local Planning Authorities themselves, and must determine the appeals of intending developers who consider themselves aggrieved by the decisions of Local Planning Authorities upon their applications for development. Further, it is his duty to mediate in any irreconcilable differences of opinion between Local Planning Authorities and the borough and district councils in their areas concerning the merits of development sponsored by the latter, and between Local Planning Authorities and government departments where the former object to development proposed to be carried out by the latter. It is to be noted that in the last-mentioned case Local Planning Authorities have no control over development by the Crown, but government departments have undertaken to consult them and to meet their wishes whenever possible.[1] Finally, the Minister has default powers to prepare a Development Plan himself if any Local Planning Authority should fail in its duty to prepare one, and he can prepare outline advisory plans, such as the Greater London Plan, in order to facilitate the unified planning of an area administered by several different Local Planning Authorities throughout which there are difficult and related problems.[2]

This brief statement of the Planning system might by itself convey the impression that the Planning powers of central and local government respectively were satisfactorily divided, but unfortunately it cannot stop at this point. Other Ministries also have powers and functions in relation to Planning.

The Board of Trade is responsible for securing the satisfactory distribution of industry, and Planning permission may not be given by a Local Planning Authority for any new industrial development, except of a very minor sort, unless the applicant has previously obtained a certificate from the Board of Trade that such development can be carried out consistently with the proper distribution of industry. Although the Local Planning Authority is free to refuse Planning permission for industrial development to take place on any particular site which may be proposed, notwithstanding a Board of Trade certificate having been issued, it is, on the other hand, unable to secure the establishment of industrial development which, on general Planning grounds, it may consider vitally necessary in a particular area if the Board of Trade withholds the necessary certificates. There is not much evidence to indicate that the Board of Trade is prepared to co-operate effectively with Local Planning Authorities, or indeed that it has any real appreciation of Planning needs. There seems every reason to suppose that its powers in relation to the distribution of industry ought to vest in appropriately constituted Regional Planning Authorities. It is also noteworthy that there is no appeal against the refusal of an Industrial Development Certificate, a unique or almost unique exception to a general rule.

From the opposite point of view industrialists are confused by and resentful of what they regard as a dual system of control. It seems absurd to many of them that, having obtained a certificate from the Board of Trade which purports to indicate that there is no objection to the location of their proposed development in relation to distribution of industry policy, they nevertheless, have to fight an appeal against a Planning refusal based solely on that policy. There may indeed often be real inconsistency here, but in other cases it may well be that the Board of Trade is justified in granting a certificate in relation to general distribution policy and the Local Planning Authority equally

---

[1] Few people seem to have much confidence in the effectiveness of this procedure.
[2] I know of no case of the Minister having even contemplated use of his default powers, nor, rather surprisingly, of a Local Planning Authority having threatened to make him do so, for a default power is a two-edged weapon and to force the use of it upon the Minister might involve him in very grave embarrassment, which would often be an excellent thing.

justified in refusing permission because of Planning objections to the actual site rather than to the general locality proposed.

The Ministry of Agriculture is concerned to secure the retention in agricultural use of as much good agricultural land as possible, and also advises Local Planning Authorities on the effect of private proposals upon agricultural land. The Ministry of Agriculture cannot prevent a Local Planning Authority from approving private development if the latter does not agree with its advice, but can, of course, make representations to the Minister of Housing and Local Government to induce him to call in an application and determine it, or if permission has already been given by the Local Planning Authority, to revoke permission.

The evidence given at appeals by officers of the Ministry of Agriculture in support of a Local Planning Authority's refusal to permit development is generally of appallingly low quality and extremely parochial. It is usually confined to a statement that the land in question is productive agricultural land; rarely if ever does it consist of the results of an investigation of the Planning Balance Sheet merits of the case based upon Wibberley's food replacement yardstick. (See p. 111). It is time that Local Planning Authorities stood on their own feet in this matter instead of relying upon the painfully limited bureaucratic rubbish usually served up by the Ministry of Agriculture, which rightly attracts the contempt of all informed people, and helps to debase the standard of Planning administration.

The Ministry of Agriculture also has the duty of ensuring that development required for the purposes of Agriculture is not unreasonably refused permission, and Local Planning Authorities must consult the Ministry before refusing permission for or imposing conditions on any such development, although, again, they need not act upon the advice given.

The Ministry of Transport is responsible for choosing and safeguarding the routes of new trunk roads and for constructing them, and may also veto any development which in its opinion might prejudice the use of an existing trunk road by causing danger or undue traffic congestion upon it. It must, therefore, be consulted by the Local Planning Authority when the latter receives an application for development likely to affect a trunk road.

The evidence normally given at appeals by the officers of the Ministry of Transport falls into much the same category as that customarily given by the Ministry of Agriculture. Apart from its generally low intrinsic quality, however, it is preposterous to perpetuate a system which assumes that Local Planning Authorities are unfit to safeguard Trunk Roads. If such an assumption is true it constitutes an impressive argument in favour of creating Local Planning Authorities of a new and better kind!

In some circumstances the Nature Conservancy must also be consulted by Local Planning Authorities.

All this makes a confusing whole. The Local Planning Authority is weighed down by the number of central government departments which it has to consult at various times. The developer—local authority or private individual—is even more depressed by these consultations with people whom he often cannot meet and whose views he frequently cannot clearly under-

stand. He is also often grievously delayed by the time each consultation takes place.

The simple, clear and reasonably logical division of responsibility between the Ministry of Housing and Local Government and Local Planning Authorities is fogged and confused by the other Ministerial fingers in the Planning pie. Where Development Plans have been submitted and approved by the Minister the situation is improved somewhat, since, before approving a Development Plan, he has to consult and reach agreement with all the government departments concerned with various aspects of the Plan, and once this agreement is reached it is possible to dispense with consultation in respect of proposals which conform to the Plan. But of course agreement is only in the degree of detail entered into by the particular stage of the Development Plan which has been reached. In some cases it may not be difficult to obtain agreement upon the broad and skeletal proposals of a County Plan, but very much more difficult to secure, for example, the Ministry of Agriculture's agreement to the staging of development within an area of comprehensive development.

To this burden is added the many consultations which a Planning department must undertake with other departments of the same council, with official and unofficial bodies not connected with central or local government, as well as with private individuals, all of which add up to a very large total.

So much, for the moment, for the present machinery of Planning. What of the preparation and content of Development Plans? It has already been said that these are prepared in stages. In the case of county councils, the first stage is a County Map which shows on a small scale the most important of the changes in land use and the construction projects which it is intended shall take place during the following 20 years. This is accompanied by another map, called a Programme Map, indicating the order in which it is expected that these events will take place. The next stage is the preparation of Town Maps and accompanying Programme Maps, in rather more detail but still quite broadly. These Town Maps are prepared in respect of areas in which considerable development is expected to take place, which may include villages and sprawling areas of sporadic development which it is proposed to tidy up, as well as town areas proper. Town Maps are not all prepared simultaneously but may be postponed until the imminence of development creates a need for them. Briefly, the *County* Map shows in which towns and villages extensive development is intended to take place, the *Town* Maps show which land is intended to be developed and the different purposes for which it is to be used.

The next stage is the preparation of Comprehensive Development Area Maps for those areas, generally within Town Map areas, where general development is imminent. These maps show in detail the intended distribution of land uses within the areas they cover. For example, they show small local shopping centres too unimportant to be shown on the Town Map, and the proposed street pattern is indicated, but without including culs-de-sac and other very minor roads, the positions and lengths of which could be changed without appreciably affecting other land.

The Development Plan (Amendment) Regulations (Statutory Instrument

No. 933, of 1954) introduced a new map, namely the Supplementary Town Map. This, in scale, notation and content, is precisely similar to the Comprehensive Development Area Map, but may be prepared in respect of any area for which a Development Plan Map at a scale of 6 inches to the mile has been prepared. There are various limitations on the land which can be included in Comprehensive Development Area Maps. The final stage consists of the preparation of layout and building Plans by intending developers shortly before development actually takes place.

The procedure is the same in county boroughs as in counties, except that, of course, no County Map is needed.

Development Plans have to be reviewed at intervals of five years,[3] and any amendments made are subject to ministerial approval and local inquiry in exactly the same way as the original Development Plan.

Before, during and after the preparation of the various stages of the Development Plan, the Local Planning Authority has to decide whether to permit, refuse or permit subject to conditions, applications for permission to carry out development within its area. It cannot postpone consideration of an application because the relevant part of the Development Plan has not been prepared, but must at once decide whether the particular proposal can take place without conflict with the Development Plan when the latter is prepared or reviewed. This is often a feat of extreme difficulty. In practice there is nothing to prevent a Local Planning Authority simply failing to determine an embarrassing application, in which case an appeal is against a failure to determine instead of against a refusal. Recently, too, it has become fashionable to refuse permission on the grounds that an application is in conflict with the Development Plan currently in operation and ought not to be given permission until the future of the area concerned is generally reconsidered in connection with a review of the Development Plan. This sounds sensible, and would be sensible if reviews in fact took place at five-yearly intervals, but when such a decision is made with reference to a Town Map prepared in the late 1940's, submitted to the Minister in 1951 and approved by him in 1958 it ceases to have any sense unless, which seems not very likely, Development Plans are going to be approved within a mere fraction of the time after submission which has so far prevailed.

We speak of Development Plans being prepared and decisions on development applications being taken by county councils and county borough councils. In practice the Plans are actually drawn up by the authority's Planning officer and his staff, who carry out many investigations and seek information and advice from other departments of the Local Planning Authority, and, in the case of a county council, from the borough and district councils of the county, from central government departments and from other sources. The Development Plan, or any particular stage of it, should seek to satisfy the needs revealed by all these investigations and discussions, resolving conflicting needs as far as possible and strengthening the mutually beneficial intention of complementary ones. It is the art of the Planner to

achieve such a synthesis after he has collected and scientifically assessed the necessary facts.

When the Plan has been prepared it has to be reported upon and explained to the lay members of the Local Planning Authority, who, after considering it and altering it in any way they think fit, approve it, after which it is submitted to the Minister for his approval.

With regard to applications for Planning permission it is the duty of the Planning staff to obtain all the information necessary for arriving at a wise decision, and to advise the members as to what that decision should be. The relationship between planning officers and members and the problems involved are discussed later.

The present system of Planning control casts its net very wide. The carrying out of practically all development of any importance requires Planning permission. Development is defined at length in Section 12 of the Town and Country Planning Act, 1947, but for the purposes of this very general résumé it may be considered to comprise all substantial changes in the use of land, except from one kind of agriculture to another, and of buildings and the erection of all buildings, except very minor ones. Control extends to the design and appearance of buildings and even in some cases to the fences, etc., which enclose their sites.

This kind of control is, by the way, no novelty, as many people seem to imagine. The scope of Planning control defined by the Planning portion of the Housing and Town Planning Act of 1909, the first enactment in this country to deal with Planning, was nearly as broad as that obtaining today, the difference under the 1909 Act being rather in the drastic restriction on the kind of land which could be made subject to control, lack of compulsion on local authorities to use Planning powers, of financial support for Planning action and of power to *enforce* any Planning control until a scheme had finally been brought into operation—a very lengthy procedure.

A Planning committee may at the same meeting have to determine applications relating to the establishment of a factory employing 5,000 people, the road layout of an estate of several hundred houses, the use of a living room of a house for a hair-dresser's business, and the erection of a front garden fence five feet high. Stated thus, the operation of Planning control might appear the *reductio ad absurdum* of bureaucracy, but it would be unwise to judge hastily. Innumerable Planning applications are given permission without question or discussion, and many activities which technically require Planning permission are begun and carried out without such permission being obtained but without interference by the Local Planning Authority, because they are obviously unobjectionable.

But quite minor development may be a real nuisance unless there is some power held in reserve to control it. For example, it might be thought that no garden wall or fence, however ugly, can justifiably be brought within the net of legal control; but consider a corrugated iron fence 12ft. high, painted in alternating irregular bands of mustard and puce. It is true that its effect would be very local, but a power, only used in extreme cases, to deal with this kind of thing may help immeasurably to keep a district seemly in appearance, and to protect the reasonable interests of its inhabitants, particularly as

---

[3] I state the law thus flatly. But it is a fiction; for various reasons Development Plans are *not* reviewed every five years mainly owing to the enormous time lag between their submission to the Minister and his approval of them. The five years starts to run from the date of approval, which may often mean that a fresh review ought to be begun before the previous review has been approved.

regards matters in which the law of nuisance affords no remedy. The justifiable and practicable lengths to which Planning control can extend is a matter of difficulty and importance. Although the legal limits of control are laid down, principally in the Town and Country Planning Act, 1947,[4] and the General Development Order of 1950, made under powers conferred by that Act, the limit to which a Local Planning Authority ought ordinarily to go in seeking to enforce control may stop some way short of the legal limit.

It will be appropriate at this point to remind readers of what was said in Chapter 20, p. 275. Since the last war we have, in relation to Development Control, pressed from a system of *controls* to a sytem of *control*. Most countries with Planning powers still operate under the former system, as we ourselves did until 1947. The enormous increase in flexibility gained by the change is slightly counterbalanced by the much higher standard of junior technical staff needed to operate it well.

22-2. THE MINISTRY OF HOUSING AND LOCAL GOVERNMENT

It has never been Government policy to make public in any detail the structure of Government Departments. The Progress Report on the work of the Ministry of Town and Country Planning (Command 8204), published in April, 1951, sets out admirably the work of the Ministry and the various problems which beset it. But even this document devotes less than two full pages (pages 19-21) to the structure of the Ministry.

It follows that no accurate and comprehensive picture can be given of the way in which the Ministry goes about its day-to-day work, since no one who has the necessary information to do so is permitted to divulge it. M. P. Fogarty, in " Town and Country Planning " gives some interesting, though out-of-date by now, information in his final chapter, " Planners at Work ", but even this is by no means comprehensive.

Since the writing of the Progress Report the Ministry has become the Ministry of Housing and Local Government, and has, in particular, absorbed the Housing functions of the Ministry of Health, so that what is said in the Report about " the Ministry " now only applies to the Planning part of it.

The Progress Report states that the Permanent Secretary and Deputy Secretary are responsible to the Minister for the functioning of the Ministry as a whole, and that the Ministry is divided into three main groups: Headquarters administration, headquarters technical directorate, and regional organisation.

The Administrative group is made up of non-specialised Civil Servants of administrative, executive and clerical, etc., grades, and there are four undersecretaries, one responsible for financial work under the Permanent Secretary, one for New Towns work and the other two for policy work on Development Plans, development proposals, the Planning system, Planning standards, National Parks, and all other aspects of the Ministry's work.

The technical staff at headquarters are in four main categories: (i) Those who deal with the main body of technical Planning work, and who, though they may not be Chartered Town Planners, have, in general, qualifications

and experience similar to their counterparts in the Local Planning Authorities; (ii) those engaged on research, who have qualifications relating to geography, geology or economics, and who investigate Planning problems of national importance within their respective fields; (iii) those who deal with the problems of public estate management, cost of land acquisition, programming, redevelopment, and so forth, and who are mostly chartered surveyors, and (iv) the inspectorate, most of whom have qualifications in Planning and/or architecture, engineering or surveying, and who preside over and report to the Minister upon all public inquiries and hearings relating to Development Plans, appeals against Local Planning Authorities' decisions, objections to orders, etc.

Until the General Election of 1951 there was quite an elaborate regional organisation, which comprehended not only Planning but various other Departments, including Health, Labour and the Board of Trade. After 1951 this organisation was progressively abandoned, until now the whole of the Planning activities of the Ministry are conducted from London. Nevertheless, for many purposes, the work of the Ministry is still organised on a regional basis. Regional Planning Officers, each with a small staff, are assigned to deal with the Ministry's Planning work for each region. These regions are not areas which bear any resemblance to Planning regions, but are simply divisions of the country into large areas. While the apparatus for consultation and policy-making at regional level which existed until 1951 has been dismantled, a great deal of interdepartmental consultation at a regional level still goes on.

It is a matter of great difficulty to give an informative account of the way in which the considerable machinery of the whole Ministry functions, because, as previously intimated, such a small proportion of its work sees the light of day. The following commentary, unavoidably mainly inferential, attempts only to mention some of the apparent merits and defects as seen by Local Planning Authorities and the public; it can be regarded as certain that, both at headquarters and regional levels, an immense amount of consultation takes place which is valuable not only in the field of land Planning but in many other ways. At regular interdepartmental meetings dealing with Physical Planning and Distribution of Industry, at many *ad hoc* meetings and conferences between officers of different Government Departments, and by means of innumerable purely informal discussions land Planning policy in broad outline is, no doubt, hammered out.

While no reasonable person would expect a detailed record of the proceedings at all these meetings to be made public it seems highly regrettable that the public in general are not given more frequent and regular account of policy decisions, and, in particular, that Local Planning Authorities and other local authorities are not more frequently consulted and made privy to the deliberations of the Ministry.

Official circulars and even speeches by the Minister are not sufficiently regular and seldom sufficiently specific for authorities and the public to feel that they are co-partners in the enterprise of Planning; rather are the Planning authorities made to feel that they are in the position of examinees who are set to do the work which is subsequently criticised and altered in the

---

[4] The Town and Country Planning Act, 1962, is now the principal enactment.

light of the superior wisdom and knowledge of the Ministry. It is, for example, particularly irritating for a County Planning Officer to carry out a substantial amount of detailed work on some particular project which appears to be demanded by current policy, only to be told, on its completion, that circumstances have meanwhile changed and that his work has been wasted.

The work of the administrative branch of the Ministry at headquarters is shrouded in almost complete mystery; the rare contacts made with it from outside, however, suggest that it contains some first-rate minds as dissimilar from the conventional popular press caricatures of Civil Servants as could be desired. Yet there is considerable evidence that the work of the technical branches which filters up through it into public view is delayed and distorted to a greater extent than is reasonable, and this, I suggest, is because, in really complicated technical matters, the unspecialised training of the administrator cannot confer judgment superior, or even equal, to that of the first-rate technologist. This is particularly so in Planning, where, as suggested in Chapter 2, a sound training teaches the Planner to take a synoptic view, which is, in fact, the administrator's special function. But the Planner's range of subjects, though wide, is limited; that of the administrator, *per se*, unlimited and not reinforced by experience of the practical application of detailed technical principles, which is essential.

One does not know exactly how Ministry publications on technical subjects are produced; whether they are written by technical officers, and merely edited by administrators, or if the whole work is done in partnership, Certainly the main defects which are apparent in these publications seem to be due to administrative rather than to technical error. These defects are principally in timing, in failing to adapt the requirements of administrative and legal detail sufficiently to technical requirements, and in lack of understanding of the machinery and mental climate of local government. The worst feature is undoubtedly the tardiness with which much needed publications are produced. There is also remarkable unevenness of quality in Ministry publications.

The notations for Planning Maps are examples of great technical skill, marred by unsuitable inclusion and exclusion of items for legal and administrative reasons and by gross delay in publication.

The Handbook on the Redevelopment of Central Areas is a highly technical document written in general terms, so that legal and administrative aspects hardly enter it. Though its details have been the subject of a good deal of controversy, no one has challenged the competence, and even the brilliance, of the work done on it. It was published in 1947, very late in the day in view of the great quantity of survey work recommended in it, and was stated to be the first of a series of handbooks on Planning technique which was to be published.

The Handbook on the Density of Residential Areas was published in 1952. Although I should personally disagree with a good many of the conclusions reached in this document, it nevertheless contains a large amount of useful information and reasoned bases from which to arrive at a sensible density policy. A tremendous amount of confused argument and many errors of judgment leading to bad development would have been avoided if it

had been published earlier. It could have been published earlier; the paper by Buchanan and Crompton, read at the Planning Summer School of 1950 and referred to in Chapter 16 contained a great deal of material which subsequently appeared almost unaltered in the Handbook. If these distinguished Ministry Officers felt confident enough in 1950 to give their views to the world there seems no good reason why the Handbook should not have been published at almost the same time.

Later Handbooks began to appear in 1955. Known as " Technical Memoranda " they were distributed to Local Authorities but not placed on sale to the public. They are extremely useful, and deal with such matters as space standards, the use of statistics and other aspects of Planning technique. The sad thing is that they appeared after most Local Planning Authorities had progressed a considerable way towards the completion of their development plans instead of beforehand when they would have been of the greatest value.

In 1962 and 1963 four " Planning Bulletins " appeared, the first, third and fourth dealing with different aspects of Town Centre Redevelopment, the second with residential density. Although none of these is without merit they have all appeared much too late, and none of them contains so much substance as to justify a long period of preparation.

One suspects that these delays may be chiefly due to excessive caution; the reluctance to give an official stamp to anything which might afterwards be shown to be untrue and thus to delay publication until everything has been checked, re-checked, chewed over, and discussed to the limit. This reluctance is very understandable, but to give way to it means greatly diminishing the eventual value of the publication; what Local Planning Authority staffs require is a clear lead on important matters so that they can go ahead with their work knowing the mind of the Ministry. Detailed imperfections hardly matter, but it is very serious to have to work in the dark and make extensive revisions at the last moment to accord with the style and content of Ministry requirements.

To take two other examples: the Memorandum on the Preservation of Trees and Woodland, issued in 1949, was a model of clarity, conciseness, and good sense, and must have been of very material help to Local Planning Authorities; it was obviously written by a person or persons with technical knowledge and experience. On the other hand, the Memorandum on the Siting of Houses in Country Areas, of 1950, betrayed abysmal ignorance, both of Planning principles and of local government, and sought to persuade Local Planning Authorities to pursue a policy vastly more delicately adjusted and subtle than could possibly be expected from them.

The Inspectorate comprises a body of men who perform their difficult, and often boring, duties with the most praiseworthy courtesy and impartiality. Unfortunately the great increase in the number of inquiries which have had to be held in recent years has demanded a commensurate increase in the number of inspectors. This has led to a general lowering of quality, and it is a fact, however regrettable, that a substantial proportion of inspectors are simply not sufficiently intelligent or sufficiently well trained to perform their very important duties adequately.

It is often ignorantly suggested that the whole inquiry system is a wrong one, because, since the inspectors are officers of the Ministry and the cases they preside over are connected with Planning, the Minister is therefore judge " in his own cause "; the cause being " Planning ". This is clearly absurd; the Minister is charged with the duty of securing good land Planning, and the vast majority of the inquiries dealt with by inspectors relate to whether a Local Planning Authority's proposals constitute Planning better than those of other persons. It is not a case of Planning v. non-Planning, an issue already decided by Parliament.

Sometimes it is true that, as in the case of New Towns Orders, the inquiry relates to proposals made by the Minister, but it has now been established in the courts that he is here acting in an administrative and not a judicial or quasi-judicial capacity. Since the New Towns Act authorised the development of new towns and the right to acquire land for the purpose, it is difficult to think of a tribunal competent to decide on technical grounds whether a site selected by the Minister is suitable or unsuitable, for the Minister has at his disposal virtually unlimited technical advice. Decisions have to be made by someone, and since there is no obvious reason why the Minister should be guided by any form of self-interest in selecting sites for New Towns, the right of appeal to any other tribunal, even if one could be found, seems redundant.

Inspectors merely preside over inquiries on behalf of the Minister, to whom they make a report on the evidence they have heard; the decision is made in the name of the Minister. In practice this procedure leads to a good deal of delay in relation particularly to appeals against Local Planning Authority's decisions which are the most numerous inquiries held.

One may be sure that an inspector's report is searchingly considered by a number of officers, both technical and administrative, before a decision is issued. The need for this is obvious; inspectors work more or less in isolation, and it is essential that similar decisions should be given in respect of cases where the circumstances are similar, whether the site is in Cornwall or Cumberland, so that inspectors' reports must be compared. Further, decisions must be in accordance with national Planning policy and must take account of all relevant factors, even though some of them may not have emerged at the inquiry. A good deal of consultation is, therefore, inevitable before the decision is issued.

Nevertheless, it is difficult not to think that the care taken is excessive. Practically everyone with experience of them agrees that Ministry inquiries are altogether admirable as regards the opportunities given to all parties to present their cases and the conduct of the inspectors, but slowness in issuing decisions seriously affects their usefulness. Even though justice may nearly always be done, it is often done too late to help the intending developer where time is of the essence of his activities, even though the final result may be favourable to him. It may well be that a year will elapse between his application for Planning permission and receipt of the Minister's decisions —two months for consideration by the Local Planning Authority, four months between refusal and the date of the inquiry and six months thereafter. This is a perfectly normal period even in relatively simple cases, and the delay may well wreck the developer's plans completely.

It has sometimes been suggested that inspectors should be given executive powers and should issue a decision on the spot at the end of an inquiry; this is probably going rather too far, for the reasons given, but it seems likely that, even at the cost of occasional errors and inconsistencies, justice would be better served by giving speedier decisions.

Since inspectors are technically qualified, they constitute expert tribunals, with great saving in time and temper to all concerned. Many appellants conduct their own cases and are quite ignorant of the technical issues involved; the inspector can, and often does, protect their interests by himself asking important questions which the appellant has failed to put in the course of cross-examination. Many an appellant who has arrived at an inquiry in a mood of surly defensiveness expecting to be browbeaten by a pin-striped trousered bureaucrat has gone away afterwards pleased and grateful at the treatment accorded him, and these feelings have even survived a subsequent adverse decision.

One further aspect of the Ministry's work should be specially emphasised because there is so much misunderstanding about it. This is the difficult task of deciding between various claims on land when either the Local Planning Authority concerned has failed to arrive at a decision which is acceptable to all parties or the problem involved is of such importance that the Ministry accept responsibility for it in the first instance. The Progress Report of the Ministry of Town and Country Planning has some very cogent things to say about this.

One could write a great deal about the defects of the Ministry of Housing and Local Government but to do so would involve entering into a wide and prolonged discussion of public administration. The defects of the Ministry are probably endemic in the British Civil Service and some limit must be set to the topics dealt with in this book. A superb essay entitled " The Apotheosis of the Dilettante " by Thomas Balogh in " The Establishment " (Anthony Bland, 1959), mercilessly exposes the inherent defects of a system in which " first rate unspecialised intellects " who may frequently move to different and quite unrelated departments, hold effective power; what he has to say is extremely relevant to the various ineptitudes of the Ministry of Housing and Local Government.

The kernel of the situation seems to me to be this. It is altogether right that the advice of technical men should be subject to the decision of elected representatives of the people at both Central and Local levels for this is of the essence of democracy. But it is not right or efficient for this advice to be filtered through the brains of high ranking administrative offices and subjected to a process of rejection and selection before it reaches the elected representatives. Still less is it right, as is clearly the case in the Ministry of Housing and Local Government for technical officers to be almost entirely subordinate to administrative officers. However eminent some of these are they may well have no more real knowledge of Planning than the Minister himself.

I once wrote to a senior administrative officer of the Ministry who had expressed regret at my low opinion of a decision he had made: " It isn't that I think badly of you but you obviously don't know enough about your job to do it properly ". This is a verdict which I would stand by as justifiable in respect of an alarming number of senior administrative officers. I have very little doubt that for Planning to succeed to an acceptable extent, technical Planners will everywhere have to occupy senior positions which enable them to deal directly with elected representatives.

22-3. LOCAL GOVERNMENT

Local government in this country is a mixture of one-tier, two-tier and three-tier systems. A county borough council is responsible for all local government functions within its area. In a municipal borough or urban district these functions are shared with the county council concerned, the latter being responsible principally for those which form part of a country-wide system, such as education and the construction and maintenance of classified roads, the former for those of more immediately local importance, such as housing. These are one-tier and two-tier systems respectively.

In rural districts the county council is responsible for an even wider range of activities than in municipal boroughs and urban districts—for unclassified as well as classified roads, for example, while each rural district is divided into parishes—the most ancient surviving unit of local government in this country—for each of which there is a parish council or parish meeting which has to be consulted, either legally or customarily, on numerous matters, and which still has some vestigial powers in its own right: a three-tier system with one of the tiers very weak. The table on this page shows the distribution of functions between different classes of local authorities.

Broadly, the policy of successive governments seems for some time to have been based on two assumptions: first, that services which have to be provided in many separate places over a large area and which, by their nature, require a complex organisation for their administration can best be provided by the larger authorities with resources adequate to engage numerically sufficient and efficient staff, and, second, that the size and efficiency of a local authority are somehow correlated.

The first assumption would probably be considered reasonable by nearly everyone not patently biased, although how functions can best be divided as between, say, a county council and a large municipal borough could be, and has been, debated endlessly. The second assumption is far more questionable; there are many rural district councils which perform their functions with great competence, but also, on the other hand, plenty of county and municipal boroughs whose affairs are in a state of chaos.

The population of a rural district is often as great as that of a large town; the total rate income is almost always far less. It has therefore been financially impossible hitherto for rural districts to perform the more expensive services out of their rate revenue. But there is not the slightest reason to suppose that the inhabitants of rural areas are any whit less competent, as persons, to administer their own local affairs than those of urban areas; indeed, it has been said that there is no authority so inefficient as a really bad county borough council. There is much to be said for a wholesale revision of legislative as well as of financial arrangements so as to make it possible for rural district councils to run all purely local services themselves, without

DISTRIBUTION OF THE FUNCTIONS OF LOCAL AUTHORITIES

	PROVISION OF SUPPLIES AND SERVICES	REGULATION BY INSPECTION OR BY CONTROL
COUNTY BOROUGHS · MUNICIPAL BOROUGHS · URBAN DISTRICTS · RURAL DISTRICTS	Cemeteries. Housing. Sewerage. Refuse Collection and Disposal. Street Lighting and Cleaning. Mortuaries. Water supply. Parks and Open Spaces.	Building By-laws. Food Sampling. Slum Clearance. Lodging-houses. Infectious Diseases. Suppression of Nuisances. Smoke Abatement. Watercourses, Sanitary Control. Slaughterhouses. Land Charges Registration.
URBAN DISTRICTS	Allotments. Baths, Swimming Baths and Washhouses. Unclassified Roads and Streets. Libraries and Museums. Electors, Registration.	Offensive Trades. Dairies, Workshops and Bakehouses. Petroleum Storage. Petrol Stations.
MUNICIPAL BOROUGHS	Child Welfare. Borough Magistrates.	By-laws, various. Shops. Weights and Measures.
COUNTY COUNCILS	Blind Welfare. Children: Adoption, Boarding-out and control of Employment. Education: Nursery, Primary, Secondary and Technical. School Medical Services. School Meals. Service of Youth. Hospitals, Maternity and Child Welfare. Midwives and Home Helps. Mental Health. Housing (Assistance in Rural Areas). Classified Roads. Bridges. Police. Public Assistance. Remand Homes. Tuberculosis. Venereal Disease. Smallholdings.	Registration of Births, Deaths and Marriages. Cinemas and Theatres. Racecourses. Fertilisers and Feeding-stuffs Analysis. Food and Drugs, Milk Sampling and Analysis. Nursing Homes Registration. Wild Birds Protection. Motor Vehicles and Drivers' Registration. By-laws for Good Government. Town and Country Planning.

altering the arrangements by which county councils are responsible for regional services. This should do much to freshen the bleak apathy regarding local affairs which is now so common.

Such a reform ought also, and this is much more directly connected with Planning, to reduce the friction between county councils and other authorities, which sometimes makes co-operation between them all but impossible. The smaller authorities often seem to look on the county council as a remote juggernaut unsympathetically and inefficiently administering powers which it has unscrupulously filched. The patronising attitude of county councils towards the smaller authorities and the extraordinary official jargon in which county clerks are apt to conduct correspondence with their lesser brethren lend plausibility to this view, but it is in many ways erroneous.

County councils are, on the contrary, often unwilling to undertake additional duties thrust upon them by legislation, and anxious to consult with and delegate their duties to borough and district councils to the maximum practicable extent. In any case, so many county councillors are also members of borough or district councils, and watch the interests of the latter so vigilantly at county committee meetings that it is possible at such meetings to get the impression that the officers in attendance are the only representatives of the county council, and that the members are solely concerned with watching the interests of the smaller authorities and are quite prepared to pass resolutions detrimental to the policy and prestige of the county council. This is an absurd state of affairs which has harmful effects in many fields, and in none more than in Planning, where co-operation and liaison between county and district councils are of special importance.

From consideration of the principal characteristics of the local government system it is a natural step to consideration of the kind of people who serve as members of local authorities. They are a very mixed bag, and range from capable, disinterested and public-spirited persons down to the ignorant, the prejudiced and the self-seeking. All members are elected by popular vote and it is, of course, mainly the fault of the electors if they fail to elect the most suitable of the candidates who present themselves for election; it is also, though to a somewhat less extent, the fault of the public collectively if, as too often happens, no one can be found to stand for election who is even remotely suitable. The burden of being a member of a local authority is not light; it involves attendance at a large number of meetings, many of them extremely lengthy and boring; in many areas the meetings are held during working hours, which means that a member who does an ordinary job of work as an employee must get leave of absence to attend, which may not be forthcoming, or, even if it is, may involve loss of pay, which is obviously a deterrent. Even if meetings are held in the evenings it is not everyone who has sufficient energy left after the day's work to be willing to attend them, or to make much of a contribution if he does attend.

The result is that membership of many local authorities is confined mainly to the retired, to those with independent means, and to those of the self-employed who are sufficiently efficient or fortunate to be able to spare plenty of time from their businesses. The members of a local authority, therefore,

seldom resemble a representative cross-section of the community, either as to age or to occupation; the youngish professional man and the experienced artisan, who would be of great value as members, are not often able to serve.

As a direct consequence of the restricted choice of members, the outlook of local authorities tends to be exceedingly narrow and their activities to be concentrated more upon maintaining and enhancing the prestige and power of the local authority itself than upon providing the best possible services for the community which the members are supposed to represent.

I do not propose to enter into a discussion of the possible ways in which better representation might be secured on local authorities. The present situation is not likely to be radically changed for a long time and has to be accepted; the poor quality of local authority members makes the Planner's task very much more difficult than it ought to be, and throws an undue emphasis upon his need for diplomatic skill rather than his technical ability.

Everyone concerned from the Minister downwards, lays stress at frequent intervals on the vital importance of local interest and participation in the Planning process, and upon the value of advice based upon local knowledge in formulating Planning proposals. Unfortunately, a local authority's expressed views about any given Planning problem are, in a staggering proportion of cases, so manifestly full of bias as to be virtually useless, and quite often are demonstrably in no way genuinely representative of local opinion.

What then, of the county councils? Are they any more competent than the smaller local authorities to administer Planning control? On the whole they seem to be; their very functions compel them to take a somewhat wider view; the very much larger population from which members are drawn tends towards a slightly higher level of competence, and every county member on a Planning committee frequently has to take a share in making decisions affecting areas wider than his own home town or district, which helps to develop a broader outlook. The county member need never lack information and advice about local matters, but when trying to decide upon a policy in respect of some matter of county-wide application the glaring inconsistency between opinion in different parts of the county often forces him to discount local views, and to decide the case on its merits, assisted by the advice of county officers.

The average county council is not an ideal Planning agency, but at least it gets away from the parish pump; there are always several men and women of really high intelligence and integrity among the members, and with the possible exceptions of substituting regional-cum-local Planning control, or of creating *ad hoc* Planning bodies with members chosen for their knowledge and experience, on the lines suggested later in this chapter, both of which are fairly revolutionary proposals, they are the only possible bodies to do the job.

Not much has so far been said about county borough councils. As Planning authorities they are self-sufficient, except that their Development Plans and the development which they themselves initiate are subject to ministerial scrutiny. They vary enormously in competence and character. Most of them suffer to a considerable extent from parochialism, partially offset, as in the case of the counties, by the comparatively wide choice of candidates for membership.

Local government officers have no powers and can give no decisions, but their influence is so great that, in order to complete the picture, they must be discussed briefly at this stage.

The function of an officer is to *advise;* on many matters his advice must necessarily be the last word. A council which rejected the advice of its engineer on road surfaces or sewer capacities or of its clerk on the interpretation of by-laws would be courting disaster, and such things seldom happen; but in other matters, where there is room for considerable divergence of opinion, the officer's position is very different.

Planning is a subject in which there is room for endless debate, and this creates an extremely difficult problem. Planning is mainly concerned with every-day things—houses, shops, roads and playing-fields, and as regards those aspects of such things with which Planning is particularly concerned there is seldom any very abstruse technical detail involved. The subject-matter lies within the experience of the lay member; he thinks he knows all about it and tends to be scornful of technical advice, which he regards as elaborate theorising. What he usually fails to realise is that the art of Planning lies in establishing satisfactory spatial and other relationships between these simple ingredients, that this is a complicated, though not a mysterious, business, and that he doesn't know as much as he thinks.

Though he would have no idea how to calculate the size of sewer required to serve a given number of houses, he feels quite competent to decide whether two shops should be permitted among a row of houses, although the latter is often the more difficult problem. He is at home when dealing with purely human, every-day problems, wisely refrains from intervening in the purely technical, and flounders hopelessly over a problem combining the two. It is most illuminating to listen to a group of members discussing with wisdom and human understanding the choice of tenants for a dozen newly completed houses, and, ten minutes later, considering some Planning applications with as much foolishness and lack of understanding.

In such matters, at all levels of local government, the quality of the officer makes a tremendous difference. Theoretically, he should give only facts to his members and direct deductions therefrom, and his purely personal opinions should be left entirely unexpressed, from which it follows that he takes no part in making policy. Yet this is seldom possible. Members come and go at far more frequent intervals than senior officers, and often they rely upon their officers to secure continuity of policy, to give them the benefit of past experience on details, and to assist them positively in formulating policy.

How do local government officers measure up to these requirements? Very variously, as might be expected.

The smaller authorities often pay badly, sometimes because of inability to do otherwise, sometimes in a short-sighted attempt to keep the expenditure of rate-income to a minimum, but occasionally because they consider competent advice unnecessary, and only want underlings. They generally get service in proportion to what they pay for it; among chief officers are to be found timid

yes-men who hardly dare to put their signatures to letters, and are utterly dominated by their members; tyrants who rule their councils with rods of iron; ignoramuses; colourless but reasonably competent 9 a.m. to 5 p.m.-ers; and men of the very highest intelligence and integrity. In almost every county there are chief officers of local authorities who fall within each of these categories, and this greatly complicates consideration of the delegation of Planning control functions.

There is one fault to which the staffs of the smaller local authorities are very prone; in a deplorably large number of cases, and for quite insufficient reasons, they seem to delight in increasing rather than minimising the friction between local authority and county council; this increases the unfortunate effects upon Planning control already described.

The staffs of the larger authorities are of rather different calibre. Although the 9 a.m. to 5 p.m.-ers are numerically strong, the more bizarrely inefficient characters to be found among the small authorities are little in evidence, and fortunately the competent and responsible are many. The affairs of the larger authority are indeed so complicated that it is virtually compelled to pay for a proper staff.

Every local authority from parish council to county council, is concerned with the Planning process and participates in it. The position of the parish councils, however, is rather different from the remainder, and their direct participation more limited; almost the only development which they initiate is the acquisition and putting into use of allotments, burial grounds and playing-fields. In order to secure government loans for these purposes they have to obtain the agreement of the county council as local Planning authority. They are vitally concerned with housing, but it is not their function to provide it, but that of the rural district council. The rural district council frequently consults the parish councils regarding suitable sites for housing, but by no means always.

Rural district councils, urban district councils, and municipal borough councils are all concerned with Planning in at least three different ways:

(1) Their own development activities, the most important of which is housing, require the approval of the county council, not only as regards choice of site, but as to layout, siting, density and external appearance of the buildings. The more efficiently the local authority prepares its development proposals and the more it is prepared to co-operate with the county council in complying with the overall Planning interest the less is delay likely to occur, the less reason will there be to complain of county council " interference ", and the more is the county council likely to be encouraged to delegate powers to district councils.

(2) In most counties some system of partial delegation to borough and district councils of development control functions in relation to private development exists, and where this is so these authorities have a real and important contribution to make to Planning; again, genuine efforts to co-operate are likely to have the very practical result of securing relatively speedy determination of applications

for Planning permission, and, even more important, of the right decision being given in a high proportion of cases.

(3) By assisting in the compilation of survey data and during the consultation which the county council is statutorily obliged to undertake with borough and district councils regarding the contents of its Development Plan, the latter, if they so wish, are able to play a direct and important part in influencing the Planning policy for their areas. Indeed, there is no limit to what they can do in this way; it is improbable that any county council would fail to welcome and make the fullest use of any information or constructive proposals, competently presented, which a local authority supplied. The fact that the 1947 Act makes the county councils the responsible authorities for Planning purposes in order to secure reasonably large Planning units in no way precludes the boroughs and districts from initiating any amount of positive Planning even as regards the " bigger picture ". As regards the " smaller picture " they will in any case be responsible for the carrying out of such development to implement the Plan as is not undertaken by private enterprise, and the bigger the share they have in Planning it the better, subject to the county council vetting their proposals in order to test their intrinsic soundness and to ensure conformity with the plan for the county as a whole.

The county councils and county borough councils, as well as being the Local Planning Authorities for their areas, also initiate a great deal of development, and it is of the greatest importance that, in order to foster and maintain public confidence in these authorities, they should, apart altogether from ministerial control over their activities, do their utmost to ensure that these conform to Planning requirements. It should not be a case of " don't do as I do, do as I say ", and this is one of the tougher problems confronting Planning officers, who often find that their colleagues in other departments of the same authority provide them with their worst headaches.

The Town and Country Planning (Authorisation of Delegation) Regulations, 1947, were extremely simple, and merely said that county councils and joint boards might, with the consent of the Minister, enter into agreements with the councils of any county district in their areas to delegate any of their functions under Part 3 of the Town and Country Planning Act, 1947, upon terms set out in the agreement and approved by the Minister. Two terms have to be included in any such agreement, namely:

(1) That the delegation may be determined or varied by agreement between the parties with the consent of the Minister and shall terminate if the Minister withdraws his consent to the delegation, and

(2) That any document issued by a district council (such as a notification of a decision to an applicant regarding a development application) shall state that the functions exercised are on behalf of the Local Planning authority.

It would be laborious and somewhat fruitless to attempt to tabulate the details of delegation agreements entered into between county councils and borough and district councils in pursuance of the Authorisation of Delegation Regulations. By far the majority combine a limited degree of direct delegation subject to a power of veto by the county council, with representation of the district councils on area sub-committees of the County Planning Committee.

The principal variations in this arrangement are those where, on each area sub-committee, the county members are in a majority and those where they are in a minority.

In the former case the arrangement operates to secure a reasonable decentralisation and division of work between members of the county Planning committee combined with the adequate representation of local views. In the latter case administration becomes extremely cumbersome at times, since the county council normally thinks it necessary to keep the situation under control by providing that, in the event of a decision being given by an area sub-committee on an important matter which is not in conformity with the recommendation of the County Planning Officer, it shall be referred to the County Planning Committee itself for final decision.

The cumbersomeness is increased by the usual arrangement that the borough or district's views on every application are sent to the county council before any sub-committee of the county council considers it.

As regards extent of delegation, one arrangement is that the district council's views are sent to the county council with each application and that the latter may determine the application in accordance with the views it has expressed unless, within a stated period, the county council (which normally authorises its Planning Officer to take action on its behalf) reserves the application to determine itself, either centrally or through the agency of an area sub-committee.

In some counties the arrangement is that the most trivial cases may be determined by the district council at their own unfettered discretion, that others slightly more important may be decided by them, provided the County Planning Officer is in agreement with the proposed decision, and that only the most important are necessarily determined by the county council. This arrangement is worked either by the County Planning Officer being authorised to inform the district council within which category he considers a particular application falls or by a somewhat elaborate description in the deed of delegation of the kinds of case of which each category is composed. The former is much the better arrangement, since it is extremely difficult to define categories clearly and concisely, and, even if this difficult feat is accomplished, the district councils have a strong tendency to stretch the definitions so as to bring an unduly large proportion of cases within the category which they can determine at their discretion.

The functioning of area sub-committees—and this seems to be a country-wide phenomenon—is greatly prejudiced by the members of borough and district councils who sit on them regarding themselves as delegates of their councils, pledged to press the views of that council to the exclusion of almost every other consideration, and not as co-opted members of a county sub-committee placed upon it to give the benefit of their local knowledge and experience in the interests of the work of the sub-committee as a whole.

Delegation seldom works really well because it is rare for delegate authorities to employ, for advice on their Planning functions, officers who possess *both* of two essential attributes: a Planning qualification combined with appropriate experience and a status which enables them to report direct to the relevant committee. It is still lamentably common for quite large delegate authorities to rely for their Planning advice upon their architect, engineer or surveyor, who, in turn, relies solely upon Building inspectors to do the donkey work of investigating and reporting upon applications for Planning permission. If a Chartered Town Planner is employed he is never of Chief Officer rank but merely does the donkey work; his views may be rejected entirely by his Chief Officer, and he may in fact have no direct contact at all with the committee.

No attempt has ever been made by the Ministry to improve this situation, and indeed it was materially worsened by Henry Brooke towards the end of his long and conspicuously unsuccessful tenure of the Ministry of Housing and Local Government.

By the Town and Country Planning (Delegation) Regulations of November, 1959, District Councils with a population of 60,000 or more were given the right to claim virtually complete delegation of Development Control functions subject to obtaining the agreement of the County Council before giving permission to any development not in accord with the Development Plan. This radical change was not accompanied by any condition that authorities claiming such powers should employ a Chartered Town Planner with Chief Officer status, which one would think a reasonable and minimum safeguard to maintain standards of control.

21-4. THE ROLE OF *AD HOC* BODIES IN PLANNING

Opinions differ widely as to the merits of *ad hoc* bodies; the B.B.C., the National Coal Board, the Tennessee Valley Authority and others have all had their detractors as well as their advocates. It is not intended here to enter into a detailed discussion of the usefulness of the *ad hoc* body in general but to consider the need for it to be employed for Planning purposes in this country at the present time, and to examine briefly the working of those at present operating in the field of Planning.

An *ad hoc* body, for the purposes of this chapter, may be defined as one set up by Government authority to deal specifically with a particular task or tasks of defined scope for the performance of which the Government has statutory responsibility.

Members of such bodies in this country are not always directly elected by popular vote, although some at least of them may be, and often are, nominated by interested local authorities, sometimes from among their members, sometimes as local residents with special knowledge of the problems involved. They are responsible not directly to the people but to the Minister responsible for the matters they deal with, who is, of course, responsible to the Government, which is responsible to Parliament, which, in turn, is responsible to the people.

The mere expression of these facts in words emphasises the somewhat remote nature of the popular control which can be exercised upon the activities of *ad hoc* bodies and it is this which has primarily led to such wide criticism of them as undemocratic. It is not easy to come to a definite and unbiased conclusion on this subject. It is true that eternal vigilance is the price of liberty, and that vigilance becomes less and less easy to exercise as responsibility becomes more remote from the directly elected local representative; at the same time, in a troubled world, democratic government can ill afford to be inefficient if it is to survive. The number of new matters which, in a civilisation becoming progressively more complicated, must inevitably become the subject of public control, necessitate control more efficient and knowledgeable than can possibly be forthcoming from the mass of, on the whole, not very distinguished amateurs who make up the membership of our local authorities.

At all events, if *ad hoc* bodies are to be used for Planning purposes it is in the highest degree desirable that the Minister of Housing and Local Government should appoint to them persons of real ability with interest in and some knowledge (not necessarily or even preferably detailed technical knowledge) of the work to be done, and that the Ministry should be highly sensitive to vigorously expressed public opinion.

Readers who wish to pursue further the subject of reconciling efficiency with democracy are urged to read Bertrand Russell's series of Reith Lectures "Authority and the Individual" (George Allen and Unwin, 6s.).

New Town Development Corporations

The Barlow Report on the Distribution of the Industrial Population suggested that decentralisation of population and industry in the form of, *inter alia*, satellite towns, should be considered, and in Sir Patrick Abercrombie's Greater London Plan of 1944 no fewer than ten New Town sites were put forward. These fruits of Ebenezer Howard's teachings paved the way for the setting up of a New Towns Committee. This, appropriately enough, was under the chairmanship of Lord Reith, who, during his all too brief tenure of office in the wartime Coalition Government, had been almost alone in perceiving and urging the need for early and detailed examination of the Planning problems of post-war development and redevelopment, so that building could begin without delay after the war in accordance with pre-arranged plans. He had been responsible for setting up the Scott and Uthwatt committees.

The New Towns Committee was set up in October, 1945, with the following terms of reference :

"To consider the general questions of the establishment, development, organisation and administration that will arise in the promotion of New Towns in furtherance of a policy of Planned decentralisation from congested urban areas; and in accordance therewith to suggest guiding principles on which such Towns should be established and developed as self-contained and balanced communities for work and living".

By March, 1946, it had produced an Interim Report (Cmd. 6759). This contained recommendations concerning the appropriate type of agency for the creation of New Towns, the establishment of a Central Advisory Commission, ownership of New Town sites, and finance.

In April, 1946, a Second Interim Report followed, and this dealt principally with powers for the acquisition of land, speed of construction desirable, and the local government status of new towns.

By July, 1946, the Final Report had been issued, and in this the emphasis was on the technical rather than the financial or administrative aspects of New Town building. Together the three documents constitute an invaluable body of informed opinion produced with remarkable speed, but, even so, legislation outstripped them, for the New Towns Act received the Royal Assent on 1st August, 1946, having been introduced to Parliament as a Bill on 17th April.

The main provisions of the Act are:

1. The Minister of Town and Country Planning (now the Minister of Housing and Local Government) may make an order designating an area as the site of a New Town. (Section 1.)

2. The Minister shall establish a Development Corporation for the purposes of the development of each New Town, the Development Corporation having powers " generally to do anything necessary or expedient for the purposes of the New Town or for purposes incidental thereto ". (Section 2.)

3. The Development Corporation shall submit various proposals for the development of land within the designated area to the Minister, who, after consultation with the local Planning authority, may approve such proposals either with or without modification. (Section 3.)

4. The Development Corporation may acquire, either by agreement or by C.P.O. approved by the Minister, any land within the designated area, or outside that area if required for purposes connected with the development of the New Town. (Section 4.)

5. The Development Corporation may dispose of land which they have acquired for the purposes of development of the New Town. (Section 5.)

6. The Development Corporation shall be deemed to be a housing association within the meaning of the Housing Act, 1936, and the Minister of Health (now the Minister of Housing and Local Government) may pay annual sums to the Development Corporation as if they were a normal local authority. (Section 8.)

7. Certain of the provisions of the Public Health Act, 1936 (relating to sewerage and sewage disposal, etc.), may be exercised by the Development Corporation consequent upon the Minister of Health (now the Minister of Housing and Local Government) making an order to this effect on application by the Development Corporation. (Section 9.)

8. The Minister may make grants to the Development Corporation for the purpose of defraying expenditure to capital account, including the provision of working capital, repayable on terms approved by the Treasury. Grants may also be made to defray other expenditure.

It is to be noted that: " It shall be a condition of the making of advances to a Development Corporation that the proposals for development submitted to the Minister under Section 3 . . . shall be approved by the Minister with the concurrence of the Treasury as being likely to secure for the Corporation a return which is reasonable, having regard to all the circumstances when compared with the cost of carrying out those proposals." (Section 12.)

9. The Minister may, by order, wind up a Development Corporation where he is satisfied that they have substantially achieved the purposes for which they were set up. The undertakings of a Development Corporation may by order thereafter be transferred to a local authority within which the designated area of the New Town lies. (Section 15.)

10. The Act also applies, with certain modifications, to Scotland.

The Designation Orders for the first New Town under the New Towns Act were made in September, 1946 (Hemel Hempstead), and November, 1946 (Stevenage), followed by Crawley (January, 1947), Harlow (March, 1947), Aycliffe (April, 1947), and East Kilbride (May, 1947). Later orders were made for areas at Bracknell, Basildon, Glenrothes, Peterlee, Cwmbran, Welwyn, Hatfield and Corby. In the case of most of the earlier mentioned, litigation delayed the setting up of the requisite Development Corporations and the commencement of their work, but Planning consultants had been appointed to prepare draft plans for these towns and were able to proceed on this work, which later became the basis of the work of the Development Corporations themselves.

Stevenage was selected as a pioneer study by the Ministry of Town and Country Planning; surveys and a master plan were prepared under the direction of Gordon Stephenson, who was the Chief Planning Officer (Technique) to the Ministry. Unhappily the time gained by this pioneer work was largely lost by the subsequent litigation on the Designation Order, which was taken to the House of Lords.

The initiative in selecting a New Town site may be exercised by the Minister in dealing with a special Planning problem not confined to the area of a single Local Planning Authority, e.g., the need to decentralise industry and population from London; by a county council as part of its Development Plan; or by a county borough hard pressed for land for new development or already too large and congested to be able satisfactorily to accommodate on its periphery population displaced by redevelopment, but the statutory process of designating land as a New Town site is the responsibility of the Minister of Housing and Local Government.

Designation which makes the land concerned liable to compulsory purchase for New Town purposes, involves making a draft order, and, if objections are received and not resolved, the holding of a public inquiry by the Minister to hear objections.

This inquiry, it has now been established, is held by the Minister in an administrative, not in a judicial or quasi-judicial capacity. After the first designation inquiry had been held in relation to Stevenage, objectors sought to have the Designation Order quashed on the grounds that the Minister had made up his mind about the objections before the inquiry was held and was therefore incapable of considering them fairly. The objectors were upheld in the High Court, but the decision was reversed by the Court of Appeal and the reversal affirmed by the House of Lords. Similar attempts were unsuccessful in the cases of Hemel Hempstead and Crawley.

Filibustering attempts to frustrate the will of Parliament on technicalities are seldom edifying, and the time taken up by litigation in these cases sadly hampered the bold attempt to tackle speedily one of the most urgent problems of post-war development which the passing of the New Towns Act represented.

When a Designation Order has been made the Minister sets up a Development Corporation; before doing so he must consult all interested local authorities, including those within whose areas the designated site lies and those from which population and/or industry is to be moved to the new town. The Corporation may consist of not more than nine members, including chairman and vice-chairman, all of whom are paid and the Minister must consider the appointment of at least one member who lives in or has special knowledge of the locality.

The organisations of the New Towns Corporations so far set up naturally vary considerably in detail, but there is a general similarity between all.

Each corporation has a general manager or chief executive officer, whose background may be administrative, legal, technical or military, and most have a chief architect who may or may not be responsible for the Planning of the town.

It has been usual for a New Town Corporation to commission the preparation of a master Plan or outline, equivalent to the Town Map stage of the Development Plan for an existing town, by an independent consultant during the first months of its life while it has been principally engaged in recruiting staff and fitting up offices, and the consultant has often been retained permanently to advise on the implementation of the Plan and/or to prepare detailed Plans for a portion of it. Other chief officers usually employed are: engineer, finance officer, estates officer, legal and administrative officer, or solicitor and public relations or social development officer. Landscape architects may also and are likely to be increasingly required on a full-time or consulting basis.

It has been generally recognised that one of the greatest dangers in building a New Town is that there may be insufficient diversity in the design of layouts and buildings because of the whole of the work being done by a comparatively small staff of Planners and architects, who, however gifted they may be, are unlikely to have a repertoire sufficiently extensive to avoid undue repetition, and to ensure liveliness.

To avoid this it is general practice for a New Town Corporation to invite selected firms of private architects each to design a portion of the town or of the buildings for a portion of it, subject to compliance with general requirements to ensure harmony between designs.

Sir Ernest Gowers, the distinguished author of "Plain Words" and Chairman of the Harlow Development Corporation, had some very plain words to say in the Corporation's report for the year ending 31st March, 1950. They have become famous, but the message they deliver is so striking that one can hardly do better than to quote them:

"Although the Corporation is given by statute the task of building the New Town, it is subject to all existing authorities who have any control over the various activities that go to building a town. In this respect its position hardly differs from that of a private developer. The County Council are responsible for roads and surface water drainage, education and certain health services. The District Council's building by-laws must be observed and that Council have statutory powers in respect of sewerage, open spaces, and sometimes water. The Parish Council are the street lighting authority. The Ministry of Health (now the Ministry of Housing and Local Government) exercise supervision over the planning and cost of houses and their approval is required to all water and sewerage schemes. The Board of Trade control the location of industry. The Ministries of Labour and Works have their hand on labour and materials.

"This multiplication of controls may be inevitable in present circumstances. To some extent it certainly is. For instance, the Corporation must be closely concerned with the provision, siting and design of schools, but no one would suggest that any authority but the Education Authority should carry the ultimate responsibility for education. Yet it may be doubted whether this great array of independent authorities or its consequences to the taxpayer are generally realised; there are few who see the picture as a whole. The Crawley Development Corporation referred to this subject in their Annual Report for 1948-49, and gave, in Appendix E, two lists, one of the 'consultations and approvals required for the execution of plans' and the other of 'authorities whose plans and projects have to be co-ordinated with those of the Corporation'. Of the contents of these formidable catalogues the Crawley Corporation said with restraint, 'they consume a great deal of time and effort'. The Harlow Corporation would be more disposed to say that they create machinery which is in some respects cumbrous almost past belief and which produces in profusion officials doing one after another work that one official could well have been trusted to do by himself. Development Corporations have too many masters.

"They have, moreover, their own particular master, the Ministry of Town and Country Planning (now the Ministry of Housing and Local Government). It is, of course, right and proper that that Ministry should exercise supervisory powers over Development Corporations. The Corporations are spending public money, and a Minister must be able to satisfy Parliament that the money is being spent wisely. The Act that created Development Corporations expressly provided that certain of their activities need approval by the Minister. But from the fact that it placed on statutory Corporations the direct responsibility for building new towns, Parliament must be presumed to have intended that the degree of Departmental control must be different from what it would have been if the Department had been directly responsible for the enterprise. Control cannot, of course, be exercised wholly by the Minister himself; it must be mostly delegated to his officials. The Corporation wishes to put on record that, in its opinion, its progress has been unnecessarily delayed and its expenses unnecessarily swollen by prolonged scrutiny on the part of Ministry officials of matters of detail which might reasonably have been left to the Corporation's discretion. As has been recorded in this report, the Corporation's proposals for the development of part of the Mark Hall neighbourhood were both with the Ministry for nearly five months before being approved and the Corporation has only just received approval (9th May, 1950) of a plan for the development of the East Industrial Estate submitted to the Ministry on the 1st December, 1949. Delays like these can cost money in two ways. So far as they may be caused by examination of detail of no great importance they mean that the time of Departmental staff is being wasted, and so far as they impose an unnecessarily long gap between the completion of a plan and starting to carry it out, they mean that staff which is ready to get on with the job cannot do so except by anticipating approval, and so risking a waste of time and labour if approval should eventually not be given. In the two cases referred to, the five months' thought devoted by the officials of the Ministry to each project ended in acceptance of both, subject to slight modifications which effected a reduction of some £3,000 in programmes estimated to cost nearly two million pounds.

" The Corporation recognises, of course, that there are two sides to this question. The problem of how much control it is proper for a Government Department to exercise over a statutory board is exceedingly difficult, and no generally accepted solution of it has yet been found. Just as there have been occasions when the Corporation felt that officials of the Minister were unwarrantably interfering with what was the Corporation's proper business, so, no doubt, there have been others when those officials felt that the Corporation was claiming a degree of independence inconsistent with their own responsibilities.

" What can hardly be questioned is that the tangled thicket of controls and overlapping duties depicted in the Crawley Corporation's Appendix contains much that serves no useful purpose, and needs to be drastically pruned if Development Corporations are to be given a chance to build new towns in reasonable time and at reasonable cost."

The Minister, in his foreword to the volume, published in November, 1950, of which this report is part, stated that many of the delays and difficulties mentioned in it had been overcome and that this should become fully evident in 1951. Some improvement has certainly been made inasmuch as the Ministry of Town and Country Planning has successively become the Ministry of Local Government and Planning and the Ministry of Housing and Local Government, and has absorbed the housing functions of the Ministry of Health. This, in itself, should simplify and shorten consultation. The whole trend of housing and Planning administration is, furthermore, towards permitting a greater degree of local autonomy in matters of detail.

The section of the Progress Report by the Ministry of Local Government and Planning on the Work of the Ministry of Town and Country Planning (Cmd. 8204) states (pages 132 and 133) :

" As a Corporation is not a Local Planning Authority, it would, in the absence of special provision, have to seek the Planning Authority's permission for all development, as well as the Minister's approval under Section 3 (1) of the New Towns Act; but this would be a duplication, since the Minister himself is required by statute to consult the Local Planning Authority before giving his approval. The Act, therefore, empowers the Minister to make a special development order freeing from the need for the authority's consent any development in a New Town area which the Minister has approved, and an order providing for this came into operation on 1st March, 1950. (This was the Town and Country Planning (New Towns Special Development) Order, 1950 (S.I. 1950, No. 152).) Previously, Development Corporations did, in fact, have to obtain dual consents, but, as the preliminary period was largely devoted to Survey and Planning, and the scale of development was small, this was not very irksome."

Surely some sharp break with traditional practice is demanded here, for observe the inherent absurdity of part of the above statement. Since a corporation is not a democratically elected body it cannot be a Local Planning Authority, and would ordinarily have to seek permission for its development from the Local Planning Authority, so the Minister, whose permission also has to be obtained, makes a Development Order dispensing with the necessity for the Local Planning Authority's consent to be obtained, leaving as the last slender thread of direct democratic control the Minister's obligation to consult (but not to follow the advice of) the Local Planning Authority regarding the Corporation's development.

If the principle of developing a New Town through the agency of an *ad hoc* body is accepted there seems to be no real objection to that body doing the job on its own and in its own way, subject to Ministerial approval of the Master Plan, agreement with outside bodies regarding aspects of the Plan, such as education and main roads, which have more than local effect, a limitation on total annual expenditure and power for the Minister to intervene if anything seriously goes wrong.

To make a Development Corporation subject to local building and street by-laws is hardly short of fantastic; many county councils, for example, which are the highway authorities in rural areas, have extremely rigid and unimaginative ideas about the appropriate widths for minor residential roads.

Since the members of the New Town Corporations are selected, and, in many cases at least, semi-expert persons, and since they are able to employ, and in fact, have employed, the most skilled professional assistance available, there seems to be no good reason for subjecting them to detailed control in any aspects of their development.

One strange anomaly in the staffing of Development Corporations must be noted. The general practice has been to appoint a Chief Architect *and* Planner for each New Town, thus suggesting something that it is to be hoped that the reader who has absorbed Parts I and II of this book will readily detect as a fallacy, namely that Town Planning is a kind of extension of architecture. In fact, of course, enormous quantities of work need to be done on the design of a New Town before architectural considerations begin to assume appreciable, still less dominant, importance. It is typical of the lack of logic and clarity in evolving Planning organisations that this should not have been recognised in setting up New Town staffs. Even though the Chief Architect/Planners who have actually been appointed have mostly been able and distinguished people it is stretching the capacities of anyone man to expect him to be responsible both for the land use Planning and much of the architecture of a New Town.

A further confusion has appeared. The Development Corporation for the recently designated New Town of Dawley, in Shropshire evidently realised that the process of preparing a Master Plan is logically separable from the working up of that Plan in detail. It therefore advertised for a Consultant Planner to prepare a Master Plan but, from a wide field of applicants, selected an Architect who is not a Chartered Town Planner! That the choice of the particular person selected may well have been a good one does not justify the extraordinary confusion of thought implied.

A new *ad hoc* body connected with Planning came into existence with the establishment of the Commission for New Towns in October, 1961. The function of this body, under powers conferred by the New Towns Act, 1959 is to take over and administer the assets of Development Corporations as and when these are dissolved on substantial achievement of the objects for which they were established.

The Town Development Act, 1952

Although, strictly speaking, this Act does not give rise to the creation of any *ad hoc* body, in the ordinary sense of the word, it is appropriate to deal with it at this point, because it allegedly provides a mechanism to supplement that of the New Towns Act.

The Conservative Government elected in 1951 considered, reasonably enough, that there was a need to facilitate the Planned expansion of towns where the expansion envisaged was substantial but not great enough to justify the use of Development Corporations under the New Towns Act.

The main purpose of the Act was stated to be to secure development in non-county boroughs, urban and rural districts so as to relieve congestion elsewhere.

Districts in which such development is to take place are called " receiving districts ". Exchequer grants are payable towards the expenses incurred by a receiving district in the course of carrying out town development on a substantial scale. (" Substantial " is not defined.)

The Act's powers can be used not only to relieve congestion in London, or in a county borough, but also in a county district in an area of continuous development adjacent to London or any other large centre of population, or in a county district outside the county in which the development is to take place.

Not only are exchequer grants payable, but contributions may be made, subject to Ministerial approval, by any local authority which has benefited by such development, and it may make such contribution conditional upon

securing that it does, in fact, get the relief from congestion by means of the proposed development which is intended.

A receiving district, may acquire compulsorily any land required in connection with development before or after a Development Plan for such land has become operative, and in the latter case may do so even if the land is not designated in the Plan as liable to compulsory purchase.

Town development does not necessarily have to be carried out by the receiving authority; the exporting authority may participate, and exchequer grants be made to it. Contributions may also be made to a participating authority by any local authorities which benefit by the development undertaken by it. The Minister may, on application by two or more authorities, set up a joint body to participate in Town Development on their behalf.

The Minister in introducing the Town Development Act to the House of Commons as a Bill said that he did not anticipate that its powers would be used in any large number of cases. Indeed they have not. The results of the Act have so far been miserably disappointing. This is probably mainly because receiving authorities have been apprehensive that an undue share of the costs of development, beyond their capacity to bear, may fall upon them. The lack of any powers (for this is no more than an enabling Act) to bring about Town Development schemes in the absence of agreement on the part of receiving authorities is also a serious weakness.

This situation strikes at the roots of real Regional Planning, the essence of which is that towns should be expanded, as regards population and/or industry, in accordance with their physical, economic and social ability to do so, rather than as the result of the outcome of haggling between authorities.

The National Parks Commission and Associated Bodies

The National Parks and Access to the Countryside Act, 1949, is a complicated measure designed to secure important but somewhat vaguely defined objects, to which end it creates a highly elaborate administrative structure operated mainly under the powers of the Town and Country Planning Act, 1947, as extended by the National Parks Act.

The objects of the Act are fivefold:

(1) To establish National Parks. These are extensive tracts of country which, because of their natural beauty and the opportunities they afford, by reason both of their character and position, are especially suitable for open-air recreation. It is the duty of the National Parks Commission to select and designate suitable areas for National Parks and, this having been done, to preserve their natural beauty and encourage open-air recreation and the study of nature within them.

(2) To confer on the Nature Conservancy and local authorities powers for the establishment of nature reserves, which are areas managed for the purpose of providing opportunities for studying and preserving wild native plant and animal life and geological and physiographical features of special interest.

(3) To record, create, maintain and improve public footpaths.

(4) To secure public access to open country.

(5) To preserve and enhance natural beauty in other ways, e.g., by the designation of areas of outstanding natural beauty other than National Parks.

The machinery designed to attain these objects is as follows :

(a) *The National Parks Commission* is principally an advisory body appointed by the Minister of Housing and Local Government. As already noted, it has the duty of selecting and designating National Park areas. When the Commission has made a Designation Order the usual opportunities are afforded to objectors and the Minister must hold an inquiry if objections are made.

After a Designation Order has been confirmed, powers of control over the National Park become the responsibility of a special Planning committee or sub-committee of the Local Planning Authority or of a Joint Board, which will be discussed shortly, the National Parks Commission's role being confined to encouragement and exhortation as regards both general policy and the handling of any special problems which may arise.

The Commission has power to designate areas of outstanding natural beauty, and the Local Planning Authorities concerned must consult the Commission regarding the Planning control exercised in such areas; in fact, they are treated in much the same way as National Parks, except that no separate Planning committee has to be set up, and the powers to provide special facilities do not apply to them. These Local Planning authorities have, of course, a right to object or to make representations regarding the designation proposals of the Commission.

The selection and establishment of long distance footpaths is the responsibility of the Commission, subject to the approval of the Minister, after which their maintenance is the responsibility of the local authorities concerned, as is also the creation of any new lengths of path required to make the route continuous.

Finally, the Commission has general advisory powers even outside the National Parks or areas of outstanding national beauty: it may be consulted by the Minister, by Local Planning Authorities, or by preservation societies concerning problems of rural land use, may, on its own initiative, appear at local inquiries and give evidence, or may bring to the attention of the Minister or of Local Planning Authorities the effect on natural beauty of development likely to be prejudicial to it.

(b) *Local Planning Authorities* have a variety of duties under the Act at least as extensive as those of the Commission. As regards National Parks, if the park is within the area of a single Local Planning Authority it must set up a special Planning Committee or sub-committee to deal with the area of the park, a wise provision to ensure adequate consideration of National Park affairs. One-third of the members of such a committee are nominated by the Minister after consultation with the National Parks Commission. Most National Parks are likely to be within the areas of two or more Local Planning Authorities, and where this is so a Joint Planning Board must be established, unless a case can be made out for the expediency of each Local Planning

Authority running its own section of the park, with a Joint Advisory Committee (also with one-third of its members nominated by the Minister) to co-ordinate their work. This fantastic arrangement has unfortunately, as a result of local political pressure, been adopted for some National Parks.

The idea of a National Park administered by, perhaps, three or four Local Planning Authorities, a Joint Advisory Committee, and the National Parks Commission, with the Minister intervening from time to time, is so awful that one is surprised that it was ever suggested, let alone used.

One-third of the members of a Joint Planning Board, or, if administration is left to individual Local Planning Authorities, of their special Planning Committees, must be nominated by the Minister, as in the case of a National Park lying wholly within the area of one Local Planning Authority.

The duties of the special committees or sub-committees of Local Planning Authorities include the preparation of Development Plans under the Town and Country Planning Act, 1947, for National Parks, and the control of development within the parks, in consultation with the Commission, under the powers of the same Act. It should be noted, in this connection, that the designation of land as a National Park does not mean that the work and other activities which previously went on it and the necessary development in connection with such activities cease, but only that special steps for its preservation and enjoyment by the public are taken.

Within twelve months of a National Park being designated, the Local Planning Authority or Joint Board concerned must formulate and notify to the Commission its proposals for the action to be taken to preserve and enhance the natural beauty of the park and to promote its enjoyment by the public during the following year, and this procedure is to be repeated annually, the period being related to the financial year of the authority. The proposals must specify the action to be taken both by the authority itself and by other parties.

Any recommendations made by the Commission with which the authority does not agree are to be made the subject of consultation with the Commission.

The proposals may include the provision of accommodation, meals and refreshments, including alcohol, camping sites and parking places, and the improvement of waterways for sailing, boating, bathing or fishing.

As already noted, Local Planning Authorities are responsible for the administration of areas of outstanding national beauty outside National Parks, subject to consultation with the Commission.

All Local Planning Authorities, other than county borough councils, are required, within three years of the 16th December, 1949 to carry out a survey of the open country in their areas to decide what rights of access to it should be provided and to give public notice of the action taken. The Minister must consider representations made by any person or body that further action is necessary and may direct the Local Planning Authority to take such action.

" Open country " means land which is predominantly mountain, moorland, heath, downland, etc. Rights of access to land may be provided by agreement with the owner, or, failing this, by making an access order; in either case the Minister's agreement is required. Compensation is payable for injurious affection caused by the making of an access order, but only after five years has elapsed, so that the effect of the order on the value of the land can be accurately assessed. Local Planning Authorities may also, in appropriate cases, buy " open country " by agreement or compulsorily. The Minister may exercise similar powers in the case of open country within a National Park or may arrange for the Ministry of Agriculture to do so if this appears more appropriate (presumably the Ministry of Agriculture would acquire where the land concerned had some value for agricultural purposes). As regards access proposals for land within a National Park the Local Planning Authority must consult the Commission.

When access to land has been secured members of the public may enter on it without being treated as trespassers but may not play organised games, and must not behave in such a way as to do damage to the land or interfere with the enjoyment of the owner or of other people using the land. Local Planning Authorities may make by-laws to enforce proper behaviour and may appoint wardens to supervise. These powers apply also to land in a National Park or area of outstanding natural beauty owned by a Local Planning Authority.

One of the most important duties in connection with the National Parks and Access to the Countryside Act is that laid on county councils to make a complete survey of all footpaths and bridleways in their areas. They must make the survey within three years of the coming into operation of the Act and must prepare a draft map showing all rights-of-way which exist or are reasonably alleged to exist. The work is to be undertaken in consultation with district and parish councils and local residents.

Objections as to the inclusion or exclusion of any ways can be made, and, in the latter case, if the county council concerned refuses to add any way to the map, an appeal may be made to the Minister. After objections have been considered, a provisional map is published and the status of disputed rights-of-way may be contested by landowners at Quarter Sessions. When these have been determined, a definitive map is published which constitutes conclusive evidence of the existence of all rights-of-way shown on it.

County councils as highway authorities become liable, under the Act, for the repair and maintenance of all public rights-of-way. They have powers to create new rights-of-way or to divert or extinguish existing ones.

The powers and duties under this part of the Act may be made to apply to parts of county boroughs if it is expedient to do so.

Nature reserves may be established and managed by local authorities with the consent of the Nature Conservancy, and, in the case of county district councils, of the appropriate county council.

To sum up, the provisions of the Act, dealing with National Parks and Areas of Outstanding Natural Beauty are administered by Local Planning Authorities or Joint Boards, with the National Parks Commission advising, intervening and informing the Minister, who, in his turn, has to approve all important actions taken, adjudicate on objections, exercise default powers and provide financial assistance.

It is difficult to think that this is a good system. In the first place, it is far too complicated ever to be comprehended by the public in general, who are more closely and beneficially affected by it than by most legislative arrangements, and whose enthusiastic co-operation is essential. In the second place, the machinery is too cumbersome for the exercise of what is, for the most part, preservation action, and there is the gravest danger of too many cooks spoiling the broth.

It seems a pity that more executive power was not given to the Commission —there seems little doubt that such a body would be well suited to exercise it—but, as things are, it has to proceed mainly by persuasion and, in the last resort, by asking the Minister to make recalcitrant Local Planning Authorities carry out its wishes, a procedure calculated to provoke far more resentment than the direct exercise of power. The Hobhouse Committee, indeed, recommended that a far greater degree of executive power should be given to the Commission but it was understandable that there should be reluctance to remove large areas of land from the control of county councils, which, in 1949, when the Act was passed, had had so brief a tenure as Local Planning Authorities.

22-5. OTHER POSSIBLE SYSTEMS

This thumbnail sketch of the contemporary Planning system being completed, we are now in a position to consider other possible systems.

The first, which I do not think would now be advocated by anyone with the slightest understanding of the matters involved, is, obviously, to have no statutory Planning system whatever, to leave development and changes of use of land to the free play of the forces of supply and demand, trusting to the efficacy of public opinion, the teachings of propagandist bodies and perhaps government exhortations, to secure satisfactory results. The arguments against such a negative policy are well known and stand around us everywhere—the ribbon of dwellings along the by-pass, the traffic jam in nearly every town centre, Peacehaven and many other anarchic messes, to mention only a few of the immediately obvious. Many of these things were done at times and places in which Planning powers were nominally in operation or available, but *nominally* is the key word, since, without some solution, however imperfect, of the compensation-betterment problem, powers of control often could not be used effectively.

In a complex modern society the physical environment is correspondingly complex, and in a very densely populated country a proper arrangement of that environment is of special importance. This cannot possibly be secured without the intervention of some impartial public agency armed with legal powers to co-ordinate and harmonise the diverse aims of various developers.

A possible system would be a return to the old pre-war method of Planning control under which no attempt was made to Plan positively or comprehensively, but each little local authority unit was given power to ensure that no grossly harmful development should take place; in other words, Planning in the form of a mild censorship rather than of a positive dynamic. There are some advocates of a return to such a system ; many smaller local authorities, for example, would like it. They feel that the administration of such matters can best be carried out on a small scale, intimate basis. The impracticability of such a policy lies in the fact that so many of the activities with which Planning is concerned affect land lying athwart local authority boundaries, that individual local authorities practically everywhere have delusions of grandeur, assume against all reason that they will have increases of population of several hundred per cent and Plan accordingly, and that even if it were possible by a gigantic effort of co-ordination for the Ministry to fit the patchwork of schemes so produced into a comprehensive whole, it is unlikely that this whole would be recognisably similar to, or as satisfactory as, a Plan produced by fitting local detail into a broad national and regional framework.

Although revolutionary proposals need to be approached with caution they are nevertheless sometimes sound, and it is worth while examining some other possibilities.

In this country democratic procedure is highly valued, and any proposal thought to be likely to weaken it is rightly regarded with suspicion. An important part of democratic method is the committee system, under which groups of popularly elected lay representatives make decisions in the light of advice tendered to them by experts.

The use made of this system varies, however. In local government it holds absolute sway, all decisions leading to corporate action being taken by a committee, but in central government the position is rather different; while the most important matters are debated upon and decided by Parliament, it would obviously be physically impossible for *every* decision to be made by Parliament, and much power is delegated to Ministers. (The recent increase of this tendency has been much criticised, but the reversal of it seems a practical impossibility.) In practice, Ministerial responsibility in all save the most important matters devolves upon senior Civil Servants, individually or in committees, who act in the Minister's name. For example, appeals against the Planning decisions of Local Planning Authorities are nominally decided by the Minister, although it is apparent that no human being could, save as a full-time task, possibly look at, let alone decide, all the appeals dealt with.

In short, the official in central government has important powers of decision, in local government none. Reliance is placed upon the vigilance of Ministers themselves, M.P.s, and the public generally for the avoidance of abuse of these powers. Even in local government, the extent to which members genuinely debate any particular matter or merely endorse the recommendations of their officers varies greatly from authority to authority and with the subject under consideration. The volume of business transacted by a large local authority is so great that it would indeed be impossible for every matter to be fully considered by the members.

It might, therefore, be in the interests of efficiency and conduce to more *genuine* democratic control if, in complicated technical subjects such as Planning, elected local government representatives confined themselves to approving a general policy, leaving detailed decisions to officers and reviewing at given intervals the effects of their policy. Certainly such a system could achieve a marked speeding up of administration, and, though it would clearly have its dangers, members would assuredly be vividly alive to them and would be likely to guard against them far more vigorously than they now

do against the concealed dangers of rubber-stamping officers' recommendations without examination.

This would be an extremely drastic change involving a break with precedent almost as great as the system operated in many American towns, under which a town manager is employed and made responsible for many of the decisions made in this country by members.

A variant of this method would be for development control officers to be appointed, not by Local Authorities, but by the Central Government, with powers and duties somewhat analogous to those of stipendiary magistrates. They would be bound by the provisions of the Development Plans in the areas in which they operated, and there would have to be an appeal from their decisions to the Minister, just as there is on the decisions of the Local Planning Authorities. Such officers, if paid sufficiently good salaries to attract able men, would almost certainly produce sounder decisions more speedily than those arrived at by Planning Committees. The idea may be startling, but it has much to commend it.

But it is necessary to consider possibilities even more radical. It is open to question whether Planning in its more general aspects ought to be entrusted to local government at all while local government retains its present structure. Many people have devised systems for dividing Britain into regions for general administrative as well as for Planning purposes, and many such systems have, either explicitly or implicitly, assumed that if such regions were formed they should be governed by authorities more closely akin to regional parliaments than to any existing local authorities. That is to say, they would have devolved to them a considerable measure of local autonomy and would be able, within a general framework laid down by national government, themselves to initiate legislation on many matters. The idea is an attractive one, which seems to me to have great merit, but consideration of it is going rather outside the scope of this book. Suffice it therefore to say that, if such a system came into being, it would greatly facilitate the good administration of Planning.

However, looking specifically at Planning, it is extraordinarily difficult to suggest a division into regions which is very meaningful. If one seeks regional boundaries to comprehend areas which shall be more or less self-supporting for Planning purposes inasmuch as they provide sufficient space for each to solve its own land use problems within its own confines, one is confronted with a baffling diversity. In the parts of Britain not yet dominated by great cities, the drawing of boundaries is comparatively simple and might not perhaps need to be very different from the present division into counties, at any rate as regards the larger counties, but if one tries to set reasonable limits to the areas of influence of the great cities, the matter is much more difficult. Where does the area of influence of each end? One finds it difficult to answer this question. For example, the boundaries of the Greater London Area presented to the Royal Commission on Local Government in Greater London in its terms of reference have been widely criticised as being much too narrowly drawn; they approximate roughly to the continuous built-up area of London. But my personal conclusion is that they are not, in fact, inappropriate. If they had been drawn wider to take in the whole of the area included in Abercrombie's Greater London Plan, they would, on the one hand, have included much land remote from strong, direct metropolitan influence, yet on the other hand, would have excluded many areas within which population and employment decentralised from Central London will need to be located.

It therefore seems to me inevitable that Planning at the most general level needs to be done for this country as a whole, that a national land use and communications Plan conceived as a single unit needs to be prepared, and it would be difficult to argue that, if this is so, the task should not be done either by the Central Government itself or by a Planning agency set up directly by Central Government. I do not see any way of escaping from this conclusion.

Below this first level of Plan-making, it would be possible, without a complete transformation of the existing local government system, to form a network of second tier Planning authorities responsible for Plans equivalent to the second stage Regional Plans described in Chapter 7, for Town Plans and for Detailed Plans, and also probably for control of major development. The success of such a system would, however, depend upon a rationalisation of boundaries of local authorities, in particular those of county boroughs. The division of the administration of a great city between, possibly, two or more all-purpose authorities in the form of county boroughs, a number of municipal boroughs, urban districts and rural districts and two or more counties makes the effective administration of Planning, in particular, and of many other aspects of local administration, an impossibility. One looks for the amalgamation within a single authority in such cases at least of the existing built-up area of the town, sufficient hinterland to include all its conceivable future urban land needs and of all communities strongly and directly influenced by it, although, as already noted in the case of the biggest cities, some arbitrary cutting short of the boundary to exclude some of the last-named may be necessary. Such a policy entails the disappearance of county boroughs as such, and their replacement by authorities fairly closely resembling county councils. It seems to me that this would be all to the good.

As suggested elsewhere in this book, we are evidently moving, if slowly, towards this policy, as the proposals for Greater London and Newcastle show.

There would still remain the tricky question of where and how to draw the line between the kinds of development to be controlled by such authorities and those which ought to be left to local units to deal with. Inevitably, the larger the units of government set up, the more remote do they become from direct and intimate influence by aggrieved individual citizens and groups of citizens. It is of the essence of successful democratic government that there should be numerous accessible offices supervised by directly elected representatives responsible for comparatively small units of population at which and to whom vigorous protest can effectively be made. The more the higher levels of Planning administration are strengthened, the more does it become necessary as a counter-balance to strengthen the lowest levels. It is, I am sure, for example, a valid criticism of the proposed new system for

Greater London Government that the new London boroughs below the Greater London authority will be much too big to function effectively in this way. Indeed, many existing local authorities are much too big.

One would therefore like to see the rationalisation of local government into much larger and physically coherent second-tier units to be accompanied by a similar rationalisation of third-tier authorities of the order of size of existing wards. But it this were done, this lowest level of authority could not possible employ full-time a Chartered Town Planner to advise it. It would be necessary to devise something rather similar to the Area Planning Officer system which already operates in some counties, in such a way that an Area Planning Officer would advise and attend the meetings of a number of the lowest tier authorities. These presumably, under such circumstances, could be entrusted with the administration of minor development control, provided they made no decisions in conflict with Development Plans, which one would hope would be much more competent, serious and detailed documents than they are at present.

To take discussion of this subject much further would be to involve ourselves too deeply in the general field of public administration and government, though it has been necessary to explore the subject thus far because the existing system is simply not constituted so as to be able to adapt itself to a rational distribution of Planning functions and Planning staff.

In the following section of this chapter, for the sake of intelligibility, discussion is confined to operations within the existing system.

22-6. THE PLANNING DEPARTMENT OF A COUNTY COUNCIL.
Preliminary

I have thought it best to confine this section to discussion of the work of county council Planning departments because they do not vary quite so widely as those of county boroughs, and also because their functioning is somewhat more complicated. The county borough council is a self-contained authority and does not have to undertake the consultations with other local authorities which form so important a part of the County Planning Department's work. While differences between, for example, the housing department and the Planning department of a county borough council may be as difficult and acrimonious as those between a County Planning Department and a local housing authority, at least, in the former case, the members concerned all belong to one authority and eventually have to come to some compromise between each other without Ministerial intervention. Further, in a deplorable number of cases, county borough councils have no separate Planning department, a state of affairs which is rare with county councils.

The reader who is primarily interested in the work of county borough councils should have no difficulty in applying the contents of this section to them.

The duties of a County Planning Department fall principally into the following divisions :—

(1) The preparation and revision of the survey and development Plan.
(2) The administration of development control.

(3) The making of tree and building preservation orders.

(4) Taking enforcement action against contraventions of Planning control.

(5) Acting as a kind of " public estate agent " by keeping records of demands for sites and sites available for development of various kinds, particularly industrial.

Each of these is on occasion likely to involve consultation with the Ministry of Housing and Local Government and other Government Departments, with other departments of the county council and with other local authorities, and every step proposed to be taken must be formally approved by members of the county council.

The work of the officers of the Planning Department resolves itself into the following categories in order to carry out these duties:

(1) *Field work.* This comprises the large amount of detailed inspection of land necessary to prepare the survey and to design the Development Plan, including special surveys to determine areas of woodland preservation, buildings worthy of preservation and areas for special control of advertisements and inspection of individual sites in respect of development applications, contemplated enforcement orders, etc.

(2) *Drawing-office work.* The presentation of survey data and proposals as drawings and models.

(3) *The preparation of written reports* for submission to members on all subjects concerning which a decision is required.

(4) *Record work.* This includes marking new development and recording the position of development applications and areas subject to Ministerial directions on maps, and other routine drawing-office work, and the keeping of records of decisions, a task normally shared with the clerk's department.

(5) *Meeting work.* Preparing for and attending committee and council meetings, conferences and discussions, and, in collaboration with the clerk of the county council, drawing up minutes of the proceedings.

(6) *Management of Staff*, including recruitment, posting, promotion and dismissal, conditions of service, departmental conferences, and the distribution of instructions and information.

(7) *Correspondence.* This ranks as a separate item because of its voluminousness, even though most of it will relate to one of the items already listed.

Public relations has not been mentioned in either of the lists given, but enters into all branches of the work, whether or not a separate public relations department is included in the county administration.

Organisation of the Department

This section must be understood to relate to a fairly large county—one with a population of a million or more, and with a reasonably even distribution of population.

Differences in total population, and its density and distribution necessarily involve differences in organisation which it would hardly be feasible to discuss but which can readily be imagined; the policy of the county council as regards number and grading of staff will also be partly determined by factors which are not directly relevant to Planning needs, so that it would be useless to try to be very specific. It must be emphasised, too, that I am describing the organisation of an entirely independent department, not one which is part of, or only semi-independent of, the county surveyor's or county architect's department.

Offices. The first problem to be solved is the relative distribution of staff between headquarters, normally located in the county hall, or whatever other name may be given to the centre of county administration, and offices elsewhere. In a county of the size in question it will certainly be necessary to have offices elsewhere because otherwise an undue proportion of working time will be spent by the staff in travelling to work in the field, and to conferences in distant parts of the country. It is also desirable that there should be an office of the department within a reasonable distance of all residents in the county for the purposes of consultation or inquiry, although, obviously, there cannot be enough offices for there to be one within easy reach of all.

There is some Planning work which can best be done for the county as a whole at headquarters and some which can as well or better be done at local offices; it is a matter of nice adjustment to allocate staff in such a way that each office can function efficiently as a unit, and the officers in it are suitable to carry out the work allocated to it.

Broadly, two systems are possible: one is to have a fairly large number of local offices, perhaps eight or nine, each with quite a small staff, which divide between them the administration of development control and enforcement and field work; the other is to have a small number of local offices, perhaps three or four, with larger staffs, under the control of a senior member of the department, and responsible for all aspects of Planning work other than those which can only properly be dealt with for the county as a whole from headquarters.

In my view, the second of these is much the better for several reasons. In the first place, the very small office, though it may be an exceptionally friendly and pleasant place in which to work, is hopelessly inflexible; usually it will have, at most, only two technical officers of any weight, a draughtsman, a typist, and, perhaps, a junior assistant who helps both the draughtsman and the typist. Illness and holidays play havoc with such a small unit and individual officers are constantly having to do two men's work, or else arrangements have to be made to borrow staff from another office, which, with all the attendant complications of travelling and unfamiliarity with the routine of a new office, usually means that two offices are functioning inefficiently.

Second, the very small office cannot embrace sufficient variety of skill and experience to produce the best results; in Planning, perhaps more than in most jobs, people in the same office derive great benefit from constant discussion and checking of each other's ideas.

Third, the variety of duties which can be assigned to such an office is so slight that monotony is likely to result, and, in any case, the inexorable flow of development applications is likely to crowd out all other work.

On the other hand, the medium-sized office, with a staff of, perhaps, about 16, is still small enough to encourage a friendly and informal atmosphere; with, say, six technical officers, three typists, five draughtsmen and a couple or so juniors, illness and holidays should not often be crippling, there is room for a variety of talents and opportunity for a variety of work to be tackled. The only danger is that with such an arrangement it may not be possible to staff headquarters adequately if, as I shall suggest is necessary, survey maps and Planning proposals are to be drawn up in their final shape at headquarters.

The boundaries of the areas with which local offices deal should be chosen, so far as possible, to coincide with those of other administrative subdivisions, whether of the county council or of other bodies, in order to simplify consultations. It is most unlikely that any boundary will be found which is entirely satisfactory, and one with the least drawbacks should be selected. On no account should the boundary chosen sever that of a district council, or the latter, the most important of consultees, is likely to be greatly hampered and confused.

Headquarters staff. The County Planning Officer. It may be taken for granted that the County Planning Officer himself will not have time, however much he may regret it, to undertake personally any substantial amount of Planning design, though of course he must direct the general lines to be followed, and constantly supervise and criticise if he is to be an effective *Planner* as well as an administrator. But the bulk of his time will inevitably be taken up by consultation with the heads of other departments; discussions on matters of policy with the Ministry of Housing and Local Government; keeping in touch with the chairman of the County Planning Committee, and briefing him on all important aspects of the department's work; attending the more important meetings of committees—and he may well be drawn in to give advice to committees other than the Planning Committee; fighting for sufficient staff, money and accommodation; resolving disputes between and giving advice to members of his staff; dealing personally with those detailed Planning matters, the delicacy or importance of which demand his personal attention (though if he is wise he will keep these to the very minimum); and fending off important busybodies with axes to grind.

In addition, if he is a prominent member of his profession, he is likely to attend and probably often to speak at professional meetings and conferences, to be invited to deliver addresses to various professional, preservationist and propaganda bodies, and to make visits to new development of special interest outside the county. All these things are important parts of his work and bear fruit in all kinds of ways.

To bear the burden of all this he needs first-rate personal assistance, and to be protected from unnecessary demands on his time; an excellent secretary is certainly indispensable, but, in addition, an intelligent junior to make unimportant phone calls on his behalf, look up references, separate the important and unimportant papers which land on his desk, and generally devil for him, can be worth his weight in gold, and perform functions outside the scope of all but the most exceptional secretaries; in the process he is himself likely to acquire a very good practical training.

The Deputy County Planning Officer's first duty is to *be* a deputy, to take the place of his chief when the latter has to be in two places at once or needs a day off. To do this properly he must, of course, be in constant touch with the County Planning Officer, know and understand his views on all subjects and be fully in the picture about all the matters with which the latter is currently concerned.

These duties, although they are likely to be too time-consuming to enable him to undertake much design work, will not completely occupy him; his other important function is to act as a liaison between the County Planning Officer and the rest of the staff, to investigate and remedy causes of friction, and to discuss their technical problems with other senior members of the department at far greater length than the County Planning Officer can spare time for.

It may be possible for the deputy, if he has some marked specialist skill and interest, to undertake the principal responsibility for one of the headquarter sections about to be discussed, provided a thoroughly competent subordinate is available, but this should not be at the expense of his general supervisory function.

Specialist Officers. Most County Planning Departments employ some senior officers to carry out duties connected with special aspects of Planning rather than those of a general practitioner, though the number of these, their specialities and the way they are used vary greatly.

Clearly, the character of a county will greatly influence the type of specialist to be employed; in an area where mineral deposits are abundant and important, the employment of a geologist on a full-time basis might be well justified; in others a forestry expert would be useful, while elsewhere, exceptionally complex industrial problems would require an economist. The employment of any particular specialist is not desirable unless the volume of work involved reaches a certain level; below this the advice of officers in some other county department, or where there is none which covers the subject concerned, of a consultant, will meet the case. Nevertheless, when full-time specialist advice is justified it should always be obtained; it is often difficult to explain to those with no experience of Planning exactly the kind of advice needed, and, in the case of other county departments, very frequent requests for advice may well meet with some resistance or the advice be given without sufficient thought and investigation, because it is, not unnaturally, made subsidiary to that department's own work.

Further, the greater the proportion of its work which the Planning department can deal with from its own resources the simpler will be its administration; multiplicity of consultation begets confusion.

In Chapter 2 the principal skills required by the Planner were listed, and discussed; obviously it would be impossible for any County Planning Department to employ specialists in each of these, and the aim should rather, in my view, be to include as many of these skills as possible among the senior members of the general Planning staff. The concept of the Planning staff as a team cannot successfully be carried too far, for almost any individual Planning problem requires the exercise to some degree of several of these skills, and to seek the views of several specialists on every problem and to synthesise these views would be utterly impracticable.

If there is a wide range of skills distributed among the staff, and if it is the regular practice for advice to be sought by officers about any problem in which a particular skill is predominantly concerned from the possessor of that skill, even if he is not employed as a specialist, satisfactory results are likely to be secured, and the essentially sound notion of the general practitioner dealing with most problems out of his own synoptic knowledge and experience is not abandoned. Although, in my view, the best training for a Planner is to study Planning from the beginning of his professional life, there will be for many years to come a large proportion of officers in any Planning staff who have previously taken some other qualification, and there will in any case always be opportunities for specialising within the wide field of Planning, even though no formal qualification is obtained in the speciality, after a Planning qualification has been secured.

It would not be uncommon to find among the senior members of a county Planning staff men with qualifications or special experience in architecture, civil engineering, chartered surveying, landscape architecture and geography, and between them they should be able to supply most of the specialist knowledge likely to be required.

If any particular officer with expert knowledge of a particular subject finds that the consultations made by his colleagues are taking up an excessive proportion of his time the moment has come to consider engaging a whole-time specialist, and in any case it will usually be necessary to have at least two full-time specialists, one to deal with *architectural control*, the other to direct *survey and research*.

Architects rightly resent any attempt by non-architects to control their work as regards its external appearance, and it is in the highest degree rash for anyone not an architect to attempt to advise on the external appearance even of designs submitted by others without an architectural qualification. It is unlikely that a Planner with an architectural qualification can be placed in each Planning office dealing with development control, and, even if this can be done, more improbable that each will have sufficient experience and standing to be able to negotiate successfully with applicants who are established architects.

It is therefore a sound arrangement to employ as a full-time specialist a Planner who is also an architect of some merit, to assign him a small staff— perhaps a qualified assistant, a draughtsman and a secretary—and to arrange for him to deal with all applications involving problems of external appearance, leaving it to the officers in charge of development control generally to decide, in the light of their own knowledge of architectural design (of which every Planner should have a fair measure), which applications should be referred to the specialist.

Survey and research is one of the aspects of the department's work which can only satisfactorily be dealt with under unified control, and the employ-

ment of a full-time specialist to do this work is practically essential. It may be best for him to have a qualification in geography, but any competent Planner of experience should be able to do the work satisfactorily and, indeed, if the choice lies between a general Planning practitioner and a geographer without Planning experience, the advantage probably lies with the former because, although his work will lack the skill and refinement of the geographer, he is likely to know better than the geographer exactly what information is vital as a basis for the Plan and what is less relevant. If a statistician can be secured as assistant to the survey specialist it will be a great advantage; competent statistical knowledge, even if not of a very advanced kind, is indispensable.

The provision of staff for the survey specialist is an awkward problem. The time-distance factor makes it essential that much of the field work involved shall be done by the staff of local offices who are under the control of the head of that office and apart from this, lengthy periods spent on field work build up an intimate local knowledge invaluable for those who are to design or help in designing the plan, which is a strong additional argument in favour of the local staff doing it.

But, as already suggested, the final survey maps must all be prepared centrally if they are to be consistent as regards colouring, strength of hatching and categorisation of borderline data. However carefully and in whatever detail notations are drawn up it is, in my experience, absolutely impossible to make sheets prepared in different offices look as if they are parts of one map. The survey specialist is therefore faced with the not very happy prospect of supervising the work of staff who are not directly under his control. The best thing he can do is to visit each local office frequently and, in particular, at the beginning of each new piece of work, to explain to the staff who are to do it exactly what is required and especially how to deal with awkward problems likely to be encountered. He may not find them very enthusiastic and can best kindle enthusiasm by taking pains to make clear the object of the survey, the information it is hoped to obtain, and the use to which it will be put in preparing the Plan.

Such explanations should, of course, only be necessary for junior staff; if the survey specialist has to use blandishments on the senior staff the department cannot be very well served. Preliminary conferences should already have been held with the senior staff of all local offices so that, so far as possible, any special requirements they may have for their own purposes as regards subject-matter and method of presentation may be catered for.

Back at headquarters the survey specialist is also likely to be faced with some difficulties; it is most improbable that the exigencies of map production will permit him to retain permanently under his control any large proportion of the drawing-office staff, for the relative volumes of work to be done in respect of Development Plan, survey and special requirements such as maps for tree preservation orders are constantly changing.

It is essential for the survey specialist to have a small permanent staff of perhaps two or three intelligent and versatile subordinates who will have, principally, the duties of collecting and presenting in rough form information for research purposes, and also carry out special surveys, such as floor space index surveys, where the work involved requires the exercise of judgment to a considerable extent as compared with mere recording, and hence must be carried out by the same staff throughout the county if a high degree of consistency is to be achieved. In addition they may often be valuable if used to set the staff of local offices on the right lines in their field work by accompanying and advising them for a short time.

The drawing-office at headquarters is an extremely important part of the department; here nearly all the most important maps are prepared and the efficiency of the department depends to a very large extent on the speed, accuracy and attractiveness of their work. It is largely true to say that the Planner is at the mercy of his draughtsmen and typists; without efficiency and conscientiousness on their part he cannot give effective expression to his work.

The drawing-office should be under the direct control of a technical officer, not necessarily yet qualified, but of high mental calibre, and with sufficient experience to be able to look at drawings as statements of fact or intentions rather than as mere areas of colour and lines, and so to detect manifest errors without delay. Few people who are primarily draughtsmen, and have not been concerned with design or development control in even a humble capacity are capable of doing this.

The demands made on the drawing-office staff will be many and varied, and it is essential that some one senior person should be responsible for deciding priority of work; this is outside the range of the officer just mentioned and can appropriately be done by the Deputy County Planning Officer, who, alone of those at headquarters, is in a position to judge relative urgency. When priority has been decided, and work begun on a particular task it is most desirable that any instructions given to draughtsmen (the senior officer concerned will often need to give instructions) should be given through, or at least in the presence of, the officer in charge of the drawing-office, so that he may not inadvertantly give subsequent conflicting instructions.

The actual allocation of work to individual draughtsmen must necessarily vary greatly according to their skill and the prevailing circumstances. The drawing-office is likely to contain all grades of draughtsmen, from artists capable of superb work down to beginners who hardly know how to hold a ruling pen. Although the need to produce high quality work must be paramount, and demands that the most difficult and important work be given to the best craftsmen, it is also important to maintain and improve the general standard of work, and the younger draughstmen should be given great encouragement to become proficient, otherwise they will soon change their jobs.

To this end, a youngster should fairly often be given a task slightly beyond his capabilities if an absolutely first-class result is not essential, and although, in the preparation of complicated maps, pressure of time may demand a sort of chain belt system, A putting on the green washes, B the red hatching, C the brown edging and so on, on each sheet, every draughtsman should be given opportunities to produce the whole of a drawing himself, which will be a source of greater satisfaction to all but the most collective-minded souls than a mere share in a drawing, however fine it may be.

Every headquarters drawing-office should have a model-making team, even though they are not particularly expert and though it may be necessary to change the composition of the team fairly frequently. For the reasons given in Chapter 3, models are of enormous value; model-making should not be confined to the occasional preparation of huge and elaborately rendered panoramas, but, on the contrary, almost every important Planning issue should be illustrated, however roughly, in three-dimensional form.

The time taken is likely to be well repaid by the greater understanding thereby given to lay members and, consequently, by the greater likelihood of a sound decision being made. Some model-making may, indeed, be done by the draughtsmen in local offices, but pressure of routine work and lack of space and apparatus makes it likely that most of it will have to be done centrally.

A good deal of work of an uninteresting kind has to be done in the headquarters drawing-office. For example, unless the work is done for the county council as a whole by some other unit, which is a possibility discussed further on in this chapter, there will be continual map revision to be done, probably on several copies of the same sheets, in order to keep maps up to date. This can be soul-destroying work, and great care should be taken to ensure that no draughtsman is kept at it continuously for too long.

Finally, the drawing-office generally has a fair number of people working in it, of whom a high proportion are likely to be young and high-spirited. Here, to a greater extent than elsewhere in the department, it is necessary to exercise reasonably firm discipline in order to avoid lowering the quality and quantity of work done.

Administrative and clerical staff. The purely administrative work of the department and the supervision of clerical staff is generally under the control of the chief clerk. He has a difficult and thankless task made particularly awkward by the fact that, subject to the final decision of the County Planning Officer, he has to exercise some control over officers senior to himself. Keeping records of leave taken, checking claims for travelling allowances and issuing equipment are three of his duties which are likely to cause disagreement and annoyance.

The duties of the chief clerk may vary widely; the besetting problem of Planning officers is how to avoid their time being frittered away on inessential detail, and the greater the amount of non-technical work which can be loaded on to the chief clerk the better. Technical officers, for their part, need to realise that the chief clerk is responsible to the County Planning Officer for the amount of money paid out on equipment and so on, and should accept the consequent limits imposed on them.

The foregoing outline simply gives an account of what appears to be a sensible organisation for a Planning department of the kind under consideration; many other equally good arrangements are, no doubt, possible, some differing only in detail from that described, others radically different. In any case it is true that good officers will do better in a badly organised department than bad officers in one which is well organised. This should discourage, not attempts at sensible organisation, but over-reliance upon machinery rather than thought.

The current (1964) emergency in relation to Development Plans suggests the need for at least temporary modification, perhaps drastic modification, of these suggested arrangements. Up-to-date Town Maps, Town Centre Plans and Supplementary Town Maps need to be produced rapidly and in large numbers if an already profoundly unsatisfactory Planning situation is not to deteriorate further into complete chaos. In these circumstances the formation of "crash teams" within County Planning Departments to prepare these Plans by more rapid and cruder methods than would otherwise be desirable seems essential, together with the employment of Town Planning Consultants. Some elaboration of these ideas is contained in my paper " Plans into Projects " reported in " Town and Country Planning," December, 1962.

The following table summarises the suggestions already made for the organisation of headquarters and those about to be made for the arrangement of staff and duties in local offices.

POSSIBLE ORGANISATION FOR THE PLANNING DEPARTMENT OF A COUNTY WITH A POPULATION OF ONE MILLION OR MORE

Headquarters
County Planning Officer—General Supervisory and Policy-making duties
Personal Assistant.
Secretary.

Deputy County Planning Officer—Varying duties.

Architectural Specialist
Technical Assistant.
Draughtsman.

Survey Specialist.
Technical Assistant (? Statistician).
Two or three Junior Technical Assistants.

Any other Specialists required.

Drawing Office : Officer in Charge.
                 8 $\pm$ Draughtsmen.
Administrative and Clerical : Chief Clerk.
                                Administrative Assistant.
                                Six Typists.

Local Offices (three or four, according to geography of county, population and amount of development control work).
Officer in Charge (Preparation of Development Plan and General Supervision).
First Technical Assistant.
Four Draughtsmen.
One Typist.

Deputy (in charge of Development Control).
Second, third and fourth Technical Assistants.
One Draughtsman.
Two Typists.

Two Junior Assistants.

Work and organisation of the local office

We shall now deal with the work of the local offices, referring also to those parts of the work at headquarters which are intimately connected with it.

The local office, if it is organised on the lines which have been suggested, will have a share of all kinds of Planning work, and the deployment of staff to deal with it effectively is bound to create recurrent problems. The head of such an office must, of course, be a thoroughly qualified and experienced Planner; he will be running what is to a very large extent an independent unit, and must not only be competent himself but be able to direct the work of others. He is in much the same position as the County Planning Officer of a small county.

The other organisational matters which are likely to raise problems are the relations of the office with its own headquarters, with other departments of the county council, particularly the Clerk's department, with the Regional Office of the Ministry of Housing and Local Government and other Government Departments, with members of the area sub-committee, or whatever the body may be called which decides the development applications dealt with by the local office, with members and officers of district councils, and with the public generally, particularly developers.

These relationships are extremely important and worth brief individual discussion.

Relations with other branches of the Planning Department. Headquarters. Relations with headquarters require the maintenance of a very delicate balance between excessive independence, which must result in each local office working without co-ordination, and, in the long run, in some glaring inconsistency between the work done in different offices and, on the other hand, excessive dependence upon the guidance of headquarters, with time wasted by the unnecessary interchange of visits, telephone calls and correspondence. It is hardly possible for this balance to be perfectly maintained all the time; frequent tilts in either direction are inevitable, but it is essential that the balance is rectified before the situation becomes serious.

There must, of course, be the highest degree of trust and confidence between the County Planning Officer and the heads of local offices: the County Planning officer should be *primus inter pares* rather than a Fuehrer, and, if this is the case, consultation and liaison are made much easier. The local head should use his judgment regarding the matters about which he seeks direction from the County Planning Officer, and the latter must be able to feel confident that nothing drastic will happen without his knowledge at a local office which might conflict with policies he has decided to recommend. On the other hand, the limited time of the County Planning Officer is likely to be seriously trespassed upon if a local officer, in all good faith, constantly seeks confirmation of views about which there is unlikely to be any difference of opinion.

The County Planning Officer can himself help to keep the balance, supplementing the regular co-ordinating activities of the Deputy County Planning Officer by means of conferences attended by the heads of local offices, and by issuing written directives laying down the general lines to be followed in preparing development plans and administering development control. Both are extremely useful; the former is of particular assistance because the interchange of views enables each local officer to shape his work in accordance with the lines followed by the others, which makes the County Planning Officer's task of co-ordination much easier.

Written directives should not be too numerous or detailed; they should be in the form of general statements wherever possible rather than of specific instructions; the local officer who has to work in accordance with a voluminous list of precise instructions detailing the circumstances in which he must consult and the exact administrative procedure to be followed on any given occasions works in chains; if he is conscientious in following his instructions most of his time is likely to be taken up in complying with the book of rules instead of in exercising his technical judgment.

However, some precise instructions are essential. The interpretation to be placed on Ministry Regulations must, for example, be the same throughout the county, and just as the Minister cannot allow contradictory decisions to be made on similar appeal cases in different parts of the country, so, but with even more urgency, there must not be contradictions between development control decisions in the same county.

The administration of development control leaves so much scope for divergences of opinion between individuals of equal skill that they simply cannot be avoided. Sooner or later the County Planning Officer, on going through lists of recommendations in respect of applications to be determined centrally, is certain to find a flat contradiction between two originating from different offices. He may or may not be able to put the matter right immediately, according to whether the recommendations have or have not already been approved by area sub-committees; but in any case he will have to make up his mind which policy is the right one and issue a directive to prevent further contradictions. He cannot hope to eliminate happenings of this kind without destroying the initiative and self-confidence of local officers, but can only aim at making them rare enough to prevent his members becoming alarmed.

The local officers' relations with the survey specialist have already been sufficiently dealt with, but those with the *architectural specialist* require further examination. The difficulty is that architectural design is often only one of several aspects of an application which require negotiation and discussion. If such an application is passed to the architectural specialist for him to deal with on his own he must be fully briefed about the other aspects before negotiating with the applicant; even so, he may often, through lack of detailed local knowledge, be unprepared for points raised during the discussion, and though it is an apparent waste of labour, it may often be better for a member of the local office also to be present at any discussion. Some discrimination is necessary, and, where the issues other than architectural are simple or the applicant is known to be timorous or surly, it may be better for the architectural specialist to tackle the job alone.

Relations with other departments of the county council can be very delicate. In the first place, the Planning department being nearly always the youngest, others tend to regard it as an upstart and to give less than full weight to its views; developing departments also find it difficult to accept the right of the upstart to require them to modify their proposals in accordance with Planning needs. These are only tendencies; very often the fullest co-operation and friendliness is given by officers of other departments, and anyone who has worked in a County Planning Department cherishes the pleasantest recollections of these.

The main difficulty is to get developing departments to understand that, though the Planning Department is part of the same organisation, its duty is to scrutinise proposals for county development with just as critical an eye as those of other developers, and to make the same efforts to have effect given to any criticisms made.

The most frequent contact is likely to be with officers of the *County Education Committee* and of the *County Architect's Department*, or its equivalent, about the siting and design of new schools. These consultations may be elaborate. The education committee determine the numbers of schools of various kinds required for each town and the villages in which schools are to be located (this is an integral part of the County Plan and not merely a matter of development control), while one section of the county architect's department may select sites and another design the buildings.

Whatever the position may be, it is essential for the local Planning officer to institute an effective system of consultation, which enables all necessary negotiations to be carried out in good time, but which does not entail the unnecessary attendance of officers not immediately concerned. One of the great curses of Planning is the number of people who sit around tables for hours at a time and who have only the slightest concern with the matters under discussion.

It is extremely important that there should be close understanding between the Planning Department and the *Roads Department*. Usually the county surveyor will ask to be consulted on all development applications which involve making an access to a county road or which are sufficiently close to a county road for future widening or sight lines at junctions and bends to be affected. These consultations can become very onerous by sheer weight of numbers since very nearly every application within rural districts is involved, and it should be possible to arrive at an understanding in accordance with which the local Planning office only passes on applications upon which there is some real chance of the Roads Department wishing to comment.

Whatever arrangements are made there is bound, sooner or later, to be a mishap, and the Planning Department will fail to consult in respect of an application which the Roads Department would wish to refuse or have modified. With mutual understanding these mishaps should be rare and if so they are a small price to pay for the avoidance of passing hundreds of files to the Roads department, and thus losing access to them for an indefinite period, so that they may be examined from the special viewpoint of the road engineer and solemnly inscribed with the words " *No objection* ".

The road proposals to be inserted in the County Plan and those portions of the road proposals in Town Plans which involve county rather than local action (i.e., generally just beyond borough and urban district boundaries) must, of course, be the subject of very close consultation with the roads department. The spheres of interest of the two departments overlap considerably, but, as already urged in Chapter 7, the Planning Department must insist that full weight be given to its views, the routes for new roads being of far more concern to it than to the Roads Department, subject to engineering difficulties being avoided.

Finally, it is important that there should be agreement between the two departments regarding carriageway and footpath widths for residential roads in rural districts, which, on completion, the county council normally take over as county roads. It has often happened that the Planning Department has readily agreed widths for footpaths and carriageways which the Roads Department have considered inadequate. The county council, no less than the Government, must speak with one voice to the outside world, and agreement must be reached on this matter. The general policy will, of course, have to be settled at headquarters, but consultation on doubtful points will be necessary locally.

Last, the *County Clerk's Department* is intimately concerned with various aspects of Planning. There are many possible sources of friction. The county clerk is, of course, invariably the chief officer of the county administration, though, even more than in other associations of senior officers, he should be no more than *primus inter pares*. There is a distinct tendency for members of his department to ascribe to themselves illusory grandeur, and to encroach upon the technical field. This is a battle which must be fought and won by the County Planning Officer himself, otherwise his subordinates will have little chance, but even if he does win there are still likely to be skirmishes to be fought further down the line; ambitious young holders of Diplomas in Public Administration are apt to see in Planning an opportunity to exercise influence on a grand scale. In pursuit of this they may tender advice to members on the wider aspects of technical Planning which are the proper field of the Planning officer, and in doing so invariably fall into the same error as that made by members, of underestimating the complexities of Planning technique.

Heads of local Planning offices will constantly be in contact with senior members of the county clerk's staff, who are often allocated to deal with the clerk's work connected with a specific local Planning office, and will do well to arrive at a clear understanding regarding the extent of their functions and those of the clerk's representative; this is particularly important in connection with the conduct of meetings, at which their harmonious functioning will often be the measure of the success achieved in terms of satisfactory decisions. Any disagreement or misunderstanding which becomes apparent will have disastrous results on the confidence of the members in their officers.

The Planning officer is responsible for recommending the technical measures to be taken by the county council to fulfil its responsibilities as Local Planning Authority, and the clerk is responsible for giving legal advice and for drawing up minutes, determinations of Planning applications, enforcement notices, preservation orders, etc., in appropriate form. Both must work closely together to ensure that the form of words the clerk uses does, in fact, accurately express the technical requirements of the matter as approved by the members. This is not always easy and it is essential that clerk and Planning

officer should establish thoroughly friendly relations or deadlock may result.

It is desirable that the Planning officer should make a practice of consulting the clerk before submitting reports containing items which have a legal aspect in order that there may be no doubt of the validity of the recommendations.

Relations with Government Departments are naturally less intimate and continuous than with other departments of the county council; the main difficulty from the Planning officer's side is usually to get Civil Servants to understand the tortuous workings of local government and, particularly, that no decision or binding opinion can be given except by resolution of the appropriate committee of members. Conversely, the Planning officer also finds difficulty in understanding the relative responsibilities of different Government Departments and of different branches of the same department; time spent in achieving sufficient mutual comprehension for practical purposes is well spent. Once this has been achieved Planning officers of the County Council and of the Ministries are often able to reach agreement easily.

One of the things which Ministry and Local Planning officers have to learn about each other's jobs is that, while in conversation they may speak with the utmost frankness, there are some things which simply must not be said in writing; for example, the local government officer hates to receive a letter the wording of which suggests that he has, in the course of discussions, in any way committed his authority to any particular course of action before the necessary resolution has been passed by members. It is most unlikely that he will have done any such thing, but a letter so worded as to suggest it, which will probably have to be read to members, is gravely embarrassing.

Similarly, the Ministry officer dislikes having ascribed to him personally anything resembling a policy statement, which, for obvious reasons, is severely frowned on in the Civil Service.

Officers of other Government Departments are often rather more difficult to work with; to the normal Civil Service ignorance of local government procedure is often added ignorance of the functions and scope of Town and Country Planning and unwillingness to admit its importance in co-ordinating development.

Relations with members of the Local Planning Authority. Which members the staff of the local Planning office will be concerned with is largely determined by the delegation arrangements made in the particular county concerned; at one extreme, meetings of the Planning committees of all district councils in the area may have to be attended as well as meetings of committees composed partly of members of district councils and partly of county council members, and meetings where county members only are present, while, at the other extreme, only county members are involved.

The relations of a local government officer with members are always delicate, and are at their most difficult at meetings where some of the members are his employers and others are not. The officer's conduct at such meetings is a real test of character. He must never forget that he is only an adviser, and must accept the most idiotic decisions made against his advice with good grace, and loyally take whatever consequential action is necessary to implement them. He may be subjected to all kinds of attacks, both from members of district councils who loathe the county council, and find him a convenient target, and from anti-Planning members of the county council, who, although they employ him, look on him as an adversary!

The prevalence of these attacks must not be exaggerated; the vast majority of members behave with courtesy and consideration towards their officers, and when there is a lapse the chairman's protection is usually forthcoming, but oblique references in general terms, though with obvious references to the officer present, to " theorists ", " red tape ", and so on can be extremely irritating.

Worst of all to a man who likes a good outspoken argument in good humour is the need to couch his remarks in decorous and impartial phrases when the members are engaging in a hearty brawl.

When the membership of committees remains substantially the same over a long period a Planning officer may be able to establish a solid relationship with his members, and be permitted, and even expected by them, to give his views in far more informal and forthright fashion than is general in local government. If this happens it is a sign that a real committee has been created rather than the bringing together of a number of individuals without a common aim.

It is most important that, whatever his relations with the rest of a committee, the officer should be on confidential terms with the chairman if the latter is any use at all. A discussion of the agenda before the meeting enables the chairman to control its conduct much more effectively and to make sure that the officer is invited to speak at appropriate moments instead of having to make desperate attempts to catch the chairman's eye when his intervention is necessary to prevent the discussion becoming irrelevant or based on misapprehension of facts.

The way in which meetings are conducted differs considerably, and it is important to reach understanding and agreement with the chairman about the procedure to be adopted. When the meeting is concerned with development control it is usual to circulate beforehand written particulars of the applications to be considered, together with the Planning officer's suggested decisions.

Sometimes the chairman simply runs through these, calling out the number of each application or the name of the applicant in turn, and assuming the members' agreement to the recommendations made unless one of them asks a question or raises an objection. At the other extreme, the chairman may read out in full the particulars and recommendations relating to each application, pause for debate, to which the Planning officer may be invited to contribute remarks in amplification of the report or explanation of points raised by members, and finally call for a motion in respect of the decision to be made, to be proposed, seconded and voted upon.

A compromise between these two is generally best; the first may result in most of the members who have not troubled to read the report leaving the meeting with no clear idea of what they have decided, which is a travesty of democracy, the second is inordinately tedious and invites controversy too conspicuously.

Good results are often achieved if the Planning officer describes the nature of each proposal briefly and informally, and explains the effect and reasons for the decisions recommended. When he has finished, the chairman merely asks " All agreed ? " and, in the absence of response, nods to the Planning officer to pass on to the next item.

It is most difficult to arrange for members to inspect quickly and conveniently drawings submitted with applications. Very often the Planning officer only displays those which are essential to make his explanation understood or if a member asks to see a particular drawing. This may work well enough, but is unlikely to satisfy the really keen member who wants to understand what he is being asked to do.

Whether all drawings or only selected ones are shown to members, the actual method of display involves difficulties. If drawings are pinned to screens before the meeting the members can inspect them at their leisure but the drawings cannot be clearly seen during the actual meeting; it is surprising at how short a distance most drawings become practically unreadable, even to people with perfect eyesight, so that, even if drawings are pinned to a screen immediately adjoining the table at which the members sit, it is unlikely that everyone will be able to see them clearly unless there are very few members present.

If the drawings are placed on the table as required there will be an uncomfortable huddling and neck-craning by the members, and they are likely to lose the thread of what is being said, while if they are passed from hand to hand either a great deal of time will be wasted or, if discussion of the proposals proceeds, someone is sure to ask a question about a drawing relating to the last application but five to have been decided upon, with hopeless confusion resulting.

Slides are nowadays so easy and cheap to make that the best method of dealing with this problem is to project onto a screen slides of all applications of a complicated or controversial kind. The expense would be very small compared with the benefits gained.

Many meetings and conferences are held on the site of a proposed development if the proposal is particularly difficult or contentious. Very often, when Government or local authority development is involved, officers of the Ministry of Housing and Local Government and of the Ministry of Agriculture, together with representatives of the developing department or members and officers of the developing authority, as the case may be, attend as well as members and officers of the Local Planning Authority.

These occasions often have a nightmare quality; in good weather the assembled gathering tends to break up into groups which wander off separately, engaged in hot argument or trivial gossip, and can only be brought together again after considerable delay and shouting; in bad weather, after a hasty inspection of the site, an inadequately considered decision is likely to be taken under a hedge if there are no buildings near by, or, if a barn is handy, everyone crowds into it, spraying water from mackintoshes and umbrellas onto maps and other documents, and discussion proceeds in thoroughly unfavourable conditions.

Every effort should be made to reduce attendance at such meetings to a minimum. The committee which considers the application initially is usually only too willing to authorise the chairman and one or two other members to attend and decide the matter on its behalf, or, in very important cases, to attend and report their opinions at the next meeting. No one should be invited unless his presence is clearly important.

Although site inspections do enable members to get a complete impression of the site concerned they consume a great deal of time, particularly in finding a date on which all concerned can attend, and they are very difficult to conduct satisfactorily. They should not be held unless there is some definite advantage to be gained, but members faced with a difficult decision which may involve them in unpopularity tend to welcome them as a legitimate reason for delaying the decision.

At these and all other conferences where several bodies are represented the Planning officer is in a difficult position regarding what he should say and when to say it. He is primarily there to advise his own members, and is far less free to express his own opinions than at a Local Planning Authority committee meeting, when, theoretically at least, only one interest is represented, and where he can give completely unfettered advice. At conferences his members are reasonably entitled to call upon him to give advice exclusively to them, and to use only those parts of it which support their own opinions. Nevertheless, and this is greatly to the credit of members, they very generally permit and invite the Planning officer to state his views fully and unreservedly, however little they may agree with him.

It will be well to mention here a right generally conceded to technical officers of local authorities. Although it may often be necessary for them to report the views of their authority, although these are contrary to their own opinions, they should not be expected to express agreement with such views.

This is of special importance in connection with the hearing of appeals to the Minister. A Planning officer giving evidence on behalf of his authority is morally bound to speak the truth, although he is not on oath; therefore, if the decision giving rise to the appeal was taken against his advice his evidence ought not to go beyond what he honestly feels to be the technical arguments in favour of that decision.

Hence, if a Planning committee refuses permission or imposes onerous conditions against the Planning officer's advice, it is his clear duty to point out to them that, in the event of an appeal, he will be unable to give effective evidence on their behalf, and that, indeed, the answers likely to be extracted from him under cross-examination would be highly damaging to their case. The committee can then either change their minds, make inquiries to find out whether some other officer of the Planning department agrees with them, and can therefore give evidence, or keep to their decision but offer no evidence at the appeal.

Relations with members and officers of other local authorities. The Planning officer can hardly function without some degree of co-operation from the district councils in his area, for he needs a great deal of information for survey purposes which can only be supplied by them; a Development Plan is unlikely to be satisfactory without some constructive comment from the district councils concerning its effect upon their areas; the district councils' own development cannot be thoroughly adapted to the plan unless they are at least prepared to discuss possible amendments to their proposals (it is better still if they positively collaborate with the Planning officer before proposals are submitted), and development control, enforcement and preservation action cannot possibly be fully effective unless the intimate local knowledge and constant inspection undertaken as a matter of routine by district councils is put at the disposal of the county council.

Where delegation arrangements require it there is little doubt that the Planning officer's attendance at the meetings of district councils is likely to promote good feeling, though it certainly increases the arduousness of his work very considerably. He is in the position of an entirely independent adviser so far as the district council is concerned; not being employed by them or even retained like a consultant, he can give them absolutely unprejudiced and candid advice. Providing that he is reasonably tactful, and the district council members are not excessively thin-skinned it is possible for a very special and valuable relationship to be built up between them which can be made use of in many directions.

If this is done the Planning officer must be particularly careful not to tread unnecessarily on the corns of the district council's own officers. Though he may often have to tender advice in direct opposition to theirs this can be done without offence, and in many ways he can assist them by giving support to their views from his own angle in matters which are connected with other subjects as well as with Planning.

Where, as will be more often the case, regular consultation is undertaken only with the surveyors of the district councils the first step, once good personal relations have been established, is to work out a system for exchanging views which is simple and clear cut. If the Planning officer and the surveyor can reach agreement it is seldom that their joint recommendations will be upset.

Discussions on the Development Plan and district councils' own development ought to be as frequent and full as time will permit.

Consultation with adjoining Local Planning Authorities, both county boroughs within the county and adjacent counties, will be necessary. In the absence of a Joint Board, or at least of some joint body of representatives meeting regularly, the former may cause great difficulty. A county borough will often wish to earmark land for future development outside its boundaries; although this may be regarded as reasonable by the Planning officer concerned, the county council itself may fear that this is no more than the opening shot in a battle for boundary extensions by the county borough, and oppose it strongly. On the other hand, on purely Planning grounds, the County Planning Officer may consider an increase of population implied by the development area proposed for the county borough to be quite unsuitable in relation to the satisfactory distribution of population in the county as a whole, and therefore oppose it.

Where differences of this kind cannot be resolved the mediation of the Ministry of Housing and Local Government should be asked for at once. It is quite futile for adjoining Local Planning Authorities to prepare Development Plans based upon entirely different assumptions as to the distribution of population, and not to approach the Ministry until they are submitted for approval, when the Ministry will, in any case, have to adjudicate. The same problem may arise, although generally in less acute form, when a town in an adjoining county is considered by that county council to require a development area which crosses the county boundary.

When, as the result of mediation or agreement, it has been determined that part of a town's development area must be located in the area of another Local Planning Authority, it is obviously sensible that the authority in which the town is situated should carry out the actual design work involved in Planning the whole of the area for future development, requesting the other authority to include the necessary proposals in its Development Plan. A good deal of consultation between the two will no doubt be necessary in respect of supplying survey data, linking any road proposals required in connection with the extension to the county's own road proposals and so on.

Even where no problems of urban development arise along the county boundary consultation will be required for the co-ordination of proposals for the pattern of rural communities, securing continuity in the boundaries of landscape and woodland preservation areas and the like. It is unlikely that these will involve any great difficulty.

It will, of course, be readily understood that, although local Planning officers will be closely concerned with all these matters, some of them are so important that the participation of the County Planning Officer will be necessary.

Relations with the public. The tolerance extended by public opinion and, hence, the co-operation and support of members of the public, to departments of central and local government is largely dependent on quite minor factors. No such department can afford to incur justified public reproach, for its effectiveness and even its existence may be threatened if it does. Civil Servants and local government officers are employed by the public, who are entitled to demand efficiency, courtesy and consideration (though not servility) from them. Accordingly, both for the sake of expediency and as a duty, great care should be taken to ensure that members of the public who visit Planning offices are properly treated. This applies both to headquarters and to local offices, but the latter are likely to receive so many more visitors that the following is written with particular reference to them.

The entrance to the office should be clearly marked with its name, and notices should be prominently displayed inside the entrance directing the visitor to the appropriate room if the layout of the building makes this necessary.

If it is not possible to arrange that the officer responsible for receiving visitors works where he can see them when they enter, though this should always be done if at all possible, a bell should be provided and a notice displayed inviting the visitor to ring for attention. It is essential that there should be a counter or other barrier so that visitors cannot penetrate into the interior of the office before being greeted, and inspect the various confidential maps and other documents which may be visible.

It should be impressed on the staff that it is a cardinal sin not to greet visitors promptly and courteously, and all senior officers should continually keep an eye and ear unobtrusively turned in this direction so that slackness

is not allowed to develop. Every reader will be thoroughly familiar with the various forms of discourtesy which are common in offices but it will be sufficient to mention the most blatant, which occurs when a visitor enters to find two members of the staff engaged in a conversation about football results or lipstick shades, which is pursued to a leisurely conclusion before his presence is acknowledged in any way.

As a matter of economy, each interview should be conducted by the most junior officer who is competent to do so, and visitors should, of course, be received by a junior assistant specially detailed for the task. It is important that he or she should be carefully instructed as to the individual officers who will conduct interviews on various subjects, and only to obtain from the visitor enough information to decide who should interview him. Sometimes, because of the subject-matter or the vagueness of the caller, it may be unavoidable that he has to tell quite a long story before this becomes apparent or the junior may inadvertently refer him to the wrong officer, so that he has to be passed on again. When this happens the visitor should be accompanied and the information he has already given passed on by the first officer to the second. Nothing is more wearisome than to have to tell a story several times; at each repetition it sounds sillier in one's own ears! When an interview is conducted by telephone the arrangement of the office telephone system and switchboard may make it inevitable for callers to have to repeat themselves on occasion, but every effort should be made to reduce this. While it is essential that junior staff should be specifically coached and instructed in dealing with visitors, a good example set by the head of the office is the most effective way of earning good results.

Visitors often ask the most surprising questions and make extraordinary demands; great care is necessary to ensure that, although the best possible service is provided, discretion is observed, and that confidential information is not disclosed. It is also essential that misleading information on matters not fully within the Planning officer's knowledge is not given, or other organisations may be embarrassed and impeded in their work, and the visitor led into error. Planning work is often made substantially more difficult by the irresponsible statements about Planning procedure and requirements made at district council offices and elsewhere, and it is important that the Planning officer himself should not commit this kind of offence in respect of other subjects.

However, almost any statement made by the Planning officer can be used as evidence against him, and cause trouble, if it is distorted and taken out of its context. This has to be faced, and should not be made the reason for adopting a clam-like attitude and refusing to give information. Some concerted policy should be worked out, preferably at headquarters, so that, in general terms, staff interviewing visitors know what they may and may not disclose. They should be encouraged to talk quite freely within wide limits; the good will derived from doing this immeasurably outweighs the harm likely to result from occasional minor indiscretions. It should be made perfectly clear to all visitors who discuss matters which may be the subject of an application for Planning permission that no opinion expressed by an officer is binding upon the members and that no action should be taken on such expressions of opinion until the members have confirmed them. It is desirable to explain this specifically at each interview. Some caution is still necessary in expressing views, since, if the committee do not subsequently endorse them, and an appeal results, the local Planning authority's case is inevitably prejudiced to some extent. Officers need to develop an aptitude for judging the characters of the people they interview, and in the light of this it is often possible to proceed confidently with discussion after receiving an assurance that views expressed on any particular subject will not be quoted in any subsequent proceedings. If this can be done, the officer's task is greatly eased, and he is not likely often to be let down.

Great patience is necessary in dealing with ignorant and inarticulate visitors: the man who wants to know what " the town planning " will let him do on a piece of land, but who cannot describe its location precisely or even locate it on a map, is a trial, but time spent in providing such people with information, helping them to fill in application forms, and even supplying them with rough tracings of sites, is well spent. This, of course, only applies to very minor development; in the case of proposals of any magnitude the man who is trying to submit his own application should be emphatically urged to seek proper professional advice. Apart from the time spent, positive advice and help given in such cases may subsequently be represented as an attempt to exercise undue influence on the applicant to his prejudice, and this cannot be risked. When a professional adviser has been engaged, however, there is no limit to the extent to which the Planning office can properly collaborate to ensure satisfactory proposals being made.

Correspondence plays an important part in the relations of the Planning officer with the public. Few people are willing to say as much on paper as in conversation, for expressions of opinion appear much starker and more uncompromising in written form, but every effort should be made to phrase letters in a clear and pleasant way; it requires very much less effort to string together official clichés, but the time spent in writing letters which sound as if they come from a person rather than a robot is well spent for the sake of the effect it has on the recipient. Sir Ernest Gowers writes a great deal of good sense about this in " Plain Words ". It is most desirable that senior officers should be allowed to sign letters in their own names, as in Government Departments. There is some nervousness about this in local government, for no very good reason so far as I can see. The common practice of signing all letters with a facsimile signature of the County Planning Officer conveys a most undesirable impression: it is impersonal, a transparent deception, and makes it harder for people who receive letters and wish to make personal contact with the writer.

Exhibitions are an important part of the public relations of a Planning department. Every important proposal should, so far as possible before it is finally adopted, be presented in the most graphic possible way and exhibited to the public. Various techniques have been described in Chapter 3.

It is also desirable that the Local Planning Authority should regularly make the public aware of its progress and intentions in other ways, and mainly by statements in the Press. This will be dealt with by the Public Relations Department, if there is one. The subjects about which statements are made should include not only explanations of various stages reached in the Development Plan, concurrently with exhibitions, but also periodical statements about development control policy. If Local Planning Authorities would regularly explain the principles that guide them in determining especially numerous or difficult types of application it is likely that the increase in public understanding secured would appreciably reduce the work involved in refusing applications, contesting appeals and negotiating amendments to proposals.[5]

Organisation of the local office. It has been suggested earlier that a typical local office may have a staff of about sixteen, comprising six technical officers, three typists, five draughtsmen, and two juniors for general duties. Of the technical officers, two at least should be corporate members of the Town Planning Institute and the others should either be preparing to qualify for membership or have some other relevant professional qualification.

A Planning department can only engage the best of the candidates who apply for posts, and it will be exceptional if there are not one or two weak links among even these sixteen, which will necessitate some arrangement of duties different from the theoretically ideal in order to cover their deficiencies. Assuming, however, that the staff is generally of a reasonably high standard, the allocations of duties described in the following pages should work well. Allowance must, however, of course be made for modifications necessitated by variations in delegation and decentralisation arrangements.

It is vital that there should be a fairly sharp cleavage between the staff working on the survey and Development Plan and those dealing with development control. The pressure of development applications is so unremitting, and some of the problems raised provide food for such extensive investigation and discussion, that nothing is easier than to reach the position where practically the whole staff of the Planning Department is spending nearly all its time on development control work. The proportion of staff to be allocated to development control should therefore be fixed, and they should only be allowed to call on the others for help in the gravest emergencies; if they are perpetually snowed under some permanent increase may have to be made. It is fatal to give any one man both survey or Development Plan work and development control work at the same time; the latter will be done because it has to be completed in time for a particular committee meeting, the former will be left because there will usually be no definite date by which it must be done. This tendency is so insidious that it is undesirable even to let the development control staff borrow a draughtsman to do a rough tracing; before you know where you are he will be doing no work at all on the Development Plan. This does not mean that staff cannot be shifted from one kind of work to another; indeed, to maintain their interest and provide them with comprehensive experience it is essential that this should be done, but they should only do one kind of work at a time.

Generally it will be best for the head of the office to be responsible for the Development Plan, and for his second in command to superintend develop-

---
[5] The admirable periodic bulletins issued by the Huntingdonshire County Planning Department are an example which ought to be widely followed.

ment control. They must, of course, develop the fullest understanding, so that the second in command informs his chief of all applications which materially affect the Development Plan, and seeks his advice about especially difficult applications but otherwise leaves him to concentrate on the Development Plan. This means that the senior officer will attend a comparatively small number of important meetings, conferences and appeals, and the second in command, together with one or more of the technical officers below him, will attend a much larger number of less important ones, which is entirely appropriate.

The allocation of staff between Development Plan and development control work must be determined by many factors, which will vary in each county. In general, development control requires a comparatively small amount of highly skilled work in order to decide and draft decisions, and to report upon them, and, proportionately, a very large amount of comparatively unskilled work devoted to collecting and summarising data upon which the decisions will be based, obtaining additional information not included in the original applications, undertaking consultations and marshalling all the necessary documents for use at committee meetings. On the other hand, the preparation of Development Plans requires comparatively little unskilled work, but a proportionately greater amount of skilled work which, however, except for the senior officer concerned, need not be of quite as high a level as that required for the skilled work in connection with development control.

Accordingly, in an average case, it would probably be suitable for the head of the office to have the assistance of the best of the technical officers below his deputy, of four of the draughtsmen and of one typist, leaving his deputy with the three junior technical officers, the least skilful draughtsman, two typists and both juniors. The most probable alteration of this allocation which is likely to be required is the transference of the most junior technical officer to Development Plan work and of a draughtsman to development control. Although a good deal of drawing is required in connection with development control much of it is very elementary—making rough tracings for record purposes and so on, and can be done by the juniors.

The large proportion of draughtsmen allocated to Development Plan work is necessary because, as will be remembered, they will periodically be diverted for field work on survey under the direction of the survey specialist.

The heads of local offices, under the conditions described, are the principal Planning designers in the department. It is therefore essential that the great majority of their time should be spent on this work, and the ancillary duties already mentioned kept to a minimum: if they cannot find time to design no one else will be able to. It follows that most of the consultations and attendance at committees in connection with development control must be undertaken by the deputies. Members and others sometimes feel that they should have the benefit of the attendance of the most senior officer concerned, and it may be necessary to explain carefully to them the impracticability of this.

Work on the Development Plan falls into several fairly distinct departments: design of the County Plan, of Town Plans and of detailed Planning proposals, and the necessary discussions, inquiries and meetings at various stages of each.

The preparation of the County Plan and of quinquennial revisions of it cannot, of course, be undertaken for the area of a local office in isolation. On the other hand, no one person is likely to have enough knowledge of the whole county to do it himself. The best procedure is, therefore, for the heads of all the local offices to meet regularly in order to dovetail their ideas. The County Planning Officer will, no doubt, often wish to preside over these meetings. The preparation of final maps must necessarily be done at headquarters.

The preparation of Town and Village Plans, on the other hand, is very suitable for individual work. The head of the office should not have to do more than prepare rough drafts, leaving his technical assistant and draughtsmen to work them up. An important part of this work is ensuring that the requirements of all authorities regarding the designation of areas for compulsory purchase and all other administrative items are properly incorporated in the maps. Responsibility for this rather prosaic work should not preclude the assistant from himself doing part of the design work, which is, in any case, sure to be more than the head of the office can tackle by himself. The latter's heavy commitments in connection with negotiations demand that he should be entirely freed from other work not involving design. The technical assistant should also be responsible for making the various calculations required for density purposes and for arriving at the total areas devoted to each use, etc.

All the necessary map work for Town Maps can be done locally, but, for the sake of uniformity, it is desirable that someone should be made responsible for co-ordinating it for the whole county as regards style of presentation. The head of the headquarters drawing office is a suitable person to do this, and it should not interfere seriously with his other duties.

The preparation of detailed Plans such as neighbourhood and central area redevelopment designs is inevitably much more of a co-operative effort; indeed, the district councils concerned may often wish to do most of the work themselves, the Planning officer providing little more than advice and possibly drafting assistance; on the other hand, councils with few resources or inefficient officers may need to have practically the whole work done for them. When they have no architect and the local Planning officer is not himself also an architect it will usually be necessary to obtain the advice of the architectural specialist at headquarters, or even for him to collaborate in preparing the plan. The increasing amount of such work to be expected in the future is likely to require substantial additions to the staff of the architectural specialist if his main duties are not to be prejudiced.

It must be made clear that this apparently inadequate recognition of the architect's role implies no slight; although the Plans referred to are "detailed" so far as land Planning is concerned, inasmuch as they involve settling the use of every parcel of land, and hence advice on the architectural implications is necessary, they do not include the design of buildings, which comes at a later stage and which is, of course, almost exclusively the concern of architects.

Development control work demands, as a first essential, bringing into operation a methodical office system made accident-proof as far as humanly possible. It is most important that applications should be decided as rapidly as possible; failure to discharge this duty satisfactorily is the accusation most commonly made by responsible persons against Local Planning Authorities; quite trivial applications, especially, take much too long to determine, it is said. No doubt there is a good deal of substance in these complaints; nevertheless, dealing with applications in strict rotation rather than selecting the simplest for immediate attention may well mean that the *average* time taken to determine applications is less. Further, even in the best-run offices, an application will occasionally escape attention quite inexplicably for a considerable time, and its determination be thus delayed out of all proportion to its complexity. One suspects that many complaints are founded upon occurrences such as these. Planning officers are understandably unlikely to volunteer the information that an accident has occured.

Applications for Planning permission are first received by the district councils of the areas to which they relate, and are then passed on to the appropriate Planning office. Subsequent procedure depends upon the delegation arrangements which have been made; it is impracticable to discuss the procedure appropriate to each of the numerous possible variants, but an important point to bear in mind is that although, when the district council's surveyor gives his views on applications his observations at the earliest possible stage are valuable, it is useless for the district council to give their formal views until the results of all necessary consultations have been obtained and made known to them. Unless they await these, applications will continually have to be referred back to them for reconsideration in the light of other views and new facts which have emerged. It is true that the district council's views are chiefly required in respect of those aspects of applications which concern their own functions but, unless they are fully informed before giving these views, good relations may be seriously impaired because of the frequency with which they have to be overridden. This particularly applies when district councils are authorised to issue decisions on applications when their views agree with those of the Planning officer. It is therefore necessary to undertake all other consultations with the utmost speed, so that the district council can be informed and give its views before its next meeting, or that of its Planning committee, if the latter has been delegated powers of decision.

Where arrangements are such that a large number of applications are customarily decided by area sub-committees of the county council at monthly meetings it is essential, to avoid delay, that the dates of its meetings are arranged in conjunction with those of the constituent district councils; preferably, the area sub-committee meeting should take place about a week after those of the district councils, so that the latter's views may be transmitted to the local Planning office in time for the necessary reports to be prepared, duplicated and distributed to members.

Speed in carrying out consultations and preparation of reports is facilitated if all applications received in the local Planning office are dealt with in standardised fashion, and *pro formas* used freely instead of letters. Each application must be given a number, and the simplest method is for each district council to be given an identifying letter or letters and for its staff to number the applications consecutively as they are received, with the allotted identification letter prefixed to each.

When they reach the Planning office the applications must be registered in a book, all essential particulars being recorded; appropriate work for a junior, who can at the same time mark the position of each on a map kept for this purpose.

The officer in charge of development control (the second in command of the office) should next see the application, for it is important that he should see all applications as early as possible in order to be fully aware of the volume and type of work in hand at any given time. All he need do at this stage is to examine the application cursorily, write on it the name of the subordinate technical officer whom he wishes to deal with the routine technical work involved, and have it passed on to him.

The application will already have been placed in a folder or envelope for protection, on which, or on a sheet attached to the application, should be printed a list of all possible consultees, with space for their observations to be noted, and also a list of all the factors which may have to be taken into account in considering the application, such as zoning proposals, density, physical characteristics of the site, situation within an area subject to a direction, etc. This list is a useful check to ensure that no aspect of the application is forgotten, and a note should eventually be written against each item to show that it has been considered. The first step to be taken by the subordinate technical officer is to arrange for consultations. Since they are the most frequent causes of delay he should make sure that none which are not statutory obligations or otherwise compulsory are made unless there is good reason to think that helpful information will follow.

Very often there will be more consultations to carry out than there are copies of the application; since as many consultations as possible should be carried out concurrently in order to avoid delay, consultees who do not require full information about all aspects of the application can be given a summary of it. Thus, neither the Ministry of Agriculture nor the Roads Department is concerned with the design of proposed buildings and can, where necessary, very often be supplied with a summary and a rough tracing of the site plan. Great care is, of course, necessary to ensure that no relevant information is omitted, and the preparation of summaries and site plans is in itself no light undertaking, but is frequently justified in the interests of speedy determination.

Summaries can best be prepared by filling in a *pro forma* which can be designed to provide suitable information for all consultees who do not require the complete application; at the foot of the *pro forma* another should be placed for replies to be given. This will have to be different for each consultee, and can best be arranged as a series of questions to ensure that all the information required is given by the consultee. For example, consultation with the Ministry of Agriculture regarding an application to erect a house for an agricultural worker on a farm and not in an area for general development should elicit replies to the following questions:

(1) Is an additional house required in connection with the work of this farm?

(2) If so, is it essential that it should be on the farm rather than in a near-by village?

(3) If so, is there any special reason why it should be built in this particular position, or could it be sited elsewhere on the farm if necessary?

(4) If the cottage is not essential for agricultural purposes, do you object to the loss of agricultural land involved by its erection?

The last question is required in order to avoid the necessity of a second consultation if the members wish to give permission irrespective of agricultural need, a regrettably frequent happening in respect of applications on sites outside development areas.

A space should, of course, be left for " any other remarks ".

While the results of consultations are being awaited the other necessary investigations which have to be carried out must proceed.

It is essential that all documents relating to an application should be attached to it as soon as they are received. If this is not done serious errors will continually occur.

A record must be kept of the date by which each application has to be determined if the maximum period permitted by the General Development Order is not to be exceeded so that special steps can be taken to determine it in time or, if this proves impossible, the need to ask the applicant for an extension of time is indicated. The value of this record, which must constantly be consulted, is increased if the consultations and the dates on which they were carried out are shown for each application.

A visit to the site of an application is usually necessary for it to receive adequate considerations. Several problems are involved in dealing with inspections. If they are made at frequent intervals, a few sites only being visited on each occasion, full information is obtained as early as possible on each case. On the other hand, the distance, time and cost involved are greatly reduced if inspection is delayed until a fair number of applications requiring inspection have accumulated, so that it may be possible to look at several which are close to each other in a single journey little longer than that which would otherwise have been required for each of them.

It is unlikely that an inspection will often provide information of sufficient importance to make the difference between recommending permission and refusal, particularly if the officers concerned know their area well, although the appropriate conditions to impose may often only become evident on inspection of the site, particularly when the nature of the application is such that the precise siting of a building is important. Generally speaking, therefore, it will be best to make a single tour of inspection just before the report is prepared for the committee; one special advantage of this is that memory will still be fresh when the applications are discussed by the committee. It must be pointed out here that many committee members ask questions about details of sites which have little or no connection with the Planning issues involved, but which it is necessary for the officer concerned to be able to answer in order to get and keep the committee's confidence. The

technical officers dealing with development control would normally draft their reports a day or two before carrying out inspections, alterations and additions being made immediately after.

The second in command of the office will have to approve all reports made by his subordinates before they are typed and distributed, as well as making his own report in respect of any applications which he deals with wholly himself, normally the most difficult. It must not, of course, be supposed that the subordinates will work in isolation the rest of the time; indeed, the great advantage of the kind of office organisation being described is that it is sufficiently compact for constant discussion and consultation to take place easily, but a review of all applications to be reported upon must be made to ensure conformity between the various recommendations made. It will be necessary for the second in command to take part in at least a proportion of the site inspections, but the arrangements made for this must depend upon the distribution of duties among the subordinate technical officers and the way in which the committee work is managed.

It is debatable whether the work of the subordinate officers should be arranged on a territorial basis, each dealing with a specific part of the office's area, or according to abilities and experience, each officer being allocated the applications he is most suited to deal with. Considerable advantages attach to the first method. Since he covers a restricted territory, each officer has an excellent chance of getting to know it really intimately, and relations with district councils are made easier if they regularly deal with the same officer instead of with two or three. Time spent in travelling is also reduced. Despite this, it will often be necessary for the second method to be adopted because wide differences between the experience and competence of officers demand that they be allotted applications according to difficulty rather than location. In addition, holidays and illness are likely to cause less dislocation.

If the first method is used the officer in charge of development control will probably be faced with as many tours of inspection as there are subordinate officers, which will be a heavy drain on his time. With the second method a grand tour can be made in which all the technical officers concerned with development control take part. This saves the time of the second in command and can be very valuable in enabling each officer to get a first-hand knowledge of his colleagues' ideas, with consequent strengthening of teamwork.

It is often difficult to decide which and how many officers should attend area sub-committee meetings, and what parts they should play. The conduct of such meetings calls for a good deal of skill and experience, including the development of a rather special technique—when to speak and when to keep quiet, how to make points most effectively, and how to summarise complicated matters effectively. An officer should not, therefore, be allowed to handle a meeting until he has attended a large number as a spectator, and thereafter been introduced to an active role by easy stages. Accordingly, it is desirable that the officer in charge of development control should nearly always take charge of the technical work of the meeting. He will probably need two others with him; a subordinate technical officer to feed him with documents at the appropriate time, to keep a check and to remind him of any points he may miss, and a junior to display drawings. The subordinate technical officers can attend meetings in rotation and thus gain experience.

However competent the officer in charge of development control may be, he cannot possibly have complete detailed knowledge of every application, and even with the help of the comprehensive notes which should be attached to the applications, will inevitably be occasionally stumped for an answer when discussion takes an unexpected course. The best way of dealing with this is frankly to admit inability to answer and to ask the chairman's permission to call in the subordinate officer who has been handling that particular application to report further.

Everything which has been said about area sub-committee meetings applies with slight modifications to meetings of the County Planning Committee. The County Planning Officer or Deputy will usually be in charge of such meetings, and will have to decide whether officers from local offices need also attend. Such attendance, because of the travelling involved, is very time-consuming but, in spite of the high level of competence to be expected from the County Planning Officer and his Deputy, the wide area covered and the small amount of time they can devote to development control work will make it very difficult for them to dispense with local help.

Before concluding this discussion of development control administration, one or two further matters must be mentioned briefly.

Applications under Section 43 and enforcement orders, although otherwise dealt with in much the same way as applications for Planning permission, require special collaboration with the County clerk because matters both of fact and law are involved. It is the duty of the County clerk to deal with the second and of the Planning department to deal with the first. The Planning officer must always remember that the facts relevant to Section 43 applications have nothing to do with the desirability or undesirability of what has been done or is proposed to be done, and he should be careful not to let his report be coloured by these considerations.

The detection of unauthorised development must be left mainly to the district councils, who have much greater opportunity, but development control staff should keep an eye open for infringements during their journeyings. Many district councils are very slack in this matter, and if numerous infringements take place unchecked a serious situation may arise. If failure to apply for Planning permission goes unchecked for any length of time the habit is likely to spread rapidly.

Members should be encouraged to do everything possible to expedite the determination of applications, and the seriousness of delay should be pointed out to them. They should never be recommended to defer a decision for any reason which is not decisive, and, provided the development control staff do their work well, the question ought seldom to arise. Efforts to accord an individual applicant the fullest possible consideration of his application by referring the matter back to the district council, or any other consultee who has raised objections, for further consideration, arranging for members to inspect the site or otherwise prolonging consideration, however beneficial they may be to that applicant, are likely to increase substantially the average time taken to determine decisions because of the additional burden placed on the development control staff.

Consultees are often dilatory. When, as will often be the case, the Planning officer concerned is clear about what the decision ought to be without the benefit of the defaulting consultee's advice, it is possible to save time by reporting to the members that the latter's views have not been received, and recommending them to make a decision " subject to no views to the contrary being received from . . . ". Notice of determination is not sent to the applicant until these views have been received, and, if they do conflict with the proposed decision, not until the comittee has considered them. When views are received only just too late for a meeting this procedure reduces the time taken to determine the application by almost a month.

It should be noted that some authorities consider that a determination is invalid if it reaches the applicant after the period allowed for determination by the Minister (two months in normal cases) has elapsed, unless, *before* this period has ended, the applicant has agreed in writing to an extension of time.

If this view is correct a Local Planning Authority could subsequently disavow an invalid decision, and take enforcement action against an applicant who had acted upon it, so that the only safe thing for the applicant to do is to submit a fresh application identical to the original one after the permitted period has expired, if the Local Planning Authority has failed to seek and obtain agreement to an extension. It seems highly improbable that the Minister would ever support on appeal a Local Planning Authority which attempted to reverse its own purported decision in this way, and that the risk of an applicant's position being prejudiced is therefore negligible, but the Planning department should find out the county clerk's views on this matter so that the development control staff can act accordingly, inviting applicants to make fresh applications when necessary if the county clerk happens to agree with the argument stated above.

Maps

The purchase, reproduction, revision and storage of maps is a subject of very special importance in the work of a Planning department. The need for having up-to-date maps to work with has been stressed in the survey chapters.

It is, therefore, essential that the arrangements made to revise maps as development takes place—and not some years later—should be carefully worked out; these will almost inevitably be somewhat elaborate, as they involve both central and local offices.

In particular, revision must be made at all scales and on all copies of maps already in use dealing with subjects which require that the map should be up to date.

Accurate maps are so important to other departments of the authority that it would usually be beneficial for a small separate department to be set up to undertake revision, and provide copies of all maps required throughout the county administration from its own photo-printing apparatus. In view of the special interest of the Planning department in maps, it would be appropriate for such a department to be under the control of the County Planning Officer.

Much of the information obtained in carrying out Planning surveys is also of importance to several other departments, and no opportunity should be lost of liaising with them so that Planning surveys may be modified, and, if necessary, extended in scope to meet the needs of other departments for similar information, thus avoiding duplication of work. Some help in carrying out the work could appropriately be given by the other departments concerned.

The storage of maps presents some awkward problems; although it is most desirable that drawings should be prepared in standard sizes, departures from these will inevitably have to be made fairly frequently. Where possible, drawings should be kept with the documents to which they relate, and this applies particularly to those relating to development applications, including any special drawings prepared in the Planning office to illustrate the problems raised by an application. Obviously, however, beyond a certain size, this is impracticable and large drawings must be stored separately and indexed and a note made on the documents to which they relate of their index numbers and place of storage.

It is most desirable that all drawings should be stored flat, not rolled, however many plan chests are needed. The physical difficulty of finding the desired drawing in a roll containing a large number, and inspecting it is considerable (often involving a spirited representation of the infant Hercules strangling the serpents) and discourages inspection unless it is absolutely essential, which is a pity, for drawings are made to be looked at.

There is hardly anything which can be said about the filing system of a Planning department which does not apply to all other offices of comparable size. The conscientiousness with which the system is operated matters much more than its details, and the matter may well be left at that.

Conclusion

Activities which the Planning department may or will have to undertake, but which, because of their infrequency or uncertainty of occurrence, cannot be specifically provided for in its staffing and organisation, must be mentioned briefly.

The boundaries of proposed national parks and of areas of countryside to which the public is proposed to be given access under the National Parks Act, proposed changes in the status and boundaries of local authorities and contemplated legislation directly or indirectly affecting Town and Country Planning, are examples of matters about which county and county borough councils are consulted or make representations, and to which, particularly if serious disputes arise, the Planning department may have to devote a great deal of work.

Similarly, the preservation of trees and woodlands, surveying routes of long-distance paths, investigating and preparing maps in connection with orders to be made imposing special restrictions in particular areas, drawing up lists of advertisements to be challenged, etc., may involve a concentration of work in time or place which cannot be dealt with within the normal organisation of the department.

It is, therefore, desirable that staffing arrangements should be so arranged that the normal and predictable work of the department does not fully extend resources, but that there is a margin left to deal with extraordinary work. It is certain that there will be enough of this to justify such a margin, even though its incidence is uncertain. Apart from this, the County Planning Officer must be continually sensitive to changes in the weight of work falling upon the various sections of the department and, should encourage his senior officers to keep him informed so that necessary changes in the organisation of the department can be made in good time.

The contents of this chapter have been written in terms of a stable and relatively unchanging programme of work because it would have been impossibly complicated to do otherwise but the quantity and kind of everyday work to be performed by a Planning department will naturally never remain the same for long.

APPENDICES

APPENDIX I

MINISTRY NOTATIONS FOR PLANNING MAPS

The official notations for survey and development plan maps are contained in Ministry of Town and Country Planning Circulars 40, 59 (as amended by Circular 70), 63 and 92. They supplement, and need to be read in conjunction with, the Town and Country Planning (Development Plans) Regulations, 1948 (S.I. 1948, No. 1767) as amended by the Town and Country Planning (Development Plans) Amendment Regulations of 1954 (No. 933) and 1959 (No. 1581).

Circular 9/55 and Circular 54/59 of the Ministry of Housing and Local Government also deal with the form and content of development plans.

Together, these documents constitute a confused and ramshackle code. It would be going beyond the proper scope of this book, which is concerned mainly to suggest appropriate planning techniques, to attempt to unravel its intricacies. Some general account of the principal components of the code and the principles on which it is based is, however, necessary. This is particularly so because, apart from B. J. Collins's " Development Plans Explained " now long out of print and in any case considerably out of date, there seems to be nowhere any full account of the system. A reader who tried to understand it by collecting and relating the original component documents would encounter great, if not insuperable difficulties in understanding them.

Perhaps the most important thing to say about the code is that it should be clearly understood that although there is a statutory obligation to comply with the development plan regulations which relate to the titles, scales and content of development plans, there is no statutory obligation whatever which governs the particular ways in which these items should be shown on maps. The Circulars which prescribe these details are actually merely advisory, and a determined local planning authority could refuse to prepare its development plan maps in accordance with them. Indeed, the development plan for the County of London and the City of Leeds Town Map have notations completely different, and in many ways superior to those officially recommended. It is regrettable that many more local planning authorities do not show a similar independent spirit, for, as suggested in Chapter 3, the standard of presentation of planning maps in this country at present is lamentably low, and there can be no doubt that slavish compliance with official notations has a great deal to do with this.

Ostensibly and superficially, the code provides for the presentation of a series of planning proposals beginning with a county map at a scale of one inch to the mile analogous to a regional plan, continuing with town maps at six inches to the mile, which, in effect, are town plans, and ending with supplementary town maps and comprehensive development area maps which show detailed planning proposals.

Unfortunately, county maps are not really Regional Plans, even if one leaves out of account altogether the fact that county boundaries are not usually suitable for this purpose. They are a weird mixture of the Plans referred to in Chapter 7 as Regional Policy Diagrams and Second Stage Regional Plans, but omit a good deal of material essential for each of these, and, on the other hand, include a number of administrative items relating to boundaries of areas which do no more than provide a sort of key to the successive amendments to the regulations which have, in fact, tended to reduce the status of the county map more and more to that of a key map, and have reduced considerably the limited amount of information about planning proposals which previously had to be included. So that even the slender resemblance to a regional plan has now virtually disappeared.

Town maps do, as regards their content, approximate fairly closely to what a proper Town Plan ought to contain. The actual methods of presenting this information are, however, seriously defective.

The essential theory of the town map notations is perfectly logical; the trouble is that it is based upon false premises and so does not work properly.

The Town Map is intended to show the town concerned as it is hoped it will be after the plan has been implemented some 20 years hence. The map therefore shows areas of existing uses which it is intended to retain and areas of intended future uses, without distinguishing between them. The map is not therefore a self-contained document, but in order to be certain of what already exists and of what is merely intended to come about, it is necessary to consult an existing land use map. From the point of view of the public this is not very satisfactory, since although town maps have to be on sale to the public, existing land use maps do not. This does not matter very much where areas at present undeveloped are intended to be developed, since the base map will show that there are no buildings at present on such areas, but where it is intended to change the use of an area already built up, the defect is serious.

The base map on which the town map proposals are shown is the six inch ordnance survey map brought up to date and printed in a light grey. The object of this is clearly to prevent the detail on the base map conflicting with and obscuring colour or hatching superimposed upon it, but the result, in fact, is often to render the base itself almost completely indecipherable, an evil which is exacerbated because, except in the case of main roads, all colours and hatchings are continued across roads instead of leaving them blank. It is really no use having a base map if one cannot read it, and the kind of base map described on page 30 is infinitely preferable, consisting as it does of a limited amount of vital information, printed at full strength, to full information printed so faintly and overlaid in such a way as to prevent it being understood.

The town map notations were substantially laid down in Circular 59 of the Ministry of Town and Country Planning. They necessitate the extensive use of colour printing and the results obtained are not at all bad if skilled draughtsmen have drawn up the maps. But it was realised not long after the publication of Circular 59 in 1948, that the numbers of maps expected to be prepared for submission to the Minister during 1951 in accordance with the Development Plan Regulations would be quite beyond the then capacity of the printing trade to deal with, if complicated colour notations were to be used. It was also no doubt realised by the Ministry that there was likely to be a good deal of grumbling from the more parsimonious local planning authorities about the cost of such a very expensive method of reproduction. Accordingly, in January, 1951, Circular 92 was issued. This includes all the notations for planning maps in Circular 59, as well as for the survey maps listed in Circular 63, but prints side by side alternative notations for full colour and monochrome maps. A great deal of trouble has sprung from this piece of emergency drafting, for although the full colour notations are reasonably legible with the faint grey base map, the monochrome notations are not, even though some uneasy compromise devices have been employed.

The full colour notations provided for the most part for zoning to be indicated by continuous areas of colour which could be sufficiently transparent for the grey ordnance map base to show through reasonably well. Such hatchings as were employed were sufficiently open for the base to show through quite legibly. With the monochrome notation, which necessitated a large variety of hatchings, some of them necessarily had to be too close for this to be possible. Another trouble was that if these hatchings were to be proportionate in intensity to the intensity of the uses they indicated, the most intense hatching would also fall on areas where the building pattern of the base map was most intense and most complicated. To get over this, shopping areas and business areas in the monochrome notation are indicated simply by an edging and the letters SA and BA respectively. A typical town map in monochrome notation shows industrial areas very prominently in heavy close hatching, residential areas at medium intensity with thin, vertical hatching, and open spaces and schools inconspicuously by means of edgings and letters. This is fairly appropriate, but the shopping and business areas shown only as intensely as schools and open spaces are often quite difficult to pick out, though they ought to be the most prominent areas on the map. Also, even though the residential hatching is not very intense, it produces a kind of dazzle effect below which it is very difficult indeed to read the base map. This last disadvantage could have been greatly minimised if the notations had provided for all streets to be left blank as previously suggested, which would have had the obvious additional advantage of enabling street names to be read. To sum up, the full colour notations, though failing to distinguish between existing uses to be retained and proposed uses, are otherwise reasonably good, but the monochrome notations are extremely bad, and could only be substantially improved by using a different base map.

If what has been said already is not sufficient to condemn this misconceived system, one need perhaps only add that the so-called monochrome notations are not, in fact, monochrome at all; their use requires three separate printings: grey for the base map, black for boundaries and some other items of administrative information and red-brown for the zoning. Though three printings are no doubt substantially cheaper than the seven or more required for full colour printing, they are still expensive. If one wants only a comparatively small number of copies as sometimes happens with, for example, a comprehensive development area map, so that the cost of colour printing is not justified, it becomes very difficult to attain sufficient accuracy with the only other practicable method of reproduction available, namely colour true-to-scale prints. One can well understand the desirability, particularly in 1951, of devising a monochrome system, but since a true monochrome system of the type illustrated in Figs. 36 and 38 is so easy to devise and prints can be made by means of the cheap dyeline process, one wonders how such an extraordinary decision can have been made.

Planning both at national and local levels, but especially at the former, is frequently and gravely impeded by the " first-rate unspecialised intellects " in the higher administrative grades. I am hardly the first to plead for first-rate specialised intellect to be given a chance. There can hardly be any doubt that the woeful system of notations which has been described owes much of its woefulness to those whom Thomas Balogh has described as " the mandarins ".

If proper Planning is to be resumed in this country, and there seems a fair chance of this happening, it will be essential that it should be aided by a proper system of map notations. Nothing but official inertia can explain the survival of the present system.

As this book goes to press a new type of notation for Town Maps, which is thought likely to become official, has made its appearance. It is of "monochrome" type, and relies entirely on edgings and letters, hatching being entirely abandoned. It enables one to locate a given site quite easily, and to see for what purpose the site is allocated, but unfortunately the last vestiges of resemblance to a PLAN have disappeared; one cannot get any idea of the pattern of proposed uses.

APPENDIX II

DEVELOPMENT AND BUILDING COSTS

(From Housing, Town Development, Land and Costs by P. A. Stone)

Ornamental gardens	£1,000 per acre
Playing fields	£500 ,, ,,
Educational	
Nursery School	£100 per pupil place
Primary School	£175 ,, ,, ,,
Secondary School	£300 ,, ,, ,,
College of Further Education	£350 ,, ,, ,,
Cultural	
Branch Library (Neighbourhood)	£3,000 per 10,000 persons
Main Library (Town Centre)	£40,000 ,, 80,000 ,,
Museum and Art Gallery	£40,000 ,, ,, ,,
Commercial	
Shop	£3 per square foot
Public House (Neighbourhood)	£10,000 for 10,000 persons
Public House (Town Centre)	£13,000 ,, 80,000 ,,
Commercial Offices	£3 per square foot
Branch Administrative Office (Neighbourhood) ...	£5,000 for 10,000 persons
Hotel (Town Centre)	£45,000 ,, 80,000 ,,
Petrol Station and Garage	£30,000 ,, ,, ,,
Restaurant and Cafés	£40,000 ,, ,, ,,
Industrial	
Service Industry	£2·5 per square foot
Factory	£2·8 ,, ,, ,,
Entertainment	
Cinema ...	£75,000 for 80,000 persons
Civic Theatre } (Town Centre)	£40,000 ,, ,, ,,
Community Centre	£10,000 ,, ,, ,,
Swimming Pool	£80,000 ,, ,, ,,
Other Buildings	
Hospital	£7,000 per bed
Health Centre (Neighbourhood)	£5,000 for 10,000 persons
Bus Station and Garage	£40,000 ,, 80,000 ,,
Fire Station	£40,000 ,, ,, ,,
Church (Neighbourhood)	£15,000 ,, 10,000 ,,
Church (Town Centre)	£40,000 ,, 80,000 ,,
Cemetery and Crematorium	£130,000 ,, ,, ,,

APPENDIX III

CONTROL OF THE HEIGHT AND SPACING OF BUILDINGS TO SECURE ADEQUATE DAYLIGHTING

The need to ensure that when a new building is erected it will receive an adequate amount of daylighting, and will not itself unduly reduce the daylight received by neighbouring buildings has long been recognised, and numerous attempts have been made to devise codes of control to ensure that these needs are catered for.

The method at present generally in use was devised by the then Ministry of Town and Country Planning shortly after the war; it seeks to ensure adequate standards of daylighting in areas of new development and where redevelopment takes place, yet, at the same time, to restrict the design and siting of buildings as little as necessary. Proposals are tested for adequacy of daylighting by means of a series of daylight indicators.

The indicators are based on certain simple assumptions, viz. that:—

(1) Daylight making an angle of less than 45° with the face of a building provides negligible illumination, and may be ignored.

(2) The remaining light may be obstructed to some extent provided that the building receives not less than a certain proportion of that available on an entirely unobstructed site. (This proportion is calculated by complicated means which need not be described.)

(3) Provided an adequate total amount of light is received by a building it does not matter whether it comes over obstructions, past them or partly over and partly past them.

It would obviously be extremely inconvenient to have to construct designs in three dimensions in order to test daylighting, and the daylight indicators are, in effect, projections onto the horizontal of pyramids of light similar to those shown in Fig. 99.

As will be seen, when daylighting requirements are just met, at a given distance from the face of the building concerned a cross-section of the "pyramid of light" received will have approximately the same *area* whatever its shape.

The method of using the indicators is described on the next page.

Allowance is made for the fact that the sill level of ground floor windows is normally some distance above ground level, so that the indicators may, for convenience, be used with reference to ground levels. It will be as well, at this point, to mention that if there are no rooms used for living or working purposes on the ground floor of a building an amount equal to the height of the floor can, for obvious reasons, be added to the permissible height of buildings facing it.

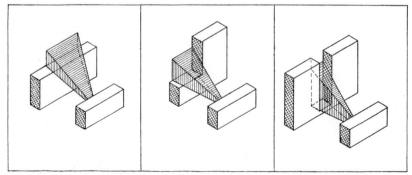

Fig. 99. On the left there is unlimited access of light laterally but it comes over a fairly tall obstacle. In the centre lateral access is restricted towards the right but the obstacle immediately in front is low enough to make up for this. On the right lateral access is restricted in both directions but the obstacle in front is so low that this does not matter.

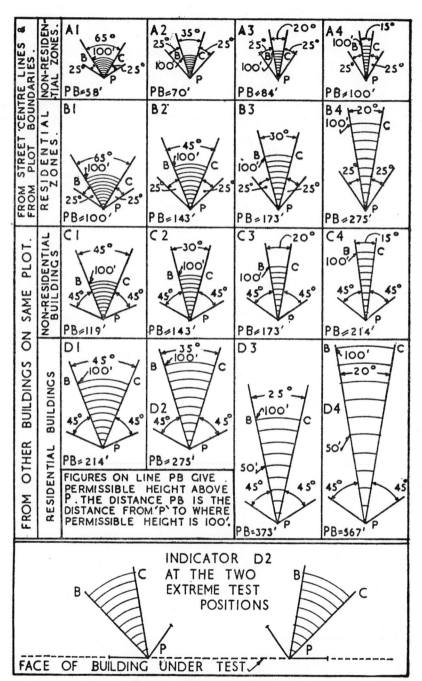

Fig. 100. The daylight indicators.

The standard indicators consist of two main groups, one for testing permissible heights from plot boundaries and centre lines of roads (A and B), the other for making tests between buildings on the same site (C and D). A and B are used to ensure that when adjoining sites come to be developed the daylighting standards of the buildings erected on them shall not be prejudiced. B and D are used for residential buildings, A and C for non-residential buildings.

A, B, C and D each consist of four indicators based upon different angles of elevation; the greater this angle is, the wider is the horizontal angle through which the access of daylight is measured.

The angles of elevation are as follows:—

A1	= 60°	A2	= 55°	A3	= 50°	A4	= 45°
B1	= 45°	B2	= 35°	B3	= 30°	B4	= 20°
C1	= 40°	C2	= 35°	C3	= 30°	C4	= 25°
D1	= 25°	D2	= 20°	D3	= 15°	D4	= 10°

The indicators are calibrated for heights up to 100 feet, but calibrations for greater heights can of course be added when necessary.

It will be seen that the requirements of non-residential buildings are less stringent than for residential buildings.

The effects of enforcing the requirements of the daylight indicators are shown in Fig. 101.

An indicator of series C or D is used by placing point P on the face of the building to be tested. Sufficient daylight will reach the building at the point examined, provided that when the indicator is placed in any position between the extremes shown on it the height of any obstruction crossed by the indicator is not greater than the permissible height shown thereby.

The positions of windows in a building under examination will not usually have been determined, so that the whole of each face of it should be tested in order to meet all eventualities. In practice, however, if certain key points on each face are tested and found satisfactory the remainder are sure also to pass the test.

The A and B series of indicators are used in a similar way at key points on plot boundaries and centre lines of roads in relation to the proposed buildings in question, which in this case are of course to be regarded as obstructions.

If, at any point tested, the first indicator of the appropriate series does not give a satisfactory reading, the remaining indicators in that series are used until one is found (if there is one) which gives a satisfactory reading. Only if none of the indicators will give a permissible reading does the point in question fail to pass the test.

The following rules for using the indicators provide for the satisfactory treatment of varying site conditions:—

(1) End walls of buildings need not be examined with C and D indicators if it is apparent that rooms adjoining them could be adequately lighted by windows in the front and/or rear walls.

(2) Buildings not exceeding 15 feet in height need not be tested with A indicators, so that low buildings can, if desired, be built against plot boundaries.

(3) Surfaces of buildings need not be examined with C or D indicators when the detailed design of the building has been prepared in accordance with one of the methods of daylighting described in " The Lighting of Buildings ", (Post-war Building Studies, No. 12), but site boundaries must, of course, be examined with A or B indicators.

(4) When a number of plots is to be developed as a single comprehensive scheme the whole area may be treated as a single site and tested with C and D indicators; centre lines of internal roads need not be tested with A or B indicators.

(5) Where it is intended to develop a length of frontage by means of a continuous façade, the first 50 feet of side elevations of individual plots need not be examined, but the indicators must not, in these circumstances, be used in such a way as to assume that light will reach a building over buildings on the plots at each side.

In residential areas the dispensations mentioned in (2) and (5) above are not given " as of right " but only if the particular circumstances make it right to do so.

Fig. 101 shows a group of buildings the testing of which for daylighting will now be described.

A and C indicators will be needed, and the first step is to draw them to the same scale as the drawing used for examination.

Testing begins at the road frontage, using A1 along the centre line of the road. The point of the indicator is placed at E, when it is seen that the main front of the building is intersected at 54 feet (F) and the higher, set-back portion at 75 feet (G). Since the heights proposed for these parts of the building are 45 feet and 65 feet respectively, the test is satisfactory. When the indicator is moved along the road, results continue to be satisfactory until H is reached, at which point the permissible height is 90 feet for the tower, for which a height of 120 feet is proposed. However, when A2 is substituted for A1 the result is satisfactory.

Between H and I the A1 indicator shows that the proposed heights are well below those permissible.

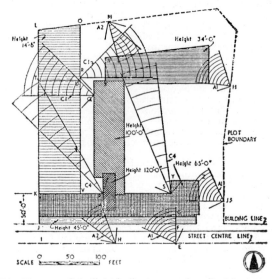

Fig. 101. The use of daylight indicators, as described in Appendix III

At JJ, on the plot boundary, the permissible height is 70 feet, using A1. Along the boundary from J to K, a distance of 50 feet, no test is necessary if continuous façades are permitted (see above). The boundary from K to L and L to O can also be ignored, since the adjoining building is less than 15 feet high (see above).

Testing along the northern boundary, the A2 indicator shows a permissible height of 86 feet at M, as compared with a proposed height of 34 feet. At N the A1 indicator shows a permissible height of 61 feet, while 34 feet only is proposed.

The C indicators are now used to determine whether any parts of the proposed building obstruct each other unduly.

The block KLOV is 14 feet 6 inches high, and most of it, KTUV, is intended for storage space only; UV need not, therefore, be tested for obstruction by the 100 feet high block parallel to it. TLOR, to be used for offices, is tested with C1, which gives 36 feet as the permissible height for the 34 feet high block. UV is similarly tested in relation to the west side of the 100-foot block and the permissible height for it is found to be 19 feet, as compared with the 14 feet proposed.

The north wall of the 65 foot block passes the test at P and S when C4 is used. YS need not be examined since rooms adjoining it can be lighted from windows in YZ, which itself passes the test.

APPENDIX IV

TYPICAL CONDITIONS AND GROUNDS OF REFUSAL IN CONNECTION WITH APPLICATIONS FOR PLANNING PERMISSION

Although it is obviously impracticable to give anything in the nature of a complete list, it may be helpful to readers who have no first-hand acquaintance with development control to give a few examples of applications commonly met and appropriate ways of dealing with them.

REFUSALS

Development Proposed	Grounds of Refusal.
Housing Estate.	(1) The site is not within an area shown on the Programme Map accompanying the Town Map as intended to be developed during the first five years of the plan.
	(2) The site is not adjacent to existing development and ought not, in the interests of orderly urban growth, to be developed until all suitable sites closer to the built-up area of the town have been substantially developed.
Industrial Development.	(1) The site is not included in the Town Map as part of any area for industrial use, and to use it for this purpose would prejudice the implementation of the Development Plan.
	(2) The development of the site for the purpose proposed would adversely affect near-by residential property.
Housing Estate.	(1) Part of the site is in an area shown on the Town Map as land to be used for shopping and business purposes, and the proposed development would prevent an important part of the Development Plan from being implemented.
	(2) The remainder of the site could not satisfactorily be developed in accordance with the road layout submitted.
	(*The applicant would be advised by letter to consult the L.P.A. and submit a revised layout for that part of the site not zoned for shops and business.*)
Conversion of House to Shop.	(1) The site is shown on the Town Map as part of an area to be used primarily for residential purposes.
	(2) Sufficient sites for shopping in the locality are included in the Town Map and the proposed development would prejudice the development of these.
	(3) The proposed development would be likely to cause annoyance to the occupants of neighbouring dwellings because of the noise and disturbance inseparable from such a use.
Housing Estate.	(1) The road layout submitted is unsatisfactory for the following reasons :—
	(a) No opportunity is provided for the proposed development to be linked eventually with similar development to the east of the site.
	(b) The safety and convenience of vehicular and pedestrian traffic are prejudiced because of the excessive number of direct crossroads and the lack of direct communication between Oak Grove and Maple Avenue.

	(c) Many of the houses are shown in positions which would result in unsatisfactory appearance from the roads upon which they front.
	(2) The elevations of the proposed houses are generally unsatisfactory in appearance.
Housing Estate.	(1) The net residential density of the proposed development is 81 habitable rooms per acre, while that shown for this part of the Bogweed Neighbourhood on the Comprehensive Development Area Map is 40 habitable rooms per acre. This difference would prevent the satisfactory development of the Bogweed Neighbourhood as a whole.
	(2) Adequate provision is made in the Comprehensive Development Area Map for development of the type proposed.
Housing Estate.	(1) The net residential density of the proposed development is 12 habitable rooms per acre, while that shown for this part of the Bogweed Neighbourhood on the Comprehensive Development Area Map is 40 habitable rooms per acre. This difference would prevent the satisfactory development of the Bogweed Neighbourhood as a whole.
	(2) As for preceding example.
Erection of Office in Central Area.	(1) The proposed development would prevent an adequate amount of daylight from reaching buildings immediately opposite the site on the south side of Fairchild Street.
	(2) Insufficient provision is made for the parking of employees' and visitors' cars off the highway.
Erection of Houses in Area of Sporadic Development.	(1) The site is not within or near any community provided with shops, schools and other essential services.
	(2) The proposed development would aggravate the already unpleasing appearance of the locality caused by similar scattered development.
	(3) The proposed development would aggravate the dangers to traffic on route B9999 caused by a multiplicity of pedestrian and vehicular accesses.
	(4) No public sewer is available and the small size of the site and the nature of the subsoil render other methods of sewage disposal dangerous to health.[1]
	(5) Adequate provision has been made in the Development Plan for necessary development in this part of Swirkit Rural District to take place in the village of Clottcher.
	(*Similar grounds of refusal would often be appropriate in respect of applications to build isolated country houses.*)
House in connection with Smallholding.	(1) The site is not within or near any community with shops, schools and other essential services.
	(2) The Ministry of Agriculture do not support the application as one which should be permitted in the interests of food production.
	(*Other grounds of refusal given in the preceding example would often also be appropriate for applications of this kind.*)
Outline Application for Development of Housing Estate.	No work to be carried out until application has been made and permission given regarding details of the routes and design of roads, and no buildings to be constructed until application has been made and permission given regarding the number, siting and design of the buildings and the boundaries of their curtilages.
	Reason: No details of the proposed development have yet been submitted.

---

[1] But, on appeal, the Minister will probably not support this ground.

Appendix IV

CONDITIONS ATTACHED TO PERMISSIONS

Conversion of Office to Factory.

(1) The proposed use shall be discontinued on or before 31st December, 1970, and all apparatus used in connection therewith removed.

(2) No industrial processes other than those connected with the trade of a radio manufacturer shall be carried on without planning permission first being obtained.

(3) No advertisement shall be erected so as to be visible from the outside of the building without planning permission being first obtained.

Reasons : (1) The site is in an area the early redevelopment of which, for residential purposes, is proposed in the Development Plan (Condition 1).

(2) To safeguard the appearance of the locality against deterioration and to protect adjoining occupiers from noise and disturbance (Conditions 2 and 3).

Conversion of House to School.

(1) The total number of pupils shall not at any time exceed 20.

(2) No sign or advertisement shall be displayed without the local planning authority's consent having first been obtained.

(3) No building or structure of any kind shall be erected without the local planning authority's consent having first been obtained.

(4) All existing trees and shrubs on the site shall be maintained[2] and any that die shall be replaced, and a screen of trees shall be planted along the eastern boundary of the site to the reasonable requirements of the local planning authority and maintained.

(5) The whole of the land between the front wall of the building and the road shall be surfaced with gravel or similar material and the existing entrance to the site shall be widened to 13ft.

Reasons: To safeguard the interests of adjoining residents and to prevent danger to traffic from the parking of vehicles.

Extraction of Sand.

(1) No excavation below the level of any road shall take place nearer than sixty feet to such road.

(2) Excavation shall proceed in an orderly manner in accordance with a programme to be agreed between the applicants and the local planning authority and no stage of such programme shall begin until the preceding stage has been completed.

(3) All top-soil removed shall be set aside and stored until it is required for respreading.

(4) The floor of the excavation shall be left so that it slopes evenly from north to south at an average gradient not exceeding 1 in 30, and no part shall have a gradient exceeding 1 in 20. The top-soil removed shall be spread evenly over the floor within six months after the completion of excavation.

(5) A close screen of trees shall be planted and maintained fifty feet from the edge of the excavation, between the points marked "A" and " B " on the attached plan.

Reasons : (1) To prevent damage to roads (Condition 1).

(2) To enable the site to be restored to agricultural use (Conditions 3 and 4).

(3) To safeguard the appearance of the locality (Conditions 2-5, inclusive).

---

[2] See footnote 1.

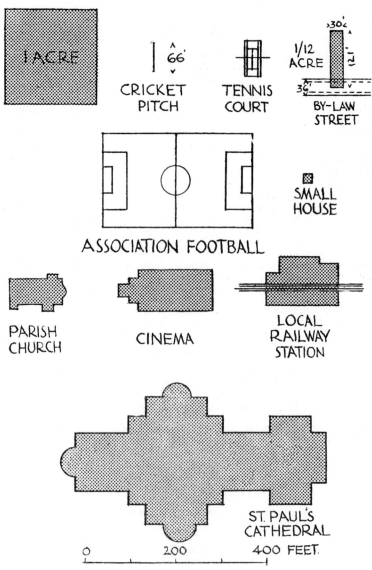

Fig. 102. Relative sizes of familiar objects. Many students of Planning experience difficulty in appreciating the relative sizes of the elements with which they have to deal. This sheet, drawn to a scale of 1/2,500, may give a little elementary assistance.

SELECT BIBLIOGRAPHY

Books mentioned in the text are listed here, but not articles from professional journals. An attempt has been made to include useful works dealing with most subjects which have a direct bearing on Planning, but to be selective rather than comprehensive. A good many of the best books listed are unhappily out of print and many excellent works are not included because of their limited relevance to Planning.

PLANNING GENERALLY

ABERCROMBIE, PATRICK. *Town and Country Planning.* (Home University Press, 1960).

ADAMS, JAMES W. R. *Modern Town and Country Planning.* (Churchill, 1952).

A.P.R.R. (Ed.). *Town and Country Planning Textbook.* (Architectural Press, 1950). (Contains a remarkable diversity of information relating to Planning).

BARLOW REPORT, The. (Royal Commission on the Distribution of the Industrial Population) Cmnd. No. 6153. (H.M.S.O., 1940).

BURNS, W. *New Towns for Old.* (Leonard Hill, 1963).

BROWN, A. J. and SHERRARD, H. M. *Town and Country Planning.* (Melbourne University Press, 1951).

FOGARTY, M. P. *Town and Country Planning.* (Hutchinson, 1948).

GALLION and EISNER. *The Urban Pattern.* (Van Nostrand, 1963).

GILLIE and HUGHES. *Some Principles of Land Planning.* (Liverpool University Press, 1950).

GIEDION, S. *Space, Time and Architecture.* (Harvard University Press, 1956).

GUTKIND, E. A. *Revolution of Environment.* (Kegan Paul, 1946).

KEEBLE, L. B. *Town Planning at the Crossroads.* (Estates Gazette, 1961).

LIVERPOOL, UNIVERSITY OF, DEPARTMENT OF CIVIC DESIGN. *Land Use in an Urban Environment.* (Liverpool University Press, 1961).

LLOYD RODWIN (Ed.). *The Future Metropolis.* (Constable, 1962).

MINISTRY OF HOUSING AND LOCAL GOVERNMENT. *Design in Town and Village.* (H.M.S.O., 1953). (Consists of three sections: Sir William Holford on Town Centres, Frederick Gibberd on Residential Design, Thomas Sharp on Villages).

RITTER, P. *Planning for Man and Motor.* (Pergamon Press, 1964).

SELF, PETER. *Cities in Flood.* (Faber, 1961).

REGIONAL PLANNING

GLIKSON, A. *Regional Planning and Development.* (Sijthoff, 1955).

HALL, P. *London 2000* (Faber, 1963.)

TOWN PLANNING

AUZELLE, R. *Documents d'Urbanisme.* (Vincent Freal, 1947-53).

COLLINS, B. J. *Development Plans Explained.* (H.M.S.O., 1952.) (Unfortunately now out of print, this little book explains the meaning and use of the Ministry map notations with wonderful clarity).

GALLION, A. B. and EISNER, S. *The Urban Pattern.* (Van Nostrand, 1950).

GIBBERD, FREDERICK. *Town Design.* (Architectural Press, 1959). (An invaluable book which touches on Town Planning but deals in detail with all aspects of more detailed Planning design.)

HOWARD, EBENEZER. *Garden Cities of Tomorrow.* (Faber, 1946). (A new edition with an introduction by Sir Frederic Osborn).

L.C.C. *A Plan to Combat Congestion.* (L.C.C., 1957).

LE CORBUSIER. *Concerning Town Planning.* (Architectural Press, 1947).

LEWIS, H. M. *Planning the Modern City.* (Chapman and Hall, 1949). (A most interesting Planning textbook written with reference to the United States).

MINISTRY OF HOUSING AND LOCAL GOVERNMENT. *Technical Memo. No. 5. Land for Residential Use.* (H.M.S.O., 1956). *Technical Memo. No. 8. The Programme.* (H.M.S.O., 1958).

MUMFORD, LEWIS. *City Development.* (Secker & Warburg, 1947). *The Culture of Cities.* (Secker & Warburg, 1946). *Technics and Civilisation.* (Routledge, 1946).

NEW TOWNS COMMITTEE. *Interim and Final Reports.* (H.M.S.O., 1946).

New Town Development Corporation Reports. (H.M.S.O., 1950 onwards).

OSBORN, F. J. and WHITTICK, A. *New Towns.* (Leonard Hill, 1963).

PARKINS, M. F. *City Planning in Soviet Russia.* (Chicago University Press, 1953).

PURDOM, C. B. *The Building of Satellite Towns.* (Dent, 1949).

SERT, J. L. *Can Our Cities Survive?* (London University Press, 1947).

SHARP, THOMAS. *Town Planning.* (Penguin Books, 1940). *English Panorama.* (Architectural Press, 1950).

STEIN, CLARENCE. *Towards New Towns for America.* (Liverpool University Press, 1951).

UNWIN, RAYMOND. *Town Planning in Practice.* (Fisher Unwin, 1920). (Long out of print and now rare, this monumental work laid the foundation for modern Planning.)

PLANNING SURVEY

JACKSON, J. N. *Surveys for Town and Country Planning.* (Hutchinson University Library, 1963).

TOWN CENTRES ETC.

MINISTRY OF TOWN AND COUNTRY PLANNING. *Advisory Handbook on the Redevelopment of Central Areas.* (H.M.S.O., 1947).

BURNS, WILFRED. *British Shopping Centres.* (Leonard Hill, 1949).

MINISTRY OF HOUSING AND LOCAL GOVERNMENT. *Planning Bulletins 1, 3 and 4.* (H.M.S.O., 1962–63).

RESIDENTIAL AREAS

ADAMS, T. *The Design of Residential Areas.* (Harvard University Press, 1934).

ALDERSON, S. *Housing.* (Penguin, 1962).

DUDLEY REPORT, The. *Design of Dwellings.* (H.M.S.O., 1944).

LE CORBUSIER. *L'Unité d'habitation de Marseille.* (Harvill Press, 1953).

MINISTRY OF HEALTH. *Housing Manual, 1949.* (H.M.S.O., 1949).

MINISTRY OF HOUSING AND LOCAL GOVERNMENT. *The Density of Residential Areas.* (H.M.S.O., 1952). *Houses, 1953.* (H.M.S.O., 1953). *Flats and Houses, 1958.* (H.M.S.O., 1958). *Planning Bulletin 2.* (H.M.S.O., 1963).

Scottish Housing Handbook: Housing Layout. (H.M.S.O., 1958).

SEGAL, W. *Home and Environment.* (Hill, 1953).

(See also Gibberd, Frederick, supra).

VILLAGE AND RURAL PLANNING
AND AGRICULTURE

BEST, R. H. and WARD, J. T.   *The Garden Controversy*.   (Wye College, 1956).

BRACEY, H. E.   *English Rural Life*.   (Routledge & Kegan Paul, 1959).

MAUGER, PAUL.   *Buildings in the Country*.   (Batsford, 1959).

ORWIN, C. S. (Ed.).   *Country Planning*.   (Oxford University Press, 1946).

ORWIN, C. S.   *The Problems of the Countryside*.   (Cambridge University Press, 1946).

SCOTT REPORT, The.   (*Report of the Committee on Land Utilisation in Rural Areas*). (H.M.S.O., 1942).

SHARP, THOMAS.   *The Anatomy of the Village*.   (Penguin Books, 1946).

STAMP, L. D.   *The Land of Britain*.   (Longmans-Green, 1950).

STAPLEDON, SIR R. G.   *The Land Now and Tomorrow*.   (1949).

WIBBERLEY, G. P.   *The Challenge of Rural Land Losses*.   (Journal of Royal Society of Fine Arts, 1954).   *Land Planning and Agriculture*.   (Wye College, 1958.) *Agriculture and Urban Growth*.   (Michael Joseph, 1960).

PLANNING HISTORY

ASHWORTH, W.   *The Genesis of Modern British Town Planning*.   (Routledge, 1954).

BURKE, G. L.   *The Making of Dutch Towns*.   (Cleaver Hume, 1956).

GEDDES, SIR PATRICK.   *Cities in Evolution*. (Williams and Norgate, 1949).

HACKETT, B.   *Man, Society and Environment*.   (Marshall, 1950). (An admirable brief summary of the subject).

HAVERFIELD, F. J.   *Ancient Town Planning*. (Oxford University Press, 1913.)

HIORNS, F. R. *Town Building in History*.   (Harrap, 1956).   (A most ambitious and compendious work).

HUGHES and LAMBORNE.   *Towns and Town Planning*. (Oxford University Press, 1923).

KORN, ARTHUR.   *History Builds the Town*.   (Humphries, 1953.)

LAVEDAN, P.   *Histoire de l'Urbanisme*.   (Laurens, 1952).

LOGIE, G.   *The Urban Scene*.   (Faber, 1954).

MUMFORD, LEWIS.   *The Culture of Cities*.   (Secker & Warburg, 1946).   *The Town in History*.   (Secker and Warburg, 1961).

RASMUSSEN, S. E.   *Towns and Buildings*.   (Liverpool University Press, 1951).   (A beautifully produced book with notable illustrations).

ROSENAU, HELEN.   *The Ideal City*.   (Routledge, 1959).

SITTE, C.   *The Art of Building Cities*.   (Reinhold, 1945).

STEWART, C.   *A Prospect of Cities*.   (Longmans, 1952).

TOUT, T. F.   *Mediaeval Town Planning*.   (Manchester University Press, 1934.)

WYCHERLEY, R. E.   *How the Greeks Built Cities*.   (Macmillan, 1949).
(See also History Section in *Town and Country Planning Textbook*, supra).

ECONOMICS, STATISTICS AND VALUATION

HANSEN, J. L.   *A Textbook of Economics*.   (Macdonald & Evans, 1956).

HENDERSON, H. D.   *Supply and Demand*.   (Cambridge University Press, 1954).

LICHFIELD, N.   *Economics of Planned Development*.   (Estates Gazette, 1956). (Frequent reference has been made herein to this very important pioneering work).

RATCLIFF, R. U.   *Urban Land Economics*. (McGraw-Hill, 1949).

HUFF, D.   *How to Lie With Statistics*.   (Gollancz, 1954).

ILERSIC, A. R.   *Statistics and Their Application to Commerce*.   (H.F.L., 1956).

MOSER, C. A. and SCOTT, W.   *British Towns*.   (Oliver & Boyd, 1961).

SOCIETY OF COUNTY TREASURERS.   *County Planning Statistics*.

STONE, P. A.   *Housing, Town Development, Land and Costs*.   (Estates Gazette, 1963).

YULE, G. U. and KENDALL, M. G.   *An Introduction to the Theory of Statistics*. (Griffin, 1950).

LAWRANCE, D. H., and REES, W. H.   *Modern Methods of Valuation*. (Estates Gazette, 1956).

PARRY, RICHARD.   *Valuation Tables*.   (Estates Gazette, 1949).

UTHWATT REPORT, The.   *Report of the Expert Committee on Compensation and Betterment*.   Cmnd. No. 6386.   (H.M.S.O., 1942).

SOCIOLOGY AND DEMOGRAPHY

BAUER, CATHERINE.   *Social Questions in Housing and Town Planning*.   (London University Press, 1952).

BLOCK, A.   *Estimating Housing Needs*.   (Architectural Press, 1946).

COLE, W. E.   *Urban Society*.   (Houghton Mifflin, 1958).

COX, PETER.   *Demography*.   (Cambridge University Press, 1950).

GIST, M. P. and HALBERT, L. A.   *Urban Society*.   (Crowell, 1956).

GLASS, RUTH.   *Social Background of a Plan*.   (Routledge, Kegan Paul, 1948). (See also *Middlesbrough Survey and Plan* and *A.P.R.R. Textbook*).

MADGE, G. H.   *The Tools of Social Science*.   (Longmans-Green, 1953).

MINISTRY OF HOUSING AND LOCAL GOVERNMENT.   *Technical Memo. No. 4. Population*.   (H.M.S.O., 1955).   *Technical Memo. No. 4. (Supplement). Guide to the Use of Local Population Statistics*. (H.M.S.O., 1955).

MUMFORD, LEWIS.   *The Condition of Man*.   (Secker & Warburg, 1944).

MOSER, K. A. *Survey Methods in Social Investigation*.   (Heinemann, 1961).

INDUSTRY AND COMMERCE

GOSS, A.   *British Industry and Town Planning*.   (Fountain Press, 1962).

LOGIE, GORDON.   *Industry in Towns*.   (Allen & Unwin, 1952).

SELF, PETER.   *The Planning of Industrial Location*.   (London University Press, 1953).

BOARD OF TRADE.   *Britain's Shops*.   (H.M.S.O., 1952).

LEVY, H. G.   *The Shops of Britain*.   (Routledge, Kegan Paul, 1948).

MINISTRY OF HOUSING AND LOCAL GOVERNMENT.   *Technical Memo. No. 2. The Use of Land for Industry*.   (H.M.S.O., 1955).
(See also: BARLOW REPORT, supra., BURNS, WILFRED, supra).

TRANSPORT

BAKER and FUNARO.   *Parking*.   (Reinhold, 1958).

BATSON, R. G.   *Roads*.   (Longmans-Green, 1950).

BRITISH ROAD FEDERATION.   *Urban Motorways*.   (Report of the London Conference, 1956).

BUCHANAN, C. D.   *The Mixed Blessing*.   (Hill, 1958).   (A fascinating analysis of the problems caused by the motor vehicle).

BUCHANAN GROUP.   *Traffic in Towns*.   (H.M.S.O., 1964).

COLLINS, H. J., and HART, C. A.   *Principles of Road Engineering*. (Arnold, 1936).

HOUNSFIELD, R. B.   *Traffic Surveys*.   (Architect & Building News, 1948).

LIEPMAN, KATE.   *The Journey to Work*.   (Kegan Paul, 1945).

TRANSPORT, MINISTRY OF WAR.   *Layouts and Construction of Roads in Built-up Areas*.   (H.M.S.O., 1946).

TRIPP, SIR ALKER. *Road Traffic and Its Control.* (Arnold, 1950). *Town Planning and Road Traffic.* (Arnold, 1942). (For clear commonsense this book cannot be excelled).

GEOGRAPHY, GEOLOGY AND MINERALS

BEST, R. H. and COPPOCK, J. T. *The Changing Use of Land in Britain.* (Faber & Faber, 1963).

DICKINSON, R. E., *City Region and Regionalism.* (Kegan Paul, 1947). *The West European City.* (Kegan Paul, 1962).

FERNSIDES and BULMAN, *Geology in the Service of Man.* (Penguin Books, 1944).

FREEMAN, T. W. *Geography and Planning.* (Hutchinson, 1958).

HAWKES, JACQUETTA. *A Land.* (Cresset, 1952).

MINISTRY OF HOUSING AND LOCAL GOVERNMENT. *Technical Memo. No. 8 (with Supplement). Mineral Working.* (H.M.S.O., 1955).

OXFORD UNIVERSITY PRESS. *Atlas of Britain.* (1963).

SMAILES, A. E. *The Geography of Towns.* (Hutchinson, 1953).

STAMP, L. D. *The Land of Britain.* (Longmans, 1948).

STAMP, L. D. and BEAVER, S. H. *The British Isles.* (Longmans-Green, 1954).

TAYLOR, T. G. *Urban Geography.* (Methuen, 1951).

WATERS REPORT, The. *Report of the Advisory Committee on Sand and Gravel.* (H.M.S.O., 1949).

LAND SURVEYING, AERIAL PHOTOGRAPHY AND MAPS

GUTKIND, E. A. *Our World from the Air.* (Chatto & Windus, 1952). (A wonderful series of aerial photographs showing development patterns of all kinds).

PARRY, R. and JENKINS, W. R. *Land Surveying.* (Estates Gazette, 1950).

HART, C. A. *Air Photography applied to Surveying.* (Longmans-Green, 1943)

HINKS, A. R. *Maps and Survey.* (Cambridge University Press, 1933).

MONKHOUSE, F. G., and WILKINSON, A. R. *Maps and Diagrams.* (Methuen, 1956). (A clear and full exposition, particularly good on presentation techniques).

ORDNANCE SURVEY. *Description of Small Scale Maps.* (Ordnance Survey, 1957). *Description of Medium Scale Maps.* (Ordnance Survey, 1955). *Description of Large Scale Plans.* (Ordnance Survey, 1954).

DRAUGHTSMANSHIP AND REPRODUCTION

REEKIE, D. F. *Draughtsmanship.* (Arnold, 1947).

CURWEN, H. *Processes of Graphic Reproduction in Printing.* (Faber, 1947).

HENDRICK, T. W. *The Modern Architectural Model.* (Architectural Press, 1957). (See also MONKHOUSE and WILKINSON, and *A.P.R.R. Textbook*, supra).

ARCHITECTURE

EDWARDS, TRYSTAN. *Good and Bad Manners in Architecture.* (Tiranti, 1946). *Style and Composition in Architecture.* (Tiranti, 1946).

GIEDION, S. *Space, Time and Architecture.* (Oxford University Press, 1956).

NAIRN, IAN. *Outrage.* (Architectural Press, 1955). *Counter-Attack.* (Architectural Press, 1957).

WATERHOUSE, P. (rev. by R. A. Cordingley). *The Story of Architecture.* (Batsford, 1950).

WITTKAUER, R. *Architectural Principles and the Age of Humanism.* (Tiranti, 1952).

LANDSCAPE DESIGN

COLVIN, BRENDA. *Land and Landscape.* (Murray, 1947).

COLVIN, BRENDA and BADMIN, S. R. *Trees for Town and Country.* (Lund Humphries, 1949).

CROWE, SYLVIA. *Tomorrow's Landscape.* (Architectural Press, 1956).

MINISTRY OF HOUSING AND LOCAL GOVERNMENT. *Technical Memo. No. 7. Derelict Land and its Reclamation.* (H.M.S.O., 1956). *Trees in Town and City.* (H.M.S.O., 1958).

SHEPHEARD, PETER. *Modern Gardens.* (Architectural Press, 1953).

OPEN SPACES ETC.

DOWER, J. *National Parks in England and Wales.* Cmnd. 6628. (H.M.S.O., 1945).

GOOCH, R. B. *Selection and Layout of Land for Playing Fields and Playgrounds.* (National Playing Fields Association, 1956).

HOBHOUSE REPORT, The. (*National Parks*). Cmnd. 7121. (H.M.S.O., 1947).

MINISTRY OF EDUCATION. *New School Playing Fields.* (*Building Bulletin No. 12*). (H.M.S.O., 1955).

MINISTRY OF HOUSING AND LOCAL GOVERNMENT. *Open Spaces. Technical Memo. No. 6.* (H.M.S.O., 1956).

SMITH, P. W. *The Planning, Construction and Maintenance of Playing Fields.* (Oxford University Press, 1950).

LAW AND ADMINISTRATION

BLUNDELL, L. and DOBRY, G. *Town and Country Planning.* (Sweet & Maxwell, 1962). *Planning Appeals and Inquiries.* (Sweet & Maxwell, 1962).

CLARKE, J. J. *An Introduction to Planning* (Cleaver Hume, 1948). *Outlines of Central Government.* (Pitman, 1958). *Outlines of Local Government of the United Kingdom.* (Pitman, 1957). *The Law of Housing and Planning.* (Pitman 1949). *The Local Government of the United Kingdom.* (Pitman, 1956). *Planning Law, 1962 (A guide to the 1962 Act).* (Franey & Co., 1962).

DELAFONS, J. *Land Use Control in the United States.* (Harvard University Press, 1963).

Encyclopaedia of the Law of Planning, Compulsory Purchase and Compensation. (Sweet and Maxwell). (Regularly revised).

FRANK, DOUGLAS, and SEWARD, G. *The Enforcement of Planning Control.* (Estates Gazette, 1958).

HAAR, C. M. *Law and Land, Anglo-American Planning Practice.* (Harvard University Press).

HEAP, DESMOND. *An Outline of Planning Law.* (Sweet and Maxwell, 1963).

JACKSON, W. E. *The Structure of Local Government in England and Wales.* (Longmans-Green, 1954).

KEKWICK, J. *Town and Country Planning Law.* (Stevens, 1947).

MANDELKAR, D. R. *Green Belts and Urban Growth.* (University of Wisconsin Press, 1962).

MINISTRY OF TOWN AND COUNTRY PLANNING (and, subsequently, Ministry of Housing and Local Government). *Bulletins of Selected Appeal Decisions.* (H.M.S.O. Issued periodically). *Progress Report, 1951.* (H.M.S.O., 1951). *Subsequent Reports on the Work of the Ministry.* (H.M.S.O. Published from time to time.)

ROBSON, W. A. *Great Cities of the World.* (Allen and Unwin, 1954).

SCHUSTER REPORT, The. (*Report on the Qualifications of Planners*). Cmnd. 8059. (H.M.S.O., 1950).

TELLING, A. E., and LAYFIELD, F. H. B. *Planning Applications, Appeals and Inquiries.* (Butterworth, 1953).

MANAGEMENT

LEECH, W. A. *Urban Estate Management.* (Estates Gazette, 1957).
WALMSLEY, R. C. *Rural Estate Management.* (Estates Gazette, 1960).

CONSTRUCTION ETC.

BLAKE, E. H. and JENKINS, W. R. (rev. by L. B. Gumbull). *Drainage and Sanitation.* (Batsford, 1951).
GOODIN, G. F. and DOWNING, J. *Domestic Sanitation.* (Estates Gazette Ltd.)
McKAY, W. B. *Building Construction.* (3 vols). (Longmans-Green, 1957).

PLANNING REPORTS, SURVEYS AND PROPOSALS

(These are but a few of the more important and interesting available).
ABERCROMBIE, PATRICK. *Greater London Plan.* (H.M.S.O., 1945)
ABERCROMBIE, PATRICK and FORSHAW, J. H. *County of London Plan.* (Macmillan, 1943).
Administrative County of London Development Plan, 1951.
First Review 1960. *County Planning Report. Vol.* 1.
ADAMS, JAMES W. R. *Planning Basis for Kent.* (Kent County Council, 1948).
BROWN, G. SUTTON. *A preliminary plan for Lancashire.* (Lund Humphries, 1951).
CHAPMAN, W. DOBSON. *County Palatine. A Plan for Cheshire.* (Country Life, 1948).
KENDALL, HENRY. *Town Planning in Uganda.* (Crown Agents for Overseas Governments, 1955).
LLOYD, T. A., and JACKSON, H. *South Wales Outline Plan.* (H.M.S.O., 1949).
NATAL PROVINCIAL ADMINISTRATION. *Tugela Basin.* (1952).
OXENBURY, T. B. *Suffolk Planning Survey.* (Cowell, 1946).
PAYNE, G. E. *A Survey of Gloucestershire.* (Gloucester County Council, 1946.) *The Tay Valley Plan.* (East Scotland Regional Planning Advisory Committee, 1950).
THOMPSON, F. LONGSTRETH. *Merseyside Plan.* (H.M.S.O., 1945).
WEST MIDLANDS GROUP. *English County.* (Herefordshire). (Faber, 1946). *Conurbation.* (Birmingham) (Architectural Press, 1948).
WINSTON, DENIS. *Sydney's great experiment. The progress of the Cumberland County Plan.* (Angus & Robertson, 1957).

TOWNS

ABERCROMBIE, P. and PLUMSTEAD, D. *Civic Survey and Plan for Edinburgh.* (Oliver & Boyd, 1949).
Basildon New Town Master Plan. (Basildon Development Corporation).
Bracknell Master Plan Report. (Bracknell Development Corporation, 1954).
Bournville Village Trust. *When we build again.* A study of Birmingham. (Allen & Unwin, 1941).
CHAPMAN, W. DOBSON and RILEY, C. F. *Granite city: a plan for Aberdeen.* (Batsford, 1952).
LE CORBUSIER. *Les plans Le Corbusier de Paris.* (Editions de Minuit, 1956).
Country town. A civic survey for the planning of Worcester. Various authors. (Murray, 1946).
Harlow New Town. (Harlow Development Corporation, 1952).
Hemel Hempstead New Town. The development of Hemel Hempstead, 1952. (Hemel Hempstead Development Corporation, 1953).

HOLFORD, W. G. *Report to the Court of Common Council of the Corporation of the City of London on the Precincts of St. Paul's.*
HOLFORD, W. G. (with HOLDEN, C. H.). *The City of London.* A record of destruction and survival. (City Corporation, 1951).
HOLFORD, W. G. (with WRIGHT, H. M.). *Cambridge Planning Proposals.* (Cambridge University Press, 1950).
LOCK, MAX. *Bedford by the River.* (Bedford Corporation, 1952). *Survey and Plan for Middlesbrough.* (Middlesbrough Corporation, 1947). *Survey and Plan for Basrah.* (1956). *Salisbury City Centre Redevelopment* (1963).
NICHOLAS, R. *City of Manchester Plan, 1945.* (Jarrold, 1945).
SENIOR, DEREK. *A guide to the Cambridge plan.* (Cambridgeshire County Planning Department, 1956).
SHANKLAND, G. *City and County Borough of Liverpool.* (Planning Consultant's Report, 1962).
SHARP, THOMAS. *A plan for Durham.* (Architectural Press, 1944). *Exeter Phoenix.* (Architectural Press, 1946). *Oxford replanned.* (Oxford City Council, 1948). *Newer Sarum: a plan for Salisbury.* (Architectural Press, 1949).
The New Town of Stevenage. (Stevenage Development Corporation, 1949).
(The Development Plans prepared by Local Planning Authorities are published and placed on sale to the public when they have been approved by the Minister. Many are now available).

PERIODICALS

Architectural Review. (Monthly). Notable for its crusade against " Subtopia ".
Architects' Journal. (Weekly).
Architect and Building News. (Weekly).
Architecture and building. (Monthly).
Builder, The. (Weekly).
Chartered Surveyor, The. (Monthly). Journal of the Royal Institution of Chartered Surveyors.
Estates Gazette. (Weekly). Reports of planning inquiries etc., and frequent well informed articles on Planning, mainly critical and written from the landowner's point of view.
Interbuild. (Monthly).
Journal of the Institute of Landscape Architects.
Journal of Planning and Property Law. (Monthly). Invaluable reports of appeals, legal cases etc. Cummulative index.
Journal of the Town Planning Institute. (Monthly).
Land Economics. (Quarterly). Published by the University of Wisconsin.
Municipal Journal. (Weekly).
News Sheet of the International Federation for Housing and Town Planning.
Planning Outlook. (Twice yearly). Journal of the School of Town and Country Planning, King's College, University of Durham.
Reports of the Town and Country Planning Summer School. (Annual). Published by the Town Planning Institute.
Town and Country Planning. (Monthly). Journal of the Town and Country Planning Association. Lively and provocative articles, many in support of the Association's decentralisation policy.
Town Planning Review. (Quarterly). Produced by an international Editorial Board. Notable for extremely fine presentation and distinction of contributions. Published by Liverpool University Press.
Urbanisme. Well illustrated French Review.
Urbanistica. Published irregularly by Instituto Nazionale Urbanistica, Torino. Notable for superb colour illustrations of Planning projects.

INDEX